Origins of Legislative Sovereignty and the Legislative State

Volume Five
(Book III)

By A. London Fell

Origins of Legislative Sovereignty and the Legislative State

Volume One	*Corasius and the Renaissance Systematization of Roman Law*
Volume Two	*Classical, Medieval, and Renaissance Foundations of Corasius' Systematic Methodology*
Volume Three	*Bodin's Humanistic Legal System and Rejection of "Medieval Political Theology"*
Volume Four	*Medieval or Renaissance Origins? Historiographical Debates and Deconstructions*
Volume Five	*Modern Origins, Developments, and Perspectives against the Background of "Machiavellism"*
	Book I: Pre-Modern "Machiavellism"
	Book II: Modern Major "Isms" (17th–18th Centuries)
	Book III: Modern Major "Isms" (19th–20th Centuries)
Volume Six	*American Tradition and Innovation with Contemporary Import and Foreground**
Volume Seven	*World Perspectives and Emergent Systems for the New Order in the New Age**
Volume Eight	*Reflections on Systems Old and New (with Bibliography and Index)**

*Forthcoming

Origins of Legislative Sovereignty and the Legislative State

Volume Five

Modern Origins, Developments, and Perspectives against the Background of "Machiavellism"

Book III: Modern Major "Isms" (19th-20th Centuries)

A. London Fell

PRAEGER

Westport, Connecticut
London

Library of Congress Cataloging-in-Publication Data

(Revised for vol. 5, 3)
Fell, A. London
  Origins of legislative sovereignty and the
legislative state.

  Vol. 5–has imprint: Westport: Praeger.
  Includes bibliographical references and indexes.
  Contents: —v. 2. Classical, Medieval,
and Renaissance foundations of Corasius' systematic
methodology —v. 4. Medieval or Renaissance
origins? Historiographical Debates and Deconstructions.
  1. Legislation—History. 2. Law—History
and criticism. 3. Political science—History.
4. Coras, Jean de, 1513–1572. I. Title.
K284.F44   1983   340´.09   81-22332
  ISBN 0-899-46140-9 (v. 1)
  ISBN 0-899-46141-7 (v. 2)
  ISBN 0-899-46142-5 (v. 3)
  ISBN 0-275-93974-X (v. 4)
  ISBN 0-275-93975-8 (v. 5, 1)
  ISBN 0-275-95689-X (v. 5, 2)
  ISBN 0-275-96753-0 (v. 5, 3)

British Library Cataloguing in Publication Data is available.

Copyright © 1999 by A. London Fell

All rights reserved. No portion of this book may be
reproduced, by any process or technique, without the
express written consent of the publisher.

Library of Congress Catalog Card Number: 81-22332
ISBN 0-275-96753-0

First published in 1999

Praeger Publishers, 88 Post Road West,
Westport, CT 06881
An imprint of Greenwood Publishing Group, Inc.

Printed in the United States of America

∞™

The paper used in this book complies with the
Permanent Paper Standard issued by the National
Information Standards Organization (Z39.48–1984).

10 9 8 7 6 5 4 3 2 1

Acknowledgements include McGraw-Hill Co., R. Palmer and J. Colton, *History of the Modern World*; Oxford Univ. Press, H. Hart, *The Concept of Law*; Mrs. J. Hallowell re J. Hallowell, *Main Currents in Modern Political Thought*; Harvard Univ. Press, N. Rosenblum, *Bentham's Theory of the Modern State*; Orion Publishers, H. Hart/ J. Austin, *The Province of Jurisprudence*; Penguin, D. Thomson, *England in the Nineteenth Century*; Harcourt Brace, G. Sabine, *History of Political Theory*; Oxford Univ. Press, M. John, *Politics and the Law in Late Nineteenth-Century Germany.*.

*To My Family
and Henry R. Fell III
in Memory*

and again

*E. Harris Harbison
in Memory*

Preface (and Press)

This third book of the fifth volume (V, 3) of *Origins of Legislative Sovereignty and the Legislative State* has been redesigned to focus on *Modern Major "Isms"* in relation to the nineteenth and twentieth centuries. The first and second books of this same volume (V, 1 and V, 2) dealt respectively with *Pre-Modern "Machiavellism"* in the sixteenth century and *Modern Major "Isms"* in the seventeenth and eighteenth centuries. This expanded coverage in three books—instead of the two books originally proposed at the outset of the Preface to Book I—was explained more fully at the outset of the Preface to Book II. Suffice it again to say that, as they now stand, the present three books of Volume V (or, in European style, 3 vols. in 1) attempt a more evenly balanced coverage of the five modern European centuries than was originally proposed on a smaller scale. As the titles of the main parts of all three books indicate, our attention has progressed from "background" (16th century) to "middle ground" (17th–18th centuries) to "foreground" (19th–20th centuries). Hence there is an overall unity of this Volume V in line with its title—*Modern Origins, Developments, and Perspectives against the Background of "Machiavellism."*

It will be useful, at this point, to follow up briefly on the kinds of "relevancy" issues in today's world that were featured in the Preface to the preceding book. The samplings to follow from the public press during the short interval since that preceding book was published in 1996 follow along the same generalized lines but need not be as numerous or developed.

First, with regard to the modern sovereign state, it is clear that the idea and reality of the national state as well as of nationalism often continue at the forefront of public and popular discussion in current events. Although some historians and journalists have been predicting the impending decline or even death of the nation-state, as supposedly in the case of the European Union, its reemergence in the domains of the former Soviet Union affords an obvious case to the contrary. Even so, despite the mistaken attempts by many experts to tie the fortunes of the state exclusively to the supposedly declining nation-state miss the mark by ignoring the legislative state that is common to smaller regional and larger supra-national entities as well as more purely national ones. Journalists, like historians, should not equate the modern state *ipso facto* with the nation-state. Indeed, the rise of the early modern state was often as closely associated with the urban and regional states of Italy and Germany as it was with the national states of France and England, not to forget the later modern imperial states under Napoleon, Bismarck, and others. The legislative state affords a model for evaluating all these types.

Headlines such as the following illustrate the ongoing vitality today of public issues concerning the nation-state: "Five Decades as a Nation, And Still the Israelis Ask, What Is Our State Now?" (*New York Times*, April 30, 1998, p. A18); "Nuclear Nationalism" (*Christian Science Monitor*, May 15, 1998, p. 16); and "New Political Tags: Global vs. National . . . . U.S. debate over Asian bailout highlights split between free traders and their critics" (the same, Dec. 22, 1997, p. 1). A brief recent speech by U.S. President Bill Clinton included this statement: "[B]y admitting Poland, Hungary, and the Czech Republic [into N.A.T.O.], we come even closer than ever to realizing a dream of a generation: a Europe that is united, democratic and secure for the first time since the rise of the nation-states on the European continent" (as printed in the *N.Y. Times* the next day, May 1, 1998, p. A24). Clearly, the European nation-states have an ongoing place in the European Union. Even if they were eventually absorbed into a European entity and became like the individual states in the United States of America, they, like them, would still be chiefly characterized as legislative states. Meanwhile, it was reported by a member of the U.S. House of Representatives (on CBS radio, June 17, 1998), as part of the debate on the reform of the U.S. tax code (and of the Internal Revenue Service), that the tax code has grown one-hundred pages in size for every year of its existence since it was first created by Congressional legislation in 1913. This is indicative of the growing massive scope of the legislative state at all levels and areas of the U.S. federal, state, and municipal governments. If a single sovereign nation-state of Europe some day emerges on the scale of the U.S. nation-state, it will then take on similar legislative characteristics.

Second, vague notions of "Machiavell*ism*," *Realpolitik*, and statecraft have continued to becloud public no less than academic debate. Indicative are the following recent headlines: "To Fight City Hall. . . . Principles of Ground-Level Realpolitik in the Age of [N.Y. mayor] Giuliani" (*N.Y. Times*, Nov. 9, 1967, sect. 14, p. 1); "The Tony Frenzy: Machiavelli Would Understand. . . . The nominations for America's best-known theater awards are pending. Will everyone please stop politicking for a moment and listen?" (same, May 5, 1996, sect. 2, p. 4); "Loyalty and Realpolitik. . . . Mandela's challenge to Clinton—to talk to U.S. 'enemies'—highlights a basic political divide. Is his advice good?" (*Christ. Sci. Mon.*, March 30, 1998, p. 12); and "Statecraft from under a Cloud. . . . Clinton gives annual address tonight amid rising doubt about his ability to lead" (same, Jan. 27, 1998, p. 1).

Third, the often obfuscating proliferation of "isms" used in the public press remains an indication of their pervasiveness in the contemporary mind (just as in academic publications). The following recent headlines are illustrative: "Clintonism. . . . Yes, there is such a thing—and it has already changed American politics" (*U.S. News & World Report*, Jan. 26, 1998, pp. 22–23); " 'Mobutuism without Mobutu'. . . . The dictator who ruled the former Zaire is gone, but is the new leader any better?" (same, Nov. 24, 1997, p. 50); "The Calculus of Me-Tooism," with regard to the Clinton vs. Dole presidential campaign (same, Oct. 21, 1996, p. 52); "Gigantism on the Yangtze," concerning China's diversion of the Yangtze River to make way for the world's biggest dam (*N.Y. Times*, Nov. 15, 1997, p. A16); and "America's Descent into Monolingualism. . . . Competence in foreign language is a sadly neglected national need" (*Christ. Sci. Mon.*, Nov. 15, 1996, p. 19). A recent instance of "isms" in academic historical debate has centered around so-called "exceptional*ism*" in relation to nationalism as expounded by Seymour Martin Lipset in his *American Exceptionalism: A Double-Edged Sword* (New York, 1996), a work debated in two review essays by J. Victor Koschmann and Mary Nolan respectively entitled "The Nationalism of Cultural Uniqueness" and "Against Exceptionalism" (*American Historical Review*, 102, 1997, pp. 758–768, 769–774).

Fourthly, there has continued to be much popular use of the term "deconstruction"—some of it serious, some not. The recent headlines to follow afford examples: "Deconstructing the Duke. . . . Gary Wills fails to capture the essence of an icon," in his new book, *John Wayne's America* (*Time*, Apr. 7, 1997); "Deconstructing Diana: A New Academic Field. . . . Princess Di is now the queen of dissertations" (*U.S. News & World Report*, Aug. 3, 1998, p. 44); and "Deconstructing His Film Crew. . . . Woody Allen's longtime staff is hit by cost-cutting efforts" (*N.Y. Times*, June 1, 1998, p. E1), in the aftermath of his 1997 film "Deconstructing Harry."

Among those who have been helpful in various academic ways in the initial preparation of this book are Professors Hans Erich Troje and Corinne Comstock Weston. My first cousin Henry R. Fell III, whose memory I cherish and whose many good qualities showed much promise, proved helpful in more personal ways. My grateful memory of Professor E. Harris Harbison at Princeton remains strong because of his inspired teaching, his kindly wisdom as research advisor, and the legendary example of his humanity and saintliness as a campus leader.

A.L.F.

Contents

Preface vii

I. *Introduction* 1

  1. Modern Origins and Modern "Isms"
    (19th-20th Centuries) 1
  2. The Great Age of "Isms" 3
  3. The Growth of "Neo-Isms" and "Anti–Neo-Isms" 4
  4. The Legislative Continuum 5

    PART ONE. MODERN "UTILITARIANISM," "POSITIVISM,"
    "IDEALISM," "SOCIALISM," AND "NATIONAL(-STAT)ISM"
    IN LEGISLATIVE AND OTHER CONTEXTS OF SOVEREIGNTY
    AND STATE: 19TH-CENTURY FOREGROUND

II. *"Utilitarianism" and "Benthamism"* 11

  1. Overture: "Advent of the 'Isms' " 11
  2. Utilitarian Perspectives 17
    Prominence and "Deconstruction" of the "Ism" 17
    Reducing "Utility" to Legislation 20
    Scholarly Non-Focus on Legislation 23
  3. Bentham's *Morals and Legislation* 26
    "The Art of Legislation" 27
    "Without legislation there would be no such thing
    as a *state*" 31

The Four Causes and the Efficient "Maker"	34
Utility, Command, and Will in the Lawmaking Power	38
Roman Law Compared	42
4. Bentham's *Laws in General*	45
"[T]he . . . *power of legislation* . . . must absorb . . . every other power . . . in a state"	46
"No Customary Law Complete"	49
"[T]he whole business of the art of legislation"	51
5. Bentham's Other Writings	53
Comment and *Fragment*	53
Principles and *Code*	55
6. J. S. Mill's Viewpoints	56
Verdicts on Bentham: Methodology	56
Verdicts on Bentham: Legislation	58
Liberty, Authority, and Laws	60
Justum, Jussum, and Utilitarian Legislation	61
7. Coda: The Emerging Dominance of Public Legislation in the Early Victorian State	65
The Victorian Legislative State, Obscured by "Isms"	65
Origins of the Modern State?	68
III. "*Positiv*ism" and "*Austinian*ism"	71
1. Imprecisions of the "Isms"	71
Anomalies and Self-"Deconstruction"	71
Dictionary Definitions	74
Clarification via Legislation	75
2. Comte's *System of Positive Polity*	76
Preliminary Contexts of a "Scientific" "System"	76
Political Parameters, "Laws" of "State"	79
Mill on Comte	82
3. Austin's *Lectures on Jurisprudence*	86
Positivist Perplexities in Historiography	86
Reducing Positive Law, Command, Utility, and Public Law to Legislation	89
Sovereignty, State, and Legislation	94
Custom, Judges, Justice, and Legislation	97
Roman Legislation and Systematization	99
Recapitulation: Austin's Legislative Legacy	101
4. Jhering and Jellinek	103
Legislation: Bodin, Bentham, and Roman Law	103
Legislation: Sovereign States as Independent Persons	106

IV. *"Idea*lism" *and* "Hegelia*n*ism" — 111

1. Diffusions of the "Isms" — 111
2. The Kantian Background — 114
   - "The Doctrine of Right" — 114
   - The Centrality of Legislation — 117
   - Reducing the State "Idea(l)" to Public Legislation — 121
   - Sovereignty and Legislation — 126
3. Hegel's *Philosophy of Right* — 129
   - Prelude — 129
   - Deification of the "Modern" State "Idea(l)" — 131
   - Exaltation of the Legislative State — 133
   - Enthronement of Sovereign Legislative Power — 135
   - Postlude — 138
4. Later Con-Fusions of "Isms" — 140

V. *"Socia*lism" *and* "Mar*x*ism" — 143

1. Reducing the Socialist State to Its "Social" Legislation — 143
2. The 1840s Background — 145
   - "Advent of the Modern Age"? — 145
   - The Frankfurt Assembly and Marx: State and Legislation — 147
   - Marx's Chronology, 1840s — 149
3. Marx's *Critique* of Hegel — 150
   - Hegel['s] . . . critical analysis of the modern state" — 150
   - "[T]he legislature is the highest development of the state" — 152
   - "[T]he modern legislature, . . . [vs.] the medieval-estates system [, is] the total [modern] state" — 155
4. Marx's *Manifesto* and *Brumaire* — 159
   - "Social," "Public," and "Common" Contexts — 159
   - Myriad "Social-*Isms*" — 160
   - State Control — 162
   - Public Law — 164
   - Legislation — 166
5. Intermezzo: Socialist Legislative State and Communist (Lawless?) Statelessness — 169
6. France and England: Social(istic) State Legislation — 172
   - Varieties of Social(istic) "Isms" — 172
   - "Bonapart*ism*" and Beyond — 173
   - "Gladstonian*ism*" and Lloyd George — 177
   - "Victorian*ism*" and "Parliamentar*ism*" — 182

VI. "National(-stat)ism" and "Bismarckianism" — 185

1. Napoleonic Empire and German National Spirit
   (*Volksgeist*) — 187
   - Napoleonic Codification and Legislation — 187
   - German Nationalist Impulses and "Romanticism" — 190
   - Folkish Customs and Legislative Leitmotifs — 195
   - Schleiermacher and Müller — 196
   - Fichte (and Hegel) — 199
2. Savigny's Historical School and German National
   History (Nationhood) — 201
   - Schools of Thought and "Isms" — 201
   - *Vocation for Legislation* — 204
   - Nation(-State?) and Legislation — 206
   - Custom and Legislation — 210
   - Codification and Legislation — 212
   - Roman Law and Legislation — 214
3. Bismarckian Developments and German National Unity
   (Nation-State) — 216
   - Legacy of "Historicism" (and "Pandectism") in
     Codification and Legislation — 216
   - "Nation-State or State-Nation?" — 219
   - National Legislative State and National
     State Legislation — 222
   - "Realism" and *Realpolitik* — 227
4. Finale on Italy: From "Mazzinianism" to "Cavourism"? — 229

PART TWO. MODERN "NEO-ISMS" AND "ANTI–NEO-ISMS"
IN LEGISLATIVE AND OTHER CONTEXTS OF SOVEREIGNTY
AND STATE: 20TH-CENTURY FOREGROUND

VII. The Growth of "Neo-Isms" — 235

1. The 20th-Century Foreground "Foreshortened" — 235
2. Encore: The Continuing Hold of 19th-Century "Isms" — 237
3. "Neo-Positivism" and "Neo-Kantianism" — 238
   - The Case of "Kelsenism" — 238
   - Kelsen's *Law and State* and "Neo-Austinianism" — 241
   - Kelsen on Legislation — 244
   - The Place of Public Law — 248
4. "Neo-Idealism" and "Neo-Hegelianism" — 251
   - The Revision of "Liberalism" — 251
   - Green's *Political Obligation*: Legislation — 253
   - Bosanquet's *Theory of State*: Legislation — 256

	Toward "Totalitarian*ism*"?	259
	The Question Answered: Hobhouse and Gentile	261
	The Fascist "Legal"-Legislative State	265
	The Rehabilitated Hegel Today	268
5.	"Neo-(Communist-)Social*ism*" and "Neo-Marx*ism*"	270
	Lenin's *State and Revolution:* Legislation	270
	The Soviet "Legal"-Legislative State	273
	"Lenin*ism*" and "Stalin*ism*"	275
6.	"Neo-(Socialist-)National*ism*" and "Neo-Bismarckian*ism*"	277
	Hitler on State and Nation	277
	Hitler on Bismarck	280
	The Nazi "Legal"-Legislative State	285
7.	"Neo-Utilitarian*ism*" and "Neo-Bentham*ism*"	289

VIII. *The Growth of "Anti–Neo-*Isms*"*   294

1.	"Anti–Neo-Positiv*ism*": Krabbe	295
	State and Sovereignty	296
	Legislation	299
2.	"Anti–Neo-Hegelian*ism*": Duguit	303
	State and Sovereignty	303
	Legislation	305
3.	"Anti–Neo-(Nationalist)Stat*ism*": Laski	309
	State and Sovereignty	309
	Legislation	313
	Bodinian Tradition and "Machiavell*ism*"	315
4.	"Anti–Neo-(Collectivist/Communal) Social*ism*": Hayek	318
	Ideology	318
	Legislation	320
5.	"Anti–Neo-Utilitarian*ism*": Rawls	323
6.	Recessional or Processional?	325

NOTES
(BIBLIOGRAPHIC, HISTORIOGRAPHIC, DOCUMENTARY)

Notes to Chapter II: "Utilitarian*ism*"	331
Notes to Chapter III: "Positiv*ism*"	376
Notes to Chapter IV: "Ideal*ism*"	396
Notes to Chapter V: "Social*ism*"	414
Notes to Chapter VI: "National(-stat)*ism*"	429
Notes to Chapter VII: "Neo-*Isms*"	459
Notes to Chapter VIII: "Anti–Neo-*Isms*"	491

Origins of
Legislative Sovereignty
and the
Legislative State

Volume Five
(Book III)

Chapter I

Introduction

1. MODERN ORIGINS AND MODERN "ISMS" (19TH–20TH CENTURIES)

We have finally reached the end point at which we were aiming in the Introduction to Volume IV in a section entitled "Sighting 19th-Century Horizon-Lines," where we looked ahead to modern perspectives on "medieval vs. Renaissance origins." Throughout that volume appeared further headings pointing toward much later "isms" like positivism and Hegelianism as appropriated by historians for interpreting the older periods. Also there, concerning issues of "ancient origins," were the headings "Bentham and Hegel as Legislative Models" and "Mommsen's Positivistic Roman State" (in Chapter II), where we looked at some historians who have anachronistically used modern models for interpreting older documents. In the first book of Volume V on Machiavellism, such headings stood out as "Modern Origins and Hegelian Absolutism" (in Chapter II). In addition, the second book of Volume V on the seventeenth and eighteenth centuries contained many references to later "isms" featured by historians when ascribing modern "origins" to earlier periods. The ideas and methods of Marx, Austin, Hegel, and many other nineteenth-century thinkers were shown in all three books to have exerted profound impacts on recent historiography on early modern Europe. Also, early-twentieth-century theorists like

Kelsen, who built on the positivist ideas of Austin and others, have greatly influenced subsequent models of state theory applied by historians to older documents of interest here.

The two main parts of this third book of Volume V continue and conclude the ongoing sequence of main parts in the two preceding books. Part I in the first book of this fifth volume dealt with issues in the "16th-Century Background." Parts I and II in the second book of this fifth volume looked at the "middle ground" of the seventeenth and eighteenth centuries respectively. In the present third book, the first and second parts study the "foreground" of the nineteenth and twentieth centuries respectively, with the twentieth-century foreground "foreshortened" for various reasons.

The place of the "isms" in historiography now changes in an important respect. The pre–nineteenth-century primary documents examined in previous books of this series made almost no mention of the extensive "isms" subsequently imposed upon them by historians of the twentieth century, who have done so often on the basis of nineteenth-century formulations of them. These "isms" include not only the types featured in this book but also an immense range of others. For the Renaissance and Reformation periods, for instance, the following examples (drawn in part from our previous books) show the massive extents to which "isms" devised in the later modern period have been used to interpret the early modern period: humanism, scholasticism, neo-Platonism, neo-Bartolism, neo-Ciceroianism, neo-Stoicism, Erastianism, Machiavellism, ultramontanism, Lutheranism, Calvinism, Anabaptism, Mennonism, Zwinglianism, Erasmianism, republicanism, civism, and so on. As for the seventeenth and eighteenth centuries, the headings in the preceding book included monarchism, radicalism, revolutionism, absolutism, constitutionalism, rationalism, empiricism, liberalism, conservatism, patriarchalism, democratism, and so on.

By contrast, many of the "isms" explored in the present book were used in the documents under discussion; they were coined or gained currency during the nineteenth century, and exerted a continuing hold over historians and theorists of the twentieth century. These "isms" include the major ones treated below: utilitarianism, positivism, idealism, socialism, and nationalism, along with the "isms" created out of the names of seminal figures associated with them (Benthamism, Austinianism, Hegelianism, Marxism, and Bismarckianism). The difficulty has been that twentieth-century historians have continued to adopt historiographical models of interpretation for pre–nineteenth-century documents on the basis of nineteenth-century paradigms. They have focused on those ideological "isms" at the expense of other more basic legislative subjects when studying nineteenth-century thought on sovereignty and the state. So saturated with these "isms" has historiography become on sovereignty and the state that scholarly attention has been diverted away from fundamental legislative and related issues, with resultant overemphasis on political ideologies.

2. THE GREAT AGE OF "ISMS"

As the "Overture" that begins the next chapter points out, the nineteenth century was the great age of "isms," or, in R. R. Palmer's notable phraseology, the century that witnessed "the advent of the 'isms' " in their modern form. It was in the nineteenth century that an immense number of new "isms," "ologies," and "schools" of thought originated and acquired a new modernity in the contexts of the new political, social, and economic forces of that age. An "ism" may here be taken as a coherent system or set of principles in the ideology of politics, law, philosophy, and so forth. As such, an "ism" is akin to an "ology" or "school." A case in point is positivism and the sociological school that at first partly grew out of the positivist school but later reacted against it. So great was the nineteenth-century interest—across a wide spectrum of "isms" in political-legal thought—in system and science, on a new, grand methodological scale, that one might be (erroneously) tempted to speak of so-called "system*ism*" and "scient*ism*."

The organization of the chapters below in Part I on the nineteenth century follows patterns of sequence that are rather new. Various other accounts of this period adhere, to greater or lesser extents, to the development of ideological "isms" with regard to state theory but usually in much different ways; by dwelling diffusively on the "isms" for their own sake, historians tend to obscure more basic legislative factors. Chapters II through VI below take up each of five major "isms" in turn—utilitarianism, positivism, idealism, socialism, and national(-stat)-ism—in connection with traditional "isms" fashioned from the names of seminal figures associated with them, namely, Benthamism, Austinianism, Hegelianism, Marxism, and Bismarckianism. The arrangements of subjects below within each chapter are also typically original. A wide variety of other related "isms" are also explored. These include, as cited in our headings, Bonapartism, Gladstonianism, Victorianism, parliamentarism, romanticism, historicism, Pandectism, realism, Mazzinianism, and Cavourism.

In the Introduction to Volume IV it was said that an aim was to "deconstruct," as it were, the nineteenth century. Our subsequent books have continued that quasi-deconstructionist effort to explode or replace the "isms" of that century that have continued to dominate historiography adversely. At the same time, attempts to exploit such "isms" and others akin to them have continued. The present book brings that endeavor to a culmination.

3. THE GROWTH OF "NEO-ISMS" AND "ANTI–NEO-ISMS"

The organization of Part II below on the twentieth century ventures an even more innovative approach to the problem of ideological "isms" in state theory. Chapter VII treats the twentieth-century in terms of "neo-isms," while Chapter VIII deals with "anti–neo-isms." In both cases, the sequences of topics closely parallel that in Part I, except for the placement of utilitarianism at the end rather than at the beginning. Under "neo-isms" are grouped many phenomena often thought to be unique or original to the twentieth century. Examples are totalitarianism and authoritarianism under Lenin, Stalin, Hitler, and Mussolini. No doubt such "isms" can indeed be studied in that light, but the present concentration is on the continuing and controlling hold of nineteenth-century paradigms in the early and mid twentieth century. Not only the generic "isms" but also the "isms" created out of corresponding names remained crucial in their "neo" forms. These center below around neo-positivism and neo-Kantianism, neo-idealism and neo-Hegelianism, neo-(Communist-)socialism and neo-Marxism, neo-(socialist-)nationalism and neo-Bismarckianism, neo-utilitarianism and neo-Benthamism. Other "isms" encountered along the way will include (in our headings): Kelsenism, liberalism, totalitarianism, Leninism, Stalinism, and (to extend the nomenclatures) Fascism, Nazism, and Hitlerism. Chapter VIII on the "anti–neo-isms" revolves, in congruent fashion, around anti–neo-positivism (Krabbe), anti–neo-Hegelianism (Duguit), anti–neo-(nationalist-)statism (Laski), anti–neo-(Communist/communal)-socialism (Hayek), and anti–neo-utilitarianism (Rawls).

The organization of Part II, closely interrelated to that of Part I, is designed to give greater coherence and clarity to the mazes of "isms" typically encountered in the secondary literature, not to mention in the primary sources themselves. In each pair of contrasting "neo-isms" and "anti–neo-isms," the continuing hold of the original nineteenth-century "isms" is apparent, albeit within the new settings and conditions of the twentieth century. For instance, the neo-Hegelianism of Green and Bosanquet, or of Fascist writers like Gentile and Rocco, as well as the anti–neo-Hegelianism of Duguit, all bear witness to the compelling impact of nineteenth-century paradigms in state theory deriving from Hegel's works and those of his immediate successors in the same century. A similar pattern holds true for "neo" and "anti-neo" Marxism in the early twentieth century. Of note is the ongoing strong influence of

Marx (and Engels) on such figures as Lenin and Stalin, who are usually studied in terms of their new revolutionary modes of political ideology. The relation of Hitlerism to Bismarckianism and neo-Bismarckianism is another illustration. The powerful impact of Bentham and Austin on Kelsen and Hart is abundantly clear as well. Such comparisons can be made at considerable length and in great detail.

In the broadest terms, then, the present book may be said to cover the span of two centuries from Bentham to Hart, thereby continuing and completing the progression of the preceding book spanning two centuries from Hobbes to Burke. Just as the Hobbes-to-Burke progression was appropriate in terms of such themes as corporatism, so too the Bentham-to-Hart trajectory is apropos of the utilitarianism and positivism that links our beginning and ending points of analysis below. Just as Hobbes' state theory in the early to mid-seventeenth century established an influential legislative paradigm for succeeding generations of political-legel theorists of state, whether pro or con Hobbes, so too the legislative models established by Bentham in the late eighteenth and early nineteenth centuries influenced later state theories, whether pro or con Bentham. In both cases, the legislative models clearly dominated amid the vicissitudes of ideology. Hobbes helped to pave the way for Locke, Rousseau, Burke, and innumerable others in these regards. Bentham, partly because of his early works prior to the beginning of the nineteenth century, impacted many other theorists at the dawn of that century.

4. THE LEGISLATIVE CONTINUUM

As in our previous books, the theme of legislation underlying sovereignty and the state unites the various chapters and sections below in a composite whole. In our preceding book on the seventeenth and eighteenth centuries, the three main sets of antitheses—the absolutist vs. constitutional state, the rationalist vs. empirical state, and the liberal vs. conservative state—were all found to have a common more fundamental foundation in the legislative state, which is the true modern state. In the present book, the legislative state is seen as crucial to the nineteenth-century ideas of the utilitarian state, positivist state, idealist state, socialist state, and nationalist state. In the sets of antitheses examined below for the twentieth century, the legislative state is likewise found to be a basic common denominator. This applies to the neo-positivist and anti–neo-positivist concepts of state, the neo-idealist and anti–neo-idealist concepts of state, the neo-socialist and anti–neo-socialist ideas of state, the neo-nationalist and anti–neo-nationalist ideas of state, and the neo-utilitarian and anti–neo-utilitarian ideas of state.

Thus the legislative factor operates as a "continuum" or "leitmotif" (among our musical metaphors) from the sixteenth-century Machiavellian notions of state to the state types just mentioned for the early and mid-twentieth century.

Among the traditional channels of thought that gave continuity amidst change in the development of state theory in the nineteenth and twentieth centuries, as in the two preceding centuries, was first and foremost the Bodinian paradigm of legislative sovereignty. It permeated, in one way or another, many of the sources to be examined below. By the end of this book, when looking back across the span of modern centuries covered in this series, the reader may feel, with the author, that there has seldom been so successful a specific paradigm in intellectual history as Bodin's model of legislative sovereignty. Sometimes explicitly, sometimes implicitly, Bodinian legislative sovereignty loomed behind and within the documents at hand.

This is not to say that the Bodinian and related legislative models, whether derived directly from Bodin or from his immediate successors, were always regarded by later writers in positive or favorable, much less uniform, ways. Bentham, for instance, had mixed feelings on the goodness and badness of the state's power, even in his central fixations on legislative topics including reform and codification. But the fact remains that for Bentham the state was characterized above all by legislation. Of course, the development of legislative themes concerning sovereignty was cumulative—as in the English progression in which Bodin influenced Hobbes, Hobbes influenced Locke, Locke influenced Blackstone, Blackstone influenced Bentham (notwithstanding Bentham's rebellion against Blackstone), and Bentham influenced Austin, and so on. At the same time, all these writers were influenced directly, as well as indirectly, by Bodin, whether in more absolutist or more constitutionalist configurations of thought. In another case, Marx's thought was profoundly shaped by Hegel, even though he reacted strongly against Hegel; in some ways Marx scorned the state as an evil (rather than deifying it), even though the state to him had a necessary interim role to play in achieving the workers' socialist control of government and society. To Marx, at any rate, the modern state was ultimately the legislative state.

Other traditional channels of thought often operating in the writings to be explored in this book include themes in Roman law, Machiavellism, and the Aristotelian four causes. Roman law continued to be closely allied to themes of legislation as interpreted both historically and theoretically in the writings of a range of theorists such as Bentham, Austin, Savigny, Jhering, Jellinek, Kelsen, Hart, and many others. At times, questions on the relationship between legislation and custom were couched in terms of Roman law, as in some of these same writers. Codification of law, another major area of concern to many writers during the periods under present discussion, was also often linked methodologically to Roman law, as were aspects of legal systematization more generally. Roman law was particularly potent as an ongoing tradition of thought in Germany. There, both the Historical School of law and the Pandectist School of law made seminal contributions toward the eventual German *Civil Code* of 1900 through their work on Roman civil law, in historical as well as theoretical modes of analysis. Machiavelli and Machiavellism made their appearance in a number of ways to be seen below, but did so usually in the more general realm of power politics than in legislation and sovereignty more specifically. The tradition of the Aristotelian four causes will also be encountered at points below, as will some related Platonic elements.

PART ONE

Modern "Utilitarian*ism*," "Positiv*ism*," "Ideal*ism*," "Social*ism*," and "National(-stat)*ism*" in Legislative and Other Contexts of Sovereignty and State: 19th-Century Foreground

Chapter II

"Utilitarian*ism*" and "Bentham*ism*"

1. OVERTURE: "ADVENT OF THE 'ISMS' "

A fitting overture to the present Part I on major "isms" of the nineteenth century relating to this series is supplied by R. R. Palmer's succinct account of "The Advent of the 'Isms'." It appears near the beginning of the perceptive chapter in his *History of the Modern World* on "Reaction vs. Progress, 1815–48," where, indicatively, it follows his synopsis of the Industrial Revolution which set loose new forces.[1] His coverage of the nomenclatures of key "isms" newly emergent in the first half of that century, particularly in England but also on the Continent, serves indirectly here to underscore the vagueness and confusion of such "isms" (many of which he necessarily omits) as well as the importance of the legislative factors of the state. Indeed, it can be shown that the major political-legal "isms" of the nineteenth century, insofar as they concerned state and sovereignty, largely revolved around legislation.

After first noting the key role of "isms" in general, Professor Palmer highlights so-called "liberal*ism*," "radical*ism*," "social*ism*," "conservat*ism*," "individual*ism*," "constitutional*ism*," "humanitarian*ism*," "monarch*ism*," "national*ism*," "commun*ism*," "capital*ism*," and "Marx*ism*." He goes so far as to assert that such newly created "isms" are among the most central categories in the makeup of Western history during the early nineteenth century and more recent times. (Historians of medieval and early modern Europe, however, have too loosely applied such "isms" to pre-nineteenth-century periods in which the "isms" had not yet emerged.)

> The combined forces of industrialization and of the French Revolution led after 1815 to the proliferation of doctrines and movements of many sorts. These broke out in a general European revolution in 1848. As for the thirty-three years from 1815 to 1848, there is no better way of grasping their long-run meaning than to reflect on the number of still living "isms" that arose at that time.
> So far as is known the word "liberalism" first appeared in the English language in 1819, "radicalism" in 1820, "socialism" in 1832, "conservatism" in 1835. The 1830's first saw "individualism," "constitutionalism," "humanitarianism," and "monarchism." "Nationalism" and "communism" date from the 1840's. Not until the 1850's did the English-speaking world use the word "capitalism" (French *capitalisme* is much older); and not until even later had it heard of "Marxism," though the doctrines of Marx grew out of and reflected the troubled times of the 1840's.
> The rapid coinage of political "isms" does not in every case mean that the ideas they conveyed were new. Men had loved liberty before talking of liberalism, and been conservative without knowing conservatism as such. The appearance of so many "isms" shows rather that people were making their ideas more systematic. They were being obliged to reconsider and analyze society as a whole. The social sciences were taking form. An "ism" (excluding such words as "hypnotism" or "favoritism") may be defined as the conscious espousal of a doctrine in competition with other doctrines. Without the "isms" created in the thirty-odd years after the Peace of Vienna it is impossible to understand or even talk about the history of the world since that event . . .[2]

Focusing first on so-called "liber*alism*," Professor Palmer gives an admirably clear and concise description. Yet the term remains one of the most unspecific, changing, and all-encompassing rubrics when applied by historians not only to pre–nineteenth-century writings that predated the term's invention but also to the nineteenth and twentieth centuries. As glimpsed by Palmer, classical liberalism related closely to the utilitarian thought of writers like Jeremy Bentham. (Bentham's liberal doctrine is prominently positioned at the beginning of a large recent anthology of nineteenth-century European writings, all grouped under the main heading of "liberalism" as the overarching theme of the whole period inclusive of so-called "Hegelian*ism*," "social*ism*," "constitutional*ism*," "authoritarian*ism*," and "national*ism*." [3]) However, as an "ism," liberalism is surely no more precise than is the diffusive topic of romanticism, notwithstanding Palmer's useful attempts to classify such concepts.

Politically, romantics could be found in all camps, conservative and radical.

The first Liberals, calling themselves by that name (though Napoleon used that word for his own system . . .), arose in Spain among certain opponents of the Napoleonic occupation. The word then passed to France, where it denoted opposition to royalism after the restoration of the Bourbons in 1814. In England many Whigs became increasingly liberal, as did even a few Tories, until the great Liberal party was founded in the 1850's. Nineteenth-century, or "classical," liberalism varied from country to country, but it showed many basic similarities.

Liberals were generally . . . of the business and professional classes, together with enterprising landowners wishing to improve their estates [, and] . . . believed in what was modern, enlightened, efficient, reasonable, and fair. They had confidence in man's powers of self-government and self-control. They set a high value on parliamentary or representative government, working through reasonable discussion and legislation, with responsible ministries and an impartial and law-abiding administration. They demanded full publicity for all actions of government, and to assure such publicity they insisted on freedom of the press and free rights of assembly. All these political advantages they thought most likely to be realized under a good constitutional monarchy. Outside of England they favored explicit written constitutions. They were not democrats; they opposed giving every man the vote, fearing the excesses of mob rule or of irrational political action. Only as the nineteenth century progressed did liberals gradually and reluctantly come to accept the idea of universal manhood suffrage. They subscribed to the doctrines of the rights of man as set forth in the American and French Revolutions, but with a clear emphasis on the right of property. . . . They favored *laissez-faire*, were suspicious of the ability of government to regulate business . . . and disapproved of attempts on the part of the new industrial laborers to organize unions. Internationally they advocated freedom of trade, to be accomplished by the lowering or abolition of tariffs. . . . They generally frowned upon the . . . landed aristocracies as obstacles to advancement. They believed in the spread of tolerance and education. . . . They wanted orderly change by processes of legislation. They shrank before the idea of revolution. Liberals on the Continent were usually admirers of Great Britain.[4]

Three other salient terms noted by Professor Palmer are so-called "radical*ism*," "republican*ism*," and "social*ism*." The first of these could be applied to Bentham in the form of "philosophical radical*ism*," which was at points intertwined with "classical liberal*ism*." The second term can be matched with both Bentham and J. S. Mill. Mill's later thought can also be understood through the third term. (A broad anthology on "Victorian liberalism" employs the categories of "liberal utilitarianism" for Bentham and "liberalism" as well as "progressivism" for J. S. Mill, along with "Gladstonianism" and the trend from "liberal-radicalism" to "conservative corporatism."[5]) The strong interest of radicals like Bentham in legislation (in contradistinction to custom), as cited by Palmer, increased among later socialist writers.

Radicalism, at least as a word, originated in England, where about 1820 the Philosophical Radicals proudly applied the term to themselves. These Radicals in the 1820's included not only the few working-class leaders who were beginning to emerge but also many of the new industrial capitalists, who were still unrepresented in Parliament. They took up where such English "Jacobins" as Thomas Paine had left off a generation earlier, before the long crisis of the French wars had discredited all radicalism as pro-French.

The Philosophical Radicals were a good deal like the French philosophes before the Revolution. They were followers of an elderly sage, Jeremy Bentham, who in prolific writings from 1776 to 1832 undertook to reform the English criminal and civil law, church, Parliament, and constitution. The English Radicals professed to deduce the right form of institutions from the very nature and psychology of man himself. They impatiently waved aside all arguments based on history, usage, or custom. . . . They wanted a total reconstruction of laws, courts, prisons, poor relief, municipal organization, rotten boroughs, and fox-hunting clergy. Their demand for the reform of Parliament was vehement and insistent. . . . Many radicals would just as soon abol-

ish royalty also; not until the long reign of Queen Victoria (1837–1901) did the British monarchy become undeniably popular in all quarters. Above all, radicalism was democratic; it demanded a vote for every adult Englishman. After the Reform Bill of 1832 the industrial capitalists generally turned into liberals, but the working class leaders remained radical democrats.
. . .
   On the Continent radicalism was represented by militant republicanism. . . . Mostly the republicans were drawn from intelligentsia such as students and writers, from working class leaders protesting at social injustice. . . . Strong believers in political equality, they were democrats demanding universal suffrage. They favored parliamentary government, but were much less primarily concerned with its successful operation than were the liberals. . . . Opposed to monarchy of any kind, even to constitutional monarchy, . . . the more militant republicans were considered by most people, including the liberals, to be little better than anarchists.
   Republicanism shaded off into socialism. Socialists generally shared the political attitudes of republicanism but added other views besides. The early socialists, those before the revolution of 1848, were of many kinds, but all had certain ideas in common. . . . All thought it improper for owners of wealth to have so much economic power. . . . All therefore questioned the value of private enterprise, favoring some degree of communal ownership of productive assets. . . . They believed that beyond the civil and legal equality brought in by the French Revolution a further step toward social and economic equality had yet to be taken.[6]

The maze of other political "isms" discussed by Professor Palmer include communism, nationalism, conservatism, and humanitarianism. Their relation to the issue of legislation remains to be treated below. On nationalism there will be seen to exist significant primary and secondary literature dealing with the nation-state in connection with legislation. On humanitarianism and communism, it will be seen that J. S. Mill and Karl Marx variously dealt with the state, including legislation, in ways that exposed (as had Bentham too) its negative aspects; in so doing, they would accentuate the central place of legislation in the state. Palmer's descriptions thus afford an insightful point of departure for the present chapters.

As for "communism," it was at this time an uncertain synonym for socialism. A small group of German revolutionaries, mainly exiles in France, took the name for themselves in the 1840's. They would have been historically forgotten had they not included Karl Marx and Frederick Engels among their members. Marx and Engels consciously used the word in 1848 to differentiate their variety of socialism from that of such utopians as St. Simon, Fourier, and Owen. But the word "communism" went out of general use after 1848, to be revived after the Russian Revolution of 1917, at which time it received a new meaning.

Nationalism . . . arose . . . largely in reaction against the international Napoleonic system. . . . It was the most pervasive and the least crystallized of the new "isms." In western Europe—Britain, France, or Spain—where national unity already existed, nationalism was not a doctrine so much as a latent state of mind, easily aroused when national interests were questioned, but normally taken for granted. Elsewhere—in Italy, Germany, Poland, the Austrian and Turkish empires—where peoples of the same nationality were politically divided or subject to foreign rule, nationalism was becoming a deliberate and conscious program. . . .

Liberalism, radical republicanism, socialism, and nationalism were after 1815 the political forces driving Europe onward toward a future still unknown. Of other "isms" less need be said. Conservatism, too, remained strong. Politically, on the Continent, conservatism upheld the institutions of absolute monarchy, aristocracy, and church, and opposed the constitutional and representative government sought by liberals. As a political philosophy, conservatism built upon the ideas of Edmund Burke, who had held that every people must change its institutions by gradual adaptation. . . . Conservatism sometimes passed into nationalism, since it stressed the firmness and continuity of national character. But nationalists at this time were more often liberals or republicans. "Monarchism" was conservative, and even reactionary. . . .

Deeper than other "isms," a feeling shared in varying ways by people of all parties, was the profound current of humanitarianism. It consisted in a heightened sense of the reality of cruelty inflicted upon others. Here the thought of the Age of Enlightenment suffered no reversal.[7]

Although, in addition, so-called "romantic*ism*" was inherently a cultural movement or a set of beliefs, it could and did become aligned with political forces, including republicanism (as in the revolts of the 1820s and 1830s) and nationalism.

> One of the "isms" was not political. It was called "romanticism," a word first used in English in the 1840's to describe a movement then half a century old. . . . Representing a new way of sensing all human experience, it affected most thinking on social and public questions. . . . The romantics, characteristically, insisted on the value of feeling as well as of reason.[8]

2. UTILITARIAN PERSPECTIVES

Prominence and "Deconstruction" of the "Ism"

Few if any English political writers exerted so great an influence in the early and mid-nineteenth century as did Jeremy Bentham and John Stuart Mill. Their importance for the early development of political as well as legal thought in Victorian England extended beyond into other disciplines, countries, and periods. They have been credited by their contemporaries and later historians with having laid the foundations of early liberalism, which is often taken to be the most all-encompassing "ism" of nineteenth-century political thought in England and Western Europe. Their ideas have been traditionally linked, more specifically, to utilitarianism, a doctrine that according to many they founded (as liberals).

Scholarly approaches to such subjects naturally vary. A few general textbook examples will suffice here. Already cited is the leading role assigned to Bentham at the beginning of a voluminous recent collection of documents of the nineteenth century centering around the topic of liberalism in a broad trajectory extending from Bentham to later factory legislation, J. S. Mill, Hegel, and so forth (in the work's first section).[9] In a monumental history of political theory, Bentham and J. S. Mill have been deemed respectively crucial for "early liberalism" (philosophical radicalism) and later "modernized liberalism."[10] The utilitarian values of Bentham and J. S. Mill occupy a central place in such coverages. One broad analysis of early–nineteenth-century Europe treats "the orders of liberalism," starting with "the principle of utility."[11] A standard survey of the history of philosophy begins its treatment of French and British philosophy of the nineteenth century with French "positivism" in Auguste Comte and proceeds to "utilitarian ethics" in

Bentham, "empiricism" in J. S. Mill, and "evolutionism" in Herbert Spencer.[12] Multitudinous books and anthologies focus on the utilitarianism of Bentham and J. S. Mill as well as of the latter's father, James Mill, a stauncher disciple of Bentham.[13] One documentary history of nineteenth-century Europe contains an initial chapter on "the rising tide of revolution." It begins with "utilitarianism" (in Bentham's *Morals and Legislation*) and proceeds to three revolutionary epicenters (Decembrists in Russia in 1825, Byron, and the July Revolution in France in 1830), Europe and the independence of Latin America, and the British Reform Bill of 1832 (which Bentham influenced through his long-developing reformist ideas prior to his death in that same year).[14] Even when Bentham and J. S. Mill have both been grouped under the rubric of "philosophical radicalism," their utilitarian values have been given particular prominence.[15]

Notwithstanding the importance traditionally assigned to utilitarianism as an "ism," as a device for interconnecting the thought of Bentham and the two Mills along with other writers of the period, one must keep in mind the indeterminate nature of all such "isms." This holds true whether the "isms" came into use during or after the periods and writings discussed in terms of them by recent historians. The utilitarianism of Bentham has been so profusely associated with other "isms" as to render it difficult to grasp precisely. These other "isms" have included the following: liberalism, radicalism, republicanism, industrialism, reformism, capitalism, Chartism, and individualism. The equally diffusive spectrum of "isms" often identified with J. S. Mill's utilitarianism include some of the above, in addition to others such as humanitarianism, collectivism, institutionalism, socialism, empiricism, idealism, representationalism, progressivism, and Victorianism. These and a host of other frequently encountered "isms" related to them are likewise shifting, having limited value as key categories of analysis for historians. Compounding the difficulty are the sweeping categories of liberalism and conservatism, two major "isms" already "exploited" and "exploded" in our preceding book in chapters on the eighteenth century. When Whiggism blended with and developed into liberalism, and Toryism into conservatism, leading respectively to the Liberal and Conservative parties in England, their status as "isms" became even more problematical. Affected also were other "isms" like utilitarianism.

An apparent contradiction to the kind of approach to Bentham cited above, which identifies him with "early liberalism," is a sprawling book on the age-old "liberal tradition" in European thought. It includes Bentham in a chapter on ideas of progress, economics, and democracy in an historical trajectory that begins with Condorcet and ends with Keynes, stretching from the eighteenth to the twentieth century. In other chapters on different liberal topics, J. S. Mill is included in lines of development leading from Spinoza and Locke to Hobhouse (on toleration and free thought), from Locke and Montesquieu to de Tocqueville and Schumpeter (on constitutionalism and democracy), and from Kant to the United Nations' "Declaration" on human rights (concerning nationalism, revolution, and international order).[16]

A more comprehensive book illustrates the historiographical disarray occasioned by the welter of "isms" surrounding "political ideas in modern Britain." It employs the following unwieldy sequence of topical headings: "friends of the modern state" (concerned with "collectivism and the growth of the modern state," "liberalism," "socialism," and "the state at home and abroad"), "pleas for liberty" (as regards "the individualist resistance to the modern state," "popular anti-statism," "conservatism and anti-socialism"), "neither state nor individual: the defence of communal and group politics" (relating to "communism and anarchism," "the reform of society," "distributism," "syndicalism," "political pluralism," "guild socialism"), "the pale of the constitution: the idea of citizenship" (concerning "democrats and élitists," "citizens, people and women," "nation, class and the style of politics"), "accommodations to the modern state: political ideas in the second quarter of the twentieth century" (in connection with "the presence of the modern state," "economists and other experts," "power and class," "culture and politics," "the foreign dimension: fascism and communism," "pessimism, caution and the possibilities of democracy"), and "arrivals and departures: political ideas in the third quarter of the twentieth century" (pertaining to "caution and consensus," "the beginning of ideology: socialism," "the beginning of ideology: libertarianism, conservatism and anarchism," and "new pluralisms"). The purported "beginning" of modern statism and modern ideology is hard to discern amid this sea of broadly defined "isms" and related contexts.[17]

If the preceding perspectives on "isms" and related topics suggest the deficiencies of imprecise "constructs" such as "utilitarian*ism*," a closer look at its definitions and uses confirms the need for "deconstruction." When applied as a label to the thought of Bentham and the two Mills, along with other writers, the term "utilitarian*ism*" tends to deconstruct or break down on its own. These three thinkers have received so many diverse criticisms from their contemporaries and later historians as to call into question the "ism" itself, despite its continued extensive use in analyses of early-nineteenth-century British thought. The complicated, unfinished, and idiosyncratic qualities of Bentham's works, together with the self-contradictory and inconsistent arguments found in J. S. Mill's works, becloud their (and our) concept of "utility." Did it represent a system or set of principles classifiable as an "ism"?

J. S. Mill prided himself on being the originator of the "ism" as a term and of certain variants. But he gave it such a diffusive universal meaning, while revealing many of his own flaws when criticizing Bentham's errors, that many historians have expressed their inability to comprehend many facets of J. S. Mill's approach. They occasionally perceive that the core concept of "utility" in Bentham and the two Mills often reduces to the topic or matrix of legislation. But this point has been heretofore insufficiently appreciated and examined.

Standard dictionary definitions of the kind set forth in the *Oxford English Dictionary* serve to suggest the incohesiveness and elusiveness of utilitarian values when presented as an "ism." There, "utilitarian" is described as follows: "One who holds, advocates, or supports the doctrine of utilitarianism, one who considers utility the standard of whatever is good for man; also, a person devoted to mere utility or material interests. . . . Of philosophy, principles, etc.; Consisting in or based upon utility; *spec.* that [which] regards the greatest good or happiness of the greatest number as the chief consideration or role of morality." Accordingly, "utilitarianism" is there defined as follows: "Utilitarian doctrines, principles, theories, or practices . . ." "Utility" signifies what is "useful or serviceable; fitness for some desirable purpose or valuable end . . ." In addition, "Benthamism" is defined by the *Oxford English Dictionary* as "[t]he philosophical system of Jeremy Bentham . . . ," in contradistinction to other variants such as "Benthamry," some of which were coined derogatorily by Bentham's critics.

Reducing "Utility" to Legislation

For utilitarians like Bentham, the notion of "utility" typically involved the medium of legislation. Yet by stressing the agelessness of utilitarian philosophy, going back to Roman concepts of *utilitas*, J. S. Mill diluted the distinctiveness of Bentham's blend of utility and legislation. The relation of "utility" to legislation needs here further introduction, with more consideration of its status as an "ism."

The factors that impeded utilitarianism as a coherent system, in conjunction with philosophical radicalism and other related "isms," are cogently outlined by George Sabine in his older but still unmatched voluminous survey of the history of political theory. Among the most general deficiencies he points out are the following:

> In point of fact no member of the group, including Bentham himself, was in any way remarkable for philosophical originality or even for a very firm grasp of philosophical principles. The formal and deductive manner of presentation which they

affected gave an appearance of system to their thought that turns out upon analysis to be deceptive. The order in which the several parts of the system appeared is significant of the fact that their relationship was practical rather than logical. . . . The alleged empiricism of the Utilitarians was in fact filled with unexamined presumptions. The greatest happiness principle in ethics might have been adopted, as it often had been in the past, without the hedonistic psychology which was supposed to support it, and the reforms advocated in the name of the greatest happiness were implied only if the principle was supplemented by a large number of premises unrelated to the system.[18]

On Bentham, Sabine astutely but insufficiently pointed out that utilitarianism involved at root an *ad hoc* concentration on utility that in ways revolved around legislation. The greatest happiness principle was to be advanced or realized in reforms through legislative processes and sovereignty. The utility of this principle depends, in Sabine's analysis, on its specific effects and benefits in the hands of legislators, who must deal with relevant circumstances rather than with past customs. Utility and legislation go hand in hand, according to Bentham's singularly important ideas, especially in criminal law. However, "utility" is there a vague term that depends on changing cases and unarticulated premises. Although dependent on the happiness principle, Bentham's "utility," says Sabine, "can be produced only by legislation," while legislative coercion is a necessary evil that produces social harmony. Bentham sought to enhance Parliament's legislative sovereignty in order to achieve reforms rather than to impose limits on sovereignty in general through bills of rights, and so on, albeit the people was ultimately sovereign. Bentham thus changed the direction of liberalism. Included by Sabine among the "isms" and ideas nascent in Bentham, are analytical jurisprudence, command-theory, and legal positivism as later developed by John Austin.[19]

On J. S. Mill, Sabine noted even more fundamental flaws of philosophy, including confusing approaches to utilitarianism. Once again, it was not a coherent system, yet often revolved around *ad hoc* issues of legislation. Going well beyond J. S. Mill's own criticisms of Bentham's philosophical radicalism, for being falsely or narrowly schematic, Sabine declares that it, too, was never a clear systematic "ism." Nor was it ever logical or empirical in the ways claimed by Bentham and his followers. Early liberalism in Bentham was philosophically deficient in its disregard for social welfare and the common good of all classes. It was imbued instead with the so-called "hedon*ism*," "sensational*ism*," and "egotistic individual*ism*" of the happiness principle, as Mill correctly underscored, according to Sabine. However, the "collectiv*ism*," of Mill, Sabine felt, was even more philosophically defective. Mill also confusingly combined anew disparate strands of other "isms," such as positivism, Kantianism, Hegelianism, idealism, and socialism. Most perplexing to Sabine were Mill's unsystematic and self-contradictory habits of mind and personality. They rendered Mill's revision of liberal utilitarianism null as a systemic "ism" and made it instead a textbook case in fallacious logic. Mill "reduced his utilitarianism to complete indefiniteness." The "root" difficulty, according to Sabine, was Mill's unwillingness to accept Bentham's "only" intended purpose in the happiness principle, which was to establish a "criterion for judging the utility of legislation." At the same time, J. S. Mill made a positive contribution by reorienting utilitarianism and liberalism away from the emphasis (by Bentham and James Mill) on good efficient government and toward liberty in the social context. J. S. Mill focused on society more than on the state, fearing the oppression of the majority more than of government, contrary to liberals like Bentham. Yet Mill maintained interest in Bentham's reform goals along with interest in law and legislation (the medium for legal rights and obligations), without which there could be no true social security and liberty. When Sabine criticizes Mill for having no clear "rule" or "criterion for defining the proper limits of legislation," but possessing only "subjective habits of judgment," he neglects to carry the point to its obvious conclusion, namely, that Mill's concept of utilitarianism reduces to the same component as in Bentham's case—legislation. Mill's understanding of social legislation rested on humanitarian grounds but without a real theory behind it. Mill suggested new relationships between legislation and the economy when criticizing classical *laissez-faire* liberalism and advocating a degree of socialist controls through legislation. Here, again, "isms" recede and legislation emerges at the forefront. Mill's far lesser interest in jurisprudence in comparison with Bentham did not prevent him from carrying forward, in more general social and institutional contexts, the legislative proclivities of Bentham. Once more, Sabine's treatment of such matters is brief and limited. The need is to examine them within the wider frameworks of this series through extended analyses of key documents and themes.[20]

A recent study of "Bentham's theory of the modern state" by Nancy L. Rosenblum also pinpoints the central role of legislation in Bentham's concept of utility (at the heart of his utilitarianism). Although her study does not focus on legislation or its relation to sovereignty and the state, it is useful in those connections more so than most other studies. Criticizing previous scholarship on Bentham for failing to appreciate the real importance and character of utility in his system, she sees it as primarily a public utility, which is geared to public necessity as distinguished from private morality, and which operates as "a rationale for legislation." The system of law that Bentham thereby provided for the state became a key to his originality and his break from tradition. But Professor Rosenblum does not sufficiently recognize in direct ways the central significance of legislation for the state and sovereignty in Bentham's thought, despite her many promising suggestions. She mistakenly dwells on Bentham's purported "anticlassic*ism*" as marking a break with the ancient and early modern idea of legislation centered around the "extraordinary" activity of great lawgivers. Rather, Bentham looked to more "ordinary" continuing systems of enactments (especially concerning codes of law). She does not take into account the kinds of early modern "ordinary" or ongoing systems of legislation examined in this series. In fact, they provided the basis of state and sovereignty that lay in the background to Bentham's theories. According to Rosenblum, Bentham's idea of utility, as a foundation for the theory of the modern state, included a higher form of supposed "individual*ism*" and "rational*ism*," which she distinguishes from older outlooks on law as a provider of ideal standards for character. Bentham's ideas of the sovereign, couched in terms of popular sovereignty and the sovereign will, lay, she argues, in the tradition of so-called "absolut*ism*" and centralization of power. In Bentham's "legal system," utility "gives the state its unity" and "legal entity." Such a focus on Bentham's purported "legal*ism*" in relation to the above and other "isms" may, for some, help to illuminate Bentham's ideas of legislation, sovereignty, and the state. Yet the author at hand could have tied her useful materials bearing on legislation, at the core of utility, more closely to the state problem, without the obscurances of myriad "isms," albeit her study is an excellent one.[21]

Scholarly Non-Focus on Legislation

To be sure, there are numerous other recent secondary works on Bentham that include significant discussions on his ideas of legislation; yet in them legislation is typically subsidiary to other topics. An impressive treatment of a broad range of problems in Bentham, giving particular attention to legislative issues, remains the collected essays on Bentham by the great authority H. L. A. Hart. Using Bentham as an historical point of departure for elaborating his own legal philosophy, Professor Hart has given important historical accounts, at the same time. However, Hart's main titles indicate his primary focal points to be other than on legislation *per se*: "The Demystification of the Law" (I), "The United States of America" (III), "Natural Rights: Bentham and John Stuart Mill" (IV), "Bentham's *Of Laws in General*" (V), "Legal

Duty and Obligation" (VI), "Legal Rights" (VII), "Legal Powers" (VIII), "Sovereignty and Legally Limited Government" (IX), and "Commands and Authoritative Reasons" (X). Particularly incisive and germane are Hart's scattered analyses of Bentham's relationships to jurists like Blackstone and Austin, with considerations of legislation and sovereignty. Topics here include volition, will, power, right, command, coercion, prohibition, and related imperative modes.[22] More directly concentrating on legislation is David Lieberman's book on "the province of legislation determined" in British legal theory of the eighteenth century. He deals first with Blackstone's *Commentaries* and then with "the Judiciary," followed by "Parliamentary statute." The final fourth chapter takes up Bentham, especially in relation to the common law, and again Blackstone. The towering accomplishments of Blackstone were criticized and minimized by Bentham but were subsequently duly recognized by constitutional historians from Maitland to Lieberman.[23] Various other related works could be cited but would again be found limited from present perspectives on legislation as central to utility and the state in utilitarian doctrines.

Far more typical are recent scholarly works on Bentham that include legislation when concentrating on much different kinds of topics in connection with nebulous "isms." Various illustrations feature the subject of utilitarianism in the main title and combine historical analysis with contemporary philosophizing. James E. Crimmins deals with "secular utilitarianism" with regard to "social science and the critique of religion" in Bentham's thought. The first part, on the "utilitarian science of society," deals with "science and religion" along with "ethics and the science of legislation." The second part, under the amusing rubric of "Church-of-England*ism*," ranges further afield of legislation *per se* when dealing with other such "isms" as anticlericalism. The third part, on "natural and revealed religion," includes such topics as "Christian asceticism."[24] P. J. Kelly's book on "utilitarianism and distributive justice" in relation to "Bentham and the civil law" concentrates in its chapter headings on such issues as "psychological hedonism and the basis of motivation" and "the principle of utility and the criterion of moral judgement." He argues that Bentham had a theory of distributive justice that enabled him to include ideals of liberty and justice engrained in "liberal*ism*" rather than merely to succumb to the "material*ism*" of "utilitarian*ism*" that would deny such higher values. (Although Kelly does not cite him, Bodin was, long before Bentham, well noted for his concept of distributive justice, which one could relate to the ideas of Blackstone in the background to Bentham and the two Mills.)[25] A book by David Lyons on "Bentham's philosophy of utility and law" pertains to "the interest of the governed." Its multiple headings exhibit a direct interest in legislation in a few cases concerning "private ethics and the art of legislation," "the basic price of legislation," and "some complexities of legislation"—as all included under the broad topic of "the convergence of interests." Here, as elsewhere, legislation often becomes an unavoidable topic for many experts on Bentham because of own his pervasive fascination with it, even though most scholars do not focus on legislation in Bentham's foundation for utility and the state.[26] Also bringing in the topic of legislation marginally in the headings is a study of Bentham's utilitarianism, in relation to his ideas of liberty, by Douglas G. Long, who devotes a chapter to " 'indirect legislation' and 'matters of place and time'."[27] Other recent books that take up legislation in Bentham within broader studies, yet without highlighting utilitarianism or utility in their main titles, include L. J. Hume on "Bentham and bureaucracy." He treats government in a wide sense, inclusive of legislative capacities as well as executive, judicial, and other administrative functions, with particular regard to a Code. Frederick Rosen examines "Bentham and representative democracy," inclusive of sovereignty as concerns democratic theory, public opinion, and the greatest happiness principle.[28]

A host of other kinds of examples could be given of scholarly nonfocus on legislation *per se* in discussions on Bentham, not to mention on the two Mills (who are included in many of the above-cited works). Broader histories of legal and political thought often yield such examples.[29] Yet studies on Bentham have been typically preoccupied with such overriding "isms" as utilitarianism and liberalism. Similar patterns hold true for the two Mills.[30]

Thus the list of topics other than legislation itself that scholars of Bentham have focused upon seems virtually endless. They include the following: judicial and executive administration, bureaucracy, codification, crime and punishment, morality, utility, sovereignty, the state, jurisprudence, reform, command, economics, philosophy, democracy, public opinion, earlier versus later Bentham, judicial procedure, fictions, public interest, majority rule, property, justice, civil law, common law, religion, liberty, education, natural law, custom, happiness, and so forth. Among the innumerable "isms" singled out by scholars for special study have been, in addition to utilitarianism and liberalism, radicalism, reformism, constitutionalism, absolutism, despotism, capitalism, parliamentarism, bureaucratism, Victorianism, positivism, individualism, collectivism, industrialism, legalism, pessimism, optimism, hedonism, Englandism, secularism, revisionism, consequentialism, asceticism, atheism, anticlericalism, and behavioralism. Such lists for J. S. Mill would perhaps be even longer.

To be sure, legislation has often figured prominently in scholarly discussions centering on the above kinds of topics; this is to be expected owing to the pervasiveness of legislative issues throughout Bentham's writings. Yet legislation itself has not received due singular attention. Nor have the earlier sources for Bentham's legislative viewpoints been sufficiently explored. Contrary to J. S. Mill's criticisms of Bentham for not taking account of traditional knowledge, Bentham was significantly influenced by a wide variety of previous writers. Many of them have been acknowledged by Bentham experts. Such sources included Beccaria, Montesquieu, Blackstone, Hume, Voltaire, D'Alembert, Helvétius, and Hobbes. It would, for instance, be instructive—from present perspectives on legislation, the state, and systematic methodology—to take a close look at William Blackstone's *Commentaries on the Laws of England* and Gaetano Filangieri's *Science of Legislation*.[31] A lengthy list could be compiled of other writers to whom Bentham has been related by historians who neglect legislation. The sections to follow cannot fill these gaps; but if they encourage other historians to do so, they will have served their purpose.

3. BENTHAM'S *MORALS AND LEGISLATION*

In view of Jeremy Bentham's great interest in legislation throughout his long, productive writing career, it was symbolically appropriate that his life (1748–1832) began and ended in years marked by a seminal event in the history of legislative thinking. The year of his birth, 1748, saw the publication of Montesquieu's *Spirit of the Laws*. It contained many sections on legislation and related topics that were to influence Bentham and late-eighteenth-century thinkers like Beccaria and Voltaire, who in turn influenced Bentham. The year of Bentham's death, 1832, saw the passage of the famous First British Reform Bill, which marked a culmination as well as a new beginning of reformist and legislative impulses in Britain. Much has been written by historians about the relationships of Bentham's writings to those of Montesquieu, Beccaria, Voltaire, Hume, Smith, and others in the eighteenth century, along with basic documents of the American and French Revolutionary eras. Even more voluminous are the studies of Bentham's great impact on nineteenth-century viewpoints both before and after the British Reform Act of 1832. However, legislation *per se* has not been as extensively investigated by historians in these connections as one might expect, considering Bentham's absorbing interest in it.

Bentham's most celebrated and classic work is *An Introduction to the Principles of Morals and Legislation*.[32] It was first printed in 1780 and then published in 1789 with a long "Concluding Note," in which he expanded or updated his thought on certain fundamental legal issues.

This work must be viewed, as is generally recognized, within the totality of Bentham's massive collected writings (which with his correspondence is projected to reach over sixty volumes through the ongoing Bentham Project). In essence, Bentham's *Morals and Legislation* was an attempt to establish or introduce principles for a penal code as part of his intended complete code of laws (criminal, civil, constitutional, international), which he worked toward throughout his writing career. His rich, wide-ranging discussions in *Morals and Legislation* on legislation and methodology are especially germane for this series. Although morals or ethics are in general less treated by him, they bear interesting relationships therein not only to legislation but also, like legislation, to utility, which is the subject highlighted at the outset of the work. For Bentham, in distinction to J. S. Mill and James Mill, the principle of utility became singularly associated with "the greatest happiness of the greatest number." In accordance with it, Bentham sought to reform the system of punishments in England and other countries. This criterion of utility in matters of legislation involved a kind of public morality, with importance for individual liberty in relation to the community, whereas private morality is distinguished from the main legislative arena. The complex and difficult organization of *Morals and Legislation* progresses, in general, from an introduction to a penal code, then to a treatment of human action, and, finally, to a consideration of utility and its opposing principles, together with classifications of pleasure and pain. Utility largely becomes public utility, and individuals share in it. Bentham supplies sets of rules for legislators in constructing a penal code. His principles are also meant to be useful for those involved in the judicial system and in the administration of justice, particularly in determining punishments.

"The Art of Legislation"

A significant phrase that frequently recurs throughout Bentham's *Morals and Legislation* is "the art of legislation." Indeed, the frequent uses, throughout his work, of the phrase "principles of legislation," as found in the full main title, are often couched in contexts of "the art of legislation," which is thus central to the work. Many diverse earlier traditions and treatises lay in the broad background to Bentham's specific appropriations of these and similar phrases. Comparisons with other writers on this topic in the immediate eighteenth-century background to Bentham could be made at length and would include jurists like Montesquieu. But it would be shortsighted not to reach further back to humanistic-classical traditions of the Renaissance, which greatly influenced writers on this same topic prior to Bentham—such as Hobbes,

Harrington, Montesquieu, Domat, Conring, and numerous others already examined in this series. The art of legislation can be traced back to sixteenth-century works by Budé, Vives, Hopperus, Corasius, and Bodin, whose humanistic discussions were typically based on classical texts in Roman legal history. In general, Bentham showed familiarity in his *Morals and Legislation* with classical thought and traditions in relation to Roman law, Aristotle, Plato (whose *Republic* he cited from the Latin edition by Marsilio Ficino[33]), Ovid, Thucydides, Caesar, Justinian, Aeneas, Lycurgus, Solon, Alexander the Great, Homer, Mark Antony, Sulla, Tacitus, Virgil, and others, albeit often in critical fashion. More specifically, Bentham's usages and concepts of phrases like "the art of legislation," along with "the principles of legislation," were *sui generis* and shaped by the exigencies of his times and treatises.

The art of legislation, in Bentham's *Morals and Legislation*, encompasses the penal (or criminal, though Bentham draws some distinctions) branch as well as the civil branch of law and jurisprudence. In Chapter XVII ("Of the Limits of the Penal Branch of Jurisprudence"), the first section is entitled "Limits between ethics and the art of legislation." There he relates the art of legislation to the subject of ethics, in keeping with the work's title. The first of the (sub)sections (consisting typically of one or more paragraphs numbered consecutively throughout the chapter) states as follows (adhering here, as elsewhere, to his stylistic modes).

> [T]hat branch which concerns the method of dealing with offences, and which is termed sometimes the *criminal*, sometimes the *penal*, branch, is universally understood to be but one out of two branches which compose the whole subject of the art of legislation; that which is termed the *civil* being the other. Between these two branches then, it is evident enough, there cannot but be a very intimate connection; so intimate is it indeed, that the limits between them are by no means easy to mark out. The case is the same in some degree between the whole business of legislation (civil and penal branches taken together) and that of private ethics . . .

In the same chapter (XVII, 2–4, 8–9) of *Morals and Legislation*, Bentham elaborates on differences and relationships between private and individual ethics, on the one hand, and, on the other, ethics in a larger public sense of the greatest happiness of the greatest number with regard to the wider community. Private ethics as the art of self-government is distinguished from the greatest happiness principle of utility. The latter involves public utility and public ethics in relation to the art of government, which is here linked to permanent measures through the art of legislation as well as to temporary administrative activities. Although the art of legislation shares many features in common with the sphere of private ethics, as does the happiness principle, it cannot, or should not, interfere with it, especially regarding punishments, a crucial area of the art of legislation. In other words, the "limits" between private ethics and the art of legislation, which are underscored by the title of the first section, together with the "limits" of the penal branch of jurisprudence, which are highlighted by the title of the chapter, pertain to Bentham's deep interest in reforming the system of criminal justice and legislation. He seeks to prevent punishments from being unfairly or improperly imposed by the state on individuals in matters that should lie outside the purview of the state, thereby restricting the punishment imposed by legislation and its judicial interpreters. Bentham's discussions result in his making close connections between the state, the public sphere, and legislation, that is, between the state and public legislation.

> Ethics at large may be defined, [*sic*] the art of directing men's actions to the production of the greatest possible quantity of happiness, on the part of those whose interest is in view. . . . Ethics, in as far as it is the art of directing a man's own actions, may be styled the *art of self-government*, or *private ethics*. . . . [T]he art of directing their actions to the above end is what we mean, or at least the only thing which, upon the principle of utility, *we ought* to mean, by the art of government: which, in as far as the measures it displays itself in are of a permanent nature, is generally distinguished by the name of *legislation:* as it is by that of *administration*, when they are of a temporary nature, determined by the occurrences of the day. . . . Private ethics concern every member, that is, the happiness and the actions of every member of any community that can be proposed; and legislation can concern no more. Thus far, then, private ethics and the art of legislation go hand in hand. The end they have, or ought to have, in view, is of the same nature. . . . Where then lies the difference? . . . In that the acts which they ought to be conversant about . . . are not *perfectly and throughout* the same. . . . [Individuals are directed toward the happiness of themselves and others,] but there are cases in which the legislator ought not (in a direct way, at least, and by means of punishment applied immediately to particular *individual* acts) to attempt to direct the conduct of the several other members of the community. . . . If legislation interferes

in a direct manner, it must be by punishment. . . . [A note by Bentham here denies that rewards are acts of legislation, unlike, we may add, the viewpoints of Renaissance writers, who saw the art of legislation as comprising both rewards and punishments.] If then there be any of these cases in which, although legislation ought not, private ethics does or ought to interfere, these cases will serve to point out the limits between the two arts or branches of science. . . . [Bentham speaks also of judges as well as legislators making use of language.] [It is thus necessary to gain a] clear idea of the limits between the art of legislation and private ethics . . .

The whole history of jurisprudence is closely aligned with the art of legislation in ensuing statements in Bentham's *Morals and Legislation* XVII, 27-29. Here Bentham alludes to his advances beyond Montesquieu and Beccaria. Moreover, customary law tends to be engulfed in the wider art of legislation, along with statute law. Yet Bentham will draw distinctions between the two types of law based on his definitions of law, which are regarded by him as a new contribution. The relationships between the civil and penal or criminal branches of jurisprudence, with which the art of legislation is concerned as regards codifications of law, require, he believes, accurate analysis through clear principles of definition and division of law. It will be remembered that the tradition of the art of legislation in Renaissance and ensuing early modern thought often revolved around principles of definition and division, notwithstanding Bentham's claims to great innovation and originality.

The most common and most useful object of a history of jurisprudence is to exhibit the circumstances that have attended the establishment of laws actually in force. But the exposition of the dead laws which have been superseded, is inseparably interwoven with that of the living ones which have superseded them. The great use of both these branches of *science* is to furnish examples for the *art* of legislation [with a note referring to Montesquieu and Beccaria]. . . . [T]he laws in question may subsist either in the form of *statute* or in that of *customary* law. . . . [T]he difference between these two branches . . . cannot properly be made appear [*sic*] till some progress has been made in the definition of *a* law. . . .

Last, the most intricate distinction of all, and that which comes most frequently on the carpet, is that which is made between the *civil* branch of jurisprudence and the *penal*, which latter is wont, at certain circumstances, to receive the name of *criminal*.

What is a penal code of laws? What a civil code? ... To answer these questions . . . , it will be necessary to ascertain what *a law* is; meaning one entire but single law: and what are the parts into which a law, as such, is capable of being distinguished . . .

Throughout Bentham's *Morals and Legislation*, there are innumerable, seemingly interchangeable uses of the words "art," "science," "method," "system," and the like in his discussions on the principles or art of legislation. They are often reminiscent of terminologies in the tradition of Renaissance humanistic jurisprudence, which, as we have already seen, carried over into the seventeenth and eighteenth centuries. Among Bentham's many diverse usages of such terms as also found in Renaissance jurisprudence are those pertaining to "distribution" and "proportion." The quest for a due "proportion" between offenses and punishments and for a proper "distribution" in such matters as rewards and punishments—topics of great concern for Bentham in his art of legislation—had newly occupied Renaissance humanistic jurists like Bodin and their successors like Domat and Montesquieu. Bentham was here indebted, directly or indirectly, to earlier traditions, which seem to have influenced him in part through the works of Montesquieu, Beccaria, Blackstone, and others in the eighteenth century.

"Without legislation there would be no such thing as a *state*"

This striking quotation that forms the heading for our examination of Bentham's legislative state in his *Morals and Legislation* is found in Chapter XVII, 18, in the midst of his disquisitions on "the art of legislation." His statement's fuller context is tied, once more, to his quest for legal and legislative reforms, which impels much of his treatise. Bentham is again *sui generis* yet builds upon tradition as much as he departs from it. The pervasiveness of legislation in a state, as well as its limits, is manifest in the following wider passage in XVII, 18. What most accrues to the state as an actual public thing, which is independent unto itself, is legislation, that is, public legislation. It is in the public arena of the state that the legislator is guided by what is expedient, while private ethics of the citizens are a separate matter.

The rules of *probity* are those, which in point of expediency stand most in need of assistance on the part of the legislator, and in which, in point of fact, his interference has been most extensive. There are few cases in which it *would* be expedient to punish a man for hurting *himself:* but there are few cases, if any, in which it would *not* be expedient to punish a man for injuring his neighbour. With regard to that branch of probity which is opposed to offences against property, private ethics depends in a manner for its very existence upon legislation. Legislation must first determine what things are to be regarded as each man's property, before the general rules of ethics, on this head, can have any particular application. The case is the same with regard to offences against the state. Without legislation there would be no such thing as a *state:* no particular persons invested with powers to be exercised for the benefit of the rest. It is plain, therefore, that in this branch the interference of the legislator cannot any where be dispensed with. We must first know what are the dictates of legislation before we can know what are the dictates of private ethics.

The centrality of legislation for the state is evident in Bentham's ensuing discussion in *Morals and Legislation* XVII, 20. He identifies the art of legislation with the public or collective affairs of men in a state or community, as distinct from private ethics of its individual members. In fact, the legislator is the guiding or determining force behind the utility of the principle of happiness and well-being in the state, without whom the state would not properly be a state.

To conclude this section, let us recapitulate and bring to a point the difference between private ethics, considered as an art or science, on the one hand, and that branch of jurisprudence which contains the art or science of legislation, on the other. Private ethics teaches how each man may dispose himself to pursue the course most conducive to his own happiness, by means of such motives as offer of themselves: the art of legislation (which may be considered as one branch of the science of jurisprudence) teaches how a multitude of men, composing a community, may be disposed to pursue that course which upon the whole is the most conducive to the happiness of the whole community, by means of motives to be applied by the legislator.

So compelling and concrete an entity is legislation for Bentham that it serves as the most substantial mainstay of jurisprudence, which otherwise for him is a fictitious entity. Jurisprudence has for its most crucial aspect the subject of legislation, as treated in a variety of ways that relate in particular to the nation-state. Even law itself is an abstract entity for Bentham, until its core relationship to legislation is duly apprehended. This means that the laws of a particular nation-state cannot be fully justified or even defined without recourse to the most elemental ingredient, legislation. Here enters Bentham's self-proclaimed originality in defining the term "law" itself, even though the various other national linguistic equivalents for it (in French, German, etc.) were of course age-old. The very definitions of "law" in all major European languages except English serve to reinforce, for Bentham, the concrete quality of legislation as distinct from the abstract quality of right and justice. He feels compelled to develop the treatise at hand in order to establish in English law and jurisprudence the central defining importance of legislation for the state. These points are brought out in *Morals and Legislation* XVII, 21–24.[34]

When Bentham calls jurisprudence a fiction and law an abstraction unless or until they are grounded in legislation, he goes to the heart of why he can say, as in the quotation that forms the heading for our present discussion, that there would be "no such thing" as a state if it were not for legislation. That is to say, the state's legislative base is what makes it a concrete public "thing" rather than a fictitious or abstract concept. Take away public legislation, and the state, like jurisprudence and law, would lack various substantial foundations. At the same time, Bentham is typically intent on giving not only newfound legislative supports to the state but also newfound legislative limitations upon it, beyond which public authority cannot encroach into private morality more than is reasonable, just, expedient, or effectual. Reforming past and current abuses was at least as much his aim in *Morals and Legislation* as was strengthening the state's hand in achieving those ends. Too often, scholars have emphasized Bentham's outlook on the state's improper encroachments on individuals without calling sufficient attention to Bentham's ultimate reliance on the state's legislative power to achieve his intended good goals. (Nevertheless, his partial indebtedness to the absolutism of Hobbes on sovereignty and state as well as to the enlightened despotism of Voltaire and others on legislation and codification has occasionally been glimpsed.[35])

Further perspectives on Bentham's understanding of the legislative state come into view in Chapter XVI of *Morals and Legislation* entitled "Division of Offences," in combination with Chapter XVII ("Limits of . . . Penal . . . Jurisprudence . . ."). At the end of the preceding chapter (XV), he terms this "a general survey of the system of offences." He aims at new solutions or systems in realization of the old commonplace about letting the punishment fit the crime (or offense). His goal is the establishment of a legislative system, science, or art that will ensure proper "proportions" between the dual elements of punishment and crime in a state or community. In various passages of Chapter XVI, Bentham propounds the main idea of the state as a public entity, in which individuals share a common or higher bond and interest, as distinct but not inseparable from each of the individuals composing it. Public offenses can pertain to a wide area of the state's sphere, including sovereignty, national interest, the public force, and religion. Government itself can be a perpetrator of mischief if it exceeds its legitimate authority, or it can be offended against by other outside activities or influences. Individuals, however, should not impede the legitimate and efficient operations of the government—which is here paired with the sovereignty of the person or group in control—in regulating the affairs of citizens and the activities of the public sphere. Here everything is directed, in one way or another, to principles of legislation. Bentham outlines the limits needing to be imposed on legislators as a check against their interfering with individuals on questions of private ethics, over which, nevertheless, legislators can ideally have a beneficial but limited guiding influence. The legislator cannot hope to extirpate such conduct as drunkenness or fornication. (Here Bentham falls far short of, say, American legislators who sought, at different points in U.S. history, to introduce prohibition against alcohol and adultery.) Legislators should not seek to regulate the lives of individuals in excessive ways that hamper their basic liberties, especially by imposing punishments in such matters where penalties have little chance of being successful deterrents. Legislators must be motivated not by their own passions and proclivities but by the rigors of a sensible system of legislation itself. A case in point is provided by religion, the terms of which are difficult and undesirable to regulate (notably after the manner of either Catholic or Protestant zealots over the centuries). The principle to follow is that which is expedient, or the utility principle, rather than such a phenonenon as sympathy (which was Hume's guiding principle and which Bentham criticizes at numerous points throughout the work in favor of utility). Here Bentham takes issue with the French king Louis XIV's revocation of the Edict of Nantes.[36]

The Four Causes and the Efficient "Maker"

Another testament to Bentham's exploitation of various traditional topics that have been studied in this series is his treatment of the four causes and in particular the efficient maker, in *Morals and Legislation*, where efficient causation becomes a vital part of the art of legislation. An illustrative passage develops the metaphor of the artist who works on the materials in order to produce a form for the sake of an end.

Bentham's metaphor involves not only the science of law but an art of legislation. The passage to follow is noteworthy for its prominent place in Bentham's Preface to the work as a whole. It is preceded or introduced by comments on Aristotle, art or science, and the logic of the will. We shall return to this close relationship between the will and the efficient maker in art with regard to Bentham's renewed interest in command, which furnished useful precedents for later writers like John Austin and for positivism as a partial outgrowth of utilitarianism. The passage on the metaphor of the artist is given below in its fuller context so as to provide a reference point for those other related topics. Here it is partly Bentham himself who becomes the artist whom he depicts as endeavoring to make a new system of the principles of legislation. Alluding to the making of a code of laws, Bentham sounds himself like a legislator-artist. Bentham's reactions to Aristotle, here and elsewhere in the treatise, on the will and other topics may belie Bentham's claims to originality and reveal a key source for his thinking on the efficient and other causes (reminiscent of Hobbes' castigations of the Aristotelians on such matters when incorporating their ideas).

> Shreds and scraps of real law, stuck on upon that imaginary ground, compose the furniture of every national code. What follows?—that he who, for the purpose just mentioned or for any other, wants an example of a complete body of law to refer to must begin with making one.
>
> There is, or rather there ought to be, a *logic* of the *will*, as well as of the *understanding:* the operations of the former faculty, are neither less susceptible, nor less worthy, than those of the latter, of being delineated by rules. Of these two branches of that recondite art, Aristotle saw only the latter: succeeding logicians, treading in the steps of their great founder, have concurred in seeing with no other eyes. Yet so far as a difference can be assigned between branches so intimately connected, whatever difference there is, in point of importance, is in favour of the logic of the will. Since it is only by their capacity of directing the operations of this faculty, that the operations of the understanding are of any consequence.
>
> Of this logic of the will, the science of *law*, considered in respect of its *form*, is the most considerable branch,—the most important application. It is, to the art of legislation, what the science of anatomy is to the art of medicine: with this difference, that the subject of it is what the artist has to work *with*, instead of being what he has to operate *upon*. Nor is the body

politic less in danger from a want of acquaintance with the one science, than the body natural from ignorance in the other. . . .

Such then were the difficulties: such the preliminaries:—an unexampled work to achieve, and then a new science to create: a new branch to add to one of the most abstruse of sciences.

Yet more: a body of proposed law, how complete soever, would be comparatively useless and uninstructive, unless explained and justified, and that in every tittle, by a continued accompaniment, a perpetual commentary of *reasons*.

More direct and elaborate use of the four causes and efficient maker in "artistic" productions occurs at the beginning of Chapter III in *Morals and Legislation* ("Of the Four Sanctions or Sources of Pain and Pleasure"). In III, 1, Bentham clearly posits the legislator to be the efficient cause (or means) that fashions or *makes* (Bentham's own emphasis in passage below) laws (which are elsewhere more explicitly identified with the forms or formal cause) for the sake of an end or final cause, which is ultimately and exclusively associated with the public entity of the state. The state is the collective community embodying the happiness of individuals taken together as the greatest happiness of the greatest number, upon which is based the principle of utility. The final cause places a necessity on the other causes directed to it. Here Bentham is following traditional Aristotelian concepts of the relationships between the four causes. (In the Renaissance the four causes were restored in their original contexts revolving around the efficient cause as maker, which had been obscured in the Middle Ages. Hobbes later adopted Aristotle's principles of the four causes and efficient maker in "artistic" productions, while in other respects criticizing Aristotle. Hobbes, again not unlike Bentham, built on principles of Roman law while in other ways attacking them.) In III, 4, Bentham closely joins his own use of the four causes with the sanction and "will of the sovereign . . . in the state" or community. In other words, will and making, as ingredients of the sovereign power of lawmaking, are interconnected with efficient causation as directed to the final cause or state itself. At the same time, the passages to follow from III, 1–2, 4 are couched in Bentham's own contexts of the principles of pleasure and pain.

It has been shown that the happiness of the individuals, of whom a community is composed, that is their pleasures and their security, is the end and the sole end which the legislator ought to have in view: the sole standard, in conformity to which each individual ought, as far as depends upon the legislator to be *made* to fashion his behaviour. But whether it be this or any thing else that is to be *done*, there is nothing by which a man can ultimately be *made* to do it, but either pain or pleasure. Having taken a general view of these two grand objects (viz. pleasure, and what comes to the same thing, immunity from pain) in the character of *final* causes; it will be necessary to take a view of pleasure and pain itself, in the character of *efficient* causes or means. . . .

There are four distinguishable sources from which pleasure and pain are in use to flow: considered separately, they may be termed the *physical*, the *political*, the *moral*, and the *religious:* and inasmuch as the pleasures and pains belonging to each of them are capable of giving a binding force to any law or rule of conduct, they may all of them be termed *sanctions*. . . . [Note: "*Sanctio*, in Latin, was used to signify the *act of binding*, and, by a common grammatical transition, *any thing which serves to bind a man:* to wit, to the observance of such or such a mode of conduct."]

If at the hands of a *particular* person or set of persons in the community, who under names correspondent to that of *judge*, are chosen for the particular purpose of dispensing it, according to the will of the sovereign or supreme ruling power in the state, it may be said to issue from the *political sanction*.

A wide variety of other passages in *Morals and Legislation* appertain to the foregoing and related topics concerning the four causes. Expounding in his Preface upon the overall divisions of the disciplines and subject-matters to be pursued in his project, Bentham calls penal law the means of achieving the ends proposed by civil law. The passage is also of value for its comments relative to science, distribution, proportion, legislation, and government.[37] In Chapter VII ("Of Human Actions in General"), the stated end of government is to secure the happiness of the members of society by a system of punishments and rewards, while the consequences of human acts provide the material (causes) with which the legislator(s) must deal.[38] In Chapter XIII ("Cases Unmeet for Punishment"), the utility principle is reaffirmed to be the true test whereby punishments in laws may be applied in order to correct actions running counter to the community's happiness, which is the end or object of legislation in general. Utility is the test by which legislators and others determine whether the basic evil of punishment *per se* is outweighed by the greater evil of the wrong committed, thereby justifying its application to the situation at hand.[39] Guided by the principle of utility, the legislator directs his laws to the end or object of preventing mischief by means of the punishments provided for by the laws. This viewpoint is expressed in Chapter XIV ("Of the Proportion between Punishments and Offences") when Bentham is emphasizing and examining the limitations or undesirability of punishments in various cases. The chapter's title bespeaks his overall concern to seek a due "proportion" between punishments and offenses, to which we alluded above. (Such terms as "proportion" and "distribution" in discussions of rewards and punishments were traditionally crucial to the art of legislation, going back to Montesquieu, Donat, Bodin, Corasius, Vives, and Budé).[40] In XVII ("... Limits of ... Penal ... Jurisprudence"), Bentham treats the form and substance of the laws of nations, including the ways in which they can be similar or vary from nation to nation. He remarks on the extent to which his treatise represents a kind of universal jurisprudence (applicable beyond the bounds merely of Britain).[41]

The placement of the "Concluding Note" in Bentham's *Morals and Legislation* is an involved story that lies outside the present scope. Yet the "Note" sheds further light on his uses of the four causes and efficient maker in relation to "artistic" productions as well as on his whole approach to legislation. Bentham labels the ever-present common law in England as being judiciary law more than legislation. He criticizes the laws of England and all other nations for being too lacking in system, too deficient in their expository matter and verbal form. This terrible situation in the existing science of legislation he compares to a science of architecture that attempts to proceed without fixed rules or nomenclatures. Neither science can truly be called a science, for each lacks a proper form as well as efficient maker. At present, he bemoans, legislators are like architects who lack a correct sense of how to build a building and of what the form of the completed structure should be. (Similar architectural analogies of how buildings should and should not be constructed were popular among Renaissance and ensuing jurists, adapting classical models devised by Aristotle and Cicero.) Too many bad laws, ill-conceived and ill-arranged, have been amassed in England and elsewhere, he believes, thereby obscuring the principle of utility (etc.) and producing enormous confusion. And nowhere is this tendency more prevalent than in the new American nation and in its various states.[42]

Utility, Command, and Will in the Lawmaking Power

Although the four causes and efficient maker have not had a *controlling* methodological role in Bentham's system, science, or art of legislation, they have helped him to shape it. They have aided him in articulating his concept of and emphasis upon the function of will and command that lie behind the act and activity of lawmaking, as directed by the principle of utility. The connection between the efficient maker and the lawmaking power has had a long history, much explored in this series. The notion that the making of law is an efficient act of making form from, or imposing it upon, matter for the sake of an end, which is identified with the state itself, went back to Renaissance jurists like Corasius and Bodin. They linked this efficient maker decisively to the notion of an inherent power residing in the lawmaker (usually seen as sovereign) and involving will and command (*arbitrium* and *iussum*); this inherent power of legally recognized bodies to make laws for their own affairs prevailed aside from questions of jurisdictional right as well as of higher laws of God, nature, and nations. Although by the time of Bentham the debate on these topics had changed, the traditional contexts just outlined remained vital in the seventeenth- and eighteenth-century background to Bentham. Like many of his predecessors, Bentham both built upon and departed from these older contexts, combining tradition and innovation in his own distinctive and influential blend.

What stands out, in accordance with the foregoing perspectives, is, in Bentham's *Morals and Legislation*, his interconnections between the three subjects of utility, command, and will in setting forth his art of legislation in its diverse modes. There is not space here to discuss the various complex ways in which Bentham's thought on this triad of subjects changed during his career or even from the original printing of *Morals and Legislation* to its final publication nearly a decade later, wherein an added "Concluding Note" addressed some new concerns. (This "Note" was originally appended as a "note" in more usual format but has been placed by the recent editors as a kind of conclusion to Bentham's main text.) Nor can his relationships to other thinkers of his period on these subjects be here recounted. It will be sufficient for present purposes to stress the well-known fact that Bentham's pronouncements on utility at times impinged on issues of command and in conjunction with will, especially in his "Concluding Note." These angles have not been as adequately pointed out by scholars as one might assume. It is above all noteworthy that the concept of command that was integral to Bentham's focus on utility became itself a focal point for jurists like Austin, who has been variously depicted by historians as a utilitarian, a command-theorist, a positivist, and a founder of the Analytical School of jurisprudence. Still instructive is H. L. A. Hart's insight that command is not the same as will in Bentham's thought but is rather one of four aspects of will.[43] The question arises from this viewpoint as to whether the command-theory of jurisprudence, which would occupy center stage in Austin's thought, originated far anterior to Bentham or Austin in the new accentuation of human will and power in Renaissance legal and political thought. Notions of command in the sixteenth century, from Machiavellian power politics to Bodinian lawmaking powers, often appeared in the context of human will.

Bentham's principle of utility in *Morals and Legislation* provides the key to governmental regulation through a system of legislation. The principle of utility promotes the greatest happiness of the greatest number in a community, which is a fictitious or abstract entity outside of its individual members, who must ultimately be bound together for the common benefit through a properly conceived system of legislation. Measurement and regulation of the ways in which human conduct augments or diminishes the community's general happiness must take into account the most defining elements of human behavior, namely, pleasure and pain, which determine all standards of right and wrong, cause and effect. Utility, in connection with a system of public legislation, which becomes the basis of the state, is the principle to be used for advancing the community's happiness. Therefore, all other values are subordinated to utility. These include what Hume had termed the principle of sympathy, to which, in his system, the concept of utility (and reason) was subordinated. According to Bentham, the opposite of sympathy, antipathy, must be regulated by a system of penal legislation that seeks to prevent mischief or criminal acts. As such, law is a dictate of utility, the only right principle (all others being wrong). Bentham is typically just as concerned to limit the state's power to do evil, which arises through bad laws not based on utility, as he is to strengthen the state's ability to promote general happiness, which is realized through good laws based on utility. Thus, Bentham can in general be seen as a "humanitarian" reformer, bent on harnessing the state's power for the noble ends of the public good rather than as someone interested in power and command in law for their own sake.[44]

The legislator's consideration of utility as the ultimate test of a law with regard to the community's happiness necessitates, according to Bentham in *Morals and Legislation*, the legislator's review of the relative goodness or badness of a given human act that the law is designed to cover. In determining the goodness or badness of an action, there must be determination of the intention or will lying behind it, the circumstances surrounding it, the person's disposition when doing it, and the consequences stemming from it. A full range of causes and effects must thus be taken into account, chiefly as to how they augment or diminish the happiness of the whole community. Such is what enables the mischievousness of an act to be determined.[45]

Although in the course of *Morals and Legislation* Bentham speaks of coercion and command,[46] it is in his "Concluding Note" that one finds the most cogent and abundant statements on these topics. Indeed, this "Note," added to the original treatise when it was finally published, redirected it along somewhat different lines, although the utilitarian and other impulses just treated remained important frameworks. Bentham opens the "Note" by asking anew what is a law and what are its parts. His concise answer represents another milestone in the history of the power to make law as traced throughout this series: "whatever is given for law by the person or persons recognized as possessing the power of making laws is *law*." This emphasis on the inherent power to make law underscores the legislative power as the law*making* power in such a way as to suggest the elements of command and will, which are indeed explicitly developed and underscored in his succeeding paragraphs. His discourses treated above on the efficient maker, in conjunction with his wider utilitarian philosophy of legislation, have obviously established a significant groundwork for statements like the one just quoted in his "Concluding Note."[47]

Bentham's "Concluding Note" in *Morals and Legislation* elaborates in detail upon the notion that laws are either coercive or non-coercive and that coercive laws are commands whereas non-coercive laws are revocations of coercive laws. Declaratory laws are not only not coercive laws. They are not even laws properly speaking, for they are "not the expression of an act of the will exercised at the time." The inherent law*making* power is thus emphatically one that performs a specific act based on will. This theme, albeit expressed here uniquely, has been a familiar one throughout the present series, especially in configurations of the efficient maker (whose action has related to the production of the formal cause and is preceded by contemplation of the end for which the form is to be created). Bentham expounds in new elaborate ways, within his utilitarian system, on how coercive laws create offenses and impose obligations. The "acts" involved in creating laws of different kinds, which establish offenses and command punishments, are more complex and even of a different quality than the efficient "acts" of law*making*. Yet the latter is a root concept not to be forgotten as Bentham's complicated but systematic classifications unfold in innovative other directions. He also distinguishes further between imperative and punatory laws in his quest for classificatory clarity and systematic comprehensiveness in the field of legislation.[48]

Bentham's "Concluding Note" marked a new key point of departure for conceptualizing the lawmaking power; at the same time, traditional relationships frequently prevail between the (efficient) maker, form, and matter in the production of "artificial" objects. This latter context has been inadequately perceived by scholars. The more elaborate systems of the four causes of law as found in earlier jurisprudence are not operative here. Yet Bentham's deceptively simple appropriations of this basic methodology must be viewed in conjunction with his fuller applications of the four causes in various (above-cited) passages earlier in his treatise, where they have likewise remained largely unnoticed by experts.

It is both the making of new legislation and the making of a code of legislation out of laws already extant that Bentham has in mind, in the "Concluding Note" of *Morals and Legislation,* when discussing command and expository elaboration with regard to the act of creating the proper form of laws from a mass of materials. For "commands endowed with the force of a public law" usually, if not always, require "the assistance of a ... [body] of matter of an expository nature." This is in particular the case when the short and simple command clause is too vague in itself to be properly expressive of what is intended or needed. Whereas "the imperative part ... of this artificial body" of "a general law" is necessarily short, the "expository appendage" needed to articulate it "may occupy a considerable volume." Bentham repeatedly employs the phraseology of material causation: the "mass of expository matter," the "masses of imperative matter" or of "commands," and the "mass(es) of legislative matter," and "expository matter." All too often, suggests Bentham, the inchoate materials of laws obscure rather than elucidate the distinctions between imperative and expository matters that are needed in order for laws to perform their function and to have their force. Every law is a command or its opposite (expressed earlier in the treatise, as cited, in terms of coercion and non-coercion or revocation). Bentham also invokes formal causation in relation to this material causation when pointing out how the "discovery" of the imperative part of laws is impeded by "the great variety of forms which the imperative part of a law may indiscriminately assume." That is, through "a multitude of forms of words" in a law, the imperative part or the command, which prohibits something, can become hidden. Thus Bentham seeks to establish a proper "method" in order not only that new legislation will be clearly made, with its commands clearly stated, but also that a new "complete body [or code] of laws" should be made to help give a proper "structure" to such matters. From the existing lack of such forms, he complains, results the current "obscurity" or confusion between civil and penal laws, as well as between imperative and expository parts of laws. To this grouping he also adds constitutional law.[49]

Roman Law Compared

There have been many direct and indirect correspondences cited above between Bentham's jurisprudence in *Morals and Legislation* and traditional jurisprudence as examined in this series. Most strikingly, they have concerned the art of legislation, the four causes and efficient maker, systematization, and the legislative state. It will naturally be asked to what extent Roman law played a part. One will recall the central place of Roman law in the disparate attempts of many earlier jurists to systematize legislation into an art or science arranged around its promulgation, forms, forces, interpretation, and the like. The question arises as to whether Bentham in *Morals and Legislation* was decidedly inspired by Roman law when dealing with these specific legislative topics. Earlier cases in point already examined have included Corasius in the sixteenth century, Donat in the seventeenth century, and Montesquieu in the eighteenth century. Against that vital backdrop, Bentham's actual references to Roman law in *Morals and Legislation* may seem a pale shadow. Yet one also remembers the diverse multitudinous examples already encountered of early modern legal and political writers for whom Roman law furnished rich topics in legislation, methodology, and so forth when formulating their own ideas. Even when they utilized Roman law as a comparative illustration for showing what was wrong about a legal system and in need of reform, as well as what was right and in need of emulation, the impact of Roman law was often crucial for them in devising their own principles. This held true for Renaissance jurists like Corasius and Bodin. On them, in matters of legislation, sovereignty, state, and system, Roman law exerted a powerful influence as a negative as well as positive model, as a system to react against as well as to build upon. The same applies to many ensuing legal writers, such as Montesquieu, in their own distinctive ways.

These historical perspectives help one in understanding Bentham's handling of Roman law, but it must be studied through specific points and passages in his *Morals and Legislation*. In the course of his discussions on legislative topics in his "Concluding Note," Roman law serves as an important if not controlling comparative model for his general treatment of the relationships between penal and civil codes of legislation, especially regarding the differences between imperative and expository matters in laws. The fuller context must be grasped. To the question, *"What parts of the total mass of legislative matter belong to the civil branch, and what to the penal?",* Bentham responds within the framework of how the "legislative matter" would be "drawn up" and "distributed" between civil and penal codes. His response is that although a civil code would necessarily include some penal laws, just as a penal code would include some civil laws, a civil code would contain expository matter while omitting imperative matter, which would be contained in the penal laws of the penal code. Bentham first illustrates these and related points with references to the recent codes of Maria Theresa of Austria and Frederick II of Prussia.[50] However, Bentham's illustration of such a code gone awry is Justinian's *Corpus Iuris Civilis*. In it the penal part was buried under the civil part, while imperative matter was smothered by expository materials. Command and will were obscured by opinions, due not only to the Roman compilers but even more so to the medieval commentators. Bentham states as follows (in "Concluding Note" #20):

> In that enormous mass of confusion and inconsistency the ancient Roman, or, as it is termed by way of eminence, the *civil* law, the imperative matter, and even all traces of the imperative character, seem at last to have been smothered in the expository. *Esto* had been the language of primeval simplicity: *esto* had been the language of the twelve tables. By the time of Justinian (so thick was the darkness raised by clouds of commentators) the penal law had been crammed into an odd corner of the civil—the whole catalogue of offences, and even of crimes, lay buried under a heap of *obligations—will* was hid in *opinion*—and the original *esto* had transformed itself into *videtur*, in the mouths even of the most despotic sovereigns.

Bentham then (in his "Note") alludes to the brief emergence of various forms (if not the substance) of imperative matter in law after the collapse of the Roman Empire; following this, he points to the need for a proper constitutional branch or code in addition to the civil and penal codes. He briefly focuses on the constitutional branch as it relates to legislation; the powers of various persons are established by permissive laws operating as exceptions to coercive laws—all of which should be aimed at the good of society.[51]

The usefulness of Roman law as a general point of comparison for Bentham is further attested in another passage of *Morals and Legislation* (XVI, 58, note). As in the passage above, the deficiencies and lack of true systems that he points out in Justinian's compilation of Roman law give impetus to Bentham's development of his own system. Whereas the above passage concerned issues in coercive or imperative legislation, along with the absence of a Roman system that could articulate them, the passage at hand in XVI, 58 revolves around deficiencies in Roman legal method or science that point up, for Bentham, what must instead be adopted in the new legal system envisioned by him. At the same time, it should be remembered that he finds most if not all other legal systems, in history and in his own era, to fall far short of his innovative approach. Bentham's new system is directed in more "universal" or "comparative" directions, beyond the bounds merely of English law, unlike, say, the methods of Coke. In this manner, Roman law supplies Bentham with useful points of comparison, in both methodology and substance, in both positive and negative ways. Occurring in a chapter indicatively entitled "Division of Offences," the passage at hand in XVI, 58, centered on Roman law, had wide applicability for Bentham on the need for "science" and "method" in arranging a new coherent system of penal legislation, which he felt had never before existed. The lack of such a system in Roman law served by inversion for him as a comparative device in pointing the way for the new system to be established. One again remembers how useful the comparisons (pro and con) with Roman law had been for innumerable previous jurists when weaving their own principles of arrangement according to systematic definitions and divisions. An interesting reference by Bentham, in connection with the passage at hand in XVI, 58, is to Johann Gottlieb Heineccius' *Elementa Iuris Civilis secundum ordinem Pandectarum* (1731). This reference, among others, serves to place Bentham's new method of reordering law, generally speaking, within long-established traditions of legal systematizations founded on Roman law, particularly Justinian's *Digest* or *Pandects*. Bentham's ready knowledge and incorporation of technical terms in Roman law further links him here and elsewhere in his treatise to civil law traditions. In addition, the age-old theme of the necessity of establishing a due proportion between punishments and offenses went back in time to Roman law and the *Digest* as well as to humanistic jurisprudence, albeit the theme was enunciated by Bentham in new modes.[52]

4. BENTHAM'S *LAWS IN GENERAL*

Originally conceived as an extension of the last chapter of his *Morals and Legislation* (XVII, ". . . Limits of . . . Penal . . . Jurisprudence"), Bentham's *Of Laws in General* was eventually projected as a separate work. Completed in 1782, two years after the former work was first printed, the latter was never published; rediscovered among Bentham's manuscripts, it was published for the first time in the mid-twentieth century. The complicated contours of its composition, dating, arrangement, scope, and place among Bentham's other works cannot be traced here. What is again required is a look at select salient features most pertinent to the present inquiry into Bentham's handling of various legislative issues. As a key factor behind sovereignty and the state, legislation is more directly and extensively taken up in Bentham's *Laws in General* than in his *Morals and Legislation*. However, because his *Laws in General* was originally unpublished and thus obscured from public view, in contrast to his acclaimed and influential *Morals and*

Legislation, it will receive somewhat less attention here. Yet its even more striking ideas on certain legislative issues, which were appropriated in his other writings, must be duly noted in ways consistent with this series.[53]

"[T]he *power of legislation* . . . must absorb . . . every other power . . . in a state"

The opening sentence of the first chapter of Bentham's *Laws in General* (I, "A Law Defined and Distinguished") firmly ties law in general to the volition of the sovereign power in a state, to which people are subjected. It reads in part: "A law may be defined as an assemblage of signs declarative of a volition conceived or adopted by the *sovereign* in a state, concerning the conduct to be observed in a certain *case* by a certain person or class of persons, who in the case in question are or are supposed to be subject to his power . . ."

What follows in this passage is one of the most sweeping or explicit ascriptions of legislative power to sovereignty and the state yet encountered in the history of thought covered by this series. Bentham himself suggests as much when going on in the same first chapter to identify legislation itself with his avowedly new application of the word "law" to broader areas than previously attempted. The "will" and "authority" of the "sovereign" is the key single element needed for a law to be a law. Law as such becomes expanded to include such phenomena as judicial orders, administrative measures, customary as well as statutory law, military and executive orders, and even domestic (household) orders, so long as they are not illegal by being forbidden by other orders.[54] Law is identified exclusively not only with legislation but also with legislative power. Legislative power is, in turn, explicitly and singularly identified with the actual act of *making* law as well as with sovereignty. Thus I, 4 (again adhering to his stylistic modes):

> Judging however from analogy, it would naturally be expected that the signification given to the word *law* should be correspondent to that of its conjugates *legislation* and *legislative power*: for what, it will be said, is legislation but the act of making laws? or legislative power but the power of making them? that consequently the term *law* should be applied to every expression of will, the uttering of which was an act of legislation, an exertion of legislative power; and that on the other hand it should not be applied to any expression of will of [*sic*] which those two propositions could not be predicated.

After elaborating on some of the ways in which various types of orders as just cited fall under the comprehensive category of legislation, Bentham in the first chapter of his *Laws in General* dwells on the commands issued by a corporate sovereign as legislative orders. Bentham expounds not only on the case of England but also of other countries, in addition to individual cities throughout Europe. His striking reductions of governmental powers to their legislative core in these cases extend as well as to ancient Rome, with material drawn from Cicero. (Citing Cicero's *De legibus*, Bentham closely associates *lex* in general with legislation and legislative command.) Similar observations by Bentham on cases where sovereign orders issue from a single person, as in France, likewise point to their legislative characteristics. The command resulting from all such acts of legislation through orders is what makes the order a law. This applies even in cases where the orders have not heretofore been clearly seen to be legislation by a sovereign, whether the sovereign be a complex corporate body or a single person; yet in fact the orders are to Bentham a form of legislation.[55]

The pervasiveness of sovereign legislative commands in the state is further demonstrated by Bentham in the first chapter of his *Laws in General*. A wide range of rules, regulations, orders, and the like that are not usually deemed to be legislation or commands issued by a legislative power are in fact just that, according to Bentham. These can be issued not only by a parliament or monarch, but by an executive as well as judicial authority, in addition to other types of authorities. Even those orders, rules, and regulations that are lacking in all but a legislative power to issue them, so as to put them on a par with actual legislation, can nevertheless, in some ways, be considered in the same category as legislation. Hence the scope of legislation in the state is all-pervasive. It includes, he believes, diverse areas of law not recognized or emphasized as such by previous juridical writers. Bentham acknowledges the considerable resistance that he will encounter by using terms like "law," "act of legislation," and "legislative power" in such areas. Rules and orders issued by a wide range of corporate bodies (towns, fraternities, etc.), no less than by magistrates, deserve to be called laws, even though they are not commonly so called. They are therefore issued by a legislative power having the inherent ability to make laws (commands) for their own affairs and deserve the name of legislation.[56]

On these latter points, the general partial parallels between Bentham and the Renaissance jurist Corasius are so striking as to raise the question of Bentham's acquaintance in some remote fashion with Corasius' thought. For it was Corasius who first underscored, as part of his new systematization of legislative topics, that any legally recognized body, be it a corporation, town, fraternity, magistrate, or whatever, has the power to make and command laws or legislation for its own affairs. Our first volume abundantly showed the great extent to which Corasius newly stressed, in these same connections, how the power to legislate revolves around the innate power to make law through acts of will and command, aside from questions of the jurisdictional right to do so. Corasius was relatively unconcerned with the higher law of God, nature, and nations when treating this specific problem. In these respects, Bentham seems less revolutionary than he declares himself to be. The pervading presence of sovereign legislative commands in the states does indeed receive fresh attention in Bentham's highly elaborate discussions. Yet Bentham's contributions form but the latest, more advanced stage in the long-developing history of thought on the legislative state. Many other general partial parallels can also be found between Bentham and Corasius, some of which we have already touched upon above in discussing the art of legislation and efficient causation. It is unlikely that Bentham was not familiar with Bodin's ideas on legislative sovereignty, especially through English writers of the seventeenth and eighteenth centuries; it is not implausible to think that the ideas of Corasius and his followers came to Bentham, however remotely, in Bodinian contexts. The indebtedness of Bentham's precursor Blackstone to such traditions opens up broad potential ways in which such ideas could have come to Bentham, albeit adapted to his own system. Yet Bentham's sweeping fixation on legislation still begs the question of a direct encounter with works by Corasius (and Hopperus).

Bentham's treatment of general vs. particular laws reveals further the comprehensive sovereign power of legislation in the state. When Bentham refers in the first chapter of his *Laws in General* to Cicero's *De legibus* (as noted above), the subject is Cicero's description of private laws in terms of their enactment as a kind of legislation (III, 19: *in privatos homines leges ferri noluerunt: id est enim privilegium*). Not altogether different was Corasius' own usage of such statements by Cicero and other classical authors on the same subject. Later on in his same treatise (IX, "The Generality of a Law"), Bentham expounds at length on the distinctions between general and particular laws, including them both under the all-embracing rubric of legislation, as enacted by the sovereign power in the state. Together they form the backbone of constitutional jurisprudence. Both types of laws are reducible to the issue of who has the power to make them. In Bentham's hands, a number of technical differentiations between types of legislation come into operation. At bottom, "the sum total of all the powers . . . in a state" reduces to the "sovereign authority" to make legislation, whether in general or particular cases. "[T]he . . . [sovereign] *power of legislation*

... must absorb ... every other power ... in a state." Once more, many further distinctions and qualifications come into operation.[57]

These latter forceful statements by Bentham on legislation's all-importance in a state prompt us to revisit briefly again some perspectives on Corasius and Bodin in the later sixteenth century, as viewed in our first three volumes. It will be remembered that Corasius newly emphasized that the power to make legislation is the highest power in a state and that this power was conjoined to the science of ruling a state through laws or legislation, as all related to aspects of command and will (*iussum, arbitrium*). Bodin vastly expanded upon Corasius' formulations. Neither jurist, however, went as far as Bentham does by insisting that legislation is not only the highest power in a state but also one that "absorbs" all others as their "sum total." Still, Bentham's far more developed formulations represent a significant advance that is at least as much a sweeping culmination as a radical departure. At the same time, few statements made prior to Bentham on the overarching importance of legislation for the state were as compelling as certain ones made by Corasius, together with his followers. In all the above cases, the conjunction between the legislative state and legislative sovereignty is apparent. It is nevertheless curious that despite the massive secondary literature on Bentham, inclusive of his legislative thought, little attention has been given to the kinds of statements highlighted in the two headings above, much less to their relationship with earlier Renaissance jurisprudence.

"No Customary Law Complete"

The striking title of Bentham's Chapter XV in *Laws in General*, "No Customary Law Complete," serves here as a rubric for grappling with his positions on custom and its relation to legislation. The two quotations utilized above in our two preceding headings indicated, respectively, the all-importance of legislation first for the state and second for sovereignty, according to Bentham. The quotation in the heading immediately above points up the counterbalancing devaluation of customary law in the hands of Bentham. Just as his heavy accent on legislation represents a new high point in the long-developing interest of jurists in that subject, his deemphasis of custom presents a milestone in the evolving subordination of custom to legislation. The earlier history of these two topics was traced in our first three volumes.

In essence, for Bentham, custom is not properly a law at all, for he defines and describes law in terms of legislation, which custom is assuredly not. He begins Chapter XV by declaring that customary law, unlike statutory law (treated in his preceding chapter, XIV, "Idea of a

Complete Law"), has no clear words, parts, rules, right or wrong, and so on. "[A]ll is uncertainty, darkness, and confusion." Customary law cannot be understood of itself, unlike statute law, without recourse to some other outside explanation. An account of it must be rendered by somebody "in the place of a legislator." Judges supposed to take account of cases that come before them never truly do so, but instead pass down this task to subordinates, who put together a history of the case in the form of a "record" as "copied from precedents of the darkest antiquity." The record thus becomes partly "imperfect," "false," "irrelevant," and "unintelligible." Judges do not inspect these records and histories with any care, and their relation to the case at hand is typically loose and indeterminate, a matter of "accident." Few of these records ever become law, and the rest become "waste paper." In addition to these "useless" "documents," there are "reports." These are rarely published, and, if they are, "nobody cares." A bookseller of such "reports" unknowingly "becomes a legislator," showing how valueless the whole exercise is. Sometimes a judge long dead is resurrected as an authority by later judges and "takes his seat on the throne of legislation, overturning the establishments of the intervening periods, like Justinian brought to life again at Amalfi." This interesting reference to the discovery of the *Corpus Iuris Civilis* in 1137 A.D. is tied here to one citing Cicero's stern criticisms of private law, which are compared to similar deficiencies in customary law. Bentham fulminates further against the heaps of records and reports that are all contradictory within and between themselves like "scattered atoms." They are so far from being laws that still another stage is necessary in order to establish some semblance of rules—the working up of "treatises." "[A]nd here again the bookseller . . . share[s] in . . . legislation." Summarizing his sarcasms against records, reports, and treatises, Bentham calls them "the shadow of the shadow of a shade" that passes for law but is not.[58]

In the same chapter of *Laws in General*, Bentham derides the practitioners of customary law who attempt to derive "general rules" from the kinds of "data" just described. Even principles or rules drawn from the "precedent" of custom that invoke the *salus reipublicae*, which is at root a term of "utility," fall short of the justice, equity, or law claimed for them, according to Bentham. He scoffs at the "enlightened reason" that produces such visions of "common or customary law" in every country. He is particularly critical of English judges who do not publish their laws and who prevent others from doing so, whereas even the Roman emperor Caligula fared better on both scores. Hence customary laws and rules of "common law" are "a fiction from beginning to end." Nobody can tell what they are.[59]

"*Utilitarianism*" *(Ch. II)* / 51

In Chapter XIII ("Signs of a Law") in his *Laws in General*, Bentham points out that law or legislation is an "expression of will," whereas customary law is not based on "an act of the will" such as a legislator manifests when making a law. On this and related points, "the nature of those laws which are here called customary" (the term itself being for Bentham an intended misnomer that points up deficiencies in the subject) "seems hardly to have been hitherto" "understood." They are, in effect, "autocratic acts" of "interpretation" that have at best the vague semblance of law. The obvious longtime fallacy of calling custom "unwritten law," when in fact it is written, is driven home by Bentham's pungent denunciation of unwritten law on grounds that it is formulated by those who can neither write nor speak and is suitable not for "civilized" people or even "barbarians" but rather for "brutes." Books of customary or so-called unwritten law are written not "by the legislator but by private individuals" and are "unauthoritative jurisprudence." The peculiar lack in the English language of the more exact distinction found in the Latin, French, and German languages between law and right (*ins-lex*, etc.) has enabled custom wrongly to be called law. Only a "forgery," he feels, could make it appear as such.[60]

"[T]he whole business of the art of legislation"

That Bentham's *Laws in General* (as an extension of his *Morals and Legislation*) revolves around the art of legislation is further attested in a separate manuscript section that was meant to provide a concluding summary of or focal point for the work.[61] Its first numbered paragraph, consisting of two long sentences, begins by noting the work's concern primarily with penal law and secondarily with civil law. The latter subject is necessary to fathom, he believes, in order to arrive at a proper understanding and arrangement of the former, "so arduous . . . is the business of arrangement." The statement thereafter made is that it is now necessary "to give a sort of analytical sketch of the whole business of the art of legislation." This is followed in the second numbered paragraph by Bentham's observation that the art of legislation is in general aimed at promoting the community's happiness. The third, lengthier paragraph states that the first of two instruments for achieving this aim is coercion, which is either physical or moral, the latter being accomplished through punishment.[62]

In these and other connections, Bentham's ensuing comments, dealing with a wide array of subjects, includes considerations of various traditional yet here reformulated categories. They are as follows: persons, things, and actions (especially with regard to one's power); duties or obligations (as fictitious entities resulting from laws or acts, which are real entities); and rights as distinct from commands (the former being a fiction resulting from duty and the latter being a more real entity connected with law). Thus laws issue commands, which create duties from which result rights, a source of power. Bentham deems his method of defining fictitious entities to be completely new and indispensable for legislators, who without it have previously stumbled in the dark with confusion.[63]

The last chapter (XIX) of Bentham's *Laws in General* is entitled "Uses of the Eighteen Preceding Chapters" and is closely related to the appended summary just cited. Here the orienting role of the art of legislation is further manifested. Bentham seeks to demarcate penal from civil law in a "complete body of laws" through a "method of division" with "natural and universal principles." Bentham seeks thereby to upgrade the "trackless wild" of the "field of legislation" and to "guide" "the legislator" in avoiding countless pitfalls. The complexities of customary laws would thus be reduced to manageable form, especially under the lead of statutory law, and the confusions of expository or interpretative jurisprudence would be put aside. By placing this new system on a comparative universal foundation, adaptable to all countries, Bentham strives to improve upon and to make available for everyone "the most important art of all, the art of legislation." The "method of teaching" it will also be enhanced and spread. Themes of command and obligation are again raised. For they are the basis of the penal branch, which together with the civil branch should form a necessary part not just of a complete "new code" of law but of each individual law. Within the "one book" containing this proposed code of laws will be found all requisite rights and duties. The "digestion" of the chaotic and ill-conceived customary laws will take place within this framework of statutory law. Further traditional adaptations of the principles of legal systematization found in Justinian's compilation of Roman law are here intimated by Bentham in calling for worldwide efforts to develop a "universal *harmony of the laws*" in "systems of legislation confronted together." Bentham's treatise is directed to the utility of legislation in conjunction with its ends, as is plain in the last sentence of Chapter XIX (and of the treatise proper).[64]

The overall organization of the chapter topics in Bentham's *Laws in General* illuminates his focus on the art of (arranging principles of) legislation. The sequence of chapter headings beginning with Chapter II conforms to the sequence of the "divisions" of law or legislation that he announced at the beginning of Chapter I when giving the "definition" of law or legislation. Those chapter headings include the following: II, "Source of a Law"; III, "Ends which a Law May Have in View"; IV, "Subjects of a Law"; V, "Objects of a Law"; XI, "Force of a Law"; XIV,

"Idea of a Complete Law"; and XVII, "Division of the Laws into Civil and Criminal." Such organizations of topics in the art of legislation recall to mind some distant parallels. The divisions of the art of legislation innovatively employed by Corasius in the sixteenth century revolved around the promulgation, forms, forces, and interpretation of legislation. They were later strongly echoed by Domat in the seventeenth century. Both cases rested on reworked principles and arrangements of Roman law.

At the same time, one must again keep in mind the immediate background to Bentham's works provided by William Blackstone's *Commentaries on the Laws of England*, published in various initial editions from 1765 to 1769. That work, too, bore many interesting relationships to earlier principles and arrangements of jurisprudence in the traditions of Roman civil law. Bentham's continuing criticisms of Blackstone are too vast and complex to be treated here. It is sufficient to note that Bentham's pervading emphasis on legislation and utility marked a signal change from Blackstone's approach, as further remains to be seen.

5. BENTHAM'S OTHER WRITINGS

Comment and *Fragment*

Bentham's *Of Laws in General* of 1782 was arranged in innovative ways around topics in the art of legislation; much differently, his unfinished earlier work, *A Comment on the Commentaries* of 1774–1776 (unpublished until the 1920s) was closely patterned around Blackstone's *Commentaries* in a kind of running critique of its flaws.[65] The title of the first part, "Of the Nature of the Laws in General," matches that of his *Laws in General* and of Section II in Blackstone's Introduction. The sequence of topics in the headings under Bentham's first part are loosely related to Blackstone's and are as follows (with uneven capitalizations): 1, "Law in General"; 2, "Law of nature"; 3, "Divine Law"; 4, "Connection of laws natural, divine, and municipal"; 5, "Law of nations"; 6, "Municipal Law"; 7, "Of Government in General"; 8, "Parts of a Law"; and 9, "Interpretation of laws."

In the course of these discussions in his *Comment*, Bentham criticizes at length Blackstone's acceptance of Justinian's principles of Roman civil law revolving around such concepts of natural law as "living honestly," "not harming another," and "giving to each his due," as found in the beginning of Justinian's *Institutes* and *Digest*. To Bentham, Justinian and others since have erred by identifying *ius* with *lex*, or the reverse, and by resting law on "right" instead of on legislation, which Bentham bases on utility and command.[66]

The second part of Bentham's *Comment*, "Of the Laws of England," is divided into discussions of statute law and common law. He faults Blackstone's main division of English law into statute or written law and common or unwritten law.[67] This, too, was a somewhat traditionalist division. Antecedents for it can be found in the (Roman) civil law tradition as well as in the (English) common law tradition.

Bearing a close, complicated relationship to his *Comment*, Bentham's *A Fragment on Government*[68] was an outgrowth of the former work. It was first published in 1776, again prior to his more developed independent treatises discussed at length above. Like his *Comment*, Bentham's *Fragment* was still primarily a lengthy discourse on aspects of Blackstone's *Commentaries*, though from a different angle. In his *Fragment*, Bentham makes ever clearer that he is largely following, as in his *Comment*, Blackstone's approach in selected parts of the latter's *Commentaries* for purposes of taking issue with it. Bentham builds his own contrary interpretations, here at the outset of his writing career, around the core provided by Blackstone. More than he cares to recognize, Bentham builds as well on a multitude of traditions to which Blackstone himself was deeply indebted, notwithstanding Bentham's critiques of Blackstone in relation to earlier jurisprudence.

After the Introduction, Bentham's *Fragment* proceeds to take up the topics of "Formation of Government" (I), "Forms of Government" (II), "British Constitution" (III), "Right of the Supreme Power to Make Laws" (IV), and "Duty of the Supreme Power to Make Law" (V). The two latter headings reflect Bentham's burgeoning concern with questions of legislative sovereignty.

It is sufficient here to note that one of Bentham's main targets in his *Fragment* is what he perceives to be Blackstone's faulty definitions and divisions with regard to topics of legislative sovereignty. Yet his manner of reacting off of Blackstone's categories concerning legislative sovereignty points up Blackstone's own understanding of it (as a topic of long standing in early modern thought). Bentham in part was using Blackstone to help clarify his own viewpoints on the subject. Bentham's detailed and complicated critiques of Blackstone on this issue are not easy to summarize. He argues that the sovereign lawmaking *power* must not be obscured, limited, or somehow split apart by such competing or alternate terms as "authority," "right," and "duty," which have been inconsistently and illogically employed by Blackstone with near disastrous results. Already at this early stage in his writing career, Bentham newly perceives and stresses in myriad ways the place of legislative power, command, and utility with regard to issues of sovereignty. The sovereign lawmaking power should not be obfuscated or hampered by vague contradictory identifications of it with rights or duties to legislate. Nor should it be confused with judicial powers, for the sovereign lawmaking power is alone responsible for abrogation of laws. As a legislative function, abrogation is not transferable to judges (a point clearly and newly established long before by Corasius).[69]

Principles and Code

The four later essays written by Bentham in 1822 as preparatory pieces for introducing his projected constitutional code are of passing interest here. Edited later under the general title *First Principles Preparatory to Constitutional Code*, they were left largely uncompleted and unpublished by Bentham. They are entitled "Economy as applied to office," "Identification of interests," "Supreme Operative," and "Constitutional Code Rationale."[70] The first essay begins by relating the constitutional branch of law to the penal and civil branches and then establishes the greatest happiness of the greatest number as the end of government. That end determines the goodness of government (otherwise inherently evil) through its enactments of law.[71] Many complicated distinctions are made by Bentham on issues of legislative, executive, judicial, and other powers, but legislative capacities remain uppermost.[72] Efficient causation is also employed but in ways less germane than previously.[73]

Despite its many interesting legislative features, Bentham's *Constitutional Code* need not detain us here; its contents lie somewhat outside the mainstreams of ideas we have been pursuing, as has *First Principles Preparatory to Constitutional Code*. Begun in 1822 and published by him in 1830, the first volume of Bentham's *Code* comprises about a quarter of the fuller work left unfinished at his death in 1832. The project marked a kind of culmination of his decades-long efforts at reform and codification. The title that he often gave when describing his projected complete code of laws was *Pannomion*. It links him somewhat to the traditions that we have traced over several centuries concerning the need for harmony and concord in laws (*eunomia*) and the drive for reducing law to an art or system. The fuller title that Bentham assigned to his *Code* in the initial installment of 1830 is linked in part to long-developing traditions of universal comparative jurisprudence—*Constitutional Code; for the Use of All Nations and All Governments Professing Liberal Opinions*. The title also again reflects Bentham's novel or idiosyncratic cast of mind.[74]

As in his earlier writings already examined, yet in different complicated ways, sovereignty and the state are ultimately legislative in Bentham's *Code*. The complex divisions of authority into constitutive, legislative, executive, judicial, and other elements pertain to ultimate sovereignty in the state. The legislative authority clearly prevails, in order of sovereignty, over the executive and judicial authorities. The constitutive authority is sovereign over them all, but in intricate ways that point not only to the actual *de facto* ascendancy of the legislative power as omnicompetent but also to the ultimate *de iure* legislative contexts of the constitutive authority as linked to the legislative authority properly speaking. Such viewpoints relate to traditions in English political thought in which, as in the case of Locke, the people as ultimate sovereign in theory squares with the Parliament as legislative sovereign in practice. They relate also to French and other traditions on the constituting of states as an activity expressive of a legislative sovereignity, according to which the great state founders were also the great lawgivers. But again, Bentham's typically weighty, multilayered categories defy easy description.[75]

6. J. S. MILL'S VIEWPOINTS

Bentham's towering stature in the areas under present discussion cast an influential shadow across a broad landscape of writers in Britain throughout the nineteenth century. Bentham's most conspicuous influences were perhaps exhibited in the writings of John Stuart Mill (1806–1873) and his father, James Mill (1773–1836). J. S. Mill was more critical of Bentham than was his father, who had been an early staunch disciple of Bentham. Yet J. S. Mill was no less than they a utilitarian philosopher, though with his own distinctive viewpoints. He prided himself as being the originator of the term "utilitarian*ism*." His collected writings (in thirty-three volumes), far larger than those of his father, represent an imposing counterbalance to the output of Bentham. They include such classics as *On Liberty*, *Utilitarianism*, and *Considerations on Representative Government*. Together, this triad of writers laid a crucial foundation for the development of Victorian thinking on multitudinous topics including legislation (one still undervalued by historians).

Verdicts on Bentham: Methodology

J. S. Mill's lengthy verdicts on Bentham appear in his *Dissertations and Discussions*.[76] Mill attributes to Bentham great importance in the realm of methodology. Although he was not a great philosopher as such, says Mill of Bentham, his methodology of amassing exhaustive classifications and details marked a momentous "revolution." Bentham's rigorously systematic method of reducing subjects in morals and politics to their constituent parts introduced a new intensity of "science" that was not evidenced in the same ways in earlier thinkers on those subjects, including even Locke and Hobbes. Here Mill is speaking largely of Bentham's *Morals and Legislation*, which Mill quotes at considerable length. For Mill, Bentham's originality lay as a great reformer and teacher in these regards, bearing much fruit for ensuing thinkers. Mill expands as well on the schools of ancient philosophy that lacked this application of scientific methodology in studying morals and politics, something that he says Bentham for the first time introduced. Subsequent British philosophers, according to Mill, have been obliged to adopt Bentham's method of detail, whether they supported or opposed Bentham's particular ideas. At the same time, Mill underscores the rich early precedents, especially classical ones, for Bentham's method of division and definition. Plato and Bacon employed a systematic method here associated with induction; yet they and their followers allegedly did not apply it to morals and politics in the same exhaustive ways pursued by Bentham. (Here one recalls the Ciceronian methods of art and science, definition and division, system and analysis, that were deployed in the Renaissance systematization of civil law and were taken up by legal thinkers of the seventeenth and eighteenth centuries.)[77]

The first of J. S. Mill's two main criticisms of Bentham's weaknesses as a philosopher is that Bentham was not only contemptuous but ignorant of previous schools of philosophy. So overconfident was Bentham of his own intellectual powers that he judged all past thinkers by his own lofty standards and found them deficient; yet in Mill's opinion it was Bentham himself who was rendered intellectually deficient by his lack of understanding about all other approaches past and present, which his superiority complex engendered. However, as we have abundantly seen, and as Mill's own somewhat self-contradictory statements cited above granted, there were many significant precedents for Bentham's methodology. Indeed, as we saw, Bentham's ideas on system, art, causation, legislation, Roman law, custom, and so forth were ripe with relationships to earlier traditions. The question of Bentham's and Mill's knowledge of those intellectual traditions is too vast to be addressed here. Although Mill's criticisms on this score were partly valid, they were also greatly exaggerated. Mill was speaking from the vantage point of his own great interest in the classics, which went back to his earliest composition written at age six on Roman history. When castigating Bentham for his misapprehensions of Plato, Socrates, and others in his *Deontology*, Mill singles out flaws that have little bearing on the kinds of relationships we have explored between Bentham's other works and previous traditions. On the topics singled out in the present chapter, traditional ideas carried far great weight for Bentham than they do for Mill. A case in point is the art of legislation. To be sure, Bentham possessed greater interest than did Mill in law and jurisprudence; therein lay Bentham's real contributions, as Mill recognized. Yet in the above contexts, Mill's criticisms of Bentham must themselves be criticized.[78]

J. S. Mill's second main criticism of Bentham, closely tied to the first, signaled where Mill's utilitarian doctrines diverged most fundamentally from Bentham's. In short, Mill probes Bentham's personal isolation from all other people, present as well as past, which resulted from the peculiar circumstances of Bentham's life and temperament. These limiting life factors conditioned Bentham's one-sided emphasis on the principle of self-interest as the key to the human motivations underlying his concepts of utility and happiness. Mill lays particular stress on the need for individuals to value the wider good of others in society. Here, Mill's critique of Bentham's weaknesses is perhaps most telling. Yet one must place it in broad perspective, including Mill's very different personality and cast of mind. Given Mill's exaggerated if perceptive view of Bentham's isolation from all past traditions, Mill's similar deprivation of Bentham's isolation from almost all genuine feelings for other human beings (due to his robust self-reliant egotism) needs to be tempered by a similar caution and objectivity. It should not be forgotten that Mill's own utilitarian philosophy was taken to task by some opponents for being too materialistic, too little concerned with higher human nature, and even too prone to self-interest if not downright selfishness—all grounds on which Mill was here faulting Bentham.[79]

Verdicts on Bentham: Legislation

J. S. Mill expressed relief that Bentham's main contribution lay in his influential jurisprudential works rather than in his weak and limited ethical inquiry.[80] Yet Mill exposed Bentham's failure to develop a truly national system of law and government. This failing was due above all, Mill believes, to Bentham's inability to appreciate the higher distinctive character of people, individually and collectively. Hence Bentham could only deal with the purely "business" side of legislation and morality in society.[81] Notwithstanding, Bentham's great merit lay in his rethinking of English law—in its philosophy, practice, and relation to other systems. In fact, it was Bentham who succeeded in resystematizing English law, which before him had been a "jumble" of "rubbish," an "Augean stable" needing to be cleaned out. (Such phraseology was also used by humanistic jurists of the sixteenth century who decried the weakened condition of Roman law as handed down by older authorities).[82]

In testifying to the chaotic condition of English law prior to Bentham, J. S. Mill cited above all the hindrances imposed on it by long-developing accretions of custom. Here he shared Bentham's particular disregard for custom in the face of legislation, which he too felt should typically override it. Older, "barbarous" customs left by the "feudal system" became outmoded but were kept layer upon layer even into the eighteenth century, although they remained unsuitable for advancing English society. Comparisons with developments in Roman law enter here. According to Mill, English law had been shackled even by the legislature, or Parliament, which was dominated by oppressive aristocratic interests, and had been alterable in significant ways only by courts of justice. The judges, in fact, lacked power to make laws, properly speaking, but on that score they were often effective in circumventing Parliament. However, such "improvements" were achieved through "old forms" that were inferior to more truly legislative modes. When English law finally began to be somewhat systematized by lawyers, it was mostly the older, barbarous portions that were brought into better order. Even then, asserts Mill, the work was inadequate. The type of systematizing results that had been achieved in later Roman law were lacking in English law. Bentham thus found English law in chaos and reduced it to order. Not even Blackstone was able to accomplish a good reform of English law, contrary to his reputation for having done so. Bentham, says Mill, was the hero of the age who actually achieved this result.[83]

One of Bentham's chief accomplishments, then, according to J. S. Mill, was his codification of laws, in which he for the first time arranged them according to clear systematic divisions and definitions, without the kind of uncertainty and disorganization of the Napoleonic code of laws. This accomplishment by Bentham overlapped with four others: his viewing of laws in practical rather than mythical ways (vs. Blackstone, *et al.*), his clearing away of the vagueness and confusion in the body of laws, his systematic understanding of the exigencies of civil society for which the code of laws was designed, and his giving a near-perfect form to judicial procedures and judicial establishments, which before had lain in a wretched condition.[84] What Mill is here referring to concerning Bentham's codification of laws is not only Bentham's actual later *Code*. Mill notes as well the entire thrust of Bentham's writings toward systematization of laws, which was also manifested in Bentham's *Morals and Legislation*. This wide-angle view of Bentham's extended efforts to systematize laws or legislation is further operative in Mill's defense of Bentham from accusations that he, Bentham, was only interested in legal systematization *per se* without regard to the changing time, place, and circumstance of the content of laws in England and other countries. Yet although Bentham did see beyond mere uniformity in the principles and form of laws, says Mill, he failed to account for different national characteristics lying behind the laws. In the opinion of Mill, Bentham's inability to discern the different national characters (English, French, German, Italian, etc.) lying behind differing national institutions was not a real drawback to his work on civil and penal law, although this failing did adversely impact his writings on constitutional legislation.[85]

Once again, despite his criticisms of Bentham's limitations, J. S. Mill (as a fellow utilitarian philosopher) points out Bentham's great growing influence at the highest governmental and judicial levels not only in England but other countries as well. Especially influential, Mill believes, have been Bentham's principles and reforms of law and legislation.[86] Mill admires Bentham's tall stature in the minds of truly "radical" philosophers who uphold the place and power of the majority against contrary tendencies in democratic and other types of government. Bentham dwelled on checks against abusers of power so as to buttress the majority's preeminence. According to Mill (who is here wrong), Bentham neglected the nature of authority and obedience to it. Mill believes that Bentham erred by not duly considering the potential for abuses by an unrestrained majority. Here Mill has in mind Bentham's *Constitutional Code*. Allowing for effective resistance to a sovereign majority is no less necessary, for Mill, than is allowing for a sovereign monarchy or aristocracy. Indeed, Mill asserts that Bentham's labors would have been better exerted in this direction, along the lines pursued by Montesquieu, of whom de Tocqueville is now a more fitting successor. (Here, as elsewhere, Mill ignores Bentham's indebtedness to Montesquieu's ideas on such topics as the art of legislation. We have explored many such areas of Bentham's links with traditional knowledge, contrary to Mill's negative verdicts on his ignorance of it.)[87]

Liberty, Authority, and Laws

These last considerations are taken up by J. S. Mill in his lengthy, most famous essay, *On Liberty* (1859). Problems of legislation in relation to the state and sovereignty arise throughout the work in ways not yet duly appreciated and in ways more subtle and less single-minded than those found in Bentham's works. Mill begins, in general fashion, by highlighting his theme of the age-old struggles, going back to ancient Greece and Rome, between liberty and authority. At first, this contest was between the civil liberty of subjects and the authority of rulers in the government; more recently, it has been between the democratic majority, which eventually came to power especially after the French Revolution, and the individuals. The tyranny of the majority must be guarded against, Mill feels, as much as that of rulers. The (legal) limits on the power of the ruler and of the majority over individuals in a society and state is what Mill seeks to determine. Because Mill is not as singularly occupied with law and legislation as was Bentham, he is less consistent in his terminology for the state, which is, as we have often seen, a topic primarily oriented around public legislation. Mill often uses somewhat interchangeably terms such as "state," "society," and "community." A more singular resort to "state" occurs in Mill, as in Bentham, when dealing with aspects of law and legislation.[88]

In *On Liberty* J. S. Mill declares as his chief aim to determine the limits of society's control over individuals—that is, the limits of collective opinion over individuals—whether through legal, physical, or moral coercion. The sole end of any such control is self-preservation.[89] This issue is directly confronted in the title of Chapter IV, "Of the Limits to the Authority of Society over the Individual." Mill begins by framing the question with reference to sovereignty.[90] Mill suggests, typically, that a proper balance must be struck between the authority of society and the liberty of the individual.

The forces of custom and legislation are decisively weighed in Mill's *On Liberty*. Of custom he makes mostly a negative assessment here, for it operates as a despotic hindrance to liberty, progress, improvement, justice, and right. The tyranny of custom is in a constant struggle with the liberty of individuals as well as with the advancement of society for the benefit of all. Eastern countries offer here useful, more extreme, parallels for Mill with Western countries like England.[91] In a number of areas, Mill believes, legislation has exerted a deleterious control when enveloped in matters of long-established customs. Legislation that prohibits drinking or selling alcohol on the sabbath is a case in point regarding the state's illegitimate interference with the liberties and rights of individuals.[92] Rather than acting in concert with unduly restrictive customs, legislation must counteract them, albeit Mill does not precisely articulate this specific difference. Another case in point from this perspective concerns the continuing despotic control of husbands over wives, a situation that the state through legislation should work to reform rather than to reinforce. The state needs proper controls over individuals in matters where it grants them control over each other. Wives deserve the same protection of law as that enjoyed by husbands. Evils should not outweigh benefits in society's collective authority over individuals.[93] Other topics of interest to Mill on issues of legislation and reform include education and the Poor Law.[94]

Justum, Jussum, and Utilitarian Legislation

It was J. S. Mill himself, rather than, as he averred above, Bentham, who focused on checks upon authority instead of on authority and obedience to it. However, subsequent to *On Liberty*, Mill's essay *Utilitarianism* (1861) offered striking statements that fell into older patterns concerning the nature of a strong central authority. Mill's utilitarian outlook especially on legislation's key role supplied the contexts.

Chapter V of Mill's *Utilitarianism* is suggestively entitled "On the Connection between Justice and Utility." Mill begins by declaring as follows: "In all ages of speculation, one of the strongest obstacles to the reception of the doctrine that Utility or Happiness is the criterion of right and wrong has been drawn from the idea of Justice. . . . [T]hat word . . . to the majority of thinkers . . . point[s] to an inherent quality in things: . . . an existence in Nature as something absolute . . . distinct from . . . the Expedient [even though many allow in practice for some interconnection between the two] . . ." On issues of one's "legal right," Mill counters, "the law which confers on him these rights, may be a bad law," granting "rights which *ought* not to have belonged to him . . ." Mill later goes on to assert the following: "In most, if not in all, languages, the etymology of the word which corresponds to Just, points distinctly to an origin connected with the ordinances of law. *Justum* is a form of *jussum*, that which has been ordered. . . . The courts of justice, the administration of justice, are the courts and the administration of law."[95]

In the foregoing passages, J. S. Mill unequivocally sets forth his basic utilitarian doctrine in terms of utility or happiness as the main criterion of what is just or right in law or legislation through orders issued by command. When thus associated with utility and happiness in contexts of expedience, justice as a term and concept arises from commands, from orders in ordinances, that is, from enacted laws (in contradistinction to custom). Judicial administration of justice is thereby that which administers the orders commanded in legislative ordinances.

Most striking of all is the way that J. S. Mill has here viewed *justum* as being etymologically and conceptually a form of *jussum* in ways that remind one of the connections made by the Renaissance jurist Corasius (as cited in our Volume I) between *ius*, *iussum*, and *institia*. Corasius, too, had posited the derivation of some aspects of justice from command. Corasius allowed for the more abstract kinds of natural justice that are rejected by Mill, who does so avowedly as an empirically minded Englishman as well as a utilitarian. But Corasius had also looked remotely ahead to command-theory by predicating many facets of natural justice on civil justice as oriented around the sovereign role of the human legislator. To present awareness, there was no such legal connection made between justice and command in specific Latin terminology—including by Domat, Hobbes, and Blackstone—from the writings of Corasius to those of Mill. It might be found that Bentham generalized or postulated thus; but to present knowledge even he, despite his burgeoning interest in command-theory, was more limited, in his Latin terminology, to the distinction between *lex* in regard to command and *ius* in regard to law and right more abstractly (as cited above in his *Morals and Legislation*). Even so, Bentham was more explicitly attuned in these areas to Latin tradition than was Mill. It may be that on that score, Bentham was influenced by Hobbes' absolutist adaptations of Bodinian legislative sovereignty in the direction of later command-theory, beyond what Bodin and Corasius had glimpsed.

J. S. Mill's overall outlook on rationalist and empiricist methodologies is curious and somewhat ambiguous, combining elements of each for his own purposes. Whereas in the regular sciences particular points precede general theories, as Mill says in *Utilitarianism*, the reverse often obtains in the practical arts like morals and legislation; there, all actions are directed to an end. Mill does not hold to *a priori* abstractions, here or in *On Liberty*, for there can be no abstract right independent of utility. To the *a priori* approach, he contrasts observation and experience, which are likewise not exactly his own methods in spite of the role of expediency in his utilitarian philosophy. By identifying utility with happiness as a higher social value, beyond what he has perceived to be Bentham's narrower focus on the self-interest of each individual, Mill has assigned a kind of higher end in the practical art of morals and legislation. The public interests of the nation-state as conveyed in its orders (commands, ordinances, legislation, etc.) take on a permanent characteristic that links Mill with older thinking encountered in this series.[96]

On concepts of "utility" and "utilitarian" legislation, J. S. Mill is at times inconsistent and even frustratingly convoluted when faulting Bentham. He criticizes Bentham's lack of novelty in appropriating age-old traditions of philosophy. At the same time, Mill takes Bentham to task for a near total ignorance of and even antagonism toward all past and contemporary wisdom. According to Mill, however, Bentham derived all his doctrines of utility from other recent thinkers. Indeed, Mill goes so far as to claim that almost all past philosophers in all ages and within all schools of thought subscribed to utilitarian beliefs. Such contradictions and exaggerations correlate with Mill's belief in his own great role as the real originator of the terms "utilitarian" and "utilitarianism." Mill projects an image of himself as standing at the apex of an august tradition of thought of which he is the (modest) patron saint.[97]

It sometimes appears that J. S. Mill distances himself from Bentham in order to offset his self-appointed role as chief spokesman for the true meaning of utilitarianism, while at the same time putting Bentham forward as the cause of much of the criticism directed against utilitarianism by outsiders. Numerous cases in point occur in Mill's crucial chapter of *Utilitarianism,* entitled "What Utilitarianism Is." Mill begins with an uncharacteristically caustic denunciation of the "ignorant blunder[s]" of opponents. They fault utilitarian doctrine for being too simplistic in its association or disassociation of utility and pleasure, as well as for being too hedonistic in its stress on pleasure or too materialistic in its accent on utility. Mill's "apology" here to critics of utilitarianism for "so absurd a misconception" tacitly blames Bentham more than himself. Further on, Mill indirectly implicates Bentham as the person responsible for the erroneous charges brought against utilitarian doctrine by antagonists who see in it only a narrow self-interest. In defense, Mill goes so far as to exalt utility as a "morality" on a par with Stoic and transcendental values together with Christian belief in the Golden Rule. Recognition of the general good or happiness of the greatest number is foundational to the respect for one's neighbors as for oneself in the preachings of Jesus (who is portrayed here as a utilitarian). Bentham is also implicated in Mill's counterargument against opponents who say that the doctrine of utility is an expediency that is contrary to Principle and Right and that inhibits the redirection of self-interest to the higher public welfare and general happiness.[98]

In the final analysis, J. S. Mill places utilitarianism on a different level than did Bentham. Utility cannot be dubbed mere opinion devoid of the standards of justice. Justice itself, Mill argues, is typically conceived with different standards by different people with different viewpoints. What is just is usually no more certain or uniform than what is useful in society. He raises utility itself to a kind of justice. It rises above the merely expedient to be imbued with what is just in human sentiment in relation to the general welfare. The traditional idea of justice as the granting to each person his due must be understood in this fashion. The age-old principle that the punishment should be proportionate to the offense—which Bentham develops on the partial basis of intellectual tradition—here attains more firmly the standard of justice itself. It combines with the principle of voluntary good conduct by individuals in society.[99] In these contexts, Mill frequently refers to figures in Christian history, including Jesus, St. Paul, Luther, and Calvin, in addition to philosophers such as Kant, Fichte, Humboldt, Rousseau, Voltaire, and Comte, with allusions to the *summum bonum.*[100] It is curious that Mill made Bentham's lack of learned critiques of traditional thinkers grounds for disqualifying his thought on utility as a substantial philosophy of utilitarianism. For in doing so, Mill inadvertently exposed his own shortcomings, judging himself as well as Bentham according to idiosyncratic standards that Mill himself could not truly meet. (Here, as elsewhere, the added complications of Mill's legendary difficult relationships to his Benthamite father cannot be fathomed.)

7. CODA: THE EMERGING DOMINANCE OF PUBLIC LEGISLATION IN THE EARLY VICTORIAN STATE

The Victorian Legislative State, Obscured by "Isms"

The triumph or predominance of the role of public legislation through the sweeping reforms and acts of Parliament in Victorian England has not been adequately explored and underscored by historians. Their relative inattention to the underlying centrality of public legislation in the Victorian state is also apparent in their manifold treatments of the diverse political, social, economic, and cultural "isms" in the broader setting and background to these parliamentary reforms and acts. Nor have historians yet duly woven together the myriad legislative themes that interconnected the writings of Bentham and the two Mills with the momentous accelerating forces of legislative change that were sweeping down their Victorian century and impacting the "isms" associated with this famed triad and related groups of writers.

By "Victorian state" we are primarily referring to public legislation of a domestic social kind in England or Britain, not only during the actual reign of Queen Victoria from 1837 to 1901 but over the wider period from roughly 1815 to 1914. The "early" part of this period is here taken to extend through the 1860s, prior to the Second Reform Act of 1867 and the beginning of William Gladstone's first ministry in 1868. This "early" Victorian period coincided with the eras of Bentham and the two Mills. It extended beyond the deaths of Bentham and James Mill respectively in 1832 and 1836 to the conclusion in 1868 of J. S. Mill's brief Parliamentary membership and his death in 1873.

Historians have not yet put together with exactitude the legislative pieces of the governmental puzzle confronting them into a focused composite picture, the main component of which has yet to be revealed by them as, indeed, legislation iself. It is, first of all, generally recognized that the three British Reform Acts of 1832, 1867, and 1884–85 (still often confusingly referred to by historians as Bills, long after their passage) were great watersheds in English history. Their reforms of Parliament gave rise to successive waves of bourgeois and working class advances. The debates in and out of Parliament before, during, and after their passage testified to the new legislative machinery that was at work in reshaping British life and thought. The legislative foundations of the Victorian state laid by these three Acts were expanded by sweeping new enactments across a wide range of activities. This process culminated in the (proto-socialist) social legislation of the later Victorian era under Prime Ministers Gladstone, Lloyd George, and others. The early part of the Victorian century witnessed such new measures as the following: the Combination Acts (1824–1825) permitting various labor organizations, the Catholic Emancipation Act (1829), the Factory Acts (1833, 1842, 1844, 1847), the New Poor Law (1834), the Municipal Corporations Act (1835), the law finally abolishing slavery (1834), and the Home Act (1847) concerning women and children but effectively limiting the working hours of adult males.

It is, furthermore, widely understood that the famous (or infamous) Corn Laws on all grains occupied an increasingly central place as a *cause célèbre* in British political, social, and economic life in the first half of the nineteenth century. Struggles intensified after 1815, the year of Napoleon's final defeat, with the aristocratic resurgence and the growing popular unrest over it. As wide protectionist measures on agriculture and trade, the Corn Laws had been cumulatively adopted over a long period of time by the aristocratic landowners who controlled Parliament. Severe new measures were passed in 1815 against importation of foreign grains in general. The Corn Laws were not repealed, with free trade established, until 1846, long after the industrial bourgeoisie became ascendant in Parliament after the first Reform Act of 1832.

Although the interests and activities of Bentham and J. S. Mill corresponding to the above events have been discussed by historians, they have again not been sufficiently tied to the problem of legislation. It has been recognized that Bentham uniquely influenced Parliament's debates and provisions leading up to the reforms of 1832, passed in the year of his death. Mill was significantly involved in the public debates over the Corn Laws, especially in the 1820s, well prior to his classics of 1859–1861—*On Liberty*, *Utilitarianism*, and *Representative Government*—and to his Parliamentary membership in 1865–1868. Mill understood the central role of legislation in his early writings on the Corn Laws, in which his attacks on the landowners' selfish insensitivity to the interests of others in society set a pattern for those later classics upholding the common good—a legislative paradigm seldom appreciated.

Thus, the wide-angle lens of legislation, encompassing the above broad perspectives, needs to be brought into sharper focus by historians of this period throughout many disciplines. Secondary works centering diffusively in their titles and contents on such rubrics as the Victorian "government" and "constitution," including "the Victorian revolution in government" (an obvious echo of G. R. Elton's "Tudor revolution in government"), generally fail to highlight the dominating role played by public legislation in the Victorian state. This oversight has no doubt been conditioned by the relative disinterest of general historians in legislation *per se* (as noted in our previous studies).

Once again, Bentham was a signal influence behind early-nineteenth-century efforts at reform through (and of) legislation. Reform and legislation became his fundamental twin concerns. Beginning with Bentham and culminating with the first three great Reform Acts, along with the massive later social legislation under Prime Ministers like Gladstone, the role of legislation became uppermost. To be sure, a steady development of interest in and emphasis on legislation can be traced over the two preceding centuries of British thinking on sovereignty and the state. Yet the cautious views of a Coke or a Burke on the characteristic gradual evolution of law, in relation to legislation as well as custom, could at times seem as typical in England as the more radical legislative viewpoints of a Hobbes or a Locke. In any case, Bentham deemed his own contributions to point in a radical new direction that gave priority to legislation over custom for purposes of achieving needed reforms. Perhaps showing their own biases, many historians have tended to overemphasize Bentham's concerns about the potential evils of unwarranted legislative and other institutional intrusions on people's lives (a reservation also voiced in distinctive ways by J. S. Mill). Nevertheless, if England during this age became "the workshop of the world," legislation became the real "workhorse" of Parliament and the people, with Bentham supplying a crucial early guiding influence in theory. In promoting legislation in order to advance reform, Bentham eventually became an avowed "radical" bent on achieving some of the social goals of the French Revolution (though not its ideas on abstract natural rights). By contrast, Burke was a "conservative" who decried the excesses even of the early phase of the French Revolution long before the execution of the king. In the final analysis, however, the theme of legislation acts as common denominator for both Burke and Bentham, no less than for the other writers examined in our preceding book and in this one, albeit their myriad modes varied widely.

Contributing to the obscurance of the legislative theme have been the kaleidoscopic "isms" through the prisms of which historians have long viewed actual affairs no less than abstract ideas in early (and later) Victorian England. Such authorities usually take "isms" to signify systems or schools of thought or activity that bear the marks of an "ology" in the form of an ideology. If properly qualified and controlled, the use of "isms" should not be discounted as a limited partial tool for historians in presenting the background to or context for Bentham and the two Mills in broad political, social, or economic terms. But it would be problematical to view these three worthies or the legislative issues just mentioned through "isms" assumed to represent a clear system, school, "ology," or ideology from anachronistic perspectives of today. Such would obscure the underlying legislative factors that give unity and focus to the topics just indicated. Secondary literature on early Victorian England, and beyond, is frequently so drawn to political "isms" for their own sake that the theme of legislation often infusing them is lost from view. Representative illustrations are given below in the composite note to this section. Readers can readily recall some of the many secondary works that orient this period and its issues around amorphous all-purpose "isms" in politics and society. These include materialism, realism, idealism, progressivism, liberalism, conservatism, Toryism, radicalism, romanticism, collectivism, and individualism. However, they are typically found to have a legislative base with regard to issues of sovereignty and state. More specific "isms" like Chartism, industrialism, and socialism can perhaps be better employed as descriptive labels, but even then uncertainty often reigns in connection with issues of sovereignty and state; the underlying legislative denominator must again typically prevail.[101]

Origins of the Modern State?

In closing, it is not surprising that Bentham, Benthamism, utilitarianism, and the Victorian state have often produced modern models for medieval historians intent on predating the diverse modern features of sovereignty and the state, including legislation, to the Middle Ages. The results, however, have not been altogether satisfactory. Cases in point arose in our Volume IV. There, in Part I, we cited, for instance, the exaggerations of Professor Walter Ullmann in vaguely comparing medieval theories and practices of legislation to Victorian social legislation represented by the great Factory Acts. An earlier chapter there pointed out the hazards of anachronistically comparing ancient ideas of legislation to those of Bentham (and Hegel). Utilitarianism and Victorianism have long supplied modernistic models for historical analysis of far anterior epochs. With attempted caution, the present chapter has pointed to some partial, limited antecedents or parallels for various nineteenth-century viewpoints in the sixteenth through eighteenth centuries. The more far-reaching kinds of comparisons just cited need to be made more circumspectly in future if they are not to become so far-fetched.

The widespread conflicts and complexities in the vast existing historiography on the origins of the modern state, covering virtually the whole range of Western Civilization, has been noted throughout this series and further complicates the question or place of the Victorian state of the nineteenth century. The sequence of chapter titles in Part I of our Volume IV pointed up the need for broad comparisons in dealing with the state's origins in early European theory and institutions. Specialists who focus on a given period usually overlook conflicting historiography on "modern origins" in other fields. Those chapter titles queried as follows: "ancient origins?," "medieval origins?," "Renaissance origins?," "Reformation origins?," "post–sixteenth-century origins?" Then, Book I of Volume V explored questions about so-called "Machiavell*ism*" and the origins of modern states or "stat*ism*" in Medici Florence and Tudor England, showing how historiographical uses of these twin "isms" have obscured the deeper issue of the legislative state. Thereupon, Book II of Volume V delineated seemingly conflicting contours of historiography on the origins of the modern state in writings of the seventeenth and eighteenth centuries from Hobbes to Burke. Obscuring the true legislative scope of the state and sovereignty was scholars' concentration on innumerable generalized "isms" centered around absolutism, constitutionalism, rationalism, empiricism, liberalism, and conservatism. For example, a chapter of Part II therein on liberalism and the French Revolution again posed the question, "origins of the modern state?" Positive answers by many of those historians to that question have often contradicted medieval as well as Renaissance historians who have diversely claimed that the modern state originated in their fields. Not surprisingly, many historians of the French Revolution have located the modern state's beginnings in their own period, long regarded as one of the greatest watersheds in Western Civilization.

Once more, then, the seemingly irresolvable impasse posed by such questions and conflicts is due largely to historians' loose or "soft" definitions and explanations of what constitutes the "modern state." A more precise focus on the state or *res-publica* as a "public thing" characterized primarily by *lex publica* or public law in the form of public legislation would better enable historians to redirect the whole question to that of the legislative state's origins. Otherwise, the "modern state" becomes an unmanageably broad rubric. It has given many historians excessive latitude for finding, usually in isolation from one another and with conflicting results, the modern state's origins in virtually every epoch of European history from the Greeks and Romans to the French Revolution and well beyond.

Much of the historiography dealing in full or in part with the modern state's origins in Victorian Britain in the nineteenth century serves to conflute the aforementioned historiography on modernity's full-fledged pre–nineteenth-century beginnings. This discrepancy is intensified by the many historians of Victorian England who have found in the Reform

Act of 1832 and in the advances of the 1840s (contemporaneous with the Continental revolutions of 1830 and 1848 in France and elsewhere) a broad new emergence of the modern state encompassing diverse areas of politics, society, law, and economics. The preceding note (#101) offers many historiographical cases in point, to which countless others could be added. Some historians have employed such headings as the "triumph," "growth," "emergence," or "beginnings" of the "bourgeois state," the "liberal state," the "centralized state," the "constitutional state," the "administrative state," the "industrial state," the "parliamentary (democratic) state," and myriad related variants including "reforms" and "isms" of state. Such signposts almost never point to the "legislative state." They are mostly taken to represent new, even revolutionary, varieties of statism that uniquely originated or developed in the nineteenth century, with relative inattention given to antecedents in earlier periods. Many such viewpoints can be found in classic surveys like R. R. Palmer's *History of the Modern World*. Indeed, many historians postdate the modern or contemporary state's real origins to the period from 1875 to 1914, that is, just prior to World War I. The present book will consider the later Victorian era under leaders like Gladstone, which some experts view in terms of the "(proto-)socialist state" and similar categories. For now, it can be concluded that any such rubrics as the "utilitarian state" or "utilitarian*ism*" are obfuscating if they deflect scholarly attention away from the legislative fulcrum of the state's sovereign power to more generalized ideological approaches.

Chapter III

"Positiv*ism*" and "Austinian*ism*"

1. IMPRECISIONS OF THE "ISMS"

Anomalies and "Self-Deconstruction"

Two major new "isms" of the early and mid-nineteenth century that have often been linked together as crucial to "modern origins" in political-legal thought are utilitarianism and positivism, both of which we seek to exploit as well as to explode. The former, associated above with Jeremy Bentham and J. S. Mill, and the latter, identified here with Auguste Comte and John Austin, had complex and often anomalous interrelationships in the writings of these four thinkers.

A few illustrations of these anomalies will suffice. As a utilitarian philosopher, Bentham had a formative influence on Austin, who has been hailed as a legal positivist but who was not truly influenced by Comte and was thus anomalously more a utilitarian than a positivist strictly speaking. Furthermore, although J. S. Mill broke with Comte, after initial agreeable correspondence with him, and never bore the positivist label, Mill was anomalously more attuned personally and philosophically to Comte than was Austin, to whom that label has long been affixed by contemporaries and historians. Not all positivists were utilitarians, just as neither group was always focused on law and jurisprudence. The discrepancies within and between so-called "utilitarian*ism*" and "positiv*ism*" cannot be explained merely by differences in the disciplines represented by these writers. Bentham and Austin dealt in their various ways with law and jurisprudence, Mill with politics and political thought more generally, and Comte with sociology and the social sciences (including politics) in broad mixtures with the physical sciences.

Such anomalies are not usually tackled directly; for historians tend to delineate these two "isms" in sharp distinction to each other and to other "isms" of the period. In the process, however, the door has opened wide to conflicting and inconclusive historiographical interpretations of the two "isms," both in their terminology and in their applications. Many twentieth-century philosophers employing these two "isms" as *neo*-"isms" have freely mixed history and current philosophy. Even when guided by the rigorous standards of historical scholarship in recent decades, many historians of utilitarianism, positivism, and other "isms" relating to Bentham, Mill, Comte, Austin, and their followers have combined historical analysis with their own contemporary philosophizing. Accordingly, utilitarianism and positivism have often become cloudier rather than clearer in meaning. To be sure, scholarly understanding of jurists like Bentham and Austin has been advancing. Yet the inadequacies of these two "isms" as terms and concepts, both in their historical and current contexts, must be better exposed.

The meaning of so-called "legal positiv*ism*" has never been truly resolved. The steadily growing body of works centered around it has intensified this irresolution. Attempts to account for what constitutes positivism in law and jurisprudence frequently take as their point of departure the thought of John Austin. His famed early-nineteenth-century paradigms of command-theory and Analytical Jurisprudence set the stage for many English, German, and other legal thinkers far into the twentieth century, in which much legal philosophy took shape by being against or "anti" the neo-positivists (often allied with the neo-utilitarians). Legal positivists have been a variegated group. They have been as divided by controversies between themselves over the meanings of their "ism," especially in relation to Austin and his relevance to later times, as they have been united as adapters of Austin's philosophy to the changing needs of their own period.

Perhaps no legal historian or legal philosopher, including even the legendary Austrian writer Hans Kelsen in the earlier twentieth century, has had greater impact on studies of legal positivism, in connection with Austin as well as Bentham, than has the British expert H. L. A. Hart. For several decades, he remained at the forefront of intensive debates on the nature and scope of legal positivism and Austinianism. Professor Hart's great accomplishments as historian and philosopher of positivism as well as of utilitarianism have been widely recognized. Yet his approaches have epitomized the aforementioned difficulties by confusing the boundaries between history and current philosophy. By projecting his own current ideologies onto the historical stage, he inevitably invited anachronisms, in addition to terminological confusions including so-called "positiv*ism*." Fortunately, Hart maintained an objectivity that saw the limitations and imprecisions of that very term and its cognates (as well as of so-called "Austinian*ism*"). Throughout a formative article of 1958 dealing with both Austin and Bentham, entitled "Positivism and the Separation of Law and Morals," [1] Hart placed quotation marks around such terms as "positivism" and "positivist," so as to underscore their inherent ambiguities in the legal realms under discussion. Much has been added since then to the understanding, historical as well as philosophical, of positivism in law and politics; but much remains the same. There is still frequent need to place the term in quotations so as to suggest its ongoing ambiguity and imprecision.

Contributing to the anomalies and uncertainties long evident in positivistic approaches have been their wide national variations—French, English, and German (as represented in sections below). For all his claims of arriving at positive certainty and scientific fact in politics and the social sciences, Comte was regarded as too abstract and abstruse by British writers like Mill and Austin in the empirical tradition. Characterizations of this sort, whether accurate or inaccurate, had often played a part in English vs. French debates in philosophy, politics, and method during the seventeenth and eighteenth centuries. The widening discrepancies between English and German positivists led in the twentieth century to noted debates between Hart and Kelsen. Controversies of various related types still continue.

Further contributing to the inherent potential for anomolous inexactitudes in the supposedly scientific positivism of Comte and Austin are the loose structures of their respectively entitled "Courses" and "Lectures," which changed and evolved over long periods of time. This parallel has never received the attention it deserves as part of the puzzlements over positivism.

If, then, the wide internal inconsistencies and uncertainties carry the potential for inducing a breakdown within positivist methodologies, what theme(s) can be held to for achieving a stablizing continuum? The question concerning anomalies becomes: the "self-deconstruction" of what into what (in our generalized use of that term)? The partially self-destructing nature of the positivist thought of a Comte or an Austin has not in itself been duly pointed out by scholars, even though the closer experts have investigated that body of knowledge the more elusive and irresolute it has often become when framed as an "ism." The reduction of "isms" to their basis in laws and legislation has yielded more reliable "constructs" for analysis in the present studies.

Dictionary Definitions

At this point, before looking more closely at individual positivists, we must consult once more the *Oxford English Dictionary* for some standard definitions and usages. The entries therein under "positivism" and its cognates are extensive and include legal as well as more general philosophical nomenclatures. This "ism" was "Comte's name for his system." Its concise definition is: "A system of philosophy elaborated by Auguste Comte from 1830 onwards, which recognizes only positive facts and observable phenomena, with the objective relations of these and the laws that determine them, abandoning all inquiry into causes or ultimate origins, as belonging to the theological and metaphysical stages of thought, held to be now superseded." This philosophy is also the basis for a new religious as well as moral system. In more generalized or diluted fashion, it is "the name given generally nowadays to the view, held by Bacon and Hume amongst others (including Comte), that every rationally justifiable assertion can be scientifically verified or is capable of logical or mathematical proof; that philosophy can do no more than attest to the logical and exact use of language through which such observation or verification can be expressed" (as also obtains for logical positivism).

Among the many older descriptions of this "ism" included in the *Oxford English Dictionary* under the above lead definitions is the following from 1892: "Positivism i.e. the representation of facts without any admixture of theory or mythology, is an ideal which in its purity perhaps will never be realized." A more recent description from 1974 states: "The much publicized juxtaposition of logic with positivism (or empiricism or 'analytic' philosophy) has burdened logic with a guilt by association." Such descriptions of this "ism" are telltale as to the widespread criticisms that have been levelled against it by writers in diverse fields. Other descriptions herein also account for positivism in physics and biology (including evolutionary positivism). The lengthy entries under "positivist" also cite "linguistic analysis, officially without metaphysical ambitions . . ." Thereunder is also an 1889 Huxley quotation: "The incongruous mixture of bad science with existential papistry, out of which Comte manufactured the Positivist religion." Various other negative as well as positive verdicts on "positive analysis" are cited.

Under "positivism" and "positivist" the *Oxford English Dictionary* provides numerous significant descriptions with respect to law and jurisprudence. They include the following: "A term derived from positive law . . . and applied to theories concerned with the enactment of law, the reaching of legal decisions, the binding nature of legal rules and the study of existing law; which postulates that legal rules are valid because they are enacted by the 'sovereign' or derive logically from existing decisions, and deny that ideal or moral considerations (such as those of natural law, or that a rule is unjust) should in any way limit the operation or scope of the law." Descriptions from a variety of earlier sources (Kelsen and others) on legal positivism include owes concerning criminal and international jurisprudence. An excerpt of 1961 taken from H. L. A. Hart's celebrated *Concept of Law* presents this "ism" as couched by him in quotations, which again suggests its elusiveness in law: "Some contemporary legal theory which is critical of the legal 'positivism' inherited from Austin." Another source from 1967 declares: "The definition of law as the command of the 'sovereign' is no doubt the most prominent example of a form of positivism. . . . Sometimes 'legal positivism' is used to refer to the view that correct legal decisions are uniquely determined by pre-existing legal rules." An opinion from 1944 aptly points out: "The number and variety of positivist legal theories is as great as that of the sciences." The same source is here reported as referring to "Austin's positivist system."

Clarification via Legislation

Two observations can be made on the above descriptions of legal positivism in the *Oxford English Dictionary*. First, it is ironic that philosophical, legal, and logical positivists strove to achieve factual scientific certainty through concrete analyses and to avoid conjectural conflict and chaos resulting from vague abstractions. For they paradoxically tended (or have been accused of tending) toward the latter negative condition as much as toward the positive former one. (An amusing but telling description of 1971 included along with the above entries is from J. H. Haddox: "To the cowardly positivists frightened by the idea of 'mental anarchy,' I say no.") Indeed, positivism has generated, far into the twentieth century, as much heated debate as has deconstructionism in recent decades.

Second, many of the foregoing definitions and descriptions of legal positivism indirectly suggest that if "positive" law lies at the heart of positivism in law and jurisprudence it reduces ultimately to legislation. This conclusion is suggested by the contexts of enacted law, sovereign command, promulgation, and so forth indicated in the preceding descriptions and remains to be elaborated in our discussions on Austin. We similarly saw, in the preceding chapter, how the "utility" lying at the core of utilitarianism revolves ultimately around legislation. It is in legislation that one finds the most "positive" or clearly identifiable foundation stone of legal positivism, especially through its key founder, Austin.

Along these lines, the *Oxford English Dictionary* is again useful. It gives the following definitions and descriptions of "Austinian" and "Austinianism": "Of or pertaining to John Austin (1790–1859) and his theory of government. Hence Austinianism. . . . 'The Austinian conception of Sovereignty has been reached through mentally uniting all forms of government in a group by conceiving them as stripped of every attribute except coercive force' [H. J. S. Maine, 1875]. . . . 'It goes back to that passionate Erastianism of Luther which was the only answer he could make to the Austinianism of [papal] Rome' [H. J. Laski, 1917]. . . . 'The unified, mechanical, Austinian State' [1921]." Needless to say, such amorphous and anachronistic predatings of Austinianism to earlier centuries (including the Middle Ages) have further beclouded the already vexed problem of what constitutes legal positivism in Austin and his followers. As Hart's 1958 article serves to show, the monolithic thought often ascribed to Austin typically breaks apart under further analysis, resulting in much perplexity among the experts, be they Austin's admirers or his detractors.

The topic of legislation affords one of the best routes (not truly pursued by Hart) for cutting through the thorny disputes over Austin's ideas concerning positive law and legal positivism. The cumulative body of interpretations on these subjects—going back well before Kelsen and continuing well beyond Hart—is more complicated than can be detailed here. But it will be further seen that legislation furnishes a core concept for disentangling the kinds of anomalies mentioned above that continue to defy satisfactory interpretations.

2. COMTE'S *SYSTEM OF POSITIVE POLITY*

Preliminary Contexts of a "Scientific" "System"

The great accomplishment of Auguste Comte (1798–1857) in establishing his novel term "positiv*ism*" on an equal footing with the new term "utilitarian*ism*" as devised by J. S. Mill should not be minimized. Together and separately the two terms have had enormous impact well into the twentieth century. The original basis of the term "positiv*ism*" in Comte's *System of Positive Polity* and other related writings sometimes appears to involve a play of words on the term "positive"—as in "positive theory"—that bore little resemblance to the uses made by legal theorists of "positive law" (an age-old term). Comte's uses of such terms as "positive theory" and "positiv*ism*" rested on his generalized and personalized views of the positive vs. negative aspects of the French

Revolution and its aftermath, as set forth in his *System of Positive Polity*. Comte clearly intended his new "ism" to represent a radical new school, system, and ideology. In addition, he made free use of other types of "isms."

In order to make sense of the pertinent essentials of Comte's massive and complicated multi-volume *System of Positive Polity* (*Système de politique positive ou Traité de Sociologie*, 1851–1854),[2] it will be helpful to adhere below to his own modes of presentation. He begins with succinct introductory overviews in Volume One (*General View of Positivism and Introductory Principles*). "Positivism," according to Comte in his introduction to the lengthy "Preliminary Discourse," "consists essentially of a Philosophy and a Polity . . .: the former being the basis, and the latter the end of one comprehensive system. . . . [T]he science of Society . . . [is] more important than any other . . ." Near the beginning of Chapter (or Part) I of his "Preliminary Discourse," Comte likewise declares: "Philosophy and Politics are the two principal functions of the great social organism. Morality, systematically considered, forms the connecting link and . . . demarcation between them."

Comte proceeds in Chapter II to flesh out the relationships of positivism to the French Revolution and its aftermath. For him, the negative first phase and positive second phase of the French Revolution opened the way for (his) current positivist philosophy; but they did so only to a degree because of the ultimately aborted and imperfect strivings of those involved. Comte's formative uses here of the terms "positive" and "positivism" stem largely from his avowed attempts to construct a new and better positive philosophy in the wake of the French Revolution and subsequent events. The first or destructive phase of the Revolution cleared away the old system, while the second or constructive phase established only an incomplete substitute, leaving the erection of a new positive social state and philosophy for future endeavors. Counter-revolution from 1794 to 1830 was followed by political stagnation between 1830 and 1848. Presently, in 1848–1850, republicanism has given prominence to the problems of subordinating politics to morals and of reconciling order with progress, while bringing the revolutionary metaphysical schools into discredit and paving the way for Comte's new positivist system. The good medieval attempts at a communal social state, in which the temporal power was first separated from the spiritual, fell short of Comte's goals. Progress and order go hand in hand for him, progress being the development of order. Comte seeks a dictatorship in which liberty of speech would be ensured and the temporal power would be more separated from the spiritual. (In Chapter I he was obliged to defend himself against critics who identify positivism variously with atheism, materialism, fatalism, and optimism, while in Chapter III he rejects communism.)

Intermixed in Comte's main title (as given above) and throughout these disquisitions in the first volume of his *Positive Polity*, as elsewhere, are the dual elements of positivism and sociology (or social science), which are often said to constitute his two main contributions to the history of ideas. Given the broadly sociological approach announced in his subtitle, together with his references to "social state" and the like, Comte's interests in the legislative criteria of sovereignty and the state may seem more tangential than those expressed by the utilitarians Bentham and J. S. Mill. However, as the birthplace of positivism, Comte's philosophical school played a key part in the background to the influential and enduring movement known as legal positivism, even though the latter pursued different agendas.

Following his "Preliminary Discourse" in the first volume of his *Positive Polity*, Comte's lengthy "Introductory Principles" takes up in Chapter I various aspects of his "scientific synthesis," inclusive of certain legal factors. A comprehensive overview of Comte's massive, all-embracing system cannot be attempted. Essentially, Comte was interested in laws of sociology rather than in laws of the state as described in this series; yet the latter did play a part and furnished many clues taken up by his followers. In Chapter I, Comte believes that "law" is "consistency amidst variation" and "implies harmony of biological and cosmological relations." "This harmony," he feels, is "variable," while "sociology deals with the laws of its variation in man." In Chapter III Comte touches at one point upon the "sociological laws in animal races." Yet, once again, Comte's prevailing concern is with a "positive" polity, in which, as stated above, politics conjoins with philosophy as keys to the social organism, with morality a connecting link; this approach hints at the protean ways in which Comte's thought could be adapted to germane questions of the state and sovereignty.

In the second volume of Comte's *Positive Polity* (*Social Statics, or the Abstract Theory of Human Order*), he begins by pairing statics and order with dynamics and progress. The "laws of positive philosophy" will in this volume, he says, be first concerned with the "laws of order," as indicated also in that subtitle. In the course of his voluminous treatment of religion and "the positive theory of human unity" in Chapter I, Comte again considers "law" as "permanence within variation," requiring that the "limits of variation must be determined."

Political Parameters, "Laws" of "State"

Building upon the general viewpoints just described, Comte turns somewhat more directly in his *Positive Polity* to political issues, with aspects more germane to sovereignty and the state. Typically, however, politics, like other disciplines including law, is subsumed under social or sociological thought. The science of politics is subordinated to Comte's new science of society.

In Chapter V of the second volume of his *Positive Polity*, Comte presents "the positive theory of the social organism." His section on the "positive theory of the social forces" takes up such matters as that "moral power is composed of command and obedience," which "correspond with character and heart." Cooperation is the necessary crux of social forces. A section on the relation of social to individual organism announces that the social is always superior to the biologic treatment. Comte's section on social organization deals with such topics as the origin of government, the government of societies that arises out of the directing forces of smaller groups, government resting on force (as Hobbes saw it), political power resting on force and other powers (intellectual, moral, and social control), the degrees of society (family, city, and church), and much more including the views of Aristotle, Decartes, Leibniz, and Bacon.

In Chapter VI on "the positive theory of social existence, systematized by the priesthood," Comte believes that "the city is the chief" and that "society has never been without the germ of religious government." Moreover, "the State must be reduced to the normal limits of the City." Other positions are also crucial: "Command tends to elevate the character"; "Moral value ... [accrues to] obedience"; "Civic duty ennobles both Obedience and Command"; "Wealth, [is] the normal source of Power"; and "Wealth [is] to be subject to moral, not to legal control." Chapter VII deals with "the general limits of variation in the order of human society." Human order is divisible into social and moral. Comte treats the "law" that progress is a development of order. General social evolution is the subject of historical sociology. Such topics here as morals and evolution provide key potential links with Jeremy Bentham and Herbert Spencer respectively.

In the third volume of his *Positive Polity*, Comte turns to "social dynamics, or the general theory of human progress." His first chapter propounds a "positive theory of human evolution, or general laws of intellectual and social progress." Here Comte singles out the focal points of unity and religion as keys to the general laws of social dynamics and evolution, which he details in typically complicated (and convoluted?) fashion. Chapter II deals with "the age of fetichism" or "the spontaneous regime of humanity," while Chapter III takes up "the theocratic state" or "conservative polytheism"—all again in a labyrinthian fashion that is *sui generis*. More germane materials are found in Chapter IV, which lays down a "positive theory of the Greek elaboration" "or general account of intellectual polytheism." Symptomatic of Comte's overall outlook is his position that the Greeks' repulse of the Persians represented a struggle between theocracy and intellectual progress," in which Athens in particular rendered a great service to humanity. After referring to Lycurgus and Alexander the Great, Comte avers that the Greeks made little progress in any useful art. Aristotle, he finds, made significant contributions to biology, sociology, and moral science, and after him Greek philosophy ended, whereas Plato is held in less esteem by Comte. Turning to the Romans in Chapter V, Comte delves partly into a range of legal and political topics including briefly the *Corpus Iuris Civilis*. Chapter VI—highlighting in its title a "positive theory," as in different variants do most other chapter headings in the work—centers on the "Catholic-feudal transition" of the Middle Ages, with particular regard to monotheism. Catholicism failed then to become a universal religion, pointing ahead to later concepts of humanity.

Comte's Chapter VII deals with the "Western revolution" in the modern period, starting with the Reformation and proceeding through the eighteenth and early nineteenth centuries. An accompanying diagram breaks the materials down into a series of "positive" and "negative" elements. This antithesis is again a controlling context of Comte's concept of "positiv*ism*" as a term at once simplistic and complex. Numerous "isms" appear, such as theologism and negativism. Figures discussed along the way are Henry VIII, Machiavelli (who represented political immorality systematized), Cusa, Decartes, Leibniz, Newton, Louis XIV, Diderot, Kant, Condorcet, Rousseau, Voltaire, Hume, Louis XVI, Robespierre, DeMaistre, and others leading up to Comte himself. Robespierre and Napoleon in different ways pursued dictatorial policies that were needed to restore order after the French Revolution; but the former, restoring deism, and the latter, Catholicism, became regressive and anti-progress. The rise of philosophical radicalism and socialism is recounted, along with other movements and events that prepared the way for positivism. Condorcet's "progress of the mind" and Diderot's encyclopedism were among the useful partial antecedents.

The fourth volume of Comte's *Positive Polity* posits his "theory of the future of man." Returning to relevant features of the French Revolution in Chapter V, centered on estimations of the present in connection with the past and the future, Comte includes positive and negative features, strengths and weaknesses, of its eventual "dictatorship." He stresses "the necessity of the adoption of the Positivist political formula: *Order and Progress.*" Comte feels that his vision of a positive utopia would be in part a realization of the medieval utopia in ways that would bind together the members of the human family. There is necessity for a common doctrine as the basis of political unity. This involves "the triumph of positivism" in worldwide frameworks.

The "General Appendix" at the end of the fourth volume of Comte's *Positive Polity* contains his earlier essays on social philosophy (1819–1828). Topics include the following (with capitalizations removed): the need for a "positive political science" (1819); "decline of the medieval and growth of the modern social system" and "first open struggle between the old and new society in the sixteenth century" (1820); "the necessity for reorganizing society" so as to overcome "social anarchy," and misconceived reorganization by people and rulers, with comments by Comte on the sovereignty of the people (1822); and the inability of constitutions to supply social reorganization and the "law of the three states" (1822). Moreover: "the growth of civilization follows laws"; "the science of positive politics is essential for social regeneration"; "scientific prevision can avert or mitigate violent revolutions," with comments by Comte on "the law of the three states" and on Montesquieu and Condorcet (1822). There are further historical surveys and philosophizing by Comte on "the law of the three states," ancient to modern (1825). Aspects of the historical and contemporary changes in the relations of temporal to spiritual power are also discussed (1828).

In broad outline, Comte's ideas pertaining to sovereignty and the state are unique and original, even idiosyncratic, yet are influenced by many other writers adapted for his own devices. Comte's "positive" notion of sovereignty, like his "positive" ideas of philosophy and society more broadly, involved what, in his mind, was real, useful, certain, precise, organic, and relative. Understanding sovereignty involves a complex consideration of the individual, the family, and the society. Society is a living organism, just as sociology more generally is linked to biological criteria. Comte's "positive" theory of sovereignty is connected to his "positive" theory of government as well as to his "positive" theory of the "law of the three states." The theological state and the sovereignty of divine law relate to the metaphysical state and popular sovereignty, while the "positive" state pertains to scientific sovereignty. In the evolution of sovereignty, the early theological state of sovereignty, relating to polytheism, involved a confusion between temporal and spiritual powers. The ensuing metaphysical state of sovereignty in the Middle Ages, associated with monotheism and Catholicism, separated the temporal and spiritual powers. This second state extended, in the sixteenth century, to the Protestant phase, with reformers and legists; it extended further beyond to the eighteenth century, in the deistic phase, with revolutionary philosophy. The third "positive" state of sovereignty connected to industry and science in the early nineteenth century. Among Comte's political principles are: the necessity of a scientific doctrine and religion, in which moral unity is the natural tendency of society; the separation of temporal and spiritual powers; the condemnation of revolutionary principles and of popular sovereignty as arbitrary and fictive; and the laws of order and progress, involving the need for material, intellectual, and moral order. Among the key influences at work on Comte were the writings of Montesquieu on laws, Condorcet on progress, Descartes on mathematics, and Saint-Simon on social theory, in addition to the revolutions in France of 1789, 1830, and 1848. Comte's laws of mental development or progress of the human mind thus hinge on rational demonstrations or proofs, knowledge of human mental organization and development, and historical verification. His three successive states or stages through which the human mind passes in history up to the present—theological or fictitious, metaphysical or abstract, and scientific or positive—are, of course, theoretical.[3]

Mill on Comte

Various points of chronology provide useful frames of reference on Comte in relation to John Stuart Mill, who attempted to square his utilitarianism with Comte's positivism. Comte's *Système de politique positive* dated back, in its original first part (of the first volume), to 1824. It was addressed by Comte in that year (while in his mid-twenties) to the Academy of Sciences, where Comte, as he later said, first placed on "public record" his "discovery" of these "laws." In 1826 Comte began teaching his course on positive philosophy at his home (and suffered a severe mental breakdown, which reoccurred at times later on). Successive volumes of his mammoth multi-volume *Cours de philosophie positive* were published from 1830 to 1842. In 1841 Comte began, from France, his early correspondence with J. S. Mill in England, each embracing much of the other's outlook. The volumes of Comte's *Système de politique positive* were published from 1851 to 1854 not long before his death in 1857. In his *Cours* Comte similarly applied his "positive doctrine" to the various disciplines—mathematics, astronomy, biology, sociology, physics, chemistry, politics, morality, and so on. The result was a kind of "social physics" or "social science," as well as a "science of politics," with references to Condorcet, Montesquieu, Hobbes, and many others.[4] These two works by Comte—the *Système* and the *Cours*—were later discussed by Mill in his lengthy two-part essay of 1865, entitled *Auguste Comte and Positivism*. By then, Mill had long since become much more critical of Comte than he had been in his enthusiastic correspondence with Comte in the early 1840s.

The complex problems of J. S. Mill's changing attitudes toward Comte in the quarter-century from 1841 to 1865 need not be investigated here; yet a few germane aspects of his *Comte and Positivism* must be pointed out in view of their great respective "isms"—utilitarianism and positivism. These two "isms" were perhaps destined by the different personalities and circumstances of their founders to diverge more than to converge. Comte and Mill have been variously depicted by scholars as tending divergently toward, respectively, the collective and the individual, the rational and the empirical, the abstract and the concrete, the uniting social force of religion and the freedom of religious conscience. Their divergent viewpoints can sometimes be attributed as much to differences in their national backgrounds, French and English, as to more purely biographical ones. The differences and similarities between their outlooks on such subjects as Benthamism and scientific methodology present vast topics in themselves not capable of apprehension here.

The first part of J. S. Mill's *Comte and Positivism* deals with Comte's *Cours de philosophie positive*. Mill first addresses himself to the unclear meaning of the basic "ism" itself when taken as a supposed "school" of thought. "For some time much has been said, in England and on the Continent, concerning 'Positivism' and 'the Positive Philosophy.' . . . It is not very widely known what they represent. . . . Indeed . . . the terms Positive and Positivism . . . are . . . better known through the enemies of that mode of thinking than through its friends. . . . Those who call themselves Positivists are indeed not numerous; but all French writers who adhere to the common philosophy . . . begin by fortifying their position against 'the Positivist school,' . . . There cannot be a more appropriate mode of discussing these points than in the form of a critical examination of the philosophy of Auguste Comte."[5] (Here one will recall the many "isms" and other types of terms that gained currency in the nineteenth century as negative labels used by critics of various groups, as in the case of so-called "impression*ism.*"

Following a look at Comte's outline of "Social Statics," J. S. Mill takes up what he says are Comte's "most eminent speculations" in the *Cours*, namely, on "Social Dynamics, or the laws of the evolution of human society." Mill addresses himself to Comte's theory that there is a "natural evolution in human affairs" and that this evolution in terms of "the social state" of "human society" represents an "improvement." Mill rejects Herbert Spencer's repudiation of Comte's ideas on these aspects of the "social state." Mill argues that despite some of Comte's weaknesses Spencer fails to do justice to Comte's positions.[6]

When in the second part of his *Comte and Positivism* Mill turns to examine Comte's "later speculations" contained in *Positive Polity* and other works, he becomes far more critical of Comte than in the first part. Characterizing this change of attitude, Mill asserts as follows: "Instead of recognizing, as in the *Cours de Philosophie Positive*, an essentially sound view of philosophy, with a few capital errors, it is in their general character that we deem the subsequent speculations false and misleading, while in the midst of this wrong general tendency, we find a crowd of valuable thoughts, and suggestions of thoughts in detail."[7]

An illuminating comprehensive summary of and objection to Comte's later social-political ideas appears at the end of the first part of Mill's *Comte and Positivism*. In Comte's concepts of "society" and the "state," there is, according to Mill, little role assigned to legal obligation as a safeguard against the political power, which for Comte is best checked by the spiritual power. Yet Comte's outlook on these two topics, as Mill recognizes, includes heavy stress on the public element. These considerations, we may add, are ironic in view of the great use made of Comte's positivism by those who have been called legal positivists. Mill's own great interest in individual liberty plays a part here in his observations on its limits or absence in Comte's system.

> A few words will sufficiently express the outline of his [Comte's] scheme. A corporation of philosophers, receiving a modest support from the state, surrounded by reverence, but peremptorily excluded not only from all political power or employment, but from all riches, and all occupations except their own, are to have the entire direction of education: together with, not only the right and duty of advising and reproving all persons respecting both their public and their private life, but also a control (whether authoritative or only moral is not defined) over the speculative class itself. . . . The temporal government which is to coexist with this spiritual authority, consists of an aristocracy of capitalists. . . . No representative system, or other popular organization, by way of counterpoise to this governing power, is ever contemplated. The checks relied upon for preventing its abuse, are the counsels and remonstrances of the Spiritual Power, and unlimited liberty of discussion and comment by all classes of inferiors. . . . [T]he general idea is, while regulating as little as possible by law, to make the pressure of opinion, directed by the Spiritual Power, so heavy

on every individual, from the humblest to the most powerful, as to render legal obligation, in as many cases as possible, needless. Liberty and spontaneity on the part of individuals form no part of the scheme. M. Comte looks on them with as great jealousy as any scholastic pedagogue, or ecclesiastical director of consciences. Every particular of conduct, public or private, is to be open to the public eye, and to be kept, by the power of opinion, in the course which the Spiritual corporation shall judge to be the most right.[8]

Mill's ensuing rebuttal of Comte's positions just outlined includes the interesting suggestion that only those persons already prone to finding them credible will be able to understand them. As for Mill, he believes Comte to be basically wrongheaded, in spite of some important contributions. This dichotomous estimate echoes Mill's opening account (cited above) of the nebulous nature of the "ism" called positivism that has become well known but little understood. Not only Comte's claims to being a pioneer in establishing a new "social science" are discredited by Mill, but also Comte's claims of having established upon it a new "political art."

This is not a sufficiently tempting picture to have much chance of making converts rapidly, and the objections to the scheme are too obvious to need stating. Indeed, it is only thoughtful people to whom it will be credible, that [Comte's] speculations leading to this result can deserve the attention necessary for understanding them. . . . M. Comte has not, in our opinion, created Sociology. Except his analysis of history, . . . he has done nothing in Sociology which does not require to be done over again, and better. Nevertheless, he has greatly advanced the study. . . . [H]is conception of its method is so much truer and more profound than that of any one who preceded him, as to constitute an era in its cultivation. If it cannot be said of him that he has created a science, it may be said truly that he has, for the first time, made the creation possible. . . . But his renown with posterity would probably have been greater than it is now likely to be, if after showing the way in which the social science should be formed, he had not flattered himself that he had formed it, and that it was already sufficiently solid for attempting to build upon its foundation the entire fabric of the Political Art.[9]

Needless to say, the vast subject of Mill's verdicts on Comte forms a large connecting link in a long and complicated chain of primary and secondary evaluations of Comte that stretches from Comte's own day into the twentieth century.[10]

3. AUSTIN'S *LECTURES ON JURISPRUDENCE*

Positivist Perplexities in Historiography

It is seldom easy to discern fixed perspectives and classifications in the shifting kaleidoscope of historiography on legal positivism and Austinianism. This elusiveness obtains even in connection with the traditionally cited key elements of command, sovereignty, positive law, rules, analytical jurisprudence, system, and the like. Historians as well as philosophers who have dealt with such topics with respect to John Austin and his followers have seldom agreed upon their significations. The inconclusiveness of academic debates results in large part from neglect of the legislative factors underlying a range of topics, including positive law. A few historiographical cases in point will help to prepare for our examination of Austin's thought on legislative and other issues in his celebrated *Lectures on Jurisprudence*.

Still one of the most substantial, comprehensive, and authoritative surveys on political thought in the nineteenth century—with chapters looking backward and forward in time and with inclusion of law and jurisprudence—is John H. Hallowell's *Main Currents in Modern Political Thought*.[11] The ninth chapter, dealing with positivism, takes up in turn the following topics as indicated in the sectional headings (with capitalizations deleted): Comte as "founder of sociology," the "logic of the moral sciences" in J. S. Mill, the "doctrine of evolution" leading up to Darwin and Spencer, the philosophy of Spencer (1820–1903), the American reception of Spencer's social-biological doctrines, the sociological thought of Ludwig Gumplowicz (1838–1909), a summary look at social Darwinism and the contexts of positivism, and "the impact of positivism upon liberalism." This concentration on the sociological beginnings and transformations of positivism leaves no room for a consideration of law and jurisprudence in connection with Austin and others, subjects that are covered instead in the much different ensuing tenth chapter on the various schools of law beginning with the historical and analytical. Even more obfuscating with regard to the place of Austinian law and jurisprudence in the development of positivism is Hallowell's orienting concern with the negative tendencies of positivism, which he associates with the demise of liberalism (or justice) and the rise of Hitlerism and tyranny.[12] In the opening paragraph of the section on the Analytical School of Jurisprudence, included in the tenth chapter on changing concepts of law, there is a passing illuminating accent on the defining role of legislation. Yet this accent, not continued, here lies in mistaken contrast to the alleged disinterest in legislation on the part of the Historical School of law and in unclear (or non) relation to positivism in Hallowell's preceding chapter.[13]

A different approach to legal positivism in relation to Austin's jurisprudence is found in a voluminous survey by Hendrik Jan van Eikema Hommes, entitled *Major Trends in the History of Legal Philosophy*. Here, the Analytical School of Austin and others is subsumed under legal positivism, the subject of Chapter VIII, which begins with German jurists like Jhering. Yet the author deemphasizes the significance of legislation in his efforts to disassociate legal positivism from its undue identifications with positive law as made, he believes, by those bent on discrediting positivism. Yet he clearly recognizes, as in the heading to section 10, that the Analytical School established by Austin centered on "the command of the habitually obeyed sovereign." Obscured from central view, we may add, in this debate over the presence or absence of higher values in positive law in Austin and legal positivism, is the core topic of legislation.[14]

Other secondary surveys divide such subjects in widely differing manners. An illustrative survey of the history of philosophy by Frank Thilly and Ledger Wood devotes a chapter to nineteenth-century French and British philosophy. Positivism in France and utilitarianism in Britain and Bentham are first treated therein, followed by empiricism in J. S. Mill and evolutionism in Spencer.[15] The classic survey of the history of political theory by George H. Sabine bypasses Austin, positivism, and the Analytical School in chapters focusing instead on liberalism. He includes Bentham in a chapter on liberalism in the form of philosophical radicalism, while including J. S. Mill in the ensuing chapter focusing on "modernized" liberalism.[16] An extensive documentary survey of the history of political as well as legal philosophy from the late eighteenth to early twentieth centuries by Margaret Spahr deals with Austin only in tandem with Bentham under the category of utilitarianism.[17] Other representative examples of such surveys, with widely varying perspectives, could be given at length.

Turning briefly to relevant examples of specialized scholarship on Austin and his legal positivism, one is often struck by the greater degree of elusiveness in his doctrines when their details are pursued at length than when wide surveys rely on brief generalizations. The continuing debates and controversies surrounding such pieces by H. L. A. Hart as the one singled out above provide good illustrations. In trying to nail down the distinguishing marks of legal positivism in relation to

Austin, Benthem, and others, Professor Hart has opened the door ever wider to divergent approaches by many others. Concentrating on the usual problem of the relationship or separation between law and morals in legal positivism, through a mixture of historical analysis and current philosophizing, Hart went far afield from the topic of legislation. Hart is instead concerned to defend legal positivism's strict separation of law-as-it-is from law-as-it-ought-to-be; he denies charges that positivism became part of the background to Nazism, although he sympathizes with those who feel thus. Nonetheless, the five key elements of legal positivism according to Hart (who has occasioned much subsequent debate) concern the following: the command or imperative theory of law, the separation of law from morals, the purely analytical study of law in contradistinction to the historical and sociological approaches, the idea of legal system as a closed logical system, and the notion of moral judgment as not being truly establishable as facts. The first three marks characterized the outlooks of both Austin and Bentham, asserts Hart, whereas the latter two did not. In trying to clear up the "great confusion" that he found in previous interpretations of legal positivism, Hart himself opened up new, still unsettled controversies. Not the least problematic were his own free-wheeling philosophical mixtures of positivism and utilitarianism, albeit both can be found in Austin as well as Bentham. The growing intricacies of academic interpretations on Austin's meanings and categories may be partly attributable to the growing details often associated with advancing modern scholarship. But in the case of this particular historical legal "ism," reputed by its founders to be "the" ultimate factual method, modern scholarship has generated as much confusion and conflict as certainty. Nevertheless, Hart's uniquely insightful and authoritative statements on Austin and legal positivism (as in the corresponding note below) have long provided helpful points of departure for others.[18]

More recent testimony to H. L. A. Hart's ongoing legacy in scholarship on Austin's legal positivism and analytical jurisprudence is found in an excellent book on this subject by Wilfrid E. Rumble. Two lengthy chapters (3–4) highlight positivistism in their titles—"Divine Law, Utilitarian Ethics, and Positivist Jurisprudence" and "Judicial Legislation and Legal Positivism." The latter chapter begins with references to Hart's five criteria of legal positivism set forth in the above-cited article as well as to controversies generated in ensuing decades by Hart's views on Austin. Professor Rumble's analysis of Austin's concept of "judiciary law," or "judicial legislation," shows the difficulties it posed for Austin's understanding of positive law; but it does not focus on legislation *per se*, which is even less in evidence in the preceding chapter intermixing positivism and utilitarianism. As the book's subtitle indicates, other issues are instead featured—"Jurisprudence, Colonial Reform, and the British Constitution." Handy for present purposes are the author's brief denials of Comte's influence on Austin and subsequent legal positivists.[19]

Even more indicative of the enormous controversies generated by Hart's interpretations of Austin's legal positivism and analytical jurisprudence is another substantial recent book on Austin by W. L. Morison. In a chapter (6) entitled "A Defence of Austin's Philosophy against Hart," Professor Morison explains as follows: "The new theory of law which Hart developed not only pays close attention to . . . Austin . . . but . . . is an empirical theory of law as well . . . which came to replace Austin. . . . The present writer wishes nevertheless . . . to defend Austin's empiricism . . . against the different [positivist] philosophy of Hart . . ."[20] A section entitled "Austinian Myth" exposes some of the factors behind the continuing confusion over Austin. (This was not resolved by Hart's attempts but rather was augmented, we may add, by his admixtures of Austinianism, neo-Benthamism, and current philosophizing.) "With the enthusiasm that scholars interested in Austin showed for revising what Austin said, usually in ways which departed from Austin's own fundamental philosophy, it was inevitable that the picture which scholars have of Austin himself would become obscured."[21]

Neither the above-cited book by Rumble nor the one by Morison has succeeded in resolving the "great confusion" over Austin's legal positivism that Hart had cited but not been able to resolve and instead intensified. This confusion may be enhanced by the widening complexities of research, but it may also cast doubt on the claims of "scientific" certainty made by positivists of different kinds, such as Austin and Comte, for their philosophical "systems." The question arises, in reaction to Morison's valuable studies, whether a new focus on legislation *per se* would now help to set straight the picture on Austin. Despite some promising efforts in that direction, Morison's interests lie far afield of legislation in itself, as indicated by his headings.[22]

Reducing Positive Law, Command, Utility, and Public Law to Legislation

It is acutely mystifying that the theme of legislation has not been better singled out for analysis by historians of (and theorists on) Austin's jurisprudence to the extent warranted by his own focus on it directly or indirectly. Austin's other core concepts of positive law, command, and utility, in addition to public law, have been among the perennial scholarly favorites. Yet the subject of legislation, around which they typically revolve in Austin's writings, has seldom been given similar close attention. This neglect is all the more puzzling in view of the usual recognition of Austin's enormous debt to Bentham's own core concepts of utility and command, which we saw above to center on legislation (the main subject of Bentham's *Morals and Legislations* and other works). It is surprising that Austin historians (and theorists), including Hart along with multitudinous others, have not looked adequately to legislation as a common unifying theme for purposes of explaining disparate topics long deemed difficult of resolution within Austin's system.

In considering now these problems in Austin's *Lectures on Jurisprudence*, it will be convenient to cite his individual continuous lectures by number rather than by the titles given to various groups of them in the form of independent works. Austin's Lectures I–VI, published in 1832 under the title *The Province of Jurisprudence Determined*, will be cited by lecture number.[23] The voluminous ensuing *Lectures* by Austin were published in 1863, a few years after his death in 1859, with various subsequent editions.[24] Austin's *Province*, his first and most celebrated work, was printed in a second edition in 1861 through his wife, who was responsible for preparing his fuller *Lectures* for publication in 1863. Although the 1832 edition of Austin's first six lectures was published as a separate work under its own title, subsequent editions after his death, beginning with the one prepared by his wife in 1861, were published in the first volume of Austin's massive two-volume *Lectures on Jurisprudence*. The original title, *Province . . .* , has been in recent decades revived in editions of Lectures I–VI by H. L. A. Hart and W. E. Rumble (cited above). The present study retains the title *Lectures* as best befitting all lectures in common. The state of the various texts and editions of these works by Austin does not hamper the present restricted approaches, but rather bolsters our case for seeing Austin's *Province* and *Lectures* as often inherently prone to anomalies in spite of Austin's so-called "analytical" or "scientific" method. (Even though he approximated it in various ways, as in "analytical," Austin himself apparently did not use the specific term "Analytical Jurisprudence," which was later employed as a descriptive label for his ideas; and he long suffered from legendary self-doubts and uncertainties.[25])

The topic of positive law looms large in Austin's *Lectures*. His titles are indicative. The title of his original pamphlet publication of 1831 (the year before his *Province* appeared) was *An Outline of a Course of Lectures on General Jurisprudence or the Philosophy of Positive Law*.[26] The fuller title of Austin's eventual voluminous two-volume work was *Lectures on Jurisprudence or the Philosophy of Positive Law*.

Positive law is crucial at the outset of Lecture I. Austin begins with a famed, oft-quoted statement: "The matter of jurisprudence is positive law: law, simply and strictly so called: or law set by political superiors to political inferiors. But positive law (or law, simply and strictly so called) is often confounded with objects to which it is related by *resemblance*, . . . *analogy*[, and] . . . by the large and vague expression *law*. To obviate . . . that confusion, I begin . . . with determining the province of jurisprudence [in contradistinction to those other areas] . . ."[27] Austin continues on in Lecture I to argue as follows (again adhering to his style):

> [T]he term *law* embraces the following objects:—Laws set by God to his human creatures and laws set by men to men. . . . [T]he laws set by God to men . . . [are] frequently styled the law of nature, or natural law. . . . But rejecting the appellation Law of Nature as ambiguous and misleading, I name those laws or rules . . . the *Divine law*, or the *law of God*. . . . [The] [l]aws set by men to men are of two . . . classes . . . often blended, although they differ extremely. . . . [S]ome are established by *political* superiors, sovereign and subject: by persons exercising supreme and subordinate *government*. . . . [O]*thers* are *not* established by political superiors . . . in that capacity . . .

These points are further clarified in Lecture V:

> Positive laws, the appropriate matter of jurisprudence, are related in the way of resemblance, or by a close or remote analogy, to the following objects. — 1. In the way of resemblance, they are related to the laws of God. 2. In the way of resemblance, they are related to those rules of positive morality which are laws properly so called. 3. By a close or strong analogy, they are related to those rules of positive morality which are merely opinions or sentiments held or felt by men in regard to human conduct. 4. By a remote or slender analogy, they are related to laws merely metaphorical, or laws merely figurative.
>
> To distinguish positive laws from the objects now enumerated, is the purpose of the present attempt to determine the province of jurisprudence.[28]

What most characterizes positive law, according to Austin's *Lectures*, is command, that is, an imperative issued by the lawmaking power in the form of legislation. Legislation has already been suggested, in the preceding passages, to lie behind the establishment of positive laws. All other types of laws are not truly positive law but rather analogous or similar to it in one fashion or another (as in the above cases of natural or divine law). These essential points must be kept in mind when one considers Austin's following complicated discussions in Lectures I and V—which also include typical references to Roman law—as well as in their continuations in the corresponding notes below. He asserts (in Lecture I, all *sic*):

> [Having] suggested the *purpose* of my attempt to determine the province of jurisprudence: to distinguish positive law, the appropriate matter of jurisprudence, from the various objects to which it is related by resemblance, and to which it is related, nearly or remotely, by a strong or slender analogy: I shall . . . state the essentials of *a law* or *rule* (taken with the largest signification which can be given to the term *properly*).
>
> Every *law* or *rule* (taken with the largest signification which can be given to the term *properly*) is a *command*. Or, rather, laws or rules, properly so called, are a *species* of commands.
>
> Now, since the term *command* comprises the term *law*, the first is the simpler as well as the larger of the two. But, simple as it is, it admits of explanation. And, since it is the *key* to the sciences of jurisprudence and morals, its meaning should be analysed with precision.
>
> Accordingly, I shall endeavour, in the first instance, to analyze the meaning of '*command:*'. . . . The elements of a science are precisely the parts of it which are explained least easily. . . .
>
> If you express or intimate a wish that I shall do or forbear from some act, and if you will visit me with an evil in case I comply not with your wish, the *expression* or *intimation* of your wish is a *command*. A command is distinguished from other significations of desire, not by the style in which the desire is signified, but by the power and the purpose of the party commanding to inflict an evil or pain in case the desire be disregarded.[29]

In addition (Lecture I):

> Like most of the leading terms in the science of jurisprudence and morals, the term *laws* is extremely ambiguous. Taken with the largest signification which can be given to the term properly, *laws* are a species of *commands*. But the term is improperly applied to various objects which have nothing of the imperative character: to objects which are *not* commands: and which, therefore, are *not* laws, properly so called. . . .

1. Acts on the part of legislatures to *explain* positive law, can scarcely be called laws, in the proper signification of the term. Working no change in the actual duties of the governed, but simply declaring what those duties are, they properly *are* acts of *interpretation* by legislative authority. Or, to borrow an expression from the writers on the Roman Law, they are acts of *authentic* interpretation.

But, this notwithstanding, they are frequently styled laws; *declaratory* laws, or declaratory statutes. They must, therefore, be noted as forming an exception to the proposition 'that laws are a species of commands.'[30]

Moreover (Lecture V):

Declaratory laws, laws repealing laws, and laws of imperfect obligation (in the sense of the Roman jurists), are merely analogous to laws in the proper acceptation of the term. Like laws imperative and proper, declaratory laws, laws repealing laws, and laws of imperfect obligation (in the sense of the Roman jurists), are signs of pleasure or desire proceeding from lawmakers. A law of imperfect obligation (in the sense of the Roman jurists) is also allied to an imperative law by the following point of resemblance.[31]

Austin's emphasis on utility in connection with legislation was aligned with the aforementioned legislative contexts of positive law and command. An illustration is the passage drawn from Austin's materials and incorporated at the outset of Lecture III by his subsequent nineteenth-century editor, Robert Campbell (who placed his editions of the *Province* at the beginning of his fuller editions of the *Lectures* published in 1869, 1873, and 1883). This passage, constituting the first paragraph of Lecture III, reads as follows (along with an ensuing second one-sentence paragraph at the beginning of the regular text):

Although it is not the object of this course of lectures to treat of the science of legislation, but to evolve and expound the principles and distinctions involved in the idea of law, it was not a deviation from my subject to introduce the principle of utility. For I shall often have occasion to refer to that principle in my course, as that which not only ought to guide, but has commonly in fact guided the legislator. The principle of utility, well or ill understood, has usually been the principle consulted in making laws; and I therefore should often be unable to explain distinctly and precisely the scope and purport of a law, without having brought the principle of utility directly before you. I have therefore done so, not pretending to expound the principle in its various applications, which would be a subject of sufficient extent for many courses of lectures; but attempting to give you a general notion of the principle, and to obviate the most specious of the objections which are commonly made to it.

In my second lecture, I examined a current and specious objection to the theory of general utility.[32]

The preceding passage bears a close relationship to Bentham's art or science of legislation—to which Austin conceived his own project as in some respects a complementary extension. In other passages on utility, however, Austin combines calculation with sentiment (contrary to impressions made by some of Austin's above-cited materials, not unlike some by Bentham cited earlier). At the same time, utility remains a key test of positive law.[33]

In a lengthy discussion of public versus private law in Lecture XLIV, Austin takes issue with this age-old antithesis, as based on Roman law and adapted especially by Continental civilian jurists over the centuries up to his own times. According to Austin, public law, pertaining to political conditions, and private law, relating to all law minus this feature, have been interfused, especially when international law and procedural law have been mixed together with public law. In other cases, certain types of law, such as criminal, have been confusedly excluded from public law. Worst of all, he believes, is when the above branches of law become jumbled together under public, as distinct from private, law. Although public law is in itself a defective rubric that has caused much classificatory uncertainty, it is best viewed from a variety of legislative perspectives.[34] Related to Austin's debunking of traditional categories of "public law," along with that rubric itself, is his partial repudiation in Lecture IV—within contexts of utility and utilitarian principles of happiness etc.—of the concept of public good or general welfare. The latter, to him, is an abstraction removed from the interests of individuals who compose the public sphere.[35]

Sovereignty, State, and Legislation

In his famed theory of sovereignty, Austin's theme of legislation, derived in part from Bentham, comes clearly to the fore. Legislation becomes again the common denominator underlying positive law (in its strict sense), command, utility, and public law. Sovereignty, in its legislative and related dimensions, becomes identified by Austin with the state itself. The two terms are repeatedly used by him nearly synonymously, especially in the frequent phrase "sovereigns or state" (appearing in the continuation of the passage below in the corresponding note). Positive laws are, for Austin, commands established or enacted by a state sovereign that entail obedience to them on the part of subjects. This fusion of sovereigns and states shapes Austin's viewpoint on "independent political society" in Lecture V and elsewhere.

> In order to [*sic*] an explanation of the marks which distinguish positive laws, I must analyze the expression *sovereignty*, the correlative expression *subjection*, and the inseparably connected expression *independent political society*. For the essential difference of a positive law (or the difference that severs it from a law which is not a positive law) may be stated thus. Every positive law, or every law simply and strictly so called, is set by a sovereign person, or a sovereign body of persons, to a member or members of the independent political society wherein that person or body is sovereign or supreme. Or (changing the expression) it is set by a monarch, or sovereign number, to a person or persons in a state of subjection to its author.[36]

Austin's main presentation of his early theory of sovereignty appears in Lecture VI. Again, as in Lecture V, he defines and describes positive laws largely in terms of legislation. And again, the legislative foundations of sovereignty and other such subjects are often stated somewhat indirectly in an implied fashion. There is good reason for this. For, as already averred by him, the main purpose of these lectures is not to discourse on the art or science of legislation, a task previously carried out by Bentham, on whose shoulders Austin's enterprise largely stands. Rather, Austin seeks to determine the province of jurisprudence with regard to positive laws. Similarly to Bentham, then, Austin conceives legislation not only in terms of promulgation, command, sovereignty, and so forth, but also in terms of the many fields upon which it directly or indirectly impinges and into which its operations extend. The following passage in Lecture VI records Austin's aims in approaching the terminologies cited immediately above. Noteworthy here are his more explicit disavowals of outside final causes and his reaffirmations of legislative frameworks within a Hobbesian mold.

> I shall finish, in the present lecture, the purpose mentioned above, by explaining the marks or characters which distinguish positive laws, or laws strictly so called. And, in order to [*sic*] an

explanation of the marks which distinguish positive laws, I shall analyze the expression *sovereignty*, the correlative expression *subjection*, and the inseparably connected expression *independent political society*. With the ends or final causes for which governments *ought* to exist, or with their different degrees of fitness to attain or approach those ends, I have no concern. I examine the notions of *sovereignty* and *independent political society*, in order that I may finish the purpose to which I have adverted above: in order that I may distinguish completely the appropriate province of jurisprudence from the regions which lie upon its confines, and by which it is encircled. . . . Every positive law, or every law simply and strictly so called, is set by a sovereign person, or a sovereign body of persons, to a member or members of the independent political society wherein that person or body is sovereign or supreme. Or (changing the expression) it is set by a monarch, or sovereign number, to a person or persons in a state of subjection to its author. Even though it sprung directly from another fountain or source, it *is* a positive law, or a law strictly so called, by the institution of that present sovereign in the character of political superior. Or (borrowing the language of Hobbes) 'the legislator is he, not by whose authority the law was first made, but by whose authority it continues to be a law.'[37]

What chiefly characterizes sovereignty as well as the state in Austin's Lecture VI is the obedience given by subjects to the commands, through positive laws and legislation, that are issued by the state sovereign(s). The members of such a state cannot be obedient to the laws or commands of other sovereign state bodies. Independence alone, therefore, does not typify such a sovereign state. Whether in contexts of international law or some other form, states are frequently guided by forces outside their own sphere. Austin builds upon, but takes issue with, Bentham, Grotius, and others on ideas of sovereignty in relation to independent political society. On these discussions and distinctions rests Austin's ensuing treatment of monarchical and aristocratic modes of government. These two chief types of sovereignty and state are viewed by him in a broad sense.[38]

For Austin in Lecture VI, legislation is the key to sovereignty and the state in a variety of other interconnected ways. The "sovereign or state" in a parliamentary form of government involves complex relationships between the electorate, the representatives, and the king; but it is largely defined or described in connection with the positive laws that are "made" and "enforced." [39] In repudiations of the separation of "legislative sovereign powers" from "executive sovereign powers," as made by his predecessors, Austin argues extensively, using British and Roman examples, that the executive as well as judicial powers are often exercised in ways that are legislatively oriented. Here, Austin is impacted by Bentham's sweeping extensions of legislation and legislative authority into many adjacent compartments; but the overall effect is Austin's heightened sense of the pervading powers of legislation throughout the commonly accepted divisions of sovereignty.[40]

Even more striking, and surely more idiosyncratic, is Austin's description, combining theory and practice, of the legislative layers of the sovereign state(s) of the United States of America. He sees the collective body of sovereign individual states as being in ways more ultimately sovereign than the U.S. federal government. The key determining force in this U.S. arrangement is the factor of legislation.[41] (One recalls the remote partial precedents set in Renaissance jurisprudence by Corasius and Bodin, who theorized that the sovereign power to make law could be exercised by any legally recognized body, regardless of competing jurisdictions, through the inherent power to make law and with strong elements of command.)

The common denominators of legislation and command underlying Austin's concept of sovereignty are further apparent in his Lecture I in connection with "the sovereign One or Number."[42]

Custom, Judges, Justice, and Legislation

Bentham tended to divorce custom from legislation, believing that custom is incomplete and different in its key attributes from legislation; Austin tends to bridge the gap by showing the legislative features accruing to customary law. In the process, Austin simultaneously recognizes the legislative features of "judge-made law." When custom is turned into law by the express or tacit consent and power of the legislative sovereign, custom can become a form of "judicial legislation." In other words, customary laws and judicial approvals of custom carry the weight, directly or indirectly, of the sovereign command of the legislative "sovereign or state," be it the "one or number." The upshot is a heightened sense, for Austin, of the legislative nature of both sovereignty and the state. Even by virtue of being reinforced, as distinct from being promulgated, by "courts of justice," customs are endowed with the weight of the imperative authority of the state—of the sovereign ruler or body—to which those courts are ultimately subordinated. Austin's intermixtures of the term "positive laws" in such discussions serve to bring out all the more their inherent legislative base. His Lectures I and V contain detailed clarifications of these ideas, while

Lectures XXIX–XXX elaborate on and revise some traditional distinctions between written and unwritten law.[43]

As in connection with customary law and judge-made law, so too in the case of justice and so-called higher laws of God and nature, Austin's *Lectures* have been widely treated by scholars; but again insufficient attention has heretofore been paid to legislation as a central context of Austin's ideas. When indicating above how Austin's ideas of positive law, along with command and utility, typically reduce to a legislative core, we presented numerous passages in which Austin's main interest in divine and natural laws lay in their analogous resemblance to positive law. Austin is interested in these traditional types of higher law not as sources of justice existing outside or above positive or human laws embodied in sovereign legislative commands. Rather, his interest lies in their analogous operations as laws, particularly in God's making or establishing of them. In this way, the legislative motif further permeates Austin's system. Positive law is not definable with precision, he declares in Lecture VI (further exposing as well the imprecision of the reputed scientific or analytical exactitude of his so-called "legal positiv*ism*"). For positive law must be delineated in relation to the higher laws that are analogous to it.[44] There, too, he declares that the end of sovereign states is to promote the greatest human happiness, this being much the same utilitarian end espoused by Bentham.[45]

These dimensions particularly of divine law, or the law of God, are highlighted in portions of Lectures II, IV–V, wherein Austin further expounds on germane facets of command, will, utility, and the like, as all part of the province of the "science" of jurisprudence. To be expected, the subject of analogy and metaphor in such contexts is intricately detailed by Austin through myriad classifications. At one point, he reduces the final causes associated with God to the final causes of positive law and jurisprudence, which we just saw to be described by Austin in terms of the utilitarian principle of the greatest happiness of the greatest number in society.[46] All in all, however, Austin's general classifications have inevitably given rise to much inconclusive scholarly debate on the degrees to which Austin can be said to include or exclude so-called higher laws. "It appears," says Austin, for instance, "that laws properly so called, with such improper laws as are closely analogous to the proper, are of three capital classes.—1. The law of God, or the laws of God. 2. Positive law, or positive laws. 3. Positive morality, rules of positive morality, or positive moral rules."[47]

Austin also criticizes and revises earlier notions about the relationships between democratic and despotic governments (the latter for him not being wholly without "free" elements),[48] between "constitutional(ism?)" and "constitutional law" (the former being for him inherently vague),[49] between *de facto* and *de iure* governments,[50] and between "right" and "law."[51] These and other such distinctions further attest to Austin's classificatory acumen as a noted analytical or scientific legal theorist; but in further determining the province of jurisprudence, they also extend, we may add, the boundaries of its uncertainties (along with the imprecisions of Austin's legal positivism).

Roman Legislation and Systematization

Stemming in large measure from his stay in Bonn, Germany, in 1827–1828, where the revived study of Roman law was gaining considerable appeal, Austin's interest in Roman law (on which he tutored J. S. Mill) was already much in evidence in his initial Lectures I–VI published in 1832.[52] For example, in Lecture IV—on the heels of a passage connecting the commands of Deity with utility, on which he continues to expound—Austin draws extensively upon the distinctions made by classical Roman jurists on civil law, natural law, and the laws of peoples. Austin builds his own case for the relation of positive law to this schema.[53] In Lecture V appear more elaborate discussions along these lines with respect to statements by the Roman jurist Ulpian included at the beginning of Justinian's *Digest* and *Institutes*.[54] In Lecture VI Austin ponders a comparative case in early Rome of a resolution that was passed by the sovereign people in the form of legislation and that was incorporated into the Twelve Tables, but that for certain reasons was not a law strictly speaking (according to his own criteria).[55]

Influenced in part by his later stay in Germany in 1841–1843, Austin's later lectures reveal the fuller weight of his knowledge of Roman law (concerning which limited excerpts appear in the corresponding notes below). These materials often pertain directly or indirectly to legislation and offer points of comparison or even building blocks for his own contemporary jurisprudence. For instance, in Lecture XXVIII dealing with "the various sources of law," Austin expressly seeks to utilize the ancient writings themselves, rather than to rely on the "countless" medieval and modern commentaries along with other writings derived from them. Austin then expounds on Roman law in relation to modern ideas and to differences between written law and unwritten law. Written law is established by the "supreme legislature"; unwritten law is not, although it receives its authority from the "sovereign or state." This is a modern distinction, according to Austin, that has been pursued by him but not by the Romans, whose ideas on the subject were taken over by Blackstone and others with results both good and bad. Drawing comparisons with the British parliament, Austin examines three kinds of laws made by the "supreme legislature" in the Roman Republic. Legislation during the Roman Empire receives also extended coverage on a comparative basis. Austin then launches into a disquisition on how judicial sovereignty was more characteristic of the Middle Ages, with legislative elements subordinated to it, and how legislative sovereignty is more characteristic of modern times, with judicial powers subsumed under it. Here again, Austin brings up his ideas on judicial legislation, including judicial decisions to which the stamp of legislative authority has been given expressly or tacitly by the sovereign legislature—an idea Austin traces back to the Romans but one often disputed by his critics.[56]

Again with extensive adaptations of Roman materials on law and legislation, Austin develops in Lecture XXIX his idea that customs and customary laws are made from customs by judges who are given express or tacit authority to do so by the sovereign legislature. Customary laws, like the judicial authority itself, is subsumed by Austin under legislative sovereignty in the state. Roman notions of written versus unwritten law are employed by him to this end.[57] A partial illustration of this orientation is found in Austin's Lecture XXX concerning the case of the Roman *paterfamilias*. The father's authority in the family was originally established by customs and then customary laws, but later through direct legislation by the praetors, people, and emperors. Austin minimizes, even belittles, the long-acclaimed importance of customary law when pointing out that it is a type of "judiciary law" produced by judges acting as subordinates of the legislative sovereign(s).[58] At the same time in Lecture XXX, Austin underscores in detail that Roman jurists or juriconsults who issued legal opinions that were later included in the compilations of the emperor Justinian were originally not themselves "legislators" (or *conditores*) or even judges acting under authority of the legislative sovereign. The subsequent imperial stamp of approval alone is what gave legislative authority to those opinions and represented the "immediate" source of legislation.[59]

Further admixtures of historicity and creativity in Austin's massive uses of Roman law in these later lectures emerge in Lecture XXXV on "legislation of the praetors." He makes abundant comparisons between Roman praetors and judges of more recent vintage in relation to judicial legislation more widely speaking. Throughout this lecture, Austin again possesses a masterful grasp of Roman law and legal history, as building blocks for his own ideas centering on legislation and legislative sovereignty. Cicero becomes here a useful source of information. The evolution of Roman praetorian edicts—which Austin traces historically up to the time of Emperor Hadrian, when they tended to be absorbed by imperial legislation—engages Austin in typically broad discourses on the Roman promulgation, forms, forces, and interpretation of legislation. Perhaps even more poignant than Austin's historical theorizing upon praetorian edicts as judicial edicts that became direct legislation are his identifications of the "equity" of praetorian legal rulings with legislative "utility" on the basis of the texts on equity near the outset of Justinian's *Digest*.[60]

This latter subject carries over into some of Austin's succeeding lectures. Lecture XXXVI studies the central place of praetorian edicts in the *Digest* and *Code*, which were compiled under Emperor Justinian and given the stamp of imperial legislation by him. Austin compares equity in praetorian edicts with equity in English law. He rejects commonly held notions that equity in both cases is not a body of laws but instead represents the pleasure or *arbitrium* of judges.[61] Roman law here becomes a comparative vehicle for Austin in instructing his contemporaries on the true nature of English law in relation to his theory of sovereign judicial legislation. In Lecture XXXVII he compares judicial legislation to statute legislation, giving succinct definitions of each along with further thoughts on legislative sovereignty.[62]

When appropriating Roman law in the above ways to support his conception of the all-importance of sovereign legislation in the state, Austin recognizes that Roman law was by no means itself a treasure trove of "legislative wisdom." The Roman jurists' contributions in these matters lay instead in their genius for legal "system." At the same time, Austin regrets that Roman law is so little understood and utilized in England.[63] In another place, he heaps scorn on the "pitiable" inabilities of the Roman lawyers to philosophize about the principles of law, in spite of their genius for reducing civil law to a coherent system. Austin attacks two key definitions of law and jurisprudence that appear at the beginning of the *Digest* and that cite justice as the pivotal point; Austin himself is more disposed toward the notion of legal "science" also cited therein.[64]

Much more could be said about Austin's proclivities toward legal systematization. For instance, in his "Notes on Criminal Law: Inconveniences of the Present State of the Criminal Law," there is included "Fragments of a Scheme of a Criminal Code."[65] In addition, Austin's "Codification and Law Reform" addresses the present and future need to "systematise" (*sic*) the "growing bulk" of English law, speaking first in respect to problems of technical reconstruction and second about matters of legislation.[66]

Recapitulation: Austin's Legislative Legacy

When all the above perspectives on legislation in Austin's works are viewed together, it becomes ever clearer that this unifying, all-embracing theme must be accorded a central place as well in the enormous legacy that he left for over a century especially in British jurisprudence (as manifested in subsequent nineteenth-century jurists like A. V. Dicey [67]). The above topics, revolving around the theme of legislation, in Austin's *Lectures on Jurisprudence* have been explored here only briefly in themselves yet with an eye rather to this theme, the overall role of which has been relatively neglected by historians of Austin's thought and its later influences. The above topics, aside from legislation *per se*, represent a cross section of his main thought that has long been treated by scholars. Legislation has been shown above to be, in one form or another, crucial in Austin's diverse treatments of positive law, command, utility, public law, sovereignty, the state, custom, judicial decisions, justice (including so-called higher laws of God, nature, and peoples), Roman law, and systematization. Additional variations on these and other topics could be examined with similar results.

Austin's legislative legacy was enmeshed with that of Bentham as well as separated from it. Their careers were, of course, only symbolically interwoven (though in apt fashion) by the chronological happenstance that 1832 was the year of Bentham's death and of the publication of Austin's *Lectures* I–VI in *Province of Jurisprudence Determined* (not to forget also the Reform Bill of 1832). Although the torch was only being figuratively passed on in that year, Bentham's ideas on legislation and related topics exerted a powerful influence on Austin's *Lectures*, which also departed from Bentham. Austin's legal positivism as well as his legal utilitarianism partly grew out of, carried on, and transformed Bentham's ideas, such as those on command in relation to legislation. The subject of their intellectual interconnections (including via the University of London) is vast. It has not been possible here to study Austin's many scattered references to Bentham—whether direct or indirect, pro or con—on the subjects at hand.[68] Nor has it been necessary to ponder their contrasting styles of intellect and personality. However, Austin's legendary underconfidence and Bentham's legendary overconfidence probably played a role in their respective weaker and stronger drives for actual reforms of state through the dominating power of legislation, one of many such points overlooked by historians.

Whether in conjunction with or independently of Bentham, Austin has continued to wield considerable influence during much of the twentieth century. If in the later nineteenth century and earlier twentieth century there was partial neglect of Austin by many, the twentieth century has witnessed great interest in Austin, both historically and philosphically. The revisionist legal neo-positivism of Hart and many others, which has in some ways supplanted Austin's original legal positivism, has often been allied with a legal neo-utilitarianism. Neo-Austinianism and neo-

Benthamism have at times been fused in the writings of Hart. Other forms of legal philosophy in the twentieth century, reaching against these neo-"isms," may be styled anti-neo-"isms," thereby further showing the continuing shaping influence of nineteenth-century thought. A case in point is the way in which twentieth-century legal neo-positivism a la Austin's command-theory has given rise to contrary ideas of justice by anti-neo-positivists. The task will become, below, to explore the common denominator of legislation underlying concepts of sovereignty, state, and so forth in such currents of thought in the twentieth century.

Thus Austin's jurisprudence must be seen in wide perspective. To be sure, the Austinian tradition that long dominated British jurisprudence in analytical or scientific directions was not the sole force infusing the development of European legal positivism. Even so, Austin, like Bentham, left an unusually strong imprint on the formation of a major new "ism" in the first half of the nineteenth century. On the Continent, the German traditions of legal positivism and neo-positivism stretched in particular from the later nineteenth to the early twentieth century. Jhering, Jellinek, Kelsen (or Kelsenism), and many others contributed to important developments in German legal thought. Just as Austin's *Lectures* were increasingly influenced by German ideas especially on Roman law, resulting largely from his stays in Germany in 1827–1828 and 1841–1843, so, too, was German legal positivism impacted by British varieties of the "ism." The difficulty remains, however, that the complexity of national varieties of positivism—British, German, and French—carries the potential for confusion and inconclusiveness. What constitutes that "ism" across national boundaries in law and jurisprudence can be approached through the common theme of legislation. Often dismissed by scholars are any real influences on Austin of France (where he visited for a time in the 1830s and also in the 1840s) and of Comte (whose death in 1857 shortly preceded Austin's own in 1859). It is thus to Germany that we must now briefly venture in order to round out and conclude our account of legal positivism and Austinianism in the nineteenth century. Later sections will consider the twentieth-century sequels to this story.

4. JHERING AND JELLINEK

Legislation: Bodin, Bentham, and Roman Law

When one turns from the relatively straightforward case of Austin in England to the more complicated cases of Jhering and others in Germany, the elusiveness of the rubric "positiv*ism*" in law and jurisprudence becomes all the more pronounced, although the centrality of legislation for sovereignty and state is again fully affirmed and indeed lends a stabilizing continuum to the "ism." Without it, secondary surveys of the relationships of positivism to other "isms" and schools of thought in Germany, England, and France vary so widely in approach as to defy easy grasp of this "ism" as a coherent doctrine, particularly in the history of legal philosophy.

In the broad historical survey by Hendrick Jan van Eikema Hommes of "major trends in the history of legal philosophy,"[69] the intricate representative treatment (Chapter VIII) of legal positivism in the nineteenth century begins most decisively with German jurisprudence, centering on the great Rudolf von Jhering (1818–1892). Organizationally, there, Jhering's jurisprudence is preceded (in Chapters III–VII) by perspectives (in turn) on Renaissance trends (in Machiavelli, Bodin, and Althusius), the "humanist theory of natural law" and "its state-absolutistic" variants (in Grotius, Hobbes, and Pufendorf), the same theory in its "individualistic currents" (in Locke and Wolff), the "ideal rational law" (in Rousseau, Kant, Fichte, and Hegel), and the "historical school of law" (in Vico, Montesquieu, Savigny, Puchta, Beseler, and Gierke). Those discussions on Jhering deal successively with his "rationalist-utilitarian view of Roman law," his "theory of legal technique" pertaining to "simplification" and so forth, his changing later thought, and his "naturalistic and radically positivistic view of law." Following a look at some other German jurists, the author turns briefly to Austin's "Analytical School of Law," which reportedly had little influence on Continental writers but much on Anglo-American ones.

The key significance of Bodinian traditions and of legislative thought in Jhering's views on the state and sovereignty is well attested in various succinct statements by Eikema Hommes. The characteritions of positivism itself, however, are more elusive (as befits the "ism"). The statements to follow (and in the corresponding note) open up further dimensions to themes featured in the present book and series.

> [L]egal positivism . . . in 19th century jurisprudence . . . [brought] the humanist natural law theory together with Jean Bodin's concept of sovereignty, which paved the way for this modern legal concept. . . . [H]umanist natural law theory, inasmuch as it was influenced by Bodin's concept of sovereignty, taught that the legislative will of the sovereign in the state was the sole and original foundation of all positive law. . . . [When the natural law tradition collapsed in the early nineteenth century under the attack against it by the Historical School, legal positivism was retained and reaffirmed, although not with the

exclusive emphasis on positive law that modern adherents of natural law have charged.] In the spirit of Bodin this school of thought regards the state's legislation as self-sufficient ground of both law's genesis and its validity. . . . [In Jhering's words, his method of "simplification"] "bring[s] to light the entire content of the legislator's will. . . . From being the legislator's porter, a collection of individual legal rules, it [jurisprudence] brings itself to the level of free art and science; to an art from which comes the material artistically . . ." His view of society, moreover, becomes radically individualistic resulting, like traditional humanist natural law theory, in a state-absolutistic conception of law. . . . Von Jhering writes: . . . "without coercion there would be neither *law* nor state . . .". . . . Law proceeds from the power . . . of the state, which he . . . calls the organized form of . . . prowess of the nation. . . . The state . . . is the *exclusive* source of law and is not itself juridically bound by law. The state's legislator is only morally, not legally, obliged to subject himself to his own legislation. Only thus law acquires its essential character as bilateral norm which also binds the state itself. . . .

In this view of positive law, a view wholly determined by Bodin's concept of sovereignty, Von Jhering does consider the legislator to be bound by general legal principles, but these again are understood as *moral*, not as juridically binding principles. . . . Material justice which Von Jhering circumscribes as "the inner equality . . . [or] *balance*" . . . between reward and . . . punishment . . . is central to these principles. If the legislator encroaches upon this principle, legislative arbitrariness results.[70]

It is not necessary here to elaborate on the wider details, textual or contextual, of Jhering's legal positivism. To be sure, it would be useful to probe his multi-volume study on Roman law (*Geist des römischen Recht*, 1852–1865). Upon Roman law, taken largely as a body of universally valid legal knowledge, Jhering built much of his own jurisprudence (in reaction to the more restricted national scope of Roman law described by Sauvigny and the Historical School). In addition, Jhering's indebtedness to the utilitarianism of Benthem could profitably be investigated for evidence of how he arrived at his own distinctive idea of utility and expediency in law. Jhering advocated a more objective or social goal in distinction to the perceived subjective or individualistic orientation of Bentham. Jhering's voluminous studies on the subjects of "purpose" (1877–1883) and "struggle" (1872) in law also formed part of his larger juristic output, the former relating to Bentham and the latter to Darwin (and social Darwinists like Spencer, along with potent German variants). Finally, there is the huge topic of Jhering's many changes in outlook from his earlier to later writings, yet one incapable of being fathomed here.[71]

For present limited purposes, it is sufficient to point out that the legislative state and legislative sovereignty reign supreme in much of Jhering's jurisprudence, as a key stage of legal positivism in nineteenth-century Germany. Indeed, as the foundation of the state, law or legislation becomes for Jhering the "machinery" and "means" by which the state organizes itself for achieving its final or higher social purpose. (A diagram in our Volume IV described the state as representing machinery or mechanism in distinction to the different functions of nation and nationalism.) Notwithstanding Jhering's distinctive concept of and emphasis upon "purpose" and "interest," he brought together elements of "utility," "command" (or compulsion), and "will." These elements have respectively been associated more usually by scholars with Bentham (as well as J. S. Mill), Austin (who, differently from Jhering, took Bentham as a starting point), and Hegel.[72]

Legislation: Sovereign States as Independent Persons

The most important legal positivist for present purposes in the generation of German jurists following Jhering, into the turn of the century, was Georg Jellinek (1851–1911). In his discussion of the Analytical School of Jurisprudence, centering on legal positivism, John Hallowell begins briefly with John Austin in England and then turns at length to three German jurists in turn—C. F. von Gerber, Paul Laband, and Georg Jellinek. He views Jellinek as a partial culmination of previous German thought, paving the way for twentieth-century trends, especially those leading to Kelsenism and also to Hitlerism (an end-product disputed by many experts yet cited by others). The triad's general outlook is depicted as follows, with the implication that German jurists were indeed significantly influenced by Austin's analytical jurisprudence.

> In Germany jurisprudence was transformed into a formal science of law through the work of men like Gerber, Laband, and Jellinek. Under the influence of positivism the study of law was confined to an analytical examination of the existing body of positive law in an effort to establish a *Staatsrechtwissenschaft* or "science of law" which would exclude all consideration of political and moral ends or purposes. Justice was discarded as a

> meta-juristic concept and compulsion was substituted for justice as the criterion of law. Having denied that there was any other law than positive law, having denied the existence of a transcendent order of law, these jurists were forced to conclude that the source of the law is the will of the state.
>
> They conceived of the state as a juristic person with a will of its own. Theoretically this subordinated the monarch to the rule of law and they were able, abstractly at least, to distinguish the will of the state from the will of the monarch.[73]

So fixated, according to Hallowell, were German analytical jurists like Jellinek on the unlimited power of positive law and public legislation in the state that their professed recognition of limitations upon sovereign powers became invalidated. In particular, he dubs Jellinek's notion of the state's "auto-limitation" as being nearly valueless. The issue of legislation, we may add, looms large behind such problems as the following (including those in the corresponding note regarding Jellinek's idea of public law as shaped by the state's personality and will or command).

> Gerber expressed it: "The State's power to will, political power, is the law of the State.". . . This distinction between the will of the state and the will of the monarch is a highly tenuous one and for practical purposes they are indistinguishable. To say, therefore, that the source of law is the will of the state as a juristic person and to say at the same time that it is only made manifest through the will of the monarch, is to say, for practical purposes, that the source of law is the will of the monarch. . . .
>
> In similar fashion Georg Jellinek declared that "a power to rule becomes legal by being limited. Law is legally limited power. The potential power of the community is greater than its actual power. Through auto-limitation it achieves the character of legal power." To say that "law is legally limited power" is like saying "law is limited by law" which means nothing. Under analysis Jellinek's conception of "auto-limitation" turns out to be no limitation at all. He defined sovereignty as "the exclusive capacity of the power of the State to give its ruling will a universally binding content, to determine its own legal order in every direction" and "the impossibility of being legally restrained by any other power against its own will." The logical implication from this is that the state, potentially at least, is omnipotent. The State can make any content binding that it desires.[74]

Issues of legislation were bound up with the propoundings of German jurists like Jellinek on the state's juristic personality existing apart from yet manifested through the organs of government (and monarchy). Sovereign legislative will and command furnish here a central point of reference. Strong statements on legislation by Laband ("The sanction is the heart of the whole process of legislation . . .") were surpassed, in the same school, by Philip Zorn ("The sanction is that public law which perfects the law. In the sanction lies the command in law: *whoever issues the command is the legislator.* The sanction is the highest and true act of legislation; therefore the right of sanction belongs only to the bearer of sovereignty.").[75] It is Hallowell's contention that German jurists like Jellinek opened the way for the possibility that a state's legislature, thus empowered to the extent of obviating individual rights and freedom, could, through legislation, end its own existence and institute a despot, as did the German Reichstag in 1933.[76]

Notwithstanding the castigations by historians like Hallowell, there remains considerable historical value in studying Jellinek's theories of the state and in particular the role of legislation. In fact, the historical surveys of political-legal thought written by Hallowell and others often reveal the culmination in the history of legislative theory represented by late-nineteenth-century German jurists such as Jellinek. This is not to deny their place in the broader intellectual background to the later power state in Germany. But one cannot ignore jurists like Jellinek on these grounds any more than historians like Meinecke, Kantorowicz, and Schramm for their supposedly proto-Hitlerian Machiavellism and Kaiserism when studying earlier European history.

Jellinek's great interest in legislation as a subject in its own right and as a crux of the state problem is reflected in his provocatively entitled *Gesetz und Verordnung: Staatsrechtliche Untersuchungen auf Rechtsgeschichtlicher und Rechtsvergleichender Grundlage.*[77] Here the close interconnection between legislation and the state in legal history and comparative or theoretical law stands out clearly in the very title. This unique symbiosis is carried throughout the work's headings and contents on a multiplicity of disparate themes and topics. His vantage point is first and foremost legislation. Jellinek's national surveys of England, France, Germany, Austria, and the Netherlands cover wide historical and contemporary ground. Intermixed at points are ancient Greek and Roman materials (on Aristotle, Cicero, and so forth). Although the historical surveys are perhaps too broad to do the subject justice, in a book of only a few hundred pages, Jellinek's overall viewpoint is what concerns us here. The legislative "foundation" of the state in history gives a powerful support for Jellinek's own state theory.

The most noted of Jellinek's later works was his vast and comprehensive *Allgemeine Staatslehre*.[78] Here his historical, comparative, and theoretical approaches to law blend together in a truly monumental achievement. Building upon his earlier work on the legislative foundation of the state and sovereignty, he erects a massive superstructure with diverse kinds of thematic materials.

The first and second books of Jellinek's *Staatslehre* treat the state in relation to such subjects as art (including in a Hegelian sense), nation, society, cause, norm, Volk, organism, authority, natural law, religion, theology, psychology, method, "ideal types," purpose (including Jhering's sense of it), will, individualism, family, limitations, legitimacy, despotism (to which Jellinek denies he opens the way), dualism, freedom, power, and right. He broadly surveys, in turn, the "Hellenic state," the "Roman state," the "medieval state," and the "modern state." Writers discussed include Aristotle, Plato, Hobbes, Locke, Pufendorf, Rousseau, Kant, Comte, Fichte, Hegel, and so on.

The third book of Jellinek's *Staatslehre* takes up issues of public and private law, sovereignty, forms of states, legislation, and the like. He broadly traces developing theories of sovereignty from antiquity and the Middle Ages to the sixteenth century (especially with regard to Bodin, the "negative character" of his ideas, and Loyseau) and beyond (featuring Hobbes, Grotius, Locke, Kant, Montesquieu, Wolff, and Sièyes). On monarchical forms of states, Jhering considers the Middle Ages, absolutism, Hobbes, Louis XIV, Frederick the Great, Leopold II, and others. Under republics he includes modern democracies. Concerning legislation he considers both theory and practice. Throughout the work are various headings citing "art" forms in ways reminiscent of Hegel (e.g., *Die Arten der Staatsorgane* and *Die Politik als Ausgewandte Staatswissenschaft und als Kunstlehre*). Other subjects in relation to the above include representation, war, fundamental law, and "administrative decentralization."

Jellinek's ideas of state and sovereignty in contexts of legislation and juristic personality can be viewed from broad historical perspectives, looking backward and forward in time. Concepts of the state as an independent entity and person can be variously found in older forms in Tudor organological metaphors, in Renaissance-medieval personifications of the king's abstract and natural bodies, and in humanistic juridical ideas of the "state itself" as the final cause of civil law. Proto-absolutist tendencies of Lutheran state theory have been said by some historians to lead in German history to Bismarck and Hitler; positivist theorists like Jellinek have been inserted by others into that line of development. What is perhaps more certain is that Jellinek and other

German jurists discussed above provide an important backdrop for understanding the neo-positivism of Hans Kelsen in the early twentieth century, to whom we will presently turn.

Chapter IV

"Ideal*ism*" and "Hegelian*ism*"

1. DIFFUSIONS OF THE "ISMS"

One of the most dominant figures in the history of political and legal thought in the nineteenth century was none other than Hegel, whom we have often encountered in previous studies. His state theory remained highly influential well into the next century among not only theorists but also, as already seen, historians. Like Bentham, Mill, Austin, Marx, and others treated in the present work, Hegel provides a *locus classicus* in theory on the legislative state that has likewise often been grouped under (obscuring) major "isms" of the nineteenth century. In addition, as in the cases of Bentham, Austin, and Marx, Hegel's name itself has frequently stood as a dominant "ism," namely, Hegelianism. The wider major "ism" with which Hegel's philosophy has been principally associated is idealism, through which he has also been connected with political "isms" such as nationalism. In the development of idealism, particularly in Germany but also more generally, Hegel's philosophical and political ideas have usually been studied against the background of his late-eighteenth-century predecessor, Kant.

Necessarily left aside below are such perennial debates as on whether Hegel, as well as Kant, possessed a genuine political theory (on the state and other subjects) or rather a more purely philosophical-metaphysical outlook. Instead, there needs to be an intensive investigation of their thought on legislation in relation to sovereignty and the state. In considering below the Kantian background to Hegel, we can also account for Kant's important state theory in its own right, which was not included in the preceding study.

Like other elusive "isms" such as utilitarianism and Benthamism as well as positivism and Austinianism, idealism and Hegelianism often self-destruct or self-"deconstruct" when used as ideological formulas by historians of political theory. By "diffusions of the isms," we primarily mean here the tendencies of the two at hand to become diffusive and dispersive through loose applications made possible by their inherent amorphousness. Such drawbacks may be glimpsed in perusals of pertinent book titles and dictionary definitions.

Few "isms" have been as widely applied by historians to thinkers in all periods, as far back as ancient Greece and Plato, as has idealism. Standard library catalogues contain scores if not hundreds of main titles bearing the words "ideal*ism*," "ideal*isme*," "ideal*ismus*," or "ideal*ismo*," to cite only four languages. Titles of this kind on Hegel and Kant (some cited below) can serve as much to confuse as to clarify. Broader rubrics diffusively incorporating this "ism" in book titles on other subjects include the following: "idealism and early wish fulfillment," "idealism and foreign policy," "idealism and naturalism," "idealism and pragmatism," "idealism and revolution," "idealism and the modern age," "idealism as a practical creed," "idealism debased from volkish ideology to national socialism," "idealism East and West," "idealism of Giovanni Gentile," "idealism past and present," "idealisme contemporain," "idealisme de Fichte," "idealisme de Marcel Proust," "idealismo e imperialismo," "idealismo e positivismo," "idealismo filosofico e realismo politico," "idealismo italiano," "idealismo scientifico di William Whewell," "idealismus und nation," "idealismus und nihilismus," "idealismus und positivismus," and "idealismus und realismus." When "ideal*ism*" in contradistinction to "real*ism*" is used as a supposed system for contrasting Hegel to Marx, More to Machiavelli, and Aristotle to Plato, the results are usually as uncertain and relativistic as when "liberal*ism*" is contrasted to "conservat*ism*".

According to the *Oxford English Dictionary*, the term "ideal*ism*," under first the category of philosophy, has the following signification, which is exceedingly broad: "Any system of thought or philosophy in which the object of external perception is held to consist, either in itself, or as perceived, of ideas (in various senses of the word: see IDEA . . . .) . . . ." The more specific varieties cited are "subjective idealism," "critical or transcendental idealism" (Kant), "objective idealism" (Schelling), and "absolute idealism" (Hegel). The earliest usages given here date from 1796 and 1803 (by W. Taylor), with numerous later ones including those describing the thought of Kant and Hegel. The second main meaning is even broader, turning from ideas to ideals and idealization: "The practice of idealizing or tendency to idealize; the habit of representing things in an ideal form, or as they might be; imaginative treatment of a subject in art or literature; ideal style or character: opp. to *realism*. Also, aspiration after or pursuit of an ideal." The earliest usage cited in these instances dates from 1829 (by I. Taylor) and 1822 (Shelley). There is thus little wonder why historians, philosophers, political theorists, and others across a broad intellectual spectrum have been enabled, by the very looseness of the term, to apply "ideal*ism*" to so many diverse subjects.

Similar exercises could be conducted for "Hegelian*ism*" and "Kantian*ism*," along with many other such words. The former term is defined in the *Oxford English Dictionary* thus: "The philosophical system of Hegel. A system of Absolute Idealism (as distinguished from the Subjective Idealism of Kant), in which pure being is regarded as pure thought, the universe as its development, and philosophy as its dialectical explication." There is, of course, a relative specificity involved when "isms" are created out of names. This holds true for "Hegelian*ism*" as well as for "Bentham*ism*," "Austinian*ism*," and "Marx*ism*." However, "post-Hegelian*ism*" and "post-Kantian*ism*" pose wider "diffusions of the isms" that are less manageable. Later "ideal*ism*" became further blurred in the complicated crosscurrents of thought among the followers and critics of Hegel and Kant in the middle to later nineteenth century. Added complications arose with so-called "neo-Hegelian*ism*" and "neo-Kantian*ism*" in the twentieth century.

In the final analysis, the term "ideal*ism*," as used to describe the thought of Hegel as well as of Kant, has opened up two pitfalls for unsuspecting historians. The first is their long-standing tendency to trace the theories of Hegel and Kant relating to this "ism" back to earlier history or to see in older theory a marked inclination toward the later uses of this "ism." Our previous studies of pre-nineteenth-century writers were frequently occupied with the task of clearing away the anachronisms of twentieth-century interpreters who predated to earlier centuries various "isms" first decisively used in the nineteenth century. But in the present study an alternate task at times is to clear away the anachronisms of nineteenth-century theorists themselves who in first decisively using an "ism" sought to justify their theorizing by conjuring forth inexact historical parallels. Thus, while Mill and Comte sought close historical parallels for their respective uses of the terms "utilitarian*ism*" and "positiv*ism*," Hegel sought historical contexts for his brand of "ideal*ism*." So, too, would Marx's views on history with regard to "social*ism*" compound the pitfalls of anachronism for later historians.

Second, frequent concentration on broad intellectual constructs like "ideal*ism*" has diverted scholarship on Hegel as well as on Kant from their more mundane views on the state's legislative foundations and has focused it instead on their alleged greater concern with philosophy and metaphysics than with political thought *per se*. Nevertheless, the state problem in Hegel and Kant must be explored here within the legislative and other contexts that have preoccupied this series. Hegel and Kant took further strides along many of the same thematic paths that we saw pursued by their predecessors.

2. THE KANTIAN BACKGROUND

"The Doctrine of Right"

In the immediate background to the development of the German philosophical school known as "ideal*ism*" in the nineteenth century, as represented most decisively in the writings of Hegel, stands the complicated, difficult, yet influential thought of Immanuel Kant (1724–1804). It has long been recognized, for instance, that the "transcendental ideal*ism*" represented in Kant's ideal rational law paved the way in German philosophical, political, and legal thought for Hegel (and others including Fichte). Notwithstanding the wide divergencies between Kant and Hegel, including the former's acceptance of various forms of "empirical real*ism*," scholars have long paired Kant and Hegel together as classic exponents of the German idealist tradition, inclusive of politics and law. However, just what the much-used scholarly rubric of "ideal*ism*" means in accounts of Kant, as well as of Hegel, is not easy to determine, especially in the broad parameters of the so-called "Platonic tradition." Similar shortcomings have befallen other "isms" ascribed to Kant, such as rationalism, realism, empiricism, and transcendentalism. Kant's political and legal thought is interwoven with his wider philosophy. His recondite "metaphysical" systems of philosophy render his political and legal ideas hard to fathom, however much experts have reduced them to idealist or other categories for purposes of analysis.[1]

Kant's legal-political philosophy relating to the state problem is most developed in Part I of his *The Metaphysics of Morals* (1797), a work laden with a complicated and difficult textual tradition. Part I constitutes his famed "Metaphysical First Principles of the Doctrine of Right" (in turn divided into two parts on "Private Right" and "Public Right"). Part II deals with "Metaphysical First Principles of the Doctrine of Virtue" (divided into two parts on "Doctrine of the Elements of Ethics" and "Doctrine of the Method of Ethics").[2] In his "Doctrine of Right,"

Kant employs the term "idea" in connection with a wide range of subjects. These include the "idea" (and rational "concept") of civil constitution, of civil union, of community of all nations, of duty, of friendship, of God, of head of state, of humanity, of original community of land, of original contract of right of nations, of the will of all united, of sovereignty—and of a state. The relationship of "idea" and "ideal" to Kant's so-called "ideal*ism*" of course looms large in the secondary literature.[3]

Kant's *Metaphysics of Morals* bears complicated relationships to his multitudinous other works, which include the following: *Critique of Pure Reason* (first edition 1781, second edition 1787), *Prolegomena to any Future Metaphysics* (1783), *Ideas towards a Universal History from a Cosmopolitan Point of View* (1784), *An Answer to the Question: What Is Enlightenment?* (1784), *Groundwork for the Metaphysics of Morals* (1785), *Metaphysical Foundations of Natural Science* (1786), *Critique of Practical Reason* (1788), *Concerning the Use of Teleological Principles in Philosophy* (1788), *Critique of Judgment* (first edition 1790, second edition 1793), *Religion within the Limits of Reason Alone* (1793), *The End of all Things* (1794), *On Perpetual Peace* (1795), *Anthropology from a Pragmatic Point of View* (1798), *Logic* (1800), and *Education* (1803). Although not attemptable here, it would be instructive to search these and other writings by Kant for his germane philosophical terminology on "legislation," the four causes, "ideas" (and "ideals"), and much else.[4]

In order to give a generalized prefatory synopsis geared to present perspectives, we may see Kant's "Doctrine of Right" as operating on two overall levels within his wider philosophy. On the metaphysical level, broadly speaking for Kant, stand the ideal rational law (replacing or superseding many traditional natural law categories) and the knowledge of things as they really are in themselves. Transcendental *a priori* forms of thought or categories of the understanding, pertaining to nature as the field for theoretical reason, involve a pure reason through which comes a universally valid moral (rational law) "legislation." Enshrining man's freedom and equality, such laws transcend the sensory experiences of pain and pleasure (emphasized contrariwise by utilitarians). They are intuited and brought to bear, by practical reason, as norms for individuals in society and for the right governance of the state through positive laws. Positive laws should ideally be guided, but in reality are not bound, by the moral norms in this metaphysical jurisprudence. Rational law "legislated" by man's practical reason should thus furnish regulatory standards—not limited to time, place, or circumstance—for all empirically based civil legislation in the state. The moral will or self is free, is capable of legislating for itself, and transcends the phenomenal world.

On the second generalized level, bearing a complicated relationship to the metaphysical level, stands, for Kant, the positive law and the empirical knowledge of things as they appear to us to be through the senses and intellect. In the final analysis, Kant, departing from traditional natural law theorists, does not stipulate that legal principles and moral legislation based on practical reason are a necessary *binding* basis for positive law or state legislation. The latter depends for its actual validity solely on the will of the sovereign state legislator(s) and cannot legitimately be resisted (much less overthrown) by subjects even when it violates the ideal rational moral law. To be sure, Kant strongly supports a moral-metaphysical basis for positive state legislation, whereby to guarantee and safeguard man's moral freedom and equality in society; but this basis has a relative or regulatory, not a constitutive, function. The ultimate result is, in part, a proto-positivistic position on sovereign state legislation that foreshadows various nineteenth-century theorists in Germany and England. Despite appearances of being rooted in rational moral law, positive law depends, in the final analysis, on the legislative will of the state sovereign, in ways that build upon concepts of (Roman) civil law and of Rousseau. Rousseau's theory of the "general will," embodying the all-embracing legislative sovereignty of the people, greatly influenced Kant. Kant's definition of the state as an association of people under law accords with traditions of civil law as much as with his own metaphysical principles of rational law. Not surprisingly, Kant condemned most aspects of the French Revolution, which violated his prohibition against resistance to empirical sovereignty in the state.

What now becomes requisite is a concentrated textual demonstration of the central role that Kant assigns to public legislation in the operations of the state and of sovereignty, with respect to both actual positive law and ideal rational law. The simple fact of legislation's centrality, already suggested above, is abundantly evident from the outset in his "Doctrine of Right," that is, in Part I of his *Metaphysics of Morals*. There is not space or need here to dwell on the complicated textual traditions of that work either in itself or in relation to Kant's other works, such as his earlier *Groundwork* (which at times experts have found to contradict or diverge from it). Nor can the weighty secondary literature pertaining to the subjects at hand be adequately explored or accounted for here. Yet it is clear that the legislative basis of the state and sovereignty in Kant's systems has not heretofore received the special attention it deserves.[5]

The Centrality of Legislation

That legislation and lawgiving or lawmaking are central to Kant's "Doctrine of Right" is clear from the start of his *Metaphysics of Morals*, in the Introduction to the work as a whole. Following revealing germane statements on his overall philosophical viewpoint,[6] Kant enters upon the complicated interconnections between positive, moral, and other types of laws. At all levels, these varied types of laws mostly revolve, in their own distinctive fashions, around the topic of lawgiving and legislation. In the course of the passages to follow, which provide general further introduction for present purposes to Kant's positions, there are numerous telling uses of terms like "idea," "art," "system," and "will," which will become clearer in scope as we proceed.

> Obligatory laws for which there can be an external lawgiving are called *external* laws (*leges externae*) in general. Those among them that can be recognized as obligatory *a priori* by reason even without external lawgiving are indeed external but *natural* laws, whereas those that do not bind without actual external lawgiving (and so without it would not be laws) are called *positive* laws. One can therefore conceive of external lawgiving which would contain only positive laws; but then a natural law would still have to precede it, which would establish the authority of the lawgiver (i.e., his authorization to bind others by his mere *choice*).
>
> A principle that makes certain actions duties is a practical law. A rule that the agent himself makes his principle on subjective grounds is called his *maxim*; hence different agents can have very different maxims with regard to the same law.
>
> The categorical imperative, which as such only affirms what obligation is, is: act upon a maxim that can also hold as a universal law. . . .
>
> Laws proceed from the will, *maxims* from choice. In man the latter is a free choice; the will, which is directed to nothing beyond the law itself, cannot be called either free or unfree, since it is not directed to actions but immediately to giving laws for the maxims of actions (and is, therefore, practical reason itself). Hence the will directs with absolute necessity and is itself *subject to* no necessitation. Only *choice* can therefore be called *free*.
>
> But freedom of choice cannot be defined—as some have tried to define it—as the ability to make a choice for or against the law . . . , even though choice as a *phenomenon* provides fre-

quent examples of this in experience.... Only freedom in relation to the internal lawgiving of reason is really an ability; the possibility of deviating from it is an inability....

A (morally practical) *law* is a proposition that contains a categorical imperative (a command). One who commands (*imperans*) through a law is the lawgiver (*legislator*). He is the author (*autor*) of the obligation in accordance with the law, but not always the author of the law. In the latter case the law would be a positive (contingent) and chosen law. A law that binds us *a priori* and unconditionally by our own reason can also be expressed as proceeding from the will of a supreme lawgiver, that is, one who has only rights and no duties (hence from the divine will); but this signifies only the idea of a moral being whose will is a law for everyone, without his being thought of as the author of the law....

The mere conformity or nonconformity of an action with law, irrespective of the incentive to it, is called its *legality* (lawfulness); but that conformity in which the idea of duty arising from the law is also the incentive to the action is called its *morality*.

Duties in accordance with rightful lawgiving can be only external duties, since this lawgiving does not require that the idea of this duty, which is internal, itself be the determining ground of the agent's choice.... On the other hand, ethical lawgiving, while it also makes internal actions duties, does not exclude external actions but applies to everything that is a duty in general. But just because ethical lawgiving includes within its law the internal incentive to action (the idea of duty), and this feature must not be present in external lawgiving, ethical lawgiving cannot be external (not even the external lawgiving of a divine will), although it does take up duties which rest on another, namely an external, lawgiving by making them, *as duties*, incentives in its lawgiving.

It can be seen from this that all duties, just because they are duties, belong to ethics; but it does not follow that the *lawgiving* for them is always contained in ethics: for many of them it is outside ethics.[7]

Succinct related statements concerning Kant's "systematic" thought in connection with his metaphysical, practical, rational, and empirical methodology, as well as with formal and final causation, appear at the beginning of his Preface to Part II on "Doctrine of Virtue."[8]

In his "Introduction to the Doctrine of Right," prior to his main treatment of that subject in Part I of *Metaphysics of Morals*, Kant begins (§ A–C) with several short sections entitled "What the Doctrine of Right Is," "What Is Right?," and "The Universal Principle of Right." The centrality of legislation and lawgiving is again abundantly evident in the complex interworkings of the myriad parts of his system. The allusion to Plato is here indicative of those elements of Kant's idealism that scholars often refer to as residing in the Platonic tradition.

> The sum of those laws for which an external lawgiving is possible is called the *doctrine of right (ius)*. If there has actually been such lawgiving, it is the doctrine of *positive right*, and one versed in this, a jurist *(iurisconsultus)*, is said to be *experienced in the law (iurisperitus)* when he not only knows external laws but also knows them externally, that is, in their application to cases that come up in experience. Such knowledge can also be called *legal expertise (iurisprudentia)*, but without both together it remains mere *juridical science (iurisscientia)*. The last title belongs to *systematic* knowledge of the doctrine of natural right *(ius naturae)*, although one versed in this must supply the immutable principles for any giving of positive law. . . .
>
> [T]he jurist . . . can indeed state what is laid down as right *(quid sit iuris)*, that is, what the laws in a certain place and at a certain time say or have said. But whether what these laws prescribed is also right, and what the universal criterion is by which one could recognize right as well as wrong *(iustum et iniustum)*, this would remain hidden from him unless he leaves those empirical principles behind for a while and seeks the sources of such judgments in reason alone, so as to establish the basis for any possible giving of positive laws (although positive laws can serve as excellent guides to this). Like the wooden head in Phaedrus's fable, a merely empirical doctrine of right is a head that may be beautiful but unfortunately it has no brain. . . .
>
> Right is therefore the sum of the conditions under which the choice of one can be united with the choice of another in accordance with a universal law of freedom. . . .
>
> "Any action is *right* if it can coexist with everyone's freedom in accordance with a universal law, or if on its maxim the freedom of choice of each can coexist with everyone's freedom in accordance with a universal law." . . .

Thus the universal law of right [*das allgemeine Rechtsgesetz*], so act externally that the free use of your choice can coexist with the freedom of everyone in accordance with a universal law, is indeed a law that lays an obligation on me. . . .

In the same "Introduction" (§ D–E), Kant briefly discusses the topic of coercion. Indicative are his headings: "Right is Concerned with an Authorization to Use Coercion" and "A Strict Right Can Also Be Represented as the Possibility of a Fully Reciprocal Use of Coercion That Is Consistent with Everyone's Freedom in Accordance with Universal Laws." Correspondingly, Kant makes use, in the ensuing "Appendix" and "Division . . . of Right," of two traditionally cited subjects in Roman law. Here he further shows his partial indebtedness, exhibited throughout the work, to civil law traditions with regard to positive law and related matters. His headings on "The Right of Necessity (*Ius Necessitatis*)" and "General Division of Duties of Right" (at the head of his "Division of the Doctrine of Right") pertain to the Roman legal maxim of "necessity knows no law," which has been encountered in our previous studies, as has the three-part maxim from Ulpian.

The motto of the right of necessity says: "Necessity has no law" (*necessitas non habet legem*). Yet there could be no necessity that would make what is wrong conform with law. . . .

One can follow Ulpian in making this division if a sense is ascribed to his formulae which he may not have thought distinctly in them but which can be explicated from them or put into them. They are the following:

(1) *Be an honorable human being (honeste vive).* . . .

(2) *Do not wrong anyone (neminem laede).* . . .

(3) (If you cannot help associating with others), *enter* into a society with them in which each can keep what is his (*suum cuique tribue*). . . .

So the above three classical formulae serve also as principles for dividing the system of duties of right into *internal* duties, *external* duties, and duties that involve the derivation of the latter from the principle of the former by subsumption. . . .

As systematic *doctrines*, rights are divided into *natural right*, which rests only on *a priori* principles, and *positive* (statutory) *right*, which proceeds from the will of a legislator.

Kant concludes ("Division" B) by tying together aspects of civil law, positive law, and public law within wider contexts, supplying further implications for the centrality of legislation and lawgiving in his system.

> The highest division of natural right cannot be the division (sometimes made) into *natural* and *social* right; it must instead be the division into natural and *civil* right, the former of which is called *private right* and the latter *public right*. For a *state of nature* is not opposed to a social but to a civil condition, since there can certainly be society in a state of nature, but not *civil* society (which secures what is mine or yours by public laws). This is why right in a state of nature is called private right.[9]

Reducing the State "Idea(l)" to Public Legislation

Our two previous chapters on utilitarianism and positivism demonstrated that the respective core concepts of "utility" and "positive" law in political-legal thought centered in distinctive ways on topics in legislation. Likewise, the present chapter on idealism, with regard first of all to Kant, shows that the state "idea" (and "ideal")—repeatedly referred to as such throughout his "Doctrine of Right"—revolves around public legislation. That this should prove to be the case throughout for Kant is already anticipated in his introductory discussions, examined above in terms of the general centrality of legislation.

Legislative criteria of the state idea are even more strongly suggested at the outset of the main body of Kant's "Doctrine of Right," in the opening listing (or table of contents) of the main headings. Most conspicuous are the titles of Parts I and II—"*Private Right* with Regard to External Objects (The Sum of Laws That Do Not Need to Be Promulgated)" and "*Public Right* (The Sum of Laws That Need to Be Promulgated)." The first chapter of Part II is on "The Right of a State" (the other two chapters dealing with "The Right of Nations" and "Cosmopolitan Right"). Here, then, promulgated laws or public legislation are already indicated to be the *raison d'être* of the state itself. Even the non-promulgated character of laws under the category of private right, as distinguished from public right of state(s), serves to accentuate legislation itself as the overriding line of demarcation in Kant's "Doctrine of Right." (The chapters and sections of Part I of his "Doctrine of Right" deal with the having and the acquiring of something external as one's own. The latter category concerns property right, contract right, rights of persons and things, and "ideal" acquisitions. Final consideration is given to acquisitions subjectively dependent upon "decisions of a public court of justice.")[10]

In Chapter I of Part I on "Private Right" in Kant's "Doctrine of Right" in his *Metaphysics of Morals*, a sectional heading (§ 8) makes a pregnant interconnection between public legislative authority and the civil state of society as the basis of rightful conditions. It reads: "It Is Possible to Have Something External as One's Own Only in a Rightful Condition, under an Authority Giving Laws Publicly, That Is, in a Civil Condition." The passage below closely associates the general will (a concept that Kant has partly borrowed from Roussseau) and public legislative authority with the power and state of the civil condition, as the context for what is meant by "external."

> Now, a unilateral will cannot serve as a coercive law for everyone with regard to possession that is external and therefore contingent, since that would infringe upon freedom in accordance with universal laws. So it is only a will putting everyone under obligation, hence only a collective general (*common*) and powerful will, that can provide everyone this assurance.—But the condition of being under a general external (i.e., public) lawgiving accompanied with power is the civil condition. So only in a civil condition can something external be mine or yours.

Under another sectional heading of Chapter I (§ 41, "Transition from What Is Mine or Yours in a State of Nature to What Is Mine or Yours in a Rightful Condition Generally"), the "idea" and "will" of public legislative authority becomes crucial for public and distributive justice in the state. Formal and material causation, along with efficient and final causation, plays a part methodologically. So, too, do artificial conditions in relation to conditions that are natural, social, and civil. Public legislation furnishes the main fulcrum for the civil state and the relations between the commanding, law-giving authority and those subjected to it.

> A rightful condition is that relation of human beings among one another that contains the conditions under which alone everyone is able to *enjoy* his rights, and the formal condition under which this is possible in accordance with the idea of a will giving laws for everyone [*eines allgemein gesetzgebenden wilens*] is called public justice. With reference to either the possibility or the actuality or the necessity of possession of objects (the matter of choice) in accordance with laws, public justice can be divided into *protective justice* (*iustitia tutatrix*), *justice in men's acquiring from one another* (*iustitia commutativa*),

and *distributive justice* (*iustitia distributiva*).—In these the law says, *first*, merely what conduct is intrinsically *right* in terms of its form (*lex iuridica*); *second*, what [objects] are capable of being covered externally by law, in terms of their matter, that is, what way of being in possession is *rightful* (*lex iuridica*); *third*, what is the decision of a court in a particular case in accordance with the given law under which it falls, that is, what is *laid down as right* (*lex iustitiae*). . . . [A] court is itself called the *justice* of a country. . . .

A condition that is not rightful, that is, a condition in which there is no distributive justice, is called a state of nature (*status naturalis*). What is opposed to a state of nature is not . . . a condition that is *social* and that could be called an artificial condition (*status artificialis*), but rather the *civil* condition (*status civilis*), that of a society subject to distributive justice. For in the state of nature, too, there can be societies compatible with rights. . . .

The first and second of these conditions can be called the condition of *private right*, whereas the third and last can be called the condition of *public right*. . . . The laws of the condition of public right, accordingly, have to do only with the rightful form of their association (constitution), in view of which these laws must necessarily be conceived as public.

The *civil union* (*unio civilis*) cannot itself be called a *society*, for between the *commander* [*befehlshaber*] (*imperans*) and the *subject* (*subditus*) there is no partnership. They are not fellow-members: one is *subordinated to*, not *coordinated with* the other; and those who are coordinate with one another must for this very reason consider themselves equals since they are subject to common laws. The civil union *is* not so much a society but rather *makes* one.

In Chapter (or Section) I § 43–45) on "The Right of a State" in Part II ("Public Right") in the "Doctrine of Right" in *Metaphysics of Morals*, Kant further identifies public legislation with public (distributive) justice as the foundation of the state "idea." According with this viewpoint are various other terms associated with the state, including "commonwealth" and "constitution." This idea of the state, uniting all people under its will through a rightful system of promulgated public legislation, provides an indispensable point of reference for Kant in considering the rights of each nation and of all nations as well as cosmopolitan rights. The state "idea" here forms a kind of "norm" for the guidance of the "actual" formation and conduct of those in a state. Rational *a priori* ideas are necessary for this system's proper operation. Yet when individuals leave the state of nature and unite under the civil laws of the state itself, so as to be free of violence and lawlessness, they subject themselves to the external and coercive legislative power of the state. (Kant's typical uses of *Gesetzgebung* and *Gesetzgeber* mean respectively "legislation" and "legislator" when the context is positive law, or "lawgiving" and "lawgiver" when it is private law.)

> The sum of the laws which need to be promulgated generally in order to bring about a rightful condition is *public right*.— Public right is therefore a system of laws for a people, that is, a multitude of human beings, or for a multitude of peoples, which, because they affect one another, need a rightful condition under a will uniting them, a *constitution* (*constitutio*), so that they may enjoy what is laid down as right.—This condition of the individuals within a people in relation to one another is called a *civil* condition (*status civilis*), and the whole of individuals in a rightful condition, in relation to its own members is called a *state* (*civitas*). Because of its form, by which all are united through their common interest in being in a rightful condition, a state is called a *commonwealth* (*res publica latius sic dicta*). In relation to other peoples, however, a state is called simply a *power* (*potentia*) (hence the word *potentate*). Because the union of the members is (presumed to be) one they inherited, a state is also called a nation (*gens*). Hence, under the general concept of public right we are led to think not only of the right of a state but also of a *right of nations* (*ius gentium*). Since the earth's surface is not unlimited but closed, the concepts of the right of a state and of a right of nations lead inevitably to the idea of a *right for all nations* (*ius gentium*) or *cosmopolitan right* (*ius cosmopoliticum*). So if the principle of outer freedom limited by law is lacking in any one of these three possible forms of rightful condition, the framework of all the others is unavoidably undermined and must finally collapse.
>
> It is not experience from which we learn of human beings' maxim of violence and of their malevolent tendency to attack one another before external legislation endowed with power appears. It is therefore not some fact that makes coercion through public law necessary. On the contrary, however well disposed and law-abiding men might be, it still lies *a priori* in the rational idea of such a condition (one that is not rightful) that before a public lawful condition is established individual human beings, peoples, and states can never be secure against

violence from one another, since each has its own right to do *what seems right* . . . and not to be dependent upon another's opinion about this. So, . . . , the first thing it has to resolve upon is the principle that it must leave the state of nature, in which each follows its own judgment, unite itself with all others (with which it cannot avoid interacting), subject itself to a public lawful external coercion, and so enter into a condition in which what is to be recognized as belonging to it is determined *by law* and is allotted to it by adequate *power* (not its own but an external power); that is, it ought above all else to enter a civil condition. . . . Hence . . . acquisition is still only *provisional* as long as it does not yet have the sanction of public law, since it is not determined by public (distributive) justice and secured by an authority putting this right into effect. . . .

A *state* (*civitas*) is a union of a multitude of human beings under laws of right. Insofar as these are *a priori* necessary as laws, that is, insofar as they follow of themselves from concepts of external right as such (are not statutory), its form is the form of a state as such, that is, of *the state in idea,* as it ought to be in accordance with pure principles of right. This idea serves as a norm (*norma*) for every actual union into a commonwealth (hence serves as a norm for its internal constitution).

In Chapter II (§ 53–55, 57, 61) on "The Right of Nations" in Part II on "Public Right," Kant makes it plain that by right of nations is really meant the right of states. This holds true for him in large part because of the legislative element involved in a state's declaration of war (war being a key component of relations between nations). When reverting to a state of nature, nations (like individuals) revert to lawlessness. War should be left behind in favor of the lawful condition of the civil state. Nations (like individuals) should rightly base themselves on the (justly promulgated) public law of the state. In this way the final goal, a "perpetual peace" among nations, can be achieved.[11]

In Chapter III (§ 62) on "Cosmopolitan Right" and the Conclusion, Kant makes it even clearer that relations between states (again his preferred vantage point for relations between nations) should depend, in an association of states, on a just system of public legislation. This pattern resembles relations among individuals in a civil condition under a civil constitution. The metaphysics of *a priori* reason meets the needs of a civil society and the final end of universal permanent peace, the way to which is not radical evolution but gradual reform.[12]

Here, as elsewhere, the words "idea" and "ideal" are extensively applied by Kant to widely different subjects revolving ultimately (whether explicitly or implicitly) around the topic of the state and its foundation in public legislation. There is little doubt that the state "idea" or "ideal" can indeed be reduced to fundamentals of public legislation.

Sovereignty and Legislation

The legislative sovereignty of the general will of the people of a state is placed by Kant over and above the threefold division of government into legislative, executive, and judicial spheres, in which the legislative factor is likewise uppermost and pervasive. Hereby the state and sovereignty are intertwined, while the reducibility of the "idea" and "ideal" of the state and sovereignty to public legislation is further attested. The state idea largely depends on the character and location of sovereignty (in the state).

These points are borne out in Chapter (or Section) I on "The Right of a State" (§ 45–47) in Part II of Kant's "Doctrine of Right" in *Metaphysics of Morals*. Not only the people's general (coercive) will (and command) is viewed by him from the perspective of legislative sovereignty and the legislative state; so, too, are a wide range of related features including citizenship, freedom, equality, constitutions, positive law, and even the original contract. Although Kant warns against inquiring too closely into the original contract, for justifying rebellion or resistance against the state, he concludes the passages below by bringing out the original contract's true nature as the expression of the people's legislative will, act, and idea in the formation of a state that is dependent upon promulgated laws.

> Every state contains three *authorities* within it, that is, the general united will consists of three persons (*trias politica*): the *sovereign authority* (sovereignty) [*Herrschergewalt (Souveränität)*] in the person of the legislator; the *executive authority* in the person of the ruler (in conformity to law); and the *judicial authority* (to award to each what is his in accordance with the law) in the person of the judge (*potestas legislatoria, rectoria et iudiciaria*). These are like the three propositions in a practical syllogism: the major premise, which contains the *law* of that will; the minor premise, which contains the *command* to behave in accordance with the law, that is, the principle of subsumption under the law; and the conclusion, which contains the *verdict* (sentence), what is laid down as right in the case at hand.

The legislative authority can belong only to the united will of the people. For since all right is to proceed from it, it *cannot* do anyone wrong by its law. . . . Therefore only the concurring and united will of all, insofar as each decides the same thing for all and all for each, and so only the general united will of the people, can be legislative.

The members of such a society who are united for giving law (*societas civilis*), that is, the members of a state, are called *citizens of a state* (*cives*). In terms of rights, the attributes of a citizen, inseparable from his essence (as a citizen), are: lawful *freedom*, the attribute of obeying no other law than that to which he has given his consent; civil *equality*, that of not recognizing among the *people* any superior with the moral capacity to bind him as a matter of right in a way that he could not in turn bind the other; and third, the attribute of civil *independence*, . . . as a member of the commonwealth. . . .

[I]t is only in conformity with the conditions of freedom and equality that this people can become a state and enter into a civil constitution. But not all persons qualify with equal right to vote within this constitution, that is, to be citizens and not mere associates in the state. . . . It follows only that whatever sort of positive laws the citizens might vote for, these laws must still not be contrary to the natural laws of freedom and of the equality of everyone in the people corresponding to this freedom. . . .

All those three authorities in a state are dignities, and since they arise necessarily from the idea of a state as such, as essential for the establishment (constitution) of it, they are *civic dignities*. They comprise the relation of a *superior* over all (which, from the viewpoint of laws of freedom, can be none other than the united people itself) to the multitude of that people severally as *subjects*, that is, the relation of a *commander* (*imperans*) to *those who obey* (*subditus*).—The act by which a people forms itself into a state is the *original contract*. Properly speaking, the original contract is only the idea of this act, in terms of which alone we can think of the legitimacy of a state. In accordance with the original contract, everyone (*omnes et singuli*) within a *people* gives up his external freedom in order to take it up again immediately as a member of a commonwealth, that is, of a people considered as a state (*universi*). And one cannot say: the human being in a state has sacrificed a *part* of his innate outer freedom for the sake of an end, but rather, he has relinquished entirely his wild, lawless freedom in order to find his freedom as such undiminished, in a dependence upon laws, that is, in a rightful condition, since this dependence arises from his own lawgiving will.

Another similar series of passages in the same Chapter I of Kant's Part II on "The Right of a State" (§ 48–49) deals with the three authorities in a state—legislative, executive, and judicial—in connection with sovereignty. Although those three authorities are interdependent, only the legislator is truly sovereign. The executive, as the ruler, is the supreme agent. As such, the executive or supreme ruler does not, strictly speaking, have a legislative capacity, which if he did could lead to despotism, but instead issues orders, ordinances, decrees, directives, and the like. The ruler is subject to the laws of the sovereign legislator, who conversely cannot be the ruler. Neither one can be judge. Citing Rousseau and Cicero, Kant, contrary to the utilitarians, believes that the goal and welfare of the citizens is not merely happiness. Although Kant assigns sovereignty outright only to one of the three authorities in the state, that is, to the legislator but not to the executive (or government, monarchy, etc.), he has tended at times elsewhere to assign to the latter a legislative-*like* capacity. At the very least, Kant has viewed it in contexts of the wider interworkings of the legislative process in terms of the execution of laws.[13]

At the same time, it becomes apparent that for Kant, near the end of Chapter I on "The Right of a State" (§ 51–52), the collective general will of the people comprising the state in its highest form tends to be an abstract legislative body, under which operates the more actual three separate authorities in the state—legislative, executive, and judicial. In other words, there appear to be three separate moral personalities within one all-embracing moral personality. (These two distinguishable legislative roles of the people as a whole and of the legislature as a body could be reconciled, we may add, with the Constitutions of France and the United States in the late eighteenth century.) The passages below dealing also with the different forms of states, especially in their legislative frameworks, offer useful insights into Kant's proclivities toward the autocratic type. He recognizes its dangers but also its simplicity and other positive features, within his "metaphysics of right" and the state "ideal" (his regard for republics being another part of the story).[14]

Lending extra weight to Kant's legislative basis of sovereignty (and the state) as both idea and actuality is his prohibition against rebellion or even resistance against the state sovereign(s) on the grounds of a violation of an original contract. Kant's prohibition rests overwhelmingly on the inviolability both of legislative sovereignty in the state and of the public legislation issuing therefrom. Kant's statements along these lines are striking in parts of Chapter I on "The Rights of a State" in Part II of his "The Doctrine of Right" in *Metaphysics of Morals.* Instead of force, he upholds "the supreme authority . . . [and] the supreme legislation that prescribes all rights." Absolute obedience to the civil law and civil constitution, viewed in these legislative contexts of sovereignty in the state, is necessary because of the commands inhering in them as ideas of practical reason. In these matters Kant obviously departs from Rousseau as well as from those who later used Rousseau to justify revolution against the French king Louis XVI. Both topics have been explored by experts on Kant but have been insufficiently linked to the legislative factor itself.[15]

Finally, there are numerous germane references to legislation scattered throughout Kant's variegated other political writings. Various passages again reveal the central role played by legislation in connection with both the state and sovereignty.[16]

3. HEGEL'S *PHILOSOPHY OF RIGHT*

Prelude

Hegelian tendencies in modern historiography on early Europe have been abundantly pointed out in our earlier studies. It is thus with special interest that we now directly turn at last to the ideas of Georg Wilhelm Friedrich Hegel (1770–1831). We again restrict ourselves to select themes.

Hegel's influential *Elements of the Philosophy of Right* (*Grundlinien der Philosophie des Rechts*),[17] published in 1821, was the outgrowth of his lectures at the Universities of Heidelberg (in academic year 1817–1818) and Berlin (in academic years 1818–1819, 1819–1820). The work was enriched by subsequent lectures at Berlin up to the time of his death. Hegel had succeeded J. G. Fichte (d. 1814) to the distinguished chair of philosophy at Berlin in 1818. Earlier, Hegel had published *The Phenomenology of Spirit* in 1807, *Science of Logic* (I–II) in 1812 and 1816, and *Encyclopaedia of the Philosophical Sciences* in 1816.

Hegel's *Philosophy of Right* bore a curious relationship to the Prussian state of his day and of later eras, including that of Bismarck. However, it would be mistaken, although it is sometimes done, to place Hegel in a direct progression of German thought extending from Luther to Bismarck to Hitler. Hegel held too many moderating viewpoints for that to be the case. These have prompted some historians to include Hegel's thought under the category of constitutional state (*Rechtsstaat*) rather than of absolutist state (*Machtstaat*). His strong nationalistic tendencies, nevertheless, gave fuel in the opposite direction for many critics and followers alike. Our attention to Hegel in previous studies was drawn to the multiplicity of flawed ways in which historians have read his state theory backward into earlier European political writers, such as Machiavelli in the Renaissance, Marsilius of Padua in the Middle Ages, and Plato in antiquity.

Such anachronistic misreadings of both history and Hegel have usually neglected the legislative component that lay at the center of Hegel's state theory. This neglect has limited much of the massive scholarship that has long been devoted to Hegel's political theory, so often studied in general terms of his nationalistic deification of the state.[18]

The numerous diverse "isms" under which Hegel's political thought has long been grouped have often not presented a satisfactory mode of analysis. These include Hegelianism, nationalism, idealism, Prussianism, liberalism, historicism, and Marxism, to mention a few. By concentrating on Hegel as a centerpiece in the intellectual tradition of so-called (German) "ideal*ism*," historians have lost sight of his more mundane legislative interests, as likewise in the case of Kant. Under that or any other rubric, it becomes even more problematic to seek the essence of Hegel's political philosophy in a sweeping progression "from Plato to Hegel," which is sometimes encountered. Also overplayed has been the generalized theme of "Hegelian*ism*" in connection with Hegel's perceived crucial role in the development of (modern) political thought culminating in the nineteenth century and shaping the next century.[19]

The similarities and differences between Hegel and Kant form too vast a subject to be explored adequately here. It has often been assumed, perhaps correctly, that Hegel was far more interested in political thought and German nationality than was Kant, who was more interested in metaphysics. Yet the state theories and "higher" political idealism of both thinkers have long fascinated historians. Hegel's well-known deification of the state in his *Philosophy of Right* set him largely apart from Kant in his "Doctrine of Right," although the similarity of these two titles suggests their general affinity in these matters of state. Hegel's uses of the terms "idea" (*Idee*) and "ideal" (*ideal, ideall*) in connection with the state (*Staat*) were not as differentiated as they sometimes were in Kant's thought, albeit Hegel's capitalization (of *Idee*) is more consistent. Not unlike Kant, Hegel deals with the state and related topics in conjunction with morals and ethics.[20]

Organizationally, Hegel's focus on the state in his *Philosophy of Right* falls under "Ethical Life," the subject of Part III, which is divided into three sections on "The Family," "Civil Society," and "The State," while Parts I and II deal with "Abstract Right" and "Morality." The section on "The State" is broken down according to the subjects of "Constitutional Law," "International Law," and "World History." The subject of "Constitutional Law" is, in brief, divided into "The Constitution" ("Crown" or "Sovereign," "Executive," "The Legislature") and "External Sovereignty." It is under "Civil Society" that Hegel includes "The Administration of Justice." Another distinctive feature is that "world history" is subsumed under "the state."

It now becomes imperative, once more, to explore the neglected theme of legislation. For it represents a common denominator linking Hegel's state theory not only with Kant in the idealist tradition but with others studied above in the utilitarian and positivist traditions.

Deification of the "Modern" State "Idea(l)"

Turning to Hegel's Section III on "The State" in Part III of his *Philosophy of Right*, one encounters passages like the one below typifying his deification of the state. Here (§ 258, in an "Addition"), the state as "Idea" is identified not only with the "march of God" but with "actual God." The state is an actualized ethical or spiritual whole that possesses its own superior form of self-conscious spirit and powerful absolute will. The Idea of the state, as the highest moral person, thus possesses its own freedom, actuality, and right, transcending individual humans and states. The latter are represented as limited "moments." On one level for Hegel, the state as a "work of art" is a misnomer and does not exist. (One recalls Burckhardt's famed adaptations of Hegelian ideas in portraying the Renaissance state, seen by him as a "work of art" in the sense of cold reflection and calculation, as distinct from an attractive picture of decorum, a sense that Hegel here casts aside.)

> The state in and for itself is the ethical whole, the actualization of freedom, and it is the absolute end of reason that freedom should be actual. The state is the spirit which is present in the world and which *consciously* realizes itself therein, whereas in nature, it actualizes itself only as the other of itself, as dormant spirit. Only when it is present in consciousness, knowing itself as an existent object . . . is it the state. Any discussion of freedom must begin not with individuality . . . or the individual self-consciousness, but only with the essence of self-consciousness; for whether human beings know it or not, this essence realizes itself as a self-sufficient power of which single individuals . . . are only moments. The state consists in the march of

God in the world, and its basis is the power of reason actualizing itself as will. In considering the Idea of the state, we must not have any particular states or particular institutions in mind; instead, we should consider the Idea, this actual God, in its own right [*für sich*]. Any state, even if we pronounce it bad in the light of our own principles, and even if we discover this or that defect in it, invariably has the essential moments of its existence . . . within itself (provided it is one of the more advanced states of our time). . . . The state is not a work of art; it exists in the world, and hence in the sphere of arbitrariness, contingency, and error, and bad behaviour may disfigure it in many respects.

Earlier in the same discussions (§ 258), Hegel depicts the state Idea as "an absolute and unmoved end in itself," in which "freedom enters into its highest right"—especially "in relation to individuals, whose *highest duty* is to be members of the state." The individual will "embodies only *one* . . . moment of the *Idea* of the rational will . . . *in itself* and *for* itself." Hegel also briefly points out the relation of his concept of will to that held by Rousseau and Fichte.[21]

Closely related statements by Hegel in his *Philosophy of Right* occur in the very brief subsections (§ 257, 259) before and after the one just cited. According to the first of these, "the state is the actuality of the ethical idea" and "*the spirit of the nation* . . . is the divine which *knows* and *wills* itself." According to the second subsection, the "Idea of the state" has a threefold quality. First of all, it "has *immediate* actuality and is the individual state as a self-related organism—the *constitution* or *constitutional law* [*inneres Staatsrecht*]." In the second place, it "passes over into the *relationship* of the individual state to other states—*international law* [*ausseres Staatsrecht*]." Third, "there is the universal Idea as a *genus* [*Gattung*] and as an absolute power in relation to individual states—the spirit which gives itself its actuality in the process of *world history*." Hegel's elaborations here on the "state" further convey his meaning of the "moment": "The state as an actual is essentially an individual state, and beyond that a particular state. Individuality should be distinguished from particularity; it is a moment within the very Idea of the state, whereas particularity belongs to history." The necessary "third factor is . . . the spirit which gives itself actuality in world history . . . and which reveals itself as the universal . . . active genius in world history." It is this spirit, with respect to the state Idea, that not only links states together on the highest levels but also confers upon them the element of divinity and deification. The ensuing subsection (§ 260, "Addition") declares: "The Idea of the state in modern times . . . is the actualization of freedom . . . in accordance with its universality and divinity." In this last passage, as in numerous others more elaborately, Hegel makes it clear that he is speaking of the new emergence of the state Idea(l) in *modern* times and history.

Exaltation of the Legislative State

Hegel's deification of the *modern* state Idea(l) is closely linked in his *Philosophy of Right* with his exaltation of what we have termed the legislative state. This crucial ingredient of legislation has long been neglected by his historians. Without it a proper or full understanding of Hegel's state theory is not possible. And without it the attempts by historians to read Hegel's state theory back into earlier centuries of political thought, an anachronistic exercise to begin with, becomes even further flawed. (Indeed, Burckhardt might have been more exact if—instead of adapting the generalized and questionable category of "state as a work of art," after the style of Hegel's followers and their *proto*-Bismarckian ideas of *Realpolitik*—he had adapted Hegel's legislative state, however difficult it is to read that model back into Machiavelli and the Italian Renaissance.)

In Hegel's subsectional discussions of "Constitutional Law" in Section III (A) on "The State" in Part III ("Ethical Life") of his *Philosophy of Right*, in the context of the "internal constitution" (§ 272, at end), he speaks of "the powers of the state" in such a way as to elevate the legislative power above the executive and judicial powers by virtue of its unique universality. "We usually speak of three powers—the legislative, the executive, and the judiciary. The first of these corresponds to universality and the second to particularity; but the judiciary is not the third constituent of the concept, because its [i.e., the judiciary's] individuality lies outside the above spheres."

The quality of universality further elevates the legislative power in Hegel's ensuing discussion (§ 273, at beginning). "The political state," he declares, "is therefore divided into three substantial elements." The first of these is "the power to deterrmine and establish the universal—the *legislative* power." Subsumed thereunder, in a lesser state role, is the executive, that is to say, "the subsumption of *particular* spheres and individual cases under the universal—the *executive power*." As the third and highest power, sovereignty, in the form of *constitutional* (therefore not truly absolutist?) monarchy, will be seen to partake of an even higher level of universality—also characterized in large measure by the legislative element. Hence: ". . . subjectivity as the ultimate decision of the will—*the power of the sovereign*, in which the different powers are united in an individual unity, which is thus the apex and beginning of the whole, i.e. of *constitutional monarchy*." Thereupon Hegel proceeds to tie this type of constitutional-monarchical state to the ultimate emergence of the state Idea and world spirit in modern history.[22]

A variety of other passages in Hegel's same discussions on "Constitutional Law" in his *Philosophy of Right* further illustrate the ultimate central, even exalted, role of legislation in the state, as thus deified in his system. "In relation to . . . civil law," he asserts (§ 261), "the state is . . . the higher power to whose nature their laws and interests [those of the family and civil society in private law] are subordinate . . . ." Following a passing reference (§ 262) to Plato's *Republic* on a point concerning freedom in relation to individuals, Hegel makes pivotal interconnections (§ 263, 265) between laws or legislation and the institutions as well as constitution of the state, with respect to the actualized rationality of spirit and Idea in public contexts. In other words, the deified state Idea is characterized in important respects by the laws that form the foundation of its institutions.[23] In another passage (§ 270), what the state as (divine) will knows is identified with its establishment of laws in an idealized fashion: "The state therefore *knows* what it wills, and knows it in its *universality* as something *thought*. Consequently, it acts and functions in accordance with known ends and recognized principles, and with laws which are laws not only in *themselves* but also for the consciousness . . . ."

It is in Hegel's treatment of the (deified) state in terms of religion, in the same discussions (§ 270) in his *Philosophy of Right* analyzed immediately above, that the real apotheosis of its laws becomes duly manifest. In the passage below, the state and its laws together receive their highest identity as divine will and Idea. As the foundational universal element in the state, legislation, like the state itself, becomes exalted.

> But the essential determinant of the relationship between religion and the state can be discovered only if we recall the concept of religion. The content of religion is absolute truth, and it is therefore associated with a disposition of the most exalted kind. As intuition, feeling, and representational cognition whose concern is with God as the unlimited foundation and cause on which everything depends, it contains the requirement that everything else should be seen in relation to this. . . . It is within this relationship that the state, laws, and duties all receive their highest endorsement as far as the consciousness is concerned, and become supremely binding upon it; for even the state, laws, and duties are in their actuality something determinate which passes over into the higher sphere as that in which its foundation lies. . . . If, then, religion constitutes the *founda-*

tion which embodies the ethical realm in general, and, more specifically, the nature of the state as the divine will, it is at the same time only a *foundation*; and this is where the two [i.e., the state and religion] diverge. The state is the divine will as present spirit, *unfolding* as the actual shape and *organization of a world*. . . . The laws, as the objective and universal element [within the state], . . . have a lasting and valid determination . . .

Enthronement of Sovereign Legislative Power

The place of sovereignty and the legislative power in the organization of Hegel's third section dealing with the state in his *Philosophy of Right* must be kept firmly in mind. Preliminary focus is on the state as ethical Idea and objective freedom, together with "moments" of the state. The first and main part deals extensively with constitutional law (followed later by international law and world history). Here, the first and main subject area falls under the heading of "The Internal Constitution" (followed later by the second on "External Sovereignty"). After initial discussion of "moments" of the rational constitution, Hegel treats the internal constitution according to the successive categories of "The Power of the Sovereign" (and Crown), "The Executive Power," and "The Legislative Power." Given Hegel's preceding deification and exaltation of the state and its legislative orientation—as uniquely rooted together in universal Ideas, in which the executive power has already been subsumed in key ways under the legislative power—it is not surprising that a similar pattern emerges in the materials at hand.

At the outset (§ 275) of his disquisitions on "The Power of the Sovereign" in *Philosophy of Right*, Hegel strikingly characterizes this subject in terms of the constitution and laws. "The power of the sovereign itself contains the three moments of the totality within itself, namely the *universality* of the constitution and laws, consultation as the reference of the *particular* to the universal, and the moment of ultimate *decision* as the *self-determination* to which everything else reverts . . ."

On the subject here of internal sovereignty (§ 278), Hegel points out its historical absence in the Middle Ages, unlike in modern times, and goes on to give a related meaning to the term "idealism." "In the *feudal monarchy* of earlier times, the state certainly had external sovereignty, but internally, neither the monarch himself nor the state was sovereign. . . . [T]he particular functions and powers of the state and civil society were vested in independent corporations and communities, so that the whole was more of an aggregate than an organism. . . . The *idealism* which constitutes sovereignty is the same determination . . . [whereby] *parts* of an animal organism are . . . members or organic moments [in the whole]." This ideal totality of sovereignty is based not on lawlessness but law(s) and lawfulness, that is, not on despotic power and arbitrariness. A variety of related ensuing disquisitions bring out further germane dimensions of these subjects.[24]

With regard to "The Executive Power" in Hegel's treatment of "The State" in *Philosophy of Right*, there is little doubt that the subject occupies a subordinate or secondary place to that of the legislative power lying at the heart of sovereignty. The legislative is related to the executive power in the context of the relation respectively of the universal to the particular, of public to private. The passages to follow (§ 287–288, 290 "Addition", 292) are indicative of Hegel's position.

> The execution and application of the sovereign's decisions, and in general the continued implementation and upholding of earlier decisions, existing laws, institutions, and arrangements to promote common ends, etc., are distinct from the decisions themselves. This task of *subsumption* in general belongs to the *executive power*, which also includes the powers of the *judiciary* and the *police*; these have more immediate reference to the particular affairs of civil society, and they assert the universal interest within these [particular] ends.
>
> The *particular* common interests which fall within civil society, and which lie outside the universal interest of the state as the interest which has being in and for itself . . . are administered by the corporations. . . . [T]he business of these administrators is to look after the *private property* and *interests* of these *particular* spheres. . . .
>
> [M]ost important . . . for the executive power is the division of functions. The executive power is concerned with the transition from the universal to the particular and individual, and its functions must be divided in accordance with its different branches. . . .
>
> [T]his subjective aspect pertains to the sovereign as the supreme [*souveränen*] and decisive power within the state.

In handling "The Legislative Power" under his more general heading of "The Sovereign Power," as outlined above, Hegel makes it plain in his *Philosophy of Right* that the sovereign power, in conjunction with the legislative power, is enthroned at the center of the (deified) state. The following initial passages (§ 298, with "Addition," and 299) illustrate this orientation.

> The *legislative power* has to do with the laws as such, in so far as they are in need of new and further determination, and with those internal concerns of the state whose content is wholly universal. This power is itself a part of the constitution, which it presupposes and which to that extent lies in and for itself outside the sphere which the legislative power can determine directly; but the constitution does undergo further development through the further evolution of the laws and the progressive character of the universal concerns of government. . . . The constitution must be in and for itself the firm and recognized ground on which the legislative power is based, so that it does not first have to be constructed. Thus, the constitution *is*, but it just as essentially *becomes*, i.e. it undergoes progressive development. . . .
>
> It is possible to distinguish in general terms between what is the object of universal legislation and what should be left to the direction of administrative bodies or to any kind of government regulation, in that the former includes only what is wholly universal in content—i.e. legal determinations—whereas the latter includes the particular and the ways and means whereby measures are *implemented*. This distinction is not entirely determinate, however, if only because a law, in order to be a law, must be more than just a commandment in general . . . , i.e. it must be *determinate* in itself. . . .

In an even more striking adjacent passage (§ 300), Hegel clearly subsumes the (derivative) monarchical and executive powers under the legislative power, thereby elevating it to the most sovereign (universal) status in the state.

> In the legislative power as a whole, the other two moments have a primary part to play, namely the *monarchy* as the power of ultimate decision, and the *executive power* as the advisory moment which has concrete knowledge [*Kenntnis*] and oversight of the whole with its numerous aspects and the actual principles which have become established within it, and knowledge of the needs of the power of the state in particular. The final element [in the legislature] is the *Estates*.

On this last-mentioned legislative role of the Estates (a subject central to the life of the state but too complex to be explained here), Hegel has much to say in his further treatment of the (sovereign) legislative power. Estates are assayed from the vantage point of legislative power.

Through participation in the legislative activities of Estates, in their different forms, the individual citizen achieves fulfillment and belonging in the state.[25] Justice itself is said to lie at the heart of the constitution and legislation (further reinforcing Hegel's assertions that his system is not reducible to arbitrariness and the like).[26]

Postlude

The relationship in Hegel's *Philosophy of Right* of the state and its laws to the nation and its customs is of interest though is not completely determinate. Generally speaking, the state is for Hegel a legal and legislative entity that emerged later on in history out of the earlier conditions of the nation expressed through customs. Hegel repeatedly refers to the "nation" as signifying the "people" or *Volk*, a term obviously oriented more to customs (of the people) than to the laws (of the state or *Staat*). The emergence of the state within this framework of law, legislation, and legality is crucial to the realization of the Idea in its own universal, divine, and rational self-existence and self-expression. Such passages as the following (§ 349–350), in the same section on "The State" as above, have not been duly appreciated by historians from the present perspectives on legislation and related topics.

> In its initial state, a nation [*Volk*] is not a state, and the transition of a family, tribe, kinship group, mass [of people], etc. to the condition of a state constitutes the *formal* realization of the Idea in general within it. If the nation, as ethical substance—and this is what it is *in itself*—does not have this form, it lacks the objectivity of possessing a universal and universally valid existence [*Dasein*] for itself and others in [the shape of] laws as determinations of thought, and is therefore not recognized; since its independence has no objective legality or firmly established rationality for itself, it is merely formal and does not amount to sovereignty.
>
> Even in the context of ordinary ideas [*Vorstellung*], we do not describe a patriarchal condition as a constitution, nor do we describe a people living in this condition as a state, or its independence as sovereignty. Consequently, the actual beginning of history is preceded on the one hand by dull innocence which lacks all interest, and on the other by the valour of the formal struggle for recognition and revenge. . . .
>
> It is the absolute right of the Idea to make its appearance in legal determinations and objective institutions, beginning with marriage and agriculture . . . , whether the form in which it is

actualized appears as divine legislation of a beneficial kind, or as violence . . . and wrong. This right is the *right of heroes* to establish states.

Nor have scholars duly appreciated that the corresponding progressive emergence of the national spirit in world history—from oriental, to Greek, to Roman, and to Germanic periods—is also ultimately viewed by Hegel in the same context of the emergence of a legal state entity in place of a more amorphous customary national body. From the custom-bound oriental realm Hegel's state "spirit" finally breaks forth into the law-dominated Germanic realm, most decisively in modern times. A further striking yet neglected feature of this final legal-legislative outcome in history is that it provides a modulus for the final "synthesis" or resolution in Hegel's famed dialectical struggle between "thesis" and "antithesis." This struggle here is between divine and human, spiritual and secular, elements.[27]

In the final analysis, for Hegel, the state, as the spirit of the nation, arises as the law-centered entity that gives new central characteristics to the nation (or nation-state) and the (formerly) custom-centered activities of its people or *Volk*. The resultant national state is a mixture of laws or legislation and customs. It is in this light that one can discern the true signification of Hegel's references to the customs as well as laws of a national state entity.[28]

Finally, there remains the issue, addressed throughout this series, of the anachronistic ways in which historians have read Hegel's state theory into earlier Western political-historical thought going as far back as Plato. The supposed modern idea of the state held by Plato has, in fact, been much discussed by some historians (as cited near the outset of our Volume IV). It is true that Hegel himself in the Preface and various passages of his *Philosophy of Right* (some discussed above) cites Plato's *Republic* as an authoritative support for the idealistic relation of philosophy to the state. But Hegel's generalized citations of Plato offer little justification for modern historians who read Hegel's state theories backward into older ideas—whether in antiquity, the Middle Ages, or early modern times—as supposedly presaging his modernity. By way of further example, the famed English historian G. R. Elton, previously seen (in Volume IV) to posit a "Meineckean Tudor state," has been said by a noted reviewer to adopt thereby Hegelian perspectives.[29]

Beyond these considerations, lies the wider issue of the categories used by historians. The continuing appeal of Hegelianism approaches illustrated by, but by no means limited to, prominent recent historians of early modern Europe who have focused on such topics as "the Machiavellian moment," "the world revolution" of the late-eighteenth century, and "philosophy and the state" in France (as all cited in our preceding book). It is not, then, only a question of historians reading Hegel's specific ideas into earlier writers but also of their adapting Hegel's ideological categories of analysis to modern historical scholarship more generally.

What the present section has endeavored to show is that the neglected legislative parameters of Hegel's state theory, taken as a topic on its own merits, comprises yet another crucial link in the long chain of development in historical theory on the legislative state and legislative sovereignty. A grasp of the yardstick of legislation will enable historians to measure more accurately Hegel's contributions on these and other matters at hand.

4. LATER CON-FUSIONS OF "ISMS"

The "diffusions of the 'isms' " cited in a heading above in connection with idealism and Hegelianism were so broad, in the first half of the nineteenth century, as to become very amorphous. The later *interfusions* of the myriad new varieties of these and many other "isms," in the second half of that century, are often so difficult to trace as to be better styled "con-fusions of 'isms'." Compounding the complications were the emerging and expanding neo-"isms" (and anti-neo-"isms") in the early twentieth century.

These complexities obtain in the development of political and legal thought, including on the state problem, no less than in philosophical and intellectual history more generally during the same periods. In the case of later British idealism and Hegelianism, their diffusions became intricately intermixed with later British utilitarianism, positivism, liberalism, socialism, and so forth. In the case of German idealism and Hegelianism, their ever-widening paths crisscrossing with Kantianism led in the early twentieth century to myriad "neo" forms in which Hegelianism and Kantianism became as often divergent as they were convergent.

Contributing to this complexity were the expanding national typologies of such "isms," in keeping with the emerging Age of Nationalism in the second half of the nineteenth century. The "isms" of the eighteenth century studied in our preceding book had a certain degree of commonality or cohesiveness extending across national lines. Those of the nineteenth century explored in this study partook less of the "international" or "cosmopolitan" qualities that had distinguished the Age of Enlightenment. Hence the national differences in the eighteenth century among varieties of rationalism as well as of empiricism were typically less striking than those in the nineteenth century among types of positivism as well as of idealism. The distinction traditionally drawn by historians of the eighteenth century between French rationalism in Voltaire, Montesquieu, and Rousseau and British empiricism in Hume and Smith has frequently involved overdone stereotypes of French proclivities toward abstraction and British inclinations toward practicality. Many recent revisionists have contrariwise underscored the interfusions between rationalism and empiricism in both France and England through the "community of letters" existing in the Age of Enlightenment. True, such interconnections of one type or another between nations can also be found in the nineteenth century, as in most other periods in intellectual history. Yet there remain, for instance, strong differences in positivism between Comte in France, Austin in England, and Jhering as well as Jellinek in Germany. With regard to idealism and Hegelianism, British varieties in the second half of the nineteenth century, and on into the next century, often diverged from German types through frequent combinations with utilitarianism, a more distinctively British "ism." Yet nineteenth-century "isms" cannot be studied in isolation from one another, Hegelianism and idealism being no exceptions.

It will be useful below to chart briefly the background to twentieth-century (neo)Hegelianism in the influential political thought of Bernard Bosanquet (1848–1923) in his *The Philosophical Theory of the State*, together with that of his predecessor Thomas Hill Green (1836–1882) in his *Lectures on the Principles of Political Obligation*. The two writers had similarities and differences too numerous to detail. Bosanquet was to adapt Rousseau's idea of the General Will in the course of approximating German types of Hegelianism that deified the state and its power. Most other Victorian English writers like him who embraced idealism lacked the strong German nationalistic tendency to glorify the state after the manner of Hegel. The individual liberty stressed by previous British liberals like J. S. Mill continued to provide restraining countercurrents in British political thought including on idealism. Assigning a lesser role to the state, in line with other British idealists, Green built his theory more on Kant than on Hegel, while deriving inspiration from both Plato and Aristotle. Green looked more to the realization of the moral self than to the power of the state, being influenced by J. S. Mill's liberal individualism. Green gave a more typically English face to idealism than did Bosanquet.

What will again become crucial to demonstrate for the present study is the legislative crux of state and sovereignty for both Bosanquet and Green. Of less concern is the greater or lesser weight they assigned on balance to the state's power, on one side, and the individual's role in society, on the other. It matters less for present purposes whether

Green saw the state to be greater potential evil as against Bosanquet's view of its benefit. More important is that both British writers (who were in many ways attuned to each other) perceived legislation to be key to sovereignty and the state. Similarly, for both J. S. Mill and Bentham, the one stressing individualism and the other more a kind of statism, the state centered on legislation. It would, of course, be instructive to explore more widely the intricate political-legal varieties of idealism, Hegelianism, Kantianism, and so forth in order to expose further the common denominator of legislation underlying their valuations of sovereignty and the state.

To Marx we must now turn for, among other reasons, an appreciation of his early approaches to Hegel. The oft-cited belief of Marx that he found Hegel standing on his head and turned him right-side-up serves to suggest the positive no less than negative views Marx held of Hegel. This metaphor is normally taken as expression of Marx's materialism concerning the struggle between socio-economic classes, in counterpoise to Hegel's idealism concerning the clash of ideas in his noted formula, adapted by Marx, of thesis, antithesis, and synthesis. More apropos are the political-legal ideas of Marx in relation to Hegel. At any rate, the admixtures of Hegelianism with Marxism by later writers further complicated the crosscurrents of "isms" operating in Germany as well as in England, where Marx, with his collaborator Engels, spent several crucial decades hammering out his doctrines.

In turning to Marx, we turn to another pair of political "isms," socialism and Marxism, remembering once more that all such "isms" are here meant to be exploded or "deconstructed" as much as to be exploited. The results will again reveal a familiar pattern—a common denominator of legislation underlying a wide range of political-legal issues on the state and sovereignty. This pattern has been generally neglected by historians, who have tended to focus on Marx's better-known fulminations against the state as ultimately in ways an "evil" that must "wither away." We thus move beyond the Hegelian heritage to a deeper appreciation not only of Marx's ideas but also of some select institutional developments. Whether at theoretical or practical levels, the diffusive doctrinal "isms" of the state and sovereignty rise and fall on the shifting surfaces of these twin problems, while the steadier singular undercurrents of legislation and related subjects flow on from one age to the next.

Chapter V

"Social*ism*" and "Marx*ism*"

1. REDUCING THE SOCIALIST STATE TO ITS "SOCIAL" LEGISLATION

Perhaps no other new "ism" in the political, legal, and social thought of the nineteenth century has had more widespread permanent impact than has socialism. And perhaps no other such "ism" can be more closely identified with legislation than can socialism. Once again, however, the topic of legislation *per se* has often been neglected by historians. This chapter attempts a new approach.

In the mid-nineteenth century, Karl Marx and others commenced what they saw as a great change—the turn away from idealistic or "utopian" types of socialism to more realistic and "scientific" approaches, with crucial lasting results for the state in relation to legislation. The development of socialism in theory and practice became closely linked to the development of the modern state across a wide spectrum of socialist state types. These have ranged from the more democratic and constitutional varieties, past and present, in Britain and Continental Europe to the more despotic forms of the twentieth century in Eastern-bloc countries of the Union of Soviet Socialist Republics and in the National Socialism of the Third Reich. Nascent or prototypical socialist states of the later nineteenth century in Germany under Bismarck, in France under Napoleon III, and perhaps in Britain under

Gladstone (as a precursor in some respects of Lloyd George) operated through the medium of domestic social legislation under varying degrees of state control. The New Deal legislation of President Franklin Roosevelt affords an American democratic example of a quasi-socialist state. In essence, the socialist state may be identified with state-sponsored social legislation.

Notwithstanding socialism's diverse definitions, varieties, and contexts, especially in combination with other "isms," its main features fall into line with present thematic perspectives. The term arose in England and France in the 1830s in conjunction with the efforts of figures like Robert Owen to promote the common interest through social organization and communal control. Much later, socialism became more recognizable in the form of the modern welfare state, in which public rather than private ownership of the means of production aimed at an equitable distribution of capital, wealth, property, and the like. Since state control provided the most characteristic medium, it was natural that state legislation became the concomitant mechanism for achieving these ends. Having arisen as a social and economic program out of conditions in the burgeoning Industrial Revolution, socialism aimed at practical action in the political sphere by harnessing and expanding the legal-legislative apparatus of the state. Indeed, "public" law or "public" legislation became the most typical means for achieving equitable "social" or "common" conditions and solutions by alleviating "private" inequalities and expanding opportunities for lesser individuals in society. In promoting the interests of the community as a whole through public ownership of production, capital, land, property, and so forth, socialists shared common ground with communists. However, strict Marxian communists believed that the (interim) proletarian socialist state would eventually "wither away" in a classless and stateless workers' paradise. If the word "social" gained in the nineteenth century a more pointed signification than it had had in the past, it remained inherently nebulous. Its usage as an "ism" has compounded the ambiguities.

The most influential theorist behind the development of modern socialism in the later nineteenth and early twentieth centuries remained none other than Marx (just as Bentham, Austin, and Hegel remained crucial for later political-legal theories of utilitarianism, positivism, and idealism, respectively). In the expanding kaleidoscope of other nineteenth-century "isms," Marxism bore complex relationships not only to socialism and communism, but also to liberalism, illiberalism, materialism, radicalism, reformism, revolutionism, industrialism, capitalism, Germanism, realism, utopianism, fetishism, Hegelianism, and so forth, not to mention Leninism and Stalinism later on. Marxism, as it related to the thought of Marx himself, revolved around socio-economic issues of class struggle, historical materialism, ownership of the means of production, the importance of labor as basic to wealth, and the like, in addition to fundamental political issues centered around the state. Marxism after Marx presents a more complicated picture, as, for instance, in the contributions of his collaborator Engels and of ensuing figures like Kautsky and Bernstein. Yet the socialist state and its social legislation were an enduring common concern across a range of socialist viewpoints. Secondary studies focusing in their titles on Marxism are often as elusive on the "ism" itself as are works on socialism more broadly. Even more than positivism and utilitarianism, Marxism in historical and theoretical studies in recent decades has tended to become an unmanageably amorphous subject, one likewise demanding here a fundamental reappraisal.

2. THE 1840s BACKGROUND

"Advent of the Modern Age"?

Before turning to Marx, it will be useful to consider briefly the broader setting in the 1840s for his early writings of that decade. Those works include, most notably, his *Critique* of Hegel in 1843 and his *Manifesto of the Communist Party* in 1848. It has long been customary to view the decisive early emergence of Marx's thought on politics and other subjects against the background of the ferment of events and ideas in the 1840s, culminating in the revolutions of 1848 in various European countries, particularly in his native Germany. Leading up to 1848 was the drive by workers, intellectuals, and others for political gains in the representative institutions controlled since 1830-1832 by the "liberal" bourgeoisie. This cause was supported by Marx along with many other writers. The failures of these mid-century revolutions to achieve their goals marked a watershed in the minds of Marx and innumerable others. The need now, they believed, was for realistic toughness of mind in political action and for rejection of unsuccessful idealistic politics. Branding most previous types of socialism as "utopian," Marx and his collaborator Engels called for a new, more "scientific" socialism.[1]

A crucial question hovered in the 1840s background to Marx. It was a far broader and weightier one than the "spectre of Communism" that he claimed in his *Manifesto* was "haunting Europe." Did that decade mark not only a watershed between the two halves of the nineteenth century (as seems reasonable to assume) but also the beginnings or advent of modern times (which is more debatable)? This question of "modern origins" has even greater importance when viewed from the perspective of many previous centuries encompassed in the present series. In Volume IV, Part I, it was asked whether the modern origins of the state and of related phenomena occurred in classical antiquity, or in the Middle Ages, or in the Renaissance, or in the Reformation, or in post-sixteenth-century periods. In Volume V, Book II, Part II, it was asked whether the state's modern origins occurred during the French Revolution. All periods have found their advocates in this regard among historians. The endlessly conflicting positive (as well as negative) verdicts on this broader question may serve to expose its futility. But since it continues to be asked so frequently by investigators of all periods, including the 1840s, it can be posed here as well in connection with a recent book on that very decade.

A masterful survey of the 1840s in Europe by Jerome Blum bears a provocative main title and an even more challenging subtitle: *In the Beginning: The Advent of the Modern Age, Europe in the 1840s*.[2] Professor Blum's chapters in Part I deal successively with the "Revolution in Communications," "Reformers and Radicals," "Romanticism, Nationalism, Realism," and "The World of Learning." He turns in chapters of Part II to "Great Britain: A New Era," "France Comes Full Circle," "Austria: Empire of Silence and Stagnation," "Germany on the Threshold of Greatness," and "Russia: Autocracy and Intelligensia." These headings reflect the broad generalized parameters of his strong claims for modernity's first emergence in the decade of the 1840s. The Introduction opens with a series of vague statements by various figures of the period who express their belief that the 1840s was indeed a great transition pointing ahead to a new age. Blum recognizes that innumerable other historical periods have also been spoken about in similar terms. In spite of his informed documentation and argumentation, however, his strong claims for this decade as marking "the advent of the modern age" are no more persuasive than are those of other historians for earlier periods.

A case in point is the topic of nationalism. It is, of course, true that new nation-states (as in Italy and Germany) emerged in the second half of the nineteenth century (but well after the 1840s). They were preceded by strong nationalist sentiments and efforts in the first half of that century. There is, however, little evidence that either nationalism or the nation-state first emerged or reemerged in the 1840s in a uniquely "modern" form. These twin phenomena were of much older standing. Citing some of the same historians of this "ism" that were cited in our previous volumes on earlier epochs, Professor Blum offers much the same generalized definitions and contexts that they presented in support of its rise during those centuries. Precisely because their uses of this "ism" have been too broad or "soft," historians of nearly all centuries of European history have been able (conflictingly) to argue for its origins in them. Beyond his broad discussions of the separate nations, Blum pays little attention to the origins or advent of modernity within specific areas of the state and sovereignty, much less legislation. Similar drawbacks concern other topics like "revolution" and "radicalism."

These criticisms are not meant to detract from the excellence of Professor Blum's broad analyses, but rather to suggest that they do not bear out the bold claims announced for them in the book's main title, subtitle, and Introduction on the origins of modernity. Indeed, Blum's exaggerations in this regard serve a useful purpose that he may have partly intended. His postdatings of modernity's beginnings to a period as recent as the mid-nineteenth century serves indirectly to expose the even greater exaggerations of other historians who point to modernity's emergence as far back as antiquity and the Middle Ages. From those perspectives, Blum's concentration on modernity's beginnings in the 1840s seems a counterbalancing *tour de force*. Was he partly reacting, somewhat playfully, to the "medieval origins of the modern state" propounded by his Princeton colleague Joseph R. Strayer? In any case, Blum's book is useful for viewing the 1840s background in the wider perspectives of this series.

The Frankfurt Assembly and Marx: State and Legislation

To the extent that the decade of the 1840s can be seen as a great turning point in the nineteenth century, or even in the broader course of European history, for the emergence of modernity, the year 1848 marked a crucial culmination. Although the revolutions of 1848 (–1849) in the various European countries failed in the short run to achieve their objectives of liberalism and nationalism, they left a rich legacy with far-reaching results, soon to be realized. Of the unsuccessful revolutions of 1848—in Germany, France, Italy, Hungary, and elsewhere— those in Germany were in certain ways the most fateful.

Although the famed *Manifesto* of 1848 by Marx and Engels was published prior to the actual outbreak of the revolutions of that year, and neither was influenced by them nor had an influence upon them, it has long been viewed in the context of the new toughness of mind born of those revolutions. In other writings, Marx had much to say about the failed Frankfurt Assembly or Parliament, which became the center of agitation in Germany in 1848 (–1849) for a new united liberal Germany. Historians have seldom appreciated the considerable extent to which the Frankfurt Assembly, in relation to Marx, can be viewed from the vantage point of legislation as well as the state.

While this is not the place for a disquisition on the complex formation, activities, and nature of the famed Frankfurt Assembly or Parliament of 1848 (–1849), it would be profitable to consider its aims as, and for, a new national legislature. Although much different and more successful, the French National (legislative) Assembly of 1789– became a kind of model for the Frankfurt Assembly (as Marx abundantly recognized). Like it, the Frankfurt Assembly issued a Declaration of Rights (although for Germans rather than for men more generally) and, after it had already begun to dissolve, a constitution, which never went into real effect for a new Germany. True, the Frankfurt Assembly, for many reasons, never gained the status of a permanent legislative Assembly, unlike its earlier French counterpart. Much of its time was spent in wrangling over proposals for the various greater or lesser territorial extents of the envisioned new unified national state of Germany (with or without Prussia, Austria, and numerous other entities). Yet there can be little doubt that the Frankfurt Assembly's many hundreds of elected representatives from throughout the German lands viewed themselves as collectively a national parliament that, in the end, would be or become, much like other parliaments, a regular permanent legislature. The legislative perspectives on the Frankfurt Assembly are not limited to its own central role in the revolutions of 1848 and to Marx's writings on it. They could be extended to the revolutionary bodies of 1848 in other countries as well.[3]

In numerous news dispatches of 1848–1849,[4] Marx followed and commented closely on the rapidly changing events in Germany (and elsewhere), including on the activities of the Frankfurt Assembly. Marx's own evolving estimations of that Assembly seemed to rise and fall with its own changing fortunes—from its encouraging rise in promoting a new German national state of the people to its demise under the stronger presence and power of the Prussian monarchical state. If at first Marx had many hopes for the success of the Frankfurt Assembly, his reservations about its orientation grew with its failures, becoming fervent denunciations with its eventual humiliation and defeat.

Marx was similarly attentive to the Berlin Assembly. It arose prior to, yet did not endure as long as, the Frankfurt Assembly. The Berlin Assembly was an elected all-Prussian legislative body allowed by the Prussian king, Frederick William IV, after agitation for it. For a time, the king considered its ideas for a Prussian-led united Germany, but with himself as head. Soon disbanded, the Berlin Assembly was less free and productive than its more famous Frankfurt counterpart, in large part because of its location in the heart of the Prussian kingdom. Yet in the end it was more highly (or less harshly) regarded in certain respects by Marx than was the Frankfurt Assembly. The latter, he felt, was betrayed (or sold out) in large measure by its own delegates over dubious "legal" considerations relating especially to issues of sovereignty and state (a telling point in its own right and in line with present perspectives).

It would thus be instructive to analyze in depth Marx's many statements on these matters in connection with issues of state, sovereignty, law, and legislation. In addition to his predictable discourses on socioeconomic class conflicts between bourgeoisie and proletarians, and on law as being conditioned by society rather than the reverse, Marx made numerous extended discussions here on the legal and legislative scope of the diverse existing and proposed types of government and state for Germany. In many passages, Marx cast aspersions on so-called "legal foundations" as being tied to jurisdictional disputes responsible for the Frankfurt Assembly caving in to Prussian authority. Here he also had in mind the professor-lawyer (intellectual-bourgeois) mentality dominating that Assembly. But in just as many other passages Marx recognized the need for a strong (properly formed) centralized national state of the German people. At this new state's center, he believed, should lie a duly conceived and functioning system of law and legislation, one in accord with his own socio-economic notions. In his discussions on the earlier stages of the Frankfurt (and Berlin) Assembly, Marx favored the nationalistic no less than liberal goals for a new unified and centralized nation-state of the German people. Although such topics cannot be further explored here, the foregoing outline furnishes a partial broad background in the 1840s to two major works of that decade by Marx, to which we must turn, placing them in the chronology of his career.

Marx's Chronology, 1840s

When in 1843 Karl Marx (1818–1883) drafted his lengthy, paradigmatic *Contribution to the Critique of Hegel's "Philosophy of Right,"* he was at the youthful and formative age of 26. He, like many others, was under the heavy influence of the political statist viewpoints of Hegel's *Philosophy of Right*, published about a dozen years earlier. Marx had not yet arrived at his partially anti-statist economic doctrines formulated in his *Manifesto of the Communist Party* in 1848, a half-decade later.

Marx had studied law at the University of Bonn in 1835–1836, at the time of the "September Laws" in France, which restricted freedom of press and banned criticism of political institutions. Moreover, he had been born a year before the "Carlsbad Decrees" in Prussia, which imposed censorship on university activities and newspapers. Thus Marx was already in 1843 well aware of the crucial role—bad rather than good in these famous or infamous cases—of law and legislation.

By 1843 Marx had just embarked on his early career as a newspaperman in Germany and elsewhere. His 1841 doctoral dissertation on aspects of classical natural philosophy for the Universities of Berlin and Jena had failed to yield an academic position. At that point, too, he had just met for the first time (in 1842) his eventual lifelong collaborator, Friedrich Engels.

In 1844—a year after drafting his *Critique* of Hegel (which was not published during his lifetime) and compiling various "Notebooks" on political history and theory—Marx published his short "Contribution to the Critique of Hegel's *Philosophy of Right:* Introduction." That year Marx made his first studies on political economy and reestablished his relationship with Engels on a permanent basis. In 1845 Marx traveled with Engels to London and Manchester, expanding his political-economic studies.

In 1847, Marx joined "The League of the Just," founded in Paris in 1836. That year it became "The Communist League" and held its first congress in London. Also in 1847, Marx helped to organize the "Brussels German Workers' Association" and attended with Engels the second congress of The Communist League in London, where he agreed to draft a program for the League. The resulting "Manifesto" was published early in the following year.

Thus, by the end of the 1840s, Marx's interests and views were to expand far beyond what they had been in the early 1840s. Yet, as he himself recognized, a pattern or paradigm for his later economic as well as political outlook was already established in his early critiques of Hegel. This is understandable considering that only a half decade separated his *Critique* and *Manifesto*.

3. MARX'S *CRITIQUE* OF HEGEL

"Hegel['s] . . . critical analysis of the modern state"

One of the most succinct and explicit statements by Marx on Hegel's theory of the state and law appears in his "Critique of Hegel . . .: Introduction" in the broader context of the historical and theoretical developments of the German state. The passage below (all *sic*) well illustrates the blend of admiration and criticism that typifies Marx's fuller critiques here of Hegel on such matters. What Marx objects to in the Hegelian-German theoretical paradigm of the modern state has more to do with its neglect of the individual or "real man" and its abstract or impractical scope than with its legal or legislative parameters. Already in this essay, Marx calls for drastic change in the modern state in its Hegelian-German form (and perhaps anticipates the revolutions of 1848). This call becomes more pronounced in other parts of the essay, in which he also attacks religion and religious authority especially in terms of German history. To the degree to which Marx is already at this early stage of his writing career attacking the modern state, it is nevertheless the Hegelian-German paradigm in legal-political theory that best characterizes for Marx the essence of the modern state.

> The criticism of the *German philosophy of state and law*, which attained its most consistent, richest and final formulation through *Hegel*, is both a critical analysis of the modern state and of the reality connected with it, and the resolute negation of the whole *German political and legal consciousness as practised* hitherto, the most distinguished, most universal expression of which, raised to the level of a *science*, is the *speculative philosophy of law* itself. If the speculative philosophy of law, that abstract extravagant *thinking* on the modern state, the reality of which remains a thing of the beyond, if only beyond the Rhine, was possible only in Germany, inversely the *German* thought-image of the modern state which disregards *real man* was possible only because and insofar as the modern state itself disregards real *man* or satisfies the *whole* of man only in imagination. In politics the Germans *thought* what other nations *did*. Germany was their *theoretical consciousness*. The abstraction and conceit of its thought always kept in step with the onesidedness and stumpiness of its reality. If therefore the *status quo of German statehood* expresses the *perfection of the ancient régime*, the perfection of the thorn in the flesh of the modern state, the *status quo of German political theory* expresses the *imperfection of the modern state*, the defectiveness of its flesh itself.
>
> Even as the resolute opponent of the previous form of *German* political consciousness, the criticism of speculative philosophy of law turns, not towards itself, but towards *problems* which can only be solved by one means—*practice*.[5]

The opening pages of Marx's more extensive *Critique* of Hegel contain many significant passages on the sovereign state in relation to laws and other elements. Here, as elsewhere, his detailed masterful commentaries on Hegel's *Philosophy of Right* often remind one in their tone of Bentham's incisive commentaries dispelling the "mysteries" of Blackstone. Marx's comments (given in the note below) relating to § 261, 269–270 in Hegel's *Philosophy of Right* illustrate Marx's modes of analyzing, pro or con, Hegel's terminologies and statements. Marx seeks not always to refute but just as often to clarify what he deems to be Hegel's illogic. Marx seeks not only to undermine but also to give better grounding to Hegel's ideas, which Marx frequently finds too abstract and speculative.[6]

Turning in his *Critique* to Hegel's treatment of "the internal constitution" in *Philosophy of Right*, Marx begins with an examination of Hegel's analysis of "the monarch's authority," following his prefatory criticisms of Hegel's abstract mystification of the whole subject.[7] Marx launches into a series of attacks on what he regards as Hegel's confused, convoluted, and defective logic concerning sovereignty as the "idealism" or "ideality" of the state. Hegel, complains Marx, jumbled together such subjects as sovereignty and monarchy, subjectivity and objectivity, personification and will (à la Louis XIV), individuality and generality, mystery and reality, and so forth with regard to the state, including legislation. Marx points in particular to Hegel's distinction between the modern state (in an abstract form suitable mostly to war, says Marx) and the medieval state (in a form based ultimately, interprets Marx, on private property). In line with his attacks elsewhere against religion, Marx is critical of Hegel's tendency toward not only mystification but deification of the state.[8]

Addressing himself next to Hegel's handling of "the executive," Marx declares that Hegel's only real originality in general was his intermixture of the executive, the police, and the judiciary, whereas previous theorists had usually separated the administration and the judiciary. Most of Hegel's thought, alleges Marx, is derived from or compatible with Prussian common law. On these points Marx seems to acknowledge somewhat receptively the traditionalism of Hegel's *legislative* ideas on sovereignty and the state. Also, Marx seems to turn the tables on himself by pointing to Hegel's grounding in Prussian practice while also criticizing Hegel for excessive abstractions. Marx again tackles Hegel's faulty logic. This includes Hegel's lack of proof for the nature of the executive as well as his defective distinction between the state and civil society, which are in the end interconnected through the bureaucracy. This bureaucracy leads to the "formalism" and "illusion" of the state idea as something resembling a theological or divine construct.[9]

"[T]he legislature is the highest development of the state"

The longest and most important section in Marx's *Critique* of Hegel takes up "the legislature" in Hegel's *Philosophy of Right*. Marx's initial attention is directed to Hegel's insistence that the constitution exists prior to and embraces the legislature, whereas Marx argues persuasively that the legislative power must in various ways be antecedent to the constitution. This latter argument not only shows Marx's own deep interest in the legislative factor in issues of sovereignty and state; it becomes the basis for Marx's more familiar ideas on revolution. It is for Marx precisely the legislature as the true representative of the people that can, as in the French Revolution, engineer the overthrow of an old constitution and institute a new one. Along the way, Marx gives high approval to Hegel's method of antithesis in such cases, but he believes that Hegel's confused intermixtures of the idea and reality of the state lay behind Hegel's erroneous belief that constitutions only precede legislatures.

> The first thing that is striking is Hegel's emphasis on the point that "this authority is itself a part of the constitution, which is antecedent to it and which lies wholly beyond direct determination by the legislature", since he has not made this remark about either the monarchical or the executive authority, though it is equally true of them. Then, however, Hegel is constructing the constitution as a whole, and, thus, cannot presuppose it. However, we recognise the profundity in Hegel precisely in the fact that he everywhere begins with and lays stress on the *opposition* between attributes (as they exist in our states).
>
> The "legislative authority is itself a part of the *constitution*" which "lies wholly beyond direct determination by the legislature". But, again, the constitution has surely not made itself spontaneously. The laws, which "require to be further determined", must surely have had to be formulated. A legislative authority *prior* to the constitution and *outside* of the constitution must exist or have existed. A legislative authority must exist beyond the actual, *empirical, established* legislative authority. But, Hegel will reply, we are presupposing an *existing* state. Hegel, however, is a philosopher of law and is expounding the genus of the state. He must not measure the idea by what exists, but what exists by the idea.
>
> The collision [sic] is simple. The *legislative power* is the power to organise the general. It is the power of the constitution. It reaches beyond the constitution.
>
> But, on the other hand, the legislative power is a constitutional power. It is therefore subsumed under the constitution. The constitution is *law* for the legislative authority. It *gave* and continues to give laws to the legislature. The legislative authority is only the legislative authority within the constitution. . . .

> How does Hegel resolve this antinomy? . . .
> That is to say, then: directly, the constitution lies beyond the reach of the legislature; but indirectly, the legislature changes the constitution. The legislature does in a roundabout way what it cannot and must not do straightforwardly. It takes the constitution apart piecemeal, because it cannot change it wholesale. . . .
> Hegel has not herewith abolished the antinomy: he has transformed it into another antinomy. He has posed the *working* of the legislature—its *constitutional* working—in antithesis to its constitutional *designation*. The opposition between the *constitution and the legislature* remains. Hegel has depicted the *actual* and the *legal* action of the legislature as constituting a contradiction, or again depicted the contradiction between what the legislature is supposed to be and what it actually is, between what it thinks it is doing and what it really does.
> How can Hegel present this contradiction as the truth? . . .
> Does the "constitution" itself, then, properly belong to the domain of the "legislative authority"? . . .
> The legislature made the French Revolution; in general, wherever it has emerged in its particularity as the dominant element, it has made the great, organic, general revolutions. It has not fought the constitution, but a particular, antiquated constitution, precisely because the legislature was the representative of the people, of the will of the species. The executive, on the other hand, has produced the small revolutions, the retrograde revolutions, the reactions. . . .
> Posed correctly, the question is simply this: Has the people the right to give itself a new constitution? The answer must be an unqualified "Yes", because once it has ceased to be an actual expression of the will of the people the constitution has become a practical illusion.
> The collision between the constitution and the legislature is nothing but a *conflict of the constitution with itself*, a contradiction in the concept of the constitution [all *sic*].[10]

In addition to the bureaucracy, explains Marx, the estates formed for Hegel a kind of intermediary device for bridging political society (that is, the state) and civil society. This device, too, feels Marx, was a further defect in Hegel's political philosophy of the state. The key point, for present purposes, is that Marx dwells on the legislative factors in relation to the estates as they existed in the Middle Ages and in modern times, as interpreted by Hegel and, in a different way, by Marx. Hegel's mysticism and formalism on the state further beclouded Hegel's vision of the relation of the legislative to the monarchical and executive elements, in the opinion of Marx. More clearly than he feels Hegel did, Marx points out the totality of legislation in the state, to which those other two powers are in fact subordinate.[11]

For Marx in his *Critique* of Hegel, the main flaw in Hegel's positions on the legislative power is that it is not, as Hegel envisioned, dependent on itself but rather on antithetical outside powers. For this reason, Hegel's idea of the modern state, according to Marx, is illusory largely because its element of legislative power is illusory. At the same time, Marx suggests that those elements in Hegel's state theory pointing to the legislative power as a "totality" in the modern state are precisely the ones that must be more centrally established and accurately developed as the true foundation of the state. This legislative basis of the modern state can be better ascertained, though, by keeping in mind the practical and conventional dimensions of the state problem, aside from Hegel's abstract metaphysical confusions and contradictions. The "absurdity" of Hegel's "Janus-faced" constructs are exemplified by the kaleidoscopic mediating legislative roles of monarch, executive, and estates. Such must be avoided or resolved through fuller concentration on the legislative element itself as the most logical and practical common denominator unifying the various components of the state problem, as seen from both Hegel's and Marx's viewpoints. Marx clearly opts, in a sense, for "a *legislative power* of the whole state" (that is, in part, of the people individually and collectively who control it) instead of "the *legislative power* of the different estates and corporations and classes over the state as a whole" (in contexts of private property and class distinctions). Says Marx: "Indeed, only the legislature is the organised, *total* political state . . . [and] the legislature is the highest development of the state . . ."[12]

"[T]he modern legislature, . . . [vs.] the medieval-estates system [, is] . . . the total [modern] state"

In a stunning series of statements, Marx poignantly perceives that Hegel's dilemma was to mix confusedly together the modern legislative state with the medieval non-legislative state. Hegel, asserts Marx, tried to use the medieval estates system based on primogeniture (the crux of which was private property as well as the family, both increasingly distrusted by Marx) as a framework for conceiving the modern state as based on legislation. Thereby, Hegel contradictorily obscured the legislative features of the modern state that he, Hegel, was seeking to highlight. Marx underscores his own belief in the "total" legislative scope of the modern state, that is, according to his own self-styled realistic (yet idealized?) version of it and without the hindrances of those propertied class elements. It might be argued that Marx's insightful historical statement here was more to the point on legislation in relation to modern versus medieval states than was Hegel in his political metaphysics. Yet however much Marx could pride himself in such matters for being more truly practical or historical than Hegel, in the end Marx was no less ideologically biased than was Hegel in his historical interpretations. Marx's political-economic viewpoints were at least as prone to ideological bias as were the political-metaphysical ideas of Marx, generally speaking.

> What an anomaly altogether, that the highest *synthesis* of the political state should be nothing but the synthesis of landed property and family life! . . .
> This is here therefore an inconsistency of Hegel *within his own* way of looking at things, and such an inconsistency is *accommodation*. In the modern sense, in the sense expounded by Hegel, the political-estates element is the *separation of civil society from its civil estate and its distinctions, assumed as accomplished.* How can Hegel turn the civil estate into a *solution* of the antinomies of the *legislature* within itself? Hegel wants the medieval-estates system, but in the modern sense of the legislature, and he wants the modern legislature, but in the body of the medieval-estates system! This is the worst kind of syncretism. . . .
> The political constitution at its highest point is therefore the *constitution of private property*. The supreme *political conviction* is the *conviction of private property. Primogeniture* is merely the *external* appearance of the *inner* nature of *landed property.* . . .
> Let us examine how the various elements conduct themselves here, in the *legislature*, the total state, the state come to actualisation and consequence, to consciousness, the *actual* political state with the *ideal*, the *logical* character and form of these elements, as they *ought to be*.[13]

Marx's extensions of his foregoing criticisms of Hegel's *Philosophy of Right* combine further negative and positive verdicts concerning issues of state. Marx inveighs at length against Hegel's presuppositions involving private property and hereditary family rights in the state. Marx refers to Roman and Germanic developments regarding such matters. Marx lauds, however, Hegel's "great merit" in uniting morality to the modern state, in the face of erroneous attacks by many others against Hegel for not separating them altogether.[14] Marx attacks Hegel's "abstract" definitions, at all levels of the state problem, as the main culprit behind Hegel's inability to pin down the elusive (legislative) essence of the state. In every sphere Hegel's state depends on supports outside itself through intricate circular antitheses that are never resolved. Yet Marx also praises the "merit" of French theorists (in an apparent allusion to Bodin and his later successors in the seventeenth and eighteenth centuries) in first developing the idea of the state as an "abstraction" or entity in its own right, regardless of mistaken later "consequences" in writers like Hegel.[15] Hence, Marx fully recognizes the necessary central places of abstraction and morality in addition to legislation in the truly modern state, notwithstanding his assaults at the same time on Hegel in connection with these elements.

The passages to follow from Marx's *Critique* of Hegel offer a summarizing mixture of Marx's presentations and criticisms of Hegel along with Marx's own views on the state problem as centered on legislation. In the process of scrutinizing Hegel's system, Marx is clearly building his own. Evident here are Marx's proclivities toward the state as a concrete actuality rather than an idealized abstraction, toward the legislature as causative as well as effectual, toward the role of individuals in the collectivity, toward a better blending of the political state with civil society, toward content as well as form, and toward a more logical realistic grasp of the legislative power. These proclivities are all worked out by Marx within the legislative framework of the state that Hegel established, however imperfectly, in his *Philosophy of Right*. The fact that Marx's own positions are not always clearly distinguishable from his presentations and evaluations, pro or con, of Hegel's work, especially on the legislative issues at hand, is further testament to the deep influences of Hegel's ideas on Marx.

> As we have seen: The state exists *only* as the *political state*. The totality of the political state is the *legislature*. To take part in the legislature is therefore to take part in the political state, is to demonstrate and put into effect one's *being* as a *member of the political state*, as a *member of the state*. Hence that *all* wish *individually* to share in the legislature is nothing but the wish of *all* to be actual (active) *members of the state*, or to give themselves a *political being*, or to demonstrate and give effect to their being as a *political* being. We have further seen that the estates element is *civil society* as legislative power, its *political being*. Hence, that civil society should penetrate the *legislative* power *in the mass*, if possible *in its entirety*, that actual

civil society wishes to substitute itself for the *fictitious* civil society of the legislative power, this is merely the striving of civil society to give itself *political* being or to make *political being* its actual being. . . .

[Moreover:] (1) It is a notion belonging to the abstraction of the political state that the *legislature* is the *totality* of the political state. Because this *single* act is the only *political* act of civil society, *all* should, and wish to, share in it at once. (2) *All* as *individuals*. In the *estates element* the legislative activity is not regarded as a *social* function, as a function of *sociality*, but rather as the act through which the individuals first enter into actual and *conscious social* function, i.e., into a political function. The *legislative power* here is no outcome, no function of society, but only its *formation*. The forming of the legislative power requires that *all* members of civil society regard themselves as *individuals*; they actually face [each other] as *individuals*. The attribute "being members of the state" is an "abstract definition", an attribute which is not realised in their actual life.

Either: Separation of political state and civil society takes place, in which case *all* cannot *individually* share in the legislative power. The political state is a phenomenon *separated* from civil society. On the one hand, civil society would abandon itself if all were legislators; on the other, the political state, which confronts civil society, can bear it only in a form appropriate to the *scale* of the political state. . . .

"Legislative" power is striven for not because of its *content* but because of its *formal* political significance. Properly speaking *executive power*, e.g., rather than legislative power, the *metaphysical* state function, must be the goal of popular desire. The *legislative* function is the will not in its practical but in its theoretical energy. Here the *will* is not to have sway *instead* of the *law*: rather, the actual law has to be *discovered* and *formulated*.

This twofold nature of the legislature as the actual *legislative* function and as the *representative, abstract-political* function gives rise to a peculiarity which comes to the fore especially in France, the land of political culture.

(In the *executive power* we always have *two* things, the actual conduct of affairs and the political considerations behind it, as a second actual consciousness which in its total structure is the bureaucracy.)

The proper content of the legislative power . . . is treated very much as separate, as a secondary matter. A question only arouses particular attention when it becomes *political,* i.e., either when it can be linked with a ministerial problem, and hence one involving the authority of the legislature over the executive, or as soon as it is in general a question of rights connected with the political formalism. . . . But Hegel is content that in the state, which he demonstrates to be the self-conscious mode of being of ethical spirit, this ethical spirit should only *as such,* in the sense of the general idea, be the *determining factor.* He does not allow society to become the actually determining factor, because that requires an *actual* subject, and he has only an abstract one—an *imaginary* one.[16]

4. MARX'S *MANIFESTO* AND *BRUMAIRE*

"Social," "Public," and "Common" Contexts

The elusiveness of socialism as an "ism" in conjunction with communism becomes apparent when one turns to a brief (re)consideration of Marx's *Manifesto of the Communist Party* in its historical setting. The work was published in January 1848 at the outset of a year of promising European revolutions. They were eventually to misfire in their efforts to achieve for the working classes what had been gained by the bourgeoisie in revolutions of the early 1830s, namely, political dominance and "social" reform especially through the medium of "public" "social" legislation by the state (the two terms being linked below in various ways, along with "public" and "common"). When writing the *Manifesto* in 1847 and its platform therein for the Communist League, Marx and his collaborator Engels considered their brand of socialism as so distinct from other varieties as to warrant the separate name of so-called "commu*nism.*"

Marx regarded his program for the triumphant struggle of the proletariat over the bourgeoisie as keynote of the hour. The treatise begins with the image of Communism as a "spectre . . . haunting Europe." In fact, the Communist League was an obscure small group of German exiles mostly in France, while their *Manifesto* itself, having no real influence on the revolutions of 1848, remained obscure long afterwards. The communist name after 1848 fell out of general use as an "ism," until it was revived with a different meaning after the Russian Revolution of 1917. When in the 1840s the League adopted the communist name for itself, it would have become forgotten if not for the eventual notoriety of Marx and Engels; after 1848 it remained largely unfamiliar to most other types of socialists for a couple of decades. The

Marxism that emerged as a name and historical force in the 1860s and 1870s (after the publication of the first volume of Marx's *Capital* in 1867) went largely under the wider banner of socialism.

Throughout the mid- and later nineteenth century, therefore, the term "commun*ism*" remained an uncertain synonym for so-called "social*ism*." This was the case despite the aims of the League and the *Manifesto* to be set apart in name as well as in program from other varieties of socialism. Yet Marxian socialism did leave an important legacy that would have a significant impact in the later nineteenth century.

It is well known that Marx considered his type of socialism to be "scientific" and "realistic," founded upon actual concrete forces in history, politics, economics, and society. Most other types of socialism he branded together as "utopian." These idealistic other types faltered or failed in their support of the lower social orders, so he felt. For they lent their support as well to the middle and even upper reaches of society. Marx faulted these other groups for not advocating a rigorous communist-style agenda for a working-class revolution and domination in an eventually classless and stateless society (comprised naturally of the workers themselves).

It is also well known that the sources of Marxian socialism included the French Revolution of 1789– and the British Industrial Revolution (the latter especially via the tutelage of Engels). Just as vital was German philosophy centered on Hegel's dialectical idealism, which became transformed into Marx's dialectical materialism. Hegel's state-centered political thought also had great impact on Marx. When these and other standard main elements are brought together in the patterns just outlined, along with more specific considerations of Marx's *Manifesto*, the place of "isms" in relation to the state problem can be viewed afresh.

Myriad "Social-*Isms*"

Aided by the foregoing observations, new light can be shed on the myriad "social-*isms*" that are set forth in the third section of Marx's (and Engel's) *Manifesto*,[17] entitled "Socialist and Communist Literature." These types of socialism are grouped according to the following headings: "I. Reactionary Socialism" ("a. Feudal Socialism"; "b. Petty-Bourgeois Socialism"; "c. German, or 'True,' Socialism"); "II. Conservative, or Bourgeois, Socialism"; and "III. Critical-Utopian Socialism and Communism."

Under these headings Marx includes a number of other such "isms." Reactionary feudal socialism, as found in writings by aristocrats, railed against the bourgeoisie that emerged triumphant in the early 1830s. The latter professed sympathy for the working classes but did so as a front for promoting their own interests. In league with feudal socialism is clerical socialism or Christian socialism. It is called "feudal" here as partly an echo of the medieval feudal aristocracy that gave rise to the bourgeoisie against which aristocrats continue to clamor.

The petty-bourgeoisie and peasant proprietors, like the feudal aristocracy, were, as Marx here explains, ruined by the greater bourgeoisie through modern industry, manufacturing, and society. This held true particularly in the aftermath of the struggles of the early 1830s. These groups agitate for the benefit of the working classes. Theirs, however, is another reactionary, utopian type of (pseudo)socialism that clings to outmoded views.

One kind of German socialism, falsely styled "true" and "scientific," has been composed of wrongheaded *literati*, according to Marx. They seek to combine French and German traditions of thought. Their anti-bourgeois (and anti-liberal) type of socialism (which is critical of "bourgeois legislation," etc.) is again reactionary and utopian. It was swept away, Engels later added in a note here, by the upheavals of 1848.

The different groups of conservative or bourgeois socialism (which seems linked here by Marx to writers such as Bentham and Mill) desire to promote the interests of the working class. Ultimately, however, those interests are subordinated to their own. In its proper sense to Marx, socialism seeks rather to benefit the working class alone, in opposition to the bourgeoisie with whom it is engaged in class warfare.

Finally, according to Marx, there is critical-utopian socialism and communism in previous forms or systems. These are associated with Saint-Simon, Fourier, Owen, and others. Their impractical albeit sympathetic "social plans" do not properly address the conditions and needs of the suffering proletariat, with which such people cannot satisfactorily identify.

The short ensuing fourth section of Marx's *Manifesto* is entitled "Position of the Communists in Relation to the Various Existing Opposition Parties." Short statements are here given on which existing political parties are supported by the Communists in the various European countries—France, Switzerland, Poland, and Germany (England and America having been included in the second section). What emerges here is a further blurring or blending of Communism with the different forms of revolutionary socialism and republicanism (as Marx defines them) with which communism is obliged to align itself under present circumstances. Yet Marx's salvos against all other such forms in the preceding section must be kept in mind.

Thus Marx's classic formulations of the diverse other forms of socialism besides his own communist brand leave an unclear picture of what constitutes socialism as an "ism," whether in itself or in relation to communism. Marx no doubt portrayed too loosely these varieties of social ideologies and political parties (such as the Social-Democrats in France) under the broad rubric of "social-*ism*," whether in opposition to or in alignment with communism. Nonetheless, in so doing Marx gave new luster to that "ism," perhaps as much as to "commun-ism" (the former appearing in English in the 1830s, the latter in the 1840s). The basic underlying question remains of how the generic term "social" can be turned into an "ism" that covers so wide a spectrum of meanings. At least in the case of "commun-*ism*," the root word "commune" conveys the suggestion of the communal or common ownership that Marx and the League advocated in place of private ownership of property and the means of production.

State Control

What unites as well as diversifies the different types of socialism under a common banner as a revolutionary "ism" is, to a greater or lesser extent in Marx's *Manifesto*, the element of state control. The first section of the *Manifesto* makes it plain that Marx is not against the state *per se* but rather against the "modern" *bourgeois* state. The latter emerged as a main engine of repression after the Middle Ages and again after the French Revolution of 1789–. It remains, in his mind, at least as repressive as the developing factory system of the Industrial Revolution.

Along these lines, Marx asserts as follows in the first section of the *Manifesto*: "Modern industry has . . . [created] the great factory of the industrial capitalist. Masses of labourers, crowded into the factory, are organized like soldiers. . . . Not only are they slaves of the bourgeois class, and of the bourgeois State; they are . . . enslaved by the machine . . ." He goes on to say: "The proletariat . . . seek[s] to restore by force the vanished status of the workman of the Middle Ages [against ongoing "feudal" repression] . . . But every class struggle is a political[!] struggle." Furthermore: "Law, morality, religion, are . . . so many bourgeois prejudices. . . . [T]he bourgeoisie is unfit any longer to be the ruling class in society, and to impose its conditions . . . upon society as an overriding law[!]."

These statements in the *Manifesto* clearly demonstrate that for Marx the state together with its elements of law and politics more broadly are at least as important as, if not more important than, more general factors of class and economics. This is particularly the case if one extends Marx's arguments to the positive (proletariat) side of the state issue, in distinction to the negative (bourgeois) side. Such a position follows logically not only from Marx's plan elsewhere in the *Manifesto* for the proletariat to seize state control as the revolutionary ruling class in society; it follows also from his earlier elaborations on the central significance of politics, law, legislation, and the state in his *Critique* of Hegel. Since Marx in the third section of the *Manifesto* criticizes all other forms of socialism for being ultimately tied in one way or another to bourgeois interests at the expense of the proletariat, it is natural for him to see the bourgeois control of the state as an underlying standard by which they are unified and diversified under this "ism."

In the second section of the *Manifesto*, entitled "Proletarians and Communists," Marx expounds more directly on the proletarian state. Near the beginning he announces: "The immediate aim of the Communist is the . . . overthrow of the bourgeois supremacy, conquest of political[!] power by the proletariat." Further on: "[Y]our jurisprudence is but the will of your [bourgeois] class made into a law[!] for all, a will, whose essential character and direction are determined by the economical conditions . . . of your class." In these ways, then, Marx is calling for a new sovereignty and state controlled by the proletariat in the political as well as legal realm. The determination of law by economic class interests is becoming more apparent here in Marx's thought, but politics and law are still as often couched by him in their own terms and contexts.

In later parts of Section II in the *Manifesto*, Marx cites the distinguishing features of the bourgeois state and society that must be eventually "abolished" in the new socialist or communist state of the proletariat. These features include the family, marriage, religion, morality, "eternal truths (freedom, justice, etc.), private property, private ownership of the means of production, and the factory system as currently structured. Notable for its absence in this sweeping list is law, to which Marx had devoted so much attention in his earlier studies and writings. At one point here, he attacks various traditional aspects of religion, morality, philosophy ("ideas" etc.), political science, and law; but law conspicuously escapes his calls for abolishment.

Marx realizes here that in the new proletarian state law will play a crucial role along with political institutions more generally. He declares that "the first step in the revolution of the working class is to raise the proletariat to the position of ruling class, to win the battle of democracy . . . [, to] use its political supremacy[!] to wrest . . . all capital from the bourgeosie, to centralize all instruments of production in the hands of the State[!], i.e., of the proletariat organized as the ruling class . . ." Thus the sovereign proletarian state seems guided first and foremost by political (and, inevitably, legal) forces and measures in the furtherance of proletarian economic goals.

Public Law

What is striking about the famed ten-point summary platform of the Communist Party that appears near the end of Section II in the *Manifesto* of Marx and Engels is its close correlation with the quasi-socialist program of state control that emerged in later Victorian England through the domestic social legislation under William Gladstone and in particular Lloyd George. The first plank of the platform is: "Abolition of property in land and application of all rent of land to public purposes." This is in ways the most extreme of the ten planks, but in various forms it would blend in with the socialist welfare state of the twentieth century. The second plank is: "A heavy progressive or graduated income tax." This proposal would become standard fare in the modern socialist state. The third plank is: "Abolition of all right of inheritance." This became a label pinned to socialist governments in twentieth century Britain by those aristocrats angered at the loss of their lands due to excessive inheritance taxes, which they complained were designed with that end in mind.

Several ensuing platform planks in the *Manifesto* center more explicitly around socialistic "state" control. Accordingly, the fifth plank stipulates: "Centralization of credit in the hands of the State[!] by means of a national bank with State capital and an exclusive monopoly." Likewise, the sixth plank is: "Centralization of the means of communication and transport in the hands of the State[!]." The seventh plank similarly includes: "Extension of factories and instruments of production owned by the State[!]. . . ." It is clear, we may add, that for Marx all such proposals for socialist "state" control must be accomplished by the proletariat, occupying the supreme political power, through the same basic mechanisms of public law and legislation that characterized the bourgeois state, which the proletarian state is designed to replace.

Once again, the above planks in the *Manifesto* were mostly congruent with aspects of the nascent socialist state in Victorian Britain, in forms compatible there with types of democracy and capitalism. The congruence of these planks with the more stringent socialist state controls exercised in the Germany of Bismarck and the France of Napoleon III is even more striking (notwithstanding Marx's disdain elsewhere for the latter ruler in his early rise to power). To be sure, there are other more extreme features of the platform that are more purely "communistic," such as the call for industrial armies as well as for forced redistribution of the population so as to abolish distinctions between town and country.

Public law is again—even though Marx does not explicitly spell it out here—the mechanism implicitly for achieving state regulation in matters of public education and child labor in the factories. The tenth and final plank of the platform in the *Manifesto* reads as follows: "Free education for all children in public schools. Abolition of children's factory labour in its present form. Combination of education with industrial production, etc., etc." The first and second of these three provisions would become wholly congruent with their counterparts in the developing social legislation of the Victorian state, not to mention in other countries as well. Earlier in Section II, Marx declared: "The Communists have not invented the intervention of society in education; they do but seek to alter the character of that intervention, and to rescue education from the influence of the [bourgeois] ruling class." Clearly, this proletarian state control of education will come through the same kinds of mechanism of public law and legislation already employed by the bourgeois state.

It is ironic that the emerging proto-socialistic Victorian state, with which such Communist planks were to prove compatible, was also, to a large extent, a bourgeois capitalist state. It was not only the negative Manchester factory model of bourgeois economic repression in England that influenced Marx. Also crucial was the positive (as well as negative) model of the proto-socialist state of Victorian England. (Marx lived and wrote in London from 1849 until his death and contributed voluminously to newspapers on current topics.)

The foregoing interpretations of Marx's *Manifesto* diverge from those of many other historians by underscoring the positive no less than negative features of the socialist-communist *state* envisioned by Marx. It is often alleged that Marx was ultimately suspicious of all law and legislation (private as well as public) and was against all political process in itself. Yet we have seen many ways in which such viewpoints must be placed in the fuller perspectives of Marx's system.

It cannot be overlooked that, at the end of the platform in Section II of the *Manifesto*, the following points are made: "When . . . class distinctions have disappeared, . . . the public[!] power will lose its political character. Political power, properly so called, is merely the organized power of one class for opposing another." Clearly, the "public" power remains in some form in the ultimate, supposedly stateless, non-"political" Communist society. Yet this third stage is little discussed further in the *Manifesto*, which concentrates instead on the realistic means needed to achieve that visionary end, as preceded by the first and second stages, namely, the bourgeois state and the proletarian state.

It would not be altogether accurate to argue backwardly from Marx's later writings or even from the *Manifesto* that Marx in his early writings was anti-law or anti-politics and anti-government.[18] Such was not the case in the *Manifesto*, much less in his earlier writings, including his *Critique* of Hegel. Marx's various synonyms for such terms in the *Manifesto* as "social use" include "public use," which gives abundant opening for public law and legislation as practical devices of socialist control in the proletarian state, prior to its eventual disappearance, at least in theory. Marx's brief *Manifesto* had not yet moved away from the heavy state-centered orientation found a half decade earlier in his detailed *Critique* of Hegel's political-legal thought; yet the *Manifesto* also looked ahead to Marx's more purely economic-social interests in his voluminous *Das Kapital* two decades later.

Legislation

Marx exhibited a different but related focus on legislation in his ensuing classic work entitled *The Eighteenth Brumaire of Louis Bonaparte*.[19] It was published in 1852 shortly after the French *coup d'état* of Napoleon III (nephew of Napoleon I) on December 2, 1851. This work is well known for its innovative applications to French history and current events of the ideas and methods of historical materialism. Marx's close and lengthy analysis of the events leading up to the *coup*–from 1848 (the year of the *Manifesto*) onward—has been little recognized as a kind of legislative history of that period, notwithstanding the work's socio-economic underpinnings. Marx clearly perceives, once again, the legislative foundation of the state entity, even if he is intent on revealing the broader materialist substructures of the society within and over which it operates. The legal-political avenues for this new Napoleon's arrival may not have been Marx's main purpose to trace in their own right. Yet their strong inroads in Marx's work remain important for an appreciation of his outlook on the state problem in history and current events.

In spite of Marx's scorn in his *Brumaire* for the new Napoleon, the latter later became, in the nearly two decades of the Second Empire (1852–1870), more of the socialist-prone benefactor of the working class than he had been during the Second Republic (1848–1852) about which Marx was writing. Marx tended to see the "dictatorship" of Napoleon III (the title adopted by Louis-Napoleon Bonaparte as the emperor of the new empire) as also that of the bourgeoisie rather than that of the proletariat. Yet Napoleon III became also a harbinger of the socialist welfare states of later times (as remains to be seen below in contexts of legislation and the term "social").

The political-legal backbone of Marx's *Brumaire* was an integral part of the story he was telling in historical as well as journalistic fashion.

"Socialism" (Ch. V) / 167

However, many other surveys of these events by more recent authorities do not dwell as pointedly as did Marx on legislative and related developments. Thus the legal-legislative aspects of this work by Marx are no less important to grasp than are the social or economic features. Even though Marx's fixation on the "bourgeois" state's legislative history becomes a sign of governmental repression of the proletariat, it nevertheless gives further fuel to present contentions.

The first of the seven sections of Marx's *Brumaire* opens with a scathing appropriation of Hegel's remark about milestones in world history occurring twice. Marx declares that Hegel neglected to add that the first occurrence is a "tragedy" and the second a "farce," alluding here respectively to Napoleon I and Napoleon III. Marx is intent on laying the background to the present story in the French Revolution of 1789– and in the "bourgeois monarchy" of King Louis Phillipe (from 1830 to 1848), which he says was replaced by a "bourgeois republic." Marx exclaims that the "social revolution of the nineteenth century cannot draw its poetry from the past, but only from the future." All such problems will here be organized, states Marx, around the three successive regimes that he portrays in terms of their legislative bodies: "Three main periods are unmistakable: *The February period*; May 4, 1848, to May 28, 1849: *the period of the constitution of the republic, or of the Constituent National Assembly*; May 28, 1849, to December 2, 1851: *the period of the constitutional republic or of the Legislative National Assembly*." The ensuing sections treating these regimes naturally trace the evolving intricate struggles between the bourgeois and proletarian classes in relation to the emergence of Napoleon III. An overriding context, at the same time, is the legislative history of the governments and constitutions around which those struggles took place. There is not the space here to detail the multitudinous specifics on this point, although the subject deserves a full study. Limited examples must suffice here.

In the fourth section of his *Brumaire*, when speaking of the predominance of the bourgeoisie during an early period of the new Napoleon's rise in late 1849, Marx states as follows: "I have not here to write the [whole] history of its legislative activity, which is summarized during this period in two laws: in the law re-establishing the *wine tax* and the *education law* abolishing unbelief." In the course of discussing this social legislation, Marx points out: "The bourgeoisie had a true insight into the fact that all the weapons which it had forged against feudalism turned their points against . . . its own civilization. . . . It understood that all the so-called bourgeois liberties and organs of progress attacked and menaced its *class rule* at its social foundation and its political summit simultaneously, and had therefore become '*socialistic*'. . . . [I]t rightly discerned the secret of Socialism, whose import and tendency it judges more correctly than so-called Socialism knows how to judge itself . . ." Subsequently turning to Napoleon directly, Marx says: "While Bonaparte's ministry partly took the initiative in framing laws in the spirit of the party of Order, and partly even outdid that party's harshness in their execution and administration, he, on the other hand, by childishly silly proposals sought to win popularity, to bring out his opposition to the National Assembly . . ." Further on, Marx discusses later laws (concerning the press, elections, etc.) of May 1850.

The general parameters of the fifth section in Marx's *Brumaire* are established at the outset: "As soon as the revolutionary crisis had been weathered and universal suffrage abolished, the struggle between the National Assembly and Bonaparte broke out again." Midway through the section Marx reiterates: "We have seen how on great and striking occasions [in late 1850] . . . the National Assembly avoided or quashed the struggle with the executive power. Now we see it compelled to take it up in the pettiest occasions." Again specific legislative contexts are recounted by Marx.

In the sixth section of his *Brumaire*, Marx traces the immediate constitutional struggles and economic crises leading up to Napoleon's final *coup* in late 1851. Marx summarizes the results as follows: "Thus the industrial bourgeoisie applauds with servile bravos the *coup d'état* of December 2, the annihilation of parliament, the downfall of its own rule, the dictatorship of Bonaparte. . . . Napoleon [I, not unlike Cromwell before the Long Parliament] . . . at least betook himself on the eighteenth Brumaire to the legislative body and read out to it . . . its sentence of death. The second Napoleon [did not do so and behaved ignominiously] . . ." Marx again outlines the main phases of the Second Republic especially in its constitutional and legislative contours.

It is in the final seventh section of his *Brumaire* that Marx makes some of his most cogent observations on the all-importance of legislation in the burgeoning state of the new Napoleon (as evidenced in the corresponding note below). In essence, the legislative power and the state machinery were to become subordinated to the authoritarian will of the Emperor himself, even though he was initially elected with wide popular support (partly because of his famous name). Thus was completed the centralization of the independent modern French state out of the lingering (medieval) feudal patchwork of decentralized authorities. In the final analysis, this new Napoleon, declares Marx, is defined by his sovereign lawmaking powers in relation to all other bodies or groups. It is through his decrees that the new Napoleon most characteristically endeavored to appease as well as to suppress both the proletariat and the bourgeoisie, playing them off against each other (but, in the end, turning them against himself). Napoleon's "decrees" may often have become simple edicts of his will rather than formal legislation. Even then, it was the legislative *nature* of his decrees that, according to Marx, best delineated Napoleon's various efforts in relation to socialist groups and their differing brands of socialism, which again provides a main medium for Marx. The new Napoleon's style of issuing decrees in such matters became, to Marx, an imperfect shadow of the first Bonaparte's.[20]

5. INTERMEZZO: SOCIALIST LEGISLATIVE STATE AND COMMUNIST (LAWLESS?) STATELESSNESS

In his noted pamphlet entitled *Socialism: Utopian and Scientific* (1880), Frederick Engels wrote as follows: "Modern socialism is . . . the recognition . . . of the class antagonism . . . between capitalists and wage-workers . . . [and] of the anarchy existing in production." He pointedly observed: "[T]he materialistic conception of history and the revelation of the secret of capitalistic production through surplus value we owe to Marx. With these discoveries socialism became a science." Further on, following headings on "*Medieval Society*" and "*Capitalist Revolution*," Engels turned to: "*Proletarian Revolution* Solution of the contradictions. The proletariat seizes the public[!] power, and by means of this transforms the socialized means of production, slipping from the hands of the bourgeoisie, into public[!] property. . . . In proportion as anarchy in social production vanishes, the political authority of the state dies out. Man, at last the master of his own form of social organization, becomes . . . free. . . . [T]his . . . is the historical mission of the modern . . . proletarian movement, scientific socialism."[21]

Along these same lines, Engels further declared elsewhere, when treating the origin of family, property, and the state: "The state is, therefore, by no means a power forced on society from without . . . [or] . . . 'the reality of the ethical idea' . . . as Hegel maintains. Rather it is a product of society at a certain stage of development . . ." In addition to territory, "[t]he distinguishing feature [of the state] . . . is the establishment of a *public*[!] *power* . . ." Engels goes on to assert: "Having public[!] power and the right to levy taxes, the officials now stand, as organs of society, *above* society. . . . [B]eing the vehicles of a power that is becoming alien to society, respect for them must be enforced by means of exceptional laws[!] by virtue of which they enjoy special sanctity and inviolability . . ." Finally: "[T]he state arose from the need to hold class antagonisms in check, but . . . it is . . . the state of the most powerful, economically dominant class, which through the medium of the state, becomes also the politically dominant class . . ."[22]

In their *The German Ideology* (1845–1846), Marx and Engels asserted that "those theoreticians who regard *might* as the basis of right were in direct contradiction to those who looked on *will* as the basis of right [as seemingly realism *vs.* idealism]. . . . If power is taken as the basis of right, as Hobbes, etc., do, then right, law, etc., are merely the symptoms, the expression of *other* relations upon which state power rests." However: "These actual relations are in no way created by the state power; on the contrary, they are the power creating it. . . . The individuals who rule in these conditions . . . have to give their will . . . as the will of the state, as law, an expression . . . of this class, as civil and criminal law[!] demonstrates . . ." In other words: "[T]he state does not exist owing to the dominant will, but the state, which arises from the material mode of life of individuals, has also the form of a dominant will." Coming then to legislation: "The most superficial examination of legislation, e.g., poor laws in all countries, shows how far the rulers got when they imagined that they could achieve something by means of their 'dominant will' alone, i.e., simply by exercising their will."[23]

In a piece dated 1852 (London) that was published in a New York City newspaper, Marx discussed "the Chartists, the politically active portion of the British *working class.*" "[T]hey . . . demand . . . universal suffrage. . . . But universal suffrage is the equivalent of political [!] power [i.e., supremacy] for the working class of England, where the proletariat forms the large majority of the population. . . . The carrying of universal suffrage in England would, therefore, be a far more socialistic [legislative] measure than anything which has been honoured with that name on the Continent."[24]

In another newspaper piece of 1855, Marx queried as follows: "But what is this British Constitution? Are its essential features to be found in the laws governing representation and the limitations imposed on the executive power? These characteristics distinguish it neither from the Constitution of the United States nor from the constitutions of the countless joint-stock companies in England. . . . The British Constitution is, in fact, only an antiquated and obsolete compromise made between the bourgeoisie, which rules in actual practice, . . . and the landed aristocracy, which forms the *official government.*" Marx then turns to the topic of legislation: "Legislative history[!] since 1831 is the history of concessions made to the industrial bourgeoisie, from the Poor Law Amendment Act to the repeal of the Corn Laws, and from the repeal of the Corn Laws to the Succession Duty on landed property." He adds: "Although the bourgeoisie . . . thus also gained general *politi-*

cal recognition as the *ruling class*, this only happened on one condition; namely, that the whole business of government[!] in all its details—including even the executive branch of the legislature, that is, the actual making of laws[!] in both Houses of Parliament—remained the guaranteed domain of the landed aristocracy."[25]

The preceding passages further establish the significance, for Marx and Engels, of public social legislation at the core of the state, conceived by them as a public entity and as the main driving force of their socialist agenda. A key byproduct of their variegated arguments above that socio-economic conditions determine political-legal factors, rather than the reverse, is their reinforcement of the traditional picture, already firmly grounded in the first half of their century, of the modern state as primarily a legal-legislative entity. The same holds true for other either-or comparisons such as will vs. might and ideas vs. material actualities. Time and time again, their criticisms of existing states and legislation wind up connecting those two topics in a unique symbiosis. Socialism and social legislation go hand in hand in their quest for a proletarian state, which, after it has been fully and finally attained, will purportedly disappear. But what is then left? Would the envisioned stateless Communist "society" and "social organization" require new forms of political as well as legal-legislative regulations and relationships, patterned after the old ones (instead of the latter merely "withering away" along with the state)?

The direct and indirect pronouncements made above on the dominant role of public social legislation and of the legislative processes in Britain, not to mention political issues more generally, are compelling testimony in themselves. Many of Marx's (and Engel's) voluminous collected writings were dispatched in reaction to British events and debates centered around Parliament and its bills, reforms, and so on. A full-length study of that subject would reveal the magnitude of their legislative concerns and efforts in that direction. To attempt a comprehensive survey of all the materials pertaining to legislation throughout the several dozen volumes of collected writings of Marx and Engels would be a much larger enterprise. Of even vaster scope is their fascination with political issues of state more generally, as is intimated in passages above.

In conclusion, it cannot be overlooked that issues of state, law, and politics have long interested historians with regard to the writings and activities of Marx (as well as Engels). But such subjects have not yet been connected by experts of Marx to legislation in the ways attempted above. As holds true for many other writers explored in this series, the interest of Marx in legislation has been unduly neglected as a topic in its own right.[26]

6. FRANCE AND ENGLAND: SOCIAL(ISTIC) STATE LEGISLATION

Varieties of Social(istic) "Isms"

Not unlike liberalism, with which it often came to be associated especially in England in the late nineteenth and early twentieth centuries, socialism has tended to be a relativistic concept capable of many diverse and divergent meanings. Not unlike liberalism, socialism has run the gamut of conceptual equivalents—from republicanism, revolutionism, and individualism to statism, nationalism, and collectivism. Socialism has been a broad and amorphous concept variously attributed by historians to Plato (*Republic*), Thomas More (*Utopia*), Rousseau (*Social Contract*), Owen (model communities), Saint-Simon (central planning), Marx, the British Labor Party, Lenin, Stalin, Hitler (National Socialism), and Franklin Roosevelt ("New Deal"). Thus socialism, at different points and times, has been found compatible with democratic and parliamentary governments as well as with communistic and totalitarian regimes.

In the second half of the nineteenth century in Western Europe, the emergence of socialism in theory and practice was subject to different meanings and interpretations, depending on the contexts involved. On one side of the political spectrum lay the case of Germany under Bismarck. There, incipient public ownership or state control of industry combined with incipient social welfare through state legislation, although Marxists disputed Bismarck's approaches. On the other side lay the England of Gladstone, foreshadowing that of Lloyd George. There, the organization of industry still accorded with private ownership and capitalism, but the growing machinery of social legislation gave early signs of the modern social-service, or welfare, state. Somewhere in between those two cases lay France under Napoleon III. There, wide latitude was given to an expanding, new rich capitalist bourgeoisie, while simultaneously a planned centralized economy was also emerging with social benefits for the working classes. In all three national varieties, a common medium was public social legislation, with greater or lesser degrees of state control in differing forms of growing bureaucratism and welfarism.

To these varieties and degrees of socialistic state legislation, or legislative states, could be added myriad other examples in the late nineteenth and early twentieth centuries. Yet the complex different modes of emergent socialism in the various European as well as non-European countries cannot be covered, much less in depth, within the present limited confines. It is appropriate rather to focus briefly on Bonapartism and Gladstonianism. Not only do they form here an extension to previous sections dealing with Marx's writings on Louis-Napoleon Bonaparte and his connections with early Victorian England, but they are also germane "isms" in their own right regarding the beginnings of the socialistic legislative state.

Although historians' ways of dividing up the topic of state socialism vary widely, the legislative base of the socialist state usually remains paramount, whether explicitly or implicitly. Some separate socialism as a topic altogether from, say, Communism, Stalinism, Fascism, and Nazism (as does the *Oxford English Dictionary*). Others use it as a broad category under which those other "isms" can be grouped. Either way, the legislative base of the socialist state still remains (as it also does in the oft-cited models of Plato, More, Rousseau, and other early theorists).

If, in the cases of France and England to follow, the relation of socialism to the state and to legislation seems at times ambiguous, ambiguity is partly inherent in the "ism," which we have sought to explode as well as to exploit. The shifting interconnections made by historians between socialism and a wide range of other "isms" have made it all the more elusive as a rubric. There seem to be few firm lines in the fluctuating interplay between socialism and those myriad other "isms" just cited. This is particularly true for three broad "isms" that have been treated by historians—Bonapartism, Gladstonianism, and Bismarckianism—in connection with a variety of socialistic "isms." The need again arises for such relativistic "constructs" to be "deconstructed" and for more fixed patterns of legislation and the state to be recognized.

It will now be useful to consider briefly the cases of France and England, reserving Germany for the next chapter dealing with nationalism. As for Bonapartism in France, its nationalistic Gallicanism harked back to the glory days of Napoleon I. Much different was the national statism of Bismarck's Germany (and its relation to illiberalism).

"Bonapart*ism*" and Beyond

Although never crystal-clear, the relationship between the Bonapartists and French socialists underwent many transformations during the Second Republic of 1848–1852 and the Second Empire of 1852–1870. Early in the Republic, of which Louis-Napoleon became the President, he and his monarchist allies ousted many of the Socialist-Republican deputies, who together with the straight republicans had at first held a substantial one-third minority of seats in the national legislative Assembly. The monarchists, split between the Orleanist and Legitimist factions, had at first held a corresponding two-thirds majority but now were even more in control. The Assembly of the Republic, which was actually anti-republican in its government, then rescinded the universal suffrage that had at first surprisingly brought the monarchists to legislative power in the wake of the destabilizing revolution of 1848. About a third of the electorate was now disenfranchised, that is, the poorest and most socialist-prone members of society. It will be remembered that the revolution of 1848 had ended the "bourgeois monarchy" of Louis-Phillipe in the Orlean line (1830–1848) and that he had been preceded by the aristocratic regimes of Louis XVIII and Charles X in the restored Bourbon line (1814–1830), which came to be championed by the "Legitimists."

In time, posing as the people's one true leader and seeking broad-based popular support, in particular from the radicals, Louis-Napoleon Bonaparte succeeded in reinstating universal suffrage and eventually becoming regarded by many socialists, especially the followers of Saint-Simon (d. 1825), as somewhat of a socialist himself. After a *coup d'état* in which the Assembly was abolished, strict public controls were imposed, and all had received the vote, Napoleon was overwhelmingly elected President for ten years. But he soon proclaimed himself Emperor. Was socialism, like republicanism, dead? As Emperor, Napoleon III (the title he gave himself in distinction to Napoleon I) became a kind of dictator, further crushing liberal parliamentary institutions. He eliminated effective universal suffrage through electoral controls, while still claiming credit for it. Yet in this respect he was akin to the Marxists, who distrusted parliamentary government and political freedom in the march toward classless material progress. Napoleon's efforts to benefit the working classes earned him the "socialist" label especially from his bourgeois critics. Socialists themselves were becoming more "realistic"; Saint-Simonians made accommodations with the expanding capitalist economy encouraged by Napoleon (for his own ends) and became pioneers in the field of investment banking. But it becomes more difficult to determine what Bonapartists and socialists stood for as "isms" than it is to identify those who fell under either group as followers or adherents ("ists").

Although even less clear, the relationships between the two corresponding "isms" often used by historians in these matters—Bonapartism and socialism—can at least be understood more distinctly in terms of the theme of public legislation. Bonapartism in French foreign affairs became typically wrapped up with Gallicanism or nationalism in evocation of the imperial glories of the first Napoleon, whom the new Napoleon sought to emulate. Bonapartism in French domestic affairs usually centered around Napoleon III as a prototype modern dictator who, in the early Empire, pushed his centralizing programs through a Legislative Body that acted in a consultative capacity but without power to initiate or veto laws. Napoleon was later forced to grant it a more "liberal" role. Napoleon III acted more like a modern "politician" than Napoleon I in the directing and manipulating of legislation to his own ends, including through extensive, often demagogic, speechmaking. It is perhaps his strong state control and central planning through public legislation, in the direction of social welfare, that best typify Napoleon III's regime as a prototype of the later social-service, or welfare, state (as well as the authoritarian state).

It is surprising that the legislative orientation of the French state under the new Napoleon has not been more specifically or extensively described by historians than has been the case. Perhaps the most explicit and detailed discussion of the legislative history *per se* of the Second Republic under Napoleon is still to be found in Marx's *Brumaire*. Even though Marx portrayed Louis-Napoleon as basically a (dangerous) buffoon, Marx's treatment of legislative issues, which has in itself attracted little scholarly attention, brought out the wide scope of the legislative state of the Second Republic. What Marx did not cover in that work was, of course, the subsequent Second Empire, in which the legislative state came ever clearer into view. It was, for instance, during the Empire that the city of Paris was reshaped into its modern design; this great enterprise was engineered by Napoleon through his authoritarian direction not only of city planning but also of state legislation. The massive public works, like the public controls, were facilitated or attained through public laws.

Napoleon III sought to be remembered not only as the heir to the great Bonaparte legend but also as a great "social" engineer; his latter ambition was more closely interwoven with French legislative history than has been commonly recognized. The modern French state not only of the Second Republic but also of the Second Empire was at bottom a legislative state. Under Napoleon III the legislative state was expressed at first more in terms of laws reflecting merely his will. Later on, there were somewhat more independent or formal legislative processes.

To the extent that the legislative history of this period is touched upon by historians, it is usually the Second Republic more than the Second Empire that is highlighted. Laws, plebiscites, constitutions, parliamentary factions, and struggles between the legislature and Napoleon are included as crucial parts of the wider political history of the period leading up to and following the *coup d'état*. But the enormous legislative activities of the Second Empire must be no less appreciated, both in the earlier muzzled phase and the later "liberalized" stage. There was a striking buildup of administrative bureaucracy through which the massive legislation of the central government was directed throughout the entire nation-state of France. Such innovations as the workers' right to unionize were among the multitudinous features of French economic, political, and social life encompassed by public legislation.

It should not be forgotten that Napoleon III developed plans (which went largely unrealized) for armies of industrial workers. Not only were his plans akin to those advanced by the Saint-Simonians, who during the Empire sometimes called him their "socialist emperor." They were also reminiscent of provisions by Karl Marx in the platform in the *Manifesto*.

Such contexts of central planning prompt one to think again of Napoleon III's rebuilding of Paris. The creation of more open "public" spaces included broad boulevards that allowed easier access for government troops to put down insurrections. Here, too, state controls can be viewed from socialistic perspectives.

Yet Napoleon and his later Saint-Simonian socialist allies did not adopt *extreme* ideas for a centrally planned industrial system and society. They allowed for private ownership in many forms. His public works and social-economic engineering provided employment opportunities for the working classes. For that element, he thereby promoted material "progress" and even "social" consciousness. Like the Marxists, he did not put a high value on individual freedom. He imposed some state controls over French intellectual and artistic life. The working classes of Paris, benefitting in employment from the rebuilding of the city, were the natural constituency of the Saint-Simonian socialists (and became the epicenter of Communistic upheavals in the Paris Commune of 1871). Along these lines, it was also during the Empire, in the decade from 1859 to 1869, that the Suez Canal was built largely through French enterprise.

There is not space here to indicate further the important legislative history of the Second Republic. Marx's legislative approach to this shorter four-year period was discussed above. Even less can the longer eighteen-year period of the Second Empire be adequately outlined here. It is to be hoped that a comprehensive study will be conducted on the legislative history *per se* of both periods, surpassing historians' usual sporadic references to it within other contexts.[27]

Vaster still is the legislative history of the ensuing seventy-year Third Republic (1870–1940), including the Paris Commune of 1871. The theme of public legislation, as the basis of state and sovereignty, emerged with even greater prominence during this epoch, along with further developments toward the modern social-service state. Thus the legislative state, as the true modern state, spanned across the Second Republic, Second Empire, and Third Republic.[28]

"Gladstonian*ism*" and Lloyd George

Early prefigurations of the socialistic legislative state of the early twentieth century in Britain began to emerge most decisively under the long liberal leadership of William Gladstone. During his four terms as Prime Minister (1868–74, 1880–85, 1886, 1892–94), and before that as Chancellor of the Exchecquer in several administrations (from 1852 to 1865), Gladstone engineered through Parliament a sweeping comprehensive program of domestic legislation, together with electoral reforms. He built upon the foundations of his predecessors to form the basis of what would become the British social-service state. On a variety of issues, his programs and policies have been discussed by some historians under the rubric of "Gladstonian*ism*."

What that term means and how it appertains to the connections at hand between socialism and state legislation (neither of which has been adequately singled out for analysis by Gladstone's historians) remain to be seen in the secondary accounts that follow. The cumulative legislative momentum toward the modern British social-service state of the early twentieth century was generally continued by both the Liberal and Conservative Parties under a succession of Prime Ministers following, respectively, Gladstone and Disraeli (the latter in 1868 and 1874–80). An early-twentieth-century culmination was reached with the rise of the liberal-socialistic Labor Party. Its early leader, David Lloyd George, became Chancellor of the Exchecquer (1908–15) and Prime Minister (1916–22).[29] The series of secondary passages to follow bring together in illustrative synoptic fashion scattered references to relevant themes at hand.

> By 1870 it was clear that if the British State was to fulfil efficiently the many new tasks it had undertaken it needed thorough overhaul and reorganization. A long series of reforms culminated in the concentrated "political engineering" achievements of Gladstone's First Ministry (1868–74). In those years the basis of the modern State was well and truly laid. So much could be achieved in so short a time only because the ground had been already prepared. . . . Three main branches of government—the civil service, the military organization, and the judiciary—were overhauled within a few years. . . . As the State could not perform the many labours of social service organization which it was assuming until its own machinery was

improved these reforms were the very basis of further change.
. . .

Lord Selborne, Gladstone's Lord Chancellor between 1872 and 1874, did for the judiciary what Cardwell did for the Army. He simplified and remodelled both the legal system and the courts which administered it. . . .

These reforms, coming so soon after the widening of the franchise in 1867 and preceding the increase in State and municipal activities in the last quarter of the century, offer some insight into the whole development of English government. They are the counterpart to the great adjustments of political and economic machinery which followed the first Reform Bill and are in part the further consequences of those earlier adjustments. Throughout the century between 1815 and 1914 there was constant interplay between the development of social-welfare legislation and the progress of parliamentary reform. Social betterment made further extension of the franchise possible and more probable, and extensions of the franchise led to fresh programmes of social improvement. The two best examples of this interplay concern public health legislation and education.

The great interest in improvement of public health between 1848 and 1874 sprang from two very dynamic forces—the cholera and Edwin Chadwick. . . . It was the Reform Bill of 1867 which gave the first real impetus to the creation of a national system of free and compulsory education. . . . The Education Act of 1870 set up locally-elected school boards which could compel attendance to the age of thirteen. . . . A quite new kind of State was quickly coming into existence. It has since come to be known as the social-service State, and is now the common pattern of political and social life in the twentieth century. . . . Because the State was being step by step democratized, new social classes claimed benefits from the State and laid claim to use the State for their own ends. Therefore the State had to adjust, extend, and develop its machinery to serve new ends of social control and public service. This meant considerable changes in the nature and functioning of Parliament.
. . . Because both were in constant interplay during the formative decades of the seventies and eighties, Liberalism was socialized and Socialism was liberalized, unlike their counterparts on the continent of Europe. There grew up a strong tradition of "Liberal Socialism" which was completely within the traditions and institutions of parliamentary government. . . .

Gladstone's first ministry laid the main foundations for the new kind of State which was to develop by 1914. The generation after 1875 built steadily on these foundations. . . . [T]he House of Commons . . . [was] becoming more completely than ever the true focus of legislative power. . . . Two Gladstonian Reform Bills of 1884 and 1885 extended the vote. . . . From 1870 onwards the habit grew of relieving the congestion of parliamentary business by providing that the details of Bills should be filled in departmentally. . . . What has come to be known as "delegated legislation," about which there has been prolonged controversy and a famous Parliamentary Committee's report, assumed large proportions. . . . Naturally, again, the spate of new social legislation produced by the Liberal Governments of 1906–14, providing old age pensions, labour exchanges, and national health insurance, meant a new and unprecedented extension of delegated legislation. That process has continued ever since. . . . The Liberal Party, influenced more and more by Lloyd George, launched its programme of social reform most of which it achieved, with the help of the Labour Party, between 1906 and 1914. The forces of social liberalism and of liberal socialism came together, and achieved a remarkable series of new measures within eight years. . . .

The three phases of Victorian development coincide respectively with the growth, supremacy, and decline of Liberalism as the operative political creed of most Englishmen.[30]

Further descriptive of the rise of British socialism through state controls and public social legislation is the following account written in 1931 at a time when the modern social-service state was becoming increasingly dominant and pervasive. Due weight is assigned to Gladstone (with emphasis on his later ministry) and the Liberal Party in the development of the Victorian legislative state, leading up to the socialistic Labor Party of Lloyd George and others. Liberalism under Gladstone was still compatible with traditional varieties of individualism and capitalism. Yet it also looked ahead to the greater collectivism and statism of the early twentieth century under Lloyd George and his followers.

When in July 1817 Robert Owen laid before a [legislative] committee of the House of Commons on the Poor Laws his plan for setting people to work in groups to fulfil one another's needs instead of either being supported in idleness or working for wages to produce goods to be sold in the open market, he started British socialism on its career as a practical plan for the general reform of society. . . .

Between 1815 and 1845 such ideas . . . spread through the community. . . . During this period the word "socialism" came into common use as descriptive of opposition to competition as a rule of economic action and legislation. . . . A declaration made in 1843 that "Socialism and Chartism pursue the same aims, they only differ in their methods," is essentially true. . . .

After about 1845 interest in socialism as a general proposal for the reorganization of society goes under a cloud, from which it scarcely emerges for forty years. . . .

Socialism came to be looked upon, notwithstanding its purely English origin and the early prevalence of socialist ideals in England, as an exotic on English soil. . . . [W]hile strong socialist political parties were growing up on the continent and international socialism was taking shape, socialism awakened in England, between 1850 and 1880, none of that robust interest so widely shown in individual reforms.

After 1880 it was different. The great current of continental socialism set, partially at least, into England. . . . Socialism, now becomes a great underlying influence upon the progress of reform.

It may be conducive to clearness to conceive of socialism as attacking the citadel of purely competitive society during this period by a threefold advance. The earliest approach was the entrance of government upon the field of industry. . . . In 1861 Mr. Gladstone, when President of the Board of Trade, established the Post Office Savings Bank, and in 1864 encouraged the trade unions to deposit their funds in it. He had certainly no realization that he was involving the government in a new policy; government was nevertheless embarking upon the banking business. . . . In 1883 the Parcel Post was instituted, the first step toward a government monopoly of the express business. In the seventies and eighties government took over the telegraph and telephone lines. . . . [T]hese [were] early and mostly unconscious intrusions of the national government into the fields of transportation, insurance, building, and general industrial development. . . . These . . . early steps of government . . . [were] all in the direction of the limitation of the field of competitive business, the socialization of certain activities previously left to private competitors. . . . The growth of government ownership is the most spontaneous form in which the modern trend toward socialism has shown itself.

A second form of approach is to be found in the socialistic element in recent humanitarian legislation. Such legislation has been increasingly based on the recognition that the competitive form of society is ineffective for general prosperity and social justice. The alleviation of various ills provided in this legislation is at the expense not only of the national treasury but of the theory of individualism. This is especially true of the social reforms . . . adopted in the decade just before the war, when the Liberal, Labour and Nationalist parties combined to introduce by parliamentary action old age pensions, labor exchanges, trade boards, and national insurance. . . . Laws implying the infeasibility of attaining general prosperity under a competitive system and establishing regulation by government in its stead could be carried to any length without further change of principle. Thus the second approach to socialism is to be found in the far-reaching social legislation of recent times.[31]

The socialistic legislative state of the early twentieth century in Britain was already emergent by the turn of the century and was hastened on by the exigencies of the first world war. Amid the swirling crosscurrents of political "isms" at the turn of the century, with particular regard to socialism, there remained the underlying continuum of the British parliament in its fundamental capacity as legislature. The legislative nexus of British socialists signaled their quest for reform instead of revolution, which to them typified Marxist Continental socialism and its disinclination toward parliamentary processes and compromises. The account continued below (and in the note) again supplies further useful summaries on issues at hand.

So we come to the third of the converging lines of socialistic influence on the reform movement. This is socialism known as such, teaching its doctrines, claiming support and urging action under its own name or some recognized equivalent of that name. It was in the troubled decade between 1880 and 1890 that the first two active and lasting modern socialist bodies, the Social Democratic Federation and the Fabian Society were established. Their members were for the most part literary men, like Shaw, Wells, and Hyndman, or artists, like Morris and Crane, or teachers, such as Webb and Wallas. . . .

The leading ideas of socialism, through their efforts and other means, percolated downward and spread widely. The first popular response to this influence was the formation in 1892 of the Independent Labour Party. . . . The Independent Labour Party may be defined as a socialist group of workingmen, striving to gain their ends by political action. It was in a certain sense a revival of the Chartism of three-quarters of a century before, though the old political ends having now been mostly reached, their objects extended further into the field of actual change. They were from the beginning satisfied with a "revisionist" attitude, their leaders having little to say about "the class war," "the revolution," or the "dictatorship of the proletariat." . . .

In 1899 the basis was at last laid for a party that should be at once numerous and socialist. . . . This was . . . the [new] Labour Party. . . .

Even before the war, then, socialism had become a large factor in thought, legislation, and discussion on reform.[32]

"Victorian*ism*" and "Parliamentar*ism*"

An earlier section discussed "the emerging dominance of public legislation in the early Victorian state" up to the Second Reform Act of 1867 and the start of Gladstone's first ministry in 1868. The legislative paradigm of the state, as we have now seen, became more sweeping and comprehensive in the later Victorian era. The rapidly expanding mass of legislation promulgated by Parliament in domestic as well as foreign affairs—in furtherance of the burgeoning modern British nation-state and its empire—was clearly a leading fixture of the Victorian Age in the nineteenth and early twentieth centuries.

There is not space here to recount adequately the many significant milestones in the cumulative mass of domestic legislation (acts, reforms, etc.) enacted by the British parliament during the heydays of Gladstone, Disraeli, and other Prime Ministers prior to Lloyd George. The legislative crux of the Victorian state has long been well documented and widely known in other contexts. But it has seldom been singled out for extensive study as a subject in its own right, including with regard to socialism and the state. There is still great need for such a study. (Some illustrations of this legislation are given below.[33]) Much has been written (and not written) about the characteristics of the Victorian Age and Victorianism during the reign of Queen Victoria (1837–1901) and in the wider scope of the century between Napoleon and World War I (1815–1914). The theme of legislation needs to be integrated into this picture more fully than has heretofore been accomplished by historians.[34]

The Victorian quest for social improvement, material progress, democratic inclusion, institutional reform, and the like was typically implemented through Parliament in public social legislation. The legislative mechanism for harnessing the power of the state through Parliament became the greatest engine of all driving the emergent social-service state. Parliament was increasingly the focal point of British life in all its aspects—political, legal, economic, social, and cultural. As the House of Commons gained ascendancy and the role of the House of Lords waned, with the steady advancements being made in the direction of universal suffrage, the modern legislative state was coming more forcefully to the fore. With the rise of "cabinet government," the Prime Ministers increasingly became the directors of the legislative processes in Parliament with regard to domestic as well as foreign affairs. The great Prime Ministers such as Gladstone, Disraeli, Palmerston, and Salisbury left defining imprints on the Victorian Age.[35]

The debates, activities, and involvements of Parliament impacted most sectors of British life, thought, and experience. Victorian writers were among those deeply interested in the social legislation being made and needing to be made by Parliament—from Bentham and J. S. Mill to Dickens, Marx, and innumerable others. If England in the Victorian Age became the world's "workshop" and the seat of an empire upon which the "sun never set," Parliament was a controlling force, chiefly through its main medium of legislation. Queen Victoria herself—giving renewed symbolic prestige to the monarchy and lending her popular name to the age—had personal involvements and influence with Disraeli, whose novels had also promoted social reform. Many vast sectors of Victorian life and thought were encompassed by such terms as "parliamentary democracy," "parliamentary politics," and ""parliamentar*ism*."[36]

In the final analysis, the maze of "isms" long used by historians in characterizing the Victorian era in Britain has often led to an unsettled picture of what constituted that period. These "isms" have included, for the second half of the nineteenth century, the following examples: Victorianism, parliamentarism, republicanism, liberalism, anti-parliamentarism, anti-liberalism, centralism, localism, conservatism, socialism, anti-socialism, (liberal) radicalism, reformism, collectivism, individualism, modernism, syndicalism, Fabianism, Gladstonianism, statism, trade unionism, illiberalism, optimism, progressivism, (conservative) corporatism, Darwinianism, constitutionalism, (liberal) utilitarianism, Benthamism, paternalism, imperialism, capitalism, and innumerable others (not to mention more purely cultural varieties).[37]

The unwieldly popular term "liberal*ism*" has long been particularly problematic. Further obfuscatory are such related terms as "liberal state," "liberal democracy," "liberal imagination," "liberal tradition," and "liberal ideal." It perhaps becomes unnecessary, by now, to cite examples of the plethora of titles and headings employing such terms in secondary literature. It has been sufficient to point out some tendencies of liberalism toward socialism in public social legislation from Gladstone to Lloyd George. Yet the term "social*istic*" or "socialist-*like*" seems the better appellation when discussing the later nineteenth century and early twentieth century prior to World War I.[38]

Chapter VI

"National(-stat)*ism*" and "Bismarckian*ism*"

When paired with so-called "stat*ism*," the rubric of "national-*ism*" provides a fitting end point in this survey of nineteenth-century "isms" in European political and legal thought. Under the category of "national(-stat)*ism*" can be grouped a variety of other related "isms." The newly formed nation-state of Germany under Otto von Bismarck marked a classic combination of nationalism and political realism (*Realpolitik*). His name has itself become an "ism" (Bismarckianism). German nationalism under Bismarck has been traced by most historians back at least to the romantic nationalist spirit that emerged in the German lands in reaction to the Empire of Napoleon. Many historians have looked further back in the history of German nationalism to Luther, in a trajectory leading on to Bismarck and Hitler.

The first section below treats the nascent German nationalist spirit expressed in the theme of *Volksgeist* in romantic political thought. The romantic German *Volksgeist* was manifested not only through folkish customs but also through legislative leitmotifs. The legal-legislative background represented by Napoleon's legal codes and various constitutional frameworks is important here in relation to Germany and in its own right. The models of Roman civil law provided links in the changing ideas from Napoleon to Savigny and to Bismarck.

The second section concentrates on Frederick von Savigny and the Historical School, including other related groups such as the Pandectist

School. Issues of legislation and codification come further to the fore. Savigny's quest for a distinctively German national history in law was a requisite, he believed, to any future codification that would serve as foundation for a new German nation-state. In the meantime, Savigny's endeavors gave further rise to a renewed sense of German nationhood.

Under Bismarck, as discussed in Section III, a culmination was reached. A new German national state became founded upon a system of public legislation and legal codification. The legislative (nation-)state and legislative sovereignty became predominant in theory as well as in institutions.

Thus the progression below, which marks a new approach, is from German "national spirit" and *Volksgeist* to German "national history" and nationhood or nationality, and finally to German "national unity" and the nation-*state* as founded on public legislation. These three stages overlapped, as in Savigny's case, and are not always easy to separate from each other, although the overall progression seems valid. Like most organizational devices of this kind, such a progression is perhaps an oversimplification. Its usefulness lies in the highlighting of themes of present interest, in particular the emergence of the legislative state. The modern major "isms" in state theory as studied in this and the preceding book revolve around topics in legislation. In different ways, the utilitarian state, the positivist state, the idealist state, the socialist state, and the national state can all be reduced to the legislative state, which is the true modern state, expressed in myriad varieties.

In a brief general survey of European legal philosophy in the nineteenth century, Guido Fassò has concentrated on a different sequence of "isms." He begins with codification (Prussian, French, etc.). He then proceeds in turn to utilitarianism (Bentham, Austin, Mill), historicism (romantics, Hugo, Savigny, Pandectists), post-Kantianism (Humboldt, Reinhold, Fichte, Schelling, etc.), Hegel, Risorgimento Italy (Rosmini, Mazzini, etc.), socialism (Marx, etc.), irrationalism (Schopenhauer, Kierkegaard, Nietzsche, Tolstoi, Dostoevski, etc.), philosophical positivism (Saint-Simon, Comte, Kirchmann, etc.), formalistic legal positivism, and anti-formalism (Jhering, Gierke, Duguit, etc.). Nationalism is conspicuously absent from that sequence of "isms." That author (like so many others) accepts such "isms" as valid constructs based on their own merits. They are not for him, unlike in the present study, questionable constructs needing to be "deconstructed." They are not reduced by him to their common legislative denominator in issues of sovereignty and the state, which are themselves obscured within the generalized coverages of those "isms." The myriad shifting lists of such "isms" in innumerable other broad surveys as well as in specialized studies serve to show their indeterminate quality.[1]

1. NAPOLEONIC EMPIRE AND GERMAN NATIONAL SPIRIT (*VOLKSGEIST*)

Napoleonic Codification and Legislation

The vast background to the legislative codifications made under Napoleon encompassed several centuries from the sixteenth through the eighteenth. Crucial, for instance, were the systematizing efforts of the seventeenth-century French jurist Dormat. In addition, the eighteenth-century Enlightened Despots made codification of legislation and legislative promulgation of codes the basics of their newly centralized state powers, while using those devices to confer more equalized systems of justice upon their peoples. As in many other respects, Napoleon viewed himself as an heir to the Enlightened Despots through his codifications of both old and new laws, which were expressive to him of his central role as great lawgiver. The cultural hegemony of France in eighteenth-century Europe through writers like Voltaire, an exponent of Enlightened Despotism in the Age of Reason, left a strong imprint of rationalism not only on Napoleon's ideas of codification but on those of French jurists who immediately preceded him. Such factors will help to explain the later reaction against Napoleon's codifications by the German Romantic School as well as the German Historical School centered around Savigny, who had much to say on legislation and codification. Studies on French legal thought prior to the Napoleonic codifications have neglected the important related topic of legislation.[2]

The series of five law codes adopted under Napoleon were substantially begun while he was First Counsul (1799–1804), prior to being Emperor (1804–1814). His leadership in the Council of State, the main agency of government, gave him ultimate control over the preparation of significant legislation. The five codes were not fully completed until after he became Emperor. Together they constituted, as he intended, the most impressive and famous codes of law since those of the imperial Romans, especially those of Justinian. The Roman civil law tradition, in conjunction wtith French law, provided a crucial context for Napoleon's codifications, which embodied both old law (pre-Revolutionary and Revolutionary) and new law (Napoleonic).

Most important was Napoleon's *Civil Code*, called simply the *Code Napoléon*, the name it received in 1807. It was mostly worked out in

1800—under the ongoing direction and supervision of Napoleon—by the Council of State in coordination with its "Commission of Legislation," composed of prominent lawyers appointed by him as draftsmen; but it was not promulgated until 1804 because of some rare opposition to certain measures, especially from the Legislative Body. Although the Revolution had swept away much of the Old Regime's legal-legislative system of privileges, it had not progressed well toward a new legal codification, which was given fresh impetus by Napoleon's great interest in order and system. The new French *Civil Code* combined egalitarian features of Revolutionary legislation, in particular equality of all citizens before the law, with authoritarian proclivities of Napoleon's regime. The latter included strong emphasis on the powers of fathers and husbands over children and spouses, as influenced in part by Roman law traditions. The French *Civil Code* of 1804 was written in a simplified and intelligible fashion for citizens to read and follow. A guiding principle (harking back to Roman law in Justinian's *Digest* I) was that legislators should lay down laws in general terms because they cannot hope to provide for all details or circumstances that may arise. In this regard, the French *Civil Code* (*Code civil des français*) bore similarities to the United States Constitution; but it was very different from the German *Civil Code* (*Bürgerliches Gesetzbuch*) that was finally completed, promulgated, and adopted under much different conditions for the new unified Germany nearly a century later in 1896/1900. The German code, influenced by Roman law traditions through the German Pandectists, was a far weightier work intended more for professionals.[3]

Of different qualities were the four other codes of law issued by Napoleon. The *Code of Civil Procedure* was promulgated in 1806, bearing various close resemblances to laws under the Old Regime. The *Code of Criminal Procedure* and the *Penal Code* were begun during the Consulate and completed in 1810. They revealed the sterner side of Napoleon's Enlightened Despotism by imposing strict penalties for political offenses and by reversing Revolutionary legislation that had given defendants the presumption of innocence until proven guilty. The *Commercial Code* of 1807 was less complete than the others and kept many of the laws of the Old Regime.

Taken together, the new codes of law under Napoleon combined features of French civil law, Roman civil law (as adapted in Southern France), and Germanic customary law (as present in Northern France). These older laws, applied during the Old Regime, were reworked under Napoleon. They were joined with elements of more recent Revolutionary and Napoleonic laws. The outcome was a distinctly national French system of law and legislation—as the basis of the new state—that was applied in different ways to other states of the Empire, including many Germanic ones. Outlasting the collapse of the Empire in 1814–1815, this system has impacted more recent legal systems in France and other countries like Canada. Napoleon is reputed to have declared in exile on St. Helena: "My glory is not to have won forty battles, for Waterloo's defeat will destroy the memory of as many victories. But what nothing will destroy, what will live eternally, is my *Civil Code*."[4]

The problem of codification links up here with traditions of legal systematization in Roman/French civil law that have been studied in our previous books, where they have been connected with topics in legislation. The compendious and intelligible nature of the Napoleonic Code of Civil Law, in particular, was a primary factor behind its enduring general impact not only in France but also in Germany and other lands where its specific provisions did not remain in force after the collapse of the Napoleonic Empire. The nineteenth century in Germany and elsewhere witnessed a great drive for codifications in large part because of the permanent methodological influence of the Napoleonic codes of law. This was the case notwithstanding Savigny's criticisms in 1814 against any new immediate codifications for Germany. The Pandectist School that partly grew out of his Historical School was instrumental in the great quest for codification of German law under Bismarck and beyond. The uniformity instilled by Napoleon's codes of law during the Empire, both inside and outside France, may have combined reactionary and progressive elements; but it clearly marked the further demise of the old feudal system of legal privileges and institutions. During the early nineteenth century, the uniform, eqalitarian, and secular state of the modern age in France was emerging. Fading away were many old vestiges of feudal, aristocratic, and ecclesiastical controls that had impeded the legal-political machinery of the central government.

Finally, it was through a complicated legislative process that the Napoleonic codes of law were originally drawn up under the Consulate. The Constitution of the Year VIII in 1799, making Napoleon virtual dictator, established a three-house legislature through the Tribunate, Legislative Body, and Senate, with the Council of State drafting much significant legislation albeit constitutionally as part of the executive branch. Striving to concentrate legislative powers more completely under himself as a despot, Napoleon promulgated the Constitution of the Year X (1802). As First Consul for life, he used the senate more as his own legislative vehicle without consulting the other legislative bodies, which in any case he directly controlled especially through his powers of appointment to them. This transformation toward Napoleon's absolute legislative sovereignty was completed by his creation as Emperor through the Constitution of the Year XII (1804), established through a *senatus consultum*. Thus by the time his codes were eventually enacted, the formal legislative process by which they had been originally drawn up was largely obviated as Napoleon himself assumed nearly all real legislative powers.

Napoleon himself, as First Consul and Emperor, clearly viewed his role in these matters as essentially that of "great lawgiver." This viewpoint is evident in the beginning of his *Civil Code*. Many scattered statements by him throughout his career on the role of legislator and legislation attest to his strong attitudes in this regard, including in express terms of sovereignty and state.[5]

Further enhancing Napoleon's position as great lawgiver were the numerous constitutions he gave to various states and territories of his Empire. The kingdoms of Italy, Naples, Holland, Spain, and Westphalia received constitutions, as did the Grand Duchies of Berg, Frankfurt, and Würzburg, along with the Illyrian Provinces. In addition, Bavaria, Baden, and Württemberg received constitutions. Actual implementation varied. Some of these constitutions were never applied in fact, others only sporadically. But some were actualized and in a few cases (notably Bavaria and Württemberg) contributed to stronger centralization and public laws.[6]

German Nationalist Impulses and "Romantic*ism*"

Especially important was the constitution that Napoleon gave in 1806 to the newly created Confederation of the Rhine, which lasted until 1815. Continuing to expand, it became one of the most important groups of dependent states in the Grand Empire. It comprised the German lands between what France had annexed to the west and what Prussia together with Austria retained to the east. This new more centralized arrangement was designed to replace the age-old jumbles of political and ecclesiastical units of the Holy Roman Empire. The latter was abolished that same year, 1806. Other areas later added to the Confederation received constitutions as well.

What in fact occurred, contrary to Napoleon's intentions, was the beginning of German nationalism. Its rise was made possible by the removal of old obstacles to national unity and the imposition of new, more centralized structures, which at first worked well for Napoleon. His codifications also left an impetus for later German efforts at devising their own codifications.[7] Napoleon thus unwittingly prepared the way for the emergence of German nationalism in the early nineteenth century, as both extension of and reaction to his unifying approaches to the Rhine Confederation of States. In doing so, Napoleon went against his own expressed aims of weakening German nationalistic impulses by controlling them and by building up Confederation lands as a buffer against Prussia (and Austria) to the east.

Writing to Talleyrand in 1802, Napoleon commented on the approaching abolition of the Holy Roman Empire: "[T]he German Empire will be effectively divided into two empires. . . . German affairs would not be administered as a single unit and . . . the opposition of interests between Berlin and Vienna [Prussia and Austria] would be greater than ever." In a letter of 1810 to Louis, King of Holland, he stated: "It was my intention to use the throne of Holland as a foundation on which I would have placed Hamburg, Osnabrück, and part of northern Germany. This would have uprooted the German national spirit still more thoroughly, and this is the chief aim of my policy."[8] This invocation of the German "national spirit," or what is commonly called the *Volksgeist*, suggests Napoleon's own early awareness of its role as a rallying point for early-nineteenth-century German romantics, who were beginning to espouse strong nationalist sentiments.

As for Prussia, it became the future engine of a more "realistic" or ruthless drive for German unification in the later nineteenth century under Bismarck. The decline and collapse of Prussia from 1797 to 1807, especially under Napoleon's successful divide-and-conquer strategy, was followed by Prussia's rebirth and reconstruction in 1807–1812. Fichte's Prussian-oriented *Addresses to the German Nation* in 1807–1808 were a part of this process. The German stage was thus being set for the participation of Prussia (along with Austria but not the Rhine Confederation) at the Congress of Vienna and for the eventual leadership of Prussia under Bismarck.

The cogent secondary account to follow underscores the centrality of romantic ideas of the *Volksgeist* in the development and spread of German nationalism in the early nineteenth century as a reaction to Napoleon and the Enlightenment. The place of Herder, Fichte, and Hegel, like that of Prussia and German history more broadly, is well known. But the *Volksgeist* as regards the laws of a nation revolving around it must be duly stressed. Through it the state achieves a national as well as historical identity. If later German nationalism under Bismarck marked the "Prussianization" of Germany, the names of Fichte and Hegel were no less significant than Stein in the earlier reconstruction of Prussia during the romantic period.

> Nationalism, as it was to be known in all the later history of Europe, developed as a movement of resistance against the forcible internationalism of the Napoleonic empire. It arose in protest against the Napoleonic idea . . . of a European Continent united by uniform law and administration. . . .

By far the most momentous national movement took place in Germany. Napoleonic Germany was a seedbed that was to fertilize, fructify, and also to poison much of the later development of Europe. The Germans rebelled not only against the Napoleonic rule but against the century-old ascendancy of French civilization. They rebelled not only against the French armies but against the philosophy of the Age of Enlightenment. The years of the French Revolution and Napoleon were for Germany the years of its greatest cultural efflorescence, the years of Beethoven, Goethe and Schiller, of Herder, Kant, Fichte, Hegel, Schleiermacher and many others. German ideas fell in with all the ferment of fundamental thinking known as "romanticism," which was everywhere challenging the "dry abstractions" of the Age of Reason. . . . In the nineteenth century the Germans came to be widely regarded as intellectual leaders, somewhat as the French had been in the century before. And most of the distinctive features of German thought were somehow connected with nationalism in a broad sense.
. . . In 1784 appeared a book by J. G. Herder, called *Ideas on the Philosophy of the History of Mankind.* . . . [He] declared that German ways were indeed different from French, but not for that reason the less worthy of respect. All true culture or civilization, he held, must arise from native roots. It must arise also from the life of the common people, the *Volk*, not from the cosmopolitan and denatured life of the upper classes. Each people, he thought, meaning by a people a group sharing the same language, had its own attitudes, spirit, or genius. A sound civilization must express a national character or *Volksgeist*. And the character of each people was special to itself. . . .

The idea of the *Volksgeist*, possibly the most significant single German idea of these agitated years, was reinforced from other and [sic] non-German sources, and soon passed to other countries in the general movement of romantic thought. . . . Good and just laws, according to the older philosophy of natural law, somehow corresponded to a standard of justice that was the same for all men. But now, according to Herder and the romantic school of jurisprudence, good laws were those that reflected local conditions or national idiosyncrasies. . . .

Herder's philosophy set forth a cultural nationalism, without political message. . . . The French Revolution made the Germans acutely conscious of the state. It showed what a people could do with a state, once they took it over and used it for their own purposes. . . . [B]ecause they had a unified state which included all Frenchmen, and one in which a whole nation surged with a new sense of freedom, they were able to rise above all the other peoples of Europe. . . .

Germans became fascinated by the idea of political unity and national greatness, precisely because they had neither. A great national German state, expressing the deep moral will and distinctive culture of the German people, seemed to them the solution to all their problems. It would . . . protect the deep German *Volksgeist* from violation. . . .

The career of J. G. Fichte illustrates the course of German thought in these years. . . . Fichte at first was practically without national feeling. He enthusiastically approved of the French Revolution, . . . and he shared Rousseau's conception of the state as the embodiment of the sovereign will of a people. . . . When the French conquered Germany Fichte became intensely and self-consciously German. He took over the idea of the *Volksgeist*. . . .

At Berlin, in 1808, Fichte delivered a series of *Addresses to the German Nation*, declaring that there was an ineradicable German spirit, a primordial and immutable national character, more noble than that of other peoples (thus going beyond Herder). . . . The Germans became interested not only in their own national history, but in history itself as a fundamental method of thought, and they thus launched an intellectual revolution, through the philosophy of Hegel and by other means. . . .

Politically, in the revolt against the French, the main transformations came in Prussia. . . . [I]n 1806, at Jena-Auerstädt, the kingdom collapsed in a single battle. . . .

The reconstruction of the state, prerequisite to the reconstruction of the army, was initiated by Baron Stein and continued by his successor, Hardenberg. . . . Deeply committed to the philosophy of Kant and Fichte, he [Stein] . . . thought that the common people must be awakened. . . . Stein's ordinance of 1807 abolished serfdom. . . . [H]is reforms endured.[9]

Some basic definitions in the *Oxford English Dictionary* are pertinent. The *Volksgeist* is defined as "the spirit or genius which makes the thought or feeling of a nation or people." Other variants further underscore the German national element of the *Volk*, as in *Volksdeutsch* pertaining to ethnically German people, and *Volkskammer* or parliament of the German Democratic Republic.

Among the germane "isms" that can be related to *Volksgeist* is nationalism, on which the same dictionary is brief and vague: "Devotion to one's nation; national aspiration; a policy of national independence." More specifically: "A form of socialism, based on the nationalizing of all industry." More lengthy are the definitions of "nation," which include: "An extensive aggregate of persons . . . associated . . . by common . . . language, . . . history, . . . race . . . , usually organized as a separate political state and occupying a definite territory." The terms "nation" and "state" here correspond sufficiently with our own respective broader and narrower concepts of them. "Statism" is more diffusively defined but again with more corresponding narrowness than in the case of nationism: "Subservience to political [sic] especially in religious matters"; "Political science, statecraft"; and "Government of a country by the state." "The state or fact of being a nation," as the definition of "nationhood," is more precise in contexts of "nation" and "nationalism" than is *Volksgeist*. The latter, as the key early-nineteenth-century expression of romantic nationalism, was to be superseded in many ways by the realistic (and ruthless) unifying nationalism of Bismarck. Defining "Germanism," the same dictionary states: "German ideas; German modes of thought or action . . . or institutions." As for romanticism: "The distinctive qualities or spirit of the romantic school in art, literature, and music." Of present concern, then, is political romanticism in contexts of nationalism and *Volksgeist* as manifested in the laws and customs indigenous to a particular country or nation, in this case, Germany.

Although the *Volksgeist* and related themes in early German nationalism were integral to romanticism in political thought, romanticism has long remained an even more elusive "ism" in the hands of historians than has nationalism. Classifications of who or what was romantic in the history of political theory have varied widely, sometimes merging with the idealist tradition in philosophy. Most scholars have included Fichte, many Hegel, and some Savigny (along with Burke) in the romantic political tradition, particularly as regards so-called "German*ism*" and German nationalism.[10] Some experts, however, have denied that Fichte, for one, was a romantic. They have found that "early" political romantics (prior to the establishment of Napoleon's Empire in 1804) favored the "organic state" (or "organic society"). Such romantics rebelled against earlier concepts of absolutism as well as liberalism. In this way, it has been argued, they marked "the genesis of modern[!] German political thought."[11] On the whole, the vast historiography on political romanticism is as elusive as the "ism" itself. It is true that uses of this "ism" as a term in literature and the arts can be found in the early nineteenth century (as cited, for instance, in the *Oxford English*

Dictionary). Yet it later gained much wider vogue as an historiographical rubric applied by scholars more broadly to the political thought of the early nineteenth century, in loose conjunction with other nebulous "isms" like liberalism.[12]

The discussions to follow concentrate as usual on restricted issues and materials. Many texts not able to be included in our main discussions will be found, once more, in the notes.

Folkish Customs and Legislative Leitmotifs

The emphasis on *Volksgeist* found in German romantic nationalist thought on the state raises questions for us on the relationship between custom and legislation. Were folkish customs the dominant concern, as some historians have claimed, or did legislation become a "leitmotif" or identifying theme of the state (to borrow a term from Wagnerian musical drama)? Or, can custom and legislation be reconciled by relating them respectively to nation and state? Was the nation a broader entity than the state insofar as it included the *Volksgeist* or distinguishing spirit and culture of a "people" in a national community? If so, was it more inclusive of custom in the political-historical ideas of the German romantics and their allies? Correspondingly, was the state a narrower entity centered on law? If so, was the state again more oriented to legislation, as in many other political "isms" already examined? If, in the political philosophy of German romantics, there was at times a tendency to blur the lines between nation and state when referring in general ways to the nation(al)-state, can the two entities nevertheless be distinguished for purposes of analysis? Must passages dealing with custom be necessarily taken as overriding those on legislation, or should they instead be interpreted in different ways? Is what historians have often loosely called the romantic "theory of state" sometimes better characterized as "theory of nation"?[13]

Those questions become more pressing in view of the kinds of assessments made by one prominent historian in particular. His excellent studies have shared in recent historiographical trends on the subject at hand (sometimes in reaction to the present series). He has argued as follows: "Law, to the Germans, was ultimately the product not of sovereign will but of custom."[14] The same distinguished author goes on at length in the same chapter to develop a strong contrast between Napoleonic legislation and the reaction against it invoking Germanic custom. Although not dwelling as such on the German Romantic School (in which Fichte has often been included), but rather on the German Historical School (centered on Savigny and extending back before Napoleon to Herder and others), the author broadly emphasizes the themes of *Volksgeist* and national Germanic spirit. He includes here the German Philosophical School (broadly associating it with Hegel, Kant, and presumably Fichte, with references also to Marx). All three Schools are somehow grouped by him under the "Germanic impulse" (or so-called "German*ism*") toward custom at the expense of legislation (as ascribed to Savigny's historical studies on Roman law in the furtherance of his "contemporary system"). However, we have previously witnessed, for example, the dominance of legislation in the state theory of Kant, Hegel, Marx, and many other German writers. In another general survey, the same author has again upheld, contrary to the present series, the predominance of custom over legislation in "the German legal tradition" of *Volksgeist* broadly associated with Herder, Fichte, Hegel, Savigny, and many others concerning history, politics, and Roman law. However, there, too, the general topic of nation and people is more operative than is the legal entity of the state in which legislation prevails over custom.[15]

Schleiermacher and Müller

An illustrative romantic address on "the concepts of different forms of the state" was delivered in 1814 by Frederich Schleiermacher (d. 1834), following his years of nationalistic exhortations against the Napoleonic occupation. He had been appointed Professor of Theology at the University of Berlin in 1810, the same year that Fichte was appointed Professor of Philosophy there. Thus he forms with Fichte a key part of the background to Hegel at Berlin.

In the course of his address, Schleiermacher gives lengthy discussions on the relationships between the legislative, executive, and judicial powers (to which he returns in the Conclusion). He elaborates on the different ways in which the legislative power is ascendant over the other two. Schleiermacher then expounds as follows on the (national) state as being essentially a legal-legislative entity that defines, identifies, and binds its people or *Volk* as a (national) group.

> For that which has always existed beforehand, the basic material of the state, so to speak, is a people, a mass which belongs together and lives together naturally. Without people there can be no state. If we think of ourselves as men who have been blown together from all the four corners of the world, and imagine that these men could have been brought under laws in the way that legend depicts the formation of ancient Rome, then we can hardly call these men a state before we can call the mass of men a people. . . . What exists in the state as right and

duty will be much the same as what was previously sense and custom; and if the citizens are held together in the state through the law, then the neighbours remained also together . . . [involving] loyalty to the fatherland. . . . In brief, the already existing sentiment and activity have been brought together and laid down in the law through the arising of the state. What existed before is now expressed, the unconscious unity and equality of the mass is transformed into a conscious unity and equality, and this arising of the consciousness of belonging together is the essence of the state. . . . First of all we would have to classify the states according to the power with which the state-forming principle seizes its object. . . . For so long as the consciousness of the regent alone is guided by his concern for the unity of the people, as has been true of all founders of great states, the subjects cannot help him in a definite form in making the law. . . . For if the end of the law were to be in these assemblies and not in the regent, anarchy would prevail. Therefore, naturally, no well-ordered legislative assembly has within its scope the whole of legislative activity; the king, however, who has been wrongly considered as being merely the executive, is really also the end of the legislative power . . . but the execution is here also completed by the totality of the laws. . . . [I]n this respect every state which has grown historically will be different from every other state, and this will belong, so to speak, to the personal character of the states.[16]

Above (and as further cited in the note) Schleiermacher suggests that when the state is formed as a legal entity, legislation takes precedence over custom. Legislation lies at the center of the founding of the state after the example of the Twelve Tables in the hero-founding of ancient Rome. The new (national) unity of the people in a legal-legislative state, who possess a patriotic (nationalistic) sense of the "fatherland," lies at the heart of the unique "spirit" or "genius" of each state. A nascent authoritarian (Prussian) orientation can also be detected even more in conjunction with Fichte. In another sense, the express "historical" orientation above to the state's origin and development places the writer somewhat in the Historical School, albeit in a more generalized way than Savigny.

A provocative lecture in 1808—as the second of his public lectures at Dresden on the "elements of politics"—was delivered by Adam Müller (d. 1829). He was a Prussian, a nationalist, and a romantic in his own way. Therein he attacked a broad range of past and current ideas about politics and law in relation to the state. Müller criticized eighteenth-century concepts of abstract natural law as supposedly separable from positive law. He believed that both together should be rendered practical and adaptable in the sphere of the state. Müller also rejected notions, which went back to writers like Hobbes, that the state is an artificial creation founded on arbitrariness. The excerpts to follow, showing reverence for the state itself as a totality of civil and public life, conjoin custom with legislation. However, as the state's primary basis, legislation must prevail over customs that run counter to it. Nevertheless, custom provides thereby a significant secondary basis of the state.

> [T]he state is not merely an artificial institution, not one of the thousand inventions for the profit and pleasure of civil life, but it is the total of this civil life itself, necessary just as soon as there are human beings. . . . [Y]ou must bring people into action and interaction; a state is to be created. The state is concerned just as much with custom as with Right; the sovereign must both stimulate as well as compel people into this great union. What does the law signify if the most sacred thing of all, the innermost affairs of man, is *hors de la loi*? . . . How is it, however, possible not merely to tolerate, but even to approve a custom which is quite alien and even contradictory to the law, a domestic virtue which is entirely opposed to civil virtue? . . . This is worse than the state within the state, this is anarchy of the mind in the midst of the legal union.[17]

In the compelling continuations of these passages, Müller connects the idea and reality of the state to that of the nation. He sees the state to be the orienting core of the nation. This nexus relates as well to the "spiritual" and "physical" configurations of the people within the nation-state as a whole. In strong fashion, Müller succinctly identifies states with legislation, and the founding of states with the creation of legislation. The state represents, in effect, the sum of legislation; the reverse also holds true. Accordingly, states are independent units. Their beginnings lie not in human arbitrariness (through positive laws separated from higher laws) but in nature and God, as according to classical writers. This position partly anticipates Hegel and Ranke. On its own ground, the state thus becomes a totality in a practical and not merely theoretical sense. Its statesmen and legislators act coordinately. There are no external forces to limit it.[18]

Fichte (and Hegel)

In light of the foregoing, it is not surprising to find similar or even stronger viewpoints expressed throughout the voluminous evolving writings of Johann Gottlieb Fichte. (The year of his death, 1814, was a crucial one in other present respects.) For Fichte, as for others, the general theme of *Volksgeist*, insofar as it was associated with "people" and "nation," could be compatible with ideas of custom. Conversely, the more specific theme of the state, as a legal phenomenon, was fastened to legislative criteria. The combined sense of nation(al)-state could include both elements, but usually with legislation prevailing over custom in the final analysis (as in the extended excerpts below).[19]

Whether or not Fichte should be considered a romantic in the early development of German nationalist thought is of lesser significance for present purposes. More crucial is his prominence as a theorist whose ideas can at points be reduced to a legislative core, with interesting relations to custom and *Volksgeist*. Those scholars who classify Fichte, along with Hegel and Savigny, under other different "isms" should still keep in mind the common denominator of legislation concerning the state and sovereignty. Some experts stress how Fichte's early *Science of Rights* (1796–1797)[20] adapted Kant's quasi-rationalism in "Doctrine of Right" (of that same year) together with Rousseau's pre-romanticism concerning freedom in the social order. Fichte's later works, as others stress, looked partly ahead to Hegel's idealism and nationalism in *Philosophy of Right*, which singled out the emerging *Volksgeist* of the German nation-state in modern history. The importance of legislation in the state theory of all four writers is abundantly evident.

In this light, the verdict of one expert (quoted above) that Fichte proclaimed the power of custom over legislation must be cast into doubt. The fuller context of that scholar's remarks is as follows: "Of all those who had been victimized by Napoleon's legislative designs, administrative impositions, and of course military intrusions, the Germans were the most reflective and articulate in their antagonism. Law, to the Germans, was ultimately the product not of sovereign will but of custom. 'In Germany all culture comes from the people,' Fichte declared in 1807, and [he] went on to deplore the 'evil associations and subversive power of vanity' that have swept the growing nation into spheres which are not its own' [from Fichte's *Addresses to the German Nation*]." The same expert adds: "The Germans had assisted the ancient Romans; they must do the same against the modern Romanizers with their false nationalism. Hardly better than the invading armies were the administrative reforms introduced by Napoleon and especially the *Code*." He goes on to treat Savigny and others as expressions of this same broad

"German impulse," which was marked in particular by its promotion of custom over legislation, of "German*ism*" over "Roman*ism*." [21]

Notwithstanding the excellence of that scholar's cogent studies, his above remarks on custom over legislation reveal a too hasty reading of the above passage from Fichte's *Addreses*. Fichte above says nothing directly or indirectly about the superiority of custom over legislation. Fichte's actual statement is generalized but self-evident. At the most, it can be said that Fichte above expresses characteristic interest in the German *Volksgeist*, which elsewhere the same expert has also assumed incorrectly to represent custom over legislation. On the contrary, the extended excerpts from Fichte's *Addresses* presented immediately above (in a note) bespeak the power of legislation over custom. This holds true both within the German framework and in relation to its outside confrontations with the French Napoleonic *Code*.

The Prussian connection links Fichte not only with Schleiermacher and Savigny in the Romantic and Historical Schools respectively, but also with Hegel in the Philosophical School (to follow again the same scholar's three-fold division). It joins them loosely together through disparate lines of developing concepts leading up to the Prussianization of Germany under Bismarck. During his early years at Jena (1793–1799), Fichte's voluminous important philosophical writings included fundamental rethinkings of Kant's idealism. Fichte's ensuing years at Berlin (1799–1814), where he delivered his *Addresses* (1807–1808), became more practical in scope. The French victories over the Prussians (in 1806) sparked his ideas for German national victory, recovery, and greatness. Fichte moved ever further away from Enlightenment rationalism than had Kant. He pointed toward the World Spirit idealized by Hegel, who identified it with the Prussian power-state. Fichte also pointed in the direction of Hegel by surpassing Herder's notion that the *Volksgeist* of each nation is equal in value. Fichte argued for the superiority of the German "national spirit," which Hegel would clearly connect to a developed legislative concept of the sovereign state. Fichte and especially Hegel, successive holders of the prestigious chair of philosophy at the University of Berlin, conceived of the long evolution of the World Spirit's self-realization in history. Not unrelatedly, the Prussian law professor Savigny proclaimed the superiority of German law, because of its long-evolutionary organic development, to the French law, as based on artificial codes, while expressing great interest in legislation *per se*, inclusive but not at the expense of custom. Fichte's uses of the title *Vocation*—as in his *Vocation of the Scholar* in 1794 and *Vocation of Man* in 1800—formed an interesting precedent for Savigny's own title, *Vocation for Legislation*, in 1814.

Fichte, Hegel, and Savigny thus form different segments in the early development of Prussian or German nationalist impulses in concepts of history, law, and the state; as such, they can be variously seen against the background of German romanticism and in turn became background for later Bismarckian concepts of the nation-state. To the extent, however, that Fichte prefigured Hegel's stronger ideas on the state, he, like Hegel, is less satisfactorily grouped with the romantics; Fichte, for instance, eventually broke with romantics like Schleiermacher at Berlin. To the degree to which Hegel and Savigny, along with others like Ranke, can be loosely included together under the rubric of "histori*cism*" in contexts of "German*ism*" or "Prussian*ism*," they can all be broadly viewed in the conceptual background to Bismarck. But Fichte is less satisfactorily included under so-called "histori*cism*," unless in loose ways together with Herder. Fichte is thus better seen in the so-called Philosophical School of German idealism with Kant and Hegel. (Hegel considered Fichte a "subjective idealist" and himself an "absolute idealist.") This viewpoint is often strongly evident in scholarship placing Fichte in the German Romantic School, whether through his later political interests in *Volksgeist* or through his earlier, more philosophical interests in transcendentalism.

We have already treated Hegel, who in philosophy and political thought tended to supplant Fichte, according to many authorities then and now. We turn next to Savigny, whose developing intellectual relation to Hegel has recently attracted some scholarly attention.

2. SAVIGNY'S HISTORICAL SCHOOL AND GERMAN NATIONAL HISTORY (NATIONHOOD)

Schools of Thought and "Isms"

Of the German "schools" of thought distinguished above—the Historical School, the Philosophical School, and the Romantic School—the works of Friedrich Carl von Savigny (1779–1861) have most often been associated by historians with the Historical School of legal studies. This school came to prominence under Savigny. Its deeper roots can be traced back, according to the same noted expert cited immediately above, to Renaissance modes of historical analysis, particularly of Roman law. At the same time, so-called "histori*cism*" of narrower and broader kinds has been associated by many historians with the Historical School of Savigny and with its antecedents in earlier centuries. Secondary works of different kinds continue to proliferate on the German Historical School of law associated with Savigny (not to mention on German historicism).[22] Less common but nonetheless vital are other studies connecting Savigny with what the same above expert (who does not include him in it) has termed the Philosophical School broadly speaking, and more particularly with the German idealist or transcendental traditions of Kant, Fichte, and Hegel.[23] Still other approaches have at times centered around the relationship of Savigny to the Romantic School, whether in specific contexts such as Roman legal studies or in generalized frameworks of so-called "romanti*cism*." Many studies on Savigny combine different features of those three "schools" or areas of interest.[24]

Some studies have focused on more restricted issues such as Savigny's outlook on legislation. One older, distinguished medieval historian has (overzealously) appropriated Savigny's famous work of 1814 on legislation to stand as a modern model for studying the Middle Ages. He positioned the Savigny model at the beginning of a book that argues strongly for the medieval origins of later modern legislative ideas related to sovereignty and the state. His assumption was (correct) that Savigny did not generally opt for the necessary priority of custom over legislation (as the same other above expert has more recently believed).[25]

As for Savigny and legal systematization, some scholars have mistakenly believed systematization to be antithetical to the methods of Savigny's Historical School.[26] Some authorities have dwelled on the transformation of jurisprudence—away from earlier rationalistic abstractions of natural-law philosophy (and transcendental theory) to the "spontaneity" of history in the Historical School. Nevertheless, there has been some recognition of the close tie of legal system to legal history, particularly in Savigny's new approaches to Roman law as systematized in Justinian's *Digest* (*Pandects*), *Code*, and *Institutes*.[27] Just as it is not true that Savigny was not generally arguing for the priority of custom and *Volksgeist* or *Volksrecht* over legislation and the state (contrary to still another historian[28]), so it is not the case that Savigny was rejecting new legal codification (together with legislation) for Germany altogether into the future. Rather, he rejected it in part for his own immediate period, while hoping and preparing for it on a firmer basis in a future era.

The Pandectist School (as described in the note below), which largely developed out of the Historical School, became a crucial influence behind the eventual German national codification of civil law that was developed under Bismarck. (In that *Code*, custom was included but legislation prevailed, as in earlier Prussian codes, no less than in Napoleon's codes, contrary again to an above expert.[29]) Indeed, strong elements of positive law and legislation (according to the same authority excerpted below) are found in Savigny's historical approach, notwithstanding his emphasis in other ways on custom or *Volksrecht*. On legislation Savigny was influenced by Bodinian-humanistic traditions and on custom by romantic ones. In turn, the Pandectist School produced even stronger positivistic legislative elements that relate not only to the eventual German *Civil Code* of 1900 but also to Jhering.[30]

Savigny's Historical School of law has been related by some experts to historicism more generally. The present concern is with select developments in what has been called "classical histori*cism*." That enterprise, from Herder on, drew attention to the uniqueness of historical subjects and conditions. Later trends in German historical scholarship were to establish it as a scientific discipline. Practitioners of the latter kind included Burckhardt, Ranke, Meinecke, and others, for whom the nation(alistic) state was a central topic.[31]

Definitions in the *Oxford English Dictionary* are again apropos. If one sees the wide trajectory of early or classical historicism as encompassing Herder as well as Hegel, along perhaps with Kant, Fichte, and even Marx, then historicism becomes loosely as follows: "A tendency in philosophy to see historical development as the most fundamental aspect of human existence, and historical thinking as the most important type of thought." Ensuing trends in historicism included the following: "The attempt, found especially among German historians since about 1850, to view all social and cultural phenomena . . . as relative and historically determined . . ."

These two contexts, of course, overlap. In the first context, Hegel, as a philosopher glorifying the state (as a legal-legislative national entity), ascribed to it a kind of historical determinism. In the second, Marx as an historian was greatly influenced by the Hegelian philosophy of the state and history. Moreover, as historians molded by historicism in various forms, Ranke, Burckhardt, Meinecke, and others were also shaped by Hegelian concepts of the nation-state. At the same time, historically oriented Pandectism in Germany unfolded systematic and other impulses that influenced the German legal codifications under Bismarck. In addition, Pandectism produced scientific methodologies that impacted those like Mommsen engaged in the professional historical study of Justinian's Roman law.

Savigny's treatise of 1814 on legislation, with its attention to Roman law and many other subjects of historical and contemporary interest, takes us further along the paths toward German ideas of the legislative nation(al)-state under Bismarck, when the Germanies finally unified under Prussian leadership. To the extent that German political romantics upheld *Volksgeist* and custom, with a generalized sense of legislation, they fell short of the legislative state, adumbrated even by

Savigny, albeit pointing in that direction. It might be more accurate, in fact, to place Fichte, with his stronger statements on legislation, in the idealist philosophical traditions leading from Kant to Hegel, both of whom underscored legislation with respect to state and sovereignty.

In part Savigny dealt with custom or *Volksrecht* in the historical development of law and *Volksgeist*. To that extent, he can be classified with generalized political-geographic notions of "nation" or *Volk* (a more fitting term in such cases than "state") held by the German Romantic School as it influenced the Historical School. But Savigny also developed a German legal-legislative history (inclusive of Roman law) as part of a German national history. In that capacity, he may be classified with the Historical School. This applies to his concepts of "state" and positive law or legislation (*Gesetz, Gesetzgebung*). Savigny's ideas of the state in wider contexts of "nationhood" looked ahead to concepts of nation-*state* as founded under Bismarck on a systematized German *Code* of civil law and legislation. That *Civil Code* finally adopted in 1900 had been prepared for methodologically by both the Germanist and Romanist wings of the Historical and Pandectist Schools of law.

Vocation for Legislation

The year in which Savigny's *Vocation of Our Age for Legislation* was produced, 1814, was a fateful one for the Germanies. It marked the collapse of Napoleon's Empire in Europe and in the Germanies more particularly. The Napoleonic codification of law was immediately thrown off as a yoke of oppression by many parts of the Germanies. In others, it was retained—as in Bavaria, Hesse-Darmstadt, the Rhenish provinces of Prussia and elsewhere, the kingdom of Westphalia, Baden, and the Hanseatic towns. Adding to this mixture were the existing Austrian and Prussian Codes (*Gesetzbuch* and *Landrecht*) made shortly before this time. The pressing question arose over how best to supply a new legal substitute especially in those areas now devoid of the French *Code*. A positive yet provocative proposal for a new code was made in 1814 by A. F. T. Thibaut, a professor of law at Heidelberg, in a tract entitled *On the Necessity of a General Civil Code for Germany*.[32] Thibaut had some defenders of his promoted "philosophical" arguments for a new (legislative) national German code, which would replace both Roman law and custom in Germany while acknowledging features of the German *Volksgeist*. But he was immediately opposed by many writers, most notably by Savigny in his *Vocation*, with its "historical" approach.

In his *Vocation*, Savigny saw the need for a period of deep historical investigation of German traditional law—Roman as well as Germanic, customary as well as legislative. Attention should be given also, he felt, to diverse methods of codification or systematization—Roman, Prussian, and Austrian. Savigny leveled his harshest criticisms against the oppressive Napoleonic codification in Germany, with its excessive orientation toward positive law as arbitrary legislative fiat. Yet Savigny believed that the Napoleonic codification would nevertheless compare more favorably alongside any new attempt at codification for Germany in the near future because of weaknesses already evident in the recent Prussian and Austrian codes, which further proved to him Germany's current unpreparedness for another new code. Long, careful preparation rather than careless haste is requisite. A new successful and lasting codification for Germany must be grounded on a more restrained legislative framework. There must be a more adequate reconciling with Germany's traditions relating to Roman law, custom, and so forth.

In his *Vocation*, Savigny agreed with Thibaut that their common aim of developing a new legal code for Germany should promote national unity as well as national freedom, despite their different means of attaining that goal. A nationalistic program underlies and unifies Savigny's combinations of philosophical and historical methods, legislation and custom, codification and non-codification, nationalism and historicism, Romanism and Germanism. It was entirely appropriate, therefore, that Savigny's treatise on legislation and codification, together with his other works on historical Roman law and its adaptations throughout German history, contributed later on to the German national codification of civil law and legislation finally adopted in 1900. Only after an exhaustive investigation of Germany's Roman law heritage, as it shaped Germany's national legal condition, could consideration be given, in his view, to moving beyond or even abandoning that Roman heritage. Here, too, Savigny was not far removed conceptually from Thibaut. They were separated more over the preparation needed for possibly superseding Roman law than over the goal in view. Savigny clearly kept the options for Germany's future more open in these respects than did Thibaut.

Because the present focus concerning Savigny's *Vocation* is on themes in legislation (the first topic indicated in his title), less attention must be given below to his views on jurisprudence (the second topic in the title) especially in relation to legal education. The full title is: *On [Of] the Vocation of Our Age for Legislation and Jurisprudence* (*Vom Beruf unsrer Zeit für Gesetzgebung und Rechtswissenschaft*).[33] Nor is it necessary below to account for two of Savigny's other great works that deal with Roman law in ways related in part to the discussions on it in his *Vocation*. These two works are his *Geschichte des römischen Rechts im Mittelalter*, the first of the seven volumes of which appeared in 1814, and his *System des heutigen römischen Rechts*, which appeared in eight volumes beginning in 1840.[34] In different ways, they employed historical as well as dogmatic approaches to Roman law in relation to Justinian, the Middle Ages, and the modern period—chiefly as pertaining to Germany.

In short, Savigny not only believed that Germany's Roman law background must be understood before it could possibly someday be abandoned; he felt that the path to the present and the future in Germany was through proper use of the past. Because Justinian's *Corpus Iuris Civilis* is the starting point for studies of Roman law, legislation, codification, and so forth, it must first be purified of the corruptions in it wrought by the post-glossators and the "reception" era more generally. Only then could the *Corpus* be a fit present-day point of departure. Savigny agreed in some ways with those like A. W. Rehberg who (in 1814) attacked Napoleon's codification and legislation as alien Romanist elements in Germany. Yet Savigny's position, contrary to Thibaut's response to Rehberg, was that the present times were not ripe for overthrowing Roman law, which had come to provide a "common law" for European nations except England, because jurisprudence in general had deteriorated. Savigny sought to restore jurisprudence, to reestablish the historical science of law, and to reconnect legal philosophy and legal history, even though the "philosophical" undertaking of a new codification for Germany was not yet feasible. It is interesting to note that Bentham entered into this wider debate in 1822 with his *Codification Proposal addressed by Jeremy Bentham to All Nations professing Liberal Opinions*.[35]

Nation(-state?) and Legislation

Savigny and his Historical School of law, in particular his *Vocation for Legislation*, are not normally studied with regard to the development of German nationalism in the early nineteenth century. Incorporating features of political romanticism and its interest in the German national spirit (*Volksgeist*), Savigny's *Vocation* and other writings sought in part to form in law and jurisprudence the basis of a new German national history (or nationhood). Before a new united Germany could have a new unified national code of civil law and legislation, at the core of a national *state*, there must first be established a national-historical foundation in law and jurisprudence. This foundation would give Germany a truer sense of its own nationhood—past, present, and future—in preparation for an eventual German *Civil Code*. Thus with respect not only to legislation but also nationalism, Savigny's Historical School and his *Vocation* in particular provided an important part of the conceptual background to the later rise of the Bismarckian national state as an entity based on legislation and as ultimately articulated in the German *Civil Code* of 1900.

Savigny's dismissal of proposals for an immediate new legislative codification for Germany has often been taken too narrowly by historians. They have not duly recognized that he was endeavoring by his historical method to prepare for the possibility of such a code in the future. Similarly, his plan in *Vocation* to revert back, with changes, to the older non-national legal structure that prevailed in the Germanies before the Napoleonic *Code* has often obscured from scholarly view his great drive for a new national legal system. Such a system, he felt, would be possible only after preparations for it were made in the field of historical research. In like manner, Savigny's interest in past custom, as crucial to the German *Volksgeist* in law and jurisprudence, has frequently diverted scholarly attention away from his great concern for legislation in Germany's future.

Savigny's nationalistic legislative focus in his famed *Vocation for Legislation* served to imprint strongly on the German and European mind, early in the nineteenth century, the centrality of the theme of legislation in affairs of state and national development. Savigny's influence in that direction was not dissimilar to what Benthem had already done in England with his *Morals and Legislation*, albeit their approaches to legislation were vastly different. These are perhaps the two most classic formative works on legislation *per se* near the dawn of the new century. Indeed, Savigny's very title, *Vocation of Our Age for Legislation*, was not merely alluding to the inadequate abilities of the German jurists of his own day for successfully preparing a new legislative codification. He was also alluding to the great zeal for the task nevertheless exhibited by many contempoary Germans, as well as the wider interest in legislation present in other European countries.

A wealth of statements in Savigny's *Vocation* can be brought to bear on these and related points. Only select examples can be given here.

In Chapter VIII ("What We Are to Do Where There Are No Codes"), a striking series of statements (excerpted below) shows clearly how greatly oriented Savigny's historical method was to the future development of a national German system of law and legislation. In this system, Roman law could be superseded, he believed, only after its historical contributions were thoroughly understood. Customary law, along with other forms of law, is to be made subservient to this ultimate goal. Only through this approach to its legal history, he felt, could the true "spirit" of a nation be expressed in more complete or concrete forms of nationhood. Speaking here of nations in general terms rather than states in particular, Savigny mixes references to law and legislation with a variety of other matters. Custom to Savigny is not something that necessarily prevails over legislation, despite its great historical value, just as his denial of the readiness of his own age for a new code does not preclude him from emphasizing the significance of properly conceived legislative activities and reforms for the future. His historical comparison of Roman edicts to what he prescribes for his own day concerning custom in relation to legislation further reveals the balance between them in his mind.[36]

In Chapter X of his *Vocation* ("General Observations"), Savigny declares the following with respect to the German nation as a whole. Not dissimilarly to those who favor a new code immediately, he seeks ultimately a unified German nation in a legal-legislative sense no less than in a political and educational sense. Indeed, Savigny avowedly aims at a more unified national entity than even Thibaut did with respect to legal arrangements. The continuation of the passage (in the note below) indicates that Savigny desires a common plan of legal study for German universities so as to enrich jurisprudence and its future potential for a new German national code. His call for an eventual national legal unification (if not an immediate codification), which would allow for regional diversities (unlike the Napoleonic codes), influenced the outcome in the Bismarckian era, namely, the German *Civil Code*.

> [E]very thing relating to the history of the individual countries of Germany has a natural interest for the whole nation. . . . [T]here are many reasons for expecting a more general interest in German history for the future, and even the study of the provincial laws will have new life infused into it thereby. . . . And thus my plan tends, by a different way, to the same object, which the advocates of the general code are aiming at; viz. the making the law the concern of the nation at large, and, at the same time, a new confirmation of its unity. Only my plan is more comprehensive, including, as it does, all the countries of Germany; while, through the proposed Code, Germany would be broken up into three great districts, the divisions of which would, by means of the law, become still more strongly marked than before; namely, Austria, Prussia, and the countries of the Code.
>
> The recognising and presupposing of this community of the law in all existing institutions, then, I hold, on account of that very union to be founded on it, to be one of the most important concerns of the nation. As there is no Prussian or Bavarian, but a German, language or literature, just so is it with the remote sources of our laws and the historical investigation of them. That it is so, is not owing to the arbitrary fiat of a prince, nor

can any prince prevent it— . . . but every mistake as to that which really belongs to the nation at large . . . is fraught with ruin.[37]

These viewpoints are expanded by Savigny in two concluding chapters of his *Vocation* (XI–XII, "Thibaut's Proposal" and "Conclusion"). Although their means diverge, Savigny recognizes the common goal he and Thibaut share for a new unified German nation, especially through a new unified all-embracing code of law and legislation. However, Savigny again believes that Thibaut's proposed code would disunite rather than unite German lands and could not be satisfactorily achieved within a few years as envisioned by Thibaut. The stumbling block, once more, for Savigny is that Germans lack a proper scientific and historical jurisprudence, one founded upon a good national system of legal education uniformly present throughout the German universities. This is a prerequisite for preparing a new national German code.[38]

In the preceding series of passages pertaining to the nation, Savigny has not specifically developed a clear concept of the state. Nor has he done so within contexts of legislation and codification, upon which he pins his hopes for a new unified German nation. So preoccupied is Savigny with preparing the legal groundwork for that future goal through new historical as well as scientific methodologies, that he has little reason or space here to discourse upon concepts of the state *per se*. Nevertheless, Savigny's absorption in matters of law and legislation, in hopes of building a new national legal system for Germany, yields much material for ideas of state, even when he is concentrating on nationhood more broadly. By acknowledging the need for eventually bringing together the disparate states or countries of the Germanies into a unified legal whole, under proper conditions, Savigny has partly in mind a national state entity, even if he does not elaborate above directly on the connections between legislation and the state. Savigny's nationalistic orientation is partly shaped by his recognition of Thibaut's own nationalistic goals for Germany in the wake of the collapse of the Napoleonic Empire. This factor helps to explain why Savigny refers more to the German nation(s) than to the German state(s). There are, however, numerous interchangeable references throughout the *Vocation* to nations and states, as will become more evident below. Nor has Savigny argued, as often suggested by scholars, for custom's necessary general priority over legislation, whether with regard to the nation or to the state. Yet he has grasped the importance of custom historically and contemporaneously for the formation of Germany's national "spirit" and regional diversification.

In the final analysis, the question of Savigny's somewhat ambiguous or incomplete concept of the state must be left in part an open one because of the paucity of direct discussions on it in his *Vocation*. Yet there are clear indications of the state's strong connections with legislation in the directions eventually pursued in the German *Civil Code*. Whether in the (overlapping) contexts of *Volksgeist* in the Romantic School or of nationhood in the Historical School, Savigny's viewpoints left a potent legacy, as did the Philosophical School of Hegel and Fichte (also influential on Savigny). All three schools were part of the background to later ideas on the German nation-state in the era of Bismarck.

Custom and Legislation

For specific points of comparison between custom and legislation, Chapter I ("Introduction") in Savigny's *Vocation* is instructive. Those who argue for the immediate adoption of a new code for Germany, he opines, commit the same error as did the blindly enthusiastic codifiers in the eighteenth century. For they subscribe to the arbitrary "accidental" power of legislation in the hands of the sovereign and to the near total eclipse of custom, which Savigny implies msut have its rightful place. Nor is Savigny satisfied with proposals for a new-old universally valid system of legislation as a way to bridge the gap between those wanting a new legal code and those advocating a return to the old legal system.[39]

Chapter II ("Origin of Positive Law") in Savigny's *Vocation* sheds further light on this issue. With the historical development of law and of national characteristics, what was originally ingrained in the consciousness of the community becomes a fixture of jurisprudence. Law contains a political as well as scientific element, that is, its connection with the people as well as with its own technical language. In the beginning, law arises generically more out of its popular than its jurisprudential base. It does so more, *like* custom, through a long-developing internal process than through external arbitrary legislation. In other words, Savigny's new historical methodology, which affords in his opinion a new concept of positive law, allows for the important role of customary law in the development of nations; it recognizes the special place of legislation, more comprehensively defined, in the life of the state. Distinctions between nation and state are not altogether clear here.[40]

In Chapter III ("Legislative Provisions and Law Books") of his *Vocation*, Savigny warns against new legislation geared simply and often corruptly to the socio-economic interests of particular groups, such as landowners. This situation arises in many cases of Roman law and, more currently, of Prussian laws (an apparent allusion to one of 1810). A more beneficial influence of legislation upon the real law, seen here as the will of the people, is when its intent is to help purify or clarify customary law, as in instances involving Roman Praetorian Edicts. Contrariwise, the types of legal codifications urged by some recent authorities would wrongly sweep away all older collections of laws (along with historical traditions inclusive of customs)—except for those provisions in them readopted in the new code side by side with the new provisions. But such new laws in Germany could not be so easily distinguished from old ones in many cases involving overlapping jurisdictions and enactments from one "nation" or "state" to another. (Those two terms are used somewhat interchangeably by Savigny in such contexts.) It is only within the framework of new codification in general, rather than with new legislation *per se*, that Savigny here addresses himself to the relationship between custom and legislation. That is, he is not here concerned so much with the altogether new recent legislation, either as a subject tied to codification or as a topic in itself extending into the future. Instead, he is occupied with the balance between older legislation and custom in a new code as well as with the legislative act of promulgating "the code as the . . . aggregate existing law, with exclusive validity conferred by the state itself [!]." Here enter two suggestions of positivistic (or Bodinian) acts of state legislation. One is explicit, in terms of enacting the new code; the other is implicit, with regard to enacting new laws on into the future.[41]

Following these disquisitions on legal content, Savigny expounds on the more apt ancient Roman models of legislation. Less than satisfactory for him are medieval modes as fit models for the legal forms needing to be adopted in a new code. He again leaves open the possibilities for positivistic legislative enactments, including in the area of completely new promulgations. He has said that his work does not much discuss new legislation so as not to deflect from the issue of new codification.

> [A]n imperfect code, however, more than any thing else, must confirm the supremacy of this dead spiritless mode of treating the law.
>
> But, besides the substance, the form of the code must be taken into consideration. . . . It is commonly required that the language of the law should be particularly distinguished by brevity. Certainly brevity may be extremely effective, as is clear from the examples of the Roman Decrees and Edicts. But there is also a dry, inexpressive brevity, adopted by him who does not understand the use of language as an instrument, and which

remains wholly ineffective; numerous examples of it are to be found in the laws and records of the Middle Ages. On the other hand, diffuseness in law authorities may be very exceptionable, nay, wholly intolerable, as in many of the constitutions of Justinian, and in most of the novels of the Theodosian Code. . . .

Putting together what has been said above concerning the requisites of a really good code, it is clear that very few ages will be found qualified for it. . . . The laws of the Middle Ages, already quoted, are examples of this . . .[42]

Codification and Legislation

On specific issues of codification and legislation in Chapter VI ("Our Vocation for Legislation") of his *Vocation*, Savigny begins by attacking those who in their rush for a completely new code reject the need for Roman law altogether as a past dead system. History is of little real direct relevance, they wrongly believe, in the face of the superiority of each new age to perfect its own new legal system. New legislative systems in themselves, Savigny counters, are not necessarily the answer to current problems if the innate traditional temper of the people and nation is not taken into careful consideration. Savigny's reservations again center around the current deficiencies in Germany of the lawmaking and juristic abilities, which must be vastly improved before a new code can be successfully undertaken. The needed "twofold scientific spirit," combining "historical" and "systematic" approaches to law, has been lacking in Germany ever since the eighteenth century. It must be elevated "for the future to the rank of a national system." The deficient books of Roman-Germanic law current in the various German lands reflect the present-day inabilities to form a good new code. As in some passages cited immediately above, Savigny here calls for a renewal of the spirit that animated the compilers of Justinian's *Pandects*, in conjunction with "the wakening spirit of [German] nationality." Better is it to refrain from the arduous task of forming a new codification because of current juristic unpreparedness than to proceed now with one and end up with the kind of grossly imperfect products rampant in the Early Middle Ages when similar deficiencies prevailed. Both ages in Germany have demonstrated unfitness for a new "general system of legislation." Once again, Savigny's incomplete conceptual focus on the state itself, as distinct from broader nationality, goes hand in hand with his incomplete concentration on new legislation as a theme itself, independently of the topic of codification.[43]

In assessing the unreadiness of his own age for a new code, Savigny points out the weaknesses as well as strengths of three major recent legal codifications in Chapter VII ("The Three New Codes") of his *Vocation*. Political more than technical elements of legislation have impacted the *Code Napoleon* and have altered existing laws more so than has been the case in the Prussian or Austrian Codes. Despite its possible formal merits as a system, Napoleon's *Code* became a tool for his despotism, particularly in Germany, thus representing a bad model for achieving successful new legislation or codification. Napoleon's *Code* went too far in introducing disliked new legislation into France, at the expense of the preexisting mixture of French customs and Roman law, which were abrogated too easily when in opposition to Napoleon's *Code*. However, the French, more so than the Germans, have wisely granted some discretion to judges in deciding cases not expressly covered in the *Code*, whether they decide in favor of more recent laws or older ones (Roman and customary). At the same time, not only are judges in France greatly limited in their ability to go against new or old law (as well as Roman law and custom); but the preexisting laws offer little protection against arbitrary powers. In the end, Savigny's prescription for France is to introduce new legislation of a good uniform kind where needed, rather than to attempt now yet another codification. Whereas the French *Code* was hastily drawn up, the Prussian *Landrecht* was more wisely designed as a legislative Code with great care and excellence of form. It either included much preexisting law and custom or provided substitutes for them where lacking. Nevertheless, the negative features of the Prussian *Landrecht*, patterned very imperfectly upon Justinian's *Pandects* as a universal model or method, shows why no new code should be presently attempted in Germany. Although the Prussian legislation in the *Landrecht* was drawn up only after much consultation with learned jurists of the age, German legal language still must be greatly improved before new codification and legislation can be launched. The Austrian *Gesetzbuch*, less complete than the Prussian *Landrecht*, shared with it a common root in mid-eighteenth-century writings on Roman law; the former received impulse under Maria Theresa, the latter under Frederick II, an arch Enlightened Despot. Taken together, these three recent codes show to Savigny the present-day unpreparedness for yet another new legislative codification. Such is, however, Savigny's ultimate future hope for Germany, once jurisprudence has been elevated to the tasks of legislation. In these discussions, Savigny views the Prussian *Landrecht* (and Austrian *Gesetzbuch*) largely in terms of legislation, as distinct from custom, contrary to the scholarly expert often cited above who has seen it (and Savigny's *Vocation*) more exclusively in terms of custom.[44]

Far from advocating the abrogation of these three existing codes because of their flaws, Savigny, in Chapter IX ("What Is to Be Done Where Codes Exist Already"), argues for their retention in Germany. Their abrogation would only cause greater confusion; it is better, he feels, to retain them until a new general code for a unified Germany becomes feasible. In order to prepare for a future code, founded upon a proper "scientific spirit," which cannot come from those three existing codes, there must nevertheless be full study of the "historical authorities" upon which they are based. But this does not mean that a new national code for Germany could or should be attempted, contrary to Thibaut, on the partial basis of the supposed scientific spirit in the three recent codes.[45]

Roman Law and Legislation

On specific points concerning Roman law and legislation, a subject already encountered in other contexts above, Savigny makes some extended observations especially in Chapter IV ("Roman Law") in his *Vocation*. The early history of ancient Roman law illustrates for him why great respect must be paid to the history of law leading up to his own times. Savigny dilates on the beneficial cumulative contributions of republican and classical jurisprudence in Rome to the eventual shaping of Justinian's post-classical compilations. Along the way, each age showed great respect for the one preceding it.[46]

In the passage to follow from the same chapter (IV), Savigny expresses an overriding interest in the organic and progressive development of law, which is revealed in Roman legal history and is crucial to his own age. The Romans made effective use of new legislation because they maintained respect for old laws and forms. These modes somewhat paralleled the long cumulative developments associated with custom. Savigny thus admires, as a potential model for his own age, the Romans' abilities in reconciling legal-legislative innovations with traditions. But he is not thereby depicting legislation as itself superseded by custom. He sees legislation rather as ideally paralleling some of custom's modes of operation.

> In the law, consequently, the general Roman character was strongly marked—the holding fast by the long-established, without allowing themselves to be fettered by it, when it no longer harmonised with a new popular prevailing theory. For this reason the history of the Roman law, down to the classical age, exhibits everywhere a gradual, wholly organic develop-

ment. If a new form is framed, it is immediately bound up with an old established one. . . .

From this representation it is plain that the Roman law, like customary law, has formed itself almost entirely from within; and the more detailed history of it shows how little, on the whole, express legislation affected it, so long as it continued in a living state. Even with regard to what has been said above of the necessity for a code, the history of the Roman law is exceedingly instructive. So long as the law was in active progression, no code was discovered to be necessary, . . .[47]

In addition, the same chapter (IV) includes a striking reference to Caesar's reported plan for reducing civil law to a system. Caesar's plan exhibited much the same modes, says Savigny, as are found in modern codes. Succeeding Roman codes or compilations, culminating with those under Justinian, aimed at overcoming certain corruptions of their ages that were similar to those that Caesar sought to correct. The ancient Roman "spirit" in law was manifested in these codes, culminating with Justinian's outstanding productions, which to Savigny are still remarkable as methodological models in spite of disagreements over their contents. The Roman codes can now be best appreciated through historical analysis of their sources. Savigny is once again drawing parallels with the modern German legal condition and "spirit" in law.[48]

Savigny's interim prescription for Germany is set forth in Chapter V ("Civil Law in Germany"). Until such future time that a new code can be fruitfully attempted, Germans should return to the system that long held sway prior to Napoleon. That system was basically a combination of modern-day Roman law embodied in the "common law" and of Germanic law especially as found in provincial laws. It is not true, he argues, that the readoption of this complicated system, particularly as it pertains to Roman law, would detract from the idea and actuality of German nationhood, as critics allege. Indeed, it would serve as an interim legal foundation for rebuilding German nationality in the wake of the collapsed Napoleonic Empire. The individual parts of the state that contribute to its existence as an organic whole should not be eliminated because of their complexity but rather must be revitalized. Similarly, the complex legal-historical materials of Roman law in Germany should not be abandoned, as some urge; instead, they must be reinvigorated in order to restrengthen German "nationality" or statehood. Those who press now for a new legal uniformity blindly ignore the traditional vitality of legal diversity. Far from having deprived Germans of their own indigenous national law, as some have complained, Roman law once was and still can be a vital part of a national

German law. The progressive development of German law would have been stymied under Napoleon even if Roman law had been absent. In any case, Roman law is a key, inextricable part of Germany's legal history and must be studied and maintained at the present time in the traditional forms of "common law" in Germany. The "political end" of the "common weal" of Germany is here a main goal for Savigny. This end was formerly reached, and still can be, by means of the "common law" that binds together "all the German nations" into an "indissoluble unity" while recognizing their "great variety and individuality."[49]

Finally, a striking point arises in Savigny's lengthy discussions on the flawed historical and technical understanding of Roman law on the part of various key French jurists instrumental in its adaptations in the *Code Napoleon*. Savigny gives an example of a misunderstood point about "public law" (*jus publicum*) as "the law concerning the state" in relation to Justinian's *Digest*. In itself, this point is too brief and indirect to reveal Savigny's outlook in his *Vocation* on the connection between public law/legislation and the state more specifically. But there is nevertheless here still another clear suggestion that he did, in fact, closely associate the two, however cursorily. Savigny deplores the traditional (unhistorical) intermingling of such topics in Justinian's Roman law with the later medieval opinions of Bartolus. Savigny also castigates the disregard for older French jurists of Roman law—such as Cujas in the sixteenth century—by recent French jurists decisive in forming the French *Code* under Napoleon. In the textual topic at hand on Roman "public law" (as in many other textual matters), Savigny seeks a precise historical understanding of the Roman law itself, freed from the unhistorical approaches of medieval postglossators like Bartolus but aided by the historical ones of Renaissance jurists like Cujas.[50]

3. BISMARCKIAN DEVELOPMENTS AND GERMAN NATIONAL UNITY (NATION-STATE)

Legacy of "Histori*cism*" (and "Pandect*ism*") in Codification and Legislation

An important recent account of the complex nineteenth-century developments leading up to the adoption of the German *Civil Code* in 1900 has extensively underscored its unique indebtedness to Savigny's German Historical School of law (or so-called legal "histori*cism*") concerning issues of codification and legislation. At the same time, the expert author, Michael John,[51] seldom mentions, and then only in passing, the contributions to the *Civil Code* made by the German Pandectist

School of law (or so-called "Pandect*ism*"), which have been noted in other ways by some historians. Nevertheless, like them, he recognizes the legacy of the German Historical School that lay behind the Pandectist School, while also pointing out that Pandectists such as Puchta represented a divergence from Savigny's School. This story of the several decades of actual debates and preparations leading up to the *Code* took place mostly during the Bismarckian era and its immediate aftermath. Although these developments were not always closely or directly linked to Otto von Bismarck himself, they typically turned around issues of so-called "national*ism*" and "stat*ism*" in wider Bismarckian contexts.

It is true that the later codifiers who adapted Savigny's viewpoints diverged at times from Savigny's original ideas, as is shown by Professor John. However, the preceding section has explored the rich discussions in Savigny's *Vocation for Legislation* that were far more positive toward future codification and legislation than many historians like John have long believed. Savigny's *Vocation* did not have to be recast by later German jurists in order for it to be a support for their efforts toward new codification or legislation. For it was already inclined in itself toward those objectives. Savigny's related tendencies toward ideals of nationalism and the nation-state have also been cited above. It is further true that Savigny also favored inclusion of particularist regional interests and traditions, as often emphasized by historians like John. Nonetheless, one should not minimize Savigny's own strong hopes for an eventual German legal unification as the foundation for a new united German national state, under apparent Prussian leadership. Here, too, Savigny left some crucial intellectual-legal precedents for the later Bismarckian period.

"In the field of jurisprudence," according to Professor John, "the dominant figure was . . . Savigny . . . , a man whose influence on subsequent patterns of German legal thought would be impossible to overestimate. In particular, his views about the nature of the law, the role of the legislator and the possibility of codification coloured attitudes to these matters until the end of the [nineteenth] century." John shows how Savigny's thought on codes and legislation was adapted as much by later codifiers in support of a new code as by their critics opposing it. "As early as the 1840s, . . . there were many calls for national codification which were based on Savigny's own theories, and after 1848 this became what might be termed the standard liberal/nationalist position. The implications of this for the way in which Germany's legal system was unified after 1871 were enormous . . ." The author connects these problems with nationalism and statism. "From the start of the nineteenth century, codification was linked to nationalism." "Nationalism," however, "was not, of course, reducible [wholly] to state formation even if the two were clearly linked in the 1860s and 1870s [under Bismarck]. At the heart of the nationalist cause lay a commitment to the unity of the people, . . . [with] emphasis . . . on ethnic and cultural aspects of 'Germanness' rather than on bureaucratic . . . state formation." Indeed, "1870 saw a marked shift towards ethnic conceptions of the *Volk* and the *Volksgeist* . . . [among] many liberal nationalists. But the relationship between this conception of nationality and the foundation of the Bismarckian state was tense and ambiguous. . . . The liberals' tendency to ignore the difficulties between ethnic nationalism and state formation left them vulnerable to attack . . . in the 1880s." At the same time: "The history of the preparation of the Civil Code [shows that] . . . the hold of the Establishment on politics could be challenged by movements from below. . . . [However,] the actual effect of these new influences on the final version of the Code was remarkably slight. . . . But, above all, the failure to introduce major reforms into the Civil Code in the 1890s was the product of the skill of the legal bureaucracy in exploiting traditional conceptions of nationalism and its mastery of the complexities of the law to head off pressure from other elements." In the final analysis: "The preparation of the Code in the 1890s suggests that successful manipulation from above and mobilization from below were hardly mutually exclusive alternatives in Wilhelmine politics."[52]

Throughout his brilliant book, Professor John elaborates at length on the many ways in which the developments toward a German *Civil Code* were closely tied not only to the changing political forces, his main focal point, but also to the changing legislative frameworks in which they typically occurred. This legislative framework is not surprising in that the *Code* was itself a monumental legislative production. The author's purpose is not primarily to reveal the legislative orientation *per se* in the *Code*'s formation over a span of several decades. Yet his rich materials on the political forces and processes operating behind the *Code*'s formation serve for present purposes to draw attention to the legislative factor itself. For at most levels of the complicated, long-developing preparations for a new code, the legislative process was a controlling context. The complex involvements of political institutions at the national, federal, and regional levels tended to be legislative in scope. These bodies included above all the regional state legislatures, the *Bundesrat* and the *Reichstag*. Because the purpose of the unified German *Civil Code* was to lay the legal-legislative foundation for the new unified German nation-state, the national legislative state becomes again for us the essence of the problems at hand. In addition, the relation of the *Code*, as a work of legislation in itself, to what is termed "special legislation," lying outside but connected with the *Code*, is treated at points by the author. His related discussions (as cited in the note below) include the following issues: so-called "German*ism*" and "Roman*ism*" (in contexts of Roman law), legal positivism (seen as congruent with the Historical School), new versus existing legislation (in connection with Savigny and Puchta), later legal arguments either against Savigny or latent in his works (distinguishing later from earlier works), questions of sovereignty and nation-state (especially concerning Prussia in relation to the rest of Germany), and the central importance of Bismarck's "revolution" (in the 1860s and 1870s).[53]

Other historians who have pointed to the more directly significant contributions of the German Pandectist School of law to the drive for codification that culminated in the German *Civil Code* of 1900 have usually seen it as an outgrowth and even culmination of the German Historical School of law. Those historians tend to focus on the role of G. F. Puchta (1798–1846). In the words of one such historian: "The legal-dogmatic character of the Historical School achieved via the work of Puchta, Von Savigny's most prominent disciple, its consummation in the Pandectist School. . . . The Pandectist movement, whose scientific results . . . had been largely incorporated by the civil law-codification of 1900, also demonstrates the continuity in legal-dogmatic method." That historian stresses the paradoxical positions of the Historical School. First, it emphasized the law's organic growth while being critical of abstract natural or universal law; yet it also promoted dogmatic scientific research into the civil law according to methods that could become another kind of abstract theoretical approach to legal logic. Second, it often purported to emphasize custom at the expense of legislation; yet it also raised to new heights the importance of legislation, at times in an absolutist or positivist manner. Savigny and Puchta shared many similar views on the key role of the national "spirit" of the people. They both had high regard for Roman law (Pandectism taking its name from Justinian's name for his *Digest*).[54]

"Nation-State or State-Nation?"

In his classic three-volume study of "Bismarck and the development of Germany," the noted historian Otto Pflanze has devoted a chapter to "nationalism and national policy." There he draws an interesting yet problematic distinction between the nation-state and the state-nation. He applies it not only to the case of Bismarck but also to wider German intellectual traditions. Accepting as genuine and not as rhetoric Bismarck's continued "expressions of German national sentiment" after 1866, Professor Pflanze poses the following question: "Was the German Reich a 'nation-state' or 'state-nation'?" He believes that the latter was primarily the case during the Bismarckian era. The German nation-state in the tradition of Herder revolved around cultural matters associated with the *Volksgeist*. The German state-nation in the (non-liberal) traditions of Hegel centered around *Weltgeist* and *Machtstaat* in political-social matters. Bismarck and his *Realpolitik* were overwhelmingly identified with the Hegelian rather than Herderian tradition.[55]

This dichotomy, however, between state-nation and nation-state tends to be idiosyncratic and obfuscating. Although Pflanze's emphasis on the state in connection with Bismarck is welcome, what is lacking is a concomitant stress by Pflanze on the legal-legislative character of the state itself. Thus the vexed problem of nationalism in the case of Bismarck and his place in the wider history of the subject is little resolved or clarified. At any rate, "nation-state" remains the traditionally preferred term that we continue to use in the present chapter according to various criteria. The term "state-nation" would no doubt appear awkward if it were extensively adopted throughout such a study. Pflanze himself does not use it much elsewhere in his own work. Indeed, Bismarck seems to have fused or blurred nation-state and state-nation in his own utterances, as had countless others before him. The main point is how the two terms are academically defined. Both can be seen in the context of the modern national legislative state.

Although state and nation are inevitably blurred together in such distinctions as the above when the connecting theme is nationalism, some useful points can be drawn. The association of the Bismarckian state/nation with the Hegelian state/nation remains instructive more generally in light of our present chapters. The intricate interconnections between ideas of *Volksgeist*, nationhood, and nation-state found in the Romantic and Historical Schools of law can also be seen in the developing efforts at codification during the Bismarckian era. The legislative traditions evident in both the Romantic and Historical Schools connect them in matters of state and sovereignty with the Bismarckian era more appropriately than do themes of *Volksgeist*. All of these traditions of thought—Hegelian, Historical, Romantic, and Bismarckian—can be said to combine elements of *Volksgeist*, nationhood, and nation-state. Yet the progressive emergence of the national state from Romantic to Historical and to Bismarckian thought finds a remote parallel in that from Herderian to Hegelian ideas. In the end, it is not surprising that in Pflanze's above-cited chapter on "nationalism and national policy" the first part on "nationalism" bears a very loose and uncertain relationship to the second part on "national policy."

The amorphorus and ambiguous nature of such distinctions as "nation-state" and "state-nation" in the debate over German nationalism before, during, and after the Bismarckian era is further evident in the statements by Bismarck cited by Professor Pflanze in support of his interpretations. In the language of German idealism, Bismarck declared in 1870 that the unification of Germany was "a development stemming from the history and spirit of the German people." Bismarck's references to the "Prussian nation," "Prussian nationality," and "north German nationality" signify, in Pflanze's words, that "Bismarck referred to the nation as closely associated with the state . . . [and that the] German nation had concrete existence for him only when united under a sovereign state." Pflanze further says that by the "German nation," to which Bismarck referred after 1871, "he meant the German Reich, not the German-speaking people of Europe." In 1881, Pflanze points out, Bismarck declared: "I am above all a royalist, then a Prussian and a German. I will defend my king and the monarchy . . . , and I will establish and leave behind me a strong and healthy Germany." Adds Pflanze: "He was able to make the transition from Prussian to German patriotism in the 1860s because the German union he brought about preserved the essential values he treasured in Prussian society and government." However: "The Germans, Bismarck often lamented, had a poorly developed national consciousness in comparison with other peoples." Overall, Pflanze here "aim[s] at a typology of . . . German nationalism in the nineteenth century," although "not . . . of nationalism as such" more broadly.[56]

The inherent complexity of German nationalistic developments in the nineteenth century heighten the uncertainties in academic admixtures like the foregoing concerning state, nation, monarchy, empire, federalism, and so forth. If state is not distinguished from nation through the legislative factor, the kaleidoscopic, multi-layered German political units become difficult of clear resolution. Nationalism and the nation-state or state-nation become inseparably interfused.

This predicament raises a series of pivotal questions about German history, further illustrating the potential confusion for historians in such cases. Is one referring to the post-Napoleonic Germanic Confederation organized in 1815 (lasting until 1866), in which general as well as particularist German nationalist strivings were hampered by Austrian influence and so-called "Metternich*ism*"? Or is one referring to the Frankfurt Assembly and Constitution (1848–1849), in which nationalism and liberalism proved largely abortive? Or is the subject instead the Prussian Constitution of 1850? Or rather Bismarck's royalist goals for the Prussia monarchy of William I (1861–), who appointed him Prussian Prime Minister in 1862? Or indeed is one thinking of the expansion of Prussia's wider sphere of hegemony under Bismarck through the incorporation or addition of further German territories after Prussia's wars against Denmark (1864) and Austria (1866)? Or perhaps the 1867

Constitution of the North German Confederation of 1867–1870 dominated by Prussia? Or the new German Empire (1871–), with Bismarck as Chancellor after more German territories were acquired through war with France (1870–1871)? Or the consolidation of the new German *Reich* under Bismarck in the 1870s and 1880s? Or the foreign colonies of the new German Empire? Or the composite diversity of all German states themselves during these periods, rather than the singular Prussianization of German states, as the essence of the emerging German national state? Or the wider scope of the Wilhelmine (or Second) *Reich* (1871–1919), the First *Reich* having been the Holy Roman Empire of the German Nation? Or the era extending from Bismarck's dismissal in 1890 by the new German Emperor, William II, to his death in 1898? Or the gradual emergence of the new German *Civil Code* (1896/1900)? Or a host of other occurrences along the way? Or the wider rule of William II (1888–1918)?

These and other myriad sectors of German nationalism have not been sufficiently distinguished by many historians. The complex nationalistic developments in other German states besides Prussia have too often been unclearly interfused. Bismarck's own shifting uses of pertinent terms serve little to clarify these issues unless they are carefully and extensively categorized along the kinds of lines indicated here.

Finally, when one speaks of German nationalism under Bismarck with regard to unification and centralization, is one referring to territory, geography, ethnicity, industry, foreign policy, domestic policy, warfare, bureaucracy, or politics? If it is one or more of these, then the "nation" is more apt to be the focal point. Or is it law, legislation, or constitution? If so, the "state" is more apropos, albeit with admixtures of the foregoing. More specifically, the sweeping scope of Bismarckian domestic national social(istic) legislation, together with the German *Civil Code* and the form of German national government during Bismarck's regime, testify to the prominence of the themes of legislative sovereignty and the legislative state.

National Legislative State and National State Legislation

In response to Professor Pflanze's provocative question above as to whether the Bismarckian *Reich* was primarily a "nation-state" or "state-nation," it will be useful here to juxtapose instead, in place of that dualism, the terms "national legislative state" and "national state legislation." This seems a better way to arrive at a satisfactory framework for viewing the essential character of the Bismarckian "state," which Pflanze feels was more at issue under Bismarck than was the "nation," though Pflanze sees the two in conjunction. Legislation has long been a subject of indirect interest to historians of this era in connection with questions of politics, bureaucracy, government, industry, codification, social welfare, and so on. However, it is surprising that the theme of legislation has not been singled out in itself in the ways proposed here with regard to the state itself. Hence the fuller term "national legislative state" can be employed here as a more exact characterization of the emerging German nation-state as a true modern state. Nonetheless, that term might seem repetitive or wordy if employed consistently throughout the present discussions. Therefore, it should be understood that many of the present uses of the simpler and more standard term "nation-state"—which as merely a *Staatsvolk* is prone to vagueness—are made with this longer version in mind.

The constitution of the North German Confederation adopted in 1867[57] is notable here in two respects. First, its chief architect was Bismarck himself. He was newly triumphant (along with the Prussian monarchy, bureaucracy, and army) after Prussian victories and territorial gains in the war of 1866 against Austria. Bismarck had already increasingly dominated the legislature established in the Prussian constitution of 1850. That durable document had been established under the Prussian king Frederick William IV (d. 1861), partly in response to the far more liberal and representative Frankfurt constitution of 1849, and it remained in effect until 1918. It had made Prussia a limited constiutional state in distinction to its older absolutist regimes. Prussia's predominance in the federated northern states of Germany after the Austro-Prussian War of 1866 was a harbinger of Prussia's predominance in the enlarged German national confederation created in 1871 when the southern German states were added to it following the Franco-Prussian (or German) War of 1870–1871. Thus it is not surprising that Bismarck assumed a singularly dominant role in the creation of the constitution of the North German Confederation, prior to its promulgation, and was aided only by his informal advisors. The process was not a representative one, unlike in the case of the Frankfurt constitution.

Second, the constitution of the North German Confederation of 1867 dealt with sovereignty and the state primarily in legislative contexts. As a step forward, from the Confederation of 1815 and toward a national federal state, the constitution of the North German Confederation made "national" legislation superior to the laws of the separate states, while equal uniform rights in civil law were granted to residents throughout the Confederation. In the first article of the constitution, the list of member states is given. Immediately thereafter, in the second article, federal laws are stipulated to take precedence over the laws of the individual states, so that federal legislation becomes the supreme law of the land. Following this, in the third article, citizenship and civil rights are provided for those living within the new Confederation. Ensuing articles of the constitution successively establish the following: the federal *Bundesrat* (or upper legislative house representing the separate states), the federal President (the Prussian king) and Chancellor (the President of the *Bundesrat* and head of the government, that is, Bismarck), the *Reichstag* (or lower house elected by universal manhood suffrage throughout the individual states and with unspecified relationship to the Chancellor), the unlimited veto power of the President of the Confederation (who had to accept all bills before their promulgation), and the requirement that the Chancellor had to countersign and take responsibility for all such laws. Thus the principles of legislative sovereignty and legislative state are abundantly affirmed.

When the new German Empire was proclaimed in 1871,[58] with the completion of German unification following the Franco-Prussian (or German) War, the above constitutional arrangement of the North German Confederation was retained. The constitution was enlarged to include the newly incorporated southern states of Germany, which were given some constitutional concessions. The Prussian king William I (ruled 1861–1888), who had also become Confederation President, now became German Emperor. Simultaneously, the federal chancellor, Bismarck, became imperial chancellor. This basic constitutional arrangement continued nearly until the end of the Empire. Bismarck (and his more authoritarian-minded emperor) largely dominated the *Bundesrat* and *Reichstag*, which were respectively more particularist and popularist in nature. The *Bundesrat* declined in relative importance.

Under Bismarck the legislature was increasingly occupied with legislative processes, which he more and more directed, especially in domestic legislation on economic, social, and other matters. In the 1880s, Bismarck's advancing programs of social(istic) legislation were spearheaded by him through the legislature. The two houses had little to do in such other matters as formulating foreign policy (in which, by contrast, the British parliament had more active direct involvement). When the *Reichstag*, for instance, resisted voting to approve subsidy bills for appropriating substantial funds for significant foreign activities by the *Reich* in other countries or territories, as in 1884–1885, Bismarck or his office could operate as overriding arbiter to obtain the desired results. Meanwhile, legal unification proceeded ahead in commercial, criminal, and civil law. A unitary state was tending to emerge in other areas as well, although obstacles remained (including in the legislature and particularly in the diverse political parties in the *Reichstag*). After Bismarck, toward the end of the Empire, various concessions were granted in the composition of the legislature, but proved too little and too late. A constitutional crisis would probably have occurred even without the pressures caused by World War I.

It is in the realm of "state socialism" in domestic legislation directed primarily by Bismarck throughout the decade of the 1880s that the new German national state achieved perhaps its greatest identity as a modern legislative state. Professor Pflanze himself devotes a substantial chapter to "state socialism,"[59] replete with detailed discussions of the massive social legislation passed under Bismarck during that decade. But Pflanze focuses on state socialism rather than on legislation *per se*. Thus he does not draw the obvious connections between socialistic state legislation and what we have termed the legislative state. Indeed, the legislative state furnishes in this regard a clearer way to depict the nature of the Bismarckian "state-nation," upon which Pflanze's own analysis of nationalism falters in his other discussions cited above. Bismarck's comprehensive legislative program of social and economic reforms is well known to historians, although the close links between state and legislation have not heretofore been adequately connected.

In the first decade of the new Empire, culminating in legislative activity against it in the later 1870s, Bismarck sought to suppress the spread of Marxist revolutionary or republican socialism in Germany.[60] Bismarck responded in particular to the formation in Germany of the Social Democratic Party in 1875, to its pro-democratic and anti-militarist positions, and to its gain of seats in the *Reichstag*, where socialist members helped to frustrate his efforts to interdict the socialist movement. Bismarck succeeded in passing anti-socialist legislation in 1878. This marked the beginning of a series of so-called "Exceptional Laws," which continued until 1890 at the end of his chancellorship. This legislation failed, however, to suppress the socialists, who continued much of their agitation underground. In fact, socialist seats in the *Reichstag* increased about three-fold from 1881 to 1890 and about another three-fold over that by 1912.

During the decade of the 1880s, Bismarck's brand of legislative state-sponsored socialism sought to undermine the socialists' own calls for social legislation.[61] The results were more successful. These and other motives of Bismarck have been much debated. He aimed at promoting the well-being of the German people as a whole largely because the abilities of his military were dependent upon them. Yet Bismarck's social conscience (or idealism) became as much a factor here as his political opportunism (realism or *Realpolitik*). Another factor was the tension between Bismarck's self-interests as aristocratic *Junker* and the working(and middle)-class interests that his legislation addressed. In addition, it must be noted that Bismarck's concern with social reform can be traced back in early form to the beginning of his appointment in 1862 by the Prussian king. In the final analysis, nonetheless, Bismarck's social reform legislation aimed mostly at reconciling labor to the state by showing that the state could care for labor's needs at least as well as could the socialists. If Bismarck expressed a sense of social justice in wanting to alleviate the exploitation of labor, he did not desire to weaken industry by burdening it with excessive regulations. He was more prone to regulate insurance companies than to compel industrialists to reduce drastically their profitability. On industry the *Reich* depended for its military strength, leaning more toward government control than toward capitalist free enterprise more typical in Britain.

The long list of significant social(istic) laws enacted under Bismarck in the 1880s,[62] though well known, needs to be more forcefully grouped under the topic of state legislation. This includes the following items (which could be greatly expanded): the medical insurance act of 1883 (his first such reform, launched in the bill of 1881), the accident insurance act of 1884, the old-age and disability insurance act of 1889, regulations of the labor of women and children in industry (1887), and the provision for a day of rest (1887). Many other laws were aimed at improving factory conditions, allowing trade-unions to grow, and providing for labor exchanges. Bismarck's endeavors to establish state monopolies of the fire and health insurance business in Prussia with regard to imperial regulation of individual companies presents another side of his legislative state socialism as well as of his partial self-interest (in using such programs to benefit estate-owners like himself). In other words, Bismarck was seeking to give to the central government the power to legislate on insurance matters, a subject that had its antecedents back in the 1860s. These and other measures reveal the intricate interrelationships between the laws and regulations of the Prussian and national German jurisdictions. But the overall result was a socialist legislative state that in ways surpassed that of Napoleon III earlier in France and inspired in part that of Lloyd George later in England.

In a wide range of other areas of industry and commerce, Bismarck embarked during the Empire on an extensive program of legislation for the benefit and control of the state, further showing his socialistic tendencies. These areas included protective tariffs, regulation of coinage, control of banks, and unification of the railroads. But one of Bismarck's greatest contributions remained his efforts toward legal reform and unification. True, the final years of revising the planned German *Civil Code*, from 1888 to 1896, took place mostly after he left government in 1890. Yet the earlier crucial stages of forming a provisional code, from 1874 to 1888, were more closely connected with the leadership of Bismarck and his government. Indeed, not only from the founding of the Empire in 1871, but from the earlier establishment of the constitution of the North German Confederation in 1867, there was a mounting drive toward legal unification, notwithstanding the many obstacles and oppositions encountered along the way.[63]

"Real*ism*" and *Realpolitik*

Taken together, then, the above subjects abundantly demonstrate that the Bismarckian state was indeed yet another illustration of the modern national legislative state. Other typologies explored by historians of the Bismarckian era often serve instead to reinforce this fundamental legislative model underlying or interconnecting them. The topics of nation-state, constitutional state (*Rechtsstaat, Verfassungsstaat*), absolutist or power state (*Machtstaat*), and other variations such as "pseudo-constitutional absolutism," can all typically be reduced to a more basic legislative state.

Along the way, we have encountered manifold instances of what historians have traditionally called the "politics of realism" or *Realpolitik*. This, too, can frequently be seen from the perspective of the legislative state. A case in point has involved Bismarck's drive toward social and economic reform. Another case above has revolved around the military dimensions of his state-building or nation-building. On this level, it cannot be denied that Bismarck's statism was closely connected to his militarism. In addition to his statecraft in foreign affairs, Bismarck's direction of domestic legislation in diverse areas displayed a prevailing sense of force or forcefulness. But whether from the perspective of force or consent, realism or idealism, the legislative state under Bismarck constituted the basic paradigm. As usual, all such "isms" fail to account for the root character of the modern national state, which is first and foremost the national legislative state. This viewpoint does not detract from such standard topics as *Realpolitik*, but provides a vantage point on them. Nationalism is the usual overarching topic for historians who examine trends from idealism and romanticism to realism and militarism in nineteenth-century German politics concerned with building a nation-state. The topic of the legislative (national) state again affords a useful common denominator for bringing together or distinguishing between such "isms" in these matters.

At the head of this chapter, in the title, stands one of the most perplexing "isms" of all—Bismarckianism. The *Oxford English Dictionary* gives a number of contemporaneous uses of the terms "Bismarckian," "Bismarckianism," and "Bismarckism." The following are telltale: "The principles of state persecution—principles which have been repudiated by the civilization of modern Europe, even though the new Bismarckian phase of that civilization seems to tend to their re-adoption" (1878, H. J. Coleridge); "The strong-minded Bismarckian man of action" (1901, G. B. Shaw); "Germany's policy is the Bismarckian policy of 'blood and iron' " (1914); "To substitute Bismarckism for Napoleonism would be a very small gain to civilization" (1870); "The general expression of the public loss . . . may serve to check a too rampant Bismarckianism" (1889); "Commercial and territorial expansion—Bismarckism in Germany, Imperialism in England" (1931, *Times Lit. Suppl.*); "It was Bismarckianism run mad for Kiderlen to suppose that Caillaux would find it easier to compromise if he was first threatened" (1954, A. J. P. Taylor).

These kinds of usages tend to interfuse all three "isms" cited in our chapter title—Bismarckianism, statism, and nationalism—through notions linked to *Realpolitik* or political (even ruthless) realism. Other equivalent "isms" could include not only Napoleonism but also Hitlerism, not to mention Machiavellism, as supposed mainstays of the modern nation-state forged through *Realpolitik*. Also relevant would be militarism, imperialism, opportunism, immoralism, materialism, and the like.

The phenomenon of *Realpolitik* has long been variously hailed and condemned as the bulwark of the modern state, the classic textbook case being Germany in the age of Bismarck. The succinct definition of *Realpolitik* in *Webster's Dictionary* is: "politics based on practical and material factors rather than on theoretical or ethical objectives." When associating *Realpolitik* with Bismarckianism, historians generally identify it with the phrase "blood and iron," which they link with militarism and industrialism at the heart of Bismarck's German state. An alternate turn of phrase, "gold and iron," has been used by one recent historian. At least as fitting would be "legislation and iron." That is, Bismarck's uses of legislation and government in tandem with industry and the military lay at the core of his modern German state. The legislative state lay behind Bismarck's domestic programs for Germany said to embody political realism or *Realpolitik*. The importance traditionally assigned to *Realpolitik* in the study of Bismarck's German state needs to be weighed in favor of legislation.

In a fine chapter on "the strategy of *Realpolitik*,"[64] Professor Pflanze focuses on Bismarck's early promotions of Prussia's interests against her ostensible ally Austria. Austria's strong presence in German confederate affairs dated back to 1815 with the emergence of so-called "Metternich*ism*." Pflanze's main sectional categories of analysis are "the art of the possible," "[seizing] the fulcrum [in the balance] of power," "the checkerboard of politics," and "the alternatives of coercion." After first giving numerous statements made by Bismarck later in life about his sense of political strategy, Pflanze concentrates skillfully on Bismarck's strategies in the 1850s in his dealings with Austria. But

Pflanze does not necessarily equate Bismarck's "strategies of *Realpolitik*" with the concept of the state itself. The real difficulty arises, however, in the many ways in which Pflanze elsewhere often tends to blur together the statesman and his statecraft with the state as centered on realistic power politics. This tendency was particularly noticeable in Pflanze's above-cited discussions in other chapters on the "state-nation" and "state socialism." These kinds of cross-connections are often found in various ways in much other historiography on such subjects concerning Bismarck.[65]

4. FINALE ON ITALY: FROM "MAZZINIAN*ISM*" TO "CAVOUR*ISM*"?

In the case of Italy, as in that of Germany, the development of nationalism from the early to the later nineteenth century has often been viewed by historians through a broad progression of "isms"—from romanticism, liberalism, and idealism to realism, opportunism, and militarism. Just as in Germany such "isms" were marked by the turn away from the liberal republicanism of the Frankfurt Assembly and toward Bismarckianism, so too in Italy there was a turn from so-called "Mazzinian*ism*" to "Cavour*ism*" in the development of Italian nationalism. This has often been tied as well to vexed questions on the Italian nation-state.

The story of Italy's unification into a modern nation-state has been typically told through the joint achievements of three protagonists. Above all, the political strategems and diplomatic maneuverings of Camillo Cavour (d. 1861) proved successful in consolidating and expanding the Kingdom of Sardinia and Piedmont in Northern and Central Italy. The military exploits and bravado of Giuseppi Garabaldi (d. 1882) secured the Kingdom of the two Sicilies in Southern Italy and Sicily. These areas were then united in 1861 under the constitutional monarchy of Victor Emmanuel II (d. 1878) as a cooperative figurehead. These activities and achievements between 1859 and 1861—when Italy gained independence from Austria and unification in all but a few areas (soon to be won over)—were expanded in the 1860s after Cavour's death. A culmination was reached in 1870–1871 with the taking of Rome and its establishment as the capital city of the new unified nation-state (or Kingdom) in Italy. The later, sterner brand of nationalism or nationalization under Cavour and Garibaldi has been variously seen by historians as either diverging from or building upon the earlier patriotic ideals and aspirations of Giuseppe Mazzini (d. 1872), who prior to 1850 through his group called "Young Italy" played a formative role.

The Italian national state in the second half of the nineteenth century, like the contemporaneous one in Germany, has not heretofore been adequately seen to have its foundation in legislation. The legal and governmental structures of the Italian state have, as to be expected, been extensively treated. But the focal point of public legislation has not yet received the full direct attention it deserves in relation to the state itself. There is neither space nor need here to detail the Italian parallels to our fuller story on Germany. It is sufficient to point the way to further investigations.

There is need for a new post-Cavourian study that would circumvent the kinds of obscuring "isms" long associated with Bismarckian Germany. Having been Prime Minister of the Kingdom of Sardinia and Piedmont (1852–1861), Cavour was deceased within three months after the main phase of Italian unification was reached in 1861, that is, long before Italian unification was completed in 1870–1871. Many historians have studied the period before 1870–1871 as the time Italy was first *becoming* a modern nation-state, while the era from then to 1915 marked Italy's development *as* a nation-state. The vast and complicated subject of Italy's developing unification of law and legislation in a new national state *after* Cavour in the post-1861 or post-1871 periods needs to be better understood than it has been in relation to the problem of the state.

The case of Italy thus differs in certain respects from that of Germany. The leadership of Bismarck as Chancellor of the new nation-state of Germany created in 1871 continued on thereafter for two decades. Historians have been able to gain a handle on the complexity of German developments by seizing on the pivotal role of Bismarck. At the same time, however, that approach to the new German state has long given rise to obscuring issues of so-called "Bismarckian*ism*" that have diverted attention away from the state itself. Such difficulty can be better avoided when one turns to the post-Cavourian Italian national state and its legislative format. Nevertheless, other issues such as political realism, power politics, and a host of "isms" associated with Cavour and "Cavour*ism*" have often continued to infuse the historical imagination.

Italy and Germany share a common historiographical pitfall. The modern Italian state after 1861 or 1871 has often been studied through long-range progressions of other "isms" usually associated with nationalism. These extend back in time to Machiavelli or ahead to Mussolini, as in liberalism-to-fascism (or Mazzini-to-Mussolini). Such historiography again typically overlooks the state's legislative foundations. It parallels historiography on the modern German nation-state in trajectories leading from Bismarck to Hitler or from Luther to Bismarck. Indeed, historiographical progressions of nationalism and statism in Italy from Renaissance to *Risorgimento* are no less problematic than those in Germany from Reformation to the Second, or Third, *Reich*.

The central place of legislation in the new Italian nation-state after Cavour revolved around several factors. At first, the laws of Piedmont were extended to other states and territories newly unified in 1861. These efforts were aimed at legal centralization throughout Italy. Beginning decisively in 1865, and continuing into the 1880s and beyond up to the Great War, a series of new legal codes were successively promulgated for the new Italian nation-state. The codes initially bore varying relationships to the earlier French legal codes under Napoleon, upon which they were at points patterned, yet they came to be influenced by the German Historical and Pandectist Schools of law. Thus the new Italian state in the second half of the nineteenth century was founded in part upon legal-legislative codifications promulgated toward its outset, whereas in the parallel case of Germany comparable national codes were not actually enacted until the end of that period. After 1871, extensive public legislation was directed at unifying and reconciling Northern and Southern Italy in such fields as transportation, communication, and education. The legislative activity under the leadership of Depretis, Crispi, Giolitti, and Victor Emmanuel III, stretching on into the next century, is a vast field of inquiry in itself. The initial roles of plebiscites in gaining popular approval and ratification for annexation in many of the newly acquired states and territories of Italy is a further part of this total picture of legislative activity.

The post-1861 form of the new Italian national government was based upon the earlier framework, established by an 1848 *statuto*, for the Kingdom of Sardinia and Piedmont. It revolved around the Parliament (with an elective Chamber and an appointive Senate), the Prime Minister (who was responsible to the Parliament and who had complete authority), and the King (as figurehead). This centralized rather than federal form of government was modeled on the British system. Parliament's function in Italy was typically that of the sovereign legislative body in the new nation-state. In 1861, it was the Italian Parliament that proclaimed the new Kingdom of Italy with Victor Emmanuel as its king. Prior to 1861, Cavour had brought about wide improvements and reforms, institutional and otherwise, for the Kingdom of Sardinia and Piedmont in his capacity as Prime Minister (1852–) under Victor Emmanuel II (1849–). These activities, too, could be studied in the framework of the legislative state and legislative sovereignty.[66]

PART TWO

Modern "Neo-*Isms*" and "Anti–Neo-*Isms*" in Legislative and Other Contexts of Sovereignty and State: 20th-Century Foreground

Chapter VII

The Growth of "Neo-*Isms*"

1. THE 20TH-CENTURY FOREGROUND "FORESHORTENED"

Because of the historical scope of this volume and series on the origins and development of legislative concepts of sovereignty and the state, there is less need here to dwell extensively on contemporary issues in the twentieth century. To do full justice to the broadening stream of complex relevant materials in the twentieth century would require an additional book or two. Fortunately, this difficulty is surmounted by focusing below in Part II on the *early* twentieth century and its continuations of nineteenth-century topics discussed at greater length in Part I. The organizational method employed aims at showing how significantly influenced the twentieth century has been by the nineteenth century in the topics under investigation. Thus it is appropriate to group together—as sections in a single chapter on the growth of neo-"isms" in the early (and mid-) twentieth century—the various extensions of the major "isms" of the nineteenth century treated above at greater length in separate chapters. This marks a new approach.

To borrow a concept from art history, the contemporary twentieth-century foreground, as viewed in Part II, has been "foreshortened." This method sets off in due proportion the earlier historical periods of which that foreground was a culmination, according to present perspec-

re remote historical background in the sixteenth century, pre-modern Machiavellism in state theory, was treated at ..erable length in Book I of this fifth volume. The middle ground of ..ie seventeenth and eighteenth centuries—with regard to the origins and development of modern state theory as expressed in modern major "isms"—was explored in Book II. Now that the nineteenth-century foreground has been surveyed in Part I of the present Book III, the closer twentieth-century foreground can be seen as carrying forward in new ways the ideological traditions of the preceding century. That intellectual debt was far greater than has been commonly recognized: most surveys of the twentieth century accentuate its radically new orientation. Thus an alternate visual metaphor for the present organization might be to say that the more distant historical origins have been "telescoped" or "elongated" at the expense of the contemporary age.

If, in the distant future, these relative relationships between what is considered background, middle ground, and foreground should seem somewhat outmoded or out of balance, the present series will still stand complete in itself. The primary design will remain that of showing the *historical* origins and development of modern state theory in its legislative profile. What is "modern" or "modernity" will undoubtedly continue to be as variable for historians in the future as it has been for them in the twentieth century. Although the cumulative weight of previous volumes has necessarily been on the side of the much older historical origins of modern state theory, ensuing studies will include further perspectives on the contemporary era in America and around the world.

It is essentially the modern legislative models of state and sovereignty in the twentieth century that must be reaffirmed here, as in the case of earlier centuries throughout this series. In the Introduction to our first volume, legislative models of the early twentieth century were brought out in statements by Hans Kelsen, Woodrow Wilson, and others. Contemporary legislative models have been cited along the way as benchmarks in our discussions of historical problems. Hence it suffices below, in the case of the twentieth century, to fasten more succinctly on the legislative components and with less attention than above to surrounding contexts.

In the series of neo-"isms" supplying the organization for this chapter, it is necessary to go immediately to the legislative heart of the matter in a few select cases that are both classic and representative. The first two neo-"isms" (neo-positivism and neo-idealism, as related respectively to neo-Kantianism and neo-Hegelianism) present another classic antithesis of the kind explored in our preceding book (namely, absolutism and constitutionalism, rationalism and empiricism, liberalism and conservatism). Once again, the legislative quality of the state and sovereignty bridges over the ideological divide often separating the two sides of such antitheses in political ideology.

2. ENCORE: THE CONTINUING HOLD OF 19TH-CENTURY "ISMS"

The following overview of early-twentieth-century problems is designed to show the continuing hold of certain nineteenth-century "isms" in political-legal thought on sovereignty and state. The issues to be explored center around the growth of neo-"isms" and anti-neo-"isms" in the early (and mid-) twentieth century. What historians have frequently regarded as radically new systems of thought in the early twentieth century stemmed in many cases from older paradigms, albeit in changed, new forms. Examples include Kelsenism, Leninism, Hitlerism, authoritarianism, and so forth, along with varieties of anti-neo-"isms" in theories of justice and the state.

The present chapter on the early (and mid-) twentieth century takes up—in an order roughly paralleling the sequence of chapters in Part I—the "neo" forms of the major "isms" in political-legal thought of the nineteenth century. Starting with neo-positivism, we proceed to neo-Hegelianism and so forth. As with the "isms" featured above, the neo-"isms" below often center around the dominating paradigmatic influence of key theorists, who are typically the same ones discussed above but now influential in new ways. Hence Leninism can be studied as not merely a radically new Russian form of communism or totalitarianism but also as a form of neo-Marxism, in which the state and sovereignty again contain a legislative core. Likewise, Kelsenism becomes here a "neo" form of Austinianism as well as of Kantianism. The list goes on to include the enduring shaping influence of Hegel, Bentham, and so on in other neo-"isms." Reacting against such neo-"isms" were a variety of corresponding anti-neo-"isms," which in their own ways likewise serve to show the continuing hold of nineteenth-century thought on the early (and mid-) twentieth century in the subjects at hand.

The ongoing impact of nineteenth-century "isms" in political-legal ideology upon historians of the twentieth century was abundantly demonstrated in our Volume IV. There, and in the first book of Volume V, Hegelian paradigms, for instance, were found to be especially powerful in shaping the views of historians in the twentieth century on a wide range of historical theorists of the state such as Plato, Marsilius of Padua, Machiavelli, and Hobbes. Such historians have included Meinecke on Machiavellian reason of state, Elton on the Henrician Tudor revolution in government, and Baron, Pocock, and Trexler on traditions of Renaissance civic humanism. The equally strong ideological impact of positivism was found to be controlling upon influential historians like Mommsen and Ehrenberg on ancient Rome and Greece, respectively. The ideological impact of Marxism on Reformation studies by Blickle and others like him in recent decades was found to shape their historiographical views on the state problem. Bismarckianism and national(-stat)ism, in addition to Hegelianism, was seen to exert a profound influence on Burckhardt's enduring historiographical paradigms on the Italian Renaissance state; these paradigms continued, in turn, to shape innumerable more recent historians like Chabod, Meinecke, and Baron. The frequently encountered historiographical trajectories of Machiavelli-to-Mussolini or Luther-to-Bismarck-to-Hitler, even at the hands of some of the most distinguished historians of the twentieth century, have been typically prompted by lasting nineteenth-century models in political-legal ideology on the state. The legislative core in those models, however, has usually been neglected by scholars, as revealed above in the present book.

These historiographical observations on Volume IV in relation to this book on the nineteenth and twentieth centuries could be readily expanded. Similar observations were made in Book I of the present Volume V with regard to Machiavellism in the Renaissance as viewed by subsequent historians writing under Hegelian and other ideological influences. Book II of Volume V pointed out further strong impacts that nineteenth-century "isms" in political ideology exerted upon twentieth-century historiography dealing with ideas of sovereignty and the state in the seventeenth and eighteenth centuries. Yet Hegelian approaches have not proved satisfactory in historiography on the many key theorists from Hobbes to Burke, as we have seen.

3. "NEO-POSITIV*ISM*" AND "NEO-KANTIAN*ISM*"

The Case of "Kelsen*ism*"

Few theorists of law and the state in the early and mid-twentieth century have been as formative as Hans Kelsen (1881–1973). His theory of the "norms" in two classic works, *General Theory of Law and State* and *Pure Theory of Law,* has commanded wide attention. Evaluations of the place of Kelsen and Kelsenism in the development of ideological "isms" have varied considerably. It is widely recognized that Kelsen combined neo-positivism and neo-Kantianism. Little appreciated is the central role of legislation in Kelsen's concepts of the state and sovereignty, whether as part of or separate from his ideas of "pure law," the "norms," and ideological "isms."

It will first be useful to consider so-called "Kelsen*ism*" in relation to so-called "neo-positiv*ism*" and "neo-Kantian*ism*." Throughout his informative book on neo-positivism in legal science, Virgilio Giorgianni devotes much attention to "Kelsenian" styles of thought. He adopts the standard focus on Kelsen's "pure theory of law," "norms," epistemology, "formal*ism*," and the like in jurisprudential science and logic. There are brief scattered remarks on legislation in terms of logical-scientific discourse but not always pertaining specifically to Kelsen.[1]

In an essay entitled "Kelsenism," which was published in 1947 and remains valid for its period, A. S. de Bustamante y Montoro has aptly proclaimed the monumental significance of the subject. "The School of Vienna," he declares, "is representative of the most important doctrine in the Philosophy of Law of our times. In spite of the lively disputes it has raised, it is the most stable of doctrines, since the more it is combated, the greater is the support it finds among jurists. . . . Kelsen is not merely the center of the School of Vienna, but its central figure. Around him and in the farthest scientific centers of the world a progeny of disciples and followers have sprung up . . ." Concentrating on Kelsen's followers, or what is termed "neo-Kelsen*ism*," the author cites first, in his list of postulates and innovations introduced by Kelsen and his school, "a Kantian conception of the world . . . with special emphasis on the dualism between 'being' (*Sein*) and 'ought to be' (*Sollen*) contrasted from a formal logical viewpoint." Also included are "absolute purity of the juridical method" and "the identity between State and Law." Commenting further on the Kantian element, the author states: "[R]ecent evaluation of Kelsen's thought implies a new emphasis upon the Neo-Kantian sources of the School of Vienna. It is reminiscent of, though does not coincide with, Stammler's conception, according to which Law should be envisaged as an autarchic will, binding in itself and internally efficacious (coercive) but in which the will—surprisingly enough—is not in essence psychological but logical." The followers of Kelsen theorized not only on the primacy of positive law but on historical relativism and on the juridical order as social technique (the latter reminiscent of Jhering on law as the policy of force).[2]

Two more recent surveys of the history of legal philosophy, already utilized above, place neo-positivism along with Kelsenism and neo-Kelsenism at the forefront of later trends of the twentieth century. According to the first survey, in a pivotal chapter devoted to the subject, Kelsen's focus on the logical structure of the norms in his legal system forms a crucial background to the neo-positivism of H. L. A.

Hart, involving issues of realism and formalism.[3] In the second survey, in a final historical chapter, neo-positivism is treated together with existentialism as key divergent trends of twentieth-century legal philosophy. The central figure in neo-positivism here is Hart, as in many other such surveys, by whom Kelsenism and the Austrian model were partly overthrown when dealing with the existence and validity of a logical legal system. Elements of Kantianism and Kelsenism are indicated at various points in this treatment of neo-positivism in the legal philosophy of Hart and others such as Julius Stone.[4] In addition, a survey of the history of philosophy, also utilized above, has two concluding chapters on the twentieth century, dealing in the one with realism and in the other with pragmatism, positivism, and analytic philosophy, again showing in general outline the ongoing significance of positivism or neo-positivism as a philosophical school and trend.[5]

Many other similar surveys could also be cited, giving broader historical perspectives on the continuing significance of positivism and neo-positivism in relation to Kant, Kelsen, Austin, Comte, and others studied above. One secondary account provides below (in the note) a succinct characterization of the relationship of Kelsenism and positivism or neo-positivism to Kantianism or neo-Kantianism. The account prompts further queries on the relation of neo-Hegelianism to this mixture.[6]

Beyond these general parameters, the subject of neo-positivism, in connection with neo-Kelsenism, neo-Kantianism, and the like is vast and complicated. It often interconnects twentieth-century historians and theorists of law and politics. Varieties of neo-positivism are extremely diverse. Although Kelsen and Hart provide pivotal points of reference, the sea of relevant literature by now perhaps engulfs even them. Fortunately, Kelsen here (and below concerning Hart) still supplies the needed frame of reference for present purposes.

Complicating the relation of positivism or neo-positivism to Kelsen and others in the twentieth century has been the shifting intermixtures of historical research and legal-political philosophy. Examples have abounded in the course of our previous studies. The positivistic models of state theory used in Mommsen's studies on ancient Rome have been developed by subsequent medieval historians such as Post, for whom Kelsen's positivistic models were also crucial. These models were blended, in the historical writings of Meinecke and his many followers, with forms of neo-Hegelianism. The historical studies on Bentham conducted by Hart have blended neo-positivism with neo-utilitarianism. In the process of building his own jurisprudential philosophy, Hart has freely conjoined historical and theoretical concerns in arriving at the true "concept of law." Once more, the slippery slopes of all such shifting amorphous "isms" in legal-political theory and historical research on the state must be avoided if the state's legislative peaks are to be reached. Such caution has not heretofore been sufficiently heeded by historians and philosophers, with some unfortunate results.

There can be little doubt that positivism or neo-positivism has become one of the most successful movements in contemporary legal philosophy, combining history and theory in enduring yet shifting mixtures. It has retained its vigor while giving rise to new forms of philosophical realism and inclusionism. These include positivist legal realism and inclusive legal positivism, along with anti-positivist viewpoints. The theories of Kelsen, like those of Austin and many others before him, have become part of a much larger sea of contemporary legal philosophy, expanding beyond them while being invigorated by them. Yet the main focus below will be on Kelsen and his ideas pertaining to the subjects featured in the present studies.[7]

Kelsen's *Law and State* and "Neo-Austinian*ism*"

In the Preface to his *General Theory of Law and State*,[8] Kelsen makes plain his debt to the Analytical School and Austin's *Lectures on Jurisprudence* in particular. This amounts, as it were, to a kind of "neo-Austinian*ism*." Kelsen pays special tribute to Austin's exclusive emphasis on positive law (in the positivist legal tradition). Kelsen seeks above all "a general theory of positive law," which "is always the law of a definite community," through "a comparative analysis of the different positive legal orders." "When this doctrine is called the 'pure theory of law'," he explains, "it is meant that it is being kept free from all the elements foreign to the specific method of a science whose only purpose is the cognition of law, not its formation." The sole specific source or model singled out in Kelsen's Preface for this pure theory is Austin's *Lectures*. "The orientation of the pure theory of law is in principle the same as that of so-called analytical jurisprudence. Like John Austin in his famous *Lectures on Jurisprudence*, the pure theory of law seeks to attain its results exclusively by an analysis of positive law. Every assertion advanced by a science of law must be based on a positive legal order . . ."

At the same time, in his Preface, Kelsen points out key differences with Austin. "[T]he pure theory of law tries to carry on the method of analytical jurisprudence more consistently than Austin and his followers. This is true especially as regards . . . the legal norm . . . and . . . legal right and . . . duty . . ." More specifically:

Austin shares the traditional opinion according to which law and State are two different entities, although he does not go so far as most legal theorists who present the State as the creator of the law, as the power and moral authority behind the law, as the god of the world of law. The pure theory of law . . . shows that the State as a social order must necessarily be identical with the law or, at least, with a specific, a relatively centralized legal order, that is, the national legal order in contradistinction to the international, highly decentralized, legal order.

In keeping with this neo-Austinian positivist approach, Kelsen's Preface further sucinctly indicates the non-political, non-ideological, and non-metaphysical nature of this pure theory of law and state. "Much traditional jurisprudence," Kelsen argues, "is characterized by a tendency to confuse the theory of positive law with political ideologies disguised either as metaphysical speculation about justice or as natural-law doctrines. . . . It is precisely by its anti-theological character that the pure theory of law proves itself a true science of law. . . . Every political ideology has its root in volition, not in cognition; in the emotional, not in the rational . . ." With regard to traditional forms of idealism: "The pure theory of law considers its subject not as a more or less imperfect copy of a transcendental idea. It does not try to comprehend the law as an offspring of justice, as the human child of a divine parent." Removal of the creation of law from subjective political and ideological forces will provide, as he further believes in the Preface, a relevant contemporary remedy:

> The political authority creating the law and, therefore, wishing to conserve it, may doubt whether a purely scientific cognition of its products, free from any political ideology, is desirable. . . . The postulate of complete separation of jurisprudence from politics cannot sincerely be questioned if there is to be anything like a science of law. . . . [T]here is [heretofore] still no influence to counteract . . . those residing in power . . . [through] a political ideology. . . . [O]ur time . . . 'is out of joint.' . . . The ideal of an objective science of law and State . . . [deserves] recognition . . .

It need not detain us here that Kelsen's critics have charged that this pure theory is unattainable because it is too formalistic and extremist, that it lays a foundation for the types of power states it seeks to avoid. More noteworthy is that his ideas on law and state represent various forms of ideological "isms" or neo-"isms" needing to be "deconstructed" and reduced to their legislative basis.

The above kinds of approaches are greatly elaborated upon in Part One on "The Law" in Kelsen's *Law and State*. His chapters (I–XII) deal in turn with "The Concept of Law" (later adopted as the title of Hart's famous book), "The Sanction," "The Delict," "The Legal Duty," "The Legal Personality," "The Legal Right," "Competence (Legal Capacity)," "Imputation (Imputability)," "The Legal Person," "The Legal Order," "The Hierarchy of the Norms," and "Normative and Sociological Jurisprudence." The first nine of these chapters concern what Kelsen calls "Nomostatics," the last three dealing with "Nomodynamics."

In his first chapter of Part One, Kelsen in *Law and State* sets forth various basic premises. "Law," he says, "is an order of human behavior. An 'order' is a system of rules. Law is not, as is sometimes said, a rule. It is a set of rules having the kind of unity we understand by a system." In rejecting the traditional dualism between positive and natural law, concentrating instead on the former, Kelsen declares: "Justice is an irrational ideal. However indispensable it may be for volition and action of men, it is not subject to cognition." He discusses "law as a coercive order." "The doctrine according to which coercion is an essential element of law is very often disputed, especially from a sociological point of view." The norms are treated in connection with Austin's commands. As part of his discussion that "[t]he element of 'coercion' . . . is essential to law" and that "the validity . . . of law" concerns "the specific existence of norms," Kelsen turns to Austin in explaining "the nature of a norm." "[L]et us provisionally assume that a norm is a command. This is how Austin characterizes law. He says: 'Every *law or rule* . . . is a *command*'. . . . On closer analysis, however, it is apparent that rules of law are 'commands' only in a very vague sense." Kelsen has said that "[r]ules of law, if valid, are norms," but he goes on to say that "not every command is a valid norm." In such ways, then, Kelsen places more value on "validity" as distinct, say, from Bentham's emphasis on "utility." Validity, for Kelsen, is found more in relation to coercion and duty (or "ought") with respect to the law or norms than in the actual command of the legislator's will expressed in positive law, as in Austin. Nevertheless, Kelsen borrows much from Austin, sometimes more than he acknowledges, and goes on to propound the theory of norms in connection with legislation.[9]

In Chapter IV of Part One in *Law and State*, Kelsen expounds at length on Austin's distinction between primary and secondary duties. "One of the main shortcomings of Austin's theory," according to Kelsen, "is the lack of clear insight into the secondary character of the norm, which stipulates the behavior of the subjects intended by the legal order. . . . In Austin's command there is no room for the sanction. And yet it is only by means of the sanction that the command is obligating. Austin's 'command' is that auxiliary concept which above has been designated as 'secondary norm.' . . ." Furthermore, "Austin is forced to introduce secondary or sanctioning commands, disguised as 'rights and duties.' However, the distinction between primary and secondary (or sanctioning) rights and duties is incompatible with his original position."[10] Such observations are further elaborated at length by Kelsen in Chapter V with regard to Austin's concept of duty: "The concept of duty developed here is the concept which Austin's analytical theory aimed at but never quite succeeded in reaching. . . . The contradictions in Austin's theory are ultimately due to his adherence to the notion of a command and his failure to reach the concept of an impersonal norm."[11]

Kelsen on Legislation

A short section of Part One in *Law and State*, under the heading "The Will of the Legislator," appertains to Kelsen's disquisitions (already cited) where he distinguishes himself from Austin. Here Kelsen further disposes of the element of "command." Command in the Austinian sense appears here to be linked with the "will" as emphasized by Hegelians. However, one might argue that the outcome for Kelsen amounts to something similar. By stressing the coercive aspect of the norms with respect to the "ought," and by making the norms controlling over laws as well as customs, Kelsen seems in ways to substitute one form of imperative for another in matters of legislation.

> If we designate a statute, decided upon by a parliament in the forms prescribed by the constitution, as a "command" or, what amounts to the same thing, as the "will" of the legislator, then a "command" in this sense has hardly anything in common with a command properly so called. A statute owing its existence to a parliamentary decision obviously first begins to exist at a moment when the decision has already been made and when—supposing the decision to be the expression of a will—no will is any longer there. Having passed the statute, the members of parliament turn to other questions and cease to will the contents of the law, if ever they entertained any such will. . . .

> The fictitious character of the common saying that a rule of law is a command is still more evident when we consider customary law. . . .
>
> Whatever may be our theory about the law-creating facts with respect to customary law, we shall never be able to contend that it is the "will" or "command" of those people whose actual conduct constitutes the custom. . . .
>
> When laws are described as "commands" or expressions of the "will" of the legislator, and when the legal order as such is said to be the "command" or the "will" of the State, this must be understood as a figurative mode of speech. . . .
>
> The comparison between the "ought" of a norm and a command is justified only in a very limited sense. According to Austin, it is the binding force of a law that makes it a "command." That is to say, when calling a law a command we only express the fact of its being a "norm." On this point, there is no difference between a law enacted by a parliament, a contract concluded by two parties, or a testament made by an individual.[12]

The complex relationship between the norms and legislation in Kelsen's *Law and State* is rendered difficult to resolve precisely because of the shifting nature (and dualistic aspects) of what he calls "the hierarchy of the norms." There are, throughout the work, wide varieties or systems of dynamic and static norms, superior and inferior norms, centralized and decentralized norms, general and individual norms, basic norms, stages of norms, and so on, including absolute and relative validity of norms. These legal orders or normative systems operate together within a formalistic legal framework grounded on the national law of a particular state, although the influence of a more abstract metaphysical framework of the Kantians also seems to be evident. Legislation is a critical part of the legal order characterized as a dynamic system of norms. Law here is always positive law, outside all natural and moral law. The creating of positive law and the creating of norms become, within this normative system, the central concern for Kelsen in curious ways that seem to shift the traditional core of legislation. He shifts it somewhat away from the domain of the human lawmaker *per se* and into the operation of the dynamic system of coercive norms, which in the end are controlling over the legislative arenas. Thus characterized, the legislative-like operations of these norms enable Kelsen to broaden his scope of what constitutes human legislation into a variety of other areas including custom, the courts, and private law. The overall effect is to broaden, not to narrow, the scope of legislation, whether in normative or more purely human and positive terms, in the state. The all-absorbing process of law-creating and law-applying boils down, it can be argued, to a different variation on the traditional modern stress on legislation. This seems to be the case notwithstanding Kelsen's revisions of Austin's command-theory of legislation, which was in ways the nineteenth-century culmination of that legislative tradition. The general norms created by positive law as well as by custom and by other means, though explicitly separated by Kelsen from coercive legislative command, seem in other ways to make room for it, as further seen in his Part One.[13]

The subject of legislation in relation to the state and sovereignty is enlarged upon more comprehensively in Part Two of Kelsen's *Law and State*, entitled "The State." Its chapter headings (I–VI) deal, in turn, with the following matters: "The Law and the State," "The Elements of the State," "The Separation of Powers," "Forms of Government: Democracy and Autocracy," "Forms of Organization: Centralization and Decentralization," and "National and International Law." It is within these broad contexts that legislation is frequently considered. That is, legislation is again essentially viewed within the broad, fluid parameters of Kelsen's normative systems concerning positive law of national states but now with more regard to government, sovereignty, and like subjects more traditionally appertaining to the state in political as well as legal terms. Nevertheless, the twin concerns of (national positive) law and the (national) secular state remain fused together as in his Part One, just as law and state are joined together in the main title of his treatise. Since the subject of legislation is more extensive in his Part Two, only selected portions and passages can be studied here (and in the corresponding notes).

After breaking apart the traditional boundaries between public law and private law, while showing that the latter also concerns the state (including in legislative contexts),[14] Kelsen proceeds more extensively to refute the long-standing doctrines of the separation of powers, particularly in connection with the legislative roles that all three branches play in the sovereign state. In considerable detail, Kelsen argues away the supposed "separation" of the legislative branch from the executive and judicial branches. Instead, the latter two become part of the law-applying function, which shares in the law-creating operations of the state that are foremost and most primary. The executive and judicial functions both share in the executing of laws enacted by the legislative power, with which they are closely associated and on which they are, in effect, dependent. (In order of operation, there must first be the enactment of laws before there can be execution of laws either by the executive or the judiciary.) Kelsen's "distinctions," rather than "separations," of the three "powers" tend to expand the central place of legislation in the state as well as in sovereignty. He is, more precisely, concerned with the legislative power as a special aspect of the function of the creation of general norms, that is, by special organs called legislative bodies. At the same time, Kelsen underscores that the created general norms do not differ essentially from legislated positive laws or statutes as promulgated by a legislative body. These laws are, in turn, akin to the other types of laws created by the other two so-called branches (orders of a court, ordinances of an executive, and so forth). Kelsen takes special aim at the U.S. Constitution. Indeed, we may add, his arguments about regulations by myriad bodies in America other than official legislatures—regulations which nevertheless represent legislation according to their own criteria—have a truthful ring for present-day America. Especially because of its treatment in the courts at the hands of judges, customary law becomes, too, a vital part as well as example of the legislative process. Courts create norms as well as, in essence, laws, through decisions and orders. These norms and laws are also applied or executed by the executive power.[15]

As usual, Kelsen's arguments in *Law and State*, here involving the constitution, are highly intricate and are capable of diverse interpretations. His attention to the legislative factor has not received proper notice. In the final analysis, Kelsen radically expands the scope of legislation and the legislative power, which encompasses diverse other functions, at the core of the truly "modern" state. He rejects long-standing claims that only an officially designated legislative body can be the source of legislation in all its varieties and manifestations. In reality, Kelsen points out, a wide spectrum of other bodies are engaged in the legislative process with regard to laws as well as norms. Kelsen's repeated uses of the modifier "so-called" when referring to a wide range of supposedly lesser normative features of his system—including the three powers in a state—cannot disguise or detract from the immense weight he assigns to legislation. Legislation remains crucial for the norms as well as for its own sake with respect to positive law, sovereignty, and the state.

The vast expanse of the subject-matters encompassed by legislation in Part Two of Kelsen's *Law and State* is further evident in his lengthy disquisitions on the forms of government or types of states. He calls this subject the traditional central problem of political theory. Democracy, for instance, is defined and discussed by Kelsen in terms of legislation. The context is largely the creation of norms by a parliament or assembly of the people. Popular initiatives, referendums, and other such popular measures are also included under the broad rubric of legislation as characterizing the modern state; here, too, current practices in present-day America no doubt confirm Kelsen's viewpoint (or, what Woodrow Wilson long ago saw as "the extraordinary scope of legislation in the modern state"—Volume I, Introduction). Not only decentralized states but also centralized states are characterized in these ways by Kelsen with respect to their legal-legislative orders.[16] The complex multi-layered legislative spheres in a federal state are elaborately described by Kelsen.

> Only the degree of decentralization distinguishes a unitary State divided into autonomous provinces from a federal State. And as the federal State is distinguished from a unitary State, so is an international confederacy of States distinguished from a federal State by a higher degree of decentralization only. . . .
> The legal order of a federal State is composed of central norms valid for its entire territory and local norms valid only for portions of this territory, for the territories of the "component (or member) States." The general central norms, the "federal laws," are created by a central legislative organ, the legislature of the "federation," while the general local norms are created by local legislative organs, the legislatures of the component States. This presupposes that in the federal State the material sphere of validity of the legal order, or, in other words, the legislative competence of the State, is divided between one central and several local authorities. On this point there exists a great similarity between the structure of a federal State and that of a unitary State subdivided into autonomous provinces. The broader the competence of the central organs, the competence of the federation, the narrower is the competence of the local organs. . . .[17]

There is much additional material in Part Two of Kelsen's *Law and State* on sovereignty and its relation to topics like legislation. These materials prompt further queries on his relation to Austin's command-theory of sovereignty.[18] Further rich discussions on positive law and legislation are found in Kelsen's voluminous Appendix, along with more perspectives on his relation to Kantianism, Austinianism, and positivism.[19]

The Place of Public Law

Further revealing of this positivistic normative emphasis on positive law in connection with the state and the legal order is Kelsen's other classic work, *Pure Theory of Law*. By "pure theory of law" Kelsen means "a theory of positive law in general, not of a specific legal order," "a science of law (jurisprudence), not legal politics." He seeks "to eliminate . . . everything that is not strictly law," in contradistinction to "the traditional science of law . . . [which] has been mixed with elements of psychology, sociology, ethics, and political theory." Much of this treatise reinvestigates matters earlier treated in *Law and State* but at times with even greater cogency. One such topic is the "traditional" distinction between public and private law, "which is so basic for the systematization of law by modern legal science." This untenable division, supposedly separating the state and individuals, involves "two [purported] methods of creating law."

> [T]he Pure Theory of Law . . . [,] always directed toward the whole of the legal order (the so-called will of the state), sees in the private legal transaction just as much as in an administrative order an act of the state, that is, a fact of law-making attributable to the unity of the legal order. By doing so, the Pure Theory of Law "relativizes" the contrast between private and public law "absolutized" by the traditional science of law. . . . The Pure Theory proves to be a true science by dissolving the ideology connected with the absolutizing of the difference in question. . . . The contrast assumed by traditional legal theory between public and private law clearly displays the fundamental dualism that dominates modern legal science and our entire social thinking: the dualism between state and law. . . . A cognition of the state free of ideology, and hence of metaphysics and mysticism, can grasp its essence. . . .[20]

In retrospect, Kelsen's attempts to deny the central place accorded to public law, in contradistinction to private law, by modern theorists of the state proved as little successful as his efforts to cast aside modern tradition on the separation of powers. It is true that Kelsen's depictions of the comprehensive qualities of legislation, which blur the lines within both sets of distinctions, have proved increasingly apropos in the course of the twentieth century, especially in the United States. Yet the enduring place of both traditional doctrines has never since been seriously challenged, much less replaced. Public law, in particular, has remained the central ingredient of the state in connection with legislation. In fact, historians no less than theorists of the modern state, including those who have adapted Kelsen's models, have mostly retained many traditional sets of distinctions rejected by Kelsen. Still basically accepted is the public-private dichotomy articulated by W. W. Willoughby in his older discussions on "the fundamental concepts of public law." Willoughby's discussions were singled out by Kelsen as typical in their flaws concerning the traditional public-private antithesis in modern theory.[21]

Kelsen himself, perhaps unintentionally, left the door open for the continuing role of the public-private dichotomy (as well as the separation of powers) by pointing to its "relativistic" rather than "absolute" quality. In this regard, Kelsen's "puristic" theories had somewhat greater permanent influence and seem less idiosyncratic. Yet his valuable emphases, as in the passages immediately above, on the centrality of law-making in the state, itself identified with law to the rejection of ideological or mystical arguments, have been neglected by many historians and theorists of the state.

Kelsen's accent on legislation's pervading presence in the state (leaving aside here his unique theorizing about the norms), together with his quest to demystify such issues, was less a break with traditional approaches than he was willing to recognize. Here, without acknowledging it, Kelsen was building on remote precedents going back to Bentham's break with Blackstone. So, too, did Kelsen adopt more from respective concepts of command and will by Austin and Hegel than he recognized.

Even those medieval historians like Gaines Post who have adopted Kelsen's model for predating the modern state and its beginnings to the Middle Ages have identified public law as the cornerstone of the state (as mentioned in the Introduction to our first volume). Some, like Post, have sidestepped Kelsen's handling of the pivotal role of legislation. Others, like Kenneth Pennington, have generalized on Kelsen's emphasis upon norms and so-called "normative" jurisprudence by using it as a device for predating the modern theory of legislation to the Middle Ages. Still others, like Ernst Kantorowicz, have seen in the "mystical" "body" of the medieval state a main element of its supposedly modern or proto-modern form. Many others have continued to read modern ideological perspectives, including Hegelian and Marxist ones, back into medieval (as well as early modern) concepts of the state. At any rate, the dominant element of public law, with or without its legislative characteristics, has tended to emerge in many such studies. The subtitle of Post's well-known book on the state problem, "Public Law and the State . . .", is especially indicative. The state as an abstract and independent "public-thing" (*res-publica*) has long been firmly established, particularly on the sixteenth-century model found in Bodin's *Republic*. Innumerable historians of the medieval and early-modern origins of the modern state have continued to adopt it directly or indirectly, with or without its legislative base, for the state no less than for sovereignty.

Kelsen's preoccupation with his "pure" system of norms, which has remained his greatest legacy, has often diverted attention away from legislation and other aspects of his state theory. Moreover, the topic of public law and legislation is, at times, fragmented in Kelsen's *Law and State* and scattered about or in places only indirectly apparent as a central force. This is another reason why Kelsen's interpreters in the realm of theory and methodology have tended (albeit with some exceptions) to neglect the legislative element. His materials on legislation have been pieced together here at the expense of a fuller consideration of the norms with which they are inextricably bound.[22]

4. "NEO-IDEAL*ISM*" AND "NEO-HEGELIAN*ISM*"

The Revision of "Liberal*ism*"

At the end of Chapter IV above on idealism and Hegelianism in political-legal theory of the state, some essential features of the thought of T. H. Green (d. 1882) and Bernard Bosanquet (d. 1923) in Britain were introduced. It was suggested that Green's idealism bore a close relationship to J. S. Mill's individualism, liberalism, and utilitarianism, whereas the idealism of Green's follower Bosanquet was more closely tied to Hegel's statism and Rousseau's corporatism. Scholarly classifications of "isms" represented in writings by these and other theorists of their period in Britain and elsewhere vary widely, often shading off into one another in shifting ideological patterns.

In general, a new form of British idealism emerged in Green's *Lectures on the Principles of Political Obligation* of 1879–1880 (published posthumously in his collected works and later issued separately with a Preface by Bosanquet). Here Green's attempt to revise the liberalism of Mill and other utilitarians can be styled a kind of "neo-ideal*ism*," with more affinity to the earlier idealism of Kant than to that of Hegel. In distinction, the neo-idealism ascribed to later American writers like Walter Lippmann (as in his *Method of Freedom*, 1934) has sometimes been grouped with the Fascist ideology of Alfredo Rocco (*Political Doctrine of Fascism*, 1925) and Giovanni Gentile (*Philosophic Basis of Fascism*, 1928); they have been depicted as widely divergent avenues in the revolt against democratic liberalism.[23]

In these and other viewpoints on so-called "liberal*ism*" and its revision in "neo" and "anti-neo" forms, that "ism" has become even more contorted than it was in works in and on the eighteenth and early nineteenth centuries. Such "isms" are relative and therefore indeterminate, hence of limited value, but need here to be taken into account.

Bosanquet built in part upon Green's idealist revision of Mill's liberalism. At the same time, the idealist revision of Hegel's ideas of the state in Bosanquet's highly influential *Philosophical Theory of the State* (1899) veered away from various traditions of British liberalism and adapted elements of German neo-idealism. In this combination, Bosanquet set some precedents for later Italian Fascist theories of the state. Instructive in this regard was the extreme and extensive criticism of Bosanquet's work made by Leonard Hobhouse, himself strongly influenced by Green, in his *Metaphysical Theory of the State* (1918), together with Bosanquet's strong lengthy defenses at the beginning of his second and third editions (1910, 1920).

The interrelationships between differing forms of idealism—British and German, neo-Hegelian and neo-Kantian, and so forth—are extremely complicated. Were ensuing ominous developments of political theory in the early twentieth century derived from them? It has sometimes been argued that whereas the neo-Kantians elevated coercive norms in their pure theory of law, the neo-Hegelians exalted the will in their pure theory of power. Both positions could be manipulated through the element of force to serve in the creation of later Fascist totalitarian ideologies. The critics and proponents of those interpretations or teleologies have their points.[24] It should be kept in mind that Hegelianism, like idealism and liberalism more loosely, is susceptible to widely divergent interpretations and applications. These range from principles of democracy and freedom to concepts of socialism or even authoritarianism with varying elements of force.

Under consideration first, then, is the idealist revision or restatement of Mill's liberalism made by Green in his *Lectures on Political Obligation*. This was the most important and influential of the British political tracts on the subject in the last two decades of the nineteenth century prior to Bosanquet's *Theory of State*. In it Green attempted to combine Mill's emphasis on individual liberty with a greater sense of social and political obligation on the part both of the individual and of the state. The individual's realization of self is achieved through, and is nearly inseparable from, the social order to which he belongs. Far from advocating a *laissez-faire* freedom of the economy from government's legislative involvement, Green favored a new, more activist role for the state. His aims blended at points with those of contemporary Fabian socialists. The milder forms of socialist Hegelian thought in Green's work were counterbalanced by the liberal individualism that continued to play its part in a revised manner. Green intended his idealist social morality to counteract the more relativist value-neutral utilitarianism behind Mill's interest in individual liberty. Green's depiction of Mill was in ways too one-sided, however; he neglected Mill's ideas on the role of society and the state—especially with regard to legislation—in contradistinction to the role of individuals. Thus Green subscribed to the mutuality between the individual self and the social good. Government and legislation must be responsive to public opinion, while individuals must look to the public interest. Morals and legislation must be intertwined, a notion partly influenced by Bentham. If this balance was at points more akin to Mill's positions than Green recognized, there is little doubt that Green sided more with the Fabians' socialist agenda. He abandoned the liberals' advocacy of free-market private enterprise in favor of the state's regulation through public legislation. Yet Green's more authoritarian or illiberal elements in line with Hegelianism were not as strong as his follower Bosanquet made them out to be when endeavoring to correct and go beyond Green in those regards.

Green's *Political Obligation:* Legislation

The essential legislative characteristic of sovereignty and the state becomes abundantly apparent in the course of Green's *Lectures on Political Obligation*.[25] Green begins by declaring his main interest to be, on the one hand, the obligation of citizens and subjects to obey the state, the sovereign, and the laws, and, on the other, the justification for a system of rights and obligations binding individuals to each other in these regards. Laws, he goes on to say, are not merely instituted for the purpose of preventing interference with the liberties of individuals. Nor must laws of the state be resisted on the grounds that they interfere with individuals' rights to do whatever they wish. The advance of civilization requires increased involvement and reforms by the state for the sake of improvement. Not absolute natural rights but relativistic moral and social duties through an ideal social or common good that must be realized in actuality is what, for Green, should motivate individuals in relation to one another in society. This stress, from the outset, on the obligations of individuals to the state and its laws, as geared to the end of the common social good, is an obvious shift in emphasis. Green moves away from the utilitarianism and individualism of J. S. Mill and turns toward the idealism and even Platonism of the Hegelians, albeit Green combines both approaches in a new mix.[26]

One of the main focal points for Green in his *Political Obligation* is Rousseau's concept of the General Will. This Green both criticizes and adapts in ways to which Bosanquet will later react pro and con. Rousseau, some say, gave rise to concepts of individual rights apart from social obligation, in opposition to others (a la Hobbes) who ignored the state's obligation to protect individual rights. Both viewpoints are fallacious to Green. Sovereignty for Rousseau, as Green points out, resided, in some vague exalted sense, in the people or state itself, whereas for Locke it had rested largely apart from the actual legislature. The main difficulty in Rousseau's theory is, Green believes, that it did not assign to the sovereign people a clear enough actual legislative power, by which the individual and social good could be promoted and safeguarded through enactments of the state. Rousseau's General Will of the people, operating in its idealized sovereign legislative capacity, tended to be, according to Green, divided or impeded by individual particular interests apart from the general welfare. Green seems ready to give Rousseau the benefit of the doubt by suggesting that Rousseau might have agreed that the General Will of the people was sovereign only *de iure* and allowed for actual *de facto* sovereignty by existing European states. Yet even this argument poses further problems for Green, who includes interesting references to the United States' situation.[27]

In disputing Rousseau's concept of sovereignty (and sovereign legislative power) residing in an indeterminate General Will of the people, Green turns to Austin's more *specific* attribution of sovereignty to a determinate body of one or more persons acting in a clear actual legislative capacity through sovereign commands in enacted positive laws.[28] A stunning series of statements ensues in support of the Austinian approach to legislative sovereignty and the legislative state (beyond what J. S. Mill could have accepted on the state's strong power). Among Green's many noteworthy points (adhering below to his style) is his thoroughgoing subordination of custom and judicial decisions to the all-important sovereign power and prerogative of legislation. It follows that, as in the cases of America and Germany, the local legislative bodies and interests must yield to the sovereign legislative power where there are discrepancies. While using Austin to dispute Rousseau, however, Green also expresses reservations over the state's too powerful role in Austin's theory of sovereignty. Green thereby leaves open the door somewhat to the more muted concepts of sovereignty variously held by Rousseau and Mill.

> If, then, those who adopt the Austinian definition of a sovereign mean no more than that in a thoroughly developed state there must be some determinate person or persons, with whom, in the last resort, lies the recognised power of imposing laws and enforcing their observance, over whom no legal control can be exercised, and that even in the most thorough democracy, where laws are passed in the assembly of the whole people, it is still with determinate persons, viz. a majority of those who meet in the assembly, that this power resides, they are doubt-

less right. So far they only need to be reminded that the thoroughly developed state, as characterised by the existence of such definite sovereignty, is even among civilised people but imperfectly established. It is perfectly established (1) where customary or "common" or "judge-made" law, which does not proceed from any determinate person or persons, is either superseded by express enactments that do proceed from such person or persons, or (as in England) is so frequently trenched upon by statute law that it may fairly be said only to survive upon sufferance, or to be itself virtually enacted by the sovereign legislature; and (2) where no question of right can be raised between local legislatures or authorities and the legislature claiming to be supreme, as in America before the war of secession, and as might perhaps be found to be the case in Germany now, if on certain educational and ecclesiastical matters the imperial legislature came to be at issue with the local legislatures. But though the organisation of the state, even in civilised and independent nations, is not everywhere complete, it no doubt involves the residence with determinate persons, or a body or bodies, of supreme i.e. legally uncontrolled power to make and enforce laws. The term "sovereign" having acquired this definite meaning, Rousseau was misleading his readers when he ascribed sovereignty to the general will. He could only be understood as meaning, and in fact understood himself to mean, that there was no legitimate sovereign except in the most thorough democracy, as just described.

But the Austinians, having found their sovereign, are apt to regard it as a much more important institution than—if it is to be identified with a determinate person or persons—it really is . . .[29]

Generally speaking, on these matters in his *Political Obligation*, Green combines ideas of Austin and Mill in British tradition with concepts of Rousseau as well as Hegel in French and German traditions. Green favors Austin over Rousseau on the location of sovereignty, placing it in a specific rather than "general" body. However, Green broadly associates Rousseau, in a manner perhaps more suggestive of Mill, with the notion that the state's greatest purpose and justification is to guarantee the individual's freedoms, liberties, and rights in society. At the same time, there can be no rights that run counter to the public good, which is one's duty to uphold and which alone is the real criterion of rights. In his own generalized way, Green adapts Rousseau's General Will in the form of a social and political will that combines with a

Hegelian will on the part of the state, through which comes true freedom. Yet Green would part company with Hegel no less than with Austin over the issue of a too powerful state.[30]

Green believes that he is the first theorist to address the issue of political obligation directly and coherently with regard to the individual's rights and duties in relation to society and the state. Previous writers on the origins of individual rights have looked too exclusively, Green contends, to natural law or a kind of free individualism divorced from the social good, on the one hand, and a coercive sovereign power, on the other. They have not properly considered the public welfare in itself as being achieved through a rightly directed sovereign power. Not force but will is the state's bulwark. This will is responsive to the common good of society, without which individuals have no real rights. This public good must ideally be kept above merely private interests. In this way, it provides the essence of public law and legislation. Yet actual circumstances are not always easy to account for in this regard. While conceiving the state, like sovereignty, in legislative contexts, Green underscores that the state is more than merely a coercive sovereign power to which subjects are subordinated, however significant that aspect may be. For the state's real orientation should be to secure the rights of individuals through a proper sense of their belonging to a social whole. "[T]he rights need definition in a general law. When such a general law has been arrived at . . . then the elementary state has been formed." This legislative state, presided over by a legislative sovereign, has as its chief continuing role the safeguarding of rights through public law and legislation. Green recognizes the place of force in the state's origins, but he assigns to the state a larger legislative role aimed at individual rights.[31]

Green's balance between private rights and the state's rights, with the state greatly accentuated in connection with individuals, is evident in the sequence of general headings pertaining to the later sectional paragraphs in his *Political Obligation*. These are, following his "Will, not force, is the basis of the state": "Private rights. The right to life and liberty"; "The right of the state over the individual in war"; "The right of the state to punish"; "The right of the state to promote morality"; and "The right of the state in regard to the family." Thus Green's accentuation of the role of the state, at the outset of his *Political Obligation*, carries over throughout the work.

Bosanquet's *Theory of State:* Legislation

As indicated in its title, Bosanquet's *The Philosophical Theory of the State*[32] singles out for special treatment the problem of the state. His predecessors in the idealist tradition of political philosophy had been much occupied with the state but had not so directly and exclusively highlighted it in their titles. What Bosanquet essentially did was to develop the strains of German political idealism—on the more authoritarian or conservative Hegelian model—that he found in British political idealism a la Green, which was more attuned to British liberal traditions centered around J. S. Mill, whom together with Green Bosanquet sought in part to correct or revise. In fact, few classic works on political thought thus far studied in this series featured the state so pointedly in the title, however prominently the state may have figured in the contents.

Bosanquet makes extensive creative uses of the history of political philosophy when constructing his *Theory of State*. The pre-modern origins of the sovereign state revolving around law and legislation, he strikingly maintains, went back to the ancient Greek city-states, after which ensued long periods of relative darkness. Only in the eighteenth century were the ancient philosophical ideals of the city-state first decisively revived, chiefly by Rousseau, in connection with the newly emergent modern nation-states. Rousseau's seminal contributions formed an intermediate stage between Hobbes and Locke, in the preceding century, and Kant and Hegel, in the next century, while Montesquieu and Vico shared a lesser place of importance in Rousseau's own century. The Sociological School of thought, inaugurated by Comte within the framework of positivism, built on Vico's earlier science of society. Alongside this school, there emerged, in the early nineteenth century, the modern idealist political philosophy of Hegel and his followers, which even more decisively restored ancient idealism and has influenced British thought. However, British writers like Bentham, reducing everything to a command in law and legislation, were disinclined to philosophical theorizing on the state, as also was J. S. Mill. Mill's resistance to governmental intervention impinged on many areas that in fact warrant it, according to Bosanquet. Mill's own writings, asserts Bosanquet, are at times in agreement not only with Victorian programs of social legislation but also with Rousseau's concept of "forcing" people to be free; Mill thereby is somewhat at odds with his own principles of individual liberty. Bosanquet addresses a range of issues concerning political obligation and self-government in relation to Green and Mill.[33]

Bosanquet's stated main purpose in *Theory of State* is to explain and adapt Rousseau's interwoven ideas of the General Will, sovereignty, the state, and public personality, which, he says, all tend to the justification of force. According to Bosanquet, Rousseau's General Will has no real existence but operates as a principle, out of which must now be fashioned a *"real* will." Rousseau's General Will, or will "in itself," as distinct from the "will of all," is identical with sovereignty. The only true laws are those issued by acts of sovereignty in conformity with the General Will or general interest. This General Will, in Bosanquet's view, not only recalls the popular sovereignty of the Greek city-states. It also expresses the essential core of the modern nation-states, in which the common good must override the private interests of individuals who compose it. Bosanquet believes that Rousseau's General Will, or will "in itself" as the *"real* will," is most fruitfully approached in connection with Rousseau's concepts of the Legislator (or sovereign) and legislation. Bosanquet voices basic agreement with Rousseau on the centrality of the role of legislators and legisation in human history concerning the topics at hand.[34]

The two culminating chapters of Bosanquet's *Theory of State* deal with the modern state conceived by Hegel, along with Kant and Fichte, as grounded on Rousseau's theories. These chapters (IX–X) are indicatively entitled "Rousseau's Theory as Applied to the Modern State: Kant, Fichte, Hegel" and "The Analysis of a Modern State. Hegel's 'Philosophy of Right'." Throughout these two chapters, there are numerous crucial contexts of legislation in regard to sovereignty and the state, that is, as derived from that triad of German idealists impacted by Rousseau (not least on the "will").

In distinction to Plato's weaker characterizations of the (ancient) state lie Hegel's stronger articulations of the modern state, according to Bosanquet in *Theory of State*. Hegel, he insists, sought to expand the paradigm of the ancient state into a more powerful modern model for the national state. For Hegel, Bosanquet continues, the modern nation-state has its own external (as well as inner) necessity in using forceful regulations for promoting the public good and for intervening in private individual affairs. As the incarnate "real" will, the state is a sovereign whole that cannot be divided in its legislative, executive, and judicial functions, as Bosanquet indicates was recognized by Rousseau and more acutely by Hegel. Nor can the sovereignty of the people be separated from the sovereignty of the state, explains Bosanquet, who criticizes the American system of divided powers, or checks and balances. So, too, does he criticize the greater powers of the U.S. Presidency, in contradistinction to the more ideal, limited executive powers conceived by Hegel as well as by Rousseau. As a prototype for Hegel and for Bosanquet himself, Rousseau's concept of the General Will, emphasizes Bosanquet, was based on a system of law and legislation. Bosanquet feels that his own pronouncements on the state's "automatic machinery" (an interesting term in view of our term "machinery" in diagrams in Volume IV to describe the state as distinct from the nation and nationalism) build upon precedents established by both Hegel and Rousseau. Bosanquet's treatment of that machinery in the state theories of Hegel and Rousseau tends to center around the legislative power and the system of law and legislation instituted by it.[35]

Toward "Totalitarian*ism*"?

There is an ominous side to Bosanquet's preoccupation, in his *Theory of State*, with the complete "identity" or identification of the individual with the "will" of the state, particularly as expressed in its law. For the individual has no "real" "self" "outside" the state and society.[36] His uncompromising uses of the word "total" can seem disturbing in light of later events. In a chapter on "the end of the state" and "limit of state action," Bosanquet rejects completely any distinction between the individual and society or the state. He drives home the "totality" of "the social or political whole," which provides the "ultimate end" for individuals. This "whole" is a "single web." Open to question, therefore, is how much real "limit" Bosanquet assigns to "state action."[37]

Any doubts about what Bosanquet here has in mind are dispelled by his ensuing ascriptions of full-fledged "absolute power" and "force" to the state and society over their individual members. There can be "no true ideal" attained by limiting the state's "individuality," to which the individual members of society are subordinated, and the state's "absolute physical power." Moreover, the state is "always" typified by the use of "force," although Bosanquet occasionally adds that this is a "lawfully exercising force." Clearly here, "will" means force to Bosanquet. Thus, whereas Green believed that will is superior to force, Bosanquet renders force superior to will by equating them in this manner. Bosanquet's example of taxation with which to illustrate the nature of the state's necessary power of compulsion cannot disguise the ultimate end, that is, the total power-state, toward which his ideas are aiming (particularly in the hands of others to follow). His assurances that the state's (lawful?) "physical force" does not entail "actual" (brute?) physical force do not change the directions where such a theory seems to be heading (whether or not as "perversion" of it).[38]

The strong advocacy of the necessity of state force and power in Bosanquet's *Theory of State* involves curious further uses of Rousseau's *Social Contract*. On the one hand, Bosanquet asserts that his concepts of state action are roughly identical to Rousseau's principles of the sovereign General Will and of "forcing men to be free."[39] Likewise, the idealist political philosophy of the modern state expounded by Hegel along with Fichte and Kant was based primarily on Rousseau's concept of freedom, which itself was modeled on the ancient ideals of the Greek city-state.[40] On the other hand, following the apparent lead of Hegel, Bosanquet rejects Rousseau's ideas of social contract because the state is an "imperative necessity" and cannot be bound by "mere agreement of certain free persons." Such a social contract involves an excessively harsh and potentially abusive "absolute rule" of law comparable to Austin's command-theory of positive law. (The acceptance of Austin's theory by Green has been surpassed elsewhere by Bosanquet in this doctrine of force.) Interestingly, Bosanquet says that such a view of law would lead to confusion of public functions with private property, as also found in the Middle Ages.[41]

What, then, was the historical place of Bosanquet's uses of Rousseau's General Will—in conjunction with Hegel's concept of the will—to justify the state's "total" (lawful) force? Some historians (rightly or wrongly) believe that Rousseau's doctrine of forcing people to be free— in the name of the sovereignty of the General Will of the people and the state—played a significant part in the distant ideological origins of modern totalitarianism. They have pointed to related precedents in the "tyranny of the majority" (and minority) associated with Robespierre's appropriations of Rousseau's ideas during the Reign of Terror. The tendency toward authoritarianism, if not totalitarianism, has been observed by numerous historians in Hegel's concepts of the state as well as of freedom. To be sure, in his *Theory of State*, Bosanquet did not have the advantages of historical hindsight on the later course taken by Fascist theories of totalitarianism in Italy and Germany. Nevertheless, he would no doubt have denied philosophical culpability for those later doctrines of the power state. Certainly he rejected Hobhouse's criticisms of his work that were perhaps pointing it in that direction, although Hobhouse himself lacked later historical hindsight in his rebuttal.

A distinction can here be drawn. There has been unsettled debate over the influence of the Hegelian idealist tradition—in British, Italian, and German writers of Bosanquet's era—upon totalitarian ideology in Hitler's Nazi Germany. A clearer affirmative verdict has been reached in the case of Mussolini's Fascist Italy. All such later uses of Hegelianism were no doubt perversions of Hegel's original ideas (and those of Rousseau as well).

Even so, the final estimation of Bosanquet's place in this line of development must remain here an open question. Is Bosanquet's neo-Hegelian distinction between lawful (absolute physical) force and illegitimate (brute) force subject to the same charge advanced by critics of the neo-positivist and neo-Austinian doctrines of theorists like Kelsen— namely, that the legal (and legislative) system can be reduced to a formalism without real relation to individual rights?

The Question Answered: Hobhouse and Gentile

The question as to whether the idealist Hegelian tradition that resulted at the turn of the century in Bosanquet's *Theory of State* paved the way for later totalitarian ideology of the state could be answered strongly in the affirmative through the attacks against Bosanquet by L. T. Hobhouse. It is not hard to imagine what Hobhouse's response would have been if his *The Metaphysical Theory of the State*, published in 1918 (London) at the end of World War I, had appeared in the next decade. His condemnations therein of the authoritarian proclivities of both Bosanquet and Hegel would have found even more fertile grounds for reproach with the emergence of the Fascist totalitarian state under Mussolini, not to mention Hitler's more extreme totalitarian state in Nazi Germany. Still, Hobhouse saw in Bosanquet's Hegelian state the ideological seeds for the evils then being wrought by the European power states, particularly Germany, in the Great War.

The Preface of Hobhouse's *Metaphysical Theory* sets the tone: "In the bombing of London [in a World War I episode,] I had just witnessed the visible and tangible outcome of a false and wicked doctrine, the foundations of which lay, as I believe, in the book [by Hegel] before me. . . . With that work began the . . . influences which have sapped the rational humanitarianism of the eighteenth and nineteenth centuries, and in the Hegelian theory of the god-state all that I had witnessed lay implicit."[42] These direct attacks on the idealist Hegelian tradition, which became in Bosanquet's treatment the immediate background to early-twentieth-century authoritarian ideology, are developed at greater length in the first of Hobhouse's five lectures or chapters. There, Hobhouse traces the German militaristic attitudes of the first world war back to the age of Bismarck, which in turn built upon the illiberal intellectual traditions of the power state cognized by Hegel. The disastrous Hegelian idealist identification of individual freedom with the law and authority of the state gained, shows Hobhouse, wide ascendancy in Britain as well as Germany and France, although the political philosophy of Green had, for Hobhouse, some redeeming features.

> Such, then, is the spirit of the metaphysical theory of society which I propose to examine in the shape given to it by its founder, Hegel, and his most modern and most faithful exponent, Dr. Bosanquet. This theory is commonly spoken of as idealism, but it is in point of fact a much more subtle and dangerous enemy to the ideal than any brute denial of idealism emanating from a one-sided science. . . . But elsewhere Dr. Bosanquet defines the state as that society "which is habitually

recognized as a unit lawfully exercising force," a definition which would apply to the rule of the Czar or Sultan. . . .

In older days we passed by the Hegelian exaltation of the state as the rhapsodical utterances of a metaphysical dreamer. It was a mistake. The whole conception is deeply interwoven with the most sinister developments in the history of Europe. It is fashionable to conceive German militarism as a product of the reaction against a beautiful sentimental idealism that reigned in the pre-Bismarckian era. Nothing could be more false. The political reaction began with Hegel, whose school has from first to last provided by far the most serious opposition to the democratic and humanitarian conceptions emanating from eighteenth-century France, sixteenth-century Holland and seventeenth-century England. It was the Hegelian conception of the state which was designed to turn the edge of the principle of freedom by identifying freedom with law. . . .

The direct connection between Bismarckian ethics and Hegelian teaching was ably worked out many years ago by a close student of the relations of ideas and facts in the political sphere, Mr. William Clark, but it is not in Germany alone that the Hegelian influence has profoundly affected the course of thought in one form or another. It has permeated the British world, discrediting the principles upon which liberal progress has been founded and in particular depreciating all that British and French thinkers have contributed. . . . [I]n the hands of T. H. Green the Hegelian theory was for a time transmuted into a philosophy of social idealism, a variant which has a value of its own and does not lack distinguished living disciples. But as a fashionable academic philosophy genuine Hegelianism has revived, and the doctrine of the state as an incarnation of the Absolute . . . has in many quarters achieved the position of an academic orthodoxy. . . . It combats the spirit of freedom . . .[43]

When attacking Bosanquet's Hegelian theory of the state, on a wide range of detailed points, Hobhouse is, in his *Metaphysical Theory*, even more devastating in his analyses of Hegel. Freedom according to Hegel, says Hobhouse, involved not restraint by the state but obedience to its will and law.[44] Not even Hegel, much less his chief British disciple in absolutist state theory, Bosanquet, went as far as Green did in recognizing a balance between the good of the state and the welfare of individuals. Bosanquet's idealist "metaphysical theory of the state" stressed allegiance to the general or real will of the state as the true realization of individual freedom. That theory was founded on Hegel's formulation of the subject, as Hobhouse points out, although the element of force arose with renewed vigor for Bosanquet.[45]

Along with Hegel's deification of the state went his glorification of war as a vital part of the state's activity, according to Hobhouse. Bosanquet's idealist development of this viewpoint provides, for Hobhouse, a direct ideological link to the first world war. War for Hegel, declares Hobhouse, carried many beneficial advantages. It instills discipline, loyalty, obedience, sacrifice, and morality in the individual citizens of the sovereign god-state. For Hegel, says Hobhouse, the ideals of peace pursued by Kant were to be abandoned, while each state is a self-justified "totality" within itself in relation to other states. Insists Hobhouse, the Hegelian militaristic state, adopted by Bosanquet, is the original ideological germ leading to Europe's suffering in the Great War. Bosanquet's own "metaphysical" formulations of the state's real self and absolute power is, to Hobhouse, a dangerous if hidden justification of the injustices of war, including murder. The Hegelian idealists led by Bosanquet have abandoned philosophy's traditional restraining impulses and thereby prepared the way for the international anarchy of the current wartime era.[46]

Hobhouse's strong ideological denunciations of Hegel and his most extreme and well-known modern disciple, Bosanquet, in the turbulent aftermath of World War I, are balanced by his wider historical assessments, lending credence to his *Metaphysical Theory*. Although rejecting the extremist elements in the state theory of Bosanquet and its originator, Hegel, Hobhouse makes some clear distinctions between Bosanquet and Green. Hobhouse finds Green's *Political Obligation* praiseworthy in some respects, especially in its departures from Hegel through recognition of citizens as individuals in the state. Hobhouse seeks to be fair to those whose ideas have derived directly from Green rather than from Hegel. Moreover, German culpability in the Great War was multifactorial. Historical forces and ideologies going back to the eras of Bismarck and Hegel, conjoined with newer and starker biological and racial outlooks, lay behind the German clamor for war. Hegel was not the seeker after naked power that Treitschke became, and he retained a certain positive idealism. Yet Hegel, Hobhouse still feels, set the framework for later even more dangerous idealizations of the state that also lay behind the recent bloody battlefields of Europe.[47]

In the Preface to his third (reprinted) edition of *Theory of State* in 1920, two years after Hobhouse's attack against it, Bosanquet sought to counterrefute Hobhouse. He paid particular attention to the question of responsibility for the ideological background to the first world war. "In the twenty years since the first publication of this book every theory of the state has been severely tested. Criticism, suggested by historical events, has attacked the writer's views among others as attributing an unreal uniqueness and a fictitious sovereignty to the state. . . . [T]he original intention of the book was neither to magnify the State nor to deny it, but to explain how its functions flow from its nature. . . . A cry has [recently] arisen for the limitations of sovereignty . . ." Already in his Introduction to the second (reprinted) edition of 1910, Bosanquet was prompted to defend his work at length from numerous critics who had argued that it was too narrow, too rigid, too negative, and too intellectual. To that Introduction Bosanquet added a section in the third edition on "How the Theory Stands in 1919." By then, a host of other critics or opponents had arisen owing to the tumult and implications of the war years. How well Bosanquet answered criticism that his abstract absolutist metaphysical theory of state was the antithesis of a liberal and practical philosophy of the state cannot be addressed here. In light of the experiences of the ensuing decades, it would seem that critics like Hobhouse had some legitimate, irrefutable points.[48]

It has long been understood that the ideology of the authoritarian or totalitarian state conceived by Mussolini and his ideologues for Fascist Italy was deeply indebted to the idealist Hegelian theories of the state adopted in the 1920s by Giovanni Gentile (1875–1944) and others. It has often been pointed out that—as a chief intellectual exponent of this ideology as well as a notable historian and theorist of philosophy and law—Gentile adulterated the Hegelian idealist tradition to serve these purposes. This point was recognized as well by Gentile's older colleague in Italian Hegelianism, the great Benedetto Croce, who became an ardent opponent of Fascism.

What has not been sufficiently underscored by historians is the degree to which the ideology of totalitarianism—which has usually been taken as one of the most unique revolutionary phenomena of the early and mid-twentieth century—was in its ideological origins an extension of the myriad neo-"isms" that were carried over from the nineteenth century. Chief among these forms of neo-"isms" was neo-Hegelianism or neo-idealism, with its abandonment of traditional liberalism for the sake of the rigidly structured corporate state. Others included neo-socialism and neo-nationalism.

Clearly, the complex and confused intellectual background to Italian (not to mention German) Fascism is very broad, encompassing German as well as British precedents. These precedents include ideas put forth by Nietzsche, Schopenhauer, Spengler, Bosanquet, Fichte, and many others, all themselves part of nineteenth-century traditions of thought. The upheavals of the war years brought not only a break with Europe's intellectual past, but renewed intensified admixtures of it in the search for new solutions to new problems. The background to totalitarianism has been much debated. Among the vast works on it are the older classic historical treatments in Hannah Arendt's *Origins of Totalitarianism* and Erich Fromm's *Escape from Freedom*. Recent research has explored the relationships between Italian and German varieties of Fascism with respect to Hegelianism—another complicated issue. The typologies and background of Italian totalitarian ideologies have been shown to be more complicated than previously understood (and more significant than Arendt believed in relation to the more "total" German and Russian models). Yet the present approach is necessarily very restricted.[49]

Gentile's *What Is Fascism* [?] (1925) was indebted to Italian as well as British and other forms of Hegelianism, with special regard to Bosanquet and the use of force. Part One presents an overview and deals with liberty and liberalism. Part Two, on "Fascism and Liberalism," begins with Gentile's own early liberalism and proceeds to Mussolini's March on Rome. Gentile then takes up, in turn, such subjects as the "Italian liberal tradition," "the liberalism of B. Croce," "From liberalism to Fascism," and "the liberalism of Cavour." Part Three concerns constitutional reforms with regard to Fascism. An Appendix is on a question of "realism and fatalism." This Fascist revolt against democratic liberalism had roots in the idealist revision of liberalism by Bosanquet and others, but it took on a far more ominous form in the wake of World War I. On the whole, Gentile's relatively superficial philosophical "polemics" are somewhat *sui generis*.[50]

The Fascist "Legal"-Legislative State

In an article published in the noted American journal *Foreign Affairs* in 1928 and entitled "The Philosophical Basis of Fascism,"[51] Gentile raised a number of pertinent issues—philosophical, political, and historical—on the concept and reality of the Italian Fascist state. There he commented upon the Fascist idealistic revival of Mazzinianism and the *Risorgimento*, the corporate nature of the new Fascist state, the rejection of liberal ideas of individualism and freedom, the state itself as the source of rights and freedom, the new idealism that enthrones the state and the individual's absorption in it for his own advantage, and much more. The "neo-idealism" of recent decades, asserts Gentile, presents a refreshing rejection of the materialistic positivism current in the second half of the nineteenth century. The latter, with its parliamentary and legalistic orientation, is termed "anti-idealistic."

Not only, according to Gentile, did Mussolini correctly see the Italians' need for idealistic and spiritual renewal through war; but

Mussolini also saw the need for a new Fascist legal-legislative state. Gentile describes the new state's birth as follows:

> More than anyone else he [Mussolini] had come to feel the necessity of a State which would be a State, of a law which would be respected as law, of an authority capable of exacting obedience but at the same time able to give indisputable evidence of its worthiness so to act. The four years between 1919 and 1923 were characterized by the development of the Fascist revolution. . . . The Fascist "squads" were really the forces of a State not yet born but on the way to being. . . . [They] transgressed the law of the old régime because it was determined [necessary] to suppress that régime as incompatible with the national State to which Fascism was aspiring. The March on Rome was not the beginning[;] it was the end of that phase of the revolution; because, with Mussolini's advent to power, Fascism entered the sphere of legality. . . . Fascism was no longer at war with the State; it *was* the State, looking about for the organization which would realize Fascism as a concept of State.[52]

Gentile's concept of the Italian Fascist state based on law and legislation takes its source and authority from the will of the people or citizens as expressed through their leader (*il duce*). The Italian Fascist state is a national state, in obedience to which lies the true freedom of its citizens. But it is to be distinguished, as a conscious creation by the citizens and their leader, from traditional aristocratic nationalistic states, which were conceived as arising somehow from preexisting conditions of nature. Not being an abstract utopian philosophy, Fascism, argues Gentile, is rather a practical and popularly based system of state in which force and freedom are inseparable. "The politic of Fascism revolves wholly about the concept of the national State." Although nationalism has points of contact with Fascism, its identification of the state with the nation, as something above and outside the will of individuals, is contrary to the Fascist state, which is the true "people's state" or "democratic State *par excellence.*"

Here Gentile has arrived at the basic fundamentals of the totalitarian state in Fascist Italy. "The Fascist State . . . exists only as . . . the citizen causes it to exist. Its formation therefore is the formation of a consciousness of it in individuals, in the masses. Hence the need of the Party, and of all the instruments of propaganda and education which Fascism uses to make the thought and will of the *Duce* the thought and will of the masses." Gentile again emphasizes that "force" and freedom are intertwined, that "[t]he authority of the State is absolute," and that "the State is a wholly spiritual creation." In addition, the "Fascist corporative State" is superior to and "freer than the old [early] liberal State." Indeed, "[t]oward it [Fascist "reform"] nationalism, . . . and even liberalism itself, were already tending in the [recent] past." By now, the partial background to Fascism represented in works by Bosanquet and others has become more fully evident.[53]

A generalized understanding of the relations of the state to law and legislation may be gleaned from Gentile's *The Fundamentals of the Philosophy of Law*.[54] This work delves, more deeply than might be expected because of the foregoing hard-line Fascist dogma, into the historical legal philosophy of Spinoza, Rousseau, Kant, Fichte, Hegel, and others. Subjects interesting Gentile include questions of force, will, authority, liberty, coercion, society, the individual, reality, objectivity, subjectivity, idealism, anti-idealism, materialism, and so forth. The "formalism" of Kant and the state theory of Hegel are also among the topics considered by Gentile.

Whereas Gentile was an idealist philosopher of international repute, who had been a liberal but became Mussolini's Minister of Education, his fellow Fascist ideologue Alfredo Rocco (1875–1935) was a jurist and a professor of law who had been an ardent nationalist. Under Mussolini Rocco became president of the Chamber of Deputies and Minister of Justice. Rocco's *The Political Doctrine of Fascism* (1925)[55] grouped liberal-democratic-socialist concepts of the state together as the antithesis of the Fascist state. There are numerous contextual references to the history of political-legal thought from the sixteenth through nineteenth centuries. Rocco, like Gentile, became not only an early avid follower of Mussolini but also another chief supplier for him of Fascist ideas of the state.

Sovereignty, according to Rocco's *Doctrine of Fascism*, is a cornerstone of the Italian Fascist state. "The state, if it exists for all, must be governed by all, and not by a small minority; if the state is for the people, sovereignty must reside in the people . . . [and] equality must be added [to liberty] . . ." Rocco goes so far as to suggest that Italian Fascism has the truest concept of sovereignty because it is the theory that is truly founded on a legal concept of the state. "Democracy rests sovereignty in the people, that is to say, in the mass of human beings. Fascism discovers sovereignty to be inherent in society when it is juridically organized as a state."[56]

This theory of sovereignty is predicated upon "public" purposes. Rocco finds in the Italian Fascist state the only real way to preserve "public order," which the socialist states have failed to achieve. Only through this state can "state justice" be promoted "both within and without the law courts," something that he believes was not achieved in Italy prior to Fascism. Of the new state Rocco declares: "Fascism replaces therefore the old atomistic and mechanical state theory with an organic and historic concept. . . . For Liberalism, the individual is the end and society the means. . . . For Fascism, society is the end, individuals the means. . . . The state therefore guards and protects the welfare and development of individuals . . . for . . . [the sake] of society as a whole." Consistent with these views is the "public" nature of sovereignty in relation to the state: "Fascism insists that the government be entrusted to men capable of rising above their own private interests and of realizing the aspirations of the social collectivity. . . . Fascism therefore . . . rejects the dogma of popular sovereignty and substitutes for it that of state sovereignty . . ." Rocco goes so far as to assert that "the great mass of citizens . . . [lack] the capacity to ignore individual private interests . . . [and] are not to be allowed to exercise any influence on the life of the state." At the same time, however, socialism errs by rejecting private property and capital, because the actual effect is to destroy capital itself, thereby potentially ruining the state.[57]

Some of the strongest statements along the above lines on the elements of the Italian Fascist state can be found in the writings and speeches of Mussolini himself. In particular, his *The Political and Social Doctrine of Fascism* (1932) contains some noteworthy viewpoints on Hegel and Germany as regards the state and nation. Differences between Italian and German brands of so-called "totalitarian*ism*" are perhaps to some extent moot points.[58]

The Rehabilitated Hegel Today

In some ways, we may say that Hegel has been "rehabilitated" in contemporary theory and historiography on politics, philosophy, and law. The harsh verdicts on Hegel's authoritarianism made by Hobhouse in his refutation of Bosanquet—which were seemingly justified in light of subsequent Fascist ideas of state—were not the end or even the center of the story of the revival of Hegel in the twentieth century. It is true that respected historians of the early twentieth century such as Meinecke added in more moderate ways to the ominously authoritarian depictions of Hegel emerging during that period. Meinecke's enormous influence on historians of early modern Europe blended, in its Hegelian slant, with that of the Burckhardtian tradition, which had its own Hegelian paradigms in political ideology on the state. At the same time, more objective and less ideological historical evaluations of Hegel's thought were developing. Even among historians of early modern Europe who employed Hegelian models of interpretation, the emphasis could be as often on the side of freedom (illustrated in works by Baron and Palmer) as on the side of authority (exemplified in works by Elton).

A measure of the continuing hold of Hegelianism on contemporary legal theory is the massive two-volume *Hegel and Legal Theory*, published in 1989 by the Cardozo Law School and based on a substantial conference there in 1988.[59] The numerous papers presented show a Hegel long since freed from the imputations of authoritarian evil made by older writers like Hobhouse, however genuinely disturbed they had been in the contexts of their own era. Here the fully "rehabilitated" Hegel is not only brought more clearly into historical light, freed from the ideologies of the war years; Hegel also still provides a powerful medium for new concepts of private law in relation to individual freedom and of public law in connection with the state. Recent trends in legal and political studies, as well as recent appraisals of contemporary liberal democratic societies, have engendered renewed interest in Hegelian methodologies. Hegel's attempts to reconcile the negative aspects of nineteenth-century liberalism with the positive features of ancient republicanism have furnished some theorists and historians with useful modes of analysis, as in cases involving civic themes.

Thus the estimation of Hegel by one of his most distinguished reinterpreters in the mid-twentieth century would still be valid in the eyes of many today: "Hegel was one of the greatest philosophers of all time, and no philosopher since 1800 has had more influence."[60] According to a current historian of Hegel and Hegelianism: "Hegelianism continues to influence the debate in a thousand ways through its impact on thinkers directly conscious of his theory or who only belong to the tradition to which he contributed."[61]

The Hegel "revival" has also been linked to ongoing interest in Marxist models. Hegelian paradigms (whether absolutist, constitutionalist, civic, or otherwise) in historiography on early modern Europe have often been linked to the continuing vogue of Marxist studies. The renewed interest in Hegel among current theorists of law, philosophy, and politics has also often had a Marxist tie. Other factors behind the "revival" of Hegel include the restoration of the reputation of British idealism, which dominated British philosophy from roughly the 1870s through the 1920s.[62] From the 1940s idealism became increasingly maligned because of its authoritarian persuasions. The Hegel of the recent Cardozo conference, however, is very different from the Hegel found in writers like Bosanquet.

5. "NEO-(COMMUNIST-)SOCIAL*ISM*" AND "NEO-MARX*ISM*"

Lenin's *State and Revolution:* Legislation

The "ideology" or polemics of the Russian Revolution as articulated in V. I. Lenin's *State and Revolution* (1917/1918)[63] was basically a new/old form of the communist-socialist ideas of Marx and Engels applied to the emerging "Soviet" state, which became a *legislative* state. Of particular importance for Lenin were the ways in which Engels had gone beyond Marx in theorizing about the state as a public power and force existing over and above society (yet also arising from it). Engels had stressed as well the need for enacting special laws or legislation to govern affairs of state and its officials. Lenin framed his theory of the proletarian (communist) state around a detailed exposition and explanation of Engel's development of Marx's more limited ideas on the subject. In addition, Lenin points out that the "withering away" of the state occurs long *after* the proletarian state has (1) replaced the bourgeois state through violent revolution and has (2) eventually fulfilled its role in bringing about the higher phase of complete communism. The "dictatorship of the proletariat," another famous phrase used by Marx, properly refers, says Lenin, building on the authority of Engels, to the proletarian (communist) state *prior* to its withering away. For Lenin, "the state power" and its special bodies bring a much needed "centralized organization of force" for the proletariat socialist society.[64]

In lengthy passages quoted from Marx's *Eighteenth Brumaire of Louis Napoleon,* Lenin finds a concrete treatment of what Marx called the "state machinery" (a term repeatedly used by Lenin), in contrast to Marx's abstract considerations of it in the *Communist Manifesto.* Like Marx, Lenin seeks the destruction of the bourgeois state machinery rather than its augmentation, which had occurred in France under the would-be socialist Napoleon III. A needed violent Russian revolution could not be achieved if "opportunistic" moderates were in charge. The dictatorship of the communist proletariat must completely replace that of the capitalist bourgeoisie.[65]

In a section entitled "What Is to Replace this Shattered State Machinery?," Lenin goes on to explain how Marx further treated the "positive" form and force of the proletarian state in his *The Civil War in France,* which paid particular attention to the Paris Commune of 1871 and its decrees. The Paris Commune appeared, for a while, to replace the shattered oppressive regimes in preceding French states with a proletarian state democracy, which attempted "the suppression of the oppressors by the *whole force* of the majority of the people—the workers and the peasants." [66]

In the ensuing section of *State and Revolution*, entitled "The Destruction of Parliamentarism," Lenin makes plain his goal of replacing the failed bourgeois parliaments, which degenerated into "talking shops," with "working bodies" of Russian soviets (or councils). The latter will conduct the business of the Russian people in the proletarian state modeled on the Paris Commune. These Russian soviets will be representative institutions directly involved in the legislative and executive processes of making and executing the laws for the proletarian state. Once more, Lenin presents his ideas as elaborations on points made by Marx but later obscured by Marx's "opportunistic" followers. Far from advocating the elimination of representative legislative bodies, Lenin sees them as foundations to the legislative business of the proletarian socialist state, prior to its eventual "withering away" into a full communist stateless society.[67]

Marx, says Lenin, was misinterpreted on the subject of the Paris Commune. Marx hailed its apparent destruction of the bourgeois state power through a projected system of communes. These would lead to national delegations of workers at Paris and thus to French national unity in a proletarian socialist state. Other writers have wrongly interpreted Marx's goal to be a federal system in its own right, declares Lenin. Federalism is bound up, in Lenin's view, with parliamentarism, which he has eschewed. Lenin insists that while Marx did not discuss positively or in detail the framework of the future proletarian state, Marx's historical analysis of the Paris Commune supplied a frame of reference for it, thereby revealing the new "machinery of state" needed to replace the old smashed version. Engels again serves as guide for Lenin in attempting to fulfill the example and promise of the Paris Commune of 1871 in the Russian Revolution of 1917.[68]

According to Lenin's *State and Revolution*, then, the writings of Marx and Engels point the way to the proletarian state as an interim form of socialist democracy. Specifically, the bourgeois capitalist state is largely broken but the fully egalitarian society of stateless communism has not yet truly emerged. This transitional or intermediate stage is marked by the retention of limited laws protecting some bourgeois rights. At the center of the "machinery" of the socialist state are the Russian Soviets of Workers' and Soldiers' Deputies. Justice and equality cannot yet be gained in full for the working people but only in part in the socialist state. Notwithstanding this defect, which Marx recognized, there is public rather than private ownership of the means of production.[69]

For Lenin in *State and Revolution*, democracy in the transitional socialist state is a lower form of communism. It exists to protect, insofar as possible, the freedoms and rights of the proletariat or people at large. The democratic socialist state eventually becomes outmoded when, in the higher kind of communism, the people can govern themselves. (Here Marx and Mill could be compared regarding their idealized social end points, in contradistinction to the practical institutions of state for which they also provided.) A formal apparatus of state machinery would then no longer be necessary for ensuring the people's rights and equality. Ultimately, Lenin emphasizes, freedom does not, for Marx, come from the state, as it did for Hegel. During the first or lower phase of communism in Russia, however, the Soviets of Workers' and Soldiers' Deputies must command full obedience through forceful means. Only as the socialist democratic state becomes more completely "public" in its ownership of production and protection of rights does it begin to outgrow its purpose and fade away. The people as a whole will then no longer need its formal rules and administration.[70]

The final section of Lenin's *State and Revolution*, in his chapter entitled "Vulgarization of Marx by the Opportunists," attacks Karl Kautsky's bourgeois parliamentarism. Kautsky's ideas for a quasi-parliament of delegates or deputies elected by the workers failed, asserts Lenin, to grasp the radical rejection by Marx and Engels of all forms of parliaments as inherently bourgeois, including all related forms of repressive state bureaucracy. Kautsky failed to understand, says Lenin, the proletarian legislative-executive functions of the Paris Commune as a working body rather than a mere talking parliamentary body. Kautsky's combination of democracy and bureaucracy is, according to Lenin, not for but against the working people. At the same time, Lenin rebuts the anarchists who seek to destroy the state machinery immediately and who will not use the modern state at all for their own purposes, whereas Lenin approves the transitional, temporary place of both.[71]

Clearly, the bodies of delegates or deputies elected to the working bodies of soviets must not, in Lenin's opinion, become mere talking bodies (shops) or parliaments. Yet it is not altogether clear how in *State and Revolution* he, like Marx and Engels before him, envisions the new soviets to act in a legislative-executive capacity different from traditional parliaments. Aside from the divergent meanings of democracy according to these perspectives on parliaments and soviets, the soviet bodies seem in ways to resemble, at least in form, the parliamentary ones not only in Lenin's *State and Revolution* but also in later developments of Soviet history.

Between Lenin's more egalitarian political theory in *State and Revolution* and the later dictatorship of Lenin and then of Stalin, there loomed a widening gulf. Near the end of his life, Lenin expressed regrets that he had not, in actual fact, followed a more egalitarian political course to match his eventual liberalization of economic policy. Amid these vicissitudes, nonetheless, the theme of legislation remained central to sovereignty and state.

The Soviet "Legal"-Legislative State

After the radical Russian Revolution of 1917, and as a result of the Bolshevik coup and dictatorship under Lenin (d. 1924), the system of "soviets" or "councils" of working peoples' delegates and deputies was set up. It replaced an abortive series of four successive "dumas" or parliamentary "councils." The latter had met from 1906 to 1916 in the wake of the more moderate 1905 revolution, although tzarist dumas had a much older history. The legislative-administrative powers of the dumas, as at first conceded to them by tzar Nicholas II, were soon in actuality greatly negated or hampered by him. The new system of soviets emerged after them as a more significant legislative-administrative institution.[72] Similarly to the term "duma," defined as "a representative council" and "the principal legislative assembly of czarist Russia," the term "soviet" is defined more briefly by Webster as "an elected government council in a Communist country" (hence "sovietism," etc.).[73]

The 1936 Constitution[74] of the Union of Soviet Socialist Republics, adopted by the Eighth Congress of Soviets of the Union of Soviet Socialist Republics, took the place of the previous Union-wide constitution, enacted in 1923 and ratified in 1924. Before the creation of the Soviet Union in 1922, each Soviet Republic had its own constitution, beginning with that of the Russian Republic promulgated in 1918. Under the U.S.S.R. Constitution of 1936, which was modified during the ensuing decades, the Supreme Soviet of the U.S.S.R. functioned as a legislative-administrative body. Thus an appropriate nomenclature was used when the Supreme Soviet of the U.S.S.R. was replaced by the "Congress" of People's Deputies of the U.S.S.R. after the Constitution was amended in 1988. This Congress functioned even more explicitly as a legislative-administrative body.

Aside from the obvious sinister orientation of the U.S.S.R. under Stalin as a totalitarian state, its formalistic legal-legislative basis is abundantly apparent in its Constitution and in the constitutions of the separate Republics within the Soviet Empire. The vast system of soviets permeated the hierarchy of the Union and its Republics, all often again with corresponding legislative functions. It is ironic that the federal structure of this socialistic communist union of states, each of which was in itself a federation of entities, as set forth in the Constitution of 1936, represented the kind of federalism and bureaucratism against which Lenin fulminated in his *State and Revolution*. Indeed, the replacement of the Supreme Soviet by the Soviet Congress in 1988 could be interpreted as putting a formal stamp of approval on the parliamentary nature of the original soviets themselves, notwithstanding Lenin's "ideological" rhetoric denouncing the dumas as talk-shops rather than working bodies. It is difficult to imagine that the heavy socialistic state machinery of the U.S.S.R. would ever have "withered away" because of its success (rather than its failure), even if it had remained the more streamlined kind envisioned at one time by Lenin. But the present emphasis remains on the legislative basis of the Soviet state set in motion by Lenin.

The U.S.S.R. Constitution of 1936 (as amended up to 1968) deserves to be quoted at key points with regard to legislation, sovereignty, and state. Article 1 declares the U.S.S.R. to be "a socialist state of workers and peasants." Article 15 announces: "The sovereignty of the union republics shall be restricted only within the limits indicated in Article 14 of the Constitution of the USSR." According to Articles 19–20: "Laws of the USSR shall have the same force in the territory of all the union republics. . . . In the event that a law of a Union Republic diverges from an all-union law, the all-union law shall prevail." Article 23 refers to the "Russian Soviet Federated Socialist Republic." Articles 30, 32–33, 37, 39–40 stipulate: "The Supreme Soviet of the USSR shall be the highest agency of state power in the USSR. . . . The legislative power of the USSR shall be exercised exclusively by the Supreme Soviet of the USSR . . . [which] shall consist of two chambers: the Soviet of the Union and the Soviet of Nationalities . . . [The two chambers] shall have equal rights . . . [and] equal powers of legislative initiative. . . . A law shall be considered confirmed if it is adopted by both chambers of the Supreme Soviet by a simple majority of the votes in each chamber . . . over the signature of the President and Secretary of the Presidium of the Supreme Soviet of the USSR." In addition, according to Article 49: "The Presidium of the Supreme Soviet of the USSR shall . . . convoke sessions [,] issue edicts [,] . . . give interpretation of the laws of the USSR in force [,] . . . annul decrees and regulations of the Council of Ministers of the USSR [,] . . . institute orders . . . [etc.]."

The subordination of the executive and administrative powers to the legislative power is manifest in Articles 64–67: "The Council of Ministers of the USSR shall be the highest executive and administrative agency of state power of the Union of Soviet Socialist Republics. . . .

[I]t shall be responsible to the Supreme Soviet of the USSR and accountable to it. . . . [It] shall issue decrees and regulations on the basis of and in execution of the laws in force and shall verify their execution. . . . Decrees and regulations of the Council of Ministers of the USSR shall be binding throughout the territory of the USSR."

Each of the Union Republics of the U.S.S.R. is patterned after this central Union model. The Supreme Soviet of each Republic is again in Article 57, "the highest agency of state power," legislative and otherwise. Likewise in Articles 79–81, the Council of Ministers in each Union Republic is the "highest executive and administrative agency of state power" and is "responsible to the Supreme Soviet of the Union Republic." These Councils "shall issue decrees and regulations on the basis of and in execution of the laws in force of the USSR and of the Union Republic, and of decrees and regulations of the Council of Ministers of the USSR, and shall verify their execution." Similar stipulations are set forth for the highest agencies of state power of Autonomous Republics.

As the "highest judicial agency," according to Article 104, the Supreme Court of the U.S.S.R. has "supervision over the judicial agencies of the USSR as well as of . . . Union republics within the limits established by law." The Supreme Court of the U.S.S.R. is "elected by the Supreme Soviet of the USSR for a term of five years." Thus the judicial as well as executive agencies are subordinated to the Supreme Soviet of the U.S.S.R. as the legislative body. Although it is true that the Supreme Soviet of the U.S.S.R. is composed of "elected" delegates put up by the Communist Party, its essential function as a legislative body remains the key point.

Finally, Article 1 of the Russian constitution[75] stipulates: "The Russian Soviet Federated Socialist Republic shall be a socialist state of workers and the peasants." The laws of the U.S.S.R. are binding on the Russian Republic as declared in Article 17. Articles 24, 26 state: "The Supreme Soviet of the RSFSR shall be the sole legislative agency of the RSFSR. . . . A law shall be considered confirmed if it is adopted by the Supreme Soviet of the RSFSR by a simple majority of the votes." And so on.

"Lenin*ism*" and "Stalin*ism*"

The relationships between so-called "Lenin*ism*" and "Stalin*ism*" have been much discussed by historians, especially with regard to "Marx*ism*." In the words of the *Oxford English Dictionary*: "*Leninism*. . . . The political and economic doctrines of Marx as interpreted and applied by Lenin to the governing of the Soviet Union . . . and to the dictatorship of the working class. So Leninism-Stalinism. Lenin's doctrines as interpreted and applied by Stalin." These are broad subjects that have been necessarily viewed above from the angle of Lenin's *State and Revolution* and the Stalinist Soviet Constitution of 1936. A host of other issues such as Lenin's other writings concerning soviets and parties could not be considered.[76]

In the process of seizing state power, Lenin not only placed political opportunism somewhat above economic dogma. Increasingly, so as to maintain his own control, he elevated the Bolshevik Communist Party above the more "democratic" soviets of the masses. Lenin ended up deviating from Marx, more than had the moderates Lenin criticized, by fostering the dictatorship of the (Bolshevik) Communist Party (and chiefly its leadership) over the dictatorship of the proletarian masses exemplified in the system of soviets. Revolutionism from below was replaced by statism from above, leading to Stalin's bureaucratic authoritarianism. The Party's near total control through the soviets was apparent in the 1936 Constitution, with Stalin as unlimited dictator in near total domination of the Party, the Union, and the Republics.

A huge divide might seem to separate Lenin's *State and Revolution* in 1917 from the Constitution of the U.S.S.R. produced in 1936 in the heyday of Stalin. After all, Lenin's economic policies in his final years were more moderating and less bureaucratic than the ruthless authoritarianism of Stalin in the 1930s during his infamous trial purges and rigid centralization and collectivization. It might furthermore be felt that the heavy emphasis on the legislative nature of sovereignty and the state in the 1936 Constitution of the U.S.S.R. represented mere window-dressing for the viewing of Western democracies. Their hopes that it signaled a new beginning were soon dashed by Stalin's despotism. The heavy bureaucratism of the legislative system may seem a sharp distinction to Lenin's original preference for swift change through violent revolution rather than slower change through legislative reform as a means for overthrowing the bourgeois state.

However, Lenin himself came to believe in the necessity of the Bolshevik Party's forceful control of the socialist state when it emerged after the 1917 Revolution. His greater accentuation of the soviet bodies in *State and Revolution* became somewhat diminished. That is, the Bolsheviks from Lenin to Stalin were increasingly compelled to replace the authoritarian bureaucratic statism of the czars with one of their own. Stalin's renewed expanded uses of soviets became a central part of this trend. Lenin came to believe that he could better control the Party than he could the soviets, not only as a revolutionary tool but also as a governing mechanism. Stalin used them both together in building a stronger totalitarian state.

It must be remembered that Lenin, as the founder of the Soviet (one-party) political state, perceived the significance of the legal-legislative scope of the socialist state, adumbrated already in his *State and Revolution*. True, Lenin in *State and Revolution* had criticized the German Social Democrat Eduard Bernstein, among others, for his Marxist revisionism and opportunistic bourgeois parliamentarism. Moreover, in his *Evolutionary Socialism* (1898),[77] Bernstein had assigned greater import to the need for constitutional legislation as a way to reform society once the violent phases of revolution had ended. In places, Bernstein seemed to prefer the latter to the former more generally. This position was naturally anathema to Lenin in his *State and Revolution* during the Russian Revolution of 1917. Lenin felt that a single party (which he could control) was a better engine for revolution than were the soviets, although he nevertheless granted a significant role to the soviets in *State and Revolution*. But the differences between Bernstein and Lenin, both as Marxist socialists, over the place of legislation in the state itself (aside from issues of reform versus. revolution) were largely over its degrees of development and ideology or its different bad and good forms in various types of states. Not only, moreover, were law and legislation crucial to the new Soviet socialist state in Lenin's *State and Revolution*. In addition, the prototypes for the later constitutions of the Soviet Union and its Republics, beginning with the Russian Republic's Constitution of 1918, went back to this period.[78]

Interesting, in light of the above observations, are the later extended criticisms by Hans Kelsen of the Communist theory of law held by Lenin and others, as well as a Communist reply to Kelsen.[79]

6. "NEO-(SOCIALIST-)NATIONAL*ISM*" AND "NEO-BISMARCKIAN*ISM*"

Hitler on State and Nation

As is well known, Adolf Hitler's *Mein Kampf*[80] was filled with hateful racial rhetoric that casts dark clouds over most if not all of his pronouncements therein on the place of state and nation in Germany and the German lands. There is a relatively substantive chapter on the state in his long, rambling work, which was set down while he was in prison in 1924 (and published in 1925) after his failed coup in Munich. In "The State" (Chapter II in Volume or Part II), Hitler basically reduces the state to a subordinate status under the nation. He sees the state not as an end in itself but as a means to the higher end centering on the nation. The state's primary aim is to preserve and promote the racial purity of the German people in a thoroughly German nation. The state becomes in part a means for the proper national educational values that will foster right thinking and proper conduct among the young. The state is thus not an independent mechanism existing for its own sake. Rather, in the true folkish state, it is a tool for promoting the interests of the people of a nation, in this case Germany.

In this chapter of *Mein Kampf* on the state, Hitler begins by referring to the then-current negative attitudes toward the state *per se* on the part of "political crooks" in the first two decades of the twentieth century. He denounces the "political law professors" in the universities who justify their jobs by writing arid tracts on the state, which seek to preserve the current "monstrosity" of state mechanisms that have failed the German people. Hitler castigates those professors who see the state as a *"voluntary grouping of people under a governmental power"* and who regard the state's end as being its own authority rather than the advancement of the people's welfare. He condemns above all those who seek a "state-people linguistically stamped and united" through an arbitrary process of Germanization (which is, in reality, he feels, a de-Germanization).[81]

Nationality or race, for Hitler, is here not a matter of language but of blood. Forcing non-blood Germans into a state, Hitler maintains, is to obviate the state's own end of existence. "The *state* in itself does not create a specific cultural level; it can only preserve the race which conditions this level." "From a dead mechanism," he asserts, "which only lays claim to existence for its own sake, there must be formed a living organism with the exclusive aim of serving a higher idea." His ensuing sentence makes plain his expansionist goals and their justification: *"The German Reich as a state must embrace all* [true] *Germans . . ."*[82] As for state and race more specifically: "The folkish state must make up for what everyone else today has neglected in this field. *It must set race in the center of all life. It must take care to keep it pure."* Maintenance of the best racial elements is the state's "first task" in promoting "the welfare of its nationality." The state's most crucial role in education relates to the racial element.[83]

Despite some of his negative opinions about the state *per se*, Hitler at points aligns himself more positively with its traditional legal-legislative, as well as political, role, aside from his heinous racial viewpoints. An ensuing chapter (IV, II) of *Mein Kampf* is entitled "Personality and the Conception of the Folkish State." He begins: "The folkish National Socialist state sees its chief task in *educating and preserving the bearer of the state*. It is not sufficient to encourage the racial elements as such . . .; the state must also adjust its own organization to this task. . . ." To be sure, Hitler rejects the view that "a folkish National Socialist state must distinguish itself from other states only in a purely mechanical sense . . ." [84] At the end of the short chapter, however, he states as follows:

> Even then it will not be possible to dispense with those corporations which today we designate as parliaments.
> Parliaments as such are necessary, because in them, above all, personalities to which special responsible tasks can later be entrusted have an opportunity gradually to rise up. . . .
> The folkish state, from the township to the Reich leadership, has no representative body which decides anything by the majority, but only *advisory bodies* which stand at the side of the elected leader. . . . [T]he folkish state . . . divides its representative bodies . . . into *political and professional chambers*. . . . [A] special *senate* of the elite always stands over them.
> In no chamber and in no senate does a vote ever take place. They are working institutions and not voting machines. . . .
> Thus the political form of the nation will be brought into agreement with the law to which it owes its greatness in the cultural and economic field.
> But it must not be believed that such a transformation can be accomplished by purely theoretical measures from above, but must permeate all other legislation [!], and indeed all civil life.[85]

Perhaps sensing that he was here somewhat contradicting his own earlier denunciations of the state *per se* by elaborating on its necessary mechanisms, Hitler makes a telling distinction. In the lengthy passage just quoted, he differentiates between mere theories of state (presumably a reference to the professorial treatises on state and law that he has detested) and practical all-embracing legislation, which together with parliament lays the foundation of the state. In fact, it is already possible to discern, in his repeated references in the chapters at hand to the National Socialist state, a harbinger of the legislative state that emerged in formalistic fashion soon after Hitler's successful rise to power in the early 1930s. The legislative element has not usually been singled out by historians of Hitler's writings and regime. The emergent Nazi state, not unlike the Soviet state, was a dictatorial socialist state framed as a legislative state. On the democratic side of the political spectrum, for instance, the proto-socialist Victorian state under Gladstone represented another kind of legislative state.

At the end of his chapter in *Mein Kampf* on "Nation and Race" (IX, I), Hitler further underscores his central interest in establishing a new National Socialist state: "[O]ur new movement . . . [aims] not only . . .

[at the goal of] halting the decline of the German people, but of creating the granite foundation upon which some day a state will rest which represents, not an alien mechanism of economic concerns and interests, but a national organism: *A German State of the German Nation.*"[86]

Hitler on Bismarck

Scattered throughout Hitler's *Mein Kampf* are numerous references to Bismarck. His final reference reveals the great impact of Bismarck's heroic exemplar on Hitler's youthful mind.

> Rumaging through my father's library, I had come across various books of a military nature; among them a popular edition of the Franco-German War of 1870–71. . . . It was not long before the great heroic struggles had become my greatest inner experience. From then on I became more and more enthusiastic about everything . . . connected with war. . . .
>
> But in another respect as well, this was to assume importance for me. . . . For the first time, . . . the question was forced upon my consciousness: Was there a difference . . . between the Germans who fought these battles and other Germans? Why hadn't Austria [his native country] taken part . . .?
>
> Are we not the same as all other Germans? . . . This problem began to gnaw at my little brain for the first time. I asked cautious questions and with secret envy received the answer that not every German was fortunate enough to belong to Bismarck's Reich.[87]

Using such terms as "German state" and "German nation" interchangeably, Hitler ponders the recovery of Germany's political power in relation to questions of German nationalism and sovereignty. He urges upon his fellow Germans the bold example of Bismarck in overcoming the resistance of the bourgeoisie and in pressing forth with "the nationalization of the . . . masses."[88] The Prussian hegemony over Germany established by Bismarck provides a model for Hitler. Yet Hitler seeks a new unitary state, rather than an older type of federated state, that would still be compatible with Bismarck's ultimate aims.

> But it is obvious that stirring up hatred against Prussia has nothing to do with federalism. And a 'federative activity' which attempts to dissolve or split up another federal state makes a weird impression. An honorable federalist, for whom quotations

of Bismarck's conception of the Reich are more than lying phrases, would hardly in the same breath want to separate portions from the Prussian state created or rather completed by Bismarck, let alone publicly support such separatist endeavors. . . . It is impossible to preach a *federalistic* form for the Reich, at the same time *deprecating, reviling, and befouling* the most essential section of such a state structure, namely, Prussia, and in short, making it, if possible, *impossible* as a *federal state*.[89]

Hitler elaborates further on Prussian hegemony in relation to what he alleges is the non-sovereign status of the other German states, both large and small. Comparing past and present conditions, he distinguishes between "so-called" and "real" sovereignty, with references to "the constitution of the old Reich." [90] Hitler then turns to Bismarck's great statesmanship in pursuing policies intended, over the long run, to strengthen the Reich's sovereignty, albeit within temporary contexts of a federated state, which, in any case, subsequently collapsed under the pressures of World War I.

At the same time, Bismarck did not act on the principle of giving to the Reich everything that could in any way be taken away from the individual states; his principle was to demand of the individual states only what the Reich absolutely needed. A principle as moderate as it was wise, which on the one hand took the highest consideration of custom and tradition, and on the other hand thereby assured the new Reich a great measure of love and joyful collaboration at the very outset. It is absolutely wrong, however, to attribute this decision of Bismarck to his conviction that the Reich thus possessed sufficient sovereign rights for all time. Bismarck had no such conviction; on the contrary, he only wanted to put off till the future what at the moment would have been hard to accomplish and to endure. He put his hope, in the gradual compromises brought about by time and the pressure of development as such, which in the long run he credited with more strength than any attempt to break the momentary resistance of the individual states at once. Thus, he best demonstrated and proved the greatness of his statesmanship. For in reality the sovereignty of the Reich steadily grew at the expense of the sovereignty of the individual states. Time fulfilled Bismarck's expectations.

With the German collapse and the destruction of the German state form, this development was necessarily accelerated. . . . A considerable number of these "state formations" lost all internal stability, to such an extent that they voluntarily renounced any further existence. . . .

And so, if the elimination of the monarchic state form and its representatives in itself administered a strong blow to the Reich's character as a federated state, this was even more true of the assumption of the obligations resulting from the "peace" treaty.[91]

Bismarck, for Hitler, provides repeated points of reference on Germany's past and present approaches to foreign affairs and alliances, chiefly with Austria and Russia. The disastrous German alliance with Austria in the Triple Alliance, cautions Hitler, cannot be justified by comparisons between Bismarck and his bungling successors, as some have attempted to do. For Bismarck maintained the ascendancy of the "German state," whereas they allowed it to sink into a "German hodgepodge."

> [T]he absurdity of the Triple Alliance [became] clear and comprehensible. . . . In alliance with Austria, to be sure, we could not undertake any military conquest, even in Europe alone. Precisely therein consisted the inner weakness of the alliance from the very first day. A Bismarck could permit himself this makeshift, but not by a long shot every bungling successor, least of all at a time when certain essential premises of Bismarck's alliance had long ceased to exist; for Bismarck still believed that in Austria he had to do with a German state. But with the gradual introduction of universal suffrage, this country had sunk to the status of an un-German hodgepodge with a parliamentary government.
>
> Also from the standpoint of racial policy, the alliance with Austria was simply ruinous. It meant tolerating the growth of a new Slavic power on the borders of the Reich . . .[92]

Bismarck's policies toward Russia must be understood as part of his nationalism and state-building, asserts Hitler. Bismarck's wider philosophy of statecraft beckons as a current guide but not in the erroneous ways it does for many others. Hitler, however, was later to reverse his own outlook on dealing with the Russians when situations became changed.

> Not only in German-National, but even in "folkish" circles, the idea of such an eastern policy is violently attacked, and, as almost always in such matters, they appeal to a higher author-

ity. The spirit of Bismarck is cited to cover a policy which is as senseless as it is impossible and in the highest degree harmful to the German nation. Bismarck in his time, they say, always set store on good relations with Russia. This, to a certain extent, is true. But they forget to mention that he set just as great store on good relations with Italy, for example; in fact, that the same Herr von Bismarck once made an alliance with Italy in order to finish off Austria the more easily. Why, then, don't they continue *this* policy? . . . It never entered Bismarck's head to lay down a political course tactically and theoretically for all time. In this respect he was too much master of the moment to tie his hands in such a way. *The question, therefore, must not be: What did Bismarck do in his time?* But rather: *What would he do today?* And this question is easier to answer. *With his political astuteness, he would never ally himself with a state that is doomed to destruction.*

Furthermore, Bismarck even then viewed the German colonial and commercial policy with mixed feelings, since for the moment he was concerned only with the surest method of internally consolidating the state formation he had created. And this was the only reason why at that time he welcomed the Russian rear cover. . . . But what was profitable to Germany then would be detrimental today.[93]

In his denunciations of Marxist or Communist socialism, which he closely tied to the perceived Jewish threat, Hitler worked his way to a domestic policy in large part through his early studies of Bismarck's anti-socialist legislation.

I studied Bismarck's Socialist legislation in its intention, struggle, and success. Gradually I obtained a positively granite foundation for my own conviction, so that since that time I have never been forced to undertake a shift in my own inner view on this question. Likewise the relation of Marxism to the Jews was submitted to further thorough examination. . . .

In the years 1913 and 1914, I . . . expressed the conviction that the question of the future of the German nation was the question of destroying Marxism.

In the catastrophic German alliance policy I saw only one of the consequences called forth by the disruptive work of this doctrine . . .[94]

At the same time, Hitler does not hesitate to point out where and why Bismarck's anti-socialist legislation proved unsuccessful. In so doing, Hitler paints himself as the would-be fulfiller of such legislative guidelines to the problem. His new philosophy is needed, he holds, to guide future approaches toward success.[95]

In Hitler's mind, Bismarck's famed statement that "politics is an art of the possible" became corrupted by succeeding German chancellors. Whereas Bismarck was willing to compromise on the means in order to attain the end, his successors failed to pursue *any* goals or definite political philosophy, compromising aimlessly without "inner laws" and good results. Rather, as in other ways, Hitler seeks to restore or to adapt Bismarck's true original strategies.[96] This is not to say that Hitler ignores Bismarck's shortcomings. He points out Bismarck's wrongheaded monetary policies, which, however, he excuses as largely set by the emperor.[97] The stature of Bismarck, he feels, stands tall when compared to the weak recent German statesmen, who also pale beside the great Mussolini (heroic combatant of Marxist internationalism in Italy).[98]

From the foregoing panegyrics on Bismarck in Hitler's *Mein Kampf*, it becomes apparent that by the early 1920s Hitler was advocating a neo-Bismarckian nationalism, statism, and socialism. By the time of Hitler's takeover of Germany a decade later, his neo-Bismarckianism became more fully evident in the establishment of the Third Reich. His boast that the Third Reich would last a thousand years was not only an allusion to what was styled the First Reich—the Holy Roman Empire (founded by Charlemagne and ended by Napoleon). As the new German chancellor, Hitler also dreamed of himself as outdistancing even Chancellor Bismarck's accomplishments, which had lasted only a few decades. It was therefore more than mere "poetic justice" that Hitler's prized battleship *Bismarck* was sunk by the British soon after it was launched. For the "greater Germany" pursued by Hitler became a horrendous catastrophic echo of Bismarck's so-called Second Reich and endured little more than a decade.

Thus Hitler's political and propagandistic appropriations of the Bismarckian legend became a powerful driving force in his own formative early thinking on statecraft. This connection has not in itself been as fully explored by historians as it deserves to be. Hitler's relationship to Bismarck on questions of German national history has produced a wide array of academic verdicts, which also point up the complex central place of German nationalism. The Bismarck-to-Hitler progression is, in the end, too enormous a subject to be treated here, beyond the issue of Hitler's own pronouncements in *Mein Kampf*.[99]

The Nazi "Legal"-Legislative State

Any such term as "legal-legislative state" applied to Hitler's Nazi regime must at first glance seem a misnomer, in view of the lawlessness that came increasingly to characterize it. His infamous subversion of the judicial process is a noted case in point. Even the Soviet Communist and Italian Fascist states were somewhat more attuned, relatively speaking, to legalistic formalism and parliamentarism in matters of government. Nevertheless, the Nazi state, no less than the Soviet and Fascist states, was, in its own way, a legislative state, as established in its early formative years. The term "legal" is again restricted.

The bureaucratic structure of the Nazi state was complex. The national government centered on the cabinet, administrative agencies, the Reichstag, and the plebiscites. State and local governments were also complicated. The Nazi Party held a monopoly within the state and government. As for law and justice, there was, of course, legal inequality, along with *ex post facto* laws, judicial review of executive acts, and the new Nazi tribunals. Nazi propaganda marshaled public opinion at all levels. There was varying control of art, literature, education, and religion, not to mention economics, political life, and foreign policy.[100]

It will be useful to identify, assemble, and reconstruct in chronological order some of the salient legal-legislative events in the formation of the Nazi state. The most decisive beginnings occurred in the years immediately following the elections to the German Reichstag in November 1932. The outcome of the elections for Hitler's National Socialist German Workers' Party, combined with ensuing events and circumstances, led to Hitler's assumption of the chancellorship early in the following year. This victory occurred through manipulation of constitutional or parliamentary channels as his party struggled to achieve a majority in the Reichstag. Although some questions remain about the legality of what Hitler as well as Hindenburg did in the transfer of power to the Nazis, especially with regard to the Weimar Constitution, there is little ambiguity about the speedy emergence of Hitler's dictatorship.

Hitler was appointed Chancellor of the German Reich on January 30, 1933, by President von Hindenburg. On the next day, January 31, 1933, Hitler prevailed upon Hindenburg to disolve the Reichstag elected on November 6, 1932, in which the Nazis had received only 196 of the 584 seats, albeit the most of any one party. The emergency presidential decree of February 4, 1933, gave the Nazi government control over political meetings and political literature that was deemed subversive. The freedom of press and association was curtailed by these decrees. They were followed later that month by other decrees further limiting political and civil rights provided in the Weimar Constitution.

After the Nazis set fire to the old Reichstag building in Berlin on February 27, 1933, a presidential decree was passed on February 28, at Hitler's urging, for the Protection of People and State. Its purpose was to prevent alleged Communist threats to Germany. By now, the Weimar Constitution was, in effect, abrogated. This emergency decree of February 28, providing for martial law throughout Germany, became a kind of "constitutional" replacement for the Weimar Constitution and set forth basic rights of citizens and powers of the government. The will of the Leader became the law of the land. This decree stipulated death for anti-Nazi crimes. It gained more sweeping scope in the law of March 29, 1933. On June 28, 1935, the statute on such matters stipulated the death penalty for a much wider range of offenses, including many others that might be alleged even though they were not specifically cited in law.

The elections to the Reichstag on March 5, 1933, gave the Nazis 288 of the 647 seats, so that they could not gain the two-thirds majority needed for constitutional changes. The Nazis declared that the Communist vote was invalid, and had already outlawed the Communist Party on February 28, 1933. When the new Reichstag met for the first time in Potsdam on March 21, 1933, it granted (by 444 to 94 votes) the Reich government's request to assume sole actual legislative power. This measure abolished parliamentary or representative government and gave rise to a dictatorship. The measure was passed in no small part because various groups of members were excluded from the session.

The formal authorization for the government to assume all real legislative prerogatives was issued in the Enabling Act of March 24, 1933, which also gave the government power to change the constitution. Although this act was supposed to remain in effect only for four years, its validity was subsequently extended. Thus on March 24, 1933, the government, meaning Hitler, was given the legislative power by the (Nazi) Reichstag. Voting in the cabinet ended several weeks later so Hitler himself could decide on matters before it. The types of legislative measures that Hitler was now empowered to dictate included laws, edicts, decrees, regulations, and commands. His public utterances became binding as a kind of law. In addition, Hitler became the sovereign judicial and executive authority in Germany. Yet, once again, the actual apparatus of state was extensive.

Hitler's sovereign legislative and executive powers were facilitated by his supreme position in relation to three Chancelleries—of the Reich, of the President, and of the Leader of the National Socialist Party. The head of the Reich Chancellery, for instance, submitted to Hitler, as Leader of Germany, the legislative proposals made by the different departments of the high government; he became, in effect, the minister for legislation concerned with the formulation of new legislation generated by various high ministerial offices. Under Hitler, in addition, were various "Representatives of Reich Sovereignty," who were rulers of the occupied and annexed territories.

In November 1933, the first all-Nazi Reichstag was elected. Subsequently it met only sporadically. Hitler and his circle were in complete control of the sessions. Those in attendance were usually given no opportunity even to speak. The meetings passed relatively few real laws and mainly provided Hitler with a forum for declarations on crucial matters of the day, particularly in foreign affairs. Those assembled were expected to give acclamation to Hitler's declarations and declamations. Here, then, the Nazi lip service to German parliamentary tradition was reduced to an empty formalism that surpassed the hollowness of the Italian Fascist and Soviet Communist parliaments. And yet the central component of legislation, however barren, was retained at the core of the Nazi state and sovereignty.

Plebiscites and *ex post facto* laws became a noted device for Hitler's government. On July 13, 1934, Hitler asked the Reichstag for an *ex post facto* law authorizing the blood purge of the Nazi party that had taken place on June 30, 1934, in which hundreds of noted Nazis were killed. After President von Hindenburg died on August 2, 1934, a plebiscite was held on August 19, 1934, to confirm the law, already passed the day before when he was near death, to combine the positions of President, Chancellor, and Leader. Thereby all control was granted to Hitler. Another such plebiscite had been held on November 12, 1933, to confirm Germany's withdrawal from the League of Nations on October 14, 1933. The circumstances of all such Nazi plebiscites were naturally tightly controlled to ensure the desired outcome.

Perhaps the most notorious Nazi legislation were the Nuremberg Laws against the Jews passed in 1935. These laws deprived Jews of German citizenship and prohibited marriage or sex between Germans and Jews. These laws were part of the extensive legislation passed between 1933 and 1938, which was the most sweeping in modern history against the Jews. In April 1933, Jews had been excluded from the civil service as well as from service in hospitals and in the judiciary. In 1936, at the time of the Berlin Olympics, however, Hitler decreed that all anti-Jewish movies should be removed from Berlin, in order not to offend establishment interests. Yet in July 1938, Jews were prohibited from engaging in commercial activities. Decrees were issued restricting the movements of Jews by means of mandatory identity cards, passports, and the like. The infamous violence against Jewish property and lives that occurred throughout Germany on the night of November

9–10, 1938, showed that such laws afforded no real protection to the Jews. Many in the high administration preferred a tidier solution and were annoyed at the violence. Nevertheless, the excesses of *Krystalnacht* pointed ahead to the calamitous paths soon to be pursued by the Nazis. The worst cases of lawlessness of their regime surfaced in crimes against humanity wrought by the "Final Solution." It need hardly be added that on June 17, 1936, Hitler had issued a decree investing Heinrich Himmler, leader of the SS and later director over the concentration camps, with the newly created office of the chief of the German police, thus enabling Himmler to realize his aim of creating a sweeping new "state protection corps."

By then the sole real legislative authority, Hitler in 1939 decreed that his only title should be "Leader" or "*Der Fuehrer.*" He dropped both "Chancellor" and "President" as titles for various reasons. His word had become the virtual law of the land. The façade of the legislative state was to continue on, but with the law and legislation of the state subordinated to or synonymous with the leadership of its sovereign, Hitler.

It is not possible here to explore the enormous wider historiographical debates. The discrepancies between Hitler's totalitarian state and the German legal-legislative tradition going back to Bismarck and before have become increasingly apparent. Historians have variously recognized elements of continuity as well as discontinuity in German history from Bismarck and his predecessors to Hitler. Such topics have been keenly debated in contexts of nationalism, socialism, and totalitarianism. Most historians would no doubt agree that the Hitlerism expressed in *Mein Kampf* was not the clear-cut case of neo-Bismarckianism that Hitler himself believed it to be. Yet his own views therein on this subject had a powerful shaping influence on Nazi ideology in the Third Reich. At the same time, the extent of his own "total" control over the state apparatus has been much debated. Some historians have concluded that the term "totalitarian*ism*" is not precisely applicable and has become outmoded in a variety of ways. The question of late-nineteenth-century German nationalism, prior to World War I and as background to the Nazi era, has long remained a controversial topic among historians, with theorists like Heinrich von Treitschke (d. 1896) sometimes occupying a significant place. The centrality of legal-legislative factors in Hitler's own discussions on the state itself, to the extent that he made them, and in his regime's state apparatus, which was at points extensive, needs much fuller exploration by historians. Pre-Nazi and Nazi writers like Carl Schmitt on sovereignty, parliamentarism, and so forth could be further examined from this perspective.[101]

7. "NEO-UTILITARIAN*ISM*" AND "NEO-BENTHAM*ISM*"

A remaining major "neo-ism" of the early and mid-twentieth century must be briefly considered because of its relationship to its nineteenth-century predecessor examined above. The so-called "utilitarian*ism*" of Jeremy Bentham, J. S. Mill, and their followers in the nineteenth century became revived in various forms of what can be called "neo-utilitarian*ism*" in the early twentieth century and beyond among various lesser-known theorists. The latter group need not detain us here. It has been succinctly cited by John Rawls under the heading of "Classical Utilitarianism" in his renowned mid-century *Theory of Justice*,[102] which may be described as a form of "anti-neo-utilitarianism," as will be further seen. More important here are the mid-twentieth-century writings by H. L. A. Hart on aspects of utilitarianism, together with positivism, as related to Bentham, Austin, and their followers. These views are found in Hart's *Essays on Bentham, Concept of Law*, and various articles.[103]

The intermixtures of neo-utilitarian and neo-positivist elements in Hart's legal philosophy are predicated in part upon the legal philosophies of Bentham and Austin, his principal points of departure in weaving a new blend of historical and contemporary themes. Here we must first recall some broad perspectives. Bentham is best known as the founder of utilitarianism in jurisprudence, with particular regard to issues of utility in legislation. J. S. Mill broadened the inquiry to include more general political, social, and humanitarian questions of the connections between institutions, government, and individuals. Austin is mostly taken as the founder of legal positivism in Britain, with special attention to doctrines of command in legislation. At the same time, however, Bentham held extensive viewpoints on command in laws, while Austin was deeply interested in utility in laws. In other words, as a utilitarian Bentham can be seen as a proto-positivist, while Austin adapted much of Bentham's utilitarian outlook. These overlappings between utilitarianism and positivism in Bentham and Austin help to explain their presence as well in the writings of Hart, who although usually recognized as a neo-positivist is also a kind of neo-utilitarian.

It will be sufficient here to discuss briefly Hart's ideas in his most famous work, *The Concept of Law*, with respect first to the legislative nature of sovereignty. This subject preoccupies Hart in the initial chapters where he accounts for traditional approaches of Austin, Bentham, and others within contexts of his own new or revised legal system. In the final analysis, it is not entirely clear to what exact extent Hart diverges from Austin and Bentham on legislative sovereignty *per se*, as distinct from related issues of absolute versus limited powers of the legislator(s). Hart's main concern lies with contexts of justice that he seeks to unite in express "new" ways with the older command-theory. Nevertheless, the sovereignty of the legislative power remains fundamental—more so than has usually been recognized—behind Hart's general concepts of law and legal system, which he goes on in subsequent chapters to develop more fully and with greater interest for followers and other experts.

At the beginning of his Chapter II on "Laws, Commands, and Orders," in his *Concept of Law*, Hart states that he will expound upon concepts inherited from Austin (and Austin's predecessor Bentham) that have exerted continued influence (including on theorists like Kelsen). It is largely the coercive nature of command lying behind their concepts of law that Hart seeks to revise with regard to legislation. In Chapter III on "The Variety of Laws," Hart declares: "What is most needed as a corrective to the model of coercive orders or rules, is a fresh conception of legislation as the introduction or notification of general standards of behavior to be followed by the society generally. The legislator is not necessarily like the giver of orders to another. . . . Like the giver of a promise he exercises powers conferred by rules . . ."[104] Nevertheless: "The enactment of a law, like the giving of an order, *is* a deliberate datable act. Those who take part in legislation consciously operate a procedure for making law. . . . Accordingly, theories which use the model of coercive orders in the analysis of law make the claim that all law can be seen . . . to have this point of resemblance to legislation and to owe its status as law to a deliberate law-creating act."[105] In the course of treating custom as a "type of law which most obviously conflicts with this claim," Hart makes the following poignant statement: "Custom is not in the modern world a very important 'source' of law. It is usually a subordinate one, in the sense that the legislature may by statute deprive a customary rule of legal status . . ."[106] Such statements are compatible with many others on custom and legislation encountered earlier in the present studies.

In Chapter IV on "Sovereign and Subject" in his *Concept of Law*, Hart turns from "criticizing the simple model of law as coercive orders" to "questions concerning the 'sovereign' person or persons whose general orders constitute, according to this conception, the law of any society."[107] Hart treats "the continuity of law-making power through a changing succession of individual legislators" as expressed in the "right to succeed," the "right to make law," and the like.[108] He distinguishes "between a simple tribal society and a [complex ongoing] modern state."[109] He later explains "[t]he incoherence of the theory that past statutes owe their present status as law to the acquiescence of the present legislature in their application by the courts . . ." Along these lines, "Hobbes, echoed here by Bentham and Austin, said that 'the legislator is he, not by whose authority the law was first made, but by whose [law-making] authority they now continue to be laws'."[110] Another area of interest to Hart "concerns the position occupied by the sovereign above the law: he creates law for others and so imposes legal duties or 'limitations' upon them whereas he is said himself to be legally unlimited. . . . [But is] this legally illimitable status of the supreme lawgiver . . . necessary for the existence of law . . . [?]"[111] Hart answers in the negative:

> [T]he theory simply asserts that there could only be legal limits on legislative power if the legislator were under the orders of another legislator whom he habitually obeyed. . . . [T]his theory as a general account of law . . . seems to give us . . . a [falsely] satisfying simple form [of explanation]. . . . [A] number of points [are] much obscured by this simple doctrine of sovereignty yet [are] vital for the understanding of the foundations of a legal system. . . . First, legal limitations on legislative authority consist not of duties imposed on the legislator to obey some supreme legislator but of disabilities contained in rules which qualify him to legislate.[112]

Hart's other points are that "in order to establish that a purported enactment is law we do not have to trace it back to the enactment . . . of a legislator who is 'sovereign' or unlimited"; that "an independent legal system . . . [does] not have to show that its supreme legislator is legally unrestructed or obeys no other person"; that "we must distinguish between a legally" unlimited legislative authority and one which, though limited, is supreme in the system"; and that the legislator's legal limits and habits of obedience are both important factors.[113]

In the ensuing section of the same chapter (IV), Hart brings to a head the thrust of his arguments under the heading "The Sovereign behind the Legislature." "There are," he begins, "in the modern world many legal systems in which the body, normally considered to be the supreme legislature within the system, is subject to legal limitations on the exercise of the legislative power: yet . . . the enactments of such a legislature within the scope of its limited powers are plainly law."[114] Hart concludes as follows: "[T]he theory treating the electorate as sovereign only provides at the best for a limited legislature in a democracy where the electorate exists. Yet there is no absurdity in the notion of an hereditary monarch like Rex enjoying limited legislative powers which are both limited and supreme within the system."[115] Summarizing his chief arguments at the beginning of the next chapter (V), Hart exclaims: "[T]he simple model of law as the sovereign's coercive orders failed to reproduce some of the salient features of a legal system. . . . [T]he analysis of law in terms of the sovereign, habitually obeyed and necessarily exempt from all legal limitations, failed to account for the continuity of legislative authority characteristic of a modern legal system, and the sovereign, person or persons could not be identified with either the electorate or the legislature of a modern state."[116]

In essence, then, Hart has criticized the simple command-theory of legislative sovereignty propounded by Bentham and Austin, according to which there could be no real limits to coercive authority; he has substituted a new theory of legislative sovereignty (as part of his wider interests in concepts of law and legal system) in which there are or can be legal limitations. In other words, despite Hart's claims to a sweeping new system within the parameters set forth by Bentham and Austin, he in part raises to new levels their own (traditional) emphasis on legislative sovereignty. Whereas for them legislative sovereignty was, at bottom, limited by their very conditions that it *not* be limited, Hart now proclaims a more far-reaching applicability of the doctrine by declaring it compatible with limitations. Hart has reaffirmed in new ways, less radical than he believes, various principles of Benthamism and Austinianism insofar as they pertain to legislative sovereignty *per se*.

Where Hart's ideas converge most conspicuously with utilitarian traditions drawn from Bentham, Austin, and Mill is in his later chapters of *Concept of Law* when endeavoring to reinstate justice and morality within conceptual systems of law and legislation. Bentham, it will be remembered, had separated morals and legislation, while J. S. Mill had largely reduced justice to questions of institutional and social utility. "Critics like Bentham and Mill," Hart maintains in Chapter IX on "Laws and Morals," "who most fiercely attacked Natural Law, often attributed their opponents' confusion . . . to the survival of the belief that the observed regularities of nature were prescribed or decreed by a Divine Governor of the Universe."[117] Even so, the justice, natural or human, that Hart reinfuses into law and legislation, minus their divine contexts, becomes more relativistic than universal, again placing him more in the camp of his nineteenth-century predecessors than he acknowledges.

The complexities of Hart's organization in *Concept of Law* are too enormous (and tangential) to treat here. So, too, are the reactions to them by numerous other theorists including Rawls, whose theory of justice diverges from that of Hart. Overall, organizationally, Hart begins with the nineteenth-century command-theory, along with its later adaptations, and then turns to the older ideals of justice and morality that that theory overthrew; he goes on to formulate an innovative conceptual system of law and legislation that conjoins central elements of both schools of thought. In the process, Hart has reinvigorated not only neo-positivism and neo-utilitarianism but has given rise to various new "anti-neo" forms.

It is at his most fundamental level of legal philosophy—in dealing with the relation of positive law and legislation to morals (morality) and justice—that Hart's neo-positivism blends in various ways with neo-utilitarianism. These were precisely the basic issues for Bentham as a utilitarian and positivist in *Morals and Legislation*; therein Bentham joined theories of utility and command when separating legislation and morals, leading on to the ideas of Austin. It is not merely the case that Hart rejects the Austinian and Benthamite models of deriving the content of positive law and legislation from material legal principles separated from morality and justice. Nor is it merely that Hart contrariwise derives the content of positive law and legislation from principles of morality inclusive of justice and even natural law. For, in fact, Hart continues to insist that law must be clearly distinguished from morality and justice, each kept within its proper sphere, and that legislative sovereignty is paramount albeit subject to limitations that Bentham and Austin failed to recognize. In these and other respects, then, Hart is more a neo-Austinian and neo-Benthamite than he acknowledges in his *Concept of Law*.

Clearly, Hart has furnished many points of departure and reaction for other writers with more purely neo-utilitarian and anti-neo-utilitarian theories of law. At the same time, a variety of recent studies, combining historical and theoretical perspectives on utilitarianism in relation to Bentham, have given fresh impetus to what may be called neo-utilitarianism and neo-Benthamism. Some defenders of neo-utilitarianism against Rawl's attacks have pointed to the integral place of justice and religion in Bentham's thought itself, with implications also for Hart's approach. Utilitarianism or neo-utilitarianism in the history of American legal thought has also been a subject of interest to scholars. Studies on legal positivism have, moreover, interconnected it to issues of Benthamism and Austinianism in conjunction with newer trends in recent legal realism.[118]

Chapter VIII

The Growth of "Anti–Neo-*Isms*"

The continuing hold of nineteenth-century "isms" upon early-twentieth-century thought on state and sovereignty is manifested not only in various so-called "neo-isms" discussed above but also in "anti–neo-isms" reacting against them—an antithesis articulated here for the first time. Notwithstanding their "new" directions, both categories are ultimately derivative or reactive in relation to their nineteenth-century prototypes. The "anti–neo-isms" in the present chapter follow roughly the same sequence of topics as the "neo-isms" treated in the preceding chapter. These similar arrangements of topics in both chapters largely parallel those for the nineteenth century adopted in Part I. The "neo-isms" of the early and mid-twentieth century were often themselves "anti–neo-isms" when reacting against one another. In general, these types of classifications are a departure from traditional organizational methods used by historians, but they are suited to the texts to be studied.

1. "ANTI–NEO-POSITIV*ISM*": KRABBE

In view of the great influence of so-called "neo-positiv*ism*" in the early and mid-twentieth century, it is not surprising that there have been equally vigorous counterattacks against it in legal-political theory as well as in philosophy more broadly. To a considerable extent, one may speak of "anti–neo-positiv*ism*." This current of thought has taken even wider diverse forms than has "neo-positiv*ism*."

One direction taken in reaction to neo-positivism was the development of the Sociological School of law, a vast field of inquiry in its own right. As an emerging "ology," it was long closely associated with positivism, pro or con, in derivative or reactive forms. As noted above, the sociological approach to philosophy, law, and other subjects arose in the nineteenth century in new ways within the parameters of the positivism of Comte, although proto-sociological methodology can be found in the preceding century in writings by Montesquieu, Vico, and others. When, however, positivism evolved along more formal lines in the study of law from Austin to Kelsen and beyond, the developing Sociological School reacted. A long series of innovative theorists reacted against legal positivism by dwelling on the social contexts of legal developments. The Historical School of law (or legal historicism) also contributed to the rise of sociological jurisprudence by building upon the Romantic School's orientation toward the "spirit of the people" (*Volksgeist*), a crucial component in the formation of national legal systems.

Two important legal theorists of the early twentieth century who were much inspired by emergent sociological viewpoints were Hugo Krabbe (1857–1936) and Léon Duguit (1859–1928). Their respective works entitled *The Modern Idea of the State* (1915) and *The Transformation of the Theory of the State* (1913) pursued social perspectives on the development of law in relation to the state and sovereignty. Their works were part of what has been called (by Spahr and others) "the liberal attack upon the sovereignty of the state." Krabbe can be classified as an anti–neo-positivist, while Duguit can be viewed as an anti–neo-Hegelian, although these categories overlap (and are used here in novel ways). Their works will be briefly treated with an eye, once again, to the underlying factor of legislation. This common denominator has likewise above linked together disparate key works on the state and sovereignty, notwithstanding the divergencies between ideological or methodological "isms" more generally. It will be seen that Krabbe, in adapting some of Duguit's ideas of objectivism in law, placed his own emphases on law's ethical ends and on the higher sense of right. Krabbe sometimes diverged from Duguit, as when detecting in him lingering elements of positivist theory that he, Krabbe, sought to move further beyond.

State and Sovereignty

The Introduction to Krabbe's *Modern Idea of the State* sets forth his fundamental points on the modern idea of the state. He reacts to German positivists and neo-positivists who still retained older ideas of the state's power in spite of their newer concepts of the state based on law and right. Krabbe also distinguishes between modern concepts of the state in actual practice and modern political theories of the state more abstractly; he subjects the latter to criticism for not keeping pace with developing political and legal realities. Positivism remains, for Krabbe, a form of absolutism, as intimated in his references to the theories of Paul Laband (1837–1918).

> The basis of the rulership (*Herrschaft*) which is essential to the idea of the state is a fundamental question which political theory must reconsider. The current conception of the state, growing out of the absolute form of government, regards it as an original manifestation of power, endowed by its very nature with the right of rulership.
> After the theory of the legal state (*Rechtsstaat*) had been developed, there arose a conflict between this conception and that of an equally original manifestation of power, the law. This leads to the theory that the state is subject to law, or, in the well-known formula of Laband, "that the state can require no performance and impose no restraint, can command its subjects in nothing and forbid them in nothing, except on the basis of a legal prescription [from *Staatsrecht des deutschen Reichs*]" . . .
> Nevertheless, political theory cannot even now bring itself to abandon the old conception of the state as an original manifestation of power. Thus it is involved in an insoluble contradiction, for it must now accept the hypothesis of a dualism of powers; namely, that of the state and that of law. The efforts to overcome this dualism and to explain the subordination of the state to law have failed to achieve their object.
> The actual course of public affairs, however, has given rise to an idea of the state which eliminates the difficulties of political theory. This, the modern idea of the state, recognizes the impersonal authority of law as the ruling power. In this respect it accepts the standpoint of the theory of the legal state as this was formulated by Laband. But it draws the ultimate conclu-

sions from the ideas which lie at the basis of this theory. It no longer holds that the state subordinates itself to the law, but insists that the authority of the state is nothing other than the authority of law. Hence there is only one ruling power, the power of law. According to this view, the state is not coerced by law, but is rather endowed with the authority of law. The law is not a superior and the state a subordinate power, but the authority inherent in the state and the authority of the law are identical, so that the basis of the rulership of the state is coincident with the binding force of the law.[1]

Chapter IX ("The State") of Krabbe's *Modern Idea of the State* reduces the state theory of Georg Jellinek (1851–1911) to its ultimate basis. That is, the state, as a group of people within a territory, centers around the relationship between the rulers who command and the ruled who obey. At the bottom of this theory, therefore, lie traditional notions of the sovereign and of sovereignty (as well as of positive law and legislation). At the same time, Krabbe points out a partial parallel here with Duguit's theory, apart from Duguit's emphasis on the higher ends of law. Implicit also is a distinction between Jellinek's idea of subjective right to rule and Duguit's noted theory of objectivism, which is joined to Duguit's social or sociological outlook on forces shaping the law of the state.

> As Jellinek correctly observes [in *Allgemeine Staatslehre*], the word "state" is scientifically very useful because it connotes nothing and therefore serves as a protection against ambiguity when it is applied to specific phenomena. But to what phenomena is it applied? . . . The Netherlands, England, Belgium, Prussia, and France are all designated as states. If we consider both the scientific and the practical meaning of this designation, we can say that universally it means an organization including a portion of mankind which occupies a definite territory. The countries mentioned above differ from one another in the details and peculiarities of their organization.
>
> But what organization is meant in this case? According to traditional political theory, the typical feature of the organization which makes a portion of mankind into a state lies in a relation between persons who command and persons who obey. Among such a portion of mankind, there emerge certain persons who issue commands; in contrast with these, all others are in a condition of obedience. Those who command are the rulers; collectively they make up the sovereign. Those who obey are

the subjects and are collectively described as the people. "Men [according again to Jellinek] who command and those who obey their commands make up the substance of the state." Political theory, however, or at any rate German political theory, is not content with this fact, but institutes a search for the *right* to command and the duty to obey. . . .

Duguit's political theory also, in explaining the organization typical of the state, starts from the fact that there are those who rule and those who are ruled. But for him the fact is enough; there is no right to command. "The truth is that political power is a fact which in itself has no quality either of legitimacy or of illegitimacy." "No one has the right to command others; neither an emperor, nor a king, nor a parliament, nor a popular majority is able to impose its will as such [*Traité de droit constitutionnel*]." How such a fact came to be is an historical question. In general, the distinction between "rulers" and "ruled" is a result of the fact that in all social groups the stronger rule. . . .[2]

In Chapter I ("The Authority of the State and the Authority of Law"), Krabbe begins with "The Opposition between the Old and the New Idea of the State" (Section I). He summarizes the changing role of the sovereign and of sovereignty, since the Middle Ages, with regard to "the subjective right to rule" and "the will of the sovereign."[3] In time, the state became the center of focus concerning sovereignty, but much remained the same. Krabbe cites various positivistic statements on the state's virtually unlimited powers carried over from the days of absolutism.

[T]he state is now recognized as the possessor of the sovereign authority; but since the state is regarded as a legal person and so requires organs for willing and acting, these organs now become bearers of the sovereign authority, and the idea of sovereignty has in fact remained undisturbed, even in its aspect of a personal right to rule. To this sovereign, or according to modern terminology to the state, is now attributed that ultimate and unlimited power so frequently referred to in the literature of the subject. The power of the state, says Maurenbrecher, is irresistible, infallible, holy. Otto Mayer speaks of the "unconditioned predominance of the state's authority," and of "the state's capacity to exercise a legally paramount will;" Jellinek speaks of the "unconditioned enforcement of its own will against others;" and Laband discusses "rulership" as the "specific prerogative of the state." All these characterizations grow directly out of the idea of absolute monarchy.[4]

Krabbe goes on in detail to describe the rise of the modern sovereign state in terms of the development of positive law, public law, the legislative power, and related matters.[5]

In Chapter II ("The Authority of the Sovereign and the Authority of the Law in Theory"), Krabbe traces the stages of historical evolution in the authority of the sovereign and of the law. He begins with earliest times in which, according to sociological and historical investigations, there was no organization externally imposed upon the community. When discussing the later rise of sovereign princes, Krabbe is especially interested in legislative powers, whether in contexts of their presence or absence, and in the laws issuing therefrom. The development of the legal state is of considerable concern to him in connection with the recent historical development of legislative organs. Krabbe refers also to the ethical ends central to ancient Greek ideas of the state in writings by Plato and Aristotle. But it is the rise of representative legislative organs since the French Revolution that have given, in Krabbe's mind, the most decisive impetus to the modern legal state over and above the sovereign.[6] In Chapter III ("The Basis of the Binding Force of Law"), Krabbe begins by treating the concept of the sovereignty of law in terms of the idea of justice and its relation to positive law and legislation.[7]

Legislation

Chapter IV of Krabbe's *Modern Idea of the State* ("The Making of Law") first sets forth the crucial place of legislative power in positivistic jurisprudence. This topic revolves around the sovereign's command and will in making law.

> So long as the idea of sovereignty alone was dominant, it was accepted as self-evident that the imperative character of the law was derived from the sovereign, whether it were king, parliament, people, or state. Because of the sovereign's inherent right to authority, his will was positive law (*Gesetz*) and as such embodied principles of right (*Recht*). The legislator, therefore, appeared as the constructive sovereign who has called the law into existence.
>
> The Positive School of Jurisprudence was content with this explanation of the imperative nature of law and of the way in which it originated or became effective. What the law might be

over and above the will and wisdom of the legislator, was regarded as belonging to the less important fields of politics or legal philosophy. For "practical" jurists law was the command of the sovereign and nothing more.[8]

According to Krabbe in the same chapter (IV), the domination by legislative command-theory in positivistic jurisprudence gave impetus as well to the systematization of law and legislation by jurists; this, he feels, became an abstract intellectual exercise.[9] Codification of law and legislation became the most satisfactory way of achieving systematization, but it, too, was removed from ordinary accessibility because it was a product of professional jurisprudence. Indeed, Krabbe's direct and indirect diatribes against legal codification in conjunction with legal positivism suggest a rejection of the Pandectist School of jurisprudence (which was linked to the Positivist as well as Historical Schools, which in Germany had culminated in various ways with the *Civil Code* of 1900).[10] Systematization of law and legislation has, however, according to Krabbe, been stymied by the unsatisfactory combination of older ideas of sovereignty in the police state and newer ideas of authority resting upon law. Only by discarding the former and embracing the latter can "public interests" be advanced through "the social sense of right," which is the real authority that "commands" a "freely given" "obedience."[11]

In the concluding sections of the same chapter on law-making, Krabbe presents short summaries comparing and contrasting older and newer ideas of the state in political theory. Concerning the binding force of law, the older view required "a sovereign over the people," whereas the new idea revolves around law as a "norm," which obtains its force from the "sense of right" (here calling to mind Kelsen's norms). Whereas the older system promoted an "omniscient legislator," whose intention and authority extends on into the future, the present view revolves around the actual legislative provisions at the time laws are made. As for the question of "the validity of statutory law," it is not merely, at present, a matter of this or that parliamentary body making legislation. The crucial factor is the people participating as a social whole in the changing "organism" of law through "a living process," on into the future, after the laws are promulgated. Krabbe urges resistance to and liberation from "the yoke of history and tradition" insofar as it impedes the ongoing social and "spiritual" development of a people's legal-legislative system. (Nonetheless, the emphasis here on a kind of living *Volksgeist* pertains in certain respects to the German Historical School of law.) In the final analysis, the new theories of the modern state as set forth here by Krabbe ultimately depend upon issues in law and legislation.[12]

A pivotal section of Krabbe's *Modern Idea of the State*, in Chapter IX ("The State"), is entitled "The Modern Theory of the State." It is immediately preceded by passages contrasting older views on sovereign power with newer ideas on the authority of the norms—in addition to observations on Duguit's distinctions between "ruler" and "ruled" as founded upon relationships rooted in law. Krabbe goes on in the section at hand (III) to place the highest premium on modern states comprising a single rather than mixed nationality. In the former, the "inner force" and "higher spiritual existence" impels the "sense of right" in "legal relations" to a high plateau (again with echoes of the Historical School and perhaps Hegel as well), especially in contrast to older sovereign powers forced upon a people. Krabbe makes it plain that the growth of "national bodies of legal relations," which give the "modern idea of the state . . . its foundation," occurred when "the people . . . recovered their share in law-making." Krabbe's implicit belief here is that a state with a single nationality can best achieve a centralized legislative activity. For he proceeds to argue that in a "state . . . [with] many . . . nationalities" the "law-making" should be as little "centralized" as possible in order for it to be "held together." In "the unitary states," moreover, the "sense of right has been organized and centralized" in a "legal system"—from all of which springs the legislative organs. "In every organ devoted to law-making, the idea of the state may be perceived . . ." Organized legislative activity stems from this independent higher quality of legal-legislative authority involved in and issuing from a proper sense of right. Actual legislatures and changing phenomena rest upon constitutions that can change. Thus actual legislation *per se* must become, for Krabbe, the manifestation of a higher legal-legislative sense of organized right lying at the heart of legal relations.[13]

Krabbe goes on in the ensuing section of Chapter IX on the state to argue that during the rise of absolute monarchy the state became transformed into a modern legal-legislative entity, with its legal relations arising chiefly from the prince's law-making activities. At the same time, the prince's sovereignty remained rooted in power. The resulting involvement of the prince in preserving public interests hampered the true idea of the modern legal state. Properly speaking, the higher independent legal-legislative entity and community of the modern state is freed from the private power of princely sovereigns.[14] The passage that continues below makes further evident the crucial part of legislation in Krabbe's theory of the state. Citing Bodin at the beginning, Krabbe develops a theory of public law as the essence of a modern state still dominated by princely rule over a subjected citizenry. This stands in contradistinction to a legal state or community where there is a higher sense of right. Nonetheless, public legislation is in both cases a pivotal factor for Krabbe.

> . . . Bodin's "true marks of sovereignty" embrace a number of princely rights with reference to certain public interests. When at a later time the need for a decentralization of the functions of government made itself felt and the theory of the separation of powers gained general acceptance, the state was regarded as a complex of three great public interests, viz., the interest of organized legislation [etc.]. . . .
>
> [There] also arose the distinction in principle between public and private law. . . . In private law representatives of interests confront each other on equal terms, but in public law they are of unequal standing, the sovereign as against the citizen-subject. Finally the same circumstance gave rise to the insoluble question whether the state can be bound by law, a question which was answered affirmatively or negatively according as the state was conceived as the possessor of a complex of public interests or as a legal community. . . .
>
> The constitutional system, at least on the Continent, made its entrance at the end of the eighteenth and beginning of the nineteenth century in the form of the constitutional monarchy. Its importance consisted for the most part in the fact that the people came to share in the exercise of the state's authority. . . . But the chief point was that the exercise of the prince's authority had to be shared with the people. . . .
>
> The most significant point, however, was the participation of the people in the exercise of legislative power. This as yet did not mean a participation in legislation throughout its entire extent, but merely a share either in establishing the civil and criminal law or with reference to certain specified objects. In particular, the competence of the people to share in legislation for public interests was long denied. . . . Hence the controversy over the extent of the ordinance-issuing power which belonged to the king alone, in comparison with the legislative power which he had to share with the legislative assembly. . . .
>
> The establishment of an organ intended solely for law-making and the subordination (required by the theory of the legal state) of monarchy with its tradition of absolutism gradually brought about in practice . . . the real essence of the state . . .[15]

Finally, Krabbe assigns great importance to legislation and legislative organs in the inevitable world state of the future. Into it, each national state will be absorbed as a province but with its own legislatures to govern it. At that point, the law, as an ethical idea at the heart of the modern state, will come to characterize the new order as well. This discussion occurs in a section on "The Rise of a World State" in Krabbe's Chapter X ("The International Legal Community"). By way of current parallels, we may add, some historians have pointed to the emerging European Union (not to mention global bodies) in which national states are subordinated. However, the eventual legislative orientation in such a larger federal entity in Europe should appear no less plausible than it is for the union of states in the United States of America, which is roughly of comparable size and which revolves around the legislative factor at all levels.[16]

2. "ANTI-NEO-HEGELIAN*ISM*": DUGUIT

State and Sovereignty

In a long article of 1917 on "The Law and the State," Léon Duguit, an almost exact contemporary of Krabbe, criticized recent German jurists like Jellinek for their mistaken neo-Hegelian doctrines of state and sovereignty. Krabbe's liberal attacks on German positivistic jurists had been mixed with his expressions of nationalistic bias, as a constitutionally minded Hollander, against the more absolutist monarchical traditions of German jurists; Krabbe also reflected a strong Germanic impulse often found in Dutch intellectual traditions in such matters. Duguit's nationalistic French bias against German absolutist tendencies are abundantly evident, even though Duguit ends up pointing to French theorists having affinities to their German counterparts. At issue for Duguit is the familiar Hegelian outlook on the state and sovereignty. Duguit's derogatory usage of the label "metaphysical" to describe Hegelian and related tendencies in political-legal thought on the state echoes Hobhouse's stronger attacks on what he called the "metaphysical theory of the state" expounded by Bosanquet in extreme absolutist (or totalitarian) neo-Hegelian fashion. Duguit's own objectivist legal philosophy is, however, different from Hobhouse's approach.

> . . . German doctrines of public law in the nineteenth century from Kant to Jhering and Jellinek were, for the most part, mere apologies for the use of force; and that under the cover of juridical theories they had only for their object the reestablish-

ment of absolutism of the State, and especially of the prince who represents it at home and abroad: while, on the contrary, the persistent effort of French juridical doctrine has ever been, from 1789 to the present time, to find the true juristic basis for legal limitation upon the power of the State, and to insure its sanction. . . . But the end in view has always been the same; namely, to prove that the powers of the State are limited by a jural principle (*une règle de droit*) superior to the State itself. . . .

I classify as metaphysical all doctrines which think of the State as a being gifted with a personality distinct from that of individuals who form the social grouping—the basic element of the State—as a personal being possessing a will which is by nature superior to individual wills, having no other will superior to it. This will receives ordinarily the name of sovereignty. . . .

Certain adherents of these doctrines have, moreover, attempted to explain and to prove the actual personality of the State and the character of superior sovereignty belonging to its will. They are, to be truthful, the French representatives of the metaphysical conception of the State. . . . Under the influence of the doctrines of the Hegelians, they have supposed the personality and the sovereign will of the State as existing *in itself* and *for itself*. They have seen in the State the synthesis of the particular and of the collective, and in this the realization of the moral idea. Without making further inquiry, they have proclaimed the conscious, willing, and sovereign personality of the State. . . . The problem of the subordination of the State to law (*le droit*), so far as the metaphysical conception is concerned, is always the same. It is this: If the State is by nature a sovereign will, that is to say, a will which commands individuals and is not subordinated to any other will, how can it be in subjection to a rule binding upon it, since by definition there is no other will capable of imposing a rule upon it? . . .

The German jurists have expressed this idea in the following formula: The State by definition possesses a will that never delimits itself except by itself, that determines the sphere of its own action, that has "jurisdiction of its own jurisdiction" (*la compétence de sa compétence*). The State would cease to be the self-determining sovereign will, it would cease to have the control of its own limitations (*la compétence de sa compétence*), it would cease to be the State, if its will were bound by a superior principle (*une règle supérieure*) fixing and limiting the extent of its action. . .[17]

In focusing on the metaphysical Hegelian tradition, Duguit points out, as had others including Hegel himself, the precedents in Rousseau's *Social Contract* for the idea of the state's sovereign will as including within itself individuals' rights and freedoms. Duguit rejects the "sheer subjectivity" of these views on the sovereign will as a "self-actualizing" individual personality existing unto itself, as the essence of the state, and as the realization of moral ideas.[18] Only in the later nineteenth century, Duguit believes, did a juridical theory of the state's public law emerge in Germany. It was distinct from, yet also an extension of, the political and moral philosophy of the Kantian-Hegelian tradition. This mixture, together with an attempt to join *Machtstaat* and *Rechtsstaat*, became a "sterile" exercise and "sophistry" in works by Jellinek and others.[19] Duguit also uses the positivist ideas of Comte to bolster his own argument that the notion of the state's subjective right involves a metaphysical viewpoint, both of which are absent in the "positive state."[20]

At the outset of his *Law in the Modern State (Transformation of the Theory of the State)*, Duguit sketches in Chapter I ("The Eclipse of Sovereignty") the doctrinal history of sovereignty. After brief looks at Roman and medieval notions, Duguit accentuates the crucial conceptual role played by Bodin, before passing on to the seventeenth and eighteenth centuries with respect to absolutist and constitutionalist doctrines. The advancing ideas of sovereignty and public law, involving subjective rights to command, were inherently absolutist, Duguit believes, even in their more constitutional frameworks in Rousseau and the French Revolution. Dogmas about national sovereignty swept all before them in the course of the nineteenth century.[21]

Legislation

In Chapter II ("Public Service"), Duguit believes that the modern state has in practice become based, in his own period, upon public services rather than upon public law in its older contexts of sovereign commands. Duguit seeks a new theory to match what he feels are the new current realities. Instead of starting from the standpoint of public law as the expression of the collective sovereign will, Duguit proceeds from the perspective of social groups, the needs of which governments must address through ever-expanding public services. The ruler's "power is imposed" on subjects in varying spontaneous ways according to "utility."[22] Public law in this new modern state theory, in the mind of Duguit, is founded on systems of rules expressed in laws or legislation for purposes of organizing "public utilities." Public law is no longer based on subjective command but rather on "objective" social functions. Government action necessarily involves "the exercise of a right to power" in order to achieve the desired public ends through public laws. Notwithstanding Duguit's new liberal objectivist theory of public law, it becomes clear, we may add, that in his system public law and legislation do indeed remain the foundation of the state and of sovereignty. Public law, in its "objective" form, still lies at the heart of the state and sovereignty, while the newer objective will replaces the older subjective will. Duguit's liberal objectivism also includes a kind of neo-utilitarianism.

> Such is the nature of the profound change that is taking place in public law. Public law is no longer a mass of rules which, applied by a sovereign person with the right to command, determine its relations between the individuals and groups on a given territory as a sovereign dealing with its subjects. The modern theory of the state envisages a mass of rules which govern the organisation of public utilities and assure their regular and uninterrupted function.
> The relations of sovereign to subject do not make their appearance. The one governmental rule is the governmental obligation to organize and control public services in such a fashion as to avoid all dislocation.
> The basis of public law is therefore no longer command but organization. Public law has become objective just as private law is no longer based on individual right or the autonomy of a private will, but upon the idea of a social function imposed on every person. So government has in its turn a social function to fulfil. . . . It follows that if governmental action is not the exercise of a right to power it has no special character. What quality it possesses, what effect it produces are derived from the end it has in view. This in its turn determines the nature of law. In all the imperialist system law is essentially the manifestation of sovereignty. It is above all a command formulated by the sovereign and so imposed upon his subjects. That is no longer the case. Law is simply the formulation of a rule, the product of a group of social facts which government believes necessary, as a rule, under the pressure of public opinion, in order to give itself the greatest possible strength. Most laws are in reality passed to organize and operate public utilities. Law is thus above all a law of public service. . . . Government is legally obliged to ensure the operation of public utilities. It issues for this purpose general rules called laws. Their character is derived from

the end government sets before itself. . . . That is to say that public utilities are institutions of objective law. . . .

Public utilities have thus an objective character. . . .

If all this is true, certain results clearly follow. The legislation and jurisprudence of such countries as are influenced by this movement ought to tend towards the organisation of a practical system which . . . relate[s] to urgent public needs. . . .

No legal bond exists between the state and the private citizen which obliges the state to fulfil his demands, but a law, that is to say, a purely general regulation, controls the operation of the service and if the state violates that law its illegal act can be annulled.[23]

Duguit's Chapter III ("Statute") makes clearer the continuing presence of public legislation as the foundation of the sovereign state in his liberal and objectivist legal system—as geared to the social needs of the citizens through public services provided by government. Statutes are no longer the expression of the sovereign will and command *per se*, but rather of the will of the people making them—whether as the leaders of the state or the members of the legislature. Once again, Duguit brands the older system "metaphysical" and "imperialist," perhaps in an unintended sign of his own biased subjectivity in developing a new "objective" legal system.

In any system of public law founded on sovereignty, statute is its clearest manifestation. Rousseau pointed this out on several occasions. . . .

It is of course clear that statutes are necessary. It is equally clear that the flavor of generality which attaches to statutes constitutes the best guarantee the individual can possess against arbitrary conduct. . . . But, . . . in Rousseau, statute was the command of the sovereign. As such it could not be unjust and was not subject to reserve or restriction. . . .

Such a conception was in clear logical accord with the imperialist system. But it is obvious that, if the theory of sovereignty is no longer the foundation of political theory, the conception is obsolete. If, then, in the legal life of the modern state we take account of facts and of situations, such as the acceptance of a jurisdiction which completely contradicts the theory of statute as an expression of sovereign will, we can show under another aspect the transformation of public law.

A statute is a general rule for governing conduct. But because we have to-day eliminated from politics the theories of metaphysics [sic] the hypothesis of national sovereignty, that of divine right and of an inheritance from God, a statute can no longer be the formulated command of sovereign power. A statute is simply the expression of the individual will of the men who make it, whether they be the leading statesmen or the private members of a legislative body. Beyond that we are in the realm of fiction. In France, for example, statute is the expression of the will of 350 deputies and 200 senators who usually form the majority in the Chamber and in the Senate. Administrative orders, which are, in fact, real laws, express the will of the statesmen or civil servants who issue them. . . . It is clear . . . that there is an objective law superior to government. As soon as a human society exists, the indispensable condition of its maintenance is a social discipline.[24]

In the same chapter on statutes (III), Duguit explains that statutes or legislation in the form of social rules are binding and compel obedience because of their inherent "normative" nature rooted in the social necessity that occasioned their promulgation. Duguit stresses that such a statute "is not, technically speaking, a command" (although it comes close to that). Public opinion is crucial in the making of legislation through "a social sanction"—a fact that Duguit believes has long been the case.[25] He sharply separates statutes from customs, while underscoring the imperative character of statutes in connection with the act of promulgation.

> It should be added that such normative law must not be confused with custom. Statute and custom are two different things. Statute is the expression of a rule which social needs are elaborating in individual consciences. . . . Often the degree that custom expresses is socially defective and the objective law is first and directly expressed in statute. . . . [A] rule of conduct . . . [i]n itself . . . is not imperative because it only becomes imperative when definitely enacted as statute. . . .
> Constructive laws are simply those which organise public services, and they form the greater part of modern legislation. . . .
> In truth, there is no statute which does not organically control some social need and derive its power therefrom. . . . This is true of all statutes . . .[26]

The weakness of Duguit's contentions that the modern state rests on public law and legislation without the element of sovereign command (when in fact he posits a kind of imperative sovereign will behind public legislation geared to social services) becomes even more apparent in his Chapter IV ("Special Statutes"). Here Duguit contends that the tendencies, in most if not all modern states, toward federalism, decentralization, and localization have precluded the element of sovereignty and sovereign command. Only in the centralized state (presumably in earlier times) can there be a true central sovereign will.[27]

On the contrary, we may add, historians have generally concluded that the trend of the modern state has been toward the unitary national state; the individual states within the national federal systems have imperative legislative powers in controlling their own affairs. The federal government of the United States of America—especially through the activities of Congress in promulgating legislation—is no less expressive of a sovereign legislative command merely because the individual states possess their own powers to legislate within their own realms. Federalism and sovereignty are not mutually exclusive, contrary to Duguit.

3. "ANTI-NEO-(NATIONALIST)STAT*ISM*": LASKI

State and Sovereignty

Whereas Duguit subscribed to the doctrine of objectivism, Harold J. Laski (1893–1950) advocated early on a doctrine of pluralism. Particularly in his early works, Laski, like Duguit, attacked traditional concepts of state and sovereignty that were founded mostly on command, coercion, and will. Laski's numerous voluminous writings took issue, in varying and changing ways, with features of liberalism, Hegelian idealism, and Austinian (as well as Comtean) positivism. Pluralism or diversity within society and the state was, for Laski, the necessary antidote to the state's all-absorbing monism and collectivism, which impeded individualism and freedom. Laski's pluralism involved complex mixtures of liberalism and anti-liberalism.

In his later writings of the 1930s and 1940s, Laski moved more in the direction of an avowed neo-Marxist-socialist set of viewpoints, while still retaining various essential features of his early pluralism in the two preceding decades. In his later works, Laski diverged from his early comprehensive indictments of traditional doctrines of the state's internal sovereignty grounded primarily on command and will in such matters as lawmaking. He also came to accommodate his ideas on the state's coercive powers to neo-Marxist socialist doctrines. He rejected the class dominance fostered by liberal capitalist society, which needed to be corrected by governmental action oriented to more equitable distributions of justice and goods for society. Nonetheless, Laski continued to condemn doctrines of sovereignty that were directed toward the nationalist egoistic statism of force and power for the state's own ends. Laski continued to reject doctrines that did not allow for popular consent or that prevented the state from fulfilling its obligation to provide social services (the state's crucial justification even more so for Duguit, who influenced Laski). Among Laski's works devoted to socialist perspectives were *Karl Marx, The Communist Manifesto: Socialist Landmark*, and *The Socialist Tradition in the French Revolution*. In the case of Marx and his followers, both Hegel's idealism and Comte's materialism can be seen as contributing to collective tendencies in socialist thinking, according to Laski.[28]

The distinctive (yet convoluted) relationships between Laski's pluralist state and the monist proclivities in the socialist state are further complicated by his changing outlook on liberalism, socialism, and Marxism. While he increasingly made use of Marx's attacks on the capitalistic liberal state, Laski continued to criticize the rigid socialist structures of the monist nationalist state in current history. Laski's more far-reaching criticisms of normative legal theories of the sovereign nationalist state-will, existing unto itself, would continue in his later works. In other respects, however, Laski's early sweeping castigations of traditional formulations of sovereignty gave way to his later recognition of the role of an ultimate sovereign power in the state for the end of achieving its mission. The changing character of British liberalism—from the more individualistic and capitalistic type espoused by J. S. Mill to the more socialistic state advocated by Lloyd George—further complicated the background to Laski's outlook. The following excerpts from Laski's later work, *The Rise of European Liberalism*, serve as sign posts with regard to liberalism and socialism.

> The nineteenth century is the epoch of liberal triumph; from Waterloo until the outbreak of the Great War no other doctrine spoke with the same authority or exercised the same widespread influence. . . . It was the prophet of industrialism; and it transformed Great Britain into the workshop of the world. . . . It established universal suffrage and parliamentarianism almost as principles of natural law. . . .
>
> [T]he victory of liberalism was an easy one. . . . On the one hand, it confronted a renovated conservatism which, in the hands of men like de Maistre and Hegel, sought to set limits to individualism in the name of . . . authority. . . . On the other, from St Simon onwards, that release of the individual which

expressed itself as the *laissez-faire* state was attacked. . . .
Comte and his disciples rejected the liberal idea in the name of
a science which, in their view, made it incumbent upon the state
to undertake the regulation of social life in the interest of an
organic community superior in its claims to any part of its
membership. . . .

But the essential attack on the liberal idea in the nineteenth
century was that of socialism. . . . There go to its making ideas
derived from the most disparate sources. . . . In its vital formulation by Marx and Engels, . . . the . . . state . . . was not a
neutral organ seeking . . . the well-being of the whole community, but a coercive power enforcing upon the working class that
social discipline required by the owners of property in their
search for profit. . . . The *laissez-faire* state . . . [for] Marx
. . . was . . . simply . . . organized subjection . . .[29]

In another later work, *The State in Theory and Practice*, Laski
affirmed the rightful central place of individual liberty in the traditional
historical liberal state, which was combatted by Hobbes, Bosanquet,
Hegel, and many others. Laski's historical interpretations typically
acquire their value and usefulness as building blocks in the construction
of his own political philosophy. Whereas in the idealist tradition Green
and Bosanquet, for instance, stressed political obligation, when expanding upon the state theory of Hegel, Laski points to limits on restraint.
Here, as occasionally elsewhere, Laski incorporates certain Marxist
viewpoints. Yet he voices with feelings about the imposition of a "common" social framework to achieve social unity. The striving of individuals in a pluralistic society toward a kind of consensus is an ideal of his
early works still partly evident here.

> The state as an organization to promote the happiness of
> individuals; . . . liberty as essentially absence of restraint . . . ;
> rights as boundary-marks which . . . the state was not normally
> entitled to invade; these were the characteristics of the history
> of political philosophy roughly from the Reformation to the
> French Revolution. The tradition they represent was, of course,
> denied hardly less seldom than it was affirmed, and the accep-
> tance of the tradition in any thorough-going way was hardly
> complete until the middle of the nineteenth century. . . . [I]n its
> making the state was never itself an end, but always a means to
> an end; . . . the individual, finite, separate, identifiable, was
> always regarded as existing in his own right, and not merely as
> a unit serving the state to which he belonged. . . .

> This tradition, which is broadly what we call the tradition of the liberal state, . . . was brilliantly attacked by Hobbes. . . . The men who made both the English and the French Revolutions announced themselves as the protagonists of the rights of man; but . . . [they really favored] the rights of that limited class of men who own the instruments of production in society. The liberal tradition, in historical fact, was an intellectual revolution primarily made in the interests of property-owners in the new (and newly significant) industrial field. . . .
>
> The idealist theory of the state . . . denied . . . that liberty meant . . . absence of restraint. . . . The idealist answer is . . . that the real will of the individual is identical with the will of the state. . . .
>
> If, indeed, we go the whole way with Hegel, . . . we are thereby denying the patent experience of mankind. For he . . . affirmed, for example, that the French state before 1789 . . . was worthy of the allegiance of its citizens[,] . . . conclusions so perverse. . . . Unity does not arise from sharing in a common world.[30]

Laski's pluralistic concept of sovereignty and the state was clearly delineated in his early *Studies in the Problem of Sovereignty* (1917). The excerpt to follow presents the contrary case, as he saw it, on the part of Hegelians and others. The Bismarckian context is extensively treated elsewhere in the same work.

> [T]he monistic theory of the State . . . —largely perhaps from its evident relation to the dominant philosophy of Hegel—has triumphed not only in modern Germany, but also, in some lesser degree, in modern Europe. . . .
>
> We have to admit, so your monist philosopher tells us, that all parts of the State are woven together to make one harmonious whole. What the Absolute is to metaphysics, that is the State to political theory. The unity is logically necessary, for were there independence, one group . . . could never act upon another. . . . Pluralism, in an ultimate sense, is therefore impossible. . . .
>
> And here clearly enough Sovereignty emerges. The State must triumph. . . . We must fight with the State whether or not we feel the justice of its cause. . . . Was not the *Kulturkampf* but the expression of Bismarck's conviction that your sovereign must be one and know no fellow?[31]

Legislation

In his same early work, *Problem of Sovereignty*, Laski discoursed at points on the key role of legislation within the contexts of the pluralistic state. The legislative sovereignty of the British parliament rests upon the consent of the governed rather than upon coercive will and forceful command. Failed notions of the omnicompetent national state held by Louis XVI and Bismarck offer useful lessons. Implicit here is Laski's combination of morality and legislation, whereas Bentham had sought to separate them. That the state should not attempt to control the church through legislative enactments is an important point in his discussions adjacent to the passages given below. Clearly, Laski's pluralism is here built not only upon traditions of parliamentary consent in British liberalism a la Locke, but also upon ethical ideas espoused a few years earlier in Duguit's seminal work concerning political-legal objectivism.

> We have nowhere the assurance that any rule of conduct can be enforced. For that rule will depend for its validity upon the opinion of the members of the State. . . . We have, therefore, to find the true meaning of sovereignty not in the coercive power possessed by its instrument, but in the fused good-will for which it stands. . . . But then law clearly is not a command. It is simply a rule of convenience. Its goodness consists in its consequences. It has to prove itself. It does not, therefore, seem wise to argue that Parliament, for example, is omnipotent in a special sense. The power Parliament exerts is situate [sic] in it not by law, but by consent, and that consent is, as certain famous instances have shown, liable to suspension. . . . Where sovereignty prevails, where the State acts, it acts by the consent of men.
>
> What guarantee have we, then, in the pluralist view that the will of the State will prevail? . . . It does not, I believe, give any more handle to anarchy than it at present possesses. . . . The monarchs of the *ancien régime* were legally the sovereign power in France, but their will was not the will of the State. . . . They confused what Rousseau would have called their "private good" with the "common good" and Louis XVI paid the penalty. . . . The will of the State obtains pre-eminence over the wills of other groups exactly to the point where it is interpreted with sufficient wisdom to obtain general acceptance, and no further. . . . There is no sanction for law other than the consent of the human mind. It is sheer illusion to imagine that the

authority of the State has any other safeguard than the wills of its members. . . . [W]hile, for example, in England, the sovereign power is Parliament, and, broadly speaking, only the rules laid down by it will be enforced by the courts, yet Parliamentary opinion, Parliamentary statute, are the result of a vast complex of forces towards which men and groups, within and without the State, make often enough valuable contributions. It seems to me that you can never find in a community any one will which is certain of obedience. . . . The sovereign is the person in the State who can get his will accepted, who so dominates over his fellows as to blend their wills with his. Clearly there is nothing absolute and unqualified about it. . . . It is not because of the force that lies behind its will, but because men know that the group could not endure if every disagreement meant a secession, that they agree to accept its will as made manifest for the most part in its law. . . . The Bishop of Exeter drew an interesting distinction between the legal and moral sovereignty of Parliament. "While according to our constitution," he said, "Parliament has unlimited power, the effect of its legislation must depend on the moral power behind it. . . ." . . . Bismarck . . . had learned that the world, even the Germanic world, is not one and indivisible. He had defined the State to himself as a power which, to maintain itself, must prove its sovereignty over every department of human life. He would have agreed with Calhoun that the division of sovereignty was its destruction. So, in one aspect, he would contend that the *Kulturkampf* was no more than the vindication for the State of rights that were in reality its own.[32]

Also in the same early work, Laski theorized about the scope of modern social legislation passed by government action to help equalize differences between economic classes. While approving of these endeavors for the sake of promoting equality, which he elsewhere believes to be as important a goal as liberty, Laski is not in favor of certain monist tendencies on the part of the state for advancing its own nationalist ends separate from the needs of the society it is meant to serve. At stake is the very conception of law and legislation, which should not be coercively imposed, however commendable the goals, although this has occurred in states of his day, as he avers here and elsewhere. Nevertheless, the state finds its most typical keynote in public legislation, whether in good or bad manifestations.

Whatever our view, the fact remains that, at least since the Industrial Revolution, the continuous tendency of modern legislation, not less in the new world than in the old, has been to soften by governmental action the harsh contrast which would otherwise obtain between the lives of the rich and the poor. And, on any long view, the ability of the state to win the loyalty of its citizens depends upon its power continuously to soften the contrast. . . .

Upon this attitude there hinges a view of law the implications of which are important. . . . Law becomes law as it goes into application; it is made law by being accepted. That is not to say that accepted law is right law; for law may be accepted by the might which is behind it.[33]

Here, in addition, Laski enumerates three types of law and legislation—the formal, the political, and the ethical. Of these only the third, resting upon consent, is truly acceptable. The first two varieties tend to revolve around sovereign will and political power, as in the example given of Hitler's decrees of 1934. At present, bemoans Laski, statist legislation in Britain and other nations is geared more to coercion and the self-interest of dominant groups than to the common welfare that such legislation is supposedly intended to promote.[34]

Bodinian Tradition and "Machiavell*ism*"

Among Laski's most enduring legacies were his noted historical accounts of sovereignty and the state in European thought. His numerous books on the subject include discussions of seminal writers in the early development of theories on the state's legislature foundation. Laski viewed Bodin as the direct forerunner of Hobbes, Rousseau, Bentham, and Austin in terms of legislative sovereignty. Notwithstanding Laski's opposition to the monist national statism inherent in the Bodinian tradition, he furnished a telling historical sketch in such passages as the following in another early work, *The Foundations of Sovereignty* (1921). Laski recognized there the logical necessity, particularly within the Bodinian tradition, of absolute legislative sovereignty, although he cast doubt on Dicey's application of it to recent British history. For Laski in this early work, such normative legal positions, however logical in themselves, result in a legal fiction. Nonetheless, Laski left behind for subsequent historians a vivid historical picture of the theoretical development of Bodinian (and related Roman) traditions on sovereignty, most notably in legislative matters.

Bodin expresses in the clearest fashion the theory to which we have moved. His book, for that very reason, is normally taken as the starting-point of modern politics; for what he teaches is, with some difference of detail, substantially the modern legal theory of the state. Nor may we deny it a logical completeness within the narrow realm it attempts to resume. "All the characteristics of sovereignty," said Bodin [*Republic* I, 8], "are contained in this, to have power to give laws to each and everyone of his subjects, and to receive none from them." The sovereign may be one or few or many, but unless it is an absolute power, it lacks the marks of *majestas*. A long history lies before those words: From Bodin and through Hobbes to Austin, every legal analysis of the state has depended upon their substance. Nor is it possible, in the sphere of positive law, to refute it. *Jus est quod jussum est* is of the essence of the state. There must be in every organized political community some definite authority not only habitually obeyed, but also itself beyond the reach of authority. . . .

So stated, Bodin's theory is unimpeachable. Yet we must not forget with what grave difficulty it made its way. To the question why men must obey the law, it answered only because the state so willed; and it therein forgot that the law, in its view, was no more than the command of the state. There were men unwilling to accept so simple a solution. Even Bodin himself, it may be remarked, has doubts of its adequacy; for he makes state-law morally bound by natural law and the law of God. . . . Bodin, in fact, was above all a practical inquirer into the political sickness of the time. The sovereignty he defined was conceived less with a view to the metaphysics of his subject, than as a weapon wherewith to make possible the special remedies of which he was the advocate. . . . [T]he monistic theory of the state goes back, in its scientific statement, to Jean Bodin. The latter became the spiritual parent of Hobbes, and thence, through Bentham, the ancestor of Austin. . . .

Legally, no one can deny that there exists in every state some organ whose authority is unlimited. But that legality is no more than a fiction of logic. No man has stated more clearly than Professor Dicey the sovereign character of the King in Parliament. . . . A history, of course, lies back of that attitude, the main part of which would be concerned with the early struggle of the modern state to be born. Nor do I think the logical character of the doctrine has all the sanction claimed for it.

It is only with the decline of theories of natural law that Parliament becomes the complete master of its destinies.[35]

According to Laski, in his early *Foundations of Sovereignty*, Machiavelli contributed to doctrines of the sovereign state by pointing out the core realities of power. Medieval thinkers had been more concerned with abstract rights and limits on power. Strong princely power within a territorial state was reaffirmed by Luther as well as by Henry VIII.[36] Subsequent to these figures and Bodin, Rousseau, following largely in Bodin's footsteps with regard to legislative sovereignty, established further paradigms that were developed by Bentham, Austin, and later theorists. Political philosophers along with legal theorists have erected a system of all-powerful state sovereignty that imposes a common unity internally without allowing for a diversity or pluralism of individual interests. Laski dwells upon internal nationalist sovereignty, which in the political philosophy of Hobbes, Hegel, Green, and Bosanquet became too monist, in Laski's opinion, whereas the national state's external sovereignty in relations with other nation-states remains necessary for defense and other purposes. Internal sovereignty typically results, according to Laski, in the rise of dominant groups and private interests rather than in a truly common public or objective good, which Laski feels can only be achieved through a process of pluralistic interests coming more freely together. To promote through coercion a statist unity is not the way to create a cohesive society of free and differing individuals. The orthodox legal theory of internal nationalist sovereignty is therefore flawed because it rests unduly on the command and will of the sovereign. This flaw has prevailed in the idealist tradition, inclusive of Hegel, Green, and Bosanquet (not to mention in positivist and other traditions). Laski's main objection to the concept of internal sovereignty is that it rests on power and coercion in ways that can be traced back not only to Bodin but also to Machiavelli.[37]

In Laski's estimation, even King Henry VIII of England, the embodiment of Machiavellian power politics, was ultimately enabled to rule in princely fashion through a kind of popular consent. Henry VIII was not able to become a despot to the extent suggested by some historians. Instead, the strong governmental powers of the centralized Tudor state, which put an end to medieval feudal ties, rested upon the control of Parliament and parliamentary cooperation through the sovereign power to make new legislation. This nationalistic power state is an antithesis of Laski's own political philosophy of pluralism, notwithstanding the element of consent that bolstered Tudor government.[38]

At the same time, in civil law countries, the revival of Roman law in the early modern period brought with it an exaltation of the secular nation-state and princely power, along with the decline of medieval canon and feudal law.[39] Although Laski has elsewhere stated that general concepts of the nation-state began to emerge in the later Middle Ages, he here believes that ideas of sovereignty in a more specific modern sense (in the Bodinian tradition) did not yet exist in the Middle Ages, where prevalent concern was more for justice and rights. In that case, not surprisingly, Laski finds more merit in medieval ideas than in modern ones on the matters at hand.[40]

Thus, while upholding the values of the state generically in contexts of pluralism (in what he calls the "pluralistic state"[41]), Laski is mostly negative toward traditional doctrines of omnicompetent nationalist sovereignty, over and above the common welfare of the citizens. He nevertheless fully recognizes the important historical place of Bodinian tradition on legislation that culminated with various nineteenth-century theorists. In using history to support his political philosophy, Laski presented a picture of the development of European statism that was not only a foil for his own anti-statism but also one that was influential upon subsequent historians of early and modern European political thought.

4. "ANTI–NEO-(COLLECTIVIST/COMMUNAL) SOCIAL*ISM*": HAYEK

Ideology

Among the classic works of the Austrian (later British) theorist Friedrich A. Hayek (1899–1992) are *The Constitution of Liberty* (1960) and *Law, Legislation and Liberty* (1973–1979). As their titles suggest, both works deal with themes of liberty and freedom (in the face of the overwhelming coercive powers of the state). These and other works by Hayek strongly criticize the "neo" varieties of state socialism prevalent in the twentieth century—that is, the totalitarian types found in Russia and Germany as well as the more limited type present in Britain and other countries. Prior to these two works, when socialism was an especially dominant force, Hayek wrote extensively on the role played by German socialism in paving the way for Hitler's National Socialism. He had warned in advance that democratic socialism would not be able to guarantee individual liberties but would be prone to limit freedoms. Communistic collectivism or communalism in political, social, and economic terms also fell under Hayek's severe scrutiny of socialist state planning. Hayek was a critic of the socialistic economic ideas of the famed British theorist John Maynard Keynes, and he won the Nobel

Prize in 1974 for his contributions to economic theory in the 1930s. Select political, legal, and social ideas of Hayek are of present note, against the backdrop of his vast collected writings.

In his *Constitution of Liberty*, Hayek declares at the outset of Chapter 9 ("Coercion and the State") that "freedom . . . [is] the absence of coercion." Coercion is "bad" insofar as it hinders the individual from using his full intellectual capacities and from contributing to the community. Yet Hayek distinguishes between different types of coercion, while recognizing the subject's complexities in the relations between individuals and the state.[42]

Chapter 17 ("The Decline of Socialism and the Rise of the Welfare State") in Hayek's *Constitution of Liberty* begins by stating that varieties of socialism have dominated efforts at social reform for about a century (including for a part of that period in the United States). During "the century of European socialism" from about 1848 to 1948, the "common aim of all socialist movements was the nationalization of the 'means of production, distribution, and exchange' . . ." However, in "the last decade . . . socialism . . . [as] a particular method of achieving social justice has collapsed . . . [and] been discredited." Yet the socialist label will be taken up by new groups for "new program[s]." Hayek is interested in new policies for a "free society." Issues of "centralization versus decentralization of governmental functions" are crucial to Hayek.[43]

In his "Postscript" ("Why I Am Not a Conservative"), Hayek makes it plain that he is not on the side of conservatives merely because he resists contemporary "progressive[s] [who typically] advocate further encroachments on individual liberty . . ." Prior to the rise of socialism, the main opponent of conservatism was liberalism. Hayek subscribes to a form of liberalism (and individual liberty in relation to the state) that is as different from conservatism as it is from socialism.[44]

As part of his broader refutations of socialism, Hayek elsewhere criticized "the [flawed] concept of social justice," in its recent parameters, for failing to achieve its goals. Having emerged as another term for distributive justice in the writings of its advocate, J. S. Mill, the term "social justice" has largely become, for Hayek, a misnomer in its applications in the twentieth century. Hayek argues that appeals to social justice have become a dominant force in political thought, but to extents that would be little recognizable to early writers like Mill. "Though the phrase has undoubtedly helped occasionally to make the law more equal for all, whether the demand for justice in distribution has in any sense made society juster or reduced discontent must remain doubtful." Hayek goes on to point out: "The various modern authoritarian or dictatorial governments have of course no less proclaimed 'social justice' as their chief aim. . . . [M]illions of men in Russia are the victims of a terror that 'attempts to conceal itself behind the slogan of social justice.' "[45] Hayek believes that "the majority of Continental liberals . . . were led more by a desire to impose upon the world a preconceived rational pattern than to provide opportunity for free growth. The same is largely true of what has called itself Liberalism in England at least since the time of Lloyd George. . . . [W]hat I have called 'liberalism' has little to do with any political movement that goes under that name today."[46]

Elsewhere, Hayek severely criticizes the harmful effects of centralized collectivist "planning" in socialist states. Not only has individual freedom in Russia, Germany, England, and other nations declined, but a dangerous nationalistic statism has been unleashed.

> There can be no freedom of thought, no freedom of the press, where it is necessary that everything should be governed by a single system of thought. In theory socialism may wish to enhance freedom, but in practice every kind of collectivism consistently carried through must produce the characteristic features which Fascism, Nazism, and Communism have in common. Totalitarianism is nothing but consistent collectivism, the ruthless execution of the principle that "the whole comes before the individual" and the direction of all members of society by a single will supposed to represent the whole. . . . [S]uch a system produces a despotic control in every sphere of life, and . . . in Germany two generations of planners have prepared the soil for Nazism. . . . [P]lanning tends to produce intense nationalism and international conflict. . . .
>
> Nothing in this situation deserves to be studied and pondered so much as the intellectual history of Germany during the last two generations. . . . Men, undoubtedly great in their way, made Germany an artificially constructed State—"organized through and through", as the Germans prided themselves. This provided the soil in which Nazism grew and in which representatives of State-organized science were found among its most enthusiastic supporters. It was the "scientific" organization of industry which deliberately created the giant monopolies and represented them as inevitable growths fifty years before it happened in Great Britain.[47]

Legislation

Of particular note in Hayek's trilogy on *Law, Legislation and Liberty* is his central focus on problems in legislation. In Volume One, bearing the subtitle *Rules and Order*, Hayek devotes a significant historical section (4) to "The Changing Concept of Law."[48] In it he sketches the historical development of concepts of law both in legislative and non-legislative matters from ancient through medieval periods and into modern times. One need not agree with Hayek's conclusions on the slow development of lawmaking, as distinguished from lawgiving, particularly during the Middle Ages, in order to appreciate the central place Hayek assigns to legislation in the modern state. His historical views on legislation are oriented to his anti-socialist political philosophy on liberty in relation to law and the state. Hayek's objections to the infringements of individual liberties by legislative promulgations are secondary, for present purposes, to the fact that he places legislation at the apex of the modern state in the matters at hand. Hayek's fundamental disagreement with the command-theory of law and legislation prompts him to distinguish it sharply from the need for more independent ways to arrive at "rules of just conduct" that will not stifle individual liberties by undue state legislative initiatives. Yet this approach does not detract from the central place, for better or worse, that he assigns to the lawmaking power as the main engine traditionally driving the modern state, as in Britain and elsewhere.

More specifically in the section at hand, Hayek decries the fallacy of long-standing "belief that there must be a supreme legislator whose power cannot be limited because this would require a still higher legislator, and so on in an infinite regress." Equally erroneous to Hayek is the age-old notion "that anything laid down by that supreme legislator is law and only that which expresses his will is law." Such concepts, from Hobbes to Austin, have applied an "absolute power" and "unlimited will" of the sovereign legislator(s) to monarchs as well as to democratic assemblies, asserts Hayek; they have assumed that "the term law is restricted to the rules guiding the deliberate and concerted actions of an organization. Thus interpreted, law, which in the older sense of *nomos* was meant to be a barrier to all power, becomes instead an instrument for the use of power." Contrary to the arguments of legal positivists, who deny "effective limits to the power of supreme legislature," Hayek contends as follows: "The authority of a legislator always rests . . . on something . . . distinguished from an act of will. . . . This source is a prevailing opinion that the legislator is authorized only to prescribe what is right, . . . [concerning not] the particular content of the rule but . . . the general attributes which any rule of just conduct must possess." The legislator's laws therefore rest not on his power but on the rights his laws are supposed, according to public opinion, to possess. Limits on the legislative power(s) may thus be arrived at through a process of public opinion.[49]

Following Hayek's ensuing section (5) entitled "Nomos: The Law of Liberty," is a section (6) of his *Law, Legislation and Liberty* entitled "Thesis: The Law of Legislation."[50] In it he further builds upon the perspectives of history in presenting his own political philosophy. "The great majority of resolutions passed by representative assemblies do not of course lay down rules of just conduct but direct measures of government. This was probably so at all times. . . . A statute (*thesis*) passed by a legislature *may* have all the attributes of a *nomos*. . . . But it *need* not . . ." In a discussion on the ambiguity of law in doctrines of the separation of powers as conceived by Montesquieu and others, Hayek goes on to cite the reaction by James Mill to Bentham's advocacy of an "omnicompetent legislature." Instead of a government under law, Mill advocated a government controlled by a free, independent popular assembly. After ensuing discussion on Napoleon I's concepts of legislation, Hayek broadly associates universal rules of just conduct with private law and links the rules of organization of government with public law. Jurists, particularly on the Continent, have apprehended law primarily in terms of public law and governmental organization. In so doing, they are responsible in large measure for the rise of legal positivism as well as of socialism and totalitarianism, according to Hayek. Constitutional law, or law dealing with the constitution, is occupied not with rules of just conduct but with rules of organization. Governmental efforts to supply particular "services" (an apparent allusion to ideas of Duguit and Krabbe) are usually connected with "infrastructures" and thereby pose "difficult problems." Hayek is critical of "the transformation of private law into public law by 'social' legislation." Social legislation attempts to direct private activities to particular ends and groups in the name of "social justice." For several generations, this "socialization of law" has been developing in Western nations. It led in Germany to harmful results.

It may be added that Hayek's *Constitution of Liberty* contains in Part II ("Freedom and the law") pertinent chapters further pertaining to legislation. The titles of Chapters 9–11 and 16 are indicative: "Coercion and the State"; "Law, Commands, and Order"; "The Origins of the Rule of Law"; and "The Decline of the Law." In addition, the second and third volumes of *Law, Legislation and Liberty* are useful and are indicatively entitled *The Mirage of Social Justice* and *The Political Order of a Free Society*.

5. "ANTI-NEO-UTILITARIA*NISM*": RAWLS

The classic work against utilitarian and neo-utilitarian doctrines is by John Rawls: *A Theory of Justice* (1971). Rawls' treatise has been aptly characterized by one commentator as follows:

> One of the major polemical concerns of John Rawls' *A Theory of Justice*—perhaps *the* major polemical concern—is to provide a satisfactory alternative to the utilitarian account of social justice. . . . Utilitarian thought, which flowered in the writings of the classical utilitarians, Jeremy Bentham, John Stuart Mill, and Henry Sedgwick, has been the dominant conception in Anglo-American moral and social philosophy for roughly the past two centuries [with roots going back to Hume and others]. . . . Rawls' book has revolutionized contemporary discussions of political theory; it seems likely to be the most profound work in the field to be published in this century. His extended argument against utilitarianism has raised important new issues. . . . But . . . [his] argument does not appear to ring the deathknell for utilitarianism; defenders of that theory . . . must feel that the battle is far from over.[51]

In an early section of his *Theory of Justice* entitled "Classical Utilitarianism," Rawls asserts: "There are many forms of utilitarianism, and the development of the theory has continued in recent years. . . . My aim is to work out a theory of justice that represents an alternative to utilitarian thought generally and not to all of these different versions of it. The main idea is that society is rightly ordered, and therefore just, when its major institutions are arranged so as to achieve the general net balance of satisfaction summed over all the individuals belonging to it."[52] According to Rawls, utilitarianism views societies as it does individuals and groups, that is, as seeking their own greatest good, interest, and well-being. Classical utilitarianism defines utility, according to Rawls, in terms of the good, conceived as the satisfaction of rational desires. "The striking feature of the utilitarian view of justice is that it does not matter, except indirectly, how this sum of satisfactions is distributed among individuals . . ." How distributions of satisfactions are made is therefore relatively unimportant and unfixed. Utilitarian distributions to different individuals and groups need not necessarily be equal if the goal of the greatest good for the greatest numbers is kept in mind.[53]

Contrasting classical utilitarianism with his own theory of justice, Rawls makes a number of intricate distinctions. In a nutshell, Rawls' own theory of social justice, or of the just society, is based on the principle of fairness and original contractual agreements. This, he feels, is more geared to what is right than to what is good, which together with happiness is instead the utilitarians' focus. Whereas utilitarianism is teleological in the sense of specifying the good to be obtained, justice as fairness does not specify the good independent from the right, which therefore takes precedence over it. "[U]tilitarian doctrine . . . relies very heavily upon the natural facts and contingencies of human life in determining what forms of moral character are to be encouraged in a just society. The moral ideal of justice as fairness is more deeply embedded in the first principles of the ethical theory. This is characteristic of natural rights views (the contractarian tradition) in conjunction with the theory of utility." Rawls goes on to suggest that classical utilitarians believed that "the imposition of disadvantages on a few can be outweighed by a greater sum of advantages enjoyed by others." Contrariwise, Rawls himself holds that "the weight of justice requires an equal liberty for all and permits only those economic and social inequalities which are to each person's interests." These basic contrasts revolve, Rawls believes, around different concepts of society.[54] Such views pertaining to social inequality are also treated in contexts of Keynesian economic doctrines.[55]

From the preceding overview of Rawls' *Theory of Justice*, it becomes apparent that he seeks a more broad-based social concept of justice than has, he feels, long dominated utilitarian viewpoints in the nineteenth and early twentieth centuries. At the same time, Rawls' theory of social or distributive justice is at odds with the theories of Hayek examined above. In certain respects, then, Rawls was less sympathetic to the individualistic utilitarian ideas of J. S. Mill than was Hayek. For Rawls, utilitarianism has long been prone at points to a hedonistic outlook due in part to the pleasure principle. One will remember the utilitarian concept of the greatest happiness for the greatest number. Rawls' idea of social justice favors society's promotion of the equality of opportunity, as distinct from ideas of utility or even of liberty.

In the final analysis, the attempt by Rawls and others to reinvigorate political theory with ideas of social justice *per se* has a wider significance in twentieth-century thought. Some experts have charged that various key nineteenth-century "isms" (such as utilitarianism, positivism, and socialism) represented different forms of materialism, to which theorists like Rawls pose a countertrend. The command-theory of Bentham and Austin, as well as the perceived absolutist state of Hegel or Bismarck, was not destined to be the sole end result of several centuries of European political and legal thought on the state and sovereignty. Elements of justice and liberty that had been waning in previous centuries have been at times reinvigorated by various twentieth-century thinkers like Rawls and Hayek. Nevertheless, "neo" as well as "anti-neo" forms of nineteenth-century utilitarianism, positivism, Hegelianism, socialism, Marxism, and the like have endured as powerful ideological influences in political-legal thinking on state and sovereignty in the twentieth century. Concepts of justice in the twentieth century have been numerous and diverse; they have been as often allied to the several "isms" just cited as they have been opposed to them. But as a separate subject in itself, the changing concepts of justice in the twentieth century are a matter for another study.

6. RECESSIONAL OR PROCESSIONAL?

Although the present Part II has concentrated on the first half of the twentieth century, it has carried the thematic materials forward at points into ensuing decades in the second half of the century. Many current legal philosophers and others believe that, beginning in the later 1960s and especially the 1970s, Western Civilization has now entered the age of postmodernism. By this "ism" they often mean the rise of new values reacting against the Enlightenment's continuing legacy of reason and rationalism, which is thereby seen as representing modernism in reaction to traditions of medievalism.[56] Other kinds of experts have typically pointed to the rise of modernism in the culture and arts of the 1920s as a reaction against traditions of Victorianism—whether or not they also view the second half of the twentieth century in terms of postmodernism. Meanwhile, historians of the modern idea of the state have continued to identify modernity with trends stretching from the Renaissance and Enlightenment to the nineteenth and twentieth centuries, on up to the current period. Previous books in this series have demonstrated the powerful continuing hold of nineteenth-century "isms" in political-legal ideology upon historians, in the second half of the twentieth century concerning all periods in European statecraft. Thus it becomes less important how experts divide up intellectual history in terms of the inevitably shifting "isms" and more crucial how one views the relevant thematic materials under discussion. To concentrate, for instance, on modernism and modernity as a feature arising in the 1920s and ending a half century later in postmodernism would place historians of the modern state in an unworkable dilemma of definitions and truncated time frames.

The wider question arises as to "what next?" for the advancing historical trends and "isms" examined in this book and series. Was a culmination reached in the early and mid-twentieth century, only then to fall into the irrelevant limbo of a past tense or to be followed by an uncertain mixture of *post-*"isms"? Already by the 1960s such rubrics as "posthistoric" and "postindustrial" were used to describe the sea changes taking place in society more generally. Or is the past a crucial prologue in this case? Although answers to such questions must await future books in this series as well as future events themselves, it has been clear for some time that Western Civilization is at a crossroads. Current history and trends remain to be examined in further studies to come, but the continuing relevance of history for the present age has been attested at numerous points in these studies (as, for instance, in the prefaces to the preceding book and the present one).

There can be little doubt that the modern (or postmodern) legislative state, of whatever size or scope, is here to stay. Even those in the United States who have called in recent years for the reduction in governmental operations at the federal and state levels have conceded that the modern legislative state is more expansive than ever and is still growing. This continued growth is no doubt unavoidable and even necessary due to the ever expanding needs of increasing populations. The broadening base of the legislative state is nowhere more evident than in the increasing flood of modern legislation at all levels of governmental administration, as in the United States. Even if, on the world stage, the nation-states of Europe (notwithstanding their linguistic differences) were to be absorbed into the European Union and have no more autonomy than the fifty states of the United States of America, and even if both the European Union and United States of America were eventually to be absorbed into a future world government in which they would all be merely provinces, the modern (or postmodern) legislative state would still not wane but become stronger. If such trends were to lead to a world state (which is by no means certain to occur), the former nation-states would, as provinces, be at least as compelled to expand their scope as a subordinated state within a federation as are the fifty states of the U.S.A. in the present federal structure. If *all* the modern nation-states of the contemporary world ceased to exist as *national* entities and were to become something else (whether bigger or smaller units), the modern state as the *legislative* state would not die because of this transformation but would continue to thrive. Again, the analogy of the fifty states of the U.S.A. is apropos in that they each constitute a legislative state, albeit within the wider federal legislative state. A future world state as a legislative state was glimpsed, as pointed out earlier in this chapter, in writings by Krabbe. With the ongoing legislative state is a continuing legislative sovereignty, about which obvious related points can also be made (as the reader by now is more than sufficiently aware).

What now recedes into the background is this series' focus on European historical studies. It has been a long, absorbing journey to this juncture. The author hopes, however, that in the journeys to come the past will indeed furnish a crucial prologue. The American materials to which we will next turn, beginning with the early revolutionary and constitutional periods, can be better understood in light of the European background. To go no further than the vast collection of handsome books from Thomas Jefferson's library now housed in the Library of Congress (not to mention his own immense writings), there is rich evidence of the powerful formative hold of European intellectual traditions upon the early American imagination in a manner not yet fully grasped by historians.

Notes
to Chapters II–VIII
(Bibliographic, Historiographic, Documentary)

Notes to Chapter II
"Utilitarian*ism*" and "Bentham*ism*"

1. R. R. Palmer, *A History of the Modern World* (New York, 1950, 1956, 1965, 1971, using here the 3rd edn.), Ch. XI, "Reaction vs. Progress, 1815–48," sect. 51, "The Advent of the 'Isms' " (= sect. 52 in 1971 edn.).
2. *Ibid.*
3. *Nineteenth-Century Europe: Liberalism and Its Critics*, edited by Jan Goldstein and John W. Boyer (Chicago, 1988), as Vol. 8 of *Readings in Western Civilization* (also cited in our Vol. V, Bk. II).
4. Palmer, *ibid.*
5. *Victorian Liberalism: Nineteenth-Century Political Thought and Practice*, edited by Richard Bellamy (London, 1990), cf. ch. headings.
6. Palmer, *ibid.*
7. *Ibid.*
8. *Ibid.*
9. *Nineteenth-Century Europe*, Sect. 1, "Early Liberal Thought and Practice."
10. George H. Sabine, *A History of Political Theory* (revised edn., New York, 1956), Ch. XXXI, "Liberalism: Philosophical Radicalism," and Ch. XXXII, "Liberalism Modernized."
11. Frederick B. Artz, *Reaction and Revolution, 1814–1832* (New York, 1934), in the Langer *Rise of Modern Europe* series, Ch. IV, "The Orders of Liberalism," sect. 1, "The Principle of Utility."
12. Frank Thilly and Ledger Wood, *A History of Philosophy* (New York, 1958, 3rd edn.), Ch. XIX, "French and British Philosophy of the Nineteenth Century," sects. 69, "Positivism in France," 70, "Utilitarian Ethics of Bentham," 72, "The Empiricism of John Stuart Mill," and 73, "The Evolutionism of Herbert Spencer."
13. E.g. *The Utilitarians* (Garden City, 1961), being a selected collection of writings by Bentham (*Morals and Legislation*) and J. S. Mill (*Utilitarianism* and *On Liberty*).

14. *Nationalism, Industrialization, and Democracy, 1815–1914*, edited by T. Barnes and G. Feldman (Boston, 1972), Ch. 2, "The Rising Tide of Revolution," with sect. titles as alluded to above.

15. William Thomas, *The Philosophic Radicals: Nine Studies in Theory and Practice, 1817–1841* (Oxford, 1979), esp. Chs. 1, 3, 4.

16. *The Liberal Tradition in European Thought*, edited by David Sidorsky (New York, 1970).

17. Rodney Barker, *Political Ideas in Modern Britain* (London, 1978), corresponding to headings of chs. and sects.

18. Sabine, *History*, pp. 675–676.

19. *Ibid.*, pp. 677, 679–682, 684–686, 690, 695: "[Bentham's] *Fragment on Government* thus laid down the chief ideas that actuated the Philosophical Radicals: the greatest happiness principle as a measure of value, legal sovereignty as an assumption necessary for reform by legislative process, and a jurisprudence devoted to the analysis and 'censure' of the law in the light of its contribution to the general happiness. . . . From Bentham's point of view any corporate body, such as society or the state, is evidently fictitious. . . . The utility of the greatest happiness principle, therefore, consists in the fact that it is the great solvent of fictions, for it means that the real significance of a law or an institution must be judged in terms of what it does, and so far as possible by what it does to specific individuals. . . .

"The greatest happiness principle, as Bentham believed, placed in the hands of the skillful legislator a practically universal instrument. . . . The legislator needs to know only the special circumstances of time and place that have produced peculiar customs and habits and he can then control behavior by allocating pains and penalties to produce the most desirable results. . . . This distrust of custom and its complete subordination to legislation were among the principal characteristics of Bentham's jurisprudence. With them was connected an indifference to, or rather a contempt for history as a factor in social studies. . . .

"Bentham's jurisprudence, which was not only the greatest of his works but one of the most remarkable intellectual achievements of the nineteenth century, consisted in the systematic application of the point of view just sketched to all branches of the law, civil and criminal, and to the procedural law and the organization of the judicial system. . . . In all cases the utility of legislation is to be measured in terms of its effectiveness, the costliness of its enforcement, and in general by its consequences in producing a system of exchanges which on the whole is advantageous to most members of the community. Utility is the only reasonable ground for making action obligatory. . . .

"In the field of the criminal law the principle of utility provided, as Bentham believed, a natural method for arriving at a rational theory of penalties. . . .

"Bentham's theory of law established the point of view of analytic jurisprudence, which was almost the only system of the subject generally known to English and American lawyers throughout the nineteenth century. This School is usually associated with the name of John Austin, but in fact Austin did little more than bring together systematically ideas that were scattered through Bentham's voluminous and not always very readable works. In political theory the chief effect of Austin's work was to attach an exaggerated importance to the theory of sovereignty, which was in fact incidental to Bentham's plan for reforming the courts by Parliamentary control. . . .

"It is certainly true, however, that Bentham's jurisprudence was not so completely determined by the principle of utility as he supposed. In fact utility is an utterly indefinite word until one specifies utility for what and for whom. The liberal elements in Bentham's philosophy resided largely in its tacit premises. . . . Far more than he realized his thought was influenced by *ad hoc* considerations, especially by the fact that legal reform in his day was so largely a matter of getting rid of obsolete practices. Nevertheless, despite obvious inadequacies in his thought, there are few thinkers in the history of social philosophy that have exercised so wide and so beneficent an influence as Bentham. . . . Utility, according to Bentham, does indeed require a harmony of interests and the greatest happiness of all, but such a condition is not natural. It can be produced only by legislation, and the significance of pleasure for a jurist is that, in addition to providing a standard of value, it makes possible the control of human behavior. Moreover, Bentham had consistently refused to name liberty as the object of law, because law exists solely to force men to do what they would not do voluntarily. From Bentham's point of view social harmony is produced by legislative coercion. . . . For even though coercion is always an evil, as Bentham believed, it is a necessary evil, and the limits of its use are set only by its power to prevent a greater evil. It is of course possible to argue on utilitarian grounds against particular restraints of trade, but some legal regulation of it is inevitable and the principle of utility can justify any amount of 'interference' with trade. . . .

"The original parts of the early utilitarian political theory were all suggested by Bentham's jurisprudence and had indeed been outlined in the *Fragment on Government*. They consisted in an extension to constitutional law of the same ideas which he used in his plans for the reorganization of the judicial system. The fundamental principle is that liberal government cannot be equated with weak government. Devices for legal limitations on sovereignty, such as bills of rights, the separation of powers, and checks and balances, Bentham regarded as confused in theory and self-defeating in practice, like the building up of formality and technicality in the law. Accordingly he accepted the complete legal sovereignty of Parliament and the need for relying upon an enlightened public opinion to insure responsibility. Ultimate political sovereignty, he believed, should inhere in the people, since only so can the interest of government be made to coincide with the general interest. . . . The significance of these political ideas lies not so much in the fact that they were more radical than any scheme of reform that was practicable in Bentham's lifetime as in the fact that he jumped, so to speak, quite over the stage of liberal thought that regarded constitutional limitations as the chief guaranties of freedom."

20. *Ibid.*, pp. 698–699, 702, 704–708, 710–714: "The criticisms commonly passed upon Philosophical Radicalism and given currency even by liberal successors like John Stuart Mill were that it neglected institutions and their historical growth and that it worked with a falsely schematic conception of human nature and motives. Both criticisms were true. Often however they were taken to imply that it was clear, rigidly logical and systematic, and merely based on premises too narrowly limited. This was not true. Its fundamental weakness was rather that as a philosophy it was never clear and never critical of its assumptions or its deductions. . . . It claimed to be empirical but it made little effort to check its premises by observation, and in effect its empiricism stopped with a crude form of sensationalism that had been derived from Locke two generations before. Hence it easily fell a victim to criticism as soon as it faced thinkers less impressed than Mill with its characteristic dogmas. Philosophical Radicalism was in truth largely an *ad hoc* philosophy, and it was also largely the spokesman for a single social interest which it identified, hastily though not hypocritically, with the well-being of the whole community. . . . Its weakness as a social philosophy can be summed up by saying that it had no positive conception of a social good, and that its egoistic individualism made it look with suspicion on the validity of any such conception, at a time when the total welfare of the community was becoming a principal object of concern. Its weakness as a political philosophy was that its theory of government was almost wholly negative, at a time when it was becoming inevitable that government should assume a larger responsibility for the general welfare. . . . Liberalism as it had been understood was on the defensive, and by a curious anomaly

legislation passed in the interest of social welfare, and therefore of the greatest happiness, ran counter to accepted liberal ideas.

This reaction against economic liberalism did not proceed from any antithetical social philosophy nor did it imply any philosophical agreement among those affected by it. What Dicey called 'collectivism' was certainly not a philosophy. It might be more accurately described as a spontaneous defense against the social destructiveness of the industrial revolution. . . . In short, a modernizing of liberal theory depended upon breaking down the intellectual isolation of Philosophical Radicalism, which was largely responsible for its dogmatism, and bringing it into touch with the outlook of other social classes, with Continental strains of thought, and with new fields of scientific investigation. Only so could liberalism claim to be a social philosophy and not merely the ideology of a special interest. . . . In the case of Mill it was the effort both to revise utilitarianism and the conception of personal liberty and also to take account of the social philosophy of Comte. It was Oxford idealism, however, that finally broke by its criticism the hold of the empirical tradition on Anglo-American philosophical thought and based itself avowedly on post-Kantian German philosophy. . . . Green submitted to drastic criticism the sensationalism and hedonism upon which the older liberalism professed to be based, but he was more clearly and more coherently liberal in his political theory than John Stuart Mill. And while idealism called itself neo-Hegelian, it contained no more than a trace, and not that in Green, of the political authoritarianism that Hegelianism connoted in Germany. . . . Mill's mind was characterized by a very high quality of candor and intellectual honesty which made him almost nervously anxious to do justice to a philosophy opposed to his own. Thus he was inclined to make concessions which implied far more than he realized and which were often more generous than critical. . . . In a broad sense, therefore, Mill's philosophy was an effort to modify the empiricism in which he was bred by taking into account the very different point of view of Kantian and post-Kantian German philosophy.

"Unfortunately Mill's candor and open-mindedness were not matched by the grasp or the originality required to bring about a really coherent synthesis of philosophies so widely divergent. . . . Mill's thought had all the marks of a transitional period in which the problems have outgrown the apparatus for their solution. Without much exaggeration it might be said that his books followed a formula. On nearly every subject he was likely to begin with a general statement of principles which, taken literally and by itself, appeared to be as rigid and as abstract as anything that his father might have written. But having thus declared his allegiance to the ancestral dogmas, Mill proceeded to make concessions and restatements so far-reaching that a critical reader was left in doubt whether the original statement had not been explained away. . . . For this reason systematic criticism is fatally easy and practically useless. The importance of Mill's philosophy consisted in its departures from the system which it still professed to support and hence in the revisions that it made in the utilitarian tradition.

"The ethical theory which Mill set forth in his *Utilitarianism* illustrates this defect of his philosophy, yet it is also the root of his revision of liberalism. . . . Mill united these propositions by an argument so patently fallacious that it became a standard exhibit in textbooks of logic. . . . This put him in the indefensible logical position of demanding a standard for the measurement of a standard, which is a contradiction in terms, and also reduced his utilitarianism to complete indefiniteness. . . . The root of all this confusion was that Mill was not willing to accept Bentham's greatest happiness principle for what in effect it was, namely, a rough and ready criterion for judging the utility of legislation[,] . . . which was the only purpose that had interested Bentham. . . . Mill's ethics was important for liberalism because in effect it abandoned egoism, assumed that social welfare is a matter of concern to all men of good will, and eregarded freedom, integrity, self-respect, and personal distinction as intrinsic goods apart from their contribution to happiness. . . . As Mill himself said . . ., the utilitarians of his father's generation had desired liberal government not for the sake of liberty but because they thought it would be efficient government, and it was indeed true that Bentham had changed nothing but details when he turned from benevolent despotism to liberalism. . . . His [Mill's] argument was addressed not to the state but to society. The essay *On Liberty* was an appeal not for relief from political oppression or for a change in political organization, but for a public opinion that is genuinely tolerant, that values differences in point of view. . . . The threat to liberty which Mill chiefly feared was not government but a majority that is intolerant of the unconventional. . . . This was a possibility that had never troubled the older generation of liberals. . . . Yet it is quite certain that Mill had not lost faith in the traditional lines of liberal reform. . . . The total impression produced by Mill's theory of liberty is therefore a little indefinite or perhaps even negative. . . . Mill's argument avoided the appearance of triviality only because it was circular. . . . The fundamental difficulty with Mill's argument was that it never really analyzed the relationship between freedom and responsibility. At times he retained the traditional view derived from Bentham that any compulsion or even any social influence is an abridgement of liberty. Yet he never supposed that there could be any important freedom without law and when he identified liberty with civilization, he did not imagine that there could be civilization without society. What Mill's theory of liberty required was a thoroughgoing consideration of the dependence of personal liberty on social and legal rights and obligations. It was this which J. H. Green tried to add to liberalism.

"The unclearness of Mill's criterion for defining the proper limits of legislation became apparent when he went on to discuss actual cases. His conclusions conformed to no rule at all but depended on quite subjective habits of judgment. Thus he regarded prohibition of the sale of alcoholic liquors as an infringement of liberty though compulsory education is not. . . . However unclear the principle, the important result emerged that Mill had abandoned economic *laissez faire*. Even Bentham's maxim that legislation is inherently bad and so must be kept at a minimum has lost the connotation that it had for Bentham. For all practical purposes Mill simply laid aside the dogma of earlier liberalism that the largest amount of freedom coincides with the absence of legislation and accepted the evident fact that there are many forms of coercion other than that exercised by the law. . . . So far as Mill was concerned, he merely accepted the need for social legislation, probably on humanitarian grounds, with no clear theory of its justifiable limits.

"Mill's economic theories showed like deficiencies of logical clarity and therefore are subject to like criticism. . . . Indeed in his later years he was willing to contemplate a degree and kind of control which he called socialism. This criticism of classical economics indicated one aspect of a general deficiency which Mill came to attribute to the social philosophy of the early liberals, namely, that it neglected the institutional nature of society. . . . Thus he opened the whole question of the relation between legislation and the economy, even its relation to the maintenance of a free market. . . .

"A just and at the same time a sympathetic estimate of Mill's liberalism is very difficult. Nothing is easier, for reasons that have been explained, than to represent it as a typical example of the futility of putting new wine into old bottles. . . . Mill's most important insights were intuitive, the outcropping of a fine moral sensitiveness and deep consciousness of social obligation . . . [yet] defects of coherence . . . marred Mill's systematic philosophy."

21. Nancy L. Rosenblum, *Bentham's Theory of the Modern State* (Camb., Mass., 1978), pp. 6–7, 9–10, 27, 55, 74, 99–100, 151–152: "Public necessity, he contended, should be genuinely public. Insight into the exigencies of the state should not be restricted to rulers in the hope that public ignorance would ensure stability or in order to spare the public conscience. Bentham would force men generally to acknowledge the painful consequences of accepting the state as the norm of order.

"This approach to Bentham's thought is also a departure from the questions ordinarily taken up by moral philosophers who have nearly monopolized Bentham studies. Often these ethical interpretations have obscured or trivialized the import of the principle of utility; they have invariably distracted readers from the purpose Bentham thought his principle would serve. . . . Private morality was always subordinate in his mind to the larger question of public utility. . . . Bentham produced the principle of utility for rulers precisely because of the inadequacy of traditional moral rules. . . .

"The chief claim Bentham advanced for utility was as a rationale for legislation. The institutional expression of public utility was, for him, a unified system of law, and law was unquestionably Bentham's main concern. Jurisprudence, model codes, and legislative programs constitute the greater part of his writings. His singular interest in law is clear in the titles of his works, in the turn of his arguments, and in his own account of his efforts: he was famous, Bentham recorded, because he had superseded everything written before him on the subject of legislation. Before he wrote, the field of law was a 'trackless wild.' . . . The state was a legal entity, Bentham explained, because it was in a unified legal system that public utility was expressed. . . .

"Bentham expounded the principle of utility chiefly as a rationale for legislation. The political contest that brought life and meaning to this work was his struggle to reform English common law, and Bentham's most potent rhetoric was invariably directed at Blackstone and the legal profession. Utilitarian legislation had another opponent in classical political thought, and Bentham was equally unsparing in his attack on this tradition. In fact, his anticlassicism and his opposition to the English legal system sometimes converged, because of the connection he discerned between classicism and aristocratic politics. . . . Bentham's main argument with classical political thought focused not on class rule, however, but on law. If utility is to serve as a rationale for legislation, then legislation itself must be made secure. That is, legislation must be acknowledged as the typical way of exercising power and social control, and lawmaking must be recognized as a continual process in response to diverse and changing desires that require adjustment. Legislation, in short, must be established as an ordinary and not extraordinary act. From this standpoint, Bentham's anticlassicism has importance apart from his attack on aristocratic government. His anticlassicism is in defense of an understanding of legislation which is clearly opposed to both the ancient view of law as custom and the ancient view of law as an instrument of education and character formation. Above all, ordinary legislation contrasts with the classical tradition of great Legislators, who more than anything else represent lawgiving as a unique and wonderful event.

"Bentham was not the first to defend the ordinary character of legislation. Political theorists before him had described the modern state as a legal entity and law as the normal way of exercising power. Hobbes, for example, had written against the common law tradition, and insisted that the changeability of statute law is necessary for order. Still, there is more to legislation than releasing rulers from the established constraints of moral and positive law, Bentham knew; the principle of utility would transform public happiness and welfare from rhetorical phrases into concrete tasks. . . . A revival of code and constitution making had brought the classical image of the Legislator to prominence once again. Codifiers modeled themselves after ancient lawgivers, and every appeal to the classical image defied the claim that legislation is an ordinary act. . . . Bentham was particularly sensitive to this revival of classicism, because he too styled himself the Legislator of his age. It was important for him to distinguish legislation from ancient lawgiving in order to make his theory of legislation comprehensible. . . .

"Bentham distinguished legislation both from law as the foundation of an ideal and unchanging order and from law as an instrument of character formation. Legislation should be understood instead as a special way of accommodating individuals' desires—as an expression of utility. Utilitarian legislation is, in this view, a higher rationality that stands above the changing and conflicting interests of men. . . .

"Bentham presented the principle of utility as a rationale for legislation. Because utility pays attention to the expectations of individuals, he claimed, it offers the best chance for legal security and for a regular course of conduct in the modern state. . . .

"Utility does not ensure agreement about laws, then. It does set out the grounds on which men could agree or disagree. . . .

"Bentham refused to accept as supreme the claims of the sovereign monarch or the sovereign state. Nevertheless, the notion of sovereignty was by no means absent from his writings. . . . Prominent in Bentham's thought is the notion of popular sovereignty. . . . Sovereignty also makes its appearance in Bentham's juristic formula 'law is an expression of the sovereign's will'. . . .

"Historically, sovereignty was part of the ideological apparatus of absolutism in an era when consolidation of the power of kings was the chief political object. . . .

"Although Bentham clearly opposed the personal character of monarchical absolutism, he was an advocate of absolutism. He rejected any limits to the matters or measures that might come within the rulers' exercise of power, and he recommended the consolidation and centralization of power. For Bentham, a new ethical basis provided absolutism with its purpose; a new rationality—utility—stripped it of its caprice. . . .

"The argument of this book is that Bentham's political thought forms a theory of the modern state. In most state theories, the state is conceived as a higher rationality which stands above the changing and conflicting interests of individuals or groups. Bentham called this rationality utility. And he explained that utility finds expression in a unified system of law. A single, rational legal system gives the state its unity, he thought. The state is a legal entity; its ethical basis is individualism. . . .

"Bentham is one of the great proselytizers for legalism as a value."

22. H. L. A. Hart, *Essays on Bentham: Studies in Jurisprudence and Political Theory* (Oxford, 1982).

23. David Lieberman, *The Province of Legislation Determined: Legal Theory in Eighteenth-Century Britain* (Cambridge, 1989). Of interest is the short published lecture by J. H. Burns entitled *The Fabric of Felicity: The Legislator and the Human Condition* (London, 1967), with comments on Bentham.

24. James E. Crimmins, *Secular Utilitarianism: Social Science and the Critique of Religion in the Thought of Jeremy Bentham* (Oxford, 1990).

25. P. J. Kelly, *Utilitarianism and Distributive Justice: Jeremy Bentham and the Civil Law* (Oxford, 1990).

26. David Lyons, *In the Interest of the Governed: A Study in Bentham's Philosophy of Utility and Law* (Oxford, 1973).

27. Douglas G. Long, *Bentham on Liberty: Jeremy Bentham's Idea of Liberty in Relation to His Utilitarianism* (Toronto, 1977).

28. L. J. Hume, *Bentham and Bureaucracy* (Cambridge, 1981), and Frederick Rosen, *Jeremy Bentham and Representative Democracy* (Oxford, 1983).

29. E.g. Michael Lobban, *The Common Law and English Jurisprudence, 1760–1850* (Oxford, 1991), Chs. 6–7 on Bentham's Code of laws and his classifications; Crane Brinton, *English Political Thought in the 19th Century* (London, 1933, etc.), Ch. II, sect. 1 on Bentham; and Robert Brown, *The Nature of Social Laws: Machiavelli to Mill* (Cambridge, 1984), Ch. 8 on J. S. Mill and "the structure of a social science."

30. E.g. William L. Davidson, *Political Thought in England: The Utilitarians, from Bentham to J. S. Mill* (London and New York, [1915–]1916, repr. 1947), covering Bentham and the two Mills; Harold J. Laski, *Political Thought in England: Locke to Bentham* (New York and London, 1920), Ch. VII on economic liberalism; Kevin Mulligan and

Robert Roth (eds.), *Regards sur Bentham et l'utilitarisme: Actes du colloque . . .* (Geneva, 1993), e.g. pp. 39 ff. on both utilitarianism and liberalism; Bhikhu Parekh (ed.), *Bentham's Political Thought* (New York, 1973), Chs. 5 and 16 on utility and the legislature respectively; *ibid.* (ed.), *Jeremy Bentham: Ten Critical Essays* (London, 1974), including essays on Bentham in relation to utility, sovereignty, and the administrative state (Chs. 5, 7, 10); Knud Haakonssen (ed.), *Traditions of Liberalism: Essays on John Locke, Adam Smith and John Stuart Mill* (New South Wales, 1988), showing the great variety of liberalism, as in the concluding ch. by Kenneth Minogue; and Maurice Cowling, *Mill and Liberalism* (Cambridge, 1990, 2nd edn.).

31. I have consulted the 1857 London edn. of the *Commentaries on the Laws of England: In Four Books* by William Blackstone (1723–1780). The first book, in Vol. I, deals with the traditional rubric of the "Rights of Persons." In the work's lengthy preliminary "Introduction," Blackstone proceeds in Sect. I according to the following headings: "On the Study of the Law," "Utility of a Knowledge of the Law," and "Neglect of this Study," followed by discussions on the origins of the Inns of Court and the plan of his work. Sect. II begins with "On the Nature of the Laws in General" and thereafter proceeds to treat in turn the laws of nature, municipal law, origins of society, forms of government, theory of the British constitution, definition of law, and interpretation of laws.

Some observations on these preliminary portions of Blackstone's *Commentaries* will be useful in relation to Bentham's handling of the work. It is, first of all, striking that at the very beginning of his work Blackstone highlights the topic of "utility." Despite Bentham's repeated continuing claims of rebellion against Blackstone through a wholly new jurisprudential philosophy of *utility*, Bentham was greatly influenced, from the outset of his writing career, by Blackstone's own new highlighting of "utility" at the beginning of his *Commentaries*. It cannot be denied that Bentham developed Blackstone's (undeveloped) initial concept of utility into a sweeping new principle, in its own right, as the cornerstone of his jurisprudence, thereby significantly departing from Blackstone. But the original core concept of utility that Bentham derived from Blackstone was not duly credited as such by Bentham and has not been duly so acknowledged by historians.

It must, secondly, be granted that Bentham was correct to point out Blackstone's traditionalism on the other kinds of topics and issues covered in Blackstone's Intro. to his *Commentaries*. This Intro. was the portion upon which Bentham concentrated in his various works criticizing and rethinking Blackstone's *Commentaries*. Blackstone's heading entitled "On the Nature of Laws in General" was duplicated in some of Bentham's own titles. What followed in that second sect. of Blackstone's Intro. did in fact correspond to traditional rubrics in the history of jurisprudential thought, particularly in the civil law traditions of Roman law (going back to Domat, Corasius, and others). Blackstone's sequence of subjects listed above is indicative of this point. At the same time, it must also be recognized that Bentham himself was far more indebted to this somewhat traditional schema in Blackstone's Intro. than he was willing to admit, esp. in the area of legislation. What Blackstone did not emphasize in his headings, unlike many earlier jurists such as Domat and Corasius, was the promulgation of legislation, whereas Bentham, in doing so, would reach back beyond Blackstone to earlier jurisprudence. Thus it is on the issue of legislation itself that Bentham's claims to newness over Blackstone had greatest import or validity.

A work much different from Blackstone's *Commentaries* was the treatise by his Italian contemporary Gaetano Filangieri (1752–1788) entitled *La scienza della legislazione*. I have consulted the 1819 Philadelphia edn. (in Italian) in 5 vols. Bk. I treats the "general rules of the legislative science" (*Delle regole generali della scientia legislativa*). Its chs. take up in turn such topics as the end of this science and the origins of society, the preservation and tranquility of human society, the relative goodness of laws, the decadence of codes, the nature of government and its types (monarchy, aristocracy, democracy, mixed, etc.), climate, and fertility of land. Succeeding bks. focus on other areas of the science of legislation including politics and economics, education and public instruction, and religion. Discussions more germane to topics and approaches pursued by Bentham deal with criminal procedure—crimes and punishments. Most noteworthy here, however, is Filangieri's concentration on "the science of legislation" itself in his title. By contrast, in the treatise of his Italian contemporary Beccaria that focused in its title on "crimes and punishments," legislation was a subordinate albeit crucial subject (as treated in our preceding book).

32. Jeremy Bentham, *An Introduction to the Principles of Morals and Legislation*, edited by J. H. Burns and H. L. A. Hart (Oxford, 1996), introduced by F. Rosen and H. L. A. Hart, and comprising a vol. in *The Collected Works of Jeremy Bentham*. As with Rousseau's *Social Contract*, Montesquieu's *Spirit of the Laws*, and various other cases in our preceding book, it is sufficient here, in citing Bentham's *Morals and Legislation*, to indicate, in the course of our main text as well as in our notes, the chapter and (sub)section numbers. The brief and easily locatable (sub)sections, or paragraphs, are numbered consecutively throughout each of Bentham's chapters from beginning to end. When presenting passages from Bentham's *Morals and Legislation* in our main text, as well as in our notes, it has been convenient, moreover, to delete the (sub)section numbers and to indicate them separately, together with chapter numbers (and titles), usually in our initial citations thereof. This approach has been adopted so as not to interrupt or complicate the flow and sequence of Bentham's often difficult materials. Chapter titles are given in citations when the need or context renders it desirable to do so, sometimes in abbreviated form especially when it has already been given in full beforehand. As in our preceding book, especially when English authors are quoted, our transcriptions adhere to the original styles of spelling, punctuation, etc., unless occasionally stated otherwise. E.g. "offences."

33. Bentham, *Morals and Legislation*, Ch. XII, n.10 (p. 146 n.).

34. *Ibid.*, Ch. XVII, 21–24: "Jurisprudence is a fictitious entity: nor can any meaning be found for the word, but by placing it in company with some word that shall be significative of a real entity. To know what is meant by jurisprudence, we must know, for example, what is meant by a book of jurisprudence. A book of jurisprudence can have but one or the other of two objects: 1. to ascertain what the *law* is: 2. to ascertain what it ought to be. In the former case it may be styled a book of *expository* jurisprudence; in the latter, a book of *censorial* jurisprudence: or, in other words, a book on the *art of legislation*.

"A book of expository jurisprudence is either *authoritative* or *unauthoritative*. It is styled authoritative, when it is composed by him who, by representing the state of the law to be so and so, causeth it so to be; that is, of the legislator himself: unauthoritative, when it is the work of any other person at large.

"Now *law*, or *the law*, taken indefinitely, is an abstract and collective term; which, when it means any thing, can mean neither more nor less than the sum total of a number of individual laws taken together. It follows, that of whatever other modifications the subject of a book of jurisprudence is susceptible, they must all of them be taken from some circumstance or other of which such individual laws, or the assemblages into which they may be sorted, are susceptible. The circumstances that have given rise to the principal branches of jurisprudence we are wont to hear of, seem to be as follow: 1. The *extent* of the laws in question in point of dominion. 2. The *political quality* of the persons whose conduct they undertake to regulate. 3. The *time* of their being in force. 4. The manner in which they are *expressed*. 5. The concern which they have with the article of *punishment*.

"In the first place, in point of extent, what is delivered concerning the laws in question, may have reference either to the laws of such or such a nation or nations in particular, or to the laws of all nations whatsoever: in the first case, the book may be said to relate to *local*, in the other, to *universal jurisprudence.*"

In a note to these discussions, Bentham declares as follows: "In most of the European languages there are two different words for distinguishing the abstract and the concrete senses of the word *law*: which words are so wide asunder as not even to have any etymological affinity. In Latin, for example, there is *lex* for the concrete sense, *jus* for the abstract: in Italian, *legge* and *diritto*: in French, *loi* and *droit*: in Spanish, *ley* and *derecho*: in German, *gesetz* and *recht*. The English is at present destitute of this advantage.

"In the Anglo-Saxon, besides *lage*, and several other words, for the concrete sense, there was the word *right*, answering to the German *recht*, for the abstract; as may be seen in the compound *folc-right*, and in other instances. But the word *right* having long ago lost this sense, the modern English no longer possesses this advantage."

35. Cf. more generally e.g. Mark Francis, "The Nineteenth Century Theory of Sovereignty and Thomas Hobbes," *History of Political Thought*, I (1980), pp. 517–540, with references to Bentham, Austin, etc.

36. Bentham's *Morals and Legislation*, Ch. XVI ("Division of Offences"), 2–4, 16–17: "The good of the community cannot require, that any act should be made an offence, which is not liable, in some way or other, to be detrimental to the community. For in the case of such an act, all punishment is *groundless*.

"But if the whole assemblage of any number of individuals be considered as constituting an imaginary compound *body*, a community or political state; any act that is detrimental to any one or more of those *members* is, as to so much of its effects, detrimental to the *state*.

"An act cannot be detrimental to a *state*, but by being detrimental to some one or more of the *individuals* that compose it. But these individuals may either be *assignable* or *unassignable*. . . .

"Public offences may be distributed under eleven divisions. 1. Offences against *external* security. 2. Offences against *justice*. 3. Offences against the *preventive* branch of the *police*. 4. Offences against the public *force*. 5. Offences against the *positive* increase of the national *felicity*. 6. Offences against the public *wealth*. 7. Offences against *population*. 8. Offences against the *national wealth*. 9. Offences against the *sovereignty*. 10. Offences against *religion*. 11. Offences against the national *interest* in general. The way in which these several sorts of offences connect with one another, and with the interest of the public, that is, of an unassignable multitude of the individuals of which that body is composed, may be thus conceived.

"Mischief by which the interest of the public as above defined may be affected, must, if produced at all, be produced either by means of an influence exerted on the operations of government, or by other means, without the exertion of such influence. . . . It is here to be observed, that if the influence exerted on any occasion by any individual over the operations of the government be pernicious, it must be in one or other of two ways: 1. by causing, or tending to cause, operations *not* to be performed which *ought* to be performed; in other words, by *impeding* the operations of *government*. Or, 2. by causing operations to *be* performed which ought *not* to be performed; in other words, by *misdirecting* them. Last, to the total assemblage of the persons by whom the several political operations above-mentioned come to be performed, we set out with applying the collective appellation of *the government*. Among these persons there *commonly* is some one person, or body of persons, whose office it is to assign and distribute to the rest their several departments, to determine the conduct to be pursued by each in the performance of the particular set of operations that belongs to him, and even upon occasion to exercise his function in his stead. Where there is any such person, or body of persons, *he* or *it* may, according as the turn of the phrase requires, be termed *the sovereign*, or the *sovereignty*.

Now it is evident, that to impede or misdirect the operations of the sovereign, as here described, may be to impede or misdirect the operations of the several departments of government as described above."

Ibid., Ch. XVII ("Of the Limits of the Penal Branch of Jurisprudence"), 15–17: "It is plain, that of individuals the legislator can know nothing: concerning those points of conduct which depend upon the particular circumstances of each individual, it is plain, therefore, that he can determine nothing to advantage. It is only with respect to those broad lines of conduct in which all persons, or very large and permanent descriptions of persons, may be in a way to engage, that he can have any pretence for interfering; and even here the propriety of his intereference will, in most instances, lie very open to dispute. At any rate, he must never expect to produce a perfect compliance by the mere force of the sanction of which he is himself the author. All he can hope to do, is to increase the efficacy of private ethics, by giving strength and direction to the influence of the moral sanction. With what chance of success, for example, would a legislator go about to extirpate drunkenness and fornication, by dint of legal punishment? Not all the tortures which ingenuity could invent would compass it: and, before he had made any progress worth regarding, such a mass of evil would be produced by the punishment, as would exceed, a thousand-fold, the utmost possible mischief of the offence. . . . [L]egislators have, in general, been disposed to carry their interference full as far as is expedient. The great difficulty here is, to persuade them to confine themselves within bounds. A thousand little passions and prejudices have led them to narrow the liberty of the subject in this line, in cases in which the punishment is either attended with no profit at all, or with none that will make up for the expense.

"The mischief of this sort of interference is more particularly conspicuous in the article of religion. The reasoning, in this case, is of the following stamp. There are certain errors, in matters of belief, to which all mankind are prone: and for these errors in judgment, it is the determination of a Being of infinite benevolence, to punish them with an infinity of torments. But from these errors the legislator himself is necessarily free: for the men, who happen to be at hand for him to consult with, being men perfectly enlightened, unfettered, and unbiassed, have such advantages over all the rest of the world, that when they sit down to enquire out the truth relative to points so plain and so familiar as those in question, they cannot fail to find it. This being the case, when the sovereign sees his people ready to plunge headlong into an abyss of fire, shall he not stretch out a hand to save them? Such, for example, seems to have been the train of reasoning, and such the motives, which led Lewis the XIVth into those coercive measures which he took for the conversion of heretics, and the confirmation of true believers [the revocation of the Edict of Nantes in 1685]. The ground-work, pure sympathy and loving-kindness: the superstructure, all the miseries which the most determined malevolence could have devised."

37. *Ibid.*, Pref. (p. 3): "An introduction to a work which takes for its subject the totality of any science, ought to contain all such matters, and such matters only, as belong in common to every particular branch of that science, or at least to more branches of it than one. Compared with its present title, the present work fails in both ways of being conformable to that rule. . . .

"Again, as an introduction to the principles of *legislation in general*, it ought rather to have included matters belonging exclusively to the *civil* branch, than matters more particularly applicable to the *penal*: the latter being but a means of compassing the ends proposed by the former. In preference therefore, or at least in priority, to the several chapters which will be found relative to *punishment*, it ought to have exhibited a set of propositions which have since presented themselves to him as affording a standard for the operations performed by government, in the creation and distribution of proprietary and other civil rights."

38. *Ibid.*, Ch. VII, 1, 3: "The business of government is to promote the happiness of the society, by punishing and rewarding. That part of its business which consists in punishing, is more particularly the subject of penal law. In proportion as an act tends to disturb that happiness, in proportion as the tendency of it is pernicious, will be the demand it creates for punishment. What happiness consists of we have already seen: enjoyment of pleasures, security from pains. . . .

"It is to be observed, that here, as well as henceforward, wherever consequences are spoken of, such only are meant as are *material*. Of the consequences of any act, the multitude and variety must needs be infinite: but such of them only as are material are worth regarding. Now among the consequences of an act, be they what they may, such only, by one who views them in the capacity of a legislator, can be said to be material,"

Also, *ibid.*, Ch. XVI, 55: "What the materials are, if so they may be called, of which conditions, or any other kind of legal possession, can be made up, we have already seen: beneficial powers, fiduciary powers, beneficial rights, fiduciary rights, relative duties, absolute duties."

39. *Ibid.*, Ch. XIII, 1–2: "The general object which all laws have, or ought to have, in common, is to augment the total happiness of the community; and therefore, in the first place, to exclude, as far as may be, every thing that tends to subtract from that happiness: in other words, to exclude mischief.

"But all punishment is mischief: all punishment in itself is evil. Upon the principle of utility, if it ought at all to be admitted, it ought only to be admitted in as far as it promises to exclude some greater evil."

40. *Ibid.*, Ch. XIV, 1–2, 7: "We have seen that the general object of all laws is to prevent mischief; that is to say, when it is worth while; but that, where there are no other means of doing this than punishment, there are four cases in which it is *not* worth while.

"When it *is* worth while, there are four subordinate designs or objects, which, in the course of his endeavours to compass, as far as may be, that one general object, a legislator, whose views are governed by the principle of utility, comes naturally to propose to himself. . . .

"Subservient to these four objects, or purposes, must be the rules or canons by which the proportion of punishments to offences is to be governed."

41. *Ibid.*, Ch. XVII, 24: "Now of the infinite variety of nations there are upon the earth, there are no two which agree exactly in their laws: certainly not in the whole; perhaps not even in any single article; and let them agree to-day, they would disagree to-morrow. This is evident enough with regard to the *substance* of the laws: and it would be still more extraordinary if they agreed in point of *form*; that is, if they were conceived in precisely the same strings of words. What is more, as the languages of nations are commonly different, as well as their laws, it is seldom that, strictly speaking, they have so much as a single *word* in common. However, among the words that are appropriated to the subject of law, there are some that in all languages are pretty exactly correspondent to one another: which comes to the same thing nearly as if they were the same. Of this stamp, for example, are those which correspond to the words *power, right, obligation, liberty,* and many others.

"It follows, that if there are any books which can, properly speaking, be styled books of universal jurisprudence, they must be looked for within very narrow limits. Among such as are expository, there can be none that are authoritative: nor even, as far as the *substance* of the laws is concerned, any that are unauthoritative. . . .

"It is in the censorial line that there is the greatest room for disquisitions that apply to the circumstances of all nations alike: and in this line what regards the substance of the laws in question is as susceptible of an universal application, as what regards the words. That the laws of all nations, or even of any two nations, should coincide in all points, would be as ineligible as it is impossible: some leading points, however, there seem to be, in respect of which the laws of all civilized nations might, without inconvenience, be the same. To mark out some of these points will, as far as it goes, be the business of the body of this work."

42. *Ibid.*, "Concluding Note," 24–27: "In countries, where a great part of the law exists in no other shape, than that of what in England is called *common* law but might be more expressively termed *judiciary*, there must be a great multitude of laws, the import of which cannot be sufficiently made out for practice, without referring to this commmon law, for more or less of the expository matter belonging to them. Thus in England the exposition of the word *title*, that basis of the whole fabric of the laws of property, is no where else to be found. And, as uncertainty is the very essence of every particle of law so denominated (for the instant it is clothed in a certain authoritative form of words it changes its nature, and passes over to the other denomination) hence it is that a great part of the laws in being in such countries remain uncertain and incomplete. What are those countries? To this hour, every one on the surface of the globe.

"Had the science of architecture no fixed nomenclature belonging to it—were there no settled names, for distinguishing the different sorts of buildings, nor the different parts of the same building from each other—what would it be? It would be what the science of legislation, considered with respect to its *form*, remains at present.

"Were there no architects who could distinguish a dwelling-house from a barn, or a side-wall from a ceiling, what would architects be? They would be what all legislators are at present. . . .

"Take, for instance, so many well meant endeavours on the part of popular bodies, and so many well meant recommendations in ingenious books, to restrain supreme representative assemblies, from making laws in such and such cases, or to such and such an effect. Such laws, to answer the intended purpose, require a perfect mastery in the science of law, considered in respect of its form—in the sort of anatomy spoken of in the preface to this work: but a perfect, or even a moderate insight into that science, would prevent their being couched in those loose and inadequate terms, in which they may be observed so frequently to be conceived; as a perfect acquaintance with the dictates of utility on that head would, in many, if not in most, of those instances, discounsel [sic] the attempt. Keep to the letter, and in attempting to prevent the making of bad laws, you will find them prohibiting the making of the most necessary laws, perhaps even of all laws: quit the letter, and they express no more than if each man were to say, *Your laws shall become* ipso facto *void, as often as they contain any thing which is not to my mind.*

"Of such unhappy attempts, examples may be met with in the legislation of many nations: but in none more frequently than in that newly-created nation, one of the most enlightened, if not the most enlightened, at this day on the globe.

"Take for instance, the *Declaration of Rights*, enacted by the state of North-Carolina, in convention, in or about the months of September, 1788, and said to be copied, with a small exception, from one in like manner enacted by the state of Virginia."

Finally, as to causation more generally, it must not be overlooked that for Bentham in *Morals and Legislation* the pain-and-pleasure principles involve certain types of "causes" of their own, not related to the four causes as we have treated them. One such instance appears in Ch. VI ("Of Circumstances Influencing Sensibility"), 1, 4. There, he removes the topic from mere metaphysics into more practical and immediate considerations and goes on to speak of the role of the "exciting cause." Thus: "Pain and pleasure are produced in men's minds by the action of certain causes. But the quantity of pleasure and pain runs not uniformly in proportion to the cause; in other words, to the quantity of force exerted by such cause. The truth of this observation rests not upon any metaphysical nicety in the import given to the terms *cause, quantity,* and *force*: it will be equally true in whatsoever manner such force be measured. . . .

"Any incident which serves as a cause, either of pleasure or of pain, may be termed an *exciting* cause: if of pleasure, a pleasurable cause: if of pain, a painful, afflictive, or dolorific cause."

43. Hart, *Bentham,* V, "Bentham's *Of Laws in General,*" pp. 105 ff. (orig. pub. 1971), on command as one of four aspects of the legislator's will expressed in a law. The other three aspects are prohibition, permission to act, and permission to refrain (cf. diagram, p. 114).

44. Bentham, *Morals and Legislation,* Ch. I, ("Of the Principle of Utility"), 1–4, 6, 8: "Nature has placed mankind under the governance of two sovereign masters, *pain* and *pleasure.* It is for them alone to point out what we ought to do, as well as to determine what we shall do. On the one hand the standard of right and wrong, on the other the chain of causes and effects, are fastened to their throne. They govern us in all we do, in all we say, in all we think. . . . The *principle of utility* recognises this subjection, and assumes it for the foundation of that system, the object of which is to rear the fabric of felicity by the hands of reason and of law. . . .

"The principle of utility is the foundation of the present work. . . . By the principle of utility is meant that principle which approves or disapproves of every action whatsoever, according to the tendency which it appears to have to augment or diminish the happiness of the party whose interest is in question: or, what is the same thing in other words, to promote or to oppose that happiness. I say of every action whatsoever; and therefore not only of every action of a private individual, but of every measure of government.

"By utility is meant that property in any object, whereby it tends to produce benefit, advantage, pleasure, good, or happiness. . . .

"The interest of the community is one of the most general expressions that can occur in the phraseology of morals: no wonder that the meaning of it is often lost. When it has a meaning, it is this. The community is a fictitious *body*, composed of the individual persons who are considered as constituting as it were its *members*. The interest of the community then is, what?—the sum of the interests of the several members who compose it. . . .

"An action then may be said to be conformable to the principle of utility, or, for shortness sake, to utility, (meaning with respect to the community at large) when the tendency it has to augment the happiness of the community is greater than any it has to diminish it. . . .

"When an action, or in particular a measure of government, is supposed by a man to be conformable to the principle of utility, it may be convenient, for the purposes of discourse, to imagine a kind of law or dictate, called a law or dictate of utility: and to speak of the action in question, as being conformable to such law or dictate."

Ibid., Ch. II ("Of Principles Adverse to That of Utility"), 1, 11, 19: "If the principle of utility be a right principle to be governed by, and that in all cases, it follows from what has been just observed, that whatever principle differs from it in any case must necessarily be a wrong one. . . .

"Among principles adverse to that of utility, that which at this day seems to have most influence in matters of government, is what may be called the principle of sympathy and antipathy. . . . Antipathy or resentment requires always to be regulated, to prevent its doing mischief: to be regulated by what? always by the principle of utility. The principle of utility neither requires nor admits of any other regulator than itself."

45. *Ibid.,* Ch. VII ("Of Human Actions in General"), 21: "So much with regard to acts considered in themselves: we come now to speak of the *circumstances* with which they may have been accompanied."

Ibid., Ch. VIII ("Of Intentionality"), 1–2: "So much with regard to the two first of the articles upon which the evil tendency of an action may depend: viz. the act itself, and the general assemblage of the circumstances with which it may have been accompanied. We come now to consider the ways in which the particular circumstance of *intention* may be concerned in it.

"First, then, the intention or will may regard either of two objects: 1. The act itself: or, 2. Its consequences."

Ibid., Ch. IX ("Of Consciousness"), 1, 3: "So far with regard to the ways in which the will or intention may be concerned in the production of any incident. . . .

"There are two points, with regard to which an act may have been advised or unadvised: 1. The *existence* of the circumstance itself. 2. The *materiality* of it."

Ibid., Ch. X ("Of Motives"), 33: "The only way, it should seem, in which a motive can with safety and propriety be styled good or bad, is with reference to its effects in each individual instance; and principally from the intention it gives birth to: from which arise, as will be shown hereafter, the most material part of its effects."

Ibid., Ch. XI ("Of Human Dispositions in General"), 1–2: "In the foregoing chapter it has been shown at large, that goodness or badness cannot, with any propriety, be predicated of motives. Is there nothing then about a man that can properly be termed good or bad, when, on such or such an occasion, he suffers himself to be governed by such or such a motive? Yes, certainly: his *disposition*. Now disposition is a kind of fictitious entity, feigned for the convenience of discourse, in order to express what there is supposed to be *permanent* in a man's frame of mind, where, on such or such an occasion, he has been influenced by such or such a motive, to engage in an act, which, as it appeared to him, was of such or such a tendency.

"It is with disposition as with every thing else: it will be good or bad according to its effects: according to the effects it has in augmenting or diminishing the happiness of the community."

Ibid., Ch. XII ("Of the Consequences of a Mischievous Act"), 1–2: "Hitherto we have been speaking of the various articles or objects on which the consequences or tendency of an act may depend: of the bare *act* itself: of the *circumstances* it may have been, or may have been supposed to be, accompanied with. . . . We now come to speak of *consequences* or tendency: an article which forms the concluding link in all this chain of causes and effects, involving in it the materiality of the whole. . . .

"The tendency of an act is mischievous when the consequences of it are mischievous; that is to say, either the certain consequences or the probable."

(Sect. ii heading: "How intentionality, etc., may influence the mischief of an act")

Ibid., Ch. XV ("Of the Properties Given to a Lot of Punishment"), 25: "The eleventh and last of all the properties that seem to be requisite in a lot of punishment, is that of *remissibility*. The general presumption is, that when punishment is applied, punishment is needful: that it ought to be applied, and therefore cannot want to be *remitted*. But in very particular, and those always very deplorable cases, it may be accident happen otherwise. It may happen that punishment shall have been inflicted, where, according to the intention of the law itself, it ought not to have been inflicted: that is, where the sufferer is innocent of the offence."

46. *Ibid.*, Ch. XIII, 13–14, covering cases where punishment is unprofitable: "Where, on the one hand, the nature of the offence, on the other hand, that of the punishment, are, *in the ordinary state of things*, such, that when compared together, the evil of the latter will turn out to be greater than that of the former.

"Now the evil of the punishment divides itself into four branches, by which so many different sets of persons are affected. 1. The evil of *coercion* or *restraint*: or the pain which it gives a man not to be able to do the act, whatever it be, which by the apprehension of the punishment he is deterred from doing. This is felt by those by whom the law is *observed*."

Ibid., Ch. XVI, 1: "So much for the division of offences in general. Now an offence is an act prohibited, or (what comes to the same thing) an act of which the contrary is commanded by the law: and what is it that the law can be employed in doing, besides prohibiting and commanding? It should seem then, according to this view of the matter, that were we to have settled what may be proper to be done with relation to offences, we should thereby have settled every thing that may be proper to be done in the way of law."

Such statements on coercion and command are revealing but are not as direct or forceful in the ways abundantly encountered in the "Concluding Note."

47. *Ibid.*, "Concluding Note," 2: "What is a law? What the parts of a law? The subject of these questions, it is to be observed, is the *logical*, the *ideal*, the *intellectual* whole, not the *physical* one: the *law* and not the *statute*. An inquiry directed to the latter sort of object, could neither admit of difficulty nor afford instruction. In this sense whatever is given for law by the person or persons recognized as possessing the power of making laws, is *law*. . . . By the word *law* then, as often as it occurs in the succeeding pages, is meant that ideal object, of which the part, the whole, or the multiple, or an assemblage of parts, wholes, and multiples mixed together, is exhibited by a statute; not the statute which exhibits them."

48. *Ibid.*, "Concluding Note," 3–7: "Every law, when complete, is either of a *coercive* or *uncoercive* nature.

"A coercive law is a *command*.

"An uncoercive, or rather a *dis*coercive, law is the *revocation*, in whole, or in part, of a coercive law.

"What has been termed a *declaratory* law, so far as it stands distinguished from either a coercive or a discoercive law, is not properly speaking a law. It is not the expression of an act of the will exercised at the time: it is a mere notification of the existence of a law, either of the coercive or the discoercive kind, as already subsisting: of the existence of some document expressive of some act of the will, exercised, not at the time, but at some former period. If it does any thing more than give information of this fact, viz. of the prior existence of a law of either the coercive or the discoercive kind, it ceases *pro-tanto* to be what is meant by a declaratory law, and assuming either the coercive or the discoercive quality.

"Every coercive law creates an *offence*, that is, converts an act of some sort or other into an offence. It is only by so doing that it can *impose obligation*, that it can *produce coercion*.

"A law confining itself to the creation of an offence, and a law commanding a punishment to be administered in case of the commission of such an offence, are two distinct laws; not parts (as they seem to have been generally accounted hitherto) of one and the same law. The acts they command are altogether different; the persons they are addressed to are altogether different. Instance, *Let no man steal;* and, *Let the judge cause whoever is convicted of stealing to be hanged*.

"They might be styled; the former, a *simple imperative* law; the other, a *punitory*; but the punitory, if it commands the punishment to be inflicted, and does not merely permit it, is as truly *imperative* as the other: only it is punitory besides, which the other is not.

"A law of the discoercive kind, considered in itself, can have no punitory law belonging to it; to receive the assistance and support of a punitory law, it must first receive that of a simply imperative or coercive law, and it is to this latter that the punitory law will attach itself, and not to the discoercive one. Example; discoercive law. *The sheriff has power to hang all such as the judge, proceeding in due course of law, shall order him to hang.*"

49. *Ibid.*, "Concluding Note," 10–16, 23: "It will happen in the instance of many, probably of most, possibly of all commands endued with the force of a public law, that, in the expression given to such a command, it shall be necessary to have recourse to terms too

complex in their signification, to exhibit the requisite ideas, without the assistance of a greater or less quantity of matter of an expository nature. . . .

"Take for instance the law, *Thou shalt not steal*: Such a command, were it to rest there, could never sufficiently answer the purpose of a law. A word of so vague and unexplicit a meaning can no otherwise perform this office. . . .

"Such then is the nature of a general law, that while the imperative part of it, the *punctum saliens* as it may be termed, of this artificial body, shall not take up above two or three words, its expository appendage, without which that imperative part could not rightly perform its office, may occupy a considerable volume.

"But this may equally be the case with a private order given in a family. . . .

"The same mass of expository matter may serve in common for, may appertain in common to, many commands, many masses of imperative matter. . . .

"Such expository matter, being of a complexion so different from the imperative, it would be no wonder if the connection of the former with the latter should escape the observation: which, indeed, is perhaps pretty generally the case. And so long as any mass of legislative matter presents itself, which is not itself imperative or the contrary, or of which the connection with matter of one of those two descriptions is not apprehended, so long and so far the truth of the proposition, *That every law is a command or its opposite*, may remain unsuspected, or appear questionable; so long also may the incompleteness of the greater part of those masses of legislative matter, which wear the complexion of complete laws upon the face of them, also the method to be taken for rendering them really complete, remain undiscovered.

"A circumstance, that will naturally contribute to increase the difficulty of the discovery, is the great variety of ways in which the imperation of a law may be conveyed—the great variety of forms which the imperative part of a law may indiscriminately assume: some more directly, some less directly expressive of the imperative quality. *Thou shalt not steal. Let no man steal.* . . . and so on. These are but part of a multitude of forms of words, in any of which the command, by which stealing is prohibited might equally be couched: and it is manifest to what a degree, in some of them, the imperative quality is clouded and concealed from ordinary apprehension.

"After this explanation, a general proposition or two, that may be laid down, may help to afford some little insight into the structure and contents of a complete body of laws. . . .

"To class *offences*, as hath been attempted to be done in the preceding chapter, is therefore to class *laws*. . . . [Such] would be to exhibit a complete collection of the laws in force: in a word, a complete body of law; a *pannomion*, if so it might be termed.

"From the obscurity in which the limits of a *law*, and the distinction betwixt a law of the civil or simply imperative kind and a punitory law, are naturally involved, results the obscurity of the limits betwixt a civil and a penal *code*, betwixt the civil branch of the law and the penal. . . .

"Thus it is, that one and the same law, one and the same command, will have its matter divided, not only between two great codes, or main branches of the whole body of the laws, the civil and the penal; but amongst three such branches, the civil, the penal, and the constitutional."

50. *Ibid.*, "Concluding Note," 16-19: "The *civil* code would not consist of a collection of civil laws, each complete in itself, as well as clear of all penal ones.

"Neither would the *penal* code (since we have seen that it *could* not) consist of a collection of punitive laws, each not only complete in itself, but clear of all civil ones. But [*sic*]

"The civil code would consist chiefly of mere masses of expository matter. The imperative matter, to which those masses of expository matter respectively appertained, would be found—not in that same code—not in the civil code—nor in a pure state, free from all admixture of punitory laws; but in the penal code—in a state of combination—involved, in manner as above explained, in so many correspondent punitory laws.

"The penal code then would consist principally of punitive laws, involving the imperative matter of the whole number of civil laws: along with which would probably also be found various masses of expository matter, appertaining, not to the civil, but to the punitory laws. The body of penal law, enacted by the Empress-Queen Maria Theresa, agrees pretty well with this account.

"The mass of legislative matter published in French as well as German, under the auspices of Frederic II of Prussia, by the name of Code Frederic, but never established with force of law, appears, for example, to be almost wholly composed of masses of expository matter, the relation of which to any imperative matter appears to have been but very imperfectly apprehended."

51. *Ibid.*, "Concluding Note," 21–22: "Among the barbarous nations that grew up out of the ruins of the Roman Empire, Law, emerging from under the mountain of expository rubbish, reassumed for a while the language of command: and then she had simplicity at least, if nothing else, to recommend her.

"Besides the civil and the penal, every complete body of law must contain a third branch, the *constitutional*.

"The constitutional branch is chiefly employed in conferring, on particular classes of persons, *powers*, to be exercised for the good of the whole society, or of considerable parts of it, and prescribing *duties* to the persons invested with those powers.

"The powers are principally constituted, in the first instance, by discoercive or permissive laws, operating as exceptions to certain laws of the coercive or imperative kind. Instance: *A tax-gatherer, as such, may, on such and such an occasion, take such and such things, without any other* TITLE."

Bentham's references to "barbarian" law that was expressive at least of the *language* of imperative matter is interesting in light of recent scholarship cited in our preceding book. For it has been shown that early Germanic customary laws at times contained some formal *words* of legislative command in order to make them *appear* official or authoritative, even though the actual content of the (expository) mass of custom represented in them was neither imperative nor legislative in nature.

Bentham's thoughts on constitutional law will be taken up in relation to other writings by him.

52. *Ibid.*, Ch. XVI, 58, note: "Imagine what a condition a science must be in, when as yet there shall be no such thing as forming any extensive proposition relative to it, that shall be at the same time a true one: where, if the proposition shall be true of some of the particulars contained under it, it shall be false with regard to others. What a state would botany, for example, be in, if the classes were so contrived, that no common characters could be found for them? Yet in this state, and no better, seems every system of penal law to be, authoritative or unauthoritative that has ever yet appeared. Try if it be otherwise, for instance, with the *delicta privata et publica*, and with the *publica ordinaria*, and *publica extra-ordinaria* of the Roman law. All this for want of method: and hence the necessity of endeavouring to strike out a new one.

"Nor is this want of method to be wondered at. A science so new as that of penal legislation, could hardly have been in any better state. Till objects are distinguished, they cannot be arranged. It is thus that *truth* and *order* go on hand in hand. It is only in proportion as the former is discovered, that the latter can be improved. Before a certain order is established, truth can be put [sic] imperfectly announced: but until a certain proportion of truth has been developed and brought to light, that order cannot be established. The discovery of truth leads to the establishment of order: and the establishment of order fixes and propagates the discovery of truth.

"See Heinecc. Elem. p. vii. § 79, 80." I.e. Johann Gottlieb Heineccius, *Elementa Iuris Civilis secundum ordinem Pandectarum* (1731), part VII, lib. xlvii, tit. I, *De privatis delictis*, sects. 79–80.

Another passage with more extensive comparative uses (pro and con) of technical terminology in Roman law occurs in Bentham, *ibid.*, Ch. IX, 17–18. It reveals further facets of the intricacies of Bentham's thinking on the subject in general. "A few words for the purpose of applying what has been said to the Roman law. Unintentionality, and innocence of intention, seem both to be included in the case of *infortunium*, where there is neither *dolus* nor *culpa*. Unadvisedness coupled with heedlessness, and mis-advisedness coupled with rashness, correspond to the *culpa sine dolo*. Direct intentionality corresponds to *dolus*. Oblique intentionality seems hardly to have been distinguished from direct; were it to occur, it would probably be deemed also to correspond to *dolus*. The division into *culpa*, *lata*, *levis*, and *levissima*, is such as nothing certain can correspond to. What is it that it expresses? A distinction, not in the case itself, but only in the sentiments which any person (a judge, for instance) may find himself disposed to entertain with relation to it: supposing it already distinguished into three subordinate cases by other means.

"The word *dolus* seems ill enough contrived: the word *culpa* as indifferently. *Dolus*, upon any other occasion, would be understood to imply deceit, concealment, clandestinity: but here it is extended to open force. *Culpa*, upon any other occasion, would be understood to extend to blame of every kind. It would therefore include *dolus*.*

"The above-mentioned definitions and distinctions are far from being mere matters of speculation. They are capable of the most extensive and constant application, as well to moral discourse as to legislative practice."

*Note: "I pretend not here to give any determinate explanation of a set of words, of which the great misfortune is, that the import of them is confused and indeterminate. I speak only by approximation. To attempt to determine the precise import that has been given them by a hundredth part of the authors that have used them, would be an endless task. Would any one talk intelligibly on this subject in Latin? let him throw out *dolus* altogether: let him keep *culpa*, for the purpose of expressing not the case itself, but the sentiment that is entertained concerning a case described by other means. For intentionality, let him coin a word boldly, and say *intentionalitas*: for unintentionality, *non-intentionalitas*."

These discussions are lengthier than the excerpts might suggest.

53. Bentham, *Of Laws in General*, edited by H. L. A. Hart (London, 1970), esp. Intro. Again, as in *Morals and Legislation*, there are consecutively numbered paragraph sects. within each ch. Again, we have deleted sect. numbers from Bentham's text and grouped them together in our initial citations. Again, all *sic*.

54. *Ibid.*, Ch. I, 3: "The latitude here given to the import of the word *law* is it must be confessed rather greater than what seems to be given to it in common: the definition being such as is applicable to various objects which are not commonly characterized by that name. Taking this definition for the standard it matters not whether the expression of will in question, so as it have but the authority of the sovereign to back it, were his by immediate conception or only by adoption: whether it be of the most public or of the most private or even domestic nature: whether the sovereign from whom it derives its force be an individual or a body: whether it be issued *propter quid* as the phrase may be, that is on account of some particular act or event which is understood to warrant it (as is the case with an order of the judicial kind made in the course of a cause); or without the assignment of any such special ground: or whether it be susceptible of an indefinite duration or whether it be *suâ naturâ* temporary and undurable: as is most commonly the case with such expressions of will the uttering of which is looked upon as a *measure of administration*: whether it be a command or a countermand: whether it be expressed in the way

of statute, or of customary law. Under the term 'law' then if this definition be admitted of, we must include a judicial order, a military or any other kind of executive order, or even the most trivial and momentary order of the domestic kind, so it be not illegal: that is, so as the issuing of it be not forbidden by some other law."

55. *Ibid.*, Ch. I, 4 (#4): "Of course the term *law* would according to the definition be applicable to any order whatsoever coming directly from the sovereign. But it is not in all cases that the issuing of any such order is looked upon as an act of legislation.

"Where the sovereign is a body corporate, there indeed, if the matter be considered with reference to the English language, there seem to be no exceptions. In Great Britain, for example, the sovereignty is in the King, Lords, and Commons in Parliament assembled: it would be hardly possible for that complex body to issue any order the issuing of which would not be looked upon as an act of legislation. What power was it that it exercised when it made the act by which the Earl of Strafford suffered death, or that by which the Earl of Clarendon was driven into banishment? The answer would I suppose be in both cases, the legislative: and in this case the command which was the result of such act of legislation would accordingly be termed a law. How would it be with a command of the like nature issued by the Diet of Poland or that of Sweden, by the sovereign councils of Berne, Venice, Genoa or Amsterdam? This would depend partly upon the political notions prevalent in the respective states, partly upon the terminology of the respective languages. As to Rome in the time of the Commonwealth we know from Cicero that the language was thus: a command was termed a *privilegium*; which being a conjugate of the word *lex*, shewed that the power of which such command was deemed the exercise, was the legislative [Cicero, *De legibus* III].

"But where the sovereignty is in a single person and the party who is looked upon as principally affected by it is an individual, neither the word *law* nor any conjugate of it seems, in common speech at least, to be employed. When the King of France orders a man to quit the metropolis, or sends him to the Bastile, the power he exercises is not spoken of as a legislative power, nor the act he performs as an act of legislation. *Lettres de cachet* are not ordinarily termed laws. They are termed *ordres souverains*, sovereign orders, or by some such name. Will it be said that the orders in question are seldom issued but on account of some offence committed or apprehended, and that therefore the power exercised by them is either of the judicial or the *phthano-paranomic* [sic] kind? Be it so. But even let the exercise of it be as far as possible from all dependence upon any particular event, as much so as any of the widest extending law can be, in short let the *sic volo* even have no other reason than the *non amo te*, still the power exercised upon the occasion would hardly be looked upon as at all the better entitled to the name of legislative."

56. *Ibid.*, Ch. I, 4 (4–7): "If the Parliament of England order money to be paid to any body it is by an act of legislation, and the command is called a law: but nobody I suppose, thinks of giving that name to a command of the like nature issued by the King of France.

"There are even cases in which although the command were in every point a general one, although it were issued *mero motu* and although the party from whom it issued were a complex body, it might be a matter of dispute whether the command itself were according to common notion entitled to the appellation of a law, or the act of issuing it to that of an act of legislation: and perhaps with not only equal but still stronger appearance of reason, whether the power in virtue of which such command was issued would admit of the appellation of the legislative power. These are the cases where either the power from whence the magistrates by whom the commands in question are issued take their official name, or that of the magistrate from whose appointment they derive their office, comes under the denomination of either of those powers which are wont to be put in contradistinction to the legislative. In England the same sets of magistrates who exercise the judicial power are allowed, many of them, to establish *ex mero motu* regulations of a durable nature, regulations that are general in all points concerning the conduct of such parties as shall chance thereafter to be anyhow concerned in litigation. These regulations, though in every other circumstance except that of their not emaning [sic] directly from the sovereign power they agree with those which are universally and without scruple termed by the name of laws, are not usually characterized by that name: they are called sometimes *orders*, sometimes by a compound sort of name *rules and orders* of the court from which they ensue: and sometimes for distinction's sake *standing orders*; nor would the magistrates who are allowed to issue them be spoken of as exercising acts of legislation or as possessing any share of legislative power.

"In the same country the magistrate whose powers taken collectively are commonly termed by the appellation of the executive power, I mean the King, is also allowed to establish of himself and *ex mero motu* a multitude of regulations; regulations which are to such a degree general that the conduct and the fate of large and numerous classes of individuals are regulated and determined by them, and which accordingly in point of duration, though limited by positive institution, are in their own nature susceptible of perpetuity. The articles of war for the government of the army and the instructions given to privateers may serve for examples. I say nothing here of the power of making treaties nor of the power of making war and peace.... These then are so many other sets of articles which the definition would comprise under the name of laws. At the same time the issuing of the commands referrable to these heads would hardly without some reluctance be acknowledged as acts of legislation; and the power in virtue of which they were issued would probably not without a still greater degree of reluctance be admitted to the title of legislative power.

"Some difficulty there may also be, though perhaps not so much, with regard to various orders (general in point of extension or perpetual in point of duration or both) which are wont to be issued by various sets of magistrates, all of whom derive their authority originally, and many of them immediately, from the King. I am speaking of those for instance, which are issued by the governing part in corporate towns and other corporations for the government of the members of the corporation: as also of those which are issued by Justices of the Peace for the levying of rates in the counties for which they are commissioned. The unwillingness to employ in these cases the terms *law, act of legislation,* and *legislative power* will probably increase as the field of dominion becomes less extensive. ... [Y]et to many it might seem odd to apply the same high sounding appellation to the powers[,] acts and operations of a fraternity of weavers or tallow chandlers in a little town or parish."

57. *Ibid.*, Ch. IX, 8–9: "The distinction between a general law or mandate and a particular law or mandate, as here explained, is more material than at first sight might be imagined. Developed and applied it will afford us a clue without which it would be scarce possible for us to find our way through the labyrinth of constitutional jurisprudence. Correspondent to the distinction which respects the laws themselves is that which respects the power of making them. The power of enacting particular laws, the power as it may be called of imperating *de singulis* is one sort of power: the power of enacting general laws, that is of imperating *de classibus*, of making laws in general terms is, as we shall see, another and a very different sort of power. The latter power, although it be susceptible of a degree of extent of which the former is not susceptible, is on the other hand liable to peculiar limitations by which its force may be diminished or even utterly destroyed. These limitations give room for other powers, which in many cases form a necessary complement as it were to the imperative power when modified as here supposed. Adding to these the autocheiristic [sic] power and dividing each into the shares into which any lot of political power upon being distributed among several hands is liable to be

divided, we have the sum total of all the powers whatever, constitutional as well as private, that can have existence in a state. . . .

"To the words *power of legislation* we naturally annex the idea of the power of enacting general laws: laws that shall be general in all points: such laws of which the bulk of the statutes, by whatever name termed, which emaning from the sovereign authority and being consigned to the press are handed down from age to age, appear to be composed. The power of issuing such laws in all cases, in such sort that no man has authority to render them invalid, and every man is bound to submit to them or obey them would naturally upon first mention of it appear to be the same thing with absolute uncontrolled power. Such power one would naturally suppose must involve in its texture, must absorb as it were into its substance, every other power that could have existence in a state: insomuch that he who had this power would have everything, and that no one without his appointment could have any thing. The possible powers in a state are reducible to two: the power of contrectation [*sic*] or impressive power as we have termed it, and the power of imperation: which latter again may be distinguished into the power of *imperation properly so called*, and the power of *de-imperation*.

"But so far from being equivalent to or coextensive with both these powers it does not include so much as what is contained in the power of imperation properly so called."

58. *Ibid.*, Ch. XV, 1–5: "If it be thus with the statute law, how is it . . . with the customary? A customary law is not expressed in words: now in what words should it present itself? It has no parts: how should it exhibit any? It is one single indivisible act, capable of all manner of constructions. Under the customary law, there can scarcely be said to be a right or a wrong in any case. How should there? Right is the conformity to a rule, wrong the deviation from it: but here there is no rule established, no measure to discern by, no standard to appeal to: all is uncertainty, darkness, and confusion.

"It is evident enough that the mute sign, the act of punishment, which is all there is properly speaking of a customary law, can express nothing of itself to any who have not some other means of informing themselves of the occasion on which it was given. . . . If then it can serve as a rule to any distance or for any length of time, some account of the case must be taken and handed down by somebody: which somebody stands then in the place of a legislator. . . .

"Under these circumstances the state of the branch of law in question where custom thus bears sway is apt to stand upon some such footing as the following. The judges who perhaps at first did take and are still supposed or rather pretended to be supposed to take an account of every case that came before them never trouble their heads about the matter: the business is left to certain officers who are under them. These officers give what is called the history of the case, which history is termed by some such name as a *record*. This record being copied from precedents of the darkest antiquity instead of being a complete history of the case of which it purports to be the record, is in fact a partial and imperfect history of a different case that was determined upon some hundreds of years before: applied to the case in question it is in consequence, partly imperfect, partly false, partly irrelevant, and partly unintelligible. . . . The trouble of finding them out is so great and the information to be got from them so scanty and indecisive that it is not above one time in a hundred that even the judge who professes to take the decisions, given in the cases of which they purport to be the histories, for the measure of his own, can endure to look at them. Whether they have weight in any case or whether they have none, depends therefore upon accident. . . . [O]ne out of a thousand becomes a law: the nine hundred and ninety nine others remain waste paper.

"These documents being become to such a degree useless, another set of documents come gradually into use under the appellation of *Reports*. . . .

"These reports are published by anybody that pleases, and by as many people as please; and where nobody publishes, nobody cares. . . . [I]f . . . accident happens to throw a copy into the hands of a bookseller: the bookseller without being aware of it and without caring about it, becomes a legislator.

"Sometimes by commission from that high authority, a judge who had been dead and forgotten for half a century or for half a dozen centuries, starts up on a sudden out of his tomb, and takes his seat on the throne of legislation, overturning the establishments of the intervening periods, like Justinian brought to life again at Amalfi.

[Note: "In the customary law, a great perhaps the greatest part of the business is done in the way of *ex post facto* law. The decisions, being formed on grounds that were inaccessible to the party previous to the act for which he was made to suffer, carry with them a great part of the mischief of the *privilegia* against which Cicero inveighs with so much justice."]

"If the series of the cases that are published is broken and interrupted, the deficiency is made up by the multitude of reports there are of the same case: all perhaps contradicting one another and contradicting what little there is of truth in the record.

"Meantime out of these scattered atoms, be the collection of them ever so copious and exact, nothing it is plain so long as they continue in the order in which they happen to be brought to light can be made, that shall wear the face I do not say of a law but of any thing that bears any perceptible relation to any thing that is entitled to that name. To give them any sort of connection with one another and with the rest of the matter of which law is made, a set of general rules must be abstracted from them and worked up into the form of a treatise. A set of treatises accordingly start up: and here again the bookseller gets another share in the prerogative of legislation.

"It is plain these general rules can have no foundation in authority any further than as they are the necessary result of some particular assignable decisions. . . . First in point of original authority comes the record: then comes the report: last of all comes the treatise: the shadow of the shadow of a shade: and it is this shadow that is worshipped as the substance."

59. *Ibid.*, Ch. XV, 9, 11: "But the general rule extracted no matter how, from these particular *data*, and which if there were a law in the case, would be the law, is after all absurd and mischievous. . . . [T]hey form themselves like the Proculians and the Sabinians of old, though on a ground of much greater extent and importance into different parties: *Stare decisis* is the maxim of the one; *salus reipublicae* or something like it, the motto of the other: both perhaps partisans of utility, though of utility viewed through a different medium: the one of the general utility which results from the adherence to established precedents: the other, of the particular utility which results from the bringing back the current of decision at any rate into the channel of original utility from which the force of precedent they suppose had drawn it aside: the one enamoured of uniformity, the mother of security and peace: the other, of Natural Justice or Equity or Right Reason or by whatever other name the phantom is best known. . . .

"From a set of *data* like these a law is to be extracted by every man who can fancy that he is able: by each man, perhaps a different law: and these then are the *monades* which meeting together constitute the rules which taken together constitute that inimitable and unimprovable production of enlightened reason, that fruit of concord, pledge of liberty in every country in which it is found, the common or customary law.

"Caligula published his laws in small characters: but still he published them: he hung them up high, but still he hung them up. English judges neither hang up their laws, nor publish them. They go further; they will not suffer it to be done by others: and if there be any dependence to be placed in any rule of common law, whosoever takes upon him to do it, well or ill, he may be punished. The rule is indeed falling into desuetude: but it has lately been recognized; it has never been disclaimed; and it may be enforced at any time. Whosoever takes upon him to do any such service to his country does it, like the Grecian lawgiver, with a halter about his neck.

"It appears then, that the customary law is a fiction from beginning to end; and it is in the way of fiction if at all that we must speak of it.

"The customary law, you say, punishes theft with hanging: be it so. But by what law is this done? who made it? when was it made? where is it to be found? what are the parts that it contains? by what words is it expressed?"

60. *Ibid.*, Ch. XIII, 1–3: "A law is an *expression* of will: that is an assemblage of signs expressive of an act of the will. These signs then may by possibility be any signs whatever which are capable of expressing such a will. . . .

"When the nature of those laws which are here called customary comes to be precisely understood, which it seems hardly to have been hitherto, the doubt above expressed will not be wondered at. These laws are nothing but so many particular autocratic acts or orders, which in virtue of the more extensive interpretation which the people are disposed to put upon them, have somewhat of the effect of general laws. . . . Written law then is the law of those who can both speak and write: traditionary law, of those who can speak but can not write: customary law, of those who neither know how to write, nor how to speak. Written law is the law for civilized nations: traditionary law, for barbarians: customary law, for brutes.

"Not but that there are plenty of books purporting to be books of customary or as it is more frequently called *unwritten* law: for if the written law is written, so is the unwritten too. But what are they? Books written not by the legislator but by private individuals: Books not of authoritative but of unauthoritative jurisprudence. In none of all these books is there so much as a single article which can with propriety receive the appellation of *a* law. It is owing rather to an imperfection which as we have seen is peculiar to the English tongue, if in that language they can with any degree of propriety be termed books of law: They contain *jus* indeed but not *leges*: *le droit*, but not *des loix*.

"If in all that has been ever written of this nature there be a single paragraph which (not being a passage copied from some statute) is seriously meant to pass for a paragraph of *a* law, I mean in the sense in which the word *law* is used in contradistinction to the word *order*, it is a forgery."

Also in the same ch., XV, 7, Bentham asserts that only a collection of customs properly composed and duly approved by legislators could be valid. "Accordingly so long as the validity of these formularies rests upon the customary law, and until a sufficient stock of them has been framed and authenticated by the proper legislator, a collection of such of them as have been drawn into question and confirmed, or passed unquestioned through the scrutiny of lawyers of eminence concerned for parties interested in their downfall, forms another branch of the customary law."

Other significant differences between legislators and judges in respect to law and custom are articulated in Ch. XI ("Force of a Law"), 3–4, with respect to the problem of "will" and "intent." "This punishment then, or this reward, whichever it be, in order to produce its effect must in some manner or other be announced: notice of it must in some way or other be given, in order to produce an expectation of it, on the part of the people whose conduct it is meant to influence. This notice may either be given by the legislator himself in the text of the law itself, or it may be left to be given, in the way of customary law by the judge: the legislator, commanding you for example to do an act: the judge in his own way and according to his own measure punishing you in case of your not doing it, or, what is much less frequent, rewarding you in case of your doing it. . . .

"But the most eligible and indeed the most common method of giving notice is by inserting a clause on purpose: by subjoining to that part of the law which is expressive of the legislator's will, another part of the office of which is to indicate the motive he furnishes you with for complying with such will.

"In this case the law may plainly enough be distinguished into two parts: the one serving to make known to you what the inclination of the legislator is: the other serving to make known to you what motive the legislator has furnished you with for complying with that inclination: the one addressed more particularly to your understanding; the other, to your will. The former of these parts may be termed the *directive*: the other, the *sanctional* or *incitative*."

61. *Ibid.*, Appendix C, as discussed by the editor in Intro., p. xxxix.

62. *Ibid.*, Appendix C, 1–3: "Thus inextricably is the penal branch of the law interwoven with the civil: that with which we are here immediately concerned, with that with which here we have no such immediate concern: in order to settle and arrange the former, it became therefore unavoidably necessary to look through all the latter: so toilsome and so arduous when pursued with care and industry is the business of arrangement. Before we conclude it may be not amiss to gather up in the way of recapitulation the broken hints that have been given in the course of this chapter and thereby to give a sort of analytical sketch of the whole business of the art of legislation.

"The art of legislation has two general objects or purposes in view: the one direct and positive, to add to the happiness of the community: the other indirect and negative, to avoid doing anything by which that happiness may be diminished.

"To enable it to compass the former of these purposes it has two great instruments or engines: 1. coercion and 2. remuneration. Coercion is either 1. physical or 2. moral, viz: by punishment."

63. *Ibid.*, Appendix C, 5, 14–19: "Now the objects in which the actions are capable of *terminating* are either *things* or *persons*. It is by causing certain actions to be abstained from on the part of other men which would lessen the advantage you are capable of reaping either for yourself or others from certain things, at the same time that you, or such and such persons of your appointment, are not caused to abstain from certain actions by which that happiness may be promoted, that you have *power* given you over those things. . . .

"When the acts you are left free to perform are such whereby the interests of other individuals is liable to be affected, you are thereby said to have a power over those individuals. . . . As to acts which, though they may be mischievous (as well as beneficial or innocent) in the first instance, are permitted, whether under the notion of their being beneficial upon the whole, or because the interests of those to whom they may be prejudicial are neglected, the performance of these acts is termed the exercise of a *power*. Power is either over persons or over things. And in both cases it is either beneficial or fiduciary.

"An act is a real entity: a law is another. A duty or obligation is a fictitious entity conceived as resulting from the union of the two former. A law commanding or forbidding an act thereby creates a duty or obligation. A right is another fictitious entity, a kind of secondary fictitious entity, resulting out of a duty. Let any given duty be proposed, either somebody is the better for it or nobody. If nobody, no such duty ought to be created: neither is there any right that corresponds to it. If somebody, this somebody is either the party bound, or some other. If it be he himself, then the duty, if such it may be called, is a duty he owes to himself: neither in this case is there any *right* that corresponds to it. If it be any other party then is it a duty owing to some other party: and then that other party has at any rate a right: a right to have this duty performed: perhaps also a *power*: a power to compel the performance of such duty.

"What is it that every article of law has in common with the rest? It issues commands and by so doing it creates *duties*, or, what is another word for the same thing, *obligations*. The notion of duty is a common measure for every article of law. It is from hence that the differences and resemblances of the various branches of law are to be traced as from this common source.

"The notion of command leads to that of duty: that of duty to that of right: and that of right to that of power. Right is either naked or armed with power. That of exemption to that of privilege: power and duty together to that of trust. . . .

"[T]he method I have just been taking here . . . is that of defining these and other names of fictitious entities not *per genus et differentiam,* nor by any other of the methods which are applicable to real entities, but by a method which I have ventured to style that of paraphrasis: a method new in itself and which therefore if mentioned at all must be mentioned by a new name. Now this method is one that most assuredly has never been taken hitherto: if therefore they are now properly explained this is the first time they have ever been so. . . . No wonder that legislators should not any where have done precisely what they ought to do when they have never hitherto had a clear understanding of what it is they themselves have actually been doing. . . .

"With regard to the powers hitherto spoken of we have seen by what operations on the part of the law they are constituted: it is in every case by *permission* only in as far as the agency of him to whom the power is given is concerned. Where the power is in its highest degree of force, a command indeed as we have seen must be superadded. But who is the person to whom such command is issued? not to you, the person to whom the power is given, but to me, the person who am commanded to assist you. . . .

"But now, besides permitting you to do the act, let the law command you to do it, and the case is very different. It is very likely that now the power given you may not be beneficial to you."

64. *Ibid.,* Ch. XIX, 1 (1–7), 2–3, 7, 11 [As to the uses of the work:] "These may be as follows [:]

"(1) To draw some sort of line between the penal and the civil branches of the law-system.

"(2) To lay the foundation for the plan of the complete body of laws supposing it to be constructed *ab origine,* according to a method of division grounded on natural and universal principles. The field of legislation is a trackless wild which how often so ever traversed has never hitherto been surveyed by rule.

"(3) To exhibit a plan to work upon, a standard to be guided by in digesting or reducing a body of customary law or a mixed body of customary and statute law together into a pure body of statutory law.

"(4) In point of matter—to exhibit a clue whereby the legislator may be guided in his endeavours to avoid the great imperfections which a body of laws is liable to fall into, weakness on the one hand, tyranny and oppressiveness on the other. Weakness from want of qualifications, tyranny from want of clearness, the one or the other as it may happen.

"(5) To restrain the licentiousness of interpretation. Legislators may travel with their eyes open over a plain and level road: instead of groping their way blindfold through a wood. Expository jurisprudence, the art of finding clear ideas to annex to the expressions of a man whose ideas were not clear, instead of being the only branch cultivated would be thrown aside. The legislator might need a censor but would need no interpreter. He would be himself his own and sole interpreter. . . .

"(6) To exhibit a common standard, by which the several systems of law prevailing in every country may respectively be compared, and thereby their mutual agreements and disagreements represented, their comparative excellences and defects exhibited to view: to the end that what is excellent in one system may be transferred into every other, that improvements in the most important art of all, the art of legislation, may like other arts make the tour of the globe, and that each legislator may add to his own wisdom the wisdom of his neighbours and contemporaries.

"(7) That the method of teaching the art of legislation may be improved, or rather that such a method may be invented, and thereby an acquaintance with the principles of this art may be diffused and rendered common among the body of the people. It is thus that in time the labours of the legislator may make room for the judgment and industry of the professor: and the fruit of Invention be made the subject of Science.

"First then, it gives the plan of a complete and regular body of statute law: and thereby . . . a complete body of law for every purpose. Laws are either obligative or de-obligative: commands or countermands. . . . It is to be remembered that by this parcelling out what relates to the several offences, the whole law is parcelled out. Not but that every law may have, and it will probably be found convenient that every law should have, a civil branch as well as a penal: a part which holds an act up to view in the character of an offence: and a part which holds not up to view any act in any such character. But the civil branch of each law, as hath been shewn, is but the *complement* of the penal: it is on the penal that every proposition which may be found in a book of law depends for its obligative force. When the imperative clause or clauses to which a clause that is not imperative relates is traced out and understood, the true nature and efficacy of such clause is clearly understood: till then, it remains in darkness. . . .

"The several laws that in a new code shall be established or that in an old one may be conceived to be established upon this plan will be the integrant or aliquot parts of that vast and complicated whole. . . . [T]hey may be connected together: and one book will hold them. On that one book any man may lay his hand and say, 'Within this cover is the sole basis of my rights, the sole standard of my duties. Duties and rights together, here I shall be sure to find them: elsewhere I have no need to look for them.'

"In the second place, it will exhibit at the same time a plan for the digestion of the customary law. The customary law as hath been shewn is not any essentially distinct branch of the body of the law, it differs not from statute law in substance, but in as far as it is at all intelligible, in as far as it has any force or efficacy, it must be considered as a miscellaneous branch of statute law ill-expressed and ill-defined. . . . Whatever then antecedently to the enactment of a new code was customary law, the same being stamped with the seal of authority, becomes statute law with the rest. At present we may boldly affirm that among all the systems of law which prevail among the several nations of the world, there is not one which does not exist more or less of it in the form of customary law: so that as yet no instance of a complete code of statute law is any where to be found. It follows not however by any means that if a complete code of that kind were given to any nation it must thereby be deprived of so much as a single article of those ancient and respected institutions to which the people in many instances with great reason are so strenuously attached. . . . By this means a set of tables might be formed exhibiting the provisions made by the several governments of the world (such of them whose policy was thought to be worth attending to) under the several heads included in the natural syllabus in question: a comparative view of the several systems of legislation confronted together in their correspondent parts and digested into one work: a work which to borrow an expression from divines might be styled a sort of universal *harmony of the laws*. [A note by Bentham allues to several 18th-century resystematizations of Justinian's compilations of Roman law, including by Heineccius.] . . .

"Such are the fruits of a method planned under the auspices of the principle of utility, in which the laws are ranged according to the ends they have in view [this being the last sentence of the chapter and treatise proper]."

65. Bentham, *A Comment on the Commentaries*, edited by J. H. Burns and H. L. A. Hart (London, 1977), with good Intro. to the work.

66. *Ibid.*, I, 2 (pp. 15–16): "But now we may expect something a little more solid: now we come at last to particulars: now we come to some specific articles of this many-titled

358 / Notes to Chapter II

law. 'Such *among others*,' continues our Author [i.e., Blackstone], 'are these principles: that we should live honestly, should hurt nobody, and should render to every one his due; to which three general precepts Justinian has reduced the whole doctrine of Law.'

"Here then we have a sample of this same Law of Nature: and a pretty large sample it should seem to be: since, according to Justinian, here is all of it. Indeed not only of *it*, not only of the Law of nature, but of everything else that is known by the name of Law: of what is called Municipal Law therefore among the rest: if '*Jus*' means Law.

"Thus, according to our Author, saith Justinian: and with Justinian our Author finds no fault. Not that he will allow it be *all* neither: since there are '*others*', it seems, that he knows of. What these '*others*' are it would have been but charity in him to have told us. The trouble surely could not have been great: here are but three: more than as many again there could not surely be. So great, so wise an emperor as Justinian, an emperor whose words are oracles, surely could not have been mistaken more than half. It is the more to be regretted our Author has not given us the rest of them, as what he has given us are such as no mortal alive, our Author himself in particular, I dare answer for him, can tell what to make of.

"Of the 1st, viz. 'we should live honestly', as obvious a sense as any is, we should do as we ought to do: which brings the precept or rather the doctrine to this incontestable one: what we ought to do we ought to do. This or 'we should not violate another's property', one or other of them, such as they are, I take to be the meaning of 'we should live honestly'. If not, let him find out what *is*, who is more fortunate than I am.

"Not that '*honeste*', which is Justinian's word, signifies 'honestly' all this while, in any other vocabulary than our Author's. In the mouth of Justinian who used it, *honeste vivere* signified, I should suppose, to live according to the rules of *decorum*: whatever according to Justinian's notion may have been decorum.

"An explanation a little more precise of this precept, if it will admit of any explanation that is at all precise, may perhaps be this. According to what *Justinian meant* by it, it signifies to act *right* (that is, what he who gave it us thought *right*) in matters wherein other men's interests *are not* directly concerned: as by abstaining from drunkenness, obscenities, and so forth. According to what *our Author has made* of it, it signifies to act *right* in matters wherein other men's interests *are* directly concerned: which gives it no imaginable distinction from the other two.

"Of the second, viz. 'we should hurt nobody', the sense, according to the best I am able to make of it is, either simply and without exception, that we *should not* give pain to any one at all; or else that we *should not*, i.e. *ought not* to give pain to any one but when we *ought*. Of these two interpretations the first would be apt, I doubt, to make it rather puzzling to us what to think of several professions hitherto thought useful ones: for example, those of the Judge, the Surgeon, the Soldier, not forgetting the Hangman. The other would, I fear, make it full as puzzling to us to find any thing in this sagacious precept that could serve a man as a rule.

"Of the 3d and last, viz. 'we should render every man his due', the meaning, I suppose, is, either, that we ought to render him what we ought to render him, we ought to do, once more, what we ought to do (for this edifying and instructive sense is all that belongs incontestably to any of them); or else that we should forbear to violate his property: that is, should forbear to deal with anything which *the Law* (as I should call, *the municipal Law* as our Author calls it) shall have declared to belong to him, in a manner which the Law shall have commanded us not to deal with it."

67. *Ibid.*, II, 1 (p. 118).

68. Bentham, *A Fragment on Government*, edited by J. H. Burns and H. L. A. Hart (London, 1977), comprising the second treatise following the *Comment* in the same edn. cited above. All *sic*.

69. *Ibid.*, Ch. IV ("Right of the Supreme Power to Make Laws"), 1, 3, 5–8, 33–34: "We now come to the third topic touched upon in the digression; namely, the *right*, as our Author [Blackstone] phrases it, which the Supreme Power has of making laws. And this topic occupies one pretty long paragraph. The title here given to it is the same which in the next succeeding paragraph he has found for it himself. This is fortunate: for, to have been obliged to find a title for it myself, is what would have been to the last degree distressing. To *intitle* a discourse, is to represent the drift of it. But, to represent the drift of this, is a task which, so long at least as I confine my consideration to the paragraph itself, bids defiance to my utmost efforts. . . .

"'Having', says our Author, 'thus cursorily considered the three usual species of government, and our own singular constitution, selected and compounded from them all, I proceed to observe, that, as the power of making laws constitutes the supreme authority, so wherever the supreme authority in any state resides, it is the right of that authority to make laws; that is, in the words of our definition, to prescribe the rule of civil action. And this may be discovered from the very end and institution of civil states. For a state is a collective body, composed of a multitude of individuals united for their safety and convenience, and intending to act together as one man. If it therefore is to act as one man, it ought to act by one uniform will. But in as much as political communities are made up of many natural persons, each of whom has his particular will and inclination, these several wills cannot by any *natural* union be joined together, or tempered and disposed into a lasting harmony, so as to constitute and produce that one uniform will of the whole. It can therefore be no otherwise produced than by a *political* union; by the consent of all persons to submit their own private wills to the will of one man, or of one, or more assemblies of men, to whom the supreme authority is entrusted: and this will of that one man, or assemblage of men is, in different states, according to their different constitutions, understood to be law.' . . .

"The obscurity in which the first sentence of this paragraph is enveloped, is such, that I know not how to go about bringing it to light, without borrowing a word or two of logicians. Laying aside the preamble, the body of it, viz. '*as* the power of making laws constitutes the supreme authority, so where-ever the supreme authority in any state resides, it is the right of that authority to make laws,' may be considered as constituting that sort of syllogism which logicians call an *enthymeme*. An *enthymeme* consists of two *propositions*; a *consequent* and an *antecedent*. 'The power of making laws', says our Author, 'constitutes the supreme authority.' This is his antecedent. From hence it is he concludes, that 'wherever the supreme authority in any state resides, it is the right of that authority to make laws.' This then is his *consequent*.

"Now so it is, that this *antecedent*, and this *consequent*, for any difference at least that I can possibly perceive in them, would turn out, were they but correctly worded, to mean precisely the same thing: for, after saying that 'the power of making laws constitutes the supreme authority', to tell us that, for that reason, 'the supreme authority' is (or has) the power (or the right) of making laws, is giving us, I take it, much the same sort of information, as it would be to us to be told that a thing is so, *because* it is so. . . .

"By the 'supreme authority' then, (we may suppose our Author to say) 'I mean the same thing as when I say the power of making laws'. This is the proposition we took notice of above, under the name of the *antecedent*. This antecedent then, we may observe, is a definition: a definition, to wit, of the phrase 'supreme authority'. Now to define a phrase is, to translate it into another phrase, supposed to be better understood, and expressive of the same idea. . . .

"Now let us consider the *consequent*; which, when detached from the context, may be spoken of as making a sentence of itself. 'Wherever', says he, 'the supreme authority in any state resides, it is the *right* of that authority to make Laws'.—By '*wherever*' I take it for granted he means, '*in whatever persons*': by '*authority*', in the former part of the sentence,—*power*; by the same word, '*authority*', in the latter part of the sentence,—*persons*. Corrected therefore, the sentence will stand thus: *In whatever persons in any state the supreme power resides, it is the right of those persons to make Laws.*

"The only word now remaining undisposed of, is the word '*right*'. And what to think of this, indeed I know not: whether our Author had a meaning in it, or whether he had none. It is inserted, we may observe, in the latter part only of the sentence: it appears not in the former. Concerning this omission, two conjectures here present themselves: it may have happened by accident; or it may have been made by design. If by accident, then the case is, that the idea annexed to the word '*right*' is no other than what was meant to be included in the former part of the sentence, in which it is *not* expressed, as well as in the latter, in which it *is*. In this case it may, without any change in the signification, be expressed in both. Let it then be expressed, and the sentence, take it altogether, will stand thus: *In whatever persons* the right of exercising *supreme power in any state resides, it is* the right *of those persons to make Laws.* . . .

"In the heat of debate, some, perhaps, would be for saying of this management that it was transferring at once the supreme authority from the legislative power to the judicial. But this would be going too far on the other side. There is a wide difference between a *positive* and a *negative* part in legislation. There is a wide difference again between a negative upon *reasons* given, and a negative without any. The power of *repealing* a law even for reasons given is a great power: too great indeed for Judges: but still very distinguishable from, and much inferior to that of *making* one.

"Let us now go back a little. In denying the existence of any assignable bounds to the supreme power, I added, 'unless where limited by express convention: for this exception I could not but subjoin. Our Author indeed, in that passage in which, short as it is, he is the most explicit, leaves, we may observe, no room for it."

Ibid., Ch. V ("Duty of the Supreme Power to Make Laws"), 1–8: "We now come to the last topic touched upon in this digression: a certain '*duty*', which, according to our Author's account, the supreme power lies under:—the *duty of making laws*.

" 'Thus far', says he, 'as to the *right* of the supreme power to make laws; but farther, it is its *duty* likewise. *For since* the respective members are bound to conform themselves to the will of the state, it is expedient that they *receive directions* from the state declaratory of that its will. . . .

"Still as obscure, still as ambiguous as ever. The '*supreme power*' we may remember, according to the definition so lately given of it by our Author, and so often spoken of, is neither more nor less than the *power to make laws*. Of this power we are now told that it is its '*duty*' to make laws. Hence we learn—what?—that it is its '*duty*' to do what it does; to be, in short, what it is. . . . 'Thus far', says our Author (recapitulating what he had been saying before) 'as to the *right* of the supreme power to make laws.'—By this '*right*' we saw, in the preceding chapter, was meant, a right to make laws *in all cases whatsoever.* 'But further', he now adds, 'it is its *duty* likewise.' Its *duty* then to do—what? to do the same thing that it was before asserted to be its *right* to do—to make laws in all cases whatsoever: or (to use another word, and that our Author's own, and that applied to the same purpose) that it is its duty to be '*absolute.*' A sort of duty this which will probably be thought rather a singular one. . . . I take it, not so much the actual *making* of laws, as the taking of proper measures to *spread abroad* the knowledge of whatever laws happen to *have been* made: a duty which (to adopt some of our Author's own words) is conversant, not so much about *issuing* 'directions', as about providing that such as *are* issued shall be '*received*'.

"Mean time to speak of the *duties* of a supreme power;—of a *legislature*, meaning a *supreme* legislature;—of a set of men acknowledged to be absolute;—is what, I must own, I am not very fond of. . . .

"I understand, I think, pretty well, what is meant by the word *duty* (political duty) when applied to myself; and I could not persuade myself, I think, to apply it in the same sense in a regular didactic discourse to those whom I am speaking of as my supreme governors. That is my *duty* to do, which I am liable to be *punished*, according to law, if I do not do: this is the original, ordinary, and proper sense of the word *duty*. Have these supreme governors any such duty? No: for if they are at all liable to punishment according to law, whether it be for *not* doing any thing, or for *doing*, then are they not, what they are supposed to be, supreme governors: those are the supreme governors, by whose appointment the former are liable to be punished.

"The word duty, then, if applied to persons spoken of as supreme governors, is evidently applied to them in a sense which is figurative and improper . . ."

70. Bentham, *First Principles Preparatory to Constitutional Code*, edited by Philip Schofield (Oxford, 1989).
71. *Ibid.*, pp. 3–4.
72. *Ibid.*, e.g. pp. 6–7, 30, 96, 101, 113, 118.
73. *Ibid.*, p. 27 (title).
74. Bentham, *Constitutional Code*, Vol. I, edited by F. Rosen and J. H. Burns (Oxford, 1983), Editorial Intro., p. xi and p. 1 of text (original title page). Article numbers are deleted in some brief extracts to follow. All *sic*.
75. *Ibid.*, Ch. III ("Sovereignty, in Whom"): "*Enactive* [a heading covering that which follows here] [:]. . . . The sovereignty is in *the people*. It is reserved by and to them. It is exercised, by the exercise of the Constitutive authority, as per Ch. iv."

Ibid., Ch. IV ("Authorities"): "*Enactive* [a heading covering that which follows here] [:]. . . . To the *Constitutive* Authority it belongs, amongst other things, to depute and *locate*, as per Ch. vi. . . .

"To the *Legislative* it belongs, amongst other things, to *locate* the *Chiefs* of the two other departments; and eventually to dislocate them: to give—not general only, but upon occasion, *individual direction* to their conduct, as well as to that of all the several functionaries respectively *subordinate* to them; eventually also to punish them, in case of noncompliance with its directions. . . .

"To the *Administrative* it belongs, amongst other things, to give execution and effect to the ordinances of the Legislative, in so far as regards the persons and things placed under its special direction, by the Legislative: to wit, in so far as litis-contestation has not place. . . .

"To the *Judiciary* it belongs, amongst other things, to give execution and effect to the ordinances of the Legislative, in so far as litis-contestation has place: to wit, either as to the question of *law*, or as to the question of *fact*. . . .

"Taken together, the *Legislative* and the *Administrative* compose the *Government*; the *Administrative* and the *Judiciary*, the *Executive*; the *Legislative* and the *Executive*, what may be termed the *Operative*, as contra-distinguished from the *Constitutive*. . . .

"So many of these supreme *authorities*, The Constitutive included, which is supreme over all the others, so many *Departments*; to each *authority*, a *department*. . . .

"The Legislature has under it as many *Sub-legislatures*, as in the territory of the state here are *Districts*: to each District, a Sub-legislature."

Ibid., Ch. V ("Constitutive Authority"): "*Enactive* [a heading covering that which follows here] [:]. . . . Subordinate to the Constitutive authority . . . are all other authorities, and thereby all other public functionaries belonging to the state.

"Those whom it cannot dislocate in an immediate, it can in an unimmediate or say interventional way; to wit, by dislocating those. . . .

"*Locative function.* Functionaries, in relation to whom this function is exercised by the members of the Constitutive authority, are as follows—

"Their *Deputies*, deputed by them to the legislature, to act as Members of the Supreme Legislature, styled collectively *the Legislature*. In relation to all these, this power is exercised by the members of the whole Constitutive body, as divided into the bodies belonging to the several Election Districts; in each District, the Members of the Constitutive electing for that District a member of the Legislature. . . .

"The members of the several Sub-Legislatures. In relation to each sublegislative body, this power is exercised by the members of the Constitutive body, belonging to its District, as divided into the bodies belonging to the several Subdistricts therein contained; the body belonging to each such Subdistrict electing a member of the Sublegislature."

Ibid., Ch. VI ("Legislature"): *"Enactive* [a heading covering that which follows here] [:].
. . . The Supreme Legislature is omnicompetent. Coextensive with the territory of the state is its local field of service; coextensive with the field of human action is its logical field of service.—To its power, there are no limits. In place of limits, it has checks. These checks are applied, by the securities, provided for good conduct on the part of the several members, individually operated upon. . . .

"The Supreme Legislative Authority has, for its immediate instrument, the Supreme *Executive*, composed of the *administrative* and the *judiciary*, acting within their respective spheres. On the will of the Supreme Constitutive, the Supreme Legislative is dependent. . . . Absolute and all-comprehensive is this dependence. So also on the will of the Legislature, the will of the Executive, and the wills of the Sublegislatures. . . .

"Variable at all times,—variable at the pleasure of the Legislature for the time being,— is every article in this and every other Code. For every moment of its duration, on its reasonableness, first in the eyes of the Legislative, then in the eyes of the Constitutive, is its sole dependence. . . .

"Of the Constitutive Authority, the constant will, (for such it cannot but be presumed to be,) is that the national felicity—the happiness of the greatest number—be maximized: to this will, on each occasion, it is the duty of the Supreme Legislature, according to the measure of its ability, to give execution and effect. . . .

"If, on any occasion, any ordinance, which to some shall appear repugnant to the principles of this Constitution, shall come to have been enacted by the Legislature, such ordinance is not on that account to be, by any judge, treated or spoken of, as being null and void: not even although its tendency, intended as well as actual, were to appear to him to be, to diminish the mass of power hereby reserved to the Constitutive Authority. . . .

"To the Constitutive Authority, and *that* alone, it belongs to enforce the observance, of contracts entered into by the Legislature. . . ."

The above provisions, like others in Bentham's *Code*, are meant to be applicable to all countries. Conversely, he has been influenced by a variety of different national models. His references throughout to the "prime minister" tend to suggest the British model. Those to the ultimate "constitutive authority" seem to borrow elements from various models of the later French Revolution, which were treated in our preceding book. Such "constitutive authority" is often legislative in nature and scope. Bentham's whole *Code* was, at its inception, written in certain regards for the state of Portugal (cf. Ed. Intro.). The government of the United States of America also has an interesting place in the *Code*, along with that of many other nations.

76. In the edn. of J. S. Mill's writings by Mary Warmock that includes his *Utilitarianism* and *On Liberty*, together with portions of Bentham's *Morals and Legislation* (New York, etc., 1974), pp. 78–125 ("Bentham"). Also in *Jeremy Bentham: Ten*

Critical Essays, edited by B. Parekh (London, 1974), p. 1 ff. ("Bentham"), and in *Mill on Bentham and Coleridge,* with Intro. by F. R. Lewis (Cambridge, 1950), pp. 39 ff. ("Mill on Bentham"). I have used the first of these three sources in the extracts to follow (all *sic*).

77. Mill, *op. cit.* (n. 76 above), pp. 84–85, 87, 89–92: "A place, therefore, must be assigned to Bentham among the masters of wisdom, the great teachers and permanent intellectual ornaments of the human race. . . . Bentham . . . was not a great philosopher, but he was a great reformer in philosophy. He brought into philosophy something which it greatly needed, and for want of which it was at a stand. It was not his doctrines which did this, it was his mode of arriving at them. He introduced into morals and politics those habits of thought and modes of investigation, which are essential to the idea of science; and the absence of which made those departments of inquiry, as physics had been before Bacon, a field of interminable discussion, leading to no result. It was not his opinions, in short, but his method that constituted the novelty and the value of what he did; a value beyond all price, even though we should reject the whole, as we unquestionably must a large part, of the opinions themselves.

"Bentham's method may be shortly described as the method of detail; of treating wholes by separating them into their parts, abstractions by resolving them into Things,— classes and generalities by distinguishing them into the individuals of which they are made up; and breaking every question into pieces before attempting to solve it. The precise amount of originality of this process, considered as a logical conception—its degree of connexion with the methods of physical science, or with the previous labours of Bacon, Hobbes or Locke—is not an essential consideration in this place. Whatever originality there was in the method—in the subjects he applied it to, and in the rigidity with which he adhered to it, there was the greatest. Hence his interminable classifications. . . . Bentham shall speak for himself on this subject: the passage is from his first systematic work, 'Introduction to the Principles of Morals and Legislation,' and we could scarcely quote anything more strongly exemplifying both the strength and weakness of his mode of philosophising. . . .

"It is the introduction into the philosophy of human conduct, of this method of detail—of this practice of never reasoning about wholes until they have been resolved into their parts, nor about abstractions until they have been translated into realities—that constitutes the originality of Bentham in philosophy, and makes him the great reformer of the moral and political branch of it. To what he terms the 'exhaustive method of classification,' which is but one branch of this more general method, he himself ascribes everything original in the systematic and elaborate work from which we have quoted. . . . The application of a real inductive philosophy to the problems of ethics, is as unknown to the Epicurean moralists as to any of the other schools; they never take a question to pieces, and join issue on a definite point. Bentham certainly did not learn his sifting and anatomising method from them.

"This method Bentham has finally installed in philosophy; has made it henceforth imperative on philosophers of all schools. By it he has formed the intellects of many thinkers, who either never adopted, or have abandoned, many of his peculiar opinions. He has taught the method to men of the most opposite schools to his; he has made them perceive that if they do not test their doctrines by the method of detail, their adversaries will. He has thus, it is not too much to say, for the first time introduced precision of thought into moral and political philosophy. . . . This is nothing less than a revolution in philosophy. Its effect is gradually becoming evident in the writings of English thinkers of every variety of opinion, and will be felt more and more in proportion as Bentham's writings are diffused, and as the number of minds to whose formation they contribute is multiplied. . . .

"Bentham's method of laying out his subject is admirable. . . . He begins by placing before himself the whole of the field of inquiry to which the particular question belongs, and divides down until he arrives at the thing he is in search of; and thus by successively rejecting all which is not the thing, he gradually works out a definition of what it is. This, which he calls the exhaustive method, is as old as philosophy itself. Plato owes everything to it, and does everything by it; and the use made of it by that great man in his Dialogues, Bacon, in one of those pregnant logical hints scattered through his writings, and so much neglected by most of his pretended followers, pronounced to be the nearest approach to a true inductive method in the ancient philosophy. Bentham was probably not aware that Plato had anticipated him in the process to which he too declared that he owed everything."

78. *Ibid.*, pp. 93–96: "Bentham failed in deriving light from other minds. His writings contain few traces of the accurate knowledge of any schools of thinking but his own; and many proofs of his entire conviction that they could teach him nothing worth knowing. For some of the most illustrious of previous thinkers, his contempt was unmeasured. In almost the only passage of the 'Deontology' which, from its style, and from its having before appeared in print, may be known to be Bentham's, Socrates, and Plato are spoken of in terms distressing to his greatest admirers; and the incapacity to appreciate such men, is a fact perfectly in unison with the general habits of Bentham's mind. He had a phrase, expressive of the view he took of all moral speculations to which his method had not been applied, or (which he considered as the same thing) not founded on a recognition of utility as the moral standard; this phrase was 'vague generalities.' . . . [I]t must be allowed, that even the originality which can, and the courage which dares, think for itself, is not a more necessary part of the philosophical character than a thoughtful regard for previous thinkers, and for the collective mind of the human race. . . .

"The hardiest assertor, therefore, of the freedom of private judgment—the keenest detector of the errors of his predecessors, and of the inaccuracies of current modes of thought—is the very person who most needs to fortify the weak side of his own intellect, by study of the opinions of mankind in all ages and nations, and of the speculations of philosophers of the modes of thought most opposite to his own. . . . A man of clear ideas errs grievously if he imagines that whatever is seen confusedly does not exist: it belongs to him, when he meets with such a thing, to dispel the mist, and fix the outlines of the vague form which is looming through it.

"Bentham's contempt, then, of all other schools of thinkers; his determination to create a philosophy wholly out of the materials furnished by his own mind, and by minds like his own; was his first disqualification as a philosopher. His second, was the incompleteness of his own mind as a representative of universal human nature."

79. *Ibid.*, pp. 96–97, 99–101: "In many of the most natural and strongest feelings of human nature he had no sympathy. . . .

"By these limits, accordingly, Bentham's knowledge of human nature is bounded. It is wholly empirical; and the empiricism of one who has had little experience. He had neither internal experience nor external; the quiet, even tenor of his life, and his healthiness of mind, conspired to exclude him from both. . . . Other ages and other nations were a blank to him for purposes of instruction. He measured them but by one standard; their knowledge of facts, and their capability to take correct views of utility, and merge all other objects in it. . . . Knowing so little of human feelings, he knew still less of the influences by which those feelings are formed. . . .

"This, then is our idea of Bentham. He was a man both of remarkable endowments for philosophy, and of remarkable deficiencies for it. . . .

"Man is conceived by Bentham as a being susceptible of pleasures and pains, and governed in all his conduct partly by the different modifications of self-interest, and the passions commonly classed as selfish, partly by sympathies, or occasionally antipathies, towards other beings. And here Bentham's conception of human nature stops. He does not exclude religion; the prospect of divine rewards and punishments he includes under the head of 'self-regarding interest,' and the devotional feeling under that of sympathy with God. But the whole of the impelling or restraining principles, whether of this or of another world, which he recognises, are either self-love, or love or hatred towards other sentient beings. That there might be no doubt of what he thought on the subject, he has not left us to the general evidence of his writings, but has drawn out a 'Table of the Springs of Action,' an express enumeration and classification of human motives. . . .

"Man is never recognised by him as a being capable of pursuing spiritual perfection as an end. . . . None of these powerful constituents of human nature are thought worthy of a place among the 'Springs of Action.' . . ."

80. *Ibid.*, p. 104: "It is fortunate for the world that Bentham's taste lay rather in the direction of jurisprudential than of properly ethical inquiry. Nothing expressly of the latter kind has been published under his name, except the 'Deontology.' . . ."

81. *Ibid.*, pp. 105–106: "A philosophy of laws and institutions, not founded on a philosophy of national character, is an absurdity. But what could Bentham's opinion be worth on national character? How could he, whose mind contained so few and so poor types of individual character, rise to that higher generalisation? All he can do is but to indicate means by which, in any given state of the national mind, the material interests of society can be protected. . . .

"We have arrived, then, at a sort of estimate of what a philosophy like Bentham's can do. It can teach the means of organising and regulating the merely *business* part of the social arrangements. . . . He committed the mistake of supposing that the business part of human affairs was the whole of them; all at least that the legislator and the moralist had to do with. Not that he disregarded moral influences when he perceived them; but his want of imagination, small experience of human feelings, and ignorance of the filiation and connexion of feelings with one another, made this rarely the case."

82. *Ibid.*, pp. 106–107: "Bentham's speculations, as we are already aware, began with law; and in that department he accomplished his greatest triumphs. He found the philosophy of law a chaos, he left it a science: he found the practice of the law an Augean stable, he turned the river into it which is mining and sweeping away mound after mound of its rubbish."

83. *Ibid.*, pp. 107–110: "[W]e may say that circumstances had made English lawyers, in a peculiar degree liable to the reproach of Voltaire, who defines lawyers the 'conservators of ancient barbarous usages.' The basis of the English law was, and still is, the feudal system. That system, like all those which existed as custom before they were established as law, possessed a certain degree of suitableness. . . . The laws which were suitable to the first of these states of society, could have no manner of relation to the circumstances of the second. . . . What was done, was done by a struggle of centuries between the old barbarism and the new civilisation; between the feudal aristocracy of conquerors, holding fast to the rude system they had established, and the conquered effecting their emancipation. The last was the growing power, but was never strong enough to break its bonds, though ever and anon some weak point gave way. Hence the law came to be like the costume of a full-grown man who had never put off the clothes made for him when he first went to school. . . . Hence all ages of English history have given one another rendezvous in English law; their several products may be seen all together, not interfused, but heaped one upon another. . . .

"In the English law, as in the Roman before it, the adaptations of barbarous laws to the growth of civilised society were made chiefly by stealth. They were generally made by the courts of justice, who could not help reading the new wants of mankind in the cases between man and man which came before them; but who, having no authority to make new laws for those new wants, were obliged to do the work covertly, and evade the jealousy and opposition of an ignorant, prejudiced, and for the most part brutal and tyrannical legislature. Some of the most necessary of these improvements, such as the giving force of law to trusts, and the breaking up of entails, were effected in actual opposition to the strongly-declared will of Parliament, whose clumsy hands, no match for the astuteness of judges, could not, after repeated trials, manage to make any law which the judges could not find a trick for rendering inoperative. . . . The result of this mode of improving social institutions was, that whatever new things were done had to be done in consistency with old forms and names; and the laws were improved with much the same effect as if, in the improvement of agriculture, the plough could only have been introduced by making it look like a spade. . . .

"When the conflicts were over, and the mixed mass settled down into something like a fixed state, and that state a very profitable and therefore a very agreeable one to lawyers, they, following the natural tendency of the human mind, began to theorise upon it, and, in obedience to necessity, had to digest it and give it a systematic form. It was from this thing of shreds and patches, in which the only part that approached to order or system was the early barbarous part, already more than half superseded, that English lawyers had to construct, by induction and abstraction, their philosophy of law; and without the logical habits and general intellectual cultivation which the lawyers of the Roman empire brought to a similar task. Bentham found the philosophy of law what English practising lawyers had made it; a jumble. . . . History will one day refuse to give credit to the intensity of the superstition which, till very lately protected this mischievous mess from examination or doubt—passed off the charming representations of Blackstone for a just estimate of the English law, and proclaimed the shame of human reason to be the perfection of it. Glory to Bentham that he has dealt to this superstition its deathblow— that he has been the Hercules of this hydra, the St. George of this pestilent dragon! The honour is all his—nothing but his peculiar qualities could have done it."

84. *Ibid.*, pp. 110–111: "To sum up our estimate under a few heads. First: he has expelled mysticism from the philosophy of law, and set the example of viewing laws in a practical light, as means to certain definite and precise ends. Secondly: he has cleared up the confusion and vagueness attaching to the idea of law in general, to the idea of a body of laws, and the various general ideas therein involved. Thirdly: he demonstrated the necessity and practicability of *codification*, or the conversion of all law into a written and systematically arranged code: not like the Code Napoleon, a code without a single definition, requiring a constant reference to anterior precedent for the meaning of its technical terms; but one containing within itself all that is necessary for its own interpretation, together with a perpetual provision for its own emendation and improvement. He has shown of what parts such a code would consist; the relation of those parts to one another; and by his distinctions and classifications has done very much towards showing what should be, or might be, its nomenclature and arrangement. What he has left undone, he has made it comparatively easy for others to do. Fourthly: he has taken a systematic view of the exigencies of society for which the civil code is intended to provide, and of the principles of human nature by which its provisions are to be tested. . . . Fifthly: (to say nothing of the subject of punishment, for which something considerable had been done before) he found the philosophy of judicial procedure, including that of judicial establishments and of evidence, in a more wretched state than even any other part of the philosophy of law; he carried it at once almost to perfection. He left it with every one of its principles established, and little remaining to be done even in the suggestion of practical arrangements."

85. *Ibid.*, pp. 112–113: "It seems proper here to take notice of an accusation sometimes made both against Bentham and against the principle of codification—as if they required

one uniform suit of ready-made laws for all times and all states of society. The doctrine of codification, as the word imports, relates to the form only of the laws, not their substance; it does not concern itself with what the laws should be, but declares that whatever they are, they ought to be systematically arranged, and fixed down to a determinate form of words. To the accusation, so far as it affects Bentham, one of the essays in the collection of his works (then for the first time published in English) is a complete answer: that 'On the Influence of Time and Place in Matters of Legislation.' It may there be seen that the different exigencies of different nations with respect to law, occupied his attention as systematically as any other portion of the wants which render laws necessary: with the limitations, it is true, which were set to all his speculations by the imperfections of his theory of human nature. For, taking, as we have seen, next to no account of national character and the causes which form and maintain it, he was precluded from considering, except to a very limited extent, the laws of a country as an instrument of national culture.... The same laws will not suit the English, who distrust everything which emanates from general principles, and the French, who distrust whatever does not so emanate. Very different institutions are needed to train to the perfection of their nature, or to constitute into a united nation and social polity, an essentially *subjective* people like the Germans, and an essentially *objective* people like those of Northern and Central Italy; the one affectionate and dreamy, the other passionate and worldly.... Bentham was little accustomed to look at institutions in their relation to these topics. The effects of this oversight must of course be perceptible throughout his speculations, but we do not think the errors into which it led him very material in the greater part of civil and penal law: it is in the department of constitutional legislation that they were fundamental."

86. *Ibid.*, pp. 111-112: "There are now even in the highest seats of justice, men to whom the claims made for him will not appear extravagant. Principle after principle of those propounded by him is moreover making its way by infiltration into the understandings most shut against his influence, and driving nonsense and prejudice from one corner of them to another. The reform of the laws of any country according to his principles, can only be gradual, and may be long ere it is accomplished; but the work is in progress, and both parliament and the judges are every year doing something, and often something not inconsiderable, towards the forwarding of it."

87. *Ibid.*, pp. 113-117: "The Benthamic theory of government has made so much noise in the world of late years; it has held such a conspicuous place among Radical philosophies, and Radical modes of thinking have participated so much more largely than any others in its spirit, that many worthy persons imagine there is no other Radical philosophy extant....

"There are three great questions in government. First, to what authority is it for the good of the people that they should be subject? Secondly, how are they to be induced to obey that authority? . . . Comes next a third question, not liable to so much variation, namely, by what means are the abuses of this authority to be checked? This third question is the only one of the three to which Bentham seriously applies himself, and he gives it the only answer it admits of—Responsibility: responsibility to persons whose interest . . . accords with the end in view—good government. . . . This one assumption being made, his 'Constitutional Code' is admirable. That extraordinary power which he possessed, of at once seizing comprehensive principles, and scheming out minute details, is brought into play with surpassing vigour in devising means for preventing rulers from escaping from the control of the majority. . . .

"But *is* this fundamental doctrine of Bentham's political philosophy an universal truth? Is it, at all times and places, good for mankind to be under the absolute authority of the majority of themselves? We say the authority, not the political authority merely, because it is chimerical to suppose that whatever has absolute power over men's bodies will not arrogate it over their minds. . . . European reformers have been accustomed to see the numerical majority everywhere unjustly depressed, everywhere trampled upon, or at the best overlooked, by governments. . . . To see these things, and to seek to put an end to them, by means (among other things) of giving more political power to the majority, constitutes Radicalism; and it is because so many in this age have felt this wish, and have felt that the realisation of it was an object worthy of men's devoting their lives to it, that such a theory of government as Bentham's has found favour with them. But, though to pass from one form of bad government to another be the ordinary fate of mankind, philosophers ought not to make themselves parties to it, by sacrificing one portion of important truth to another. . . . There must, we know, be some paramount power in society; and that the majority should be that power, is on the whole right, not as being just in itself, but as being less unjust than any other footing on which the matter can be placed. . . . A centre of resistance, round which all the moral and social elements which the ruling power views with disfavour may cluster themselves, and behind whose bulwarks they may find shelter from the attempts of that power to hunt them out of existence, is as necessary where the opinion of the majority is sovereign, as where the ruling power is a hierarchy or an aristocracy. . . . Surely when any power has been made the strongest power, enough has been done for it; care is thenceforth wanted rather to prevent that strongest power from swallowing up all others. Wherever all the forces of society act in one single direction, the just claims of the individual human being are in extreme peril. . . . If Bentham had employed himself in pointing out the means by which institutions fundamentally democratic might be best adapted to the preservation and strengthening of those two sentiments, he would have done something more permanently valuable, and more worthy of his great intellect. Montesquieu, with the lights of the present age, would have done it; and we are possibly destined to receive this benefit from the Montesquieu of our own times, M. de Tocqueville.

"Do we then consider Bentham's political speculations useless? Far from it. We consider them only one-sided."

88. Using Mill's *On Liberty* in *ibid.* (as cited above, n. 76), pp. 126–250. Here, pp. 126–129: "The subject of this Essay is not the so-called Liberty of the Will, so unfortunately opposed to the misnamed doctrine of Philosophical Necessity; but Civil, or Social Liberty: the nature and limits of the power which can be legitimately exercised by society over the individual. . . .

"The struggle between Liberty and Authority is the most conspicuous feature in the portions of history with which we are earliest familiar, particularly in that of Greece, Rome, and England. But in old times this contest was between subjects, or some classes of subjects, and the Government. By liberty, was meant protection against the tyranny of the political rulers. . . . The aim, therefore, of patriots was to set limits to the power which the ruler should be suffered to exercise over the community; and this limitation was what they meant by liberty. . . .

"But, in political and philosophical theories, as well as in persons, success discloses faults and infirmities which failure might have concealed from observation. The notion, that the people have no need to limit their power over themselves, might seem axiomatic, when popular government was a thing only dreamed about, or read of as having existed at some distant period of the past. Neither was that notion necessarily disturbed by such temporary aberrations as those of the French Revolution. . . . In time, however, a democratic republic came to occupy a large portion of the earth's surface, and made itself felt as one of the most powerful members of the community of nations. . . .

"Like other tyrannies, the tyranny of the majority was at first, and is still vulgarly, held in dread, chiefly as operating through the acts of the public authorities. But reflecting persons perceived that when society is itself the tyrant . . ."

89. *Ibid.*, pp. 130, 135: "There is a limit to the legitimate interference of collective opinion with individual independence: and to find that limit, and maintain it against encroachment, is as indispensable to a good condition of human affairs, as protection against political despotism. . . .

"The object of this Essay is to assert one very simple principle, as entitled to govern absolutely the dealings of society with the individual in the way of compulsion and control, whether the means used be physical force in the form of legal penalties, or the moral coercion of public opinion. That principle is, that the sole end for which mankind are warranted, individually or collectively, in interfering with the liberty of action of any of their number, is self-protection."

90. *Ibid.*, p. 205: "What, then, is the rightful limit to the sovereignty of the individual over himself? Where does the authority of society begin? How much of human life should be assigned to individuality, and how much to society?"

91. *Ibid.*, pp. 200–201: "The despotism of custom is everywhere the standing hindrance to human advancement, being in unceasing antagonism to that disposition to aim at something better than customary, which is called, according to circumstances, the spirit of liberty, or that of progress or improvement. . . . The progressive principle, however, in either shape, whether as the love of liberty or of improvement, is antagonistic to the sway of Custom, involving at least emancipation from that yoke; and the contest between the two constitutes the chief interest of the history of mankind. The greater part of the world has, properly speaking, no history, because the despotism of Custom is complete. This is the case over the whole East. Custom is there, in all things, the final appeal; justice and right mean conformity to custom; the argument of custom no one, unless some tyrant intoxicated with power, thinks of resisting."

92. *Ibid.*, pp. 222, 233: "Another important example of illegitimate interference with the rightful liberty of the individual, not simply threatened, but long since carried into triumphant effect, is Sabbatarian legislation. Without doubt abstinence on one day in the week, so far as the exigencies of life permit, from the usual daily occupation . . . is a highly beneficial custom. . . .

"A further question is, whether the State, while it permits, should nevertheless indirectly discourage conduct which it deems contrary to the best interests of the agent; whether, for example, it should take measures to render the means of drunkenness more costly, or add to the difficulty of procuring them by limiting the number of the places of sale."

93. *Ibid.*, pp. 238, 248: "The State, while it respects the liberty of each in what specially regards himself, is bound to maintain a vigilant control over his exercise of any power which it allows him to possess over others. . . . The almost despotic power of husbands over wives needs not be enlarged upon here, because nothing more is needed for the complete removal of the evil than that wives should have the same rights, and should receive the protection of law in the same manner, as all other persons. . . .

"To determine the point at which evils, so formidable to human freedom and advancement, begin, or rather at which they begin to predominate over the benefits attending the collective application of the force of society, . . . is one of the most difficult and complicated questions in the art of government."

94. *Ibid.*, p. 249: "The powers of administrative coercion and subordinate legislation possessed by the Poor Law Board (but which, owing to the state of opinion on the subject, are very scantily exercised by them), though perfectly justifiable in a case of first rate national interest, would be wholly out of place in the superintendence of interests purely local."

95. Mill's *Utilitarianism* in *ibid.* (cited above, n.76), pp. 251–321, here pp. 296, 298, 302.

96. *Ibid.*, pp. 252, 253, 257: "The truths which are ultimately accepted as the first principles of a science, are really the last results of metaphysical analysis, practised on the elementary notions with which the science is conversant. . . . But though in science the particular truths precede the general theory, the contrary might be expected to be the case with a practical art, such as morals or legislation. All action is for the sake of some end, and rules of action, it seems natural to suppose, must take their whole character and colour from the end to which they are subservient. . . . According to the one opinion, the principles of morals are evident *à priori*, requiring nothing to command assent, except that the meaning of the terms be understood. According to the other doctrine, right and wrong, as well as truth and falsehood, are questions of observation and experience. . . .

"The creed which accepts as the foundation of morals, Utility, or the Greatest Happiness Principle, holds that actions are right in proportion as they tend to promote happiness, wrong, as they tend to produce the reverse of happiness. By happiness is intended pleasure, and the absence of pain; by unhappiness, pain, and the privation of pleasure."

Mill, *On Liberty*, pp. 136, 246: "It is proper to state that I forego any advantage which could be derived to my argument from the idea of abstract right, as a thing independent of utility. I regard utility as the ultimate appeal on all ethical questions; but it must be utility in the largest sense, grounded on the permanent interests of a man as a progressive being. Those interests, I contend, authorise the subjection of individual spontaneity to external control, only in respect to those actions of each, which concern the interest of other people. . . . In countries of more advanced civilisation and of a more insurrectionary spirit, the public, accustomed to expect everything to be done for them by the State, or at least to do nothing for themselves without asking from the State not only leave to do it, but even how it is to be done, naturally hold the State responsible for all evil which befalls them, and when the evil exceeds their amount of patience, they rise against the government, and make what is called a revolution; whereupon somebody else, with or without legitimate authority from the nation, vaults into the seat, issues his orders to the bureaucracy, and everything goes on much as it did before; the bureaucracy being unchanged, and nobody else being capable of taking their place."

97. Mill, "Bentham," pp. 90, 118, 120–121: "The generalities of his philosophy itself have little or no novelty: to ascribe any to the doctrine that general utility is the foundation of morality, would imply great ignorance of the history of philosophy, of general literature, and of Bentham's own writings. He derived the idea, as he says himself, from Helvetius; and it was the doctrine no less, of the religious philosophers of that age. . . . In all ages of philosophy one of its schools has been utilitarian—not only from the time of Epicurus, but long before. It was by mere accident that this opinion became connected in Bentham with his peculiar method. The utilitarian philosophers antecedent to him had no more claims to the method than their antagonists. . . . The greatest service rendered by him to the philosophy of universal human nature, is, perhaps, his illustration of what he terms 'interest-begotten prejudice'—the common tendency of man to make a duty and a virtue of following his self-interest. The idea, it is true, was far from being peculiarly Bentham's. . . . This was one of Bentham's leading ideas, and almost the only one by which he contributed to the elucidation of history: much of which, except so far as this explained it, must have been entirely inexplicable to him. The idea was given him by Helvetius. . . . Bentham's philosophy . . . [centered around] the 'principle of utility,' or, as he afterwards named it, 'the greatest-happiness principle'. . . . It is probable, however, that to the principle of utility we owe all that Bentham did. . . . Whether happiness be or be not the end to which morality should be referred . . . is essential to the very idea of moral philosophy. . . . That the good or evil of those consequences is measured solely by pleasure or pain, is all of the doctrine of the school of utility, which is peculiar to it. . . . [A] . . . cold,

mechanical, and ungenial air . . . characterises the popular idea of a Benthamite. This error, or rather one-sidedness, belongs to him not as a utilitarian, but as a moralist by profession, and in common with almost all professed moralists, whether religious or philosophical . . ."

Mill, *Utilitarianism*, p. 257 n.: "The author of this essay has reason for believing himself to be the first person who brought the word utilitarian into use. He did not invent it, but adopted it from a passing expression in Mr. Galt's *Annals of the Parish*. . . ."

98. *Ibid.*, pp. 256, 268–269, 274: "A passing remark is all that needs be given to the ignorant blunder of supposing that those who stand up for utility as the test of right and wrong, use the term in that restricted and merely colloquial sense in which utility is opposed to pleasure. An apology is due to the philosophical opponents of utilitarianism, for even the momentary appearance of confounding them with any one capable of so absurd a misconception; which is the more extraordinary, inasmuch as the contrary accusation, of referring everything to pleasure, and that too in its grossest form, is another of the common charges against utilitarianism. . . .

"Meanwhile, let utilitarians never cease to claim the morality of self devotion as a possession which belongs by as good a right to them, as either to the Stoic or to the Transcendentalist. The utilitarian morality does recognise in human beings the power of sacrificing their own greatest good for the good of others. It only refuses to admit that the sacrifice is itself a good. . . .

"I must again repeat, what the assailants of utilitarianism seldom have the justice to acknowledge, that the happiness which forms the utilitarian standard of what is right in conduct, is not the agent's own happiness, but that of all concerned. . . . In the golden rule of Jesus . . . [is] the complete spirit of the ethics of utility. To do as you would be done by and to love your neighbour as yourself, constitute the ideal person of utilitarian morality. . . . [Mill seeks] to establish in the mind of every individual an indissoluble association between his own happiness and the good of the whole; especially between his own happiness and . . . the general good. . . .

"Again, Utility is often summarily stigmatised as an immoral doctrine by giving it the name of Expediency, and taking advantage of the popular use of that term to contrast it with Principle. But the Expedient, in the sense in which it is opposed to the Right, generally means that which is expedient for the particular interest of the agent himself; as when a minister sacrifices the interests of his country to keep himself in place."

99. *Ibid.*, pp. 311, 317–318: "We are continually informed that Utility is an uncertain standard, which every different person interprets differently, and that there is no safety but in the immutable, ineffaceable, and unmistakable dictates of Justice, which carry their evidence in themselves, and are independent of the fluctuations of opinion. One would suppose from this that on questions of justice there could be no controversy; that if we take that for our rule, its application to any given case could leave us in as little doubt as a mathematical demonstration. So far is this from being the fact, that there is as much difference of opinion, and as much discussion, about what is just, as about what is useful to society. Not only have different nations and individuals different notions of justice, but in the mind of one and the same individual, justice is not some one rule, principle, or maxim, but many, which do not always coincide in their dictates, and in choosing between which, he is guided either by some extraneous standard, or by his own personal predilections. . . . The principle, therefore, of giving to each what they deserve, that is, good for good as well as evil for evil, is not only included within the idea of Justice as we have defined it, but is a proper object of that intensity of sentiment, which places the Just, in human estimation, above the simply Expedient.

"Most of the maxims of justice current in the world, and commonly appealed to in its transactions, are simply instrumental to carrying into effect the principles of justice which

372 / Notes to Chapter II

we have now spoken of. That a person is only responsible for what he has done voluntarily, or could voluntarily have avoided; that it is unjust to condemn any person unheard; that the punishment ought to be proportioned to the offence, and the like, are maxims intended to prevent the just principle of evil for evil from being perverted to the infliction of evil without justification."

100. Cf. *ibid.*, index, and p. 251 (*summum bonum*).

101. The following miscellaneous listing of telltale headings in secondary works indicates representative examples of the historiographical and documentary patterns outlined in the above sect. 6 on the Victorian state in terms of legislation, reform, and "isms." Examples include: Oliver MacDonagh, *Early Victorian Government, 1830–1870* (London, 1977), e.g. Ch. 2, "Early Factory Legislation," Ch. 3, "The Factory Act of 1833," Ch. 4, "Later Factory Reform," Ch. 6, "The Poor Law," and Ch. 9, "Law and Public Order"; Peter Stansky (ed.), *The Victorian Revolution: Government and Society in Victoria's Britain* (New York, 1973), esp. Oliver MacDonagh, "The Nineteenth-Century Revolution in Government: A Reappraisal," pp. 5 ff., G. Kitson Clark's rejoinder to MacDonagh, pp. 29 ff., D. C. Moore, "The Corn Laws and High Farming," pp. 119 ff., and David Roberts, "Tory Paternalism and Social Reform in Early Victorian England," pp. 147 ff.; Jonathan Parry, *The Rise and Fall of Liberal Government in Victorian England* (New Haven, 1993), Pt. I, "Liberalism and Reform, 1820–1832" (esp. on "liberal Toryism"), with later discussions of the rise of "Gladstonianism" and the Liberal Party; R. J. Evans, *The Victorian Age, 1815–1914* (2nd. edn., London, 1968), e.g. Ch. 6, sect. 1, "The Coming of the Modern State" (in the 1840s, as per ch. title); George Woodbridge, *The Reform Bill of 1832* (New York, 1970, new edn.), comprehensive on both the first and second bills as well as on the act itself in 1832; Llewellyn Woodward, *The Age of Reform* (2nd. edn., Oxford, 1962); F. B. Smith, *The Making of the Second Reform Bill* (London, 1966); J. R. Dinwiddy, *From Luddism to the First Reform Bill: Reform in England 1810–1832* (Oxford, 1986), esp. Chs. 1–2, "Whig and Middle-Class Reformism c. 1810–29" and "Popular Radicalism c. 1810–29"; Paul Smith, *Disraelian Conservatism and Social Reform* (London, 1967); Eric J. Evans, *Britain Before the Reform Act: Politics and Society, 1815–1832* (London, 1989), e.g. Ch. 9, " 'Liberal Toryism' . . ."; Stewart Angas Weaver, *John Fielden and the Politics of Popular Radicalism, 1832–1847* (Oxford, 1987), e.g. Ch. 5, "Factory Laws and Poor Laws," and Ch. 7, "Towards Popular Liberalism"; C. R. Fay, *The Corn Laws and Social England* (Cambridge, 1932), remaining one of the best and fullest treatments of the whole subject; and H. J. Hanham (ed.), *The Nineteenth-Century Constitution* (Cambridge, 1969), Ch. 1, "The Theory of the Constitution" (p. 1: "The British constitution during the nineteenth century was . . . the yardstick and exemplar for liberals all over the world, the pattern of a constitutional monarchy and a liberal state."), and Ch. 3, "Parliament."

In addition, Crane Brinton, *English Political Thought in the 19th Century* (London, 1933, repr. 1962), Ch. II, "The Revolution of 1832," sect. 1, "Bentham," states as follows (p. 14): "[S]carcely an English thinker has left more definite trace upon English legislation than Jeremy Bentham . . ." In Ch. II, "Chartism," sect. 1, "Mill," Brinton employs a superabundance of "isms" as descriptive labels for Mill's variegated, changing ideas and influences on actual politics. These include: rationalism, emotionalism, transcendentalism, pessimism, optimism, individualism, liberalism, egotism, instrumentalism, empiricism, Manicheanism, collectivism, socialism, spiritualism, etc., all within only about a dozen pages. Also, Sidney W. Jackman (ed.), *The English Reform Tradition, 1790–1910* (Englewood Cliffs, 1965), includes Ch. I, "Parliamentary Reform," Ch. 5, "The Chartist Movement," and Ch. 8, "The Repeal of the Corn Laws." Edward P. Cheyney, *Modern English Reform: From Individualism to Socialism* (Philadelphia, 1931, repr. 1962), e.g. Ch. VI, "British Socialism, 1817–1930," takes a broad view of the subject that begins in the early nineteenth century with Robert Owen. Elie Halévy, *England in 1815* (translated by E. Watkin and D. Barker, London, 1924, etc.), Pt. I, Ch. I, "The Legislature and the Supremacy of Public Opinion," cites (e.g. p. 200 and passim) Montesquieu's verdicts on the British "mixed" constitution. Halévy's *The Triumph of Reform, 1830–1841* (translated by E. Watkin, London, 1961), e.g. Pt. I, includes Ch. II, sects. II–III, "The Liberalism of the Government" and "The Beginnings of Administrative Centralization." These two bks. by Halévy form parts (I, III) of his *History of the English People in the Nineteenth Century*. James B. Conacher (ed.), *The Emergence of British Parliamentary Democracy in the Nineteenth Century: The Passing of the Reform Acts of 1832, 1867, and 1884–1885* (New York, 1971), takes up, intricately in turn, each of the three Acts. Robert C. Binkley, *Realism and Nationalism, 1852–1871* (New York, 1935, etc.), incorporates a wide variety of "isms" centered around the two in the title, including in relation to British history. Charles Breunig, *The Age of Revolution and Reaction, 1789–1850* (New York, 1970), includes Ch. 6, "The Industrial Revolution and the Triumph of the Bourgeoisie," sect. 2, "The Triumph of Economic Liberalism in Great Britain." Frederick B. Artz, *Reaction and Revolution, 1814–1832* (New York, 1934), includes Ch. IV, "The Creeds of Liberalism," sects. I–V, "The Principle of Utility," "Laissez-faire Economics and the Bourgeois State," "Constitutionalism," "Anti-clericalism and State Education," and "Aspirations for National Unity and Freedom." W. E. Lunt, *History of England* (3rd edn., New York, 1945), includes Ch. XXXIV, "An Epoch of Reform, 1830–1846." David Thomson, *England in the Nineteenth Century, 1815–1914* (Baltimore, 1950, etc.), includes Pt. III, "The Third Phase: 1875–1914," Ch. IX, "The Growth of the Modern State."

J. S. Mill's significant writings of the 1820s on the Corn Laws are contained in *Collected Works of John Stuart Mill*, Vol. IV (edited by J. M. Robson, Toronto, 1967)— *The Corn Laws (1825)*, pp. 45 ff. and *The New Corn Law (1827)*, pp. 141 ff. Mill refers to "this most important of all commercial reforms" (p. 60). He argues that the landlords' economic self-interest depends in large part on the economic benefit of the whole community or nation. Mill declares (p. 64): "The landlord should consider, that if he has an interest opposed to that of the community, he has also an interest in common with them. . . . [L]et him throw the happiness of . . . his countrymen into the scale. . . . [Instead of believing that] the robbery of the public . . . [is] gain to themselves . . . [landlords should realize that] what is a blessing to all the rest of the community [will be a blessing no less to themselves]." What is in the landlords' best interest, Mill believes, is to benefit England as a trading commercial nation by allowing complete free trade on all grains, etc. For Parliament merely to substitute new Corn Laws, or amendments, which set import duties, for old Corn Laws, which ban imports, is no improvement; his arguments (e.g. p. 143) are addressed to the members and ministers of Parliament who have believed the contrary. "Freed from the trammels of sinister interest," the "ministers" of the "government," Mill urges (p. 70), "should have . . . sympathy with the public . . . [and] succeed in relieving the community from the intolerable scourge of our Corn Laws . . ." Mill cites (p. 149) Adam Smith on behalf of the need for complete free trade, without so-called "protection to agriculture." In various places, Mill argues that all of England will suffer, including the landlords, if, in future times of scarce domestic supplies of grain, foreign countries will not sell grain to England because a dependable long-standing market had not already been established in England.

Arguments like the foregoing by J. S. Mill show the great influence of his early writings on the Corn Laws—that is, on legislation relating to importation of foreign grain— upon his burgeoning ideas on the public interest of the whole community, as distinct from mere self-interest. Here one might see Mill's concept of public interest, in terms of the whole community, as shaped in large measure by his concept of what should constitute and motivate true public legislation. This specific early context has generally been lost

374 / Notes to Chapter II

from scholarly view. Yet it has long been recognized that Mill's distinctive emphasis on the interest of the whole community differed from Bentham's stress on a more individualistic—or, as Mill declared, egotistic—orientation. In the passages given above in this note, Mill uses the word "happiness," possibly echoing Bentham's discussions of the happiness principle. Yet Mill also uses the word "sympathy" in ways that suggest the likely influence of Hume. Bentham rejected Hume's guiding principle of sympathy as the key to what motivates human thought and behavior, involving caring for others in society. Mill, however, seems to have re-incorporated it here in a possible early reaction not only to Bentham but also to his father, James Mill, who long remained a staunch disciple of Bentham.

Of peripheral interest here, in light of observations made in our main text, are various other items in J. S. Mill's *Collected Writings*. These include his *Autobiography* and "Juvenilia" on the history of Rome (1812–13?) (Vol. I); his essays on French history and historians (Vol. XX); and the comprehensive chronological data on Mill's collected writings (Vol. XXXIII). Also, Iris Wessel Mueller, *John Stuart Mill and French Thought* (Urbana, 1956), deals with the French Revolutions of 1830 and 1848, the influence of Comte and de Tocqueville, etc.

Although there has not been space in this study to investigate the writings of James Mill, the father of J. S. Mill, a recent collection is especially useful—*James Mill: Political Writings* (edited by Terence Ball, Cambridge, 1992). The sects. entitled "Government" (pp. 1 ff.) and "Jurisprudence" (pp. 43 ff.), as well as the disputes with Macaulay (Appendix), are esp. interesting. The sect. on "Government," for instance, begins with a short discourse on "The End of Government . . ." in relation to Locke (I), followed by brief discussions on "The Means of attaining the End of Government; viz, Power . . ." (II) and on securities against "Abuse of Power" (III), and so forth. The sect. on "Jurisprudence" begins with a treatment of "The end of Jurisprudence, viz. the Protection of Rights . . ." (I), with ensuing thoughts on the "Penal Code" (IV), the "Code of Procedure" (VI), and the "Judicial Establishment" (VII). (All *sic* according to his style.) In general, James Mill adopts a narrower rendition of Bentham's thought than would be acceptable to his son J. S. Mill and is of less interest here than either of the other two authors. Perhaps more germane are his disputes with Macaulay.

The vast subject of the Victorian "revival" styles in literature, architecture, art, domestic interiors, etc. is not irrelevant here. It is well known, for instance, that Victorian writers in Britain, such as John Ruskin (1819–1900) and Walter Pater (1839–1894) were profoundly interested in reviving and adapting Renaissance Italian aesthetics, as were the pre-Raphaelite painters, along with many others. The Renaissance "revival" style in Victorian architecture and interior decoration was likewise extensive. With the Victorian Renaissance "revival" went the Victorian classical "revivals" of Greece and Rome. At the same time, one must not forget the Victorian medieval "revival" styles, chiefly the Romanesque and Gothic, as well as Victorian rococo "revival" styles, again in literature, art, architecture, and interior decorations. It has been observed by many, though by no means all, intellectual historians of Victorian styles that they were predominantly eclectic and derivative. Earlier patterns were put together into new hybrid mosaics. The great Victorian interests in history extended, of course, to new intensive approaches to historical research. For present purposes, it can be underscored that the rich influences on the Victorians of the historical past, esp. of Renaissance-Classical thought, offer useful though seldom recognized perspectives for historians of Victorian political-legal theory. For historians have often overemphasized the Victorian political thinkers' break with the past to the neglect of their considerable debt to earlier traditions. To take but one case of recent scholarship with regard to cultural matters, there is Frank M. Turner, *The Greek Heritage in Victorian Britain* (New Haven, 1981). He gives extensive materials on "Victorian humanistic Hellenism" in relation to the Athenian constitution and revivals of Plato, Aristotle, etc. The work provides an illustration here of the great spirit of so-called "revival*ism*" that infused Victorian culture, including the "revival" of Renaissance ideas. Useful literary anthologies with excerpts from Pater, Ruskin, *et al.* include William E. Buckler (ed.), *Prose of the Victorian Period* (Boston, 1958), and E. D. H. Johnson (ed.), *The World of the Victorians: An Anthology of Poetry and Prose* (New York, 1964). The present author remains deeply grateful to Professor Johnson for his inspired and masterful approaches in an undergraduate course on Victorian literature and thought in their broad dimensions.

Finally, the relation of Victorian political thought to Enlightenment and Romantic thought has been discussed by M. Francis and J. Morrow, *A History of English Political Thought in the Nineteenth Century* (London, 1994), with inclusion of Bentham and J. S. Mill. They view this period as a new "modern" patchwork of ideas, breaking from old "civic" ideas.

Notes to Chapter III
"Positiv*ism*" and "Austinian*ism*"

1. H. L. A. Hart, "Positivism and the Separation of Law and Morals," *Harvard Law Review*, 71 (1958), pp. 593–629.
2. Auguste Comte, *Système de politique positive ou Traité de sociologie*, 4 vols., in *Oeuvres d'Auguste Comte*, Vols. VII–X (Paris, 1969–1970), reimpression of Paris edn. of the work in 4 vols., 1851–1854. Also the influential English version by J. H. Bridges (London, 1876–1877, in 4 vols.) under the title of *System of Positive Polity*.
3. Cf. André Millet, *La souveraineté d'après Auguste Comte: Étude sociologique* (Poitiers, 1905).
4. Comte's *Cours de philosophie positive* is in *Oeuvres* Vols. I–.
5. Using the repr. of John Stuart Mill's *Auguste Comte and Positivism* published in Ann Arbor, 1961, 1965, pp. 1–3.
6. *Ibid.*, pp. 5, 100–103.
7. *Ibid.*, p. 5.
8. *Ibid.*, pp. 122–123.
9. *Ibid.*, pp. 123–124.
10. For discussion of J. S. Mill's views on Comte, there is Iris Wessel Mueller, *John Stuart Mill and French Thought* (Urbana, 1956), Ch. 4, "The Influence of Auguste Comte," showing how intricate and complicated the whole subject is. Cf. e.g.: p. 98 on positivism and Benthamism; p. 100 on Mill's reactions to Macaulay's attacks on his father's (James Mill's) Benthamist viewpoints and with regard to Mill's outlook on Comte's views on Benthamism; p. 132 on the place of Saint-Simon; pp. 128 ff. on the ultimately irreconcilable differences separating Comte and Mill; p. 133 on the differences between Comte and Mill on religion; and, in general, the overall progression of the ch. from early to later stages of the intellectual relationships between Mill and Comte.

A variety of secondary works on Comte can be usefully cited here.

An insightful division of subject matter is found in Arline Beilein Standley, *Auguste Comte* (Boston, 1981), Chs. 3–4, "Positive Philosophy: Old Wine in New Bottles" and "Positive Polity: New Wine in Old Bottles." The latter ch. makes use of Comte's final version of the motto in *Positive Polity*—"The principle, Love; The basis, Order; the End, Progress." She explains as follows (p. 100): "Like the Utilitarians, then, Comte determined value by the standard of usefulness even though he rejected their materialism (their measuring of value solely in terms of economic well-being) and their encouragement of the egoistic instincts (their attempt to build a social theory on a psychological base of self-interest). Usefulness is, however, as problematical in the context of Positivism as it is in that of Utilitarianism."

Mary Pickering, *Auguste Comte: An Intellectual Biography*, Vol. I (Cambridge, 1993), treats Comte's relationships with Saint-Simon (Chs. 2–5) and J. S. Mill (Chs. 12–13). On p. 706 she declares: "In reacting against commercial self-interest as a motive for human action, Comte glorified society, not God, the monarchy, or the state itself [a task, we may add, left for Hegel]." This was the case in part because (p. 708) "Comte's [all-enbracing] sociology was a mixture of history, moral philosophy, political economy, political theory, anthropology, aesthetics, religion, international relations, philosophy of science, biology, and the inorganic sciences."

Other pertinent works relating to Comte etc. include the following: W. M. Simon, *European Positivism in the Nineteenth Century* (Ithaca, 1963), comprehensive yet detailed; Willard Wolfe, *From Radicalism to Socialism* (New Haven, 1975), including Comte's influences on Fabian socialism; Herbert Spencer, *Reasons for Dissenting from the Philosophy of M. Comte* (Berkeley, 1968, repr. of his 19th-century work); Boris Sokoloff, *The "Mad" Philosopher Auguste Comte* (New York, 1961), notable for its curious yet telltale title; F. J. C. Hearnshaw, *The Social and Political Ideas of Some Representative Thinkers of the Age of Reaction and Reconstruction, 1815–65* (London, 1932), Ch. VII on Comte (also Chs. III, VI, and VIII on Hegel, J. S. Mill, and Austin); Robert Brown, *The Nature of Social Laws: Machiavelli to Mill* (Cambridge, 1984), Ch. 7, "Comte and the Objective Knowledge of Social Stages," e.g. sects. 2, 5, "The Law of Social Evolution" and "Empirical Laws and Metaphysical Causes," along with Ch. 8, "J. S. Mill: The Structure of a Social Science"; and L. Levy-Bruhl, *The Philosophy of Auguste Comte* (London, 1903, transl., repr. 1973), e.g. Bk. I, Ch. II, "The Law of the Three States," an older study but still of interest.

11. John H. Hallowell, *Main Currents in Modern Political Thought* (New York, 1950), esp., for present purposes, Ch. 9, "Positivism," and Ch. 10, "Changing Concepts of Law in the Nineteenth and Twentieth Centuries."

12. *Ibid.*, pp. 290–291, 326–327: "With the rise of positivism in the nineteenth century the only task left to social science and jurisprudence is the description of events and the induction from these events of general laws of causality—the evaluation of the goodness or badness, justice or injustice, of particular events being regarded not only as irrelevant but as being incompatible with scientific methods and 'ideals.' In an effort to confine himself to the 'pure' description of empirically observable 'facts,' the positivist substitutes the inductive reasoning of the physical scientist for the 'right reason' of the seventeenth-century philosopher. . . . It represents the complete victory of empiricism. . . . It is an attempt to repudiate all metaphysical speculation and ethical evaluation in the interest of 'scientific objectivity.'

"Positivism became, in the nineteenth century, the dominant climate of intellectual opinion and only very recently has it been seriously challenged. The name of positivism is intimately associated with that of Auguste Comte for he was one of the first to use the term. . . .

"[W]hen the test of legality, moreover, is ultimately conceived as the force behind the law, freedom from illegal compulsion amounts to no more than freedom to do whatever the state does not forbid. This is a conception of freedom much more congenial to tyranny than to the preservation of the inalienable rights of man.

"But the conception of the inalienable rights of man no more survived the scrutiny of positivism than did the concept of justice. Viewed from the perspective of positivism the rights of man were conceived no longer as natural rights but as legal rights. Properly speaking, according to the positivist view, man has no rights at all; what the liberals have traditionally called rights are actually only concessions granted by the state or society. Whatever rights men have are those guaranteed by the law and since the rights are the product of the law they are not, properly speaking, rights at all but concessions to claims which the individual makes and the state recognizes. As concessions, it follows, of course, that they can be withdrawn to the extent that the state deems such withdrawal of its recognition compatible with the interests of the 'general welfare.'

"Of the many factors which have contributed to the decline of liberalism in the modern world no single factor has been more important than the rise of positivism and its infiltration into every sphere of thought. For it was the liberal, positivistic jurists long before Hitler who taught (explicitly or implicitly) that might makes right and that rights are not attributes which individuals have by virtue of their humanity but simply claims which the state may or may not choose to recognize. Unwittingly, it may be, such liberals prepared the way for Lidice and Dachau. When the liberals were finally confronted with totalitarian dictatorship most of them could not find words of condemnation. For how can you condemn a tyrant as unjust when you have purged the word justice from your vocabulary? . . . The liberals who were under the influence of positivism had neither the convictions nor the will to identify injustice or to combat it. It was not because they were any less courageous than their liberal predecessors but because their liberal convictions were less firmly and deeply rooted. The liberal vocabulary and slogans alone remained, emptied, by positivism, of all substantive content."

13. *Ibid.*, p. 336: "Unlike the historical school which thought of law as something which was found and not made the analytical jurists regarded the law as something which was consciously made by the lawgiver. Whereas, the historical jurists saw the social pressure behind the law as the sanction of the law, the analytical jurists saw primarily force and constraint. Thus, for the latter, there could be no law apart from some agency capable of enforcing it. Law was embodied most typically for the historical jurists in custom [a common misconception seen below in new light], it was embodied most typically for the analytical jurists in statutory law. Whereas, the philosophical basis of historical jurisprudence was idealistic and principally Hegelian, the philosophical basis of analytical jurisprudence was utilitarianism."

14. Hendrik Jan van Eikema Hommes, *Major Trends in the History of Legal Philosophy* (Amsterdam, 1979), p. 208: "Legal positivism should never be identified with the conception that all law is positive law. Such an identification is continually advanced by modern adherents of the traditional theory of natural law. They construe a dilemma between natural law theory and juridical positivism, so that he who rejects natural law is reckoned among the legal positivists. However, this dilemma is false. There are various legal theories—my own among them—which only acknowledge positive law to be valid law, but which nevertheless bind such valid law to a supra-arbitrary foundation (legal principles), without which positive law cannot be called law in a proper sense."

15. Thilly and Wood, *History of Philosophy*, Ch. XIX.

16. Sabine, *History of Political Theory*, Chs. XXXI–XXXII.

17. Margaret Spahr (ed.), *Readings in Recent Political Philosophy* (New York, repr. 1941).

18. Hart, "Positivism," esp. pp. 601–602. Following Hart's article is another of good merit on this subject by Lon L. Fuller, "Positivism and Fidelity to Law—A Reply to Professor Hart," *Har. Law Rev.*, 71, pp. 630–672. Fuller criticizes Hart for ignoring the internal "morality of order" necessary to the creation of all law (introductory synopsis). According to Fuller (pp. 638–639): "Professor Hart emphatically rejects 'the command theory of law,' according to which law is simply a command backed by a force sufficient to make it effective. He observes that such a command can be given by a man with a loaded gun, and 'law study is not the gunman situation writ large.' There is no need to dwell here on the inadequacies of the command theory, since Professor Hart has already revealed its defects more clearly and succinctly than I could. His conclusion is that the foundation of a legal system is not coercive power, but certain 'fundamental accepted rules specifying the essential lawmaking procedures.' . . . I found Professor Hart leaving completely untouched the nature of the fundamental rules that make law itself possible, and turning his attention instead to what he considers a confusion of thought on the part of the critics of positivism. Leaving out of account his discussion of analytical jurisprudence, his argument runs something as follows: Two views are associated with the names of Bentham and Austin. One is the command theory of law, the other is an insistence on the separation of law and morality. Critics of these writers came in time to perceive— 'dimly' Professor Hart says—that the command theory is untenable. By a loose association of ideas they wrongly supposed that in advancing reasons for rejecting the command theory they had also refuted the view that law and morality must be sharply separated. This was a 'natural mistake,' but plainly a mistake just the same."

Particularly useful are H. L. A. Hart's cogent characterizations of Austin's doctrines in his noted Intro. to an edn. (Weidenfeld, 1954) of parts of Austin's *Lectures—The Province of Jurisprudence Determined* (1832) and *The Uses of the Study of Jurisprudence* (1863). Hart there explains as follows (pp. x–xii, xvi): "The essence of Austin's doctrine in *The Province* may be shortly stated. His object in this avowedly preliminary work is to identify the distinguishing characteristics of positive law and so to free it from the perennial confusion with the precepts of religion and morality which had been encouraged by Natural Law theorists and exploited by the opponents of legal reform. To effect his purpose Austin uses two notions: the first is that of a *command* which he analyses as an expression of desire by a person who has the purpose, and some power, to inflict an evil in case the desire be disregarded; the second is that of a *habit of obedience* to a determinate person. In terms of these two elements he defines successively *being under a duty* or *obligation* (being liable to an evil from the person commanding in the event of disobedience): *sanction* (the evil which will probably be incurred in case a command be disobeyed): *a superior* (a person or persons who can compel others to obey): *independent political society* (a society of which the bulk are in a habit of obedience to a determinate common superior who is in no such habit of obedience to another): and *sovereign* (a determinate human superior not in a habit of obedience to a like superior but in receipt of habitual obedience from the bulk of a given society). *Laws properly so called* are defined as commands which oblige a person or persons to a course of conduct and the 'essential difference' of *positive law* is found to be that it is set by a sovereign to the members of an independent political society. . . .

"Criticisms of Austin's doctrine have, regrettably, come to be better known than the doctrine itself. . . .

"[A] legal system is a system of rules within rules; and to say that a legal system exists entails not that there is a general habit of obedience to determinate persons but that there is a general acceptance of a constitutional rule, simple or complex, defining the manner in which the ordinary rules of the system are to be identified. We should think not of sovereign and independent *persons* habitually obeyed but of a rule providing a sovereign or ultimate *test* in accordance with which the laws to be obeyed are identified. . . .

"[I]t is now clear that Austin's influence on the development in England of the subject has been greater than that of any other writer. For English jurisprudence has been and still is predominantly analytical in character; other influences . . . have been secondary. It is true that there is little original in Austin: he was inspired above all by Bentham from whom he inherited hatred of mysticism and unreality and a triple passion for classification, legislation and codification. The main doctrines of *The Province of Jurisprudence Determined* can be easily identified in Austin's predecessors: the definitions of 'law,' 'sovereign' and 'political society' can be found almost verbatim in Bentham and Hobbes, and the conception of the rules of morality as based on the principle of Utility itself the index of God's commands is to be found in Paley and Berkeley, and in a less definite form, in Locke and Hobbes. Austin's achievement was to segregate these doctrines from the political and philosophical discussions in which they were embedded and to restate them with a new firmness, grasp of detail and precision. . . . Similarly, . . . the analysis and classification of legal notions in the lectures was in the main derived from Roman and pandect law . . ."

19. Wilfrid E. Rumble, *The Thought of John Austin: Jurisprudence, Colonial Reform, and the British Constitution* (London, 1986), pp. 109 ff. on Hart and pp. 53–54 relating to Austin's brief encounter with Comte in France. ("Comte . . . had no influence upon Austin's philosophy of law, and little or no impact upon subsequent legal positivism. . . . Austin was critical of Comte's dogmatism and . . . contempt for religion [and] '. . . all which has been done by others.' ")

20. W. L. Morison, *John Austin* (Stanford, 1982), Ch. 6, p. 178. Cf. also not only that ch. in full but also Appendix I, "Recent Commentaries on Austin."

21. *Ibid.*, p. 170.

22. Morison's non-focus on legislation is evident in his numerous headings (without standard capitalizations), which deal with quite different subjects. These extraneous subjects include: "jurisprudence and moral sciences," "the analysis of laws generally," "the analysis of positive law," "legal positions of persons," "sources of law," "the map of a legal system," "the uses of the study of jurisprudence," Austin as "conservative or reformer?," "Austin's motivations," the "practical consequences" and "enduring theoretical value" of Austin's works, the "scholarly reception" of Austin, the "Austinian tradition," and, at the book's beginning, the "personal," "social," and "literary" "influences" on Austin.

23. In edn. of Austin's *Lectures on Jurisprudence*, Lectures I–VI, *The Province of Jurisprudence Determined*, edited by Wilfrid E. Rumble (Cambridge, 1995), with Intro. on textual and interpretative matters. Rumble has done a good job of identifying and placing in brackets those passages added to the *Province* by Austin's editor Robert Campbell (cf. n. 24 below) on the basis of Austin's own other materials. I have avoided quoting those portions for crucial documentation here, unless otherwise stated (as in passage above corresponding to this n.).

24. I have used the London edn. of 1873 in 2 vols. of Austin's subsequent *Lectures*, edited by Robert Campbell.

25. Cf. Rumble's edn. of Austin's *Province*, p. xii and passim (editorial Intro.).

26. *Ibid.*, p. xxviii.

27. *Ibid.*, pp. 18–19 (Lect. I).

28. *Ibid.*, pp. 115–116 (Lect. V).

29. *Ibid.*, pp. 20–21 (Lect. I). Furthermore (pp. 21, 24–25, 28–29): "If you cannot or will not harm me, in case I comply not with your wish, the expression of your wish is not a command, although you utter your wish in imperative phrase. If you are able and willing to harm me in case I comply not with your wish, the expression of your wish amounts to

a command, although you are prompted by a spirit of courtesy to utter it in the shape of a request. '*Preces* erant, sed *quibus contradici non posset.*' Such is the language of Tacitus, when speaking of a petition by the soldiery to a son and lieutenant of Vespasian. . . . But it is only by the chance of incurring *evil*, that I am *bound* or *obliged* to compliance. It is only by conditional *evil*, that duties are *sanctioned* or *enforced*. . . .

"If we put *reward* into the import of the term *sanction*, we must engage in a toilsome struggle with the current of ordinary speech. . . .

"It also appears from what has been premised, that *command, duty,* and *sanction* are inseparably connected terms: that each embraces the same ideas as the others, though each denotes those ideas in a peculiar order or series. . . .

"Commands are of two species. Some are *laws* or *rules*. The others have not acquired an appropriate name, nor does language afford an expression which will mark them briefly and precisely. I must, therefore, note them as well as I can by the ambiguous and inexpressive name of '*occasional* or *particular* commands.'

"The term *laws* or *rules* being not unfrequently applied to occasional or particular commands, it is hardly possible to describe a line of separation which shall consist in every respect with established forms of speech. But the distinction between laws and particular commands may, I think, be stated in the following manner. . . .

"Now where it obliges *generally* to acts or forbearances of a *class*, a command is a law or rule. But where it obliges to a *specific* act or forbearance, or to acts or forbearances which it determines *specifically* or *individually*, a command is occasional or particular. . . .

"A different line of separation has been drawn by Blackstone and others. According to Blackstone and others, a law and a particular command are distinguished in the following manner.—A law obliges *generally* the members of the given community, or a law obliges *generally* persons of a given class. A particular command obliges a *single* person, or persons whom it determines *individually*.

"That laws and particular commands are not to be distinguished thus, will appear on a moment's reflection.

"For, *first*, commands which oblige generally the members of the given community, or commands which oblige generally persons of given classes, are not always laws or rules. . . .

"And, *secondly*, a command which obliges exclusively persons individually determined, may amount, notwithstanding, to a law or rule. . . .

"Laws established by political superiors, and exclusively binding specified or determinate persons, are styled, in the language of the Roman jurists, *privilegia*. . . .

"Laws and other commands are said to proceed from *superiors*, and to bind or oblige *inferiors*. I will, therefore, analyze the meaning of those correlative expressions; and will try to strip them of a certain mystery, by which that simple meaning appears to be obscured."

30. *Ibid.*, p. 31 (Lect. I). The passage continues as follows (pp. 32–33): "It often, indeed, happens (as I shall show in the proper place), that laws declaratory in name are imperative in effect: Legislative, like judicial interpretation, being frequently deceptive; and establishing new law, under guise of expounding the old.

"2. Laws to repeal laws, and to release from existing duties, must also be excepted from the proposition 'that laws are a species of commands.' In so far as they release from duties imposed by existing laws, they are not commands, but revocations of commands. They authorize or permit the parties, to whom the repeal extends, to do or to forbear from acts which they were commanded to forbear from or to do. And, considered with regard to *this*, their immediate or direct purpose, they are often named *permissive laws*, or, more briefly and more properly, *permissions*.

"Remotely and indirectly, indeed, permissive laws are often or always imperative. . . .

"3. Imperfect laws, or laws of imperfect obligation, must also be excepted from the proposition 'that laws are a species of commands.' . . .

"The imperfect laws, of which I am now speaking, are laws which are imperfect, in the sense of *the Roman jurists.*"

31. *Ibid.*, p. 156 (Lect. V). The passage goes on to state (p. 157): "Declaratory laws, and laws repealing laws, ought in strictness to be classed with laws metaphorical or figurative: for the analogy by which they are related to laws imperative and proper is extremely slender or remote. Laws of imperfect obligation (in the sense of the Roman jurists) are laws set or imposed by the opinions of the law-makers, and ought in strictness to be classed with rules of positive morality. But though laws of these three species are merely analogous to laws in the proper acceptation of the term, they are closely connected with positive laws, and are appropriate subjects of jurisprudence. Consequently I treat them as improper laws of anomalous or eccentric sorts, and exclude them from the classes of laws to which in strictness they belong."

32. *Ibid.*, p. 58 (Lect. V).

33. *Ibid.*, pp. 52–53 (Lect. II): "To think that the theory of utility would *substitute* calculation for sentiment, is a gross and flagrant error: the error of a shallow, precipitate understanding. He who *opposes* calculation and sentiment, opposes the rudder to the sail, or to the breeze which swells the sail. Calculation is the guide, and not the antagonist of sentiment. Sentiment without calculation were blind and capricious; but calculation without sentiment were inert.

"To crush the moral sentiments, is not the scope or purpose of the true theory of utility. It seeks to impress those sentiments with a just or beneficent direction: to free us of *groundless* likings, and from the tyranny of senseless antipathies; to fix our love upon the useful, our hate upon the pernicious.

"If, then, the principle of utility were the presiding principle of our conduct, our conduct would be determined immediately by Divine *rules*, or rather by moral *sentiments* associated with those rules. . . .

"But these conclusions (like most conclusions) must be taken with limitations. . . .

"For example, If we take the principle of utility as our index to the Divine commands, we must infer that obedience to established government is enjoined generally by the Deity. For, without obedience to 'the powers which be,' there were little security and little enjoyment."

Ibid., pp. 74–75 (Lect. III): "If utility be the proximate test of positive law and morality, it is simply impossible that positive law and morality should be free from defects and errors. . . .

"For, *first*, positive law and morality, fashioned on the principle of utility, are gotten by observation and induction from the tendencies of human actions. . . .

"And, *secondly*, if utility be the proximate test of positive law and morality, the defects and errors of *popular* or *vulgar* ethics will scarcely admit of a remedy."

34. *Lectures*, Vol. II, pp. 776–777, 780–781 (Lect. XLIV): "[T]he division of law into *jus publicum* and *jus privatum* involves . . . absurdity. For *jus publicum* is the law of political conditions, and *jus privatum* is all the law, *minus* the law of political conditions. The opposed terms public and private law tend moreover, in my opinion, to generate a complete misconception of the real ends and purposes of law. Every part of the law is in a certain sense public, and every part of it is in a certain sense private also. There is scarcely a single provision of the law which does not interest the public, and there is not one which does not interest, singly and individually, the persons of whom that public is composed. . . .

"Endeavouring to explain its import, as taken with its large and vague signification, I will advert to the distinction between *jus publicum et privatum* as drawn by the Roman lawyers: that being the model or pattern upon which the modern distinctions into public and private law have all of them been formed.

"The Roman lawyers divide the *corpus juris* into two opposed departments: — the one including the law of political conditions, and the law relating to crimes and criminal procedure: the other including the rest of the law. The first they style *jus publicum*, the second they style *jus privatum*. . . .

"Nothing can be more varying than the views taken by some modern writers of the distinction between public and private law. Some include in public law, besides the law of political conditions, and of crimes and criminal procedure, the whole law also of civil procedure. As the distinction between public and private law rests upon no intelligible basis, there is certainly no reason why public law should not include this, or any other portion of the *corpus juris*. If these writers had any particular reason for including it, their reason probably was, that public law is administered by public persons, namely by judges, and other ministers of justice, and that the law of civil procedure is administered by the same persons. But a great deal of the law of civil procedure comprises rights vested in private persons: namely, rights vested in the parties to the cause as against the judges. . . .

"From the utter impossibility of finding a stable basis for the division, others exclude criminal law. They see that a multitude of crimes affect individuals as directly as the delicts which are styled civil.

"But the greatest logical error of all is that committed by many continental jurists, who include in public law, not only the law of political conditions, of crimes, and of civil and criminal procedure, but also *international* law; which is not positive law at all, but a branch of positive morality. . . .

"Every division of law into which this detestable word enters must be indefinite. . . .

"The phrase *public law* has at least four or five totally different meanings. 1st; it has either of the two meanings above adverted to: its strict or definite and its large or vague sense. 2ndly; it sometimes means the law which proceeds either from the supreme legislature, or from subordinate political superiors, as distinguished from what have been termed laws *autonomic*, that is, laws set by private persons in pursuance of legal rights with which they are invested. These laws which proceed indirectly from the sovereign legislature, through rights with which it has invested private persons, are called private laws, and all other public laws. 3rdly; public laws are sometimes opposed to laws creating *privilegia*. Laws of this kind are sometimes called *jus singulare*, and *jus publicum*, as opposed to them, is called *jus commune*. . . . 4thly; under public law are sometimes classed definite and obligatory modes of performing certain transactions. . . . 5thly; by public laws are sometimes meant the laws called *prohibitive* or *absolutely* binding, as opposed to the laws called dispositive or *provisional*. The legislator in certain instances determines absolutely what shall be the effect of a given transaction, namely, determining what effect the transaction shall have, if the parties do not provide otherwise. Now, when the legislature determines absolutely the effect of a transaction, the law is called *public*: when he leaves a certain latitude to the parties, it is called dispositive or provisional . . ."

35. *Province*, pp. 94–95 (Lect. IV): "Strictly speaking, therefore, utility is not the *measure* to which our conduct should conform, nor is utility the *test* by which our conduct should be tried. It is not in itself the source or spring of our highest or paramount obligations, but it guides us to the source whence these obligations flow. It is merely the *index* to the measure, the *index* to the test. . . . Accordingly, I style the Divine commands the *ultimate* measure or test: but I style the principle of utility, or the general happiness or good, the *proximate* measure to which our conduct should conform, or the *proximate* test by which our conduct should be tried.

"Now, though the general good is that proximate *measure*, or though the general good is that proximate *test*, it is not in all, or even in most cases, the *motive* or *inducement* which ought to determine our conduct. . . .

"When I speak of the public good, or of the general good, I mean the aggregate enjoyments of the single or individual persons who compose that public or general to which my attention is directed. . . .

"'Mankind,' 'country,' 'public,' are concise expressions for a number of individual persons considered collectively or as a whole. In case the good of those persons considered singly or individually were sacrificed to the good of those persons considered collectively or as a whole, the general good would be destroyed by the sacrifice. The sum of the particular enjoyments which constitutes the general good, would be sacrificed to the mere name by which that good is denoted. . . . For example, That notion of the public good which was current in the ancient republics supposes a neglect of the truism to which I have called your attention. Agreeably to that notion of the public good, the happiness of the individual citizens is sacrificed without scruple in order that the common weal may wax and prosper. The only substantial interests are the victims of a barren abstraction, of a sounding but empty phrase."

36. *Ibid.*, pp. 116–117 (Lect. V). The passage subsequently continues: "Positive laws, or laws strictly so called, are established directly or immediately by authors of three kinds: — by monarchs, or sovereign bodies, as supreme political superiors: by men in a state of subjection, as subordinate political superiors: by subjects, as private persons, in pursuance of legal rights. But every positive law, or every law strictly so called, is a direct or circuitous command of a monarch or sovereign number in the character of political superior: that is to say, a direct or circuitous command of a monarch or sovereign number to a person or persons in a state of subjection to its author. And being a *command* (and therefore flowing from a *determinate* source), every positive law is a law proper, or a law properly so called.

"Besides the human laws which I style positive law, there are human laws which I style positive morality, rules of positive morality, or positive moral rules. . . . Laws set by subjects as subordinate political superiors, are positive laws: they are clothed with legal sanctions, and impose legal duties. They are set by sovereigns or states in the character of political superiors, although they are set by sovereigns circuitously or remotely. Although they are made directly by subject or subordinate authors, they are made through legal rights granted by sovereigns or states, and held by those subject authors as mere trustees for the granters."

37. *Ibid.*, p. 165 (Lect. VI).

38. *Ibid.*, pp. 167, 172, 180–182, 184–185 (Lect. VI): "In order that a given society may form a society political and independent, the two distinguishing marks which I have mentioned above must unite. The *generality* of the given society must be in the *habit* of obedience to a *determinate* and *common* superior: whilst that determinate person, or determinate body of persons must *not* be habitually obedient to a determinate person or body. It is the union of that positive, with this negative mark, which renders that certain superior sovereign or supreme, and which renders that given society (including that certain superior) a society political and independent. . . .

"The definition of the abstract term *independent political society* (including the definition of the correlative term *sovereignty*) cannot be rendered in expressions of perfectly precise import, and is therefore a fallible test of specific or particular cases. The least imperfect definition which the abstract term will take, would hardly enable us to fix the class of every possible society. It would hardly enable us to determine of every *independent* society, whether it were *political* or *natural*. . . .

"Having tried to determine the notion of sovereignty, with the implied or correlative notion of independent political society, I will produce and briefly examine a few of the definitions of those notions which have been given by writers of celebrity.

"Distinguishing *political* from *natural* society, Mr. Bentham, in his Fragment on Government, thus defines the former. . . .

"In his great treatise on international law, Grotius defines sovereignty in the following manner. . . . Now in order that an individual or body may be sovereign in a given society, two essentials must unite. The generality of the given society must render habitual obedience to that certain individual or body: whilst that individual or body must not be habitually obedient to a determinate human superior. . . . But if perfect or complete independence be of the essence of sovereign power, there is not in fact the human power to which the epithet *sovereign* will apply with propriety. Every government, let it be never so powerful, renders occasional obedience to commands of other governments. Every government defers frequently to those opinions and sentiments which are styled international law. . . .

"Every society political and independent is therefore divisible into two portions: namely, the portion of its members which is sovereign or supreme, and the portion of its members which is merely subject. In case that sovereign portion consists of a single member, the supreme government is properly a *monarchy*, or the sovereign is properly a *monarch*. In case that sovereign portion consists of a number of members, the supreme government may be styled an *aristocracy* (in the generic meaning of the expression). . . . Changing the phrase, every supreme government is a *monarchy* (properly so called), or an *aristocracy* (in the generic meaning of the expression)."

39. *Ibid.*, pp. 194–195 (Lect. VI): "The trust imposed by the electoral body upon the body representing them in parliament, is tacit rather than express. . . .

"If a trust of the kind in question were enforced by legal sanctions, the positive law binding the representative body might be made by the representative body and not by the electoral. For example: If the duties of the commons' house towards the commons who appoint it were enforced by legal sanctions, the positive law binding the commons' house might be made by the parliament: that is to say, by the commons' House itself in conjunction with the king and the peers. Or, supposing the sovereignty resided in the commons without the king and the peers, the positive law binding the commons' house might be made by the house itself as representing the sovereign or state.—But, in either of these cases, the law might be abrogated by its immediate author without the direct consent of the electoral body. . . . For the king and the lords with the electoral body of the commons, or the electoral body of the commons as being exclusively the sovereign, would form an extraordinary and ulterior legislature: a legislature superior to that ordinary legislature which would be formed by the parliament or by the commons' house. A law of the parliament, or a law of the commons' house, which affected to abrogate a law of the extraordinary and ulterior legislature, would not be obeyed by the courts of justice."

40. *Ibid.*, pp. 196–197 (Lect. VI): "From the exercise of sovereign powers by the sovereign directly, and also by the sovereign through political subordinates or delegates, I pass to the distinction of sovereign, and other political powers, into such as are *legislative*, and such as are *executive* or *administrative*.

"It seems to be supposed by many writers, that legislative political powers, and executive political powers, may be distinguished precisely, or, at least, with an approach to precision: and that in every society whose government is a government of a number, or, at least, in every society whose government is a limited monarchy, the legislative sovereign powers, and the executive sovereign powers, belong to distinct parties. According, for example, to Sir William Blackstone, the legislative sovereign powers reside in the parliament: that is to say, in the tripartite sovereign body formed by the king, the members of the house of lords, and the members of the house of commons. But, according to the same writer, the executive sovereign powers reside in the king alone.

"Now the distinction of political powers into such as are *legislative*, and such as are *executive*, scarcely coincides with the distinction of those powers into such as are *supreme* and such as are *subordinate*: for it is stated or assumed by the writers who make the former distinction, that sovereign political powers (and, indeed, subordinate also) are divisible into such as are legislative and such as are executive. If the distinction of political powers into legislative and executive have any determinate meaning, its meaning must be this: The former are powers of establishing laws, and of issuing other commands: whilst the latter are powers of administering, or of carrying into operation, laws or other commands already established or issued. But the distinction, as thus understood, is far from approaching to precision. For of all the instruments or means by which laws and other commands are administered or executed, laws and other commands are incomparably the most frequent: insomuch that most of the powers deemed executive or administrative are themselves legislative powers, or involve powers which are legislative . . . are mainly administered through judgments or decrees: that is to say, through commands issued in particular cases by supreme or subordinate tribunals. And, in order that the law so administered may be administered well, they must be administered agreeably to laws which are merely subservient to that purpose. Thus: all laws or rules determining the practice of courts, or all laws or rules determining judicial procedure, are purely subsidiary to the due execution of others.

"That the legislative sovereign powers, and the executive sovereign powers, belong, in any society, to distinct parties, is a supposition too palpably false to endure a moment's examination. Of the numerous proofs of its falsity, which it were easy to produce the following will more than suffice. — 1. Of the laws or rules made by the British parliament, or by any supreme legislature, many are subsidiary, and are intended to be subsidiary, to the due execution of others. . . . 2. In almost every society, *judicial* powers, commonly esteemed *executive* or *administrative*, are exercised directly by the supreme legislature."

41. *Ibid.*, pp. 199, 209–210 (Lect. VI): "Of all the larger divisions of political powers, the division of those powers into *supreme* and *subordinate* is perhaps the only precise one. The former are the political powers, infinite in number and kind, which, partly brought into exercise, and partly lying dormant, belong to a sovereign or state: that is to say, to the monarch properly so called, if the government be a government of one: and, if the government be a government of a number, to the sovereign body considered collectively, or to its various members considered as component parts of it. . . .

"The supreme government of the United States of America, agrees (I believe) with the foregoing general description of a supreme federal government. I believe that the common government, or the government consisting of the congress and the president of the united states, is merely a subject minister of the united states' governments. I believe that none of the latter is properly sovereign or supreme, even in the state or political society of which it is the immediate chief. And, lastly, I believe that the sovereignty of each of the states, and also of the larger state arising from the federal union, resides in the states' governments *as forming one aggregate body*: meaning by a state's government, not its ordinary legislature, but the body of its citizens which appoints its ordinary legislature, and which, the union apart, is properly sovereign therein. If the several immediate chiefs of the several united states, were respectively single individuals, or were respectively narrow oligarchies, the sovereignty of each of the states, and also of the larger state arising from the federal union, would reside in those several individuals, or would reside in those several oligarchies, *as forming a collective whole*."

42. *Ibid.*, pp. 26–27 (Lect. I): "As issued by a sovereign legislature, and as wearing the form of a law, the order which I have now imagined would probably be *called* a law. And

hence the difficulty of drawing a distinct boundary between laws and occasional commands. . . . If made by a sovereign assembly deliberately, and with the forms of legislation, it would probably be called a law. If uttered by an absolute monarch, without deliberation or ceremony, it would scarcely be confounded with acts of legislation, and would be styled an arbitrary command. Yet, on either of these suppositions, its nature would be the same. It would not be a law or rule, but an occasional or particular command of the sovereign One or Number."

43. *Ibid.*, pp. 34–36 (Lect. I): "According to an opinion which I must notice *incidentally* here, though the subject to which it relates will be treated *directly* hereafter, *customary laws* must be excepted from the proposition 'that laws are a species of commands.'

"By many of the admirers of customary laws (and, especially, of their German admirers), they are thought to oblige legally (independently of the sovereign or state), *because* the citizens or subjects have observed or kept them. Agreeably to this opinion, they are not the *creatures* of the sovereign or state, although the sovereign or state may abolish them at pleasure. Agreeably to this opinion, they are positive law (or law, strictly so called), inasmuch as they are enforced by the courts of justice: But, that notwithstanding, they exist as *positive law* by the spontaneous adoption of the governed, and not by position or establishment on the part of political superiors. Consequently, customary laws, considered as positive law, are not commands. And, consequently, customary laws, considered as positive law, are not laws or rules properly so called.

"An opinion less mysterious, but somewhat allied to this, is not uncommonly held by the adverse party: by the party which is strongly opposed to customary law; and to all law made judicially, or in the way of judicial legislation. According to the latter opinion, all judge-made law, or all judge-made law established by *subject* judges, is purely the creature of the judges by whom it is established immediately. To impute it to the sovereign legislature, or to suppose that it speaks the will of the sovereign legislature, is one of the foolish or knavish *fictions* with which lawyers, in every age and nation, have perplexed and darkened the simplest and clearest truths.

"I think it will appear, on a moment's reflection, that each of these opinions is groundless: that customary law is *imperative*, in the proper signification of the term; and that all judge-made law is the creature of the sovereign or state.

"At its origin, a custom is a rule of conduct which the governed observe spontaneously, or not in pursuance of a law set by a political superior. The custom is transmuted into positive law, when it is adopted as such by the courts of justice, and when the judicial decisions fashioned upon it are enforced by the power of the state. But before it is adopted by the courts, and clothed with the legal sanction, it is merely a rule of positive morality: a rule generally observed by the citizens or subjects; but deriving the only force, which it can be said to possess, from the general disapprobation falling on those who transgress it.

"Now when judges transmute a custom into a legal rule (or make a legal rule not suggested by a custom), the legal rule which they establish is established by the sovereign legislature. A subordinate or subject judge is merely a minister. The portion of the sovereign power which lies at his disposition is merely delegated. The rules which he makes derive their legal force from authority given by the state: an authority which the state may confer expressly, but which it commonly imparts in the way of acquiescence. For, since the state may reverse the rules which he makes, and yet permits him to enforce them by the power of the political community, its sovereign will 'that his rules shall obtain as law' is clearly evinced by its conduct, though not by its express declaration.

"The admirers of customary law love to trick out their idol with mysterious and imposing attributes. But to those who can see the difference between positive law and morality, there is nothing of mystery about it. . . . But, considered as moral rules turned into positive laws, customary laws are established by the state: established by the state directly, when the customs are promulged in its statutes; established by the state circuitously, when the customs are adopted by its tribunals.

"The opinion of the party which abhors judge-made laws, springs from their inadequate conception of the nature of commands.

"Like other significations of desire, a command is express or tacit. If the desire be signified by *words* (written or spoken), the command is express. If the desire be signified by conduct (or by any signs of desire which are *not* words), the command is tacit.

"Now when customs are turned into legal rules by decisions of subject judges, the legal rules which emerge from the customs are *tacit* commands of the sovereign legislature. . . .

"My present purpose is merely this: to aprove that the positive law styled *customary* (and all positive law made judicially) is established by the state directly or circuitously, and, therefore, is *imperative*. I am far from disputing, that law made judicially (or in the way of improper legislation) and law made by statute (or in the properly legislative manner) are distinguished by weighty differences."

Ibid., p. 141 (Lect. V): "Customary laws are positive laws fashioned by judicial legislation upon pre-existing customs. Now, till they become the grounds of judicial decisions upon cases, and are clothed with legal sanctions by the sovereign one or number, the customs are merely rules set by opinions of the governed, and sanctioned or enforced morally."

Cf. Lects. XXIX–XXX for Austin's criticisms of Blackstone and others over the differences between written and unwritten law, that is, between legislation and custom.

44. *Ibid.*, p. 288 (Lect. VI): "The definition, therefore, of a positive law, which is assumed expressly or tacitly throughout the foregoing lectures, is not a perfectly complete and perfectly exact definition. . . . To determine the province of jurisprudence is to distinguish positive law (the appropriate matter of jurisprudence) from the various objects (noted in the foregoing lectures) to which it is allied or related in the way of resemblance or analogy."

45. *Ibid.*, p. 242 (Lect. VI): "The proper purpose or end of a sovereign political government, or the purpose or end for which it ought to exist, is the greatest possible advancement of human happiness."

46. *Ibid.*, p. 87 (Lect. IV): "That these inscrutable sentiments are signs of the Divine will, is an inference which we necessarily deduce from our consideration of *final causes*. Like the rest of our appetites or aversions, these sentiments were designed by the Author of our being to answer an appropriate end. And the only pertinent end which we can possibly ascribe to them, is the end or final cause at which I have now pointed.

"Now, supposing that the Deity has endowed us with a moral sense or instinct, we are free of the difficulty to which we are subject, if we must construe his laws by the principle of general utility. According to the hypothesis in question, the inscrutable feelings which are styled the moral sense arise directly and inevitably with the thoughts of their appropriate objects."

Also e.g. pp. 38, 79, 81, 106–109, and 156 (Lects. II, IV–V).

47. *Ibid.*, p. 136 (Lect. V).
48. *Ibid.*, e.g. pp. 225–227 (Lect. VI).
49. *Ibid.*, e.g. pp. 214–215 (Lect. VI).
50. *Ibid.*, e.g. pp. 281–284 (Lect. VI).
51. *Ibid.*, p. 34 (Lect. I).
52. *Ibid.*, pp. ix–x (ed. Intro.).
53. *Ibid.*, pp. 91–92 (Lect. IV): "According to the hypothesis which I have now stated and examined, the moral sense is our *only* index to the tacit commands of the Deity.

According to an intermediate hypothesis, compounded of the hypothesis of utility and the hypothesis of a moral sense, the moral sense is our index to *some* of his tacit commands, but the principle of general utility is our index to *others*. . . .

"By modern writers on jurisprudence, positive law (or law, simply and strictly so called) is divided into *law natural* and *law positive*. By the classical Roman jurists, borrowing from the Greek philosophers, *jus civile* (or positive law) is divided into *jus gentium* and *jus civile*. Which two divisions of positive law are exactly equivalent.

"By modern writers on jurisprudence, and by the classical Roman jurists, positive morality is also divided into *natural* and *positive*. For, through the frequent confusion (to which I shall advert hereafter) os positive law and positive morality, a portion of positive morality, as well as of positive law, is embraced by the *law natural* of modern writers on jurisprudence, and by the equivalent *jus gentium* of the classical Roman jurists."

54. *Ibid.*, pp. 151 ff.(Lect. V).

55. *Ibid.*, p. 213 (Lect. VI): "The sovereign Roman people solemnly voted or resolved, that they would never pass, or even take into consideration, what I will venture to denominate a *bill of pains and penalties*. . . . This solemn resolution or vote was passed with the forms of legislation, and was inserted in the twelve tables in the following imperative terms: *privilegia ne irroganto*. But although the resolution or vote was passed with the forms of legislation, although it was clothed with the expressions appropriate to a law, and although it was inserted as a law in a code or body of statutes, it scarcely was a law in the proper acceptation of the term, and certainly was not a law simply and strictly so called."

56. *Lectures*, Vol. II, pp. 528–530, 532–534, 536 (Lect. XXVIII): "Law considered with reference to its sources, is usually distinguished into law written and unwritten.

"The distinction between written and unwritten law in the modern acceptation of the term, is this: *Written* law is law which the supreme legislature establishes directly. Unwritten law is not made by the supreme legislature, though it owes its validity, or *is law* by the authority, expressly or tacitly given, of the sovereign or state. . . .

"According to the same division, the edicts of the Prætors and other judicial functionaries, the rules introduced by the practice of the tribunals, the writings and opinions of jurisconsults, and laws established by custom, were unwritten law, or *jus non scriptum*. For although law originating in any of these sources, owed its validity to the assent of the supreme legislature, it was not made by the supreme legislature, directly and immediately.

"The distinction between written and unwritten law, as drawn by the modern Civilians, was adopted by Hale, and imported by Blackstone into his Commentaries. . . .

"By the Roman Lawyers themselves, little importance was attached to the distinction between written and unwritten law. And, in every instance in which they take the distinction, they understand it in its literal sense. When they talk of *written* law, they do not mean law proceeding directly from the supreme Legislature, but law which was committed to writing at its origin. . . . And accordingly they include in written law, not only the laws of the *Populus* and *Plebs*, with the Senatus-consulta and the Constitutions of the Emperors, but also the Edicts of the Prætors and other Magistrates, and the Responses of the jurisconsults. . . .

"An example of laws made by the sovereign body directly and immediately, is that of our own Acts of Parliament, which are made directly by the supreme legislature in its three branches, the King, the House of Lords, and the House of Commons. . . .

"In Rome under the Commonwealth, or in *liberâ* republicâ, laws established by the supreme legislature were of three kinds: there were three distinct bodies whose decrees were considered as made by the sovereign or supreme legislature. . . .

"This legislative power was sometimes exercised by the people, as collected in a single assembly. At other times, it was exercised by the same people as divided into two bodies: — namely, *by* the *plebs*, with the concurrence of the senate; or *by* the senate, with the concurrence of the *plebs*. And, in either of these last-mentioned cases, the joint act of the parts into which the whole was divided, was equivalent to an act of that sovereign whole as united in one assembly. If our House of Lords and House of Commons sometimes sat and voted in one assembly, and sometimes separately as at present, they would afford an exact parallel to the manner in which the sovereignty was divided in the Roman Republic. Acts passed by the two bodies assembled in one house, would correspond to *leges curialae* and *centurialae*; acts originating in the one House and adopted by the other, would be *plebiscita* or *senatus-consulta*. . . .

"From the accession of Hadrian, and perhaps from an earlier period, the Emperors openly assumed the supreme legislative power which they had before exercised covertly. Instead of emitting their laws through the *populus*, *plebs*, or *senate*, they began to legislate avowedly as monarchs and autocrators, and to notify their commands to their subjects in *Imperial Constitutions*.

"These imperial constitutions (which are not unfrequently styled *principum placita*) were general or special. . . .

"A third class of these Special Constitutions, and the most important and remarkable, consisted of those decretes and rescripts which were made by the Emperors, not in their quality of sovereign legislators, but in their quality of sovereign judges. . . . For, although in modern Europe the judicial power residing in the sovereign is commonly delegated by him to individuals called judges, the Roman emperors were themselves judges in the last resort.

"I find this a convenient opportunity to observe that sovereignty, being unlimited and incapable of any legal limitation, includes the judicial as well as the legislative power. The judicial powers implied in sovereignty are in our own times commonly delegated wholly or in part; but in the nations of antiquity and in the Middle Ages the person or body of persons composing the supreme legislature was also the judge in the last resort, or even in the first instance. The *populus* of Rome, which was the supreme legislative body, was also the judge in capital cases. . . . [I]t is from the *Aula Regis* that our House of Lords, although no longer the same assembly, and not now the sovereign, but a branch of the supreme legislature, derives the judicial power which it still exercises. I cannot remember that Parliament in its collective capacity ever exercised judicial power. . . . Indeed, the judicial power seems to have been more completely detached from the legislative in our own country than in any other."

57. *Ibid.*, Vol. II, pp. 544–545 (Lect. XXIX): "The distinction between written and unwritten law, in the improper or juridical sense, or between promulged and unpromulged law in the same improper sense, is founded on difference of source. For written or promulged law in this sense is law emanating directly from the supreme legislator: unwritten or unpromulged law in the same sense is law made immediately by a subordinate authority. But the distinction between written and unwritten law, taking the terms in their grammatical meaning, is built exclusively upon a difference in the mode in which they originate. Written law is law which exists in writing at or before its origin; unwritten law is law which neither exists in a written state previously, nor is committed to writing at its origin. . . .

"Such, at least, is the *only* distinction between *written* and *unwritten* law, that appears to be known to the Roman lawyers. Lex, Plebiscita, Senatus-consulta, Principum Placita, are ranked by Justinian with *jus scriptum*, not because they emanated directly from the sovereign authority, but because they existed in a written form at their origin. . . .

"Customary Law is, according to Justinian, *jus non scriptum*."

58. *Ibid.*, Vol. II, p. 560 (Lect. XXX): "In Rome, the absolute dominion of the *paterfamilias* over his wife and descendants, arose from custom and consequent customary law, and was gradually abridged by direct legislation: namely, by the edicts of the Praetors, the laws of the People, and the edictal constitutions of the Emperors.

"Let us turn our eyes in what direction we may, we shall find that there is no connection between customary law, and the well-being of the many.

"In spite, then, of the grandiloquous talk by which it has been extolled and obscured, customary law has nothing of the magnificent or mysterious about it. It is but a *species* of *judiciary* law, or of law introduced by sovereign or subordinate judges as properly exercising their judicial functions. And it differs from other species of the same kind of law merely by this peculiarity; that it is formed or fashioned by the judges, who are its sources or immediate authors, upon pre-existing rules observed spontaneously, or wholly deriving their imperfect obligatory force from the religious or moral sanctions."

59. *Ibid.*, Vol. II, p. 561 (Lect. XXX): "By the Roman Lawyers, these merely private though respected jurisconsults are styled *conditores* or founders of law. And by modern Civilians generally, and apparently by the Roman Lawyers, they are deemed the sources of the law, or the immediate authors of the law, which really was formed upon their opinions by legislators or judges. . . .

"But merely private jurisconsults, respected for their knowledge and judgment, are not *conditores* or founders of Law, although the weight of their opinions may determine *others* to found it. If their opinions determine the legislator, the influence of those opinions is a *remote* cause of the Law, of which the Legislator himself is exclusively the *immediate* cause, or is exclusively the *source*. . . . Justinian legislated by the advice of Tribonian. He also legislated at the instance of his Empress. And the blandishments of the wife, as well as the responses of the legal oracle, were *remote causes* of laws emanating from the Emperor as their *source*.

"Nay, the writings of private lawyers are not law, although it be declared by the legislator that they shall thereafter be law. For they are not law as being the production of the writers, but by virtue of the Legislator's adoption. Such, for example, is the case with those excerpts from the writings of jurists, of which Justinian's Digest is almost exclusively composed. As forming parts of those writings, they were not law; but as compiled and promulged by Justinian, they took the quality of law immediately proceeding from the sovereign."

60. *Ibid.*, Vol. II, pp. 616, 618, 624 (Lect. XXXV): "But though most of the law, formed by judicial decisions, was made by the Praetors (as judges), and *might* have been *styled* 'praetorian,' the term '*jus praetorium*' was exclusively applied to the law which they made by their general edicts in the way of direct legislation. . . .

"Inasmuch as the body of law, formed by the *Praetores Urbani*, was partly derived from the *jus gentium*, and was partly fashioned upon Utility (as conceived by the Praetors and the public), it was naturally styled the *Equity* of the Praetors. . . . For . . . the *jus gentium* was styled *jus aequumm*, whilst general utility (or principles of legislation supposed to accord with it) was often styled 'Aequitas.'

"It is said in a passage of the Digests (referring to a certain rule of the *jus praetorium*). . . . That is to say, the rule was commended by general utility (or equity). . . .

"But the Praetorian Edict, as promulged by the command of Hadrian, was styled '*perpetual*,' in another signification of the epithet. . . .

"Whether the Praetors after this change under Hadrian, continued to legislate *directly* (or to legislate by *general* edicts), is an agitated and doubtful question. It would rather appear that Hadrian, in making the change, intended (amongst other objects) to obviate the necessity and demand for the subordinate legislation of the magistracy."

61. *Ibid.*, Vol. II, p. 640 (Lect. XXXVI): "Another very common error is to suppose that equity is not a body of laws or rules, but is moulded at the pleasure of the tribunals: that, in short, equity as meaning law, is equity as meaning the *arbitrium* of the judge. This is an error of which, strange as it may appear, even English lawyers of considerable reputation have been guilty."

62. *Ibid.*, Vol. II, p. 641 (Lect. XXXVII): "Statute law may proceed directly from subject, or subordinate authors: whilst a monarch or supreme body may exercise the judicial powers inhering necessarily in the Sovereign, and therefore may be directly the author of law made in the judicial manner.

"By the opposed expressions 'statute law' and 'judiciary law,' I point at a difference (not between the *sources* from which law proceeds, but) between the *modes* in which it begins. By the term 'statute law,' I mean any law (whether it proceed from a subordinate, or from a sovereign source) which is made directly, or in the way of proper legislation. By the term 'judiciary law,' I mean any law (whether it proceed from a sovereign, or a subordinate source) which is made indirectly, or in the way of judicial or impoper legislation."

63. *Ibid.*, Vol. II, p. 1115 ("On the Use of the Study of Jurisprudence"): "It is much to be regretted that the study of the Roman Law is neglected in this country, and that the real merits of its founders and expositors are so little understood. . . .

"Nor is the Roman law to be resorted to as a magazine of legislative wisdom. The great Roman Lawyers are, in truth, expositors of a positive or technical system. Not Lord Coke himself is more purely technical. Their real merits lie in their thorough mastery of that system . . ."

64. *Province*, pp. 160–161 (Lect. V): "Those who know the writings of the Roman lawyers only by hearsay are accustomed to admire their philosophy. Now this, in my estimation, is the only part of their writings which deserves contempt. Their extraordinary merit is evinced not in general speculation, but as expositors of the Roman law. They have seized its general principles with great clearness and penetration, have applied these principles with admirable logic to the explanation of details, and have thus reduced this positive system of law to a compact and coherent whole. But the philosophy which they borrowed from the Greeks, or which, after the examples of the Greeks, they themselves fashioned, is naught. Their attempts to define jurisprudence and to determine the province of the jurisconsult are absolutely pitiable, and it is hardly conceivable how men of such admirable discernment should have displayed such contemptible imbecility.

"At the commencement of the digest is a pasage attempting to define jurisprudence. . . . 'Jurisprudence,' says this definition, 'is the knowledge of things divine and human; the science which teaches men to discern the just from the unjust.' . . . In the excerpt from Ulpian, which is placed at the beginning of the Digest, it is attempted to define the office or province of the jurisconsult. 'Law,' says the passage, 'derives its name from justice, *justitia*, and is the science or skill in the good and the equitable. . . .' . . .

"Were I to present you with all the criticisms which these two passages suggest, I should detain you a full hour. . . . Now jurisprudence, if it is anything, is the science of law . . ."

65. *Lectures*, Vol. II, pp. 1075 ff., 1086 ff.

66. *Ibid.*, Vol. II, pp. 1128 ff., 1133 ff.

67. The British jurist A. V. Dicey (1835–1922) was greatly influenced by Austin's ideas of legislative sovereignty even when criticizing them in his *Introduction to the Study of the Law of the Constitution* (first published in London, 1885; 8th edn. pub. in 1915, being the last one prepared by Dicey himself).

In Pt. I ("The Sovereignty of Parliament"), Ch. I ("The Nature of Parliamentary Sovereignty"), Dicey begins by stating that his threefold purpose in this ch. is to show that the British Parliament's sovereignty is a legally recognized fact, that none of the alleged limitations on parliamentary sovereignty have any real existence, and that Parliament is "an absolutely sovereign legislature" as provided for by "the British constitution" (p. 3). Dicey criticizes Austin (pp. 25–29) in relation to these propositions, arguing that Austin was wrong to view King, Lords, and Commons together as the legislative sovereign, since only Parliament itself can be considered the legislative sovereign. Austin, he believes, is too abstract in his theory, whereas he, Dicey, reaffirms what the British (so-called) constitution declares about parliamentary legislative sovereignty, which Dicey insists has often not been duly recognized by writers. Wider questions of the electorate's or people's sovereignty are "political" perspectives but not "legal" ones, in the sense that, e.g., the courts do not recognize the people's (abstract) will but only the (concrete) acts of Parliament. Austin's theory of sovereignty, according to Dicey, is a generalization drawn from English law, which Austin would have done well to recognize as such by assigning to Parliament its proper central legislatively sovereign role as set forth therein. Austin's analysis of law in the abstract is in fact an examination of English criminal law that is somewhat warped. Austin's theory is marred by internal inconsistencies as well, Dicey declares, that point instead to the true nature of Parliament's legislative sovereignty.

However, in spite of or indeed because of Dicey's criticisms of Austin, it becomes clear that he is reapplying much of Austin's emphasis on the absolute legal sovereignty of the legislative power to Parliament itself instead of to the broader King-Lords-Commons version, which had a long, widely-accepted history in political-legal theory. Dicey's Ch. II ("Parliament and Non-Sovereign Law-Making Bodies") takes up further features of law-making authority in relation to sovereignty or non-sovereignty.

68. Austin's multitudinous references to Bentham, dealing with such subjects as legislation and utility, include the following germane instances in Austin's *Province*: p. 23 (Lect. I), p. 105 (Lect. IV), p. 155 (Lect. V), and p. 163 (Lect. V). Such references further on in Austin's *Lectures*, Vol. II, include: p. 665 (Lect. XXXVIII, "the important business of legislation"), p. 722 (Lect. XLI), p. 725 (Lect. XLI), and p. 727 (Lect. XLI). It would be useful to compile a detailed descriptive listing of such references by Austin to Bentham on the different issues at hand, as well as to other authorities like Hobbes (e.g. *Province*, pp. 228–229, Lect. VI), Locke, and Sidney.

69. Eikema Hommes, *op. cit.*

70. *Ibid.*, pp. 207–208, 212–213, 215–216. Also, pp. 216–217: "This entire view is typical of the state-absolutistic legal positivism of the previous century and that of our own. Violation of the (morally binding) general principles of law does not affect the *legal* character of legislation nor its formal-legal validity. Even when the state does not subject itself voluntarily to its own legislation and, indeed, deviates from it arbitrarily (unilaterally binding legal norm) the rule issuing from the state's plenitude of power nevertheless remains a legal rule. . . . 'Now the legislative power . . . transcends the law; every law which it proclaims, no matter what the content of that law, is in a juridical sense a perfectly legal act . . .'

"Von Jhering adheres to this juridical positivism in his subsequent discourses on the *content* of legislation as far as this content is determined by the societal purpose of law and state. Von Jhering considers this purpose to be the protection of the vital conditions of society . . . , but he does not conceive of these conditions in an *objective* sense, as do the sociological positivists. His concern is only the legislator's subjective representation of these vital conditions. . . .

"Von Jhering's influence on the development of legal philosophy and jurisprudence of his day was considerable. His theory of concept-construction became the starting point for the so-called 'general theory of law' although his 'cult of the logical' was rejected; his theory of the social purpose as source of law inspired later [jurists] . . ."

394 / *Notes to Chapter III*

71. Cf. in particular Rudolf von Jhering's *Geist des römischen Rechts auf den verschiedenen Stufen seiner Entwickelung* (3 vols. in 4, Leipzig, 1852–1865; later edns. of each of the 4 vols., respectively those of 1907, 1894, 1898, and 1906, were reprinted in 1968), e.g. Vol. I, pp. 1 ff. on the significance of Roman law for the "modern world"; *Die Entwickelungsgeschichte des römischen Rechts* (Leipzig, 1894); *Der Zweck im Recht* (Vienna, 1880, 6th edn.; 1st edn. Leipzig, 1877–1883, 2 vols.); *Law as a Means to an End* (transl. of *Der Zweck*, Vol. I, by I. Husik, Boston, 1913, with general intro.), esp. Pt. I, Ch. III, sect. 5, "The State and the Law" ("The organization of purpose attains its highest point in the State . . . in reference to what is the purely external element of the machinery by which the purpose is realized"; "The organization of the purpose of the State is characterized by the extended application of law."); and *Der Kampf um's Recht* (Regensburg, 1872).

On Jhering there are three notable recent publications. The essays by various authorities in *Privatrecht heute und Jherings evolutionäres Rechtsdenken* (edited by Okko Behrends, Cologne, 1993) cover a broad range of topics relating (but not restricted) to Jhering's legal evolutionism. In addition to the expected considerations therein of Darwin, Savigny, Roman law, and a host of other such subjects, there are interesting discussions relative to positivism and the *Rechtsstaat* (pp. 131 ff.). Even wider material on Jhering's life, career, works, and correspondence is presented in *Rudolf von Jhering: Beiträge und Zeugnisse aus Anlass der einhundertsten Wiederkehr seines Todestages am 17.9.1992* (edited by Okko Behrends, Gottingen, 1992). Finally, there is *Jherings Rechtsdenken* (edited by Okko Behrends, Gottingen, 1996), which is fuller still.

72. See preced. n.

73. Hallowell, *Main Currents*, p. 338.

74. *Ibid.*, pp. 338–340. Also p. 341: "In effect, Jellinek declares that the legality of an action depends not upon the content of an action but upon the *form* which it takes. Anything can be done if it is done in accordance with some prescribed legal procedure. . . . The limitation he envisages, therefore, is purely formal, technical and procedural. He recognizes no substantive limitations to the power of the State. Jellinek would agree with Laband when he declared that 'there is no idea which could not be made into a law.' Such a theory of the law and of the State would appear to be more congenial to despotism than to the preservation of freedom but the analytical jurists did not think so because they put their faith in procedural limitations. They could not, apparently, envisage a situation in which that procedure might be used to give an illiberal content to the law. . . . There can be rights against the State only when the individual and the State are both subordinated to the same order of law. But when the State is conceived as the source of law and hence above the law, there can be no rights against it. . . . 'Only as a member of the State,' Jellinek declared, '. . . is man the bearer of rights.' 'Personality,' in fact, he wrote, 'is *juris publici.*'"

75. *Ibid.*, p. 339 (with above quotations).

76. *Ibid.*, pp. 342–343: "Whereas, [*sic*] classical liberalism declared that the individual ought to be free from all *unjust* compulsion, the analytical jurists argue that an individual can claim freedom only from *illegal* compulsion. . . .

"In effect, the analytical jurist says that the legality of an action depends not upon the content of the action but upon the form of the action. . . . Such a theory, however much a jurist like Jellinek may have doubted it, and he did, prepares the way for despotism. With such a theory despotism may, indeed, be legislated into existence—as it was in Germany in 1933. The legislature may decide, as the German *Reichstag* did, to legislate itself out of existence and to adopt a new procedure for the enactment of legal prescriptions that dispenses with its services as a deliberative body altogether. If the State itself determines its own competency, the extent of its own power and the content of its own law, who, indeed, is to say that the State is wrong? By abolishing from jurisprudence all conceptions of right and wrong, justice and injustice, Jellinek and the other analytical jurists might consistently answer that the question is invalid and irrelevant. From *their* point of view the question is invalid and irrelevant; from the point of view of the classical liberals, however, the question is not only relevant but crucial.

"It is a short step from the conception of law as the product of the will of the state . . . to the notion that law is the command of the stronger."

77. Georg Jellinek, *Gesetz und Verordnung: Staatsrechtliche Untersuchungen auf Rechtsgeschichtlicher und Rechtsvergleichender Grundlage* (Freiburg, 1887).

78. *Ibid., Allgemeine Staatslehre* (Berlin, 1900, etc.).

Notes to Chapter IV
"Idealism" and "Hegelianism"

1. Secondary works of a general kind that connect Kant with Hegel under the topic of idealism include the following examples: Hallowell, *Main Currents*, Ch. 8, "Idealism," dealing at length first with Kant, then with Hegel, and finally with T. H. Green; Spahr, *Readings*, Ch. V, "German Idealism," presenting lengthy excerpts first from Kant and then from Hegel; and Eikema Hommes, *Major Trends*, Ch. VI, "The Ideal Rational Law ("Rederecht") of Rousseau, Kant, Fichte, and Hegel"; and Thilly and Wood, *History of Philosophy*, Ch. XVI, "The Critical Philosophy of Immanuel Kant," with sects. on "The Transcendental Method" and "Idealism...," together with Ch. XVII, "The Development of German Idealism" (Fichte, Hegel, etc.). Other books that concentrate at length on Kant with regard to the term "idealism" in their titles include: Wilhelm Metzger, *Gesellschaft, Recht und Staat in der Ethik des deutschen Idealismus* (edited by E. Bergmann, Heidelberg, 1917); Henry E. Allison, *Kant's Transcendental Idealism: An Interpretation and Defense* (New Haven, 1983) and ibid., *Idealism and Freedom: Essays on Kant's Theoretical and Practical Philosophy* (Cambridge, 1996), treating transcendental idealism in Pt. I on theoretical philosophy and freedom as well as obligatory ends in Pt. II on practical philosophy.

The following excerpts from Thilly and Wood (*op. cit.*, pp. 414–418, 423, 427–431, 437, 439–440) provide a useful overview here for purposes of introducing Kant's complex wider philosophy (with some references to notions of "thesis" and "antithesis" along with the four causes): "The fundamental problem for Kant is the problem of knowledge: What is knowledge, and how is it possible? What are the boundaries of human reason? In order to answer these questions, we must examine human reason, or subject it to criticism. Knowledge always appears in the form of judgments in which something is affirmed or denied.... Universality and necessity have their source not in sensation or perception, but in reason, in the understanding itself....

"Kant's claim, then, is that knowledge consists of synthetic a priori judgments. Analytic judgments are always a priori; we know without going to experience. . . . Kant's formulation of the transcendental method is perhaps the first attempt in modern philosophy to devise a distinctively philosophical method. Bacon, Hobbes, Descartes, and Leibniz before him were enthusiastic methodologists, but they were satisfied to adapt to philosophy methods already achieved by the special sciences, rather than to invent new and unique methods of philosophical inquiry. . . .

"The argument from experience to its necessary presuppositions is the crux of the transcendental method, and at this point Kant's procedure diverges widely from that of traditional empiricists. . . . The starting-point of the critical investigation is experience. . . . Experience is, to be sure, a notoriously ambiguous term for Kant and his Idealistic successors. . . .

"The analysis of experience proceeds in accordance with the traditional distinction between matter and form. . . . Form apparently embraces everything structural and relational in experience; matter pertains to the qualia subsumed under the forms. . . . The understanding by itself cannot intuit or perceive anything; the senses by themselves cannot think anything. Knowledge is possible only in the union of the two. The science of the rules of sensibility is called 'Transcendental Esthetic'; the science of the rules of the understanding is called 'Transcendental Analytic.'

"The understanding has different forms of conceiving, relating or connecting percepts; they are called pure concepts or categories of the understanding, because they are a priori and not derived from experience. The understanding expresses itself in judgment; indeed, understanding is a faculty of judgment: to think is to judge. . . . As has been pointed out, we cannot transcend our experience or have a priori knowledge of the supersensible, of things-in-themselves, of things as they are apart from the way they affect consciousness. Knowledge involves perception, but things-in-themselves cannot be perceived by the senses: in sense perception we know only the way things appear to consciousness, not what they are in themselves. . . .

"It is evident, therefore, that we cannot have universal and necessary or a priori knowledge of anything non-perceivable. Hence, we cannot have a metaphysics that transcends experience, a metaphysics of things-in-themselves, a metaphysics that can offer us genuine knowledge of a non-phenomenal world in which reside free will, immortality, and God. But we can have an a priori science of the phenomenal order. . . . His rejection of metaphysics is not, however, absolute and unqualified. There are several senses in which he regards metaphysics as possible. . . . [H]e rejects 'dogmatic' or speculative metaphysics of the kind advanced by his rationalistic predecessors. The understanding can know only what can be experienced; but reason strives to go beyond the confines of the understanding, and attempts to conceive the supersensible, that for which we have no objects in perception, that which is merely thought. . . . He calls the principles which are applied within the confines of possible experience *immanent* principles, those which transcend these limits *transcendent* principles, or concepts of reason, or *Ideas*. . . . Such Ideas, however, are transcendent, beyond experience: they can never be empirically fulfilled or exemplified. Thus, we can never represent the Idea of an absolute Totality in the form of an image; it is a problem without a solution. Yet these Ideas have their value and use as guides to the understanding; they lead it onward in its pursuit of knowledge; they are, in Kant's language, regulative rather than constitutive. . . . Though the transcendental Ideas produce an irresistible illusion, they are as natural to reason as are the categories to the understanding. . . . The transcendental Ideas have their immanent use in guiding inquiry, but when they are mistaken for concepts of real things, they are transcendent and deceptive in their application. . . .

"The Ideas of the reason, then, are not mere fictions of the mind but are highly useful, indeed necessary methodological ideals. . . .

398 / Notes to Chapter IV

"Human knowledge begins with percepts, proceeds to concepts, and ends with Ideas. It has a priori sources of knowledge with respect to all three elements. A complete criticism shows that reason, in its speculative use, can never go beyond the field of possible experience with respect to these elements. . . . Among the Ideas which reason applies in the contemplation of nature is the Idea of purpose, or the teleological Idea. This Idea Kant subjects to careful criticism in a separate work called *The Critique of Judgment*. . . . The understanding conceives every existent whole of nature solely as the effect of the concurrent moving forces of its parts. . . . Every part is both a means and an end and, in cooperating to make the whole possible, is determined by the Idea of the whole. . . . When so interpreted, the thesis invites us to seek for mechanical causes in material nature wherever possible; the antithesis, to search for final causes or purposes in certain cases . . ."

As for the legendary difficulty of Kant's philosophy in general, the present writer recalls the approach of James Ward Smith in his popular undergraduate survey course at Princeton on the history of modern philosophy. When he came to Kant, Professor Smith announced in the lecture hall that some of his colleagues had warned him that to include Kant in an introductory survey course "cannot be done" because of the difficulties involved. Whereupon Smith proceeded to hand out voluminous outlines and summaries to show that it *could* be done. These materials were gratefully received but did leave a lasting impression of the unique complexities involved. I remain grateful for his renowned inspired teaching long ago.

2. A recent reliable introduction to the textual traditions and terminological complexities of Kant's *The Metaphysics of Morals* (*Die Metaphysik der Sitten*) is found in the beginning of the version by Mary Gregor (transl. and ed., Cambridge, 1996). This version is based on a variety of previous German and English versions, particularly the German edn. by Paul Natorp in Vol. 6 (1907) of the German Academy of the Sciences edn. of Kant's collected works (*Gessamelte Schriften*, Berlin, 1900–) and the 1991 English version in the Cambridge Texts in German Philosophy series. Those and other twentieth-century versions at times vary significantly among themselves in relation to the earliest versions, both German and English, that were produced during Kant's lifetime. A problem has been that the second German edn. (1803)—published with changes soon after the first edn. (1797) and sometimes used in its place—apparently did not receive Kant's scrutiny, thereby complicating some subsequent English versions (the first being issued in 1799). Meanwhile, later published as a separate work, *The Doctrine of Right* has long been recognized as "corrupted" in certain parts and has been partly redone in the version of *Rechtslehre* edited by Bernd Ludwig (Hamburg, 1986), as detailed (but not adopted) by Gregor. The translation of Kant's *Doctrine of Right* by William Hastie in 1887 (Edinburgh), under the title *The Philosophy of Law: An Exposition of the Fundamental Principles of Jurisprudence as the Science of Right by Immanuel Kant* (repr. 1974), has numerous drawbacks and has been the source of some misinterpretation by the many scholars who have used it. The two halves of Kant's *Metaphysics of Morals* were issued about six months apart and hence gave impetus to the publications of *Rechtslehre* (inclusive of the subjects of *Staatsrecht* and *Staatslehre* in Pt. II of "Doctrine of Right") as a separate work.

Kant's (German) text is frequently interspersed with equivalent Latin terms in parentheses. These often show his extensive debt to and adaptation of Roman law (as well as e.g. Cicero). In the passages to follow, I have deleted a number of them where not sufficiently pertinent.

3. On "ideas" and "ideals" in Kant's philosophy, see this ch. nn. 1 (toward end of excerpts from Thilly and Wood, *op. cit.*) and 4 (in connection with Kant's *Critique of Pure Reason*).

"Idealism" / 399

4. In Kant's *Critique of Judgment* (translated by J. Bernard, New York, 1951), sects. IV and IX of the Intro. bear the respective titles "Of Judgment as a Faculty Legislating *a priori*" and "Of the Connection of the Legislation of Understanding with That of Reason by Means of the Judgment." The following statements in sect. IV are indicative: "Judgment in general is the faculty of thinking the particular as contained under the universal. If the universal (the rule, the principle, the law) be given, the judgment which subsumes the particular under it . . . is *determinant*. . . .

"The determinant judgment only subsumes under universal transcendental laws given by the understanding; the law is marked out for it, *a priori*, and it has therefore no need to seek a law for itself in order to be able to subordinate the particular in nature to the universal. But the forms of nature are so manifold, and there are so many modifications of the universal transcendental natural concepts left undetermined by the laws given, *a priori*, by the pure understanding . . . that there must be laws for these [forms] also. . . .

"Now the concept of an object, so far as it contains the ground of the actuality of this object, is the *purpose*; and the agreement of a thing with that constitution of things which is only possible according to purposes is called the *purposiveness* of its form. Thus the principle of judgment, in respect of the form of things of nature under empirical laws generally, is the *purposiveness of nature* in its variety."

Cf. e.g. John H. Zammito, *The Genesis of Kant's "Critique of Judgment"* (Chicago, 1992), esp. concerning Kant's influence on German idealism; and H. W. Cassirer, *A Commentary on Kant's "Critique of Judgment"* (New York, 1970, repr.), Ch. III, "The Critique of Teleological Judgment."

In his *Critique of Pure Reason* (translated by N. Smith, New York, 1933, 2nd edn.), Kant distinguishes at the outset (Intro. I) "between pure and empirical knowledge." Pts. I and II deal respectively with "Transcendental Doctrine of Elements" and "Transcendental Doctrine of Method." Kant's uses of such words as "idea," "ideal" (also "concept" and "category") are often not clearly distinguishable in meaning from each other. In Pt. I Kant discusses, for instance, "pure concepts of the understanding, or categories." Under "concepts of pure reason," he treats "the ideas in general" and "transcendental ideas." Elsewhere there, he treats "the ideals of pure reason," under which he discusses "the ideal in general" and "transcendental ideals." In Pt. II Kant deals with "the ideal of the highest good as a determining ground of the ultimate end of pure reason."

More generally, see W. H. Walsh, *Kant's Criticism of Metaphysics* (Edinburgh, 1975), dealing with "the necessity of categories," "the application of categories," and "reason and metaphysics"; and H. J. Paton, *Kant's Metaphysics of Experience*, Vol. I (London, 1936, etc.), esp. Bk. XII, "Transcendental Idealism."

5. Secondary works on Kant's political thought, in general, is voluminous. Examples include the following: Ulrich Sassenbach, *Der Begriff des Politischen bei Immanuel Kant* (Wurzburg, 1992), Pt. 3 on the state, but typically without focus on public legislation; Howard Williams, *Kant's Political Philosophy* (Oxford, 1983), with chs. on e.g. moral and political worlds, metaphysic of justice, property, contract, liberalism, philosophical foundations, authority, Marxism, and international peace (highest moral and political good), but not concerning public legislation; Hans Saner, *Kant's Political Thought: Its Origins and Development* (translated by E. Ashton, Chicago, 1973), centering on Kant's metaphysics in terms of polemics and peace-making; William James Booth, *Interpreting the World: Kant's Philosophy of History and Politics* (Toronto, 1986), esp. with regard to the place of the individual in a political and social community; Patrick Riley, *Kant's Political Philosophy* (Totowa, 1983); Aris Reinhold, *History of Political Thought in Germany from 1789 to 1815* (London, 1936), inclusive of Kant; R. Beiner and W. Booth (eds.), *Kant and Political Philosophy: The Contemporary Legacy* (New Haven, 1993); and Jeffrey G.

Murphy, *Kant: The Philosophy of Right* (LaSalle, 1970). Kant's political thought and particularly his Enlightenment belief that practical politics should be guided by reason, is seen as a key background to nineteenth-century German political thought (in terms of three "isms"—liberalism, romanticism, and conservatism) in Frederick C. Beiser's *Enlightenment, Revolution, and Romanticism: The Genesis of Modern German Political Thought, 1790–1800* (Camb., Mass., 1992).

Among the multitudinous secondary studies dealing with Kant's legal thought are the following examples: Allen D. Rosen, *Kant's Theory of Justice* (Ithaca, 1993), with Ch. 3, "Types of Rights, Duties, and Laws," touching briefly on topics concerning legislation; *Philosophie und Rechtswissenschaft: Zum Problem ihrer Beziehung im 19. Jahrhundert*, edited by J. Blüdorn and J. Ritter (Frankfurt, 1969), Pt. A on Kant's influence on nineteenth-century ideas of civil and criminal law, *Staatsrecht*, and *Staatslehre*, while Pt. B contains discussions particularly on "system" and with regard to humanist jurisprudence, Kant, Savigny, and Jhering; Eggert Winter, *Ethik und Rechtswissenschaft* (Berlin, 1980), with some preliminary discussions on Kant; Gerhard Dulckeit, *Naturrecht und positives Recht bei Kant* (Aalen, 1973); and Ernst J. Weinrib, "Law as a Kantian Idea of Reason," *Columbia Law Rev.*, LXXXVII (1987).

Concentrating generally on Kant's ideas relating to state and society are e.g. Richard Saage, *Eigentum, Staat und Gesellschaft bei Immanuel Kant* (Stuttgart, 1973), including materials on state forms and constitutions; Kurt Borries, *Kant als Politiker: Zur Staats- und Gesellschaftslehre des Kritizismus* (Leipzig, 1928); Gottfried Dietze, *Kant und der Rechtsstaat* (Tubingen, 1982); George Peabody Gooch, "German Views of the State," in *The German Mind and Outlook* (edited by Gooch, etc., London, 1945); and Metzger, *Gesellschaft und Staat*.

Among the specific themes in Kant's political thought that have been singled out for study in recent decades are property, political judgment, morality, the republican constitution, the French Revolution, rejection of rebellion, obedience to government, and so on. Various recent issues of *History of Political Thought* have carried pieces on Kant: XVII (1996), pp. 379–407, "Values behind the Market: Kant's Response to the *Wealth of Nations*," by Samuel Fleischacker; XIV (1993), pp. 103–132, "Kant's Judgment on Frederick's Enlightened Absolutism," by Georg Cavallar ("Kant devalues reformed Enlightened Absolutism to a mere transitory phase in this process toward republicanism [p. 104]"); and X (1989), pp. 719–731, "Kant's Theory of Political Authority," by Craig L. Carr, with regard to justice, freedom, coercion, Hobbes, etc., in *Metaphysical Elements of Justice* (translated by J. Ladd, Phila., 1965). Again, however, legislation has been little appreciated as a central subject in its own right for Kant.

6. Kant, *Metaphysics of Morals*, Preface: "The critique of *practical* reason was to be followed by a system, the metaphysics of morals, which falls into metaphysical first principles of the *doctrine of right* and metaphysical first principles of the *doctrine of virtue*. . . .

"For the doctrine of right, the first part of the doctrine of morals, there is required a system derived from reason which could be called the *metaphysics of right*. But since the concept of right is a pure concept that still looks to practice (application to cases that come up in experience), a *metaphysical system* of right would also have to take account, in its divisions, of the empirical variety of such cases, in order to make its division complete (as is essential in cosntructing a system of reason)."

Ibid., Introduction (to the work as a whole), sects. I–III: "It has been shown elsewhere that for natural science, which has to do with objects of outer sense, one must have *a priori* principles and that it is possible, indeed necessary, to prefix a system of these principles, called a metaphysical science of nature, to natural science applied to particular experiences, that is, to physics. . . .

"But it is different with moral laws. They hold as laws only insofar as they can be *seen* to have an *a priori* basis and to be necessary. . . .

"If the doctrine of morals were merely the doctrine of happiness it would be absurd to seek *a priori* principles for it. . . .

"If, therefore, a system of *a priori* cognition from concepts alone is called *metaphysics*, a practical philosophy, which has not nature but freedom of choice for its object, will presuppose and require a metaphysics of morals, that is, it is itself a *duty to have* such a metaphysics, and every human being also has it within himself, though in general only in an obscure way; for without *a priori* principles how could he believe that he has a giving of universal law within himself? . . .

"The counterpart of a metaphysics of morals, the other member of the division of practical philosophy as a whole, would be moral anthropology. . . .

"As for the higher division under which the division just mentioned falls, namely that of philosophy into theoretical and practical philosophy, I have already explained myself elsewhere (in the *Critique of Judgment*), and I have explained that practical philosophy can be none other than moral wisdom. . . . Hence philosophy can understand by its practical part (as compared with its theoretical part) no *technically practical* doctrine but only a *morally practical* doctrine; and if the proficiency of choice in accordance with laws of freedom, in contrast to laws of nature, is also to be called *art* here, by this would have to be understood a kind of art that makes possible a system of freedom like a system of nature, truly a divine art. . . .

"In contrast to laws of nature, laws of freedom are called *moral* laws. As directed merely to external actions and their conformity to law they are called *juridical* laws. . . .

"The concept of *freedom* is a pure rational concept, which for this very reason is transcendent for theoretical philosophy, that is, it is a concept such that no instance corresponding to it can be given in any possible experience, and of an object of which we cannot obtain any theoretical cognition: the concept of freedom cannot hold as a constitutive but solely as a regulative and, indeed, merely negative principle of speculative reason. . . .

"On this concept of freedom, which is positive (from a practical point of view), are based unconditional practical laws, which are called *moral*. For us, whose choice is sensibly affected and so does not of itself conform to the pure will but often opposes it, moral laws are imperatives (commands or prohibitions) and indeed categorical (unconditional) imperatives. As such they are distinguished from technical imperatives (precepts of art), which always command only conditionally. By categorical imperatives certain actions are *permitted* or *forbidden*, that is, morally possible or impossible. . . .

"The following concepts are common to both parts of *The Metaphysics of Morals*.

"*Obligation* is the necessity of a free action under a categorical imperative of reason.

"An imperative is a practical rule by which an action in itself contingent is *made* necessary. An imperative differs from a practical law. . . .

"*Duty* is that action to which someone is bound. . . .

"A categorical imperative, because it asserts an obligation with respect to certain actions, is a morally practical *law* . . . that either commands or prohibits . . ."

7. *Ibid.*, Intro. (to the work as a whole), sects. III–IV.

8. *Ibid.*, Preface to Pt. II, "Doctrine of Virtue": "A *philosophy* of any subject (a system of rational knowledge from concepts) requires a system of *pure rational* concepts independent of any conditions of intuition, that is, a *metaphysics*. — The only question is whether every *practical* philosophy, as a doctrine of duties, and so too the *doctrine of virtue* (ethics), also needs *metaphysical first principles*, so that it can be set forth as a genuine science (systematically) and not merely as an aggregate of precepts sought out one by one (fragmentarily). — No one will doubt that the pure doctrine of right needs metaphysical first principles; for it has to do only with the *formal condition* of choice that

is to be limited in external relations in accordance with laws of freedom, without regard for any *end* (the matter of choice). Here the doctrine of duties is, accordingly, a mere *scientific doctrine*. . . .

"But in this philosophy (the doctrine of virtue) it seems directly contrary to the idea of it to go all the way back to *metaphysical first principles*, so as to make the concept of duty, though purified of anything empirical (any feeling), the incentive."

9. From here on, it is sufficient for purposes of citation in our main text to rely mostly on the divisions of Kant's *Metaphysics of Morals* as there given, so as to avoid needless duplications of citations in unnecessary corresponding notes.

10. Further pertinent discussion on public distributive justice and law in Pt. I of "Doctrine of Right" in Kant's *Metaphysics of Morals* appears in Ch. III ("On Acquisition That Is Dependent Subjectively upon the Decision of a Public Court of Justice"—§ 36, 39, 42): "If by natural right is understood only non-statutory right, hence simply right that can be cognized *a priori* by everyone's reason, natural right will include not only the *justice* that holds among persons in their exchanges with one another . . . but also distributive justice (*iustitia distributiva*), insofar as it can be cognized *a priori* in accordance with the principle of distributive justice how its decisions (*sententia*) would have to be reached.

"The moral person that administers justice is a *court (forum)* and its administration of justice is a *judgment (iudicium)*. . . .

"Here again reason giving laws with regard to rights comes forth with a principle of *distributive justice*, of adopting as its guiding rule for the legitimacy of possession, not the way it would be judged *in itself* by the private will of each (in the state of nature), but the way it would be judged before a *court* in a condition brought about by the united will of all (in a civil condition). . . .

"From private right in the state of nature there proceeds the postulate of public right: when you cannot avoid living side by side with all others, you ought to leave the state of nature and proceed with them into a rightful condition, that is, a condition of distributive justice. — The ground of this postulate can be explicated analytically from the concept of *right* in external relations, in contrast with *violence* . . ."

11. Kant, *Metaphysics of Morals*, "Doctrine of Right," Pt. II, Ch. II (§ 53–55, 57, 61): "The right of *states* in relation to one another (which in German is called, not quite correctly, the *right of nations*, but should instead be called the right of states, *ius publicum civitatum*) is what we have to consider under the title the right of nations. Here a state, as a moral person, is considered as living in relation to another state in the condition of natural freedom and therefore in a condition of constant war. . . . In this problem the only difference between the state of nature of individual men and of families (in relation to one another) and that of nations is that in the right of nations we have to take into consideration not only the relation of one state toward another as a whole, but also the relation of individual persons of one state toward the individuals of another, as well as toward another state as a whole. . . .

"The elements of the right of nations are these: (1) states, considered in external relation to one another, are (like lawless savages) by nature in a non-rightful condition. (2) This non-rightful condition is a *condition* of war (of the right of the stronger). . . . (3) A league of nations in accordance with the idea of an original social contract is necessary . . . to protect against attacks from without. (4) This alliance must, however, involve no sovereign authority (as in a civil constitution). . . .

"[C]itizens of a state . . . must always be regarded as co-legislating members of a state (not merely as means, but also as ends in themselves), and must therefore give their free assent, through their representatives, not only to waging war in general but also to each particular declaration of war. . . .

"The greatest difficulty in the right of nations has to do precisely with right during a war; it is difficult even to form a concept of this or to think of law in this lawless state without contradicting oneself. . . . [Cicero, *Pro Milone*, IV, 10]. . . .

"Since a state of nature among nations, like a state of nature among individual human beings, is a condition that one ought to leave in order to enter a lawful condition, before this happens any rights of nations, and anything external that is mine or yours which states can acquire or retain by war, are merely *provisional*. Only in a universal *association of states* (analogous to that by which a people becomes a state) can rights come to hold *conclusively* and a true *condition of peace* come about. . . . So *perpetual peace*, the ultimate goal of the whole right of nations, is indeed an unachievable idea. Still, the political principles directed toward perpetual peace, of entering into such alliances of states, which serve for continual *approximation* to it, are not unachievable. . . .

"Such an *association* of several *states* to preserve peace can be called a *permanent congress of states*, which each neighboring state is at liberty to join."

12. *Ibid.*, "Doctrine of Right," Pt. II, Ch. III (§ 62) and Conclusion: "This rational idea of a *peaceful*, even if not friendly, thoroughgoing community of all nations on the earth that can come into relations affecting one another is not a philanthropic (ethical) principle but a principle *having to do with rights*. . . .

"It can be said that establishing universal and lasting peace constitutes not merely a part of the doctrine of right but rather the entire final end of the doctrine of right within the limits of reason alone; for the condition of peace is the only condition in which what is mine and what is yours are secured under *laws* for a multitude of human beings living in proximity to one another and therefore under a constitution. But the rule for this constitution, as a norm for others, cannot be derived from the experience of those who have hitherto found it most to their advantage; it must, rather, be derived *a priori* by reason, from the ideal of a rightful association of human beings under public laws as such. For all examples (which only illustrate but cannot prove anything) are treacherous, so that they certainly require a metaphysics. Even those who ridicule metaphysics admit its necessity, though carelessly, when they say for example, as they often do, 'the best constitution is that in which power belongs not to men but to the laws.' For what can be more metaphysically sublimated than this very idea, which even according to their own assertion has the most confirmed objective reality, as can also be easily shown in actually occurring cases? The attempt to realize this idea should not be made by way of revolution, by a leap, that is, by violent overthrow of an already existing defective constitution (for there would then be an intervening moment in which any rightful condition would be annihilated). But if it is attempted and carried out by gradual reform in accordance with firm principles, it can lead to continual approximation to the highest political good, perpetual peace."

13. *Ibid.*, "Doctrine of Right," Pt. II, Ch. I, (§ 48–49): "Accordingly, the three authorities in a state are, *first*, coordinate with one another . . . as so many moral persons, that is, each complements the others to complete the constitution of a state. . . . But, *second*, they are also *subordinate* . . . to one another, so that one of them, in assisting another, cannot also usurp its function; instead, each has its own principle, that is, it indeed commands in its capacity as a particular person, but still under the condition of the will of a superior. *Third*, through the union of both each subject is apportioned his rights.

"It can be said of these authorities, regarded in their dignity, that the will of the *legislator* (*legislatoris*) with regard to what is externally mine or yours is *irreproachable* . . . ; that the executive power of the *supreme ruler* (*summi rectoris*) is *irresistible*; and that the verdict of the highest *judge* . . . is *irreversible* (cannot be appealed).

"The *ruler* of a state (*rex, princeps*) is that (Moral or natural) person to whom the executive authority (*potestas executoria*) belongs. He is the *agent* of the state, who appoints the magistrates and prescribes to the people rules in accordance with which each of them can acquire something or preserve what is his in conformity with the law (through subsumption of a case under it). Regarded as a moral person, he is called the *directorate*, the government. His *directives* to the people, and to the magistrates and their superior (the minister) whom he charges with *administering the state* (*gubernatio*), are ordinances or *decrees* (not laws); for they are directed to decisions in particular cases and are given as subject to being changed. A *government* that was also legislative would have to be called a *despotic* as opposed to a *patriotic* government; but by a patriotic government is understood not a *paternalistic* one . . . , which is the most despotic of all (since it treats citizens as children), but one *serving the native land*. . . . In it the state (*civitas*) does treat its subjects as members of one family but it also treats them as citizens of the state, that is, in accordance with laws of their own independence: each is in possession of himself and is not dependent upon the absolute will of another alongside him or above him.

"So a people's sovereign (legislator) cannot also be its *ruler*, since the ruler is subject to the law and so is put under obligation through the law by *another*, namely the sovereign. The sovereign can also take the ruler's authority away from him, depose him, or reform his administration. But it cannot *punish* him . . . for punishment is, again, an act of the executive authority, which has the supreme capacity to *exercise coercion* in conformity with the law. . . .

"Finally, neither the head of state nor its ruler can *judge*, but can only appoint judges as magistrates. . . .

"There are thus three distinct authorities (*potestas legislatoria, executoria, iudiciaria*) by which a state (*civitas*) has its autonomy, that is, by which it forms and preserves itself in accordance with laws of freedom. — A state's *well-being* consists in their being united (*salus rei publicae suprema lex est* [Cicero, *De legibus* III, 8]). By the well-being of a state must not be understood the *welfare* of its citizens and their *happiness*; for happiness can perhaps come to them more easily and as they would like it to in a state of nature (as Rousseau asserts) or even under a despotic government."

14. *Ibid.*, "Doctrine of Right," Pt. II, Ch. I (§ 51–52): "The three authorities in a state, which arise from the concept of a *commonwealth* as such (*res publica latius dicta*), are only the three relations of the united will of the people, which is derived *a priori* from reason. They are a pure idea of a head of state, which has objective practical reality. But this head of state (the sovereign) is only a *thought-entity* (to represent the entire people) as long as there is no physical person to represent the supreme authority in the state and to make this idea effective on the people's will. . . . In other words, the *form of a state* is either *autocratic, aristocratic,* or *democratic*. (The . . . autocrat is the sovereign, whereas the monarch merely represents the sovereign.) — It is easy to see that the autocratic form of state is the *simplest*, namely the relation of one (the king) to the people, so that only one is legislator. The aristocratic form of state is already *composed* of two relations: the relation of the nobility (as legislator) to one another, to constitute the sovereign, and then the relation of this sovereign to the people. But the democratic form of state is the most composite of all. . . . It is true that . . . the simplest form is also the best. With regard to right itself, however, this form of state is the most dangerous for a people, in view of how conducive it is to despotism. . . .

"The different forms of states are on the *letter* (*littera*) of the original legislation in the civil state, and they may therefore remain as long as they are taken, by old and long-standing custom (and so only subjectively), to belong necessarily to the machinery of the constitution."

15. *Ibid.*, "Doctrine of Right," Pt. II, Ch. I (§ 49, in "General Remark On the Effects with Regard to Rights That Follow from the Nature of the Civil Union," sect. A): "A peo-

ple should not *inquire* with any practical aim in view into the origin of the supreme authority to which it is subject, that is, a subject *ought not to reason subtly* for the sake of action about the origin of this authority, as a right that can still be called into question . . . with regard to the obedience he owes it. . . . Whether a state began with an actual contract of submission . . . as a fact, or whether power came first and law arrived only afterwards, or even whether they should have followed in this order: for a people already subject to civil law these subtle reasonings are altogether pointless and, moreover, threaten a state with danger. . . . A law that is so holy (inviolable) that it is already a crime even to call it in doubt *in a practical way*, and so to suspend its effect for a moment, is thought as if it must have arisen not from human beings but from some highest, flawless lawgiver; and that is what the saying 'All authority is from God' means. This saying is not an assertion about the *historical basis* of the civil constitution; it instead sets forth an idea as a practical principle of reason: the principle that the presently existing legislative authority ought to be obeyed, whatever its origin. . . .

"Therefore a people cannot offer any resistance to the legislative head of a state which would be consistent with right, since a rightful condition is possible only by submission to its general legislative will. There is, therefore, no right to *sedition* . . . , still less to *rebellion* . . . , and least of all is there a right against the head of a state as an individual person (the monarch). . . . The reason a people has a duty to put up with even what is held to be an unbearable abuse of supreme authority is that its resistance to the highest legislation can never be regarded as other than contrary to law, and indeed as abolishing the entire legal constitution. For a people to be authorized to resist, there would have to be a public law permitting it to resist, that is, the highest legislation would have to contain a provision that it is not the highest and that makes the people, as subject, by one and the same judgment sovereign over him to whom it is subject. . . .

"A change in a (defective) constitution, which may certainly be necessary at times, can therefore be carried out only through *reform* by the sovereign itself, but not by the people, and therefore not by *revolution*; and when such a change takes place this reform can affect only the *executive authority*, not the legislative. — In what is called a limited constitution, the constitution contains a provision that the people can legally *resist* the executive authority and its representative (the minister) by means of its representatives (in parliament). Nevertheless, no active resistance (by the people combining at will to coerce the government to take a certain course of action, and so itself performing an act of executive authority) is permitted, but only *negative* resistance. . . .

"Moreover, once a revolution has succeeded and a new constitution has been established, the lack of legitimacy with which it began and has been implemented cannot release the subjects from the obligation to comply with the new order of things as good citizens, and they cannot refuse honest obedience to the authority that now has the power."

Ibid., Appendix (to "The Doctrine of Right"), "Explanatory Remarks on The Metaphysical First Principles of the Doctrine of Right," "Conclusion": "If then a people united by laws under an authority exists, it is given as an object of experience in conformity with the idea of the unity of a people *as such* under a powerful supreme will, though it is indeed given only in appearance, that is, a rightful constitution in the general sense of the term exists. And even though this constitution may be afflicted with great defects and gross faults and be in need eventually of important improvements, it is still absolutely unpermitted and punishable to resist it. For if the people should hold that it is justified in opposing force to this constitution, however faulty, and to the supreme authority, it would think that it had the right to put force in place of the supreme legislation that prescribes all rights, which would result in a supreme will that destroys itself.

"The *idea* of a civil constitution as such, which is also an absolute command that practical reason, judging according to concepts of right, gives to every people, is *sacred* and irresistible. And even if the organization of a state should be faulty by itself, no subordinate authority in it may actively resist its legislative supreme authority; the defects attached to it must instead be gradually removed by reforms the state itself carries out. . . . [T]he authority which already exists, under which you live, is already in possession of legislative authority, and though you can indeed reason publicly about its legislation, you cannot set yourself up as an opposing legislator."

It is not necessary here to cite the scattered references, direct and indirect, to Rousseau and Louis XVI in Kant's "Doctrine of Right." Nevertheless, the following passage—which concludes Ch. I (§ 52) on "The Right of a State" in Pt. II on "Public Right" in *Metaphysics of Morals*—presents the whole issue of the overthrow of Louis XVI in contexts of legislative sovereignty in the state: "A powerful ruler in our time [Louis XVI] therefore made a very serious error in judgment when, to extricate himself from the embarrassment of large state debts, he left it to the people to take this burden on itself and distribute it as it saw fit; for then the legislative authority naturally came into the people's hands, not only with regard to the taxation of subjects but also with regard to the government, namely to prevent it from incurring new debts by extravagance or war. The consequence was that the monarch's sovereignty [*Herrschergewalt*] wholly disappeared (it was not merely suspended) and passed to the people, to whose legislative will the belongings of every subject became subjected. Nor can it be said that in this case one must assume a tacit but still contractual promise of the National Assembly not to make itself the sovereign but only to administer this business of the sovereign and, having attended to it, return the reins of government into the monarch's hands; for such a contract is in itself null and void. The right of supreme legislation in a commonwealth is not an alienable right but the most personal of all rights. Whoever has it can control the people only through the collective will of the people; he cannot control the collective will itself, which is the ultimate basis of any public contract. A contract that would impose obligation on the people to give back its authority would not be incumbent upon the people as the legislative power, yet would still be binding upon it; and this is a contradiction, in accordance with the saying 'No one can serve two masters.' "

Further contexts of Kant's ascriptions of great inviolable power to sovereigns and commanders in the state in matters of civil law and even reason of state occur in *ibid.*, Ch. I on "The Right of a State," in Pt. II of "Doctrine of Right" (§ 49, "General Remark," sects. B–C): "Can the sovereign [*Beherrscher*] be regarded as the supreme proprietor (of the land), or must he be regarded only as the one who has supreme command over the people by law? Since the land is the ultimate condition that alone makes it possible to have external things as one's own, and the first right that can be acquired is possession and use of such things, all such rights must be derived from the sovereign as *lord of the land*, or better, as the supreme proprietor of it. . . . The people, the multitude of subjects, also belong to him (they are his people). But they belong to him not as if he owned them (by a right to things); they instead belong to him as their supreme commander [*Oberbefehlshober*] (by a right against persons). — This supreme proprietorship is, however, only an idea of the civil union. . . .

"To the supreme commander there belongs *indirectly*, that is, insofar as he has taken over the duty of the people, the right to impose taxes on the people for its own preservation. . . .

"The general will of the people has united itself into a society which is to maintain itself perpetually; and for this end it has submitted itself to the internal authority of the state in order to maintain those members of the society who are unable to maintain themselves. For reasons of state the government is therefore authorized to constrain the wealthy to provide the means of sustenance to those who are unable to provide for even their most necessary natural needs."

Finally, when criticizing at length Beccaria's arguments against capital punishment, Kant once again dwells on various legislative factors (in the same "General Remark," sect. E, "On the Right to Punish and to Grant Clemency," sect. I). Kant was, of course, strongly in favor of the death penalty for diverse kinds of resistance to authority.

16. The following further illustrative passages concerning legislation, sovereignty, the state, causation, etc., are from *Kant: Political Writings*, edited by Hans Reiss and translated by H. B. Nisbett (2nd edn., Cambridge, 1991).

(1.) *Idea for a Universal History with a Cosmopolitan Purpose*, Seventh Proposition, pp. 47–48: "*The problem of establishing a perfect civil constitution is subordinate to the problem of a law-governed external relationship with other states, and cannot be solved unless the latter is also solved.* What is the use of working for a law-governed civil constitution among individual men, i.e. of planning a *commonwealth?* The same unsociability which forced men to do so gives rise . . . to . . . unrestricted freedom. . . .

"Whether we should firstly expect that the states, by an Epicurean concourse of efficient causes, should enter by random collisions (like those of small material particles) into all kinds of formations which are again destroyed by new collisions, until they arrive *by chance* at a formation which can survive in its existing form (a lucky accident which is hardly likely ever to occur) . . ."

(2.) *On the Common Saying: "This May Be True in Theory, But It Does Not Apply to Practice,"* Sect. I, pp. 65–66: "[T]he general concept of duty . . . acquires an *object* in the shape of an ideal of pure reason. [Note: The necessity of assuming as the ultimate end of all things a *highest good* on earth, which it is possible to achieve with our collaboration, is not a necessity created by a lack of moral incentives, but by a lack of external circumstances within which an object appropriate to these incentives can alone be produced as an end in itself, as an *ultimate moral end*. For there can be no *will* without an end in view, although we must abstract from this end whenever the question of straightforward legal compulsion of our deeds arise . . ."] For in itself, duty is nothing more than a *limitation* of the will within a universal legislation which was made possible by an initially accepted maxim."

(3.) *Ibid.*, Sect. II, "On the Relationship of Theory to Practice in Political Right (Against Hobbes)," pp. 73, 77–81: "And the end which is a duty in itself in such external relationships, and which is indeed the highest formal condition . . . of all other external duties, is the *right* of men *under coercive public laws* by which each can be given what is due to him. . . . And *public right* is the distinctive quality of the *external laws* which make this constant harmony possible. Since every restriction of freedom through the arbitrary will of another party is termed *coercion*, it follows that a civil constitution is a relationship among *free* men who are subject to coercive laws, while they retain their freedom within the general union with their fellows. Such is the requirement of pure reason, which legislates *a priori*, regardless of all empirical ends (which can all be summed up under the general heading of happiness). . . .

"Anyone who has the right to vote on this legislation is a *citizen (citoyen*, i.e. citizen of a state . . .). . . .

"Those who possess this right to vote must agree *unanimously* to the law of public justice, or else a legal contention would arise between those who agree and those who disagree. . . .

"This, then, is an *original contract* by means of which a civil and thus completely lawful constitution and commonwealth can alone be established. But we need by no means assume that this contract . . . based on a coalition of the wills of all private individuals in a nation to form a common, public will for the purposes of rightful legislation, actually exists as a *fact*, for it cannot possibly be so. . . . It is in fact merely an *idea* of reason, which nonetheless has undoubted practical reality; for it can oblige every legislator to frame his laws in such a way that they could have been produced by the united will of a whole nation. . . . For we are not concerned here with any happiness which the subject might expect to derive from the institutions or administration of the commonwealth, but primarily with the rights which would thereby be secured for everyone. And this is the highest principle from which all maxims relating to the commonwealth must begin. . . . No generally valid principle of legislation can be based on happiness. . . . The doctrine that *salus publica suprema civitatis lex est* retains its value and authority undiminished; but the public welfare which demands *first* consideration lies precisely in that legal constitution which guarantees everyone his freedom within the law, so that each remains free to seek his happiness in whatever way he thinks best, so long as he does not violate the lawful freedom and rights of his fellow subjects at large. If the supreme power makes laws which are primarily directed towards happiness . . . , this cannot be regarded as the end for which a civil constitution was established, but only as a means of *securing the rightful state*. . . .

"It thus follows that all resistance against the supreme legislative power, all incitement of the subjects to violent expressions of discontent, . . . is the greatest and most punishable crime in a commonwealth, for it destroys its very foundations. This prohibition is *absolute*. And even if the power of the state or its agent, the head of state, has violated the original contract by authorising the government to act tyrannically, and has thereby, in the eyes of the subject, forfeited the right to legislate, the subject is still not entitled to offer counterresistance."

(4.) *Perpetual Peace*, Appendix II, Sect. II, "On the Agreement between Politics and Morality According to the Transcendental Concept of Public Right," p. 125: "If in considering public right as the jurists usually conceive of it, I abstract from all its *material* aspects (as determined by the various empirically given relationships of men within a state, or of states with one another), I am left with the *formal attribute of publicness*. For every claim upon right potentially possesses this attribute, and without it, there can be no justice (which can only be conceived of as *publicly knowable*) and therefore no right, since right can only come from justice.

"Every claim upon right must have this public quality. . . . [I]t provides us with a readily applicable criterion which can be discovered *a priori* within reason itself. If it cannot be reconciled with the agent's principles, it enables us to recognise at once the falseness (i.e. unrightfulness) of the claim . . . in question, as if by an experiment of pure reason."

(5.) *Critique of Pure Reason*, Appendix ("Transcendental Logic," II, "Dialectic," I, 1: "Of Ideas in General"), p. 191: "A constitution allowing the *greatest possible human freedom* in accordance with laws which ensure *that the freedom of each can co-exist with the freedom of all the others* (not one designed to provide the greatest possible happiness, as this will in any case follow automatically), is at all events a necessary idea which must be made the basis not only of the first outline of a political constitution but of all laws as well. It requires that we should abstract at the outset from present hindrances, which . . . are . . . occasioned by neglect of genuine ideas in the process of legislation. . . . The more closely the legislation and government were made to harmonise with this idea, the rarer punishments would become, and it is thus quite rational to maintain (as Plato does) that none would be necessary at all in a perfect state. Even if the latter should never come about, the idea which sets up this maximum as an archetype, in order to bring the legal constitution of mankind nearer and nearer to its greatest possible perfection, still remains correct."

In excerpt #1, law is clearly the foundation of the state or commonwealth with respect to its civil constitution. This basis provides the framework for relationships between states. Efficient and formal causation also enters into Kant's discussions.

In excerpt #2, the elements of duty and universal legislation are wrapped up with considerations of final causation and the necessity of highest good.

In excerpt #3, when refuting Hobbes, Kant interconnects the higher public right with coercive public legislation as the bases of the state or commonwealth and its civil constitution as regards duties and the final cause or end. Here, pure reason itself legislates as well. Strikingly, citizenship in a state is also defined along legislative lines. The ideals of public will, public justice, and public legislation, as ideas of pure reason with practical applications, should act as models for actual legislators in a nation-state. Public welfare rather than individual happiness is not only the true end or final cause but embodies a system of rights through legislation in the rightful state. In these contexts, the sovereignty of the legislator is what gives primary orientation to Kant's prohibition against rebellion and approval of original contract.

In excerpt #4, distinguishing as usual between rationally-based ideals and empirically-based actualities, Kant squarely plants justice and right upon the public basis of a state, consistent with *a priori* reason and its practical applications. The sect. title connecting politics and morality to transcendental public right epitomizes a key aim of Kant.

In excerpt #5, Kant links the freedom as well as happiness of each individual to the proper legislative process and its publicly oriented laws. He promotes a kind of Platonic idealism with respect to the laws that form the groundwork of the state. (It will be remembered from materials in our previous vols. that various ancient writers like Plato and Cicero depicted laws as the sinews of the state.)

17. The fuller original double title of Hegel's *Philosophy of Right* was *Naturrecht und Staatswissenschaft im Grundrisse* and *Grundlinien der Philosophie des Rechts (Natural Law and Political Science in Outline; Elements of the Philosophy of Right)*, published in 1821. The version of the *Elements of the Philosophy of Right* by Allen W. Wood and H. B. Nisbet (transl. and ed., Cambridge, 1991) gives the correct date of 1821 on p. xxxiv; but on the opposite page (xxxv) it is given as 1820, under the title *Rechtsphilosophie*, in the context of its repro. in Vol. VII of Hegel's *Werke*, edited by E. Moldenhauer and K. Michel (Frankfurt, 1970). On the correctness of the 1821 dating, cf. e.g. the version of *Philosophy of Right* by T. M. Knox (transl., Oxford, 1952, etc.), p. v (n.).

Here, as in the case of our preceding citations of Kant, the references in our main text to Hegel's own sectional and subsectional divisions will largely suffice, in lieu of duplicated citations in unnecessary corresponding notes. In general, I have relied on the Wood-Nisbet version.

18. On Hegel's views on the state, cf. e.g. Sabine, *History of Political Theory*, Ch. XXX on Hegel (centering in large part on nationalism esp. regarding the state); Shlomo Avineti, *Hegel's Theory of the Modern State* (Cambridge, 1972); Michael Mitias, *The Moral Foundation of the State in Hegel's "Philosophy of Right"* (Amsterdam, 1984); Franz Rosenzweig, *Hegel und der Staat* (2 vols., Munich, 1920); Ernst Cassirer, *The Myth of the State* (transl., Garden City, 1955); J. D. Mabbott, *The State and the Citizen: An Introduction to Political Philosophy* (London, 1948, 1952, etc.), Ch. V, "Hegel and the Hegelians" (with preceding chs. on Hobbes, Locke, and Rousseau); Joannes Mattern, *Concepts of State, Sovereignty and International Law: With Special Reference to the Juristic Conception of the State* (Baltimore, 1928), Ch. IV, "The Theories of Kant, Hegel, and Fichte" (with Ch. I on "Bodin's Theory of Sovereignty" and Ch. V on "The Austinian or Analytical School"); and Charles Taylor, *Hegel* (Cambridge, 1975, etc.), Pt. IV, Ch. XVI, "The Realized State."

Concerning aspects of Hegel's political thought more generally, there is e.g. Bernard Cullen, *Hegel's Social and Political Thought* (New York, 1979); Eugène Fleischmann, *La philosophie politique de Hegel* (Paris, 1964); Hans-Friedrich Fulda, *Das Recht der Philosophie in Hegels Philosophie des Rechts* (Frankfurt, 1968); Charles Taylor, *Hegel and Modern Society* (Cambridge, 1979); Reinhart Albrecht, *Hegel und die Demokratie* (Bonn, 1978); Laurence Dickey, *Hegel: Religion, Economics, and the Politics of Spirit, 1770–1807* (New York, 1987), regarding Hegel's early intellectual development; *Hegel's Philosophie des Rechts: Die Theorie der Rechtsformen und ihre Logik*, edited by D. Henrich and R.-P. Horstmann (Stuttgart, 1982), Pts. I–II; *Hegel's Social and Political Thought: The Philosophy of Objective Spirit*, edited by D. Verene (Sussex, 1980), "Hegel's Theory of Sovereignty," pp. 137 ff.; Mark Tunick, *Hegel's Political Philosophy: Interpreting the Practice of Legal Punishment* (Princeton, 1992), regarding Hegel's *Philosophy of Right* as practical theory; A. Biral et al., *Per una storia del moderno concetto di politica: Genesi e sviuppo della separazione tra "politico" e "sociale"* (Padua, 1977), with sects. on Hegel, Kant, etc.; and Patrick T. Murray, *Hegel's Philosophy of Mind and Will* (Queenstown, 1991). Also, see articles on Hegel in several recent issues of *Hist. of Pol. Tht.*: XVII (1996), by Robert Bruce Ware, pp. 253 ff., "Hegel's Metaphilosophy and Historical Metamorphosis"; XIII (1992), by Kenneth Kierans, pp. 417 ff., "The Concept of Ethical Life in Hegel's *Philosophy of Right*"; XII (1991), by Zdravko Planinc, pp. 305 ff., "Family and Civil Society in Hegel's *Philosophy of Right*"; and XII (1991), by Mark Tunick, pp. 482 ff., "Hegel's Justification of Hereditary Monarchy."

19. On Hegel in relation to Plato, cf. e.g. Huntington Cairns, *Legal Philosophy from Plato to Hegel* (Baltimore, 1949); Gary K. Browning, *Plato and Hegel: Two Modes of Philosophizing about Politics* (London, 1991), stressing the importance of Hegel's philosophical method for an understanding of his political thought; *ibid.*, "The Night in which All Cows Are Black: Ethical Absolutism in Plato and Hegel," *Hist. of Pol. Tht.*, XII, pp. 392 ff., with interesting treatment of the "ism" in that title; and Michael B. Foster, *The Political Philosophies of Plato and Hegel* (New York, 1984).

Examples of the approaches to "isms" as alluded to above include those in both Hallowell and Spahr, *op. cit.*, for Hegel in relation to Kant and idealism; and Sabine, *op. cit.* concerning Hegelianism and nationalism. Other varieties abound. Cf. e.g. for other "isms"—Steven B. Smith, *Hegel's Critique of Liberalism: Rights in Context* (Chicago, 1989), Ch. 5, "The Hegelian Rechtsstaat"; Frederick C. Beiser, *The Cambridge Companion to Hegel* (Cambridge, 1993), Chs. 9, 13, "Hegel's Historicism" and "Hegel and Marxism"; T. M. Knox, "Hegel and Prussianism," *Philosophy* (1940); and John Edward Toews, *Hegelianism* (Cambridge, 1980). Titles on Hegel's political and other idealism can be expanded upon at length. E.g. George A. Kelly, *Idealism, Politics and History: Sources of Hegelian Thought* (Cambridge, 1972).

20. For Hegel in relation to Kant, there is, in addition to works already cited, e.g. Lew Hinchmann, *Hegel's Critique of the Enlightenment* (Tampa, 1984); and Stephen Priest (ed.), *Hegel's Critique of Kant* (Oxford, 1987).

21. Hegel, *Philosophy of Right*, Pt. III, Sect. III, "The State" (§ 258): "As far as the search for this concept is concerned, it was the achievement of Rousseau to put forward the *will* as the principle of the state, a principle which has *thought* not only as its form (as with the social instinct, for example, or divine authority) but also as its content, and which is in fact *thinking* itself. But Rousseau considered the will only in the determinate form of the *individual* . . . will (as Fichte subsequently also did) and regarded the universal will not as the will's rationality in and for itself, but only as the *common element* arising out of this individual will *as a conscious will*."

22. *Ibid.* (§ 273): "The development [*Ausbildung*] of the state to constitutional monarchy is the achievement of the modern world, in which the substantial Idea has attained infinite form. The *history* of this immersion of the world spirit in itself or—and this amounts to the same thing—this free development in which the Idea releases its moments (and they are only its moments) from itself as totalities, and in so doing contains them in that ideal unity of the concept in which real rationality consists [*besteht*]—the history of this true formation [*Gestaltung*] of ethical life is the concern [*Sache*] of universal world history."

Hegel's continuing passages contain some substantial references to Montesquieu (also Fichte) especially on forms of governments and states. Elsewhere (§ 261) Hegel treats Montesquieu's ideas concerning laws in relation to the character of the state.

23. *Ibid.* (§ 263, 265): "If we compare these natural relations . . . with those of spirit, we must liken the family to sensibility and civil society to irritability. Then the third factor is the state, the nervous system itself [*für sich*], with its internal organization; but it is alive only in so far as both moments—in this case, the family and civil society—are developed within it. The laws which govern them are the institutions of that rationality which manifests itself within them. . . . But the ground and ultimate truth of these institutions is the spirit, which is their universal end. . . .

"These institutions together form the *constitution*—that is, developed and actualized rationality—in the realm of *particularity*, and they are therefore the firm foundation of the state and of the trust and disposition of individuals towards it. They are the pillars on which public freedom rests, for it is within them that particular freedom is realized and rational; hence the union of freedom and necessity is present *in itself* within these institutions."

In the same segment (§ 270), the state, as a problem first and foremost in law generally speaking, enters into the following further passages: "Nevertheless, the state, too, has its doctrine, for its institutions and whatever it recognizes as valid in relation to right, to the constitution, etc. are present essentially in the form of *thought* as law. And since the state is not a mechanism but the rational life of self-conscious freedom and the system of the ethical world, the *disposition* [of its citizens], and so also the[ir] consciousness of this disposition in *principles*, is an essential moment in the actual state. . . .

"[T]he development of this Idea has established the truth [of the proposition] that spirit, as free and rational, is inherently [*an sich*] ethical, that the true Idea is *actual* rationality, and that it is this rationality which exists as the state. It has further emerged just as plainly from this Idea that the ethical *truth* which it embodies is present for *thinking* consciousness as a *content* on which the form of *universality* has been conferred—i.e. as *law*—and that the state in general *knows* its ends . . ."

It is interesting to note that in his adjacent discussion (§ 272, near beginning) on methodology Hegel makes one of his strongest criticisms of some fellow German predecessors and contemporaries: "The constitution is rational in so far as the state *differentiates* and determines its activity within itself *in accordance with the nature of the concept.* It does so in such a way that *each* of the *powers* in question is in itself the *totality*, since each contains the other moments and has them active within it, and since all of them, as expressions of the differentiation . . . of the concept, remain wholly within its ideality and constitute nothing but *a single individual* whole.

"In recent times, we have an endless amount of empty talk both about the constitution and about reason itself. The most vapid of this has come from those in Germany who have persuaded themselves that they have a better understanding than anyone else—especially governments—of what a constitution is, and who believe that all their superficialities are irrefutably justified because they are alledgedly based on religion and piety. It is no wonder that such talk has made reasonable men . . . sick of the words 'reason', 'enlightenment', 'right', etc., and likewise of the words 'constitution' and 'freedom', and that one is almost ashamed to enter into any further discussion of political constitutions. But it may at least be hoped that such excesses will lead to a more widespread conviction that philosophical *cognition* of such subjects cannot come from ratiocination . . ."

24. *Ibid.* (§ 278): "Since sovereignty is the ideality of every particular authority . . . , it is easy to fall into the very common misunderstanding of regarding this ideality as mere power and empty arbitrariness, and of equating sovereignty with despotism. But despotism signifies the condition of lawlessness in general, in which the particular will as such, whether of a monarch or of the people (ochlocracy), counts as law (or rather replaces law), whereas sovereignty is to be found specifically under lawful and constitutional conditions as the moment of ideality of the particular spheres and functions [within the state]."

Also *ibid.* (§ 285): "The *third* moment in the power of the sovereign concerns the universal in and for itself, which is present subjectively in the *conscience* of the *monarch* and objectively in the *constitution* and *laws* as a *whole*. To this extent, the power of the sovereign presupposes the other moments, just as it is presupposed by each of them."

Various other adjacent discussions treat such topics as the sovereign power as will and moral personality.

(In § 299 occurs another of Hegel's references to Plato's *Republic*.)

25. *Ibid.* (§ 301–303, 308): "The proper significance of the Estates is that it is through them that the state enters into the subjective consciousness of the people, and that the people begins to participate in the state.

"Viewed as a *mediating* organ, the Estates stand between the government at large on the one hand and the people in their division into particular spheres and individuals on the other. Their determination requires that they should embody in equal measure both the *sense* and *disposition* of the *state* and *government* and the *interests* of *particular* circles and *individuals*. . . .

"It is integral to the definition of the *universal* estate—or more precisely, the estate which devotes itself to the *service of the government*—that the universal is the end of its essential activity; and in the *Estates*, as an element of the legislative power, the private estate attains a *political significance* and function. . . . Only in this respect is there a genuine link between the *particular* which has actuality in the state and the universal.

"This runs counter to another prevalent idea according to which, if the private estate is raised to the level of participating in the universal interest [*Sache*] via the legislative power. . . .

"The idea [*Vorstellung*] that *all* individuals ought to participate in deliberations and decisions on the universal concerns of the state . . . seeks to implant in the organism of the state a *democratic* element *devoid of rational form*, although it is only by virtue of its rational form that the state is an organism. . . . Each member of the state is a *member* of an *estate* of this kind, and only in this objective determination can he be considered in relation to the state. His universal determination in general includes two moments, for he is a *private person* and at the same time a *thinking* being with consciousness and volition of the *universal*."

26. *Ibid.* (§ 317): "Public opinion therefore embodies . . . the eternal and substantial principles of justice—the true content and product of the entire constitution and legislation and of the universal condition in general—in the form of *common sense* . . ."

27. *Ibid.* (§ 346–347, 352–355, 358, 360): "Since history is the process whereby the spirit assumes the shape of events and of immediate natural actuality, the stages of its development are present as *immediate natural principles*. . . .

"The nation [*Volk*] to which such a moment is allotted as a *natural* principle is given the task of implementing this principle in the course of the self-development of the world spirit's self-consciousness. This nation is the *dominant* one in world history for this epoch. . . .

"The concrete Ideas of national spirits [*Völkergeister*] have their truth and destiny [*Bestimmung*] in the concrete Idea as *absolute universality*, i.e. in the world spirit. . . .

"The principle of the *fourth* configuration [*Gestaltung*] is the transformation of this spiritual opposition in such a way that the spirit . . . produces and knows its own truth as thought and as a world of legal actuality.

"In accordance with these four principles, the world-historical realms are four in number: 1. the Oriental, 2. the Greek, 3. the Roman, 4. the Germanic. . . .

"The world-view of this first realm . . . is a theocracy, the ruler is also a high priest or a god, the constitution and legislation are at the same time religion, and religious and moral commandments—or rather usages—are also laws of right and of the state. . . . The distinctions which develop between the various aspects of customs, government, and the state take the place of laws, and even where customs are simple, these distinctions become ponderous, elaborate. . . . Consequently, the Oriental state lives only in its movement, and . . . nothing in it is stable.

"[In the Germanic realm lies] the *turning point*. . . . The spirit now grasps the *infinite positivity* of its own inwardness, the principle of the unity of divine and human nature. . . . The task of accomplishing this reconciliation is assigned to the Nordic principle of the *Germanic peoples*. . . .

"In the hard struggle between these two realms . . . the spiritual realm brings the existence [*Existenz*] of its heaven down to earth in this world, to the ordinary secularity of actuality and representational thought. The secular realm, on the other hand, develops its abstract being-for-itself to the level of thought and to the principle of rational being and knowing, i.e. to the rationality of right and law."

28. E.g. *ibid.* (§ 274): "Since spirit is actual only as that which it knows itself to be, and since the state, as the spirit of a nation [*Volk*], is both the law which *permeates all relations within it* and also the customs and consciousness of the individuals who belong to it, the constitution of a specific nation will in general depend on the nature and development [*Bildung*] of its self-consciousness; it is in this self-consciousness that its subjective freedom and hence the actuality of the constitution lie."

Also *ibid.* (§ 339, "Addition"): "The European nations [*Nationen*] form a family with respect to the universal principle of their legislation, customs, and culture [*Bildung*], so that their conduct in terms of international law is modified accordingly in a situation which is otherwise dominated by the mutual infliction of evils. The relations between states are unstable, and there is no praetor to settle disputes; the higher praetor is simply the universal spirit which has being in and for itself, i.e. the world spirit."

The preceding passages prompt one to note that in *ibid.* (§ 324) Hegel points out critically that "Kant proposed a league of sovereigns to settle disputes between states." Hegel (§ 329), however, maintains (over and above this) the state sovereigns (and the universal national-world spirit). Cf. also § 336. Furthermore (§ 342): "in world history . . . spirit in and for itself is *reason* . . ." In this way, the state as law emerges in the context of reason or rationality. Here, one recalls Kant's rational concept of law cited above, a partial precedent for Hegel.

29. Arthur J. Slavin, "G. R. Elton and his Era: Thirty Years On," *Albion*, 15 (1983), pp. 207 ff.

Notes to Chapter V
"Social*ism*" and "Marx*ism*"

1. On 1848 and the 1840s more generally, the following titles are representative: François Fejtö (ed.), *The Opening of an Era: 1848* (transl., New York, 1973), esp. the opening essay by A. J. P. Taylor and the detailed initial chronology; Peter N. Stearns, *1848: The Revolutionary Tide in Europe* (New York, 1974), both comprehensive and detailed; Priscilla Robertson, *Revolutions of 1848: A Social History* (New York, 1952), etc.), even lengthier and arranged by country; Lewis Namier, *1848: The Revolution of the Intellectuals* (Garden City, 1964, repr.), older yet suggestively entitled; and Jonathan Sperber, *The European Revolutions, 1848–1851* (Cambridge, 1994), a broad synthesis with detailed chronology and with chs. on the social and political background.

2. Jerome Blum, *In the Beginning: The Advent of the Modern Age, Europe in the 1840s* (New York, 1994).

3. On the revolution of 1848(–1849) in Germany and on contexts of the Frankfurt Assembly (May 1848–May 1849) see Michael Wettengel: *Die Revolution von 1848/1849 im Rhein-Main-Raum: Politische Vereine und Revolutionsalltag im Grossherzogtum Hessen, Herzogtum Nassau und in der Freien Stadt Frankfurt* (Wiesbaden, 1989), a well-documented study not distorted by an entrenched Marxist-Leninist viewpoint; Gunther Hildebrandt, *Politik und Taktik der Gagern-Liberalen in der Frankfurter Nationalversammlung, 1848–1849* (Berlin, 1989), who takes a rigorous Marxist-Leninist approach in line with the DDR, albeit with good documentation; V. Valentin, *Geschichte der deutschen Revolution von 1848–1849* (2 vols., Berlin, 1930); P. K. Noyes, *Organization and Revolution: Working Class Associations in the German Revolution of 1848–1849* (Princeton, 1966); F. Eyck, *The Frankfurt Parliament 1848–1849* (New York, 1968), who strikingly refers (e.g. p. 1) to the "first German National Assembly . . . known as the Frankfurt Parliament"; E. N. and P. R. Anderson, *Political Institutions and Social Change in Continental Europe in the Nineteenth Century* (Berkeley, 1967);

T. S. Hamerow, *Restoration, Revolution, Reaction* (Princeton, 1958); J. J. Sheenhan, *German Liberalism in the Nineteenth Century* (Chicago, 1978); Manfred Hamisch, *Für Fürst und Vaterland: Legitimitätsstiftung in Bayern zwischen Revolution 1848 und deutscher Einheit* (Munich, 1991), a study of Maximilian with relevance to Bismarck; and Jonathan Sperber, *Rhineland Radicals: The Democratic Movement and the Revolution of 1848–1849* (Princeton, 1991), stressing the revolution's character as a mass political phenomenon.

4. Cf. Karl Marx, *The Revolutions of 1848*, in his *Political Writings*, Vol. I (edited by D. Fernbach, London, 1973).

5. Karl Marx, "Contribution to the Critique of Hegel's 'Philosophy of Law [=Right]': Introduction," in *Collected Works* of Karl Marx and Friedrick Engels, Vol. 3 (trans., New York, 1975), pp. 175–187 (at p. 181). A standard collected edn. of *Werke* by Marx and Engels is that of Berlin, 1957–1968 in 41 vols.

6. Karl Marx, *Contribution to the Critique of Hegel's "Philosophy of Law {=Right]*," in *Works*, pp. 3–129 (at pp. 6, 11, 14, 17–18, in relation to § 261, 269–270 in Hegel's *Philosophy of Right*, with Marx's quotations from Hegel; all *sic* here and below): "'External necessity' can only be taken to mean that where a collision occurs, the 'laws' and 'interests' of family and society must give way to the 'laws' and 'interests' of the state; that they are subordinate to it; that their existence is dependent on its existence; or again that its will and its laws appear to their 'will' and their 'laws' as a necessity!

"However, Hegel is not here speaking of empirical collisions: he is speaking of the relation of the '*spheres* of civil law and personal welfare, the family and civil society' to the state. What is at issue is the *essential relationship* of these spheres themselves. Not only their 'interests', but also their 'laws', their 'fundamental characteristics' are 'dependent' on the state, 'subordinate' to it. It stands to their 'laws and interests' as 'superior *authority*'. Their 'interest' and 'law' stand as its 'subordinate'. They live in 'dependence' on it. . . .

"The political constitution is the organism of the state, or the organism of the state is the political constitution. That the various aspects of an organism stand to one another in a necessary connection arising out of the nature of the organism is sheer tautology. . . .

"In truth, Hegel has done nothing but dissolve the 'political constitution' into the general abstract idea of 'organism'; but in appearance and in his own opinion he has evolved something determinate from the 'general idea'. . . .

"The 'purpose of the state' and the 'state authorities' are mystified since they are presented as 'modes of existence' of 'substance' and cut off from their real mode of existence, from 'mind knowing and willing itself, educated mind'.

"The concrete content, the actual definition, appears as something formal; the wholly abstract formal definition appears as the concrete content. The essence of the definitions of the state is not that they are definitions of the state, but that in their most abstract form they can be regarded as logical-metaphysical definitions. Not the philosophy of law but logic is the real centre of interest. Philosophical work does not consist in embodying thinking in political definitions, but in evaporating the existing political definitions into abstract thoughts. Not the logic of the matter, but the matter of logic is the philosophical element. The logic does not serve to prove the state, but the state to prove the logic."

7. Marx, *Critique*, p. 19, the first page of Marx's treatment of Hegel's "internal constitution" (in relation to Hegel's § 272–273): "The constitution is thus rational insofar as its elements can be dissolved into abstractly logical elements. The state has to differentiate and define its activity not in accordance with its specific nature, but in accordance with the nature of the concept, which is the mystified movement of abstract thought. The rationale of the constitution is thus abstract logic and not the concept of the state. In place of the concept of the constitution we get the constitution of the concept. Thought does not conform to the nature of the state; but the state to a ready-made system of thought. . . .

"All that follows from Hegel's argumentation is that a state in which there is a contradiction between 'character and development of self-consciousness' and 'constitution' is no true state.... Hegel here is a *sophist.*"

8. *Ibid.*, pp. 20 (first page of Marx's treatment of Hegel's "monarch's authority"), 22–26, 32, 34, 39 (in relation to Hegel's § 275, 278–280, etc.): "What Hegel really wants to establish, however, is only that 'the general element of the constitution and the laws' is the monarchical authority, the sovereignty of the state. It is wrong, then, to make the *monarchical authority* into the *subject*, and to make it seem, since the monarchical authority can also be taken as referring to the authority of the monarch, as if he, the monarch, were the master of *this* element, its subject. . . .

"This idealism is therefore not developed into a conscious rational system. In *peaceful* conditions it appears either merely as an external constraint imposed on the prevailing power, on private life by 'direct influence from above', or as a blind, unconscious result of self-seeking. This ideality finds its 'own proper actuality' only when the state is in a 'condition of war or emergency'. . . .

"*Sovereignty*—the idealism of the state—exists, therefore, only as *inner* necessity, as *idea*. Hegel is satisfied even with this, for all that is at issue is the *idea*. Sovereignty thus exists, on the one hand, only as *unconscious, blind substance*. . . .

"If Hegel had set out from real subjects as the bases of the state he would not have found it necessary to transform the state in a mystical fashion into a subject. 'In its truth, however,' says Hegel, 'subjectivity exists only as *subject*, personality only as *person*.' This too is a piece of mystification. . . .

"So in this case sovereignty, the essential feature of the state, is treated to begin with as an independent entity, is objectified. Then, of course, this objective entity has to become a subject again. This subject then appears, however, as a self-incarnation of sovereignty; whereas sovereignty is nothing but the objectified mind of the subjects of the state.

"Leaving aside this fundamental defect of the exposition, let us consider this first proposition of the paragraph. . . .

"But whereas Hegel conceives of sovereignty as the idealism of the state, as the actual regulation of the parts by the idea of the whole, now he makes it 'the will's *abstract* and to that extent *unfounded* self-determination with which lies the final decision. This is the state's *individuality* as such'. . . . As determining the general the citizen is legislator; as the maker of individual decisions, as *actually* exercising his will, he is king. What is the meaning of [saying that] *the individuality of the state's will* is 'one *individual*', one particular individual distinct from all others? The element of *generality*, legislation, also has an 'explicitly actual and separate form'. One could therefore conclude that 'the legislature are these particular individuals'. . . .

"Hegel converts all the attributes of the constitutional monarch in the Europe of today into the absolute self-determinations of *the will*. . . .

"Hegel mixes up the two subjects—sovereignty "as subjectivity sure of itself' *and* sovereignty 'as the will's *unfounded* self-determination, as the individual will', so as to construe the 'idea' as '*one* individual'. . . .

"Hegel here defines the monarch as 'the personality of the state, the state's certainty of itself'. The monarch is 'personified sovereignty', 'sovereignty incarnate', political consciousness in the flesh. . . . At the same time, however, Hegel knows of no other content to give to this '*souveraineté personne*' than the 'I will', the element of arbitrary choice within the will. 'Political reason' and 'political consciousness' are a 'single' empirical person to the exclusion of all others; but this personified reason has no content other than the abstraction of the 'I will'. *L'état c'est moi*. . . .

"The abstraction of the *state as such* belongs only to modern times, because the abstraction of private life belongs only to modern times. The abstraction of the *political state* is a modern product.

"In the Middle Ages there were serfs, feudal estates, merchant and trade guilds, corporations of scholars, etc.: that is to say, in the Middle Ages property, trade, society, man are *political*. . . . In the Middle Ages the political constitution is the constitution of private property, but only because the constitution of private property is a political constitution. In the Middle Ages the life of the nation and the life of the state are identical. Man is the actual principle of the state—but *unfree* man. It is thus the *democracy of unfreedom*. . . .

"Hegel is saying that the transformation of state sovereignty (of a self-determination of the will) into the body of the born monarch (into existence) is *on the whole* that transition of content in general effected by the will in order to *realise*, to translate into existence, a purpose *entertained in thought*. . . . [I]t is the essence of the will as a mystical subject that makes decisions. . . .

"Another consequence of this mystical speculation is that a *particular* empirical existent, one individual empirical existent in distinction from the others, is regarded as the *embodiment of the idea*. Again, it makes a deep mystical impression to see a *particular* empirical existent posited by the idea, and thus to meet at every stage an incarnation of God."

9. *Ibid.*, pp. 41 (second page of Marx's treatment of Hegel's "executive"), 44–46, 52 (in relation to Hegel's § 287–297, etc.): "The only thing that can be said to be *original* in Hegel is that he *links* the *executive*, the police and the *judiciary*, whereas usually the administration and the judiciary are treated as antithetical. . . .

"Hegel has not *fully set forth executive authority*. But even taking this into account, he has not proved that the executive power is more than *one function*, one *attribute*, of state citizens as such. He has deduced the executive as a *particular, separated* power only by looking at the 'particular interests of civil society' as such, which 'lie outside the intrinsically and explicitly general character of the state'. . . .

"What Hegel says about the 'executive' does not deserve to be called a philosophical exposition. Most of the paragraphs could stand word for word in the Prussian Common Law. And yet, the administration proper is the most difficult point of all in the exposition. . . .

"Hegel proceeds from the *separation* of the 'state' and 'civil' society, from 'particular interests' and the 'intrinsically and explicitly general'; and indeed bureaucracy is based on *this separation*. . . .

"The *corporations* are the materialism of the bureaucracy, and the bureaucracy is the *spiritualism* of the corporations. The corporation is the bureaucracy of civil society; the bureaucracy is the corporation of the state. . . .

"The 'bureaucracy' is the '*state formalism*' of civil society. It is the 'state consciousness', the 'state will', the 'state power'. . . .

"The 'state formalism' which bureaucracy is, is the 'state as formalism'; and it is as a formalism of this kind that Hegel has described bureaucracy. Since this 'state formalism' constitutes itself as an actual power and itself becomes its own *material* content, it goes without saying that the 'bureaucracy' is a web of *practical* illusions, or the 'illusion of the state'. The bureaucratic spirit is a jesuitical, theological spirit through and through. The bureaucrats are the jesuits and theologians of the state. . . . The sovereignty dwelling in the monarch is taken here in a clearly mystical sense, just as theologians find the personal God in nature. It was also stated that the monarch is the subjective aspect of the sovereignty dwelling in the *state*. . . ."

10. *Ibid.*, pp. 54 (first page of Marx's treatment of Hegel's "legislature"), 55, 57 (in relation to Hegel's § 298 etc.).

11. *Ibid.*, 60, 63, 65, 72–73, 78 (in relation to Hegel's § 300–301, etc.): "The monarchical authority and the executive authority are . . . legislative authority. If, however, the legislative authority is the *totality*, monarchical and executive authority would, rather, have to be elements of the legislative authority. The supervening *estates* element is legislative authority *alone*, or the legislative authority in *distinction* from the monarchical and executive authority. . . . It is significant that Hegel, who has such a great respect for the state spirit, for the ethical spirit, for state consciousness, positively despises it when it confronts him in an actual, empirical form.

"This is the enigma of mnysticism. The same fantastic abstraction, which rediscovers *state consciousness* in the inadequate form of the *bureaucracy*, a hierarchy of knowledge. . . .

"In modern states, as in Hegel's philosophy of law, the *conscious*, the *true actuality* of *matters of general concern is merely formal*; or, *only what is formal is an actual matter of general concern*.

"Hegel is not to be blamed for depicting the nature of the modern state as it is, but for presenting that which is as the *nature of the state*. That the rational is actual is proved precisely in the *contradiction* of *irrational actuality*, which everywhere is the contrary of what it asserts, and asserts the contrary of what it is. . . .

"The constitutional state is the state in which the state interest as the actual interest of the nation exists *only* formally but, at the same time, as a *determinate form* alongside the actual state. . . . The *estates* element is the *sanctioned, legal lie* of constitutional states, the lie that the *state* is the *nation's interest*, or that the *nation* is the *interest of the state*. This lie reveals itself in its *content*. It has established itself as the *legislative* power, precisely because the legislative power has the general for its content, and, being an affair of knowledge rather than of will, is the *metaphysical* state *power*; whereas in the form of the executive power, etc., this same lie would inevitably have to dissolve at once, or be transformed into a truth. The metaphysical state power was the most fitting seat for the metaphysical, general illusion of the state. . . .

"The identity Hegel is asserting was at its most complete, as he himself admits, in the *Middle Ages*. Here the *estates of civil society* as such and the *estates in the political sense* were identical. . . .

"Hegel, however, takes as his starting point the *separation* of '*civil society*' and the '*political state*' as two fixed opposites, two really different spheres. This separation does indeed *really* exist in the *modern* state. The identity of the civil and political estates was the *expression* of the *identity* of civil and political society. This identity has disappeared. Hegel takes it to have disappeared. . . . Hegel is dealing here with *political* estates in a quite different sense from that of the *political* estates of the Middle Ages whose identity *with the estates of civil society* is asserted.

"Their whole existence was political. Their existence was the existence of the state. Their *legislative activity*, their *voting of taxes for the Empire*, was only a *particular* expression of their *general* political significance and effectiveness. . . . In the Middle Ages the estates of civil society were as estates of *civil society* at the same time legislative estates, because they were *not* civil estates, or because the *civil estates* were political estates. The medieval estates did not acquire a new character as a political-estates element. They did not become *political* estates because they participated in legislation; on the contrary, they participated in legislation because they were *political* estates. What have they in common, then, with Hegel's *civil estate*, which as a *legislative* element attains a political aria di bravura, an ecstatic condition, an outstanding, striking, exceptional political significance and effectiveness?

"All the *contradictions* characteristic of Hegel's presentation are to be found together in the exposition of this question.

"1) He has presupposed the *separation* of civil society and the political state (a modern condition), and expounded it as a *necessary element of the idea*, as absolute rational truth. He has presented the political state in its *modern* form—in the form of the *separation* of the various powers. . . .

"2) Civil society as *civil estate* is counterposed by Hegel to the political state.

"3) He characterises the *estates* element of the legislature as the mere *political formalism* of civil society. . . .

"But Hegel here confuses the state as the whole of the existence of a people with the political state. This particular is not the *'particular in'* but rather *'outside* the state', namely, the political state. Not only is it not 'the really particular in the state', it is rather the *'unreality'* of the state'."

12. *Ibid.*, pp. 84, 87, 90, 92–93: "First, let us notice with regard to this whole exposition that the 'mediation' which Hegel here wants to effect is not a demand he derives from the *essence of the legislative power*, from its own character; it is rather derived from *consideration* for an existence which lies outside its essential character. . . . The legislature in particular is only derived from consideration for a third thing. It is therefore pre-eminently the *construction of its formal being* which lays claim to all the attention. The legislature is constructed very *diplomatically*. This follows from the *false*, illusory . . . *political* position which the legislature occupies in the modern state (whose interpreter is Hegel). It follows as a matter of course that this state is no *true* state, since in it the *political attributes*, one of which is the legislature, have to be considered not in and for themselves, not theoretically, but practically, not as independent powers, but as powers afflicted with an antithesis, not according to the nature of things, but according to the rules of convention. . . .

"In the legislature, the monarch had therefore to constitute the middle term between the executive and the estates element; but the executive is the middle term between him and the estates element, and the estates element is the middle term between him and civil society. How is he to mediate between what he needs for his middle term in order not to be a one-sided extreme? Here all the absurdity of these extremes which in turn play the role now of the extreme, now of the middle term, becomes obvious. They are Janus-faced, show themselves now from the front, now from the back and have different characters front and back. That which originally was defined as the middle term between two extremes now appears itself as an extreme, and one of the two extremes which through it was mediated with the other, now appears again as the middle term (because it is regarded in *its distinction* from the other extreme) between its extreme and its middle term. . . .

"On the other hand: The legislature is a totality. . . . As we have seen, civil society becomes organised as *political* existence only as the 'estates' element. The 'estates' element is its *political* existence, its *transubstantiation* into the political state. Only the 'legislature' is therefore, as we have seen, the *political state* proper in its totality. . . . The 'estates' element is 'the *civil society of the political state*', of the 'legislature'. . . .

"Hegel therefore . . . made the political-estates element arise from the corporations and the distinct estates to no good purpose. This would only be meaningful if the distinct estates as such were legislative estates, hence if the distinctions of civil society, the civil character, were in reality the political character. Then we would have not a *legislative power* of the whole state, but the *legislative power* of the different estates and corporations and classes over the state as a whole. The estates of civil society would not acquire a political determination, but on the contrary they would determine the political state. . . .

"The estates are supposed to be 'mediation' between monarch and executive on the one hand and the nation on the other, but they are not that, they are rather the organised *political* opposite of civil society. The 'legislature' requires *mediation* within itself, namely, as has been shown, a mediation on the part of the estates. The presupposed *moral* harmony of the two wills, of which one is the will of the state as the monarchical will and the other the will of the state as the will of civil society, is not sufficient. Indeed, only the legislature is the organised, *total* political state, but precisely because the legislature is the highest development of the state, it is there that the uncovered contradiction of the *political state* with itself becomes evident. Hence the *appearance* of an *actual identity* between the monarchical will and the will of the estates must be established."

13. *Ibid.*, pp. 95, 98, 100.

14. *Ibid.*, pp. 105, 107–108, 110 (in relation to Hegel's § 307 etc.): "Here therefore *participation in the legislature* is an *innate* human right. Here we have *born legislators*, the *born mediation of the political state with itself*. There has been much sneering at *innate human rights*, especially by the owners of entailed estates. Is it not even stranger that the right to the supreme dignity of the legislative authority is entrusted to a particular race of men? Nothing is more ridiculous than the fact that the appointment by 'birth' of legislators, representatives of the citizens, should be opposed by Hegel to their appointment by 'the fortuitousness of elections'. . . . Hegel descends everywhere from his political spiritualism into the crassest *materialism*. At the summits of the political state it is everywhere birth which makes certain individuals the incarnations of the supreme offices of state. The supreme state activities coincide with the individual by birth, much as the position of the animal. . . . In its supreme functions the state acquires the reality of an *animal*. . . . The political state and the *legislative authority* in it, as we have seen, is the unveiled mystery of the *true value and essence* of the elements of the state. The significance which *private property* has in the political state is its *essential*, its *true*, significance; the significance which *differences of estate* have in the political state is the *essential significance* of differences of estate. . . .

"Thus, when 'independent private property' has in the political state, in the legislature, the *significance* of *political independence*, then it is the *political independence* of the state. 'Independent private property' or '*real* private property' is then not only the 'pillar of the constitution' but the '*constitution itself*'. And surely the pillar of the constitution is the constitution of constitutions, the primary, real constitution? . . . Similarly, in primogeniture the right of this abstract personality, its *objectivity*, 'abstract private property', comes into being as the supreme objectivity of the state, as its *supreme law*.

"That the state is a hereditary monarch, an abstract personality, means nothing but that the personality of the state is abstract, or that it is the state of the abstract personality; just as the Romans expounded the royal prerogative purely within the norms of civil law, or civil law as the supreme norm of constitutional law.

"The *Romans* are the rationalists, the Germans the *mystics* of sovereign private property.

"Hegel describes civil law as the *right of abstract personality* or as *abstract right*. And, in truth, it must be expounded as the *abstraction* of right and thus as the *illusory right of abstract personality*, just as the morality expounded by Hegel is the *illusory being of abstract subjectivity*. . . . Hegel has been often attacked for his exposition of morality. He has done no more than expound the morality of the modern state and of modern civil law. People have wanted to separate morality more from the state, to emancipate it more. What have they proved thereby? That the separation of the present-day state from morality is moral, that morality is apolitical and the state is immoral. Rather, it is a great merit of Hegel to have assigned to modern morality its proper position, although in one respect this is an unconscious merit (namely, in that Hegel passes off the state which is based on such a morality for the actual idea of ethical life). . . .

"It is really the Romans who first developed the *law of private property*, abstract right, civil law, the right of the abstract person. *Roman civil law* is *civil law* in its *classical form*. But nowhere do we find among the Romans that the law of private property is mystified, as is the case with the Germans. It nowhere becomes the *law of the state* either."

15. *Ibid.*, pp. 113–115: "Since in modern times the idea of the state could not appear except in the *abstraction* of the *'merely* political state' or the *abstraction of civil society from itself*, from its actual condition, it is a merit of the French to have defined, produced this *abstract actuality*, and in so doing to have produced the *political* principle itself. The abstraction for which they are blamed is therefore not an abstraction but the true consequence and product of the *rediscovered political conviction*, rediscovered it is true in an antithesis, but in a necessary antithesis. . . .

"In the modern sense the *existence* of the *assembly of the estates* is the *political existence* of civil society, the *guarantee* of its political being. To cast doubt on its existence is therefore to *doubt the existence of the state*. Just as previously 'political conviction', the essence of the legislature, finds its guarantee according to Hegel in 'independent private property', so its *existence* finds a guarantee in the 'privileges of the corporations'. . . .

"Thus Hegel everywhere sinks to that level where the 'political state' is not described as the highest actuality of social being, existing in and for itself, but where a precarious reality is granted to it, one which is *dependent on something else*; and where the political state is not depicted as the true being of the other sphere, but rather as something which finds in the other sphere *its true being*. Everywhere it requires the guarantee of spheres which lie outside it. It is not realised power. It is *supported* impotence, it is not power over these supports but the power of the support. The support is the paramount power.

"What kind of august aspect is this whose existence requires a guarantee from outside itself, while it is itself supposed to be the *general* existence of this guarantee, and thus its actual guarantee? In general, in expounding the legislature Hegel everywhere falls back from the philosophical standpoint to that other standpoint where the matter is not dealt with *in its own terms*. . . .

"Firstly, Hegel calls 'being a member of the state' an *'abstract* definition', although according to the *idea*, the *view* of his own expounding, it itself is the highest, *most concrete* social definition of the legal person, the member of the state. . . . But that the 'definition of being a member of the state' is an *'abstract'* definition is not the fault of that thinking but of Hegel's exposition and of the actual modern conditions which presuppose the separation of real life from the life of the state and make belonging to a state an 'abstract definition' of the real member of the state."

16. *Ibid.*, pp. 118–120, 122.

17. I have used a standard version (Penguin, London, 1967, based on older transl.) of the *Manifesto of the Communist Party* (more usually rendered as *The Communist Manifesto*) by Karl Marx and Friedrick Engels. Because the treatise itself is so short (around forty small pages in this version), and conveniently divided into numerous parts with ample headings, it is convenient to cite Marx's own divisions in our main text above, in lieu of unnecessary page citations in additional notes. It is also less cumbersome to refer usually to the *Manifesto* under the authorship of Marx rather than to cite Engels as well at every turn. Also cf. *Manifesto* in *Marx: Later Political Writings* (edited by T. Carver (Cambridge, 1996), pp. 1 ff. For a useful synopsis of Marx and Marxism cf. Palmer, *History*, pp. 434 ff., 495 ff.

18. As is the tendency in Palmer, *History*, Ch. XII, sect. 61 (citing a later Marxist position of 1875 but without consideration of Marx's early *Critique* of Hegel a half decade prior to his *Manifesto*).

19. Karl Marx's *The Eighteenth Brumaire of Louis Bonaparte* was first published in the United States (New York, 1852), the version here being of New York, 1973. The Eighteenth Brumaire of Napoleon I occurred on November 9, 1799. On December 10, 1848 Louis-Napoleon was elected president of the French Republic by universal vote, but his term was fixed by the constitution to four years.

20. *Ibid.*, sect. VII (pp. 120–125, 130–133, 135): " '*C'est le triomphe complet et définitif du socialisme!*'. Thus Guizot characterized December 2. But if the overthrow of the parliamentary republic contains within itself the germ of the triumph of the proletarian revolution, its immediate and palpable result was *the victory of Bonaparte over parliament, of the executive power over the legislative power, of force without phrases over the force of phrases*. In parliament the nation made its general will the law, that is, it made the law of the ruling class its general will. Before the executive power it renounces all will of its own and submits to the superior command of an alien will, to authority. The executive power, in contrast to the legislative power, expresses the heteronomy of a nation, in contrast to its autonomy. France, therefore, seems to have escaped the despotism of a class only to fall back beneath the despotism of an individual, and, what is more, beneath the authority of an individual without authority. The struggle seems to be settled in such a way that all classes, equally impotent and equally mute, fall on their knees before the rifle butt. . . .

"This executive power . . . sprang up in the days of the absolute monarchy, with the decay of the feudal system, which it helped to hasten. The seignorial privileges of the landowners and towns became transformed into so many attributes of the state power, the feudal dignitaries into paid officials and the motley pattern of conflicting medieval plenary powers into the regulated plan of a state authority whose work is divided and centralized as in a factory. The first French Revolution, with its task of breaking all separate local, territorial, urban and provincial powers in order to create the civil unity of the nation, was bound to develop what the absolute monarchy had begun: centralization, but at the same time the extent, the attributes and the agents of governmental power. Napoleon perfected this state machinery. The Legitimist Monarchy and the July Monarchy added nothing but a greater division of labour, growing in the same measure as the division of labour within bourgeois society created new groups of interests, and, therefore, new material for state administration. Every *common* interest was straightway severed from society, counterposed to it as a higher, *general* interest, snatched from the activity of society's members themselves and made an object of government activity. . . . Finally, in its struggle against the revolution, the parliamentary republic found itself compelled to strengthen, along with the repressive measures, the resources and centralization of governmental power. All revolutions perfected this machine instead of smashing it. The parties that contended in turn for domination regarded the possession of this huge state edifice as the principal spoils of the victor.

"But under the absolute monarchy, during the first Revolution, under Napoleon, bureaucracy was only the means of preparing the class rule of the bourgeoisie. Under the Restoration, under Louis Philippe, under the parliamentary republic, it was the instrument of the ruling class, however much it strove for power of its own.

"Only under the second Bonaparte does the state seem to have made itself completely independent. As against civil society, the state machine has consolidated its position so thoroughly. . . .

"And yet the state power is not suspended in midair. Bonaparte represents a class, and the most numerous class of French society at that, the *small-holding . . . peasants.*

"Just as the Bourbons were the dynasty of big landed property and just as the Orleans were the dynasty of money, so the Bonapartes are the dynasty of the peasants, that is, the mass of the French people. Not the Bonaparte who submitted to the bourgeois parliament, but the Bonaparte who dispersed the bourgeois parliament is the chosen of the peasantry . . . and in cheating the peasants out of the restoration of the empire. The election of December . . . 1848, has been consummated only by the *coup d'état* of December 2, 1851. . . .

"Historical tradition gave rise to the belief of the French peasants in the miracle that a man named Napoleon would bring all the glory back to them. And an individual turned up who gives himself out as the man because he bears the name of Napoleon. . . .

"But let there be no misunderstanding. The Bonaparte dynasty represents not the revolutionary, but the conservative peasant; not the peasant that strikes out beyond the condition of his social existence, the small holding, but rather the peasant who wants to consolidate this holding. . . . It represents not the enlightenment, but the superstition of the peasant; not his judgment, but his prejudice; not his future, but his past. . . . But the parody of the empire [*des Imperialismus*] was necessary to free the mass of the French nation from the weight of tradition and to work out in pure form the opposition between the state power and society. With the progressive undermining of small-holding property, the state structure erected upon it collapses. The centralization of the state that modern society requires arises only on the ruins of the military bureaucratic government machinery which was forged in opposition to feudalism.

"The condition of the French peasants provides us with the answer to the riddle of the *general elections of December 20 and 21*, which bore the second Bonaparte up Mount Sinai, not to receive laws, but to give them.

"Manifestly, the bourgeoisie had now no choice but to elect Bonaparte. . . .

"As the executive authority which has made itself an independent power, Bonaparte feels it to be his mission to safeguard 'bourgeois order.' . . . He looks on himself, therefore, as the representative of the middle class and issues decrees in this sense. Nevertheless, he is somebody solely due to the fact that he has broken the political power of this middle class and daily breaks it anew. . . . But by protecting its material power, he generates its political power anew. . . . But this cannot pass off without slight confusions of cause and effect, since in their interaction both lose their distinguishing features. New decrees that obliterate the border line. As against the bourgeoisie, Bonaparte looks on himself, at the same time, as the representative of the peasants and of the people in general, who wants to make the lower classes of the people happy within the frame of bourgeois society. New decrees that cheat the 'True Socialists' of their statecraft in advance. But, above all, Bonaparte looks on himself as the chief of the Society of December 10. . . . And he vindicates his position as chief of the Society of December 10 with decrees, without decrees and despite decrees.

"This contradictory task of the man explains the contradictions of his government, the confused groping about which seeks now to win, now to humiliate first one class and then another and arrays all of them uniformly against him, whose practical uncertainty forms a highly comical contrast to the imperious, categorical style of the government decrees, a style which is faithfully copied from the Uncle. . . . The people are to be given employment. Initiation of public works. But the public works increase the obligations of the people in respect of taxes. . . .

"Bonaparte would like to appear as the patriarchal benefactor of all classes. But he cannot give to one class without taking from another. . . . He would like to steal the whole of France in order to be able to make a present of her to France or, rather, in order to be able to buy France anew with French money. . . . Bonaparte throws the entire bourgeois economy into confusion, violates everything that seemed inviolable to the Revolution of 1848, makes some tolerant of revolution, others desirous of revolution, and produces actual anarchy in the name of order, while at the same time stripping its halo from the entire state machine, profanes it and makes it at once loathsome and ridiculous."

21. In *The Marx-Engels Reader* (edited by Robert C. Tucker, New York, 1978, 2nd edn.), pp. 683 (I), 700 (II), and 717 (III)—from *Socialism: Utopian and Scientific* by Friedrick Engels.

22. In *Marx and Engels on Law* (edited by Maureen Cain and Alan Hunt, London, 1979), pp. 156–157—from *Origin of the Family, Private Property and the State* by Friedrick Engels.

23. In *ibid.*, pp. 153–154—from Marx and Engels, *The German Ideology*.

24. In *Political Writings* of Karl Marx, Vol. 2, *Surveys from Exile* (edited by D. Fernbach, London, 1973, 1992), p. 264. Cf. p. 277 on the "Labour Parliament" held in Manchester in 1854, as part of the unsuccessful Chartist attempt to create a broad workers' organization.

25. In *ibid.*, pp. 281–282.

26. On law in relation to Marx and the Marxists, there is, in addition to Cain and Hunt, *Marx and Engels on Law* (with excerpts from the sources), Piers Beirne and Richard Quinney (eds.), *Marxism and Law* (New York, 1982), esp. Ch. 3, "Law and State"; and Hugh Collins, *Marxism and Law* (Oxford, 1982), Ch. I, sect. 2, "Is There a Marxist Theory of Law?", and Ch. 2, "Law as an Instrument of Class Oppression." In particular, there is Donald R. Kelley, "The Metaphysics of Law: An Essay on the Very Young Marx," *Amer. Hist. Rev.* 83 (1978), pp. 350–367, who briefly yet instructively underscores Marx's continuing debt in his mature writings to the rich legal-philosophical knowledge gained in his younger years especially as a law student. Kelley cites, for instance, Marx's references to Roman classical jurisprudence with regard to such topics as "true philosophy" and an original communal property (notwithstanding Marx's eventual dislike for existing legal systems as repressive of the proletariat and for abstract philosophizing a la Hegel). The state itself, of whatever form in Marx's thought, is passed over but not without brief allusions to legislation. Of more restricted interest is Rinaldo Orecchia (ed.), *Problemi della sanzione: Societè e diritto in Marx* (Rome, 1978) [= Società italiana di filosofia giuridica e politica].

On the state there is e.g. David Wells, *Marxism and the Modern State: An Analysis of Fetishism in Capitalist Society* (Brighton, 1981), Ch. IV, sect. 2, "Marx's Early Writings on the State," and Ch. V, "The Genesis and Early Development of the Capitalist State" (progressing from the neo-feudalism of the absolutist state to the bourgeois liberal state, in which law is a "fetish"). The author combines historical analysis of Marx and of Marxist writers more broadly with his own theorizing, yet the parameters even of the most relevant topics differ greatly from the present ones. Other works on the state include W. A. Turetzki, *Die Entwicklung der Anschauungen von Marx und Engels über der Staat* (Berlin, 1956), Ch. I, tracing chronological developments in Marx's early views on the state in the 1840s; *Marxistisch-leninistische Staats- und Rechtstheorie: Lehrbuch* (Berlin, 1975), a state publication of the DDR, e.g. Chs. 9–11 on the "socialist states"; and Paul Thomas, *Alien Politics: Marxist State Theory Revisited* (New York, 1994), who in a positive way explores Marx's idea of the state as alien to civil society, while taking issue with Marx's notion of the proletariat as a universal class.

Relating to political as well as social and ideological thought more generally are: Shlomo Avineri, *The Social and Political Thought of Karl Marx* (Cambridge, 1968); H. L. Adams, *Karl Marx in His Earlier Writings* (New York, 1965, 2nd edn.); Richard N. Hunt, *The Political Ideas of Marx and Engels* (2 vols., London, 1974–1984), esp. Vol. I, Ch. I, "The Origins of the State"; Joseph O'Malley (ed.), *Marx: Early Political Writings* (Cambridge, 1994), Intro.; G. Teeple, "The Doctoral Dissertation of Karl Marx," *Hist. of Pol. Tht.*, XI (1990), pp. 81–118, dealing with the oft-cited problem of Marx's early transition from idealism to materialism; Daniel Doveton, *ibid.*, XV (1994), pp. 555–591, relating the historical subject to current ideological debates; George E. McCarthy (ed.), *Marx and Aristotle: Nineteenth-Century German Social Theory and Classical Antiquity* (Savage, Md., 1992), covering a broad range of Marx's sources; Harold Mah, *The End of Philosophy, the Origin of "Ideology": Karl Marx and the Crisis of the Young Hegelians* (Berkeley, 1988), on the transition from Hegelianism to Marxism; John M. Maguire, *Marx's Theory of Politics* (Cambridge, 1978), with much on ideology in Marx's politics; Alan Gilbert, *Marx's Politics: Communists and Citizens* (Oxford, 1981), for Marx's pre-1853 political involvements and ideological tensions; and Jerrold E. Seigel, *Marx's Fate: The Shape of a Life* (Princeton, 1978), with psychological approaches.

27. Secondary literature on Napoleon III, the Second Empire, and the Second Republic is immense, as to be expected. A broad representative overview is by Roger L. Williams, *The World of Napoleon III, 1851–1870* (New York, 1957), with Chs. I–II on ". . . the Renascence of Bonapartism" and ". . . the Genesis of Parliamentarianism." On Bonapartism there is e.g. *Le Bonapartisme: Phénomène historique et mythe politique* (edited by K. Hammer and P. C. Hartmann, 1977), and Palmer, *History*, Ch. XII, sect. 62. A detailed partial chronology of crucial events, laws, etc. for this and adjacent periods in French history is in François Furet, *Revolutionary France, 1776–1880* (transl., Oxford, 1992), Appendix I. On the city of Paris cf. David H. Pinkney, *Napoleon III and the Rebuilding of Paris* (Princeton, 1958, etc.), under "Legislative Body" in index.

In his own writings, Louis-Napoleon had much to say on Napoleonism and legislation. Cf. *The Political and Historical Works of Louis Napoleon Bonaparte* (2 vols., New York, 1972, repr.), Vol. I, pp. 247 ff. ("Ideas of Napoleonism"), and Vol. II, esp. pp. 262, 265, 267, 282, 295, and passim, concerning law, legislation, sovereignty, etc.

On broader issues of French political thought in the nineteenth century, during the periods in question and adjacent ones, the following works provide useful points of reference, esp. on such subjects as liberalism: André Jardin, *Histoire du libéralisme politique: De la crise de l'absolutisme à la constitution de 1875* (Paris, 1985); Roger Henry Soltau, *French Political Thought in the 19th Century* (New York, 1959), Bk. II, "The Reassertions of Authority (1848–1875)"; Rudolf von Albertini, *Freiheit und Demokratie in Frankreich: Die Diskussion von der Restauration bis zur Resistance* (Munich, 1957), with Chs. centering sequentially on key "isms" (liberalism, Catholicism, republicanism, socialism, positivism, radicalism, nationalism, syndicalism, and personalism); and George Armstrong Kelly, *The Humane Comedy: Constant, Torqueville and French Liberalism* (Cambridge, 1992). On history and historians in relation to larger public issues, there is A. J. Becker, *Geschichtsinteresse und historischer Diskurse: Ein Beitrage zur Geschichte der französishen Geschichtswissenschaft im 19. Jahrhundert* (Stuttgart, 1986); and Linda Orr, *Headless History: Nineteenth-Century French Historiography on the Revolution* (Ithaca, 1990).

On early nineteenth-century legislative and parliamentary issues in France, cf. Thomas D. Beck, *French Legislators, 1800–1834: A Study in Quantitative History* (Berkeley, 1974), with the revolution of 1830 as the focal center; and Irene Collins, *Napoleon and His Parliaments, 1800–1815* (London, 1979). Relating to the "public sphere" is William M. Reddy, "Marriage, Honor, and the Public Sphere in Postrevolutionary France: *Separations de Corps, 1815–1848*," *Jour. of Mod. Hist.*, 65 (1993), pp. 437–472. In other respects: Ronald Aminzade, *Ballots and Barracades: Class Formation and Republican Politics in France, 1830–1871* (Princeton, 1993); Arthur Mizman, *Michelet, Historian: Rebirth and Romanticism in Nineteenth-Century France* (New Haven, 1990); and Rainer Riemenschneider, *Dezentralisation und Regionalismus in Frankreich um die Mitte des 19. Jahrhunderts: Politische Bewegungen gegen den Verwaltungszentralismus im Umkreis von Februarrevolution 1848 und napoleonischer Restauration 1851* (Bonn, 1985).

28. Cf. e.g. H. S. Jones, *The French State in Question: Public Law and Political Argument in the Third Republic* (New York, 1993); Jack D. Ellis, *The Physician-Legislators of France: Medicine and Politics in the Early Third Republic, 1870–1914* (Cambridge, 1990); Soltau, *French Political Thought*, Bk. III, "The Republican Era (1875–1914)," e.g. Ch. XIV, "The Syndicalist Challenge to the Sovereign State"; William Logue, *From Philosophy to Sociology: The Evolution of French Liberalism, 1870–1914* (De Kalb, 1983), e.g. Ch. I, "French Liberalism, Old and New"; Patricia Mainardi, *The End of the Salon: Art and the State in the Early Third Republic* (New York, 1993); Marie-Claude Genet-Delacroix, *Art et état sous la IIIe République: Le système des*

Beaux-Arts, 1870–1940 (Paris, 1992); Steven D. Kale, *Legitimism and the Reconstruction of French Society, 1852–1883* (Baton-Rouge, 1992); Jeremy Jennings, *Syndicalism in France: A Study of Ideas* (Basingstoke, 1990).

29. On Gladstonianism cf. Parry, *Rise and Fall of Liberal Government*, Pt. IV, "The Gladstonian Liberal Party, 1868–1886," Ch. 11, sect. 3, "Gladstonianism in Practice, 1868–74"; and Richard Bellamy (ed.), *Victorian Liberalism: Nineteenth-Century Political Thought and Practice* (London, 1990), Ch. 9, "Gladstonianism, the Provinces, and Popular Political Culture, 1860–1906," with other headings dealing with liberal utilitarianism, illiberalism, liberal radicalism, and conservative corporatism.

Further germane secondary works concerning Gladstone and his era are by Michael Barker, *Gladstone and Radicalism: The Reconstruction of Liberal Policy in Britain, 1885–94* (New York, 1975), with inclusion of issues in legislature; and Eugenio F. Biagini, *Liberty, Retrenchment and Reform: Popular Liberalism in the Age of Gladstone, 1860–1880* (Cambridge, 1992), with inclusion of the Factory Acts, socialism, and the Education Act of 1870. Biagini also views "British support for the [Paris] Commune [of 1871 as a] . . . 'prelude to socialism' spearheaded by the Positivist intellectuals [p. 63]." He regards "the style of Gladstone's electoral campaigns [, in addressing the masses, as overtaking] . . . any Continental model, whether republican, socialist or Bonapartist [p. 420]." Cf. also J. P. Parry, *Democracy and Religion: Gladstone and the Liberal Party, 1867–1875* (New York, 1986).

Additional works of interest in the broader setting, including with regard to liberalism and socialism, are Peter Mandler, *Aristocratic Government in the Age of Reform: Whig and Liberal, 1830–1852* (Oxford, 1990), with inclusion of issues in legislation; Alice Russell, *Political Stability in Later Victorian England: A Sociological Analysis and Interpretation* (Sussex, 1992), Pt. I, "Paternalists and Their Strategies: Leaders, Socialization and Social Control," with relevance to the early beginnings of socialism, which is treated in a variety of ways; T. R. Gourvish and Alan O'Day (eds.), *Later Victorian Britain, 1867–1900* (Boundmills, 1988), with consideration of social reform; Miles Taylor, *The Decline of British Radicalism, 1847–1860* (Oxford, 1995), with discussion of the Reform Party; Corrine Comstock Weston, *The House of Lords and Ideological Politics: Lord Salisbury's Referendal Theory and the Conservative Party, 1846–1922* (Philadelphia, 1995), with extended discussions of Gladstone and Lloyd George along with Ch. 4, " 'Legislating by Picnic' "; Stansky (ed.), *Victorian Revolution*, with treatment of social reform and social control in later as well as earlier Victorian England; Conacher (ed.), *Emergence of Parliamentary Democracy*, Pts. II–III on the second and third Reform Acts of 1867 and 1884 respectively; Elie Halévy, *Imperialism and the Rise of Labour* (transl. and repr., New York, 1961), covering the period from 1895 to 1905 as background to "the rule of democracy" from 1905 to 1914; Peter Clarke, *Liberals and Social Democrats* (Cambridge, 1978), with attention to the "modern state" and Fabian socialism; Margot C. Finn: *After Chartism: Class and Nation in English Radical Politics, 1848–1874* (New York, 1993); Douglas Newton, *Labour, European Socialism, and the Struggle for Power, 1889–1914* (New York, 1985); Richard Shannon, *The Age of Disraeli, 1868–1881* (New York, 1992); E. D. Steele, *Palmerston and Liberalism, 1855–1865* (Cambridge, 1991); C. E. Hill, "Sidney Webb and the Common Good: 1887–1889," *Hist. of Pol. Tht.*, XIV (1993), pp. 591 ff., on Fabian socialism, etc.; Julian Stapleton, "Localism versus Centralism in the Webbs' Political Thought," *ibid.*, XII (1991), pp. 147 ff.; Rodney Barker, *Political Ideas in Modern Britain* (London, 1978), with headings on "Collectivism and . . . the modern state," "Liberalism," "Socialism," "Popular anti-socialism," "Conservatism and anti-socialism," "Communism and Anarchism," "Distributism," "Syndicalism," "Political pluralism," "Guild socialism," and "Pessimism . . . ," along with other "isms" and references to "modern state"; W. H. Greenleaf, *The British Political*

Tradition, Vol. I, *The Rise of Collectivism* (New York, 1983); and Patrick Joyce, *Visions of the People: Industrial England and the Question of Class, 1848-1914* (New York, 1991).

30. Thomson, *England in the Nineteenth Century*, pp. 130-131, 133-136, 175, 178-179, 193, 224.

31. Cheyney, *Modern English Reform*, pp. 197, 202-207, 209, 211.

32. *Ibid.*, pp. 211-214. Passages continued (pp. 215-216, 218): "But the most distinctive influence of the war and of Bolshevism was to force socialists, and specifically the Labour party, to clarify their principles and aims. They needed to distinguish their position from that of the Communists on the one hand and the Conservatives and Liberals on the other. . . . [T]he platform of the party in 1928, 'The Constitution of a Socialist State,' . . . differed from the pronouncement of 1918 only in being more concrete in their proposals. . . . [Therefrom are] derived the predominating characteristics of modern British socialism so far as that is embodied in the Labour party.

"It is gradual, not revolutionary[,] . . . '. . . by the use of the ordinary machinery of democratic government.' Parliament as it stands is good enough for their purposes, though they would probably introduce proportional representation on an industrial basis, and would certainly abolish the House of Lords; the monarchy is apparently not especially distasteful to the majority of English socialists, though an appreciable number would prefer a republic. . . . The ultimate objects of this socialist party of the twentieth century are not very different from the hopeful visions of the Utopian socialists of the early nineteenth, or the bitter creed of the Marxian socialists of the middle of that century. It is its gradual methods, its realism, and what appears to be its favorable opportunity that are different."

33. For a brief useful synopsis in a standard wider survey cf. Norman Rich, *The Age of Nationalism and Reform, 1850-1890* (2nd edn., New York, 1977), Ch. 6, sect. 1, "Great Britain in the Mid-Nineteenth Century." Also Parry, *Rise and Fall*, "Chronology," pp. 312 ff. The following illustrations of legislation have been culled from these two sources and arranged chronologically, with a few additions at the end.

For the second half of the nineteenth century, the following legislative items can be cited. In 1850: a Factories Act. In 1855: a Civil Service Commission. In 1858: an act ending property qualifications for members of Parliament. In 1867: the Second Reform Act passed (further extending suffrage). In 1869: the Disestablishment Act. In 1870: Elementary Education Act, Irish Land Act, an Order in Council extending reform of the civil service, and Army Enlistment Bill. In 1871: Trade Union Act and University Tests Act. In 1872: Licensing Act and Ballot Act. In 1873: Judicature Act (simplifying the British legal system and ending abuses described in Dickens' *Bleak House* two decades earlier). In 1874: Public Worship Regulation Act. In 1875: Employers and Workmen Bill, Trade Union Act, a Factory Act, Public Health Act, Artisans Dwelling Act, Sale of Food and Drugs Act, and Agricultural Holdings Act. In 1880: Employers' Liability Act, elementary education made compulsory, Ground Grave Act, and Burials Act. In 1881: Irish Land and Coercion Acts. In 1882: Games Act and Arrears Act. In 1883: Agricultural Holdings Act, Corrupt and Illegal Practises Act. In 1884: Third Reform Act passes (further extending suffrage). In 1885: Redistribution Act. In 1886: First Home Rule Bill for Ireland, defeated. In 1888: Local Government Act, Affirmation Bill passed. In 1891: school fees for public education abolished. These prime examples have been assembled here from disparate sources.

Germane seminal dates of the early twentieth century include the following. In 1906-11: social insurance and Parliamentary reform. In 1918: universal suffrage established. In 1924: first Labor coalition government. In 1945: Labor election victory. In 1945-51: Labor government in power. In 1964: Labor wins election.

34. The wide diffusive parameters of the characteristics of the Victorian Age and Victorianism have been suggested by some of the secondary citations above. Legions of

works have variously dealt with the Victorian "frame of mind," such as Walter E. Houghton's *The Victorian Frame of Mind* (New Haven, 1957).

35. On "cabinet government" cf. *Nineteenth-Century Constitution*, Ch. 2, "Cabinet Government" (on the monarchy, Prime Minister, the cabinet and ministry), followed by Ch. 3, "Parliament" (Commons, Lords), etc. A classic older work on the subject was by Walter Bagehot, *The English Constitution* (repr. Ithaca, 1976), originally published as early as 1867 and dealing in turn with the cabinet, monarchy, Lords, Commons, and so forth including the "prerequisites of cabinet government." (It is interesting to note that this famous term seems echoed in that of "congressional government" in a book title by Woodrow Wilson, who took an interest in Bagehot's writings.)

36. Cf. also e.g. W. C. Lubenow, *Parliamentary Politics and the Home Rule Crisis: The British House of Commons in 1866* (New York, 1988); Arthur P. Monahan, *Consent, Coercion, and Limit: The Medieval Origins of [Modern] Parliamentary Democracy* (Montreal, 1987).

37. For some examples of such "isms" cf. above n.29, this ch. and nn. at end of Ch. II concerning the early Victorian state.

38. Cf. *ibid.* concerning uses of "liberalism" and "liberal."

Notes to Chapter VI
"National(-stat)*ism*" and "Bismarckian*ism*"

1. Guido Fassò, *Storia della filosofia del diritto*, Vol. III, *Ottocento e Novecento* (Bologna, 1970).
2. Cf. André-Jean Arnaud, *Essai d'analyse structurale du Code civic français: La régle du jeu dans la paix bourgeoise* (Paris, 1973), replete with refs. to older literature. Paul Dubouchet, *La pensée juridique avant et après le Code civil* (Lyons, 1994), deals briefly in the first book with traditions esp. of Roman law (ancient, medieval, and early modern including Dormat and Kant). The second book concentrates on the nineteenth century (Fichte, Hegel, Historical School, etc.). The third book is on the twentieth century (Pound, Duguit, Kelsen, etc.). There are extensive refs. to older bibliog. Paul Ourliac and Jean-Louis Gazzaniga, *Histoire du droit privé français de l'an mil au Code civil* (Paris, 1985), devotes Pt. I to the formation of French private law in Roman, medieval, and early modern eras. John Henry Merryman, *The Civil Law Tradition: An Introduction to the Legal Systems of Western Europe and Latin America* (2nd edn., Stanford, 1985), includes Chs. II ("Roman Civil Law, Canon Law, and Commercial Law"), III ("The Revolution"), IV ("The Sources of Law"), and V ("Codes and Codification"). Giovanni Tarello, *Le ideologie della codificazione nel secolo XVIII: Corso di filosofia del diritto* (Genoa, 1971), includes discussion of Domat, Leibniz, Wolff, Voltaire, Montesquieu, Prussia, Austria, and America. Donald R. Kelley, *Historians and the Law in Postrevolutionary France* (Princeton, 1984), Ch. 4 ("History and the Civil Code"), deals briefly with background to and parallels with Napoleon's *Code* in traditions of Roman law and Renaissance jurisprudence. He gives suggestions of Napoleon as a kind of new Justinian.
3. Useful general discussions on Napoleon's codes of law and on their historical contexts can be found in e.g. Robert B. Holtman, *The Napoleonic Revolution* (New York, 1967), Ch. IV ("The Lawgiver"); Owen Connelly, *The Epoch of Napoleon* (New York, 1972), Ch. 5 ("The Enlightened Proconsuls"); Mary Ann Glendon, *et al.*, *Comparative Legal Traditions in a Nutshell* (St. Paul, 1982), Pt. I, Ch. I, sect. 9 ("Codification");

Charles Breunig, *The Age of Revolution and Reaction, 1789–1850* (New York, 1970), pp. 68–70; René David, *English Law and French Law* (London, 1980), "Codified Law and Case Law," pp. 16 ff.; *The Progress of Continental Law in the Nineteenth Century*, by various authors (Boston, 1918), in The Continental Legal History Series, passim; and Bernard Schwartz (ed.), *The Code Napoleon and the Common-Law World* (Westport, 1975, repr.), e.g. Ch. 3 ("Codification and National Unity"), passim.

4. Cited by Holtman, *op. cit.*, p. 88.

5. The beginning of Napoleon's *Civil Code* makes plain his view of himself as great lawgiver, in *The Code Napoleon; or, The French Civil Code* (transl., New York, 1941), Preliminary Title, "Of the Publication, Effect, and Application of the Laws in General," Article 1: "The laws are executory throughout the whole French territory, by virtue of the promulgation thereof made by the Emperor . . . [and] shall be executed in every part of the Empire. . . .

"The promulgation made by the Emperor shall be taken to be known in . . . the seat of government. . . .

"The judges are forbidden to pronounce, by way of general and legislative determination, on the causes submitted to them."

I have substituted "Emperor" and "Empire" above for "First Counsel" and "Republic" on the basis of the German-*French* version of the *Code Napoléon* (repr. Frankfurt, 1982), entitled *Napoleons Gesetzbuch (Grand-Duché de Berg)*, as meant to be applied in that German area. The *Code* deals first with persons and then more extensively with property, the main subject of the work along with family. More generally, as a measure of the strong lasting influence of Napoleon's *Code* on the modern French *Civil Code*, cf. *The French Civil Code*, revised edn. 1994, translated by J. Crabb (Deventer, 1995), having roughly the same overall topical approaches.

Useful collections of Napoleon's statements—arranged according to various topics ("political order," "law and the social order," "the art of ruling," "nations and peoples," etc.)—can be found in *The Mind of Napoleon* (edited by J. Herold, New York, 1955, 1961). The following excerpts are illustrative (pp. 71–75, 80–81, 98, 160, 162): "[Manuscript, 1786] Laws are established either by a nation when it submits to a ruler or by the ruler himself. In the first case, the ruler is obliged by the very nature of his office to carry out the agreed-upon laws without exception. In the second case, the laws must serve the end of government, which consists in the peace and well-being of the people. If not, it is evident that the people resumes its original status and that the government, by not furthering the aim of the social compact, dissolves itself. We shall go even further: the compact by which a people places sovereign authority in the hands of some political body is not a contract. That is to say, the people has the right to take back at will the sovereignty which it has transferred. Men in the state of nature do not form a government. In order to establish one, it was necessary for each individual to give his consent to the change. . . . All men thus pledged have made the laws. Thus they have been sovereign. . . . There are no prior laws that the people (which under any government whatsoever must be regarded as intrinsically sovereign) has not the right to abrogate. . . .

"[Stenographic transcript, Conseil d'État, 1805] I say: we have had a jubilee. The social order has been overthrown; the king, who was the apex of all legislation, has been guillotined. . . . Everything has been uprooted. . . .

"[Conversation, 1804] Liberty means a good civil code. The only thing modern nations care for is property. . . .

"[Letter to his brother Jérôme, then king of Westphalia, 1807] What the peoples of Germany desire most impatiently is that . . . an intermediate hierarchy between the sovereign and the lowest class of the people should be completely abolished. The benefits of the Code Napoléon, the publicity of judicial procedure, the creation of juries must be so many distinguishing marks of your monarchy. . . . I count more firmly on their effects for the enlargement and consolidation of your kingdom than on the results of even the greatest military victories. Your people must enjoy a degree of freedom, equality, and prosperity unknown to the people of the Germanies, and this liberal regime must produce, in one way or another, the most salutary changes affecting the politics of the Confederation of the Rhine and the power of your monarchy. This manner of governing will give you a more powerful shield against Prussia than the Elbe, fortifications, and French protection. . . . Be a constitutional king. . . .

"[1803; on the democratic cantons] . . . Free nations have never tolerated any attempt to deprive them of the direct exercise of their sovereignty. They neither know nor care for the modern invention of representative government, which destroys the essential attributes of a republic. The only limitation permissible to legislators is the kind of restriction which, without taking away from the people the semblance of directly exercising its sovereignty, apportions political influence according to education and property. . . .

"All legislation must favor the property owner. He must find his profit in putting to use his property; otherwise he will abandon his enterprises. He must be given great freedom of action, for whatever hinders the free use of property irks the citizen. . . .

"[Manuscript, 1791] . . . To this end you will warn the legislator not to sanction laws that would enable a few to own everything. The lawgiver must solve his political problem in such a way that even the poorest own something. . . .

"[Conversation, April 1815] Don't talk to me of goodness, of abstract justice, of natural law. Necessity is the highest law; public welfare is the highest justice. Unto each day the evil thereof; to each circumstance its own law; each man according to his nature. . . .

"[Conversation, 1800s] It is for the sake of a remote, indeterminate goal, which they themselves do not fully apprehend, that men become heroes and that the inspired minority triumphs over the inert masses. Those lawgivers who have influenced history most were very much aware of this."

In addition, Holtman, *op. cit.*, pp. 94–95, quoting from Napoleon's instructions to Louis in Holland about applying the *Civil Code* there: "Having the same civil laws . . . tightens the bond of nations. . . . The Romans gave their laws to their allies—why should not France have hers adopted in Holland?"

6. Holtman, *op. cit.*, p. 81.

7. Concerning the Confederation of the Rhine and its Constitution, see John A. Hawgood, *Modern Constitutions since 1787* (London, 1939), Ch. VI ("The Napoleonic Spheres of Influence"), pp. 74–77. His Ch. V, "The Constitutional Absolutism of the Year VIII," uses in its title the same term often applied by historians to Bismarck, and treats Napoleon's constitutional positions more broadly with particular regard to legislation. Ernst Rudolf Huber (ed.), *Dokumente zur deutschen Verfassungsgeschichte*, Vol. I (Stuttgart, 1961), has a useful first part ("Das Ende des alten Reichs"), pp. 1 ff. (various documents). Werner Schubert, *Französisches Recht in Deutschland zu Beginn des 19. Jahrhunderts: Zivilrecht, Gerichtsverfassungsrecht und Zivilprozessrecht* (Cologne, 1977), Ch. III, examines contexts of the *Code Napoleon*. Ensuing chs. deal with the various Confederation entities (Berg, Bavaria, Baden, etc., including those cited above in our main text). Also: *Progress of Continental Law in the Nineteenth Century*, Chs. V–VII concerning Napoleon and Germany; Breunig, *Age of Revolution*, pp. 76 ff.; Palmer, *History*, pp. 378 ff., 388 ff.; Stuart Woolf, *Napoleon's Integration of Europe* (London, 1991), passim; and later portions of Hanns Gross, *Empire and Sovereignty: A History of the Public Law Literature in the Holy Roman Empire, 1599–1804* (Chicago, 1973), including the final sect. on "Hegel's Criticism of the Empire's Public Law" in the concluding Ch. 12.

8. As quoted in *Mind of Napoleon*, pp. 181–182.

9. Palmer, *History*, pp. 401–408.

10. E.g. H. S. Reiss (ed.) and A. Hayward (transl.), *The Political Thought of the German Romantics, 1793–1815* (New York, 1955), includes in turn Fichte, Novalis, Adam Müller, Schleiermacher, and Savigny. Reinhold Aris, *History of Political Thought in Germany from 1789 to 1815* (New York, 1965), Pt. II ("The Romantic Movement"), includes discussion of Herder, Burke, Novalis, F. Schlegel, and the "organic theory." Early Fichte, the Jacobin, is explored in Pt. I ("Enlightenment and Revolution"). Later Fichte, the nationalist, is treated in Pt. III ("The Reconstruction of Prussia"). The *Introduction to Contemporary Civilization in the West: A Source Book* (Columbia University), Vol. II (2nd edn., New York, 1954, etc.), Pt. I ("The Romantic Outlook and Its Expressions"), includes selections from Burke, Goethe, Chateaubriand, Fichte, and Hegel. Carl Schmitt, *Political Romanticism* (translated by G. Oakes, Camb., Mass., 1996), pp. 109 ff., takes up changing and diverse concepts of the state.

11. E.g. Frederick C. Beiser (ed. and transl.), *The Early Political Writings of the German Romantics* (Cambridge, 1996), Intro. Ibid., *Enlightenment, Revolution, and Romanticism: The Genesis of Modern German Political Thought, 1790–1800* (Camb., Mass., 1992), Pt. I ("Liberalism"), discusses Kant, Schiller, Humboldt, etc. Pt. II ("Herder and Early German Romanticism") has sects. on "The Politics of Historicism" (Herder), "The Organic Concept of Society," and "The . . . Romantic State" (Novalis), with Pt. III ("Conservatism") on Wieland. Also ibid., *The Face of Reason: German Philosophy from Kant to Fichte* (Camb., Mass., 1987), e.g. Ch. 5 ("Herder's Philosophy of Mind").

12. One of the more interesting studies connecting romanticism with liberalism, broadly speaking, is by Nancy Rosenblum, *Another Liberalism: Romanticism and the Reconstruction of Liberal Thought* (Camb., Mass., 1987). It includes J. S. Mill, Wordsworth, Thoreau, Humboldt, Locke, Kant, Hegel (as romantic), Rawls, Coleridge, and Novalis. When dealing with literature and the arts, historians of romanticism are sometimes on firmer footing (than those of political thought) in characterizing this "ism." They cite such ingredients as heroic genius, return to nature, pantheism, emotions, irrationality, and ideals of golden age. An example of a more specific thematic treatment of the transition from neoclassicism to romanticism in art is by Robert Rosenblum, *Transformations in Late Eighteenth Century Art* (Princeton, 1967). An example of a broader "century" approach to romanticism is Jacques Barzun's magisterial *Berlioz and the Romantic Century* (2 vols., Boston, 1950, etc.). Of course the elusiveness of romanticism in historiography on the literature and arts of the early nineteenth century is heightened by the elusive traits often cultivated by the romantics themselves.

Several German works of the early and later nineteenth century that included political thought when dealing with the German Romantic School were as follows: Heinrich Heine, *Die romantische Schule*, originally published in 1833 (new edn., Stuttgart, 1976); Rudolf Haym, *Die romantische Schule* (Berlin, 1870, repr. 1977); and Ricarda Huch, *Blüthezeit der Romantik* (Leipzig, 1899). Among the pertinent works of the early twentieth century, when studies on German romantics as an "ism" blossomed, are Oskar Walzel, *German Romanticism* (New York, 1932, transl. of 1908 Ger. edn., which lacked the "ism" in the title *Deutsche Romantik*); Walter Silz, *Early German Romanticism* (Camb., Mass., 1929); and Robert Maximilian Wernaer, *Romanticism and the Romantic School in Germany* (London, 1910, repr. 1966). On the nation-state in German romantic thought, older studies include: Paul Kluckhohn, *Persönlichkeit und Gemeinschaft: Studien zur Staatsauffassung der deutschen Romantik* (Halle, 1925); Friedrich Meinecke, *Weltbürgertum und Nationalstaat* (Munich, 1928); A. D. Verschoor, *Die ältere deutsche Romantik und die Nationalidee* (Paris, 1928); and G. Holstein, *Die Staatsphilosophie Schleiermachers* (Bonn, 1923). For the 1960s there is e.g. Jacques Droz, *Le romantisme allemand et l'état* (Paris, 1966); Hans Wolfgang Kuhn, *Der Apokalyptiker und die Politik: Studien der Staatsphilosophie des Novalis* (Freiburg, 1961); and Jerry Dawson, *Friedrich*

Schleiermacker: The Evolution of a Nationalist (Austin, 1966). Works on the state theories of Fichte and Hegel are more numerous.

13. As cited in preceding note.
14. Kelley, *Historians of the Law*, Ch. 6 ("The German Impulse"), pp. 72–73, ff.
15. Kelley, *Human Measure*, pp. 245–246, 252 ff., 268–269, and passim.
16. In *Political Thought of the German Romantics*, pp. 183–184, 188, 199–201. Excerpts from Schleiermacher are also found briefly in *Early German Romantics* by Beiser, who as already noted does not regard Fichte as a romantic.

Included in the latter work edited by Beiser are extensive excerpts from Novalis and Schlegel. According to Novalis (*Faith and Love*, pp. 38, 43), "law . . . is . . . the expression of the will of . . . the mystical sovereign," while "the state depends upon the public ethos." Such words as "romantic" and "pantheism" can be found passim in Novalis. Excerpts from Schlegel include his discussions passim on legislation, sovereignty, the states, constitutions, religion, transcendentalism, Fichte, the French Revolution, and the Middle Ages. (P. 166: "The genuine true Middle Ages is perhaps that of the Neoplatonic philosophy. Then and only then had mysticism manifested itself in great measure.") In general, Beiser's studies are not interested in themes of sovereignty and the state along present lines.

17. In *Political Thought of the German Romantics*, pp. 145, 148–149 (from Adam Müller's second lecture).
18. *Ibid.*, pp. 150, 152–153, 155, 157 (from Adam Müller): "The first basic fallacy of the current political systems is refuted: the state is not a mere factory, a farm, an insurance institution, or mercantile society, it is the intimate association of all physical and spiritual needs, of the whole of physical and spiritual wealth, of the total internal and external life of a nation into a great, energetic, infinitely active and living whole. . . . But states, definite, positive states are legal institutions; to create a state—according to the concepts of this age—means to create law, i.e. a law in face of law and outside the law. . . . It is that *idea of law* has two elements: a physical or a positive element and a spiritual or universal and universally valid element, and it was this second element which those people called 'natural law.' Now they thought that this spiritual element could be separated from the physical or positive element. . . .

"The state, however, is a large definite locality, its legislation is the sum of the formulae belonging to this locality. Anyone who considers both, locality and formulae, in their interaction, and therefore in movement, grasps the idea of the state. . . . The state is entirely autonomous; independent of human caprice and invention, it arises directly and immediately from where man himself comes from—from Nature—from *God*, the ancients said. . . .

"Let us now sum up all the details of our consideration. *The state is the totality of human affairs, their union into a living whole.* . . .

"The universal form in which the idea of the state appears here must not frighten us. . . . [T]he true limits, which do not hinder but further the movement of the state, can be pointed out and established. These limits exist, they are about us in all actual states; they determine the actions of the practical statesman and legislator. . . .

"We must above all correct the theory, since it is here our concern to reconcile theory with practice. . . . Do you still think that there is something outside the state, for the sake of which the state exists, and which the state must serve as the scaffolding supports the building and as the shell protects the core?

19. It is not possible here to explore the changing concepts of Fichte over the course of his vast writing career from the 1790s to 1814 as well as beyond (in posthumous publications). The excellent extended excerpts in *ibid.*, pp. 44–125, show Fichte's transformations from rationalism (in the tradition especially of Kant) to romanticism (in the background to

Novalis, Schlegel, Hegel, etc.). It is sufficient here to point out the continuing legal-legislative framework of state and sovereignty throughout these changing "isms" in Fichte's thought from the late eighteenth to early nineteenth century. It is convenient to employ below the titles as they appear in *ibid.*

In the first excerpt from Fichte below ("The Foundations of Natural Law according to the Principles of the Theory of Science," pp. 44 ff.; here pp. 45–47, 50–54, 73, 75–76), Fichte is concerned with natural law and reason when speaking of legislation in philosophical terms reminiscent somewhat of Kant. Fichte's methodology of thesis-antithesis-resolution prefigures that of Hegel. Fichte's concept or system of "right" involves positive law and legislation lying at the heart of the state as a legal as well as organic entity. The state, with its sovereign, is not arbitrary but derived from nature and reason, and is an autonomous abstract concept.

Hence excerpt #1 from Fichte: "At this stage we are able to say only so much about the legislator, that it is Nature that required a number of rational and free beings to co-exist in the world of sense in that it was Nature that produced a number of bodies capable of being educated to reason and to freedom. This does not mean: Nature possesses reason and will. . . . If free beings as such are to co-exist, then every one among them must impose upon himself the law which has been described above. . . . [I]f they are to co-exist, then all must impose this law upon themselves, and if they do not do so, they cannot co-exist. This presupposition, therefore, is the only reason for a philosopher to accept such a legislation.

"From this we draw the following conclusions. The law is conditioned, and any possible being who may impose this law upon himself, as far as we can see at this stage, imposes it only as a conditional law.

". . . *Thesis:* The freedom of the individual is according to the law of Right. . . .

"*Antithesis:* According to a valid conclusion from that same law of Right each individual must alienate his power and his judgement of right completely and unconditionally, if a legal state among free beings is ever to be possible. . . . Such norms are called *positive laws;* the system of all norms is called *the* (positive) *law.*

". . . All positive laws are more or less contained within the rule of Right. They contain no arbitrariness. . . . They must be of such a form that every rational and informed person would necessarily make the same laws. . . . The legal judgement must already be contained in the law, if legislation is to be clear and complete, as it should be. . . .

"*Result.* According to reason, we can alienate our power and our judgement of right only to the necessary will of the law that is incapable of any exception. . . . In the organic body every part continuously preserves the whole and by preserving it the part is itself preserved; the citizen's relationship to the state is precisely the same. . . .

"It is a proof that the state is not an arbitrary invention, but is demanded by nature and reason. . . . [E]ach will do this by demanding that the other should subject himself immediately to his sovereign. This demand: 'subject yourself immediately to my sovereign' is made by each of them with the same right; for each is in a legal organization.

". . . All relationships between states are founded on the legal relationship between their citizens. The state itself is nothing but an abstract concept: only the citizens as such are real persons. . . .

"Each state has, according to this, the right to judge the legality of another state with whose citizens its own citizens come into contact. . . . Its inner constitution is no one else's concern and no state has any right of judgement with respect to it. Herein consists the mutual *independence* of states. . . .

"States are necessarily independent of one another and autonomous."

In the second excerpt below ("The Closed Commercial State," pp. 86 ff.; here pp. 86–87, 91), Fichte discourses on the relationship of the rational state and pure constitutional law to the actual state and politics with particular regard to public law, which in its pure constitutional form is the "end." The wider context of laws governing public commerce makes it plain that Fichte is referring throughout to public law as public legislation. The state is, indeed, as he strongly suggests, founded squarely on legislation. The Hegelian three-fold methodology is further anticipated.

Hence excerpt #2 from Fichte: "Pure constitutional law openly permits the rational state to arise according to the concepts of Right. . . .

"It is here not merely a question of what is *right*, as it is with the rational state, but of how much of what is right can be *carried out* under the given conditions. If the science of governing in the actual state according to the maxim I have just described is called politics, then these politics will lie half-way between the actual state and the rational state; it will describe the straight line by which the former changes into the latter, and it will end in pure constitutional Public Law.

"Anyone who undertakes to show which laws in particular shall govern public commerce in the state, has first to examine what is right with respect to commerce in the rational state; then he has to describe what the custom in existing actual states is, and finally he has to show the way in which a state may change over from the latter condition to the former. . . .

"A false thesis is usually superseded by an equally false antithesis; only later do we find the truth which lies in the middle. That is the fate of science. . . . [T]hey may believe that no single aspect of my theory is applicable to the state, and yet I should never deny it the name of a legal state for that reason. The decrees about commerce and trade would then merely be questions of expediency, of wisdom and in that respect they would be quite arbitrary, but in no way objects of strict law. . . . [I]f [a nation] . . . is governed from its own midst and if its rulers have no other education beyond that which can be attained in such a nation, a wise legislation and a wise arrangement of the state can hardly be expected."

In the third excerpt below ("Addresses to the German Nation," Thirteenth Address, pp. 102 ff.; here pp. 102–106, 108, 110), Fichte turns away from eighteenth-century rationalism and looks in the direction of early-nineteenth-century romanticism. His German nationalist positions include much material on concepts of nation and state, these two topics often being blurred together. His continuing regard for the state, as now the nation-state of Germany, is a topic first and foremost in law and legislation. Yet his approaches here differ greatly from his former ones. When stressing the inner, even spiritual, frontiers of nations, Fichte is concerned at bottom with the problem of *Volksgeist*. The unique nature or spirit of the people of each nation gives shape even to its boundaries in the form of language, territory, and so forth. The special *Volksgeist* of the German nation in historical and contemporary perspective is superior to that of other nations and justifies its territorial expansion at the expense of other nations. The German will, nature, and reason must guide Germany toward a new unified nation-state in which the forces of human law and divine order help to bind it together. The dream of universal monarchy (and Holy Roman Empire) must fade away. The German fatherland, in a new patriotic call to arms, must rise up and throw out the occupying forces (of Napoleon).

Hence excerpt #3 from Fichte: "The first, original and truly natural frontiers of all states are undoubtedly their inner frontiers. Those who speak the same language are linked together, before human intervention takes a hand, by mere nature . . . are . . . one indivisible whole. No other nation of a different origin and language can try to appropriate and absorb such a people without becoming confused itself in the first place. . . . This inner frontier, drawn by the spiritual nature of man, first gives rise to outward frontiers of territories as a direct consequence. . . .

"Thus the German nation which was sufficiently united by a common language and mode of thought and sufficiently clearly separated from other nations, was situated in the centre of Europe as a dividing wall between unrelated tribes. It was a nation sufficiently large in numbers and also sufficiently brave to protect its frontiers against any foreign attack. . . . A nation which has remained faithful to nature may, if its territory has become too small, desire to enlarge it by conquering the neighbouring territory in order to gain more space. . . . Was there not in the centre of Europe the all-powerful German nation? . . . The German states, whose separate existence was anyhow against nature and reason, had to become subsidiary weights to supplement the main weights in the balance of European equilibrium so that they might become of some significance. They followed the moves of the foreign nations blindly and without a will of their own. . . . Germany did not belong to this Europe where the rule of law did not prevail and which had become divided. If only this country had remained united, it would have been dependent upon itself in the centre of the civilized world just like the sun in the centre of the cosmos; it would have kept itself and hence its environment in peace. . . .

"Finally, let us have the courage to recognize in all its despicableness and irrationality the dream image of a universal monarchy, a dream image which for some time has been increasingly offered as an object of public veneration to replace the dream image of a balance of power. . . . Only in so far as each one of these nations, left to itself, develops and takes shape in accordance with its own peculiarities, . . . is the phenomenon of divinity reflected in the way it should be, and only a person who lacked any conception of legality and Divine order . . . could dare to intervene in that highest law of the spiritual world. . . . We are a conquered nation. . . . The war with arms is decided; now a new war of principles, of morals and of character begins, and this is a war that we want.

"Let us give our guests a portrait of loyal attachment to fatherland . . ."

In the fourth excerpt below ("Comments on the Theory of the State," pp. 118 ff.; here pp. 118–123), Fichte writes on the state and sovereignty from various perspectives that involve legislation, including ones that are somewhat Platonic. The realization of the state idea is achieved, in particular, through an elite of sovereign lawgivers, whose purpose is to educate the people to a proper understanding and recognition of law. This viewpoint recalls to mind Plato's *Republic* and looks ahead somewhat to Hegel's *Philosophy of Right*. Fichte's concept of right in connection with the state has many points of comparison with that of Hegel, including on such topics as compulsion, freedom, and power, although there are differences as well. Fichte's notions of inner freedom of the people or citizens, individually and collectively, can again be reconciled with his understanding of the *Volksgeist*, especially in connection with Germany. Fichte makes various distinctions when discussing the legislators, the people, the educators, the sovereigns, the government, and so on. He tends in the end, however, to place legislation at the forefront of his considerations of the state, more strictly speaking, as distinct from the nation and its *Volksgeist*. The legislator-rulers, as the elite educators of the people regarding law, are the ones best guided by supreme reason. They are thus best suited to compel others to obey the dictates of law and reason.

In summary, Fichte remains interested here in "the creation of the rational state." His early cosmopolitanism and republicanism became largely superseded by his later German nationalism. Yet his rationalism and utopianism continued on throughout his intellectual career, blending with romanticism. The subject of Fichte's transformations of Kant's rationalism is too complex to be explored here.

Hence excerpt #4 from Fichte: "Any creation of the state and of the law of Right proceeds from a paradox, and is the *real* solution of this paradox.

"To be subjected to the law means to be subjected to our own insight. But—All of us may compel others to execute this right, our own right or the general right, and we may do so by virtue of our own conscience. . . .

"Only that state is a true (rightful) state which effectively solves this contradiction. The mediating term has already been found: it is the education of all to the insight of what is right. Only if the state which is based on compulsion fulfils this condition, does it possess itself the *right* to exist, for it prepares its own *abolition.*

"This is an important point—*Compulsion* is itself education—education towards the recognition of moral ends. . . . What is suppressed by the law is not at all the state's true freedom, but a force of nature. . . . [F]orces of nature shall be brought into agreement, the contradiction between them shall be removed. Each one receives the sphere which is guaranteed to him. . . . The introduction of external right by compulsion for ever contradicts the inner right. No state can be brought about except through the insight of all. Insight can only be achieved in the *peace* of the state. . . .

"The purpose of the kingdom—let me explain this by examples. At first the most general and permanent purpose is the education of the people to the recognition of the law. This means really the protection of the *inner* freedom of the citizens and implies guardianship. . . .

"Here the more general question arises: how does this reside in the concept of Right itself? . . .

"The freedom of man in this respect, as far as he can extend it intensively, is therefore just as much his right, as is his inner freedom, and no one else may interfere with this freedom through negligence or omission. . . .

"Compulsion is justified only by education for future insight; this alone permits the person who compels to take it on his own conscience. He can therefore be only the most educated person or he whom all must consider to be the most educated person. Only thus can he obtain a right to power. This produces the whole conception of the state *in nuce*. . . . This task here becomes a historico-practical one to prove what kind of element is found in this given condition, an element that irresistibly moves beyond that condition and towards the goal of realizing the state.

"On the other hand, the question remains unsolved there (in the *Theory of the State*). It is that of the necessary creation of the Republic of Scholars who, from among themselves, are to elect the sovereign ruler. He will always be an elderly man but he has been thinking about the state during the whole of his life, about its idea and its immediate relations in which this idea is realized. He knows the state and the things which need be done next. . . . Planned education of the people and planned government are one and the same thing; legislation pronounces in accordance with those things to which the scholars educated the legislators. . . . They have . . . proved themselves the best educators of the people, and this gives them the right and the claim to govern the people as well. Therefore, the supreme ruler, too, can come only from this council of the highest educators of the people. . . . [T]he supreme direction of affairs can reside only with the educators.—The mistake in our states is merely that the method of popular education is missing in the constitution and creation of the legal regent. . . . Man is afraid of subordinating his subjectivity to the laws of reason: he prefers tradition or arbitrariness.

"No one has an external right against reason. The supreme reason has therefore the right to compel all to follow its insight."

It should be noted that excerpts #1 and #2 above are from Fichte's *Sämmtliche Werke* (edited by I. H. Fichte, 8 vols., Leipzig, 1845–1846), Vol. III, while excerpts #3 and #4 are from Vol. VII. Excerpt #4 refers to the third sect. of Fichte's *Die Staatslehre*, in Vol. IV, which constituted lectures delivered in 1812 and first published in 1820. I have consulted the 1808 Berlin edn. of Fichte's *Reden an die deutsche Nation*, e.g. pp. 407 ff., Thirteenth "Address" (the common but perhaps inexact equivalent usually given by scholars for Fichte's *Rede*).

In addition to germane secondary works already cited that deal with Fichte, there is e.g. Gustav Adolf Walz, *Die Staatsidee des Rationalismus und der Romantik und die Staatsphilosophie Fichtes: Zugleich ein Versuch zur Grundlegung einer allgemeinen Sozialmorphologie* (Berlin, 1928). Bk. II is on rationalist/romantic views of the state, and

438 / Notes to Chapter VI

Bk. III is on Fichte's state theory. As the main title suggests, the perspective is "social philosophy" more generally speaking, rather than legislation more specifically. There is interesting discussion of Machiavellism in the struggles of Germany against Napoleon, pp. 587 ff. Douglas Moggach, "Fichte's Engagement with Machiavelli," *Hist. of Pol. Tht.*, XIV (1993), pp. 573–589, shows the importance of Machiavellian realism in Fichte's concepts of right and so forth in such works as *Addresses to the German Nation*. Mattern, *Concepts of State*, gives a broad survey beginning with Bodin, and continuing with Hobbes, Rousseau, etc. He then proceeds to Kant, Hegel, and Fichte, before dwelling at greater length on early-twentieth-century ideas. A useful collection is by Daniel Breazeale (ed. and transl.), *Fichte: Early Philosophical Writings* (Ithaca, 1988), covering the period 1794–1799. The same expert is ed. and transl. of Fichte's *Foundations of Transcendental Philosophy (Wissenschaftslehre) Nova Methodo (1796/99)* (Ithaca, 1992), with useful apparatus.

Part of the difficulty with broader concepts of *Volk* and of the *Staat* in modern historiography and political thought is how they have been blurred together by some experts within wider diffusions of other related topics. An example is *Volk und Staat* by Johann Wilhelm Mannhardt (Vienna, 1973). He employs a welter of other rubrics such as land, race, society, and nation, but with little pertaining to legislation directly.

20. Fichte's *Grundlage des Naturrechts nach Principien der Wissenschaftslehre—Foundation of Natural Right*—has often been known as *Science of Rights*, as in the version by A. E. Kroeger (London, 1970, revised edn.).

21. Kelley, *Historians and the Law*, pp. 72–73.

22. On the German Historical School and Savigny, there is e.g. Kelley, *Human Measure*, pp. 253 ff.; ibid., *Historians and the Law*, Ch. 6; Hallowell, *Main Currents*, pp. 329 ff.; Eikema Hommes, *Major Trends*, Ch. VII; and Spahr (ed.), *Recent Political Philosophy*, Ch. IV. The Historical School is traced back to the Renaissance by Kelley, and to Vico and Montesquieu by Eikema Hommes.

23. On Savigny's relation to German idealism, Hegelianism, and so forth, cf. Joachim Rückert, *Idealismus, Jurisprudenz und Politik bei Friedrich Carl von Savigny* (Ebelsbach, 1984), passim on Hegel, Kant, and Fichte, with extensive bibliog. Also by ibid., *August Ludwig Reyschers Leben und Rechtstheorie, 1802–1880* (Berlin, 1974), with discussions on Savigny, Hegel, and Kant.

24. E.g. James Q. Whitman, *The Legacy of Roman Law in the German Romantic Era: Historical Vision and Legal Change* (Princeton, 1990), with extensive bibliog. There are voluminous considerations of Savigny and some briefer ones on the later German *Civil Code* (pp. 229–232). See other citations above on romanticism with regard to Savigny.

25. Sten Gagnér, *Studien zur Ideengeschichte der Gesetzgebung* (Upsala, 1960), pp. 15 ff. ("Eine Position von Jahre 1814"). Also more generally, e.g. Dieter Strauch, *Recht, Gesetz und Staat bei Friedrich Carl von Savigny* (Bonn, 1960), a broad pertinent coverage. The maze of terminologies here serves to show, though Strauch does not draw the point directly, that for Savigny the state relates primarily to law and legislation; the nation pertains mainly to the *Volk* or people in a looser political-geographic sense.

26. Hallowell, *Main Currents*, pp. 329 ff. is one of those who tends to regard the Historical School, in addition to the Analytical School, as antithetical to systematization.

27. Cf. passages from Eikemma Hommes, *Major Trends*, in note immediately below, showing the congruence of the Historical School with systematization. On system in relation to history in Savigny, there is the suggestively entitled work by Aldo Mazzacane, *Savigny e la storiografia giuridico tra storia e sistema* (Naples, 1976). He supplies background on the centuries preceding Savigny and discussion of the later German *Civil Code*. Also Hans-Ulrich Stühler, *Die Diskussion um die Erneuerung der Rechtswissenschaft von 1780–1815*, e.g. Pt. A (on Savigny), II, 2 ("Die systematische Methode"); and Giuliano

Marini, *Friedrich Carl von Savigny* (Naples, 1978), Ch. III ("La storia e il sistema"). In Chs. II–III, Marini deals with transformations in jurisprudence—from ideas of national law and transcendental abstractions in philosophy to the historical approach and "spontaneity" of history found in Savigny.

28. E.g. Hallowell, *Main Currents*, pp. 329–330: "Under the influence of Romanticism and Idealism historical jurisprudence found one of its earliest and most distinctive expressions in the writing of the German jurist, Frederick von Savigny. . . . Savigny found the folk spirit embodied in law. Law, he declared, is peculiar to particular places, peoples, and times; it is the product of a particular folk-mind or folk-spirit. Law, essentially, is *Volksrecht* or custom. . . . For Savigny the development of the law, however, was an organic and not a progressive one, it was simply the unfolding of that idea of the law which was contained in embryonic form in the very beginning of a peoples' history. . . .

"Law, for Savigny, is inseparably bound up with nationality. 'Law grows with the growth, and strengthens with the strength of the people, and finally dies away as the nation loses its nationality.' "

29. Kelley, *loc. cit.*

30. On the Pandectist School, there is a useful synopsis by Eikema Hommes, *Major Trends*, pp. 192–195 ff.: "Renewal and unification of German civil law is to be expected only from a historical-scientific understanding of the organic development of law which alone enables us to distinguish what is dead from what is alive in present law. The call of the times, according to Von Savigny, in the area of civil law, is not for legislation (codification), but for (historical) legal science. . . .

"Von Savigny gained success with his arguments, for it was not until 1900 that a general code of civil law was introduced in Germany. A curious feature, however, is that this codification became feasible through the systematic and dogmatic efforts of the German *Pandectists*, direct heirs of the Historical School of Law.

"This somewhat paradoxical situation is due to the fact that the programme of the Historical School not only involved legal-historical research . . . but above all it encouraged legal-dogmatic research into common civil law, its foundations and basic concepts. It may be said that legal-historical research took place in the service of legal dogmatics. . . .

"Von Savigny proceeded on the assumption that classical Roman law had been correctly represented by the Justinian codification. . . . [H]e . . . wished to maintain the purity of this law . . . A consequence of Von Savigny's appreciation of Justinian law was that a critical investigation of the sources, essential to true legal-historical research, was not extended to the Justinian texts themselves. . . . Finally, only the legal-dogmatic bent of the Historical School can explain why they, at least the Romanistic wing, hardly paid any attention to national German law, instead focusing all attention upon Justinian law. This Justinian law, it was thought, needed to be purged of the corruptions of the Reception-era in order to serve in its purified form as the basis for systematic research into the foundations of civil law in Germany. . . . Precisely because, lacking a codification, the fundamentals of civil law had to be derived from other sources than the fragmented national law, jurisprudence resorted to Justinian law which contained a codification of differentiated Roman civil law. . . . The legal-dogmatic character of the Historical School achieved via the work of Puchta, Von Savigny's most prominent disciple, its consummation in the Pandectist School. . . . The Pandectist School represents the supreme form of 'conceptual jurisprudence.' . . .

"The Pandectist movement, whose scientific results, as observed, had been largely incorporated by the civil law-codification of 1900, also demonstrates the continuity in legal-dogmatic method between humanist natural law theory and the Historical School. Both considered Roman law as *'ratio scripta.'* . . .

"Thus the Historical School evidences a curious paradox. On the one hand we find an emphasis upon the historical, organic development of law, issueing from a supra-individual (irrationally conceived) national Spirit and a concomitant rejection of abstract, universally valid natural law; on the other hand we encounter dogmatic scientific research into civil law and its 'logical' foundations by means of a method as abstractly-theoretical as that employed by natural law theorists.

"Parallel to it, we find a second paradox, namely, a strong emphasis upon customary law as the direct, immediate expression of law as alive in the national Spirit, and hence a depreciation of the significance of legislation, on the one hand; on the other, we are confronted by an absolutization of state-legislation as the exclusive source of positive law and its validity, on the pattern of Bodin and the humanistic natural law theories. . . .

"Puchta relates legislation to the state. He distinguishes between people in the natural sense, that is the national community as determined by natural and spiritual kinship . . . and the people as unified within the state in the form of an organized public-legal unity. . . . Just as the natural, national community of the people is foundational to the community of the state, so the latter presupposes the former. The natural community of the people possesses no legal capacity and needs an organisation of state to acquire the same. A corresponding distinction is that between the natural consciousness of law (within the national community in the natural sense) and validation of this law by the organs of state. . . . Puchta finds himself in the state-absolutistic bedding of humanist natural law theory and of juristic positivism. For though he does say that state-legislation is a more formal source of law than are 'custom' and jurisprudence . . . , yet he also makes it impossible to check the content of legislation against popular law as it lives in the nation."

31. Concerning German historicism in its broader contexts and background, cf. Peter Hanns Reill, *The German Enlightenment and the Rise of Historicism* (Berkeley, 1975), Intro.; Friedrich Engel-Janosi, *The Growth of German Historicism* (Baltimore, 1944), dealing in turn with Herder, Humboldt, Goethe, Niebuhr, the Romantic School, Hegel, Ranke, Marx, Schopenhauer, and Burckhardt; Georg G. Iggers, *The German Conception of History: The National Tradition of Historical Thought from Herder to the Present* (Middletown, 1969), progressing from Herder in Ch. II ("The Origins of German Historicism"), through Humboldt, Ranke, and others, to the "crisis of historicism" in the early twentieth century (Chs. VI–VII), and beyond; Isaiah Berlin, *Vico and Herder: Two Studies in the History of Ideas* (London, 1976), pp. 143 ff. on "Herder and the Enlightenment"; and F. M. Barnard, *Self-Direction and Political Legitimacy* (Oxford, 1988), Pt. II ("From Individual Self-Direction to National Self-Determination").

Of parallel interest is the English Historical School led by Henry Maine. His earliest book, *Ancient Law*, became a classic and remained in ways his most famous work. Cf. Spahr, *op. Cit.*, pp. 146 ff. Also, George Feaver, *From Status to Contract: A Biography of Sir Henry Maine 1822–1888* (London, 1969), Ch. 5 ("Ancient Law").

32. A. F. T. Thibaut, *Ueber die Nothwendigkeit einer allegemeinen bürgerlichen Rechts für Deutschland* (Heidelberg, 1814). Of related interest is J. Stern, *Thibaut und Savigny* (Darmstadt, 1959); Werner Schubert, *Französisches Recht in Deutschland zu Beginn des 19. Jahrhunderts* (Cologne, 1977); Reinhart Koselleck, *Preussen zwischen Reform und Revolution* (Stuttgart, 1967); A. W. Rehberg, *Ueber den Code Napoleon und desen Einführung in Deutschland* (Hannover, 1814), a work that attacked Napoleon's *Code* and that Savigny praised in his *Vocation*.

33. Using the standard version of Savigny's *Vocation* by Abraham Hayward (London, 1831), along with consultation of the German edn. of 1828.

34. Savigny's *Geschichte* . . . in 6 vols. (Heidelberg, 1815–1831), or in 7 vols. in 5 (Heidelberg, 1834–1851), and his *System* in 8 vols. (Berlin, 1840–).

35. Cf. in general Kelley, *Historians and the Law*, Ch. 6. Bentham's *Codification Proposal* . . . was published in London in 1822. On Rehberg see citation immediately above.

36. Savigny, *Vocation*, Ch. VIII, pp. 131–137, 141–144, 151–155 (as usual, all *sic*): "With regard, in the first place, to the authorities, to which even the proposed code was to conform, the same mixed system of common-law and provincial-law, which formerly prevailed throughout the whole of Germany, ought, in my opinion, to be substituted for the code, or retained where the code was not in force: I hold these authorities to be sufficient, nay, excellent, provided jurisprudence does what it ought to do, and what can only be done by means of it. For if we consider our actual condition, we find ourselves in the midst of an immense mass of juridical notions and theories which have descended, and been multiplied, from generation to generation. At present, we do not possess and master this matter, but are controlled and mastered by it, whether we will or not. This is the ground of all the complaints of the present state of our law, which I admit to be well-founded: this, also, is the sole cause of the demand for codes. . . . People might think to annihilate it, by severing all historical associations, and beginning an entirely new life. But such an undertaking would be built on a delusion. . . . There is . . . no mode of avoiding this overruling influence of the existing matter; it will be injurious to us so long as we ignorantly submit to it; but beneficial, if we oppose to it a vivid creative energy,—obtain the mastery over it by a thorough grounding in history, and thus appropriate to ourselves the whole intellectual wealth of preceding generations. . . . The historical spirit, too, is the only protection against a species of self-delusion. . . . In the history of all considerable nations we find a transition from circumscribed, but fresh and vigorous, individuality, to undefined universality. The law undergoes the same, and in it, likewise, the consciousness of nationality may, in the end, be lost. . . . History, even in the infancy of a people, is ever a noble instructress, but in ages such as ours she has yet another and holier duty to perform. For only through her can a lively connection with the primitive state of the people be kept up; and the loss of this connection must take away from every people the best part of its spiritual life. . . . [T]he strict historical method of jurisprudence . . . is to trace every established system to its root, and thus discover an organic principle, whereby that which still has life, may be separated from that which is lifeless and only belongs to history. But the subject matter of jurisprudence . . . [is] with regard to the common law, threefold. . . . Roman law, German law, and new modifications of the two. . . . The foundation must certainly be laid in the lectures of the universities. . . . A hundred years ago, far more time and trouble were devoted to the Roman law in Germany than now; and it is undeniable that no such progress in the proper knowledge of it could be made as is now practicable with good teachers. Moreover, there is no great reason to be afraid of critical difficulties, which Thibaut speaks of as insurmountable. . . . This opinion is . . . particularly where, on the establishment of new codes, the Roman law was to be no more than an ancillary pursuit:—the same when the education of future legislators was the question. The painful study of details was believed to be useless for these purposes; people might rest satisfied with what was termed the spirit of this law. . . .

"I have above assumed three things to be necessary:—law-authorities, ministry of justice, and forms of procedure, all in good condition. . . . In this [third] respect many countries of Germany require a speedy and effectual reform. . . . To remedy these, the aid of legislation will be required; general consultation and communication between the states of Germany on the subject is also highly desirable. . . .

"According to this view, therefore, no code, it is true, would be formed in countries where the common law prevails; but it by no means follows that civil legislation would be altogether dispensed with. . . . [B]ut the Code Napoleon, young as it is, may already . . . be placed alongside of the Roman law. . . .

"The second object of legislation would be the recording of customary law, which might in this manner be subjected to a superintendance, such as that effected by means of the edict in Rome. . . . For in this customary law, that only will be comprised which has been decided in actual practice, and this, now that the legislator has the decisions before him, will, beyond a doubt, be thoroughly comprehended; the code, on the contrary, is obliged to speak on every subject. . . . Every one must see that this is not the place for speaking of the mode of carrying into execution the remaining branches of civil legislation. . . . The historical matter of law, which now hems us in on all sides, will then be brought under subjection, and constitute our wealth. We shall then possess a truly national law, and a powerful expressive language will not be wanting to it. We may then give up the Roman law to history, and we shall have, not merely a feeble imitation of the Roman system, but a truly national and new system of our own."

37. *Ibid.*, Ch. X, pp. 172–174. After remarks on the need for seeking a "common study" of law throughout the German universities, Savigny's passage continues (pp. 175–176): "Austria, Bavaria, and Wirtemberg, those excellent, purely German races, have not (partly from of old, partly at present) that freedom of intercourse, as regards their universities, with the rest of Germany, which is so highly advantageous to the other countries; this intercourse is impeded, partly by custom, partly by restrictive enactments. The experience of the period that has just elapsed, has shown what confidence the nations of Germany may place in each other, and that their only safety is in the closest union. The time therefore appears to be arrived, for this intercourse to be not merely established, but favoured and encouraged in every way. . . . But not only in a political point of view . . . but . . . for the intrinsic scientific excellence of the universities themselves."

38. *Ibid.*, Ch. XI, pp. 176–177: "Thibaut assures us, in the beginning of his work, that he speaks as a warm friend of his country, and he has certainly a right to say so. For, at the time of the Code, he maintained the honour of German jurisprudence in a series of articles, while many were hailing the new wisdom—many, the very despotism to which it led—with senseless jubilees. The object of his proposal, also, the firmer and closer union of the nation, is an additional proof of the goodness of his intentions, which I acknowledge with pleasure. Up to this point, therefore, we are agreed, and our contest therefore is not a hostile one; we have the same object earnestly at heart, and are deliberating about the means. As to these means, however, our views differ very widely indeed. . . .

"Thibaut assumes that the proposed code may be formed in two, three, four years, not as a mere make-shift, but as a finished work."

Ibid., Ch. XII, pp. 182–183: "I shall sum up in a few words in what my view agrees with that of the advocates of a code, and in what they differ.

"We are agreed as to the end in view: we desire a sound system of law, secure against the encroachments of caprice and dishonesty; as also, the unity of the nation, and the concentration of its scientific efforts upon the same object. For this end, *they* are anxious for a code, which, however, would only produce the desired unity for one half of Germany, and separate the rest by a line of demarcation, more strongly marked than before—*I* see the proper means in an organically progressive jurisprudence, which may be common to the whole nation.

"In the opinions we form of our present condition, also, we coincide, for we both regard it as defective. *They*, however, see the cause of the evil in the sources of law, and believe that they could remedy it by a code—*I*, on the other hand, find it in ourselves, and believe, for this very reason, that we are not qualified to frame a code."

39. *Ibid.*, Ch. I, pp. 20, 22–23: "Of two opinions as to the establishment of the law, with which I am acquainted, the one inclines to the restoration of the old system [Rehberg], the other to the adoption of a general code for all the states of Germany. To illustrate this second opinion, some observations are necessary here; as it must be considered in a twofold historical connection.

"In the first place, it is connected with many plans and experiments of the kind since the middle of the eighteenth century. During this period the whole of Europe was actuated by a blind rage for improvement. . . . In the second place, those plans are connected with a general theory of the origin of all positive law, which was always prevalent with the great majority of German jurists. According to this theory, all law, in its concrete form, is founded upon the express enactments of the supreme power. Jurisprudence has only the contents of the enactments for its object. Accordingly, legislation itself, and jurisprudence as well, are of a wholly accidental and fluctuating nature; and it is very possible that the law of tomorrow may not at all resemble the law of today. A complete code is, consequently, of primary importance, and it is only in case of its defectiveness that we can ever be exposed to the lamentable necessity of making shift with customary law as an uncertain kind of supplement. This theory is of much greater antiquity than the theory abovementioned. . . . The conviction that there is a practical law of nature or reason, an ideal legislation for all times and all circumstances, which we have only to discover to bring positive law to permanent perfection, often served to reconcile them . . ."

40. *Ibid.*, Ch. II, pp. 24, 28–31: "We first inquire of history, how law has actually developed itself among nations of the nobler races. . . .

"This difficulty leads us to a new view of the development of law. With the progress of civilization, national tendencies become more and more distinct, . . . the jurists now become more and more a distinct class of the kind; law perfects its language, takes a scientific direction, and, as formerly it existed in the consciousness of the community, it now devolves upon the jurists, who thus, in this department, represent the community. . . . For the sake of brevity, we call, technically speaking, the connection of law with the general existence of the people—the political element; and the distinct scientific existence of law—the technical element.

"At different times, therefore, amongst the same people, law will be natural law (in a different sense from our law of nature), or learned law, as the one or the other principle prevails, between which a precise line of demarcation is obviously impossible. . . . The sum, therefore, of this theory is, that all law is originally formed in the manner in which, in ordinary but not quite correct language, customary law is said to have been formed: i.e. it is first developed by custom and popular faith, next by jurisprudence,—everywhere, therefore, by internal silently-operating powers, not by the arbitrary will of a lawgiver. . . . It will likewise appear, that a partial influence of legislation on jurisprudence may sometimes produce a beneficial, and sometimes an injurious, effect. Lastly, there are great variations within the limits of the validity and application of the law. For, as the same nation branches off into many stocks, and states are united or disunited, the same law may sometimes be common to several independent states; and sometimes, in different parts of the same state."

41. *Ibid.*, Ch. III, pp. 32–35: "Legislation, properly so called; not unfrequently exercises an influence upon particular portions of the law; but the causes of this influence vary greatly. In the first place, the legislator, in altering the existing law, may be influenced by high reasons of state. When, in our time, unprofessional men speak of the necessity of new legislation, they commonly mean that only of which the settlement of the rights of land-owners is one of the most striking examples. The history of the Roman law, also, supplies examples of this kind. . . . That enactments of this kind easily become a baneful corruption of the law, and that they should be most sparingly employed, must strike any one who consults history. . . . Of a much less doubtful character is a second influence of legislation upon the law. . . . Here a kind of legislation may be introduced, which comes to the aid of custom, removes these doubts and uncertainties, and thus brings to the light, and keeps pure, the real law, the proper will of the people. The Roman government had, for this purpose, an excellent institution in the Praetorian Edicts. . . .

"But these kinds of partial influence are not intended when, as in our times, the necessity of a code is spoken of. Rather, in this case, the following is meant:—The nation is to examine its whole stock of law, and put it into writing, so that the book, thus formed, shall henceforth be not one amongst other legal authorities, but that all others which have been hitherto in force, shall be in force no longer. . . . The substance of a code would, accordingly, be two-fold; it would be composed partly of the existing law, and partly of new provisions. So far as the last are concerned, their occurrence on the occasion of a code, is obviously a matter of accident. . . . In Germany, in particular, these new provisions would often be but apparently new, since that which was new in one state might have been already in force in another; so that the question would relate, not to new laws, but to already existing laws of kindred nations, with a mere change of jurisdiction. Not, therefore, to confuse our enquiry, we will lay new laws entirely aside, and look only to the essentials of the code. In this case we must consider the code as the exposition of the aggregate existing law, with exclusive validity conferred by the state itself."

42. *Ibid.*, Ch. III, pp. 41–42.

43. *Ibid.*, Ch. VI, pp. 61–67, 69: "Very recently, the opponents of the Roman law have not unfrequently laid particular stress upon such arguments as the following:—Reason is common to all nations and ages alike, and as we have, moreover, the experience of former times to resort to, all that we do must infallibly be better than all that has been done before. But even this opinion, that every age has a vocation for every thing, is a prejudice of the most dangerous kind. . . . But the hope which they here found upon legislative enactments, I hold to be altogether groundless. If, at any time, a decided and commendable tendency be distinguishable in the public mind, this may be preserved and confirmed, but it cannot be produced, by legislation; and where it is altogether wanting, every attempt that may be made to establish an exhaustive system of legislation will but increase the existing uncertainty, and add to the difficulties of the cure. . . . Our taking this view . . . is itself a proof of a state of the public mind in which the law-making faculty is deficient. . . .

"Unluckily, during the whole of the eighteenth century Germany was very poor in great jurists. . . . A two-fold spirit is indispensable to the jurist; the historical, to seize with readiness the peculiarities of every age and every form of law; and the systematic, to view every notion and every rule in lively connection and co-operation with the whole. . . . This twofold scientific spirit is very rarely found amongst the jurists of the eighteenth century; and, in particular, some superficial speculations in philosophy had an extremely unfavourable effect. A just appreciation of the time in which one lives is very difficult: still, unless all signs deceive, a spirit has come upon our science, capable of elevating it for the future to the rank of a national system. Little, indeed, of this improvement is yet produced, and upon this ground I deny our capacity for the production of a good code. . . . I challenge them to show me one out of the no small number of systems of Roman-Germanic law . . . for of such we have many—but which is really good as a book. . . . Thus, for example, in the Roman law, the point would be to catch the method of the old jurists, the spirit which animates the Pandects. . . . I maintain that, in our age, a good code is not practicable. . . .

"If then, we have really nothing which is necessary to the formation of a good code, we are not to believe that the actual undertaking would be nothing more than a disappointment. . . . [T]his danger would be great in proportion to the vastness of the undertaking and its connection with the wakening spirit of nationality. . . . I will refer to the time immediately following the decline of the Roman empire in the West, where an imperfect state of legal knowledge was fixed exactly in this manner. . . . But the similarity is not to be mistaken in this: that there was then a mass of historical matter to be expressed, which was not comprehended. . . .

"I have hitherto investigated the fitness of our times for a general system of legislation, as if nothing of the kind had ever been undertaken. I now turn to the codes which recent times have actually produced."

44. *Ibid.*, Ch. VII, pp. 70–74, 93–95, 98–99, 101–102, 108–109, 111, 114, 126, 128: "[T]he question here does not turn so much on the particular merits of these codes, as on the prospect they hold out to us of the success or ill success of a new undertaking of the kind. . . . I take the Code Napoleon first, because on it alone detailed treatises have been published, directly applicable to my purpose.

"At the composition of this code, the political element of legislation had a greater influence than the technical; and, for that reason, it altered the existing law more than the German codes. . . . As soon as Napoleon had subjected every thing to a military despotism, he greedily held fast that part of the revolution which answered his purpose and prevented the return of the ancient constitution. . . . This, when the code was framed, was, in theory, republican in the revolutionary sense; but all, in reality, inclined to the recently developed despotism. . . .

"It would be difficult to imagine a state of public affairs, more unfavourable for legislation than this. . . . But as regards Germany, the Code . . . was consequently more pernicious and ruinous than to France herself. . . . The code served him as a bond the more to fetter nations: and for that reason it would be an object of terror and abomination to us, even had it possessed all the intrinsic excellence which it wants. . . . [T]he . . . pre-existing law, however, is partly Roman, partly French (*coutumes*), so that the code introduced a system of law, of which one half was new, into every particular part of France, and was welcome nowhere. . . .

"The pre-existing law is notoriously abrogated, not only where it comes into opposition with the code, but in all matters comprised in the Code (Art. 4), consequently, as good as totally abrogated. However, the French are more in the light as to the meaning of this abrogation than the Germans, who, from antipathy or partiality to the Roman law, have disputed a good deal about it. The former take it for granted, that the judge is permitted to follow the Roman law, as well as the *coutumes*, but that he is not enjoined to do so; that is to say, an equitable decision cannot be quashed for being contrary to this source of law. . . . Undoubtedly, it is not supposed that every judge in a case left undetermined by the code, may choose between the Roman law and any custom whatever, for this would be giving him too unlimited a power; but each is to follow the law which formerly prevailed in the vicinity, i.e. either the Roman law . . . or some special custom. . . . [T]he Court of Cassation is only to quash in cases where any provision of the code, or any new enactment, has been contravened: consequently, a decision for or against *loi naturelle*, Roman law, *coutume* or *jurisprudence*, is beyond the jurisdiction of this court. Lastly, . . . in all the parts of the code which were produced by the Revolution, the pre-existing law affords no protection against the blindest exertion of arbitrary power. . . . [P]ermit the various existing laws to remain, and only introduce new and uniform law through the whole of France in certain fixed parts; that is to say, make no code at all. . . .

"I now come to the Prussian Landrecht. . . . The materials of the whole new legislation are still in a great measure extant. . . . The French code was to be got ready at a moment's warning, to alleviate many pressing evils of the revolution, and to place every thing on an equal footing, while the Landrecht was framed with no other end or desire than that of accomplishing something excellent, without any imperative external necessity. What I regard as a second great advantage of the Landrecht, is the relation which it bears to the local sources of law. It was introduced merely as a subsidiary law in the place of 'the Roman Law, the Saxon common law, and other foreign subsidiary laws and ordinances;' and all provincial laws were to retain their authority, but were to be reduced into particular codes within three years. . . .

"If, however, we regard the composition of the Landrecht, it confirms my opinion, that no code should be undertaken at the present time. Every one knows the plan on which it was prepared. The Justinianean law was to be to such a degree the groundwork of the whole. . . . And in that respect the method of the Landrecht is in direct contrast with that, above described, which we find in the extant works of the Roman jurists; not, in my opinion, to the advantage of the Landrecht. . . . That this difference exists, will be allowed by every one, who, without prejudice, compares the Landrecht with the Pandects, and such a comparison is certainly allowable here, since we are obviously not discussing the peculiar constitution of Rome, but the universal method. . . . However, it must not be overlooked that a great . . . difficulty presented itself in the present state of the German language, which, generally speaking, is not juridically formed, and least of all for legislation. . . .

"Every government is to blame which is ignorant of, or disregards, the intelligence of its age. In this respect, however, the Prussian legislation is certainly not open to reproach. The voices, not merely of professional men, but of all the learned of Germany, were invoked and listened to. . . .

"The history of the Austrian Gesetzbuch is so far similar to that of the Prussian Landrecht, that each received its first impulse about the middle of the last century, so that the very same state of German juridical literature could operate on each. The groundwork was a manuscript work of eight large folios, mostly extracted from the commentators on the Roman law, and completed as early as 1767. . . . It has been already observed, that the completeness, aimed at in the Landrecht, was not even attempted in the Gesetzbuch. . . .

"If this judgment upon the three new codes be well founded, it forms a confirmation of my argument, that the present time has no aptitude for the undertaking of a code; and a very strong confirmation indeed."

45. *Ibid.*, Ch. IX, pp. 156, 168–169: "I now come to those countries of Germany, in which codes exist already; it is clear that only the Prussian Landrecht and the Austrian Gesetzbuch can be comprised under this head; not the French code, which must be regarded as a subdued political malady, from which indeed we shall still feel many evil consequences.

"I have already given my opinion on these German codes, but I should be misunderstood were I supposed to think their abrogation desirable. On the contrary, they are rather to be treated as occurrences new and unprecedented in the history of law, and their abrogation would . . . merely be followed by great confusion. . . . Besides, a large proportion of the evil which a general code would [at this time] produce, is not to be apprehended from these, so long as the common law is left in other countries of Germany. . . .

"If, once again, we consider the three Codes above-named together, and with particular reference to the study of the law, it is clear that a peculiar scientific spirit cannot spring from them, and that, even co-existently with them, a scientific spirit will only be kept alive in proportion as the historical authorities of these Codes remain the constant object of all juridical studies. The same, however, could not fail to be the case, should we resolve on framing a Code for Germany. Thibaut, who advises this, does not wish . . . to do away with scientific jurisprudence; indeed, he expects it to be greatly improved. He does not clearly explain what is to form the basis . . ."

46. *Ibid.*, Ch. IV, pp. 44, 47: "If, in the first place, we consider the juridical works of Justinian, consequently, that form in which the Roman law has come down to modern Europe, we cannot but remark a season of decline in them. The nucleus of these codes is a compilation from the works of a classical age, which must now be regarded as lost and

irrecoverable, and Justinian himself does not conceal this. This classical age, therefore, the age of Papinian and Ulpian, is that to which we have now to look. . . .

"This highly cultivated state of jurisprudence amongst the Romans at the beginning of the third century of the Christian era, is so well worthy of note, that we must also pay some attention to its history. It would be very wrong to regard it as the pure creation of a highly favoured age, unconnected with the preceding. On the contrary, the materials of their science were handed down to the jurists of this time, a great part of them even from the time of the free republic."

47. *Ibid.*, Ch. IV, pp. 48–50.

48. *Ibid.*, Ch. IV, pp. 51–52: "But when, at an earlier period Caesar, in the consciousness of his power and of the corruption of the age, resolved on being absolute in Rome, he is said to have formed the conception of a code in our meaning of the term. [Note: "Sauetonius, Caesar, c.44. Jus civile ad certum modum redigere, atque ex immensâ diffusáque legem copiâ, optima quaeque et necessaria in paucissimos conferre libros."] And when, in the sixth century, all intellectual life was dead, the wrecks of better times were collected to supply the demand of the moment. Thus, within a very short period, several compilations of the Roman law were formed; the Edict of Theodoric, the Breviarium of Alaric, the Responsiones Papiani, and the legal productions of Justinian. Hardly would works on the Roman law have been preserved, but for these compilations; and hardly would the Roman law have found entrance into modern Europe, had not Justinian's works been amongst them; in which alone, of all these, the spirit of the Roman law is discernible. The idea of these codes, however, was evidently suggested only by the extreme decay of the law.

"As to the value of the substance of the Roman law, there may be many different opinions, but as to its superiority in juridical method, all are undoubtedly unanimous who have a voice in the matter. But such a voice can only be allowed to those who read the sources of the Roman law without prejudice, and in a scientific spirit."

49. *Ibid.*, Ch. V, pp. 53–56, 58–59: "Up to a very recent period a uniform system of law was in practical operation throughout the whole of Germany under the name of the common law, more or less modified by the provincial laws, but no where altogether without force. The principal sources of this common law were the law-books of Justinian, the mere application of which to Germany had of itself already introduced important modifications. To this common law, the scientific activity of the German jurists had been always principally devoted. But it is this very foreign element of our law which has long occasioned bitter complaints. The Roman law, it is said, has deprived us of our nationality, and nothing but the exclusive attention paid to it by jurists, has hindered our indigenous law from attaining to an equally independent and scientific condition. Complaints of this kind have a degree of hollowness and groundlessness about them. . . . Even without the intermixture of the Roman law, an undisturbed progressive formation of German law would have been impossible. . . .

"The importance of the Roman law as an example of juridical method, has been shown in a former chapter; historically, also, it is now of great importance to Germany, on account of its relation to the common law. It is a palpable mistake to limit this historical importance of the Roman law to the cases immediately decided by it. . . . This historical importance, however, the Roman law shares with the German law which is every where preserved in the provincial laws. . . .

"Of this extremely complicated state of the sources of law in Germany, arising from the connection of the common law (very complicated in itself) with the provincial laws, the loudest complaints have been raised. . . .

"The most important argument urged in favour of the uniformity of the law, is, that our love for our common country is enhanced by it, but weakened by a multiplicity of particular laws. . . .

"The well-being of every organic being (consequently of states) depends on the maintenance of an equipose between the whole and its parts—on each having its due. . . . It is, therefore, an error to suppose that the common weal would gain new life by the annihilation of all individual relations.

"Indeed, for this political end, no state of law appears more favourable than that which was formerly general in Germany: great variety and individuality in particulars, but with the common law for the general foundation, constantly reminding all the Germanic nations of their indissoluble unity."

50. *Ibid.*, Ch. VII, pp. 76–79, 81: "The . . . Code . . . is and remains the very hasty work of the known redactors—of jurists, properly so called. Now what was the state of jurisprudence in France, when these jurists were formed? It is universally known, that, with regard to Roman law, Pothier is the pole-star of the modern French jurists, and that his works exercised the most immediate influence upon the code. I am far from undervaluing Pothier; rather might the jurisprudence of a nation in which he was one of many, be expected to turn out well. But a juridical literature in which he stands alone, and is almost revered and studied as the source, must, notwithstanding, be pitiable. . . . Very significant, to go no farther, are such phenomena as Desquiron, who talks about a Roman jurist, one Justus Lipsius, soon after the Twelve Tables. . . . But we will turn at once to the framers of the Code, to Bigot Preameneu, Portalis, and Maleville. . . . [O]f Portalis the following may suffice:—The sixth article contains the rule, *jus publicum privatorum pactis mutari non potest*. It had been objected that *jus publicum* meant, not the law concerning the state, but every law without distinction, every *jus publice stabilitum*. To this Portalis replies, that in general the word might have two meanings, but the question is what it means in this particular part of the Roman law. . . . I will not say that here *jus publicum* is superficially and erroneously interpreted; but I ask what this general rule had to do with the question how the Romans understood a similar rule? and . . . how it was possible to prove the forms of speech in use amongst the Romans from a passage of Bartolus . . . ? . . . Maleville . . . at the redaction of the code . . . was one of the representatives of the Roman law. . . . This state of juridical learning, however, is not to be regarded as pride or obstinacy. . . . Neither can this literary simplicity be laid to the charge of any national prejudice, for there were notoriously many individuals in France in the sixteenth century, from whom Roman law may still be learned. But I myself have heard a law professor in Paris say, that the works of Cujas, it was true, could not be omitted in a complete library, but that they were no longer necessary, because all that was good in them is to be found in Pothier.

"So much for the soil on which the Code has grown."

51. Michael John, *Politics and the Law in Late Nineteenth-Century Germany: The Origins of the Civil Code* (Oxford, 1989).

52. *Ibid.*, Intro., pp. 6—7, 9–10.

53. *Ibid.*, Ch. 2 ("The Theory and Practice of Codification, 1814–1867"), pp. 15, 21–25, 28, 38–41: "The campaign for a national legal system was a prominent feature of political debate in nineteenth-century Germany. In the second and third decades of the century, it occupied the attention of some of the most famous writers of the day such as Hegel, Savigny, and Anselm von Feuerbach. From the days of the Wars of Liberation of 1813–14 until the foundation of the North German Confederation in 1867, the call for legal unity was intimately connected with the liberal/nationalist movement and it shared the fortunes of that movement. . . . This movement resulted in the completion of the first great national code of the century—the Commercial Code (*Handelsgesetzbuch*) of 1861. Shortly afterwards, work on other codes—of criminal law, civil and criminal procedure, and the law of obligations—began, and was completed in the very different political atmosphere of the period after 1867. The Civil Code, on the other hand, was produced entirely under the auspices of the 1871 Reich.

"Nevertheless, the Civil Code was essentially the product of developments in politics and jurisprudence before 1867. . . .

"There is the further question of why it was that Savigny's ideas should later have been taken up by most of the supporters of the liberal-nationalist cause when they called for a codification. There are a number of reasons for this, not the least important of which was the rapidly established intellectual hegemony of Savigny's Historical School in the law faculties of the universities of northern Germany. . . . Savigny's theory of the origins of the law (later known as the *Volksgeistlehre*) did not necessarily involve the rejection of all attempts at codification. . . . Savigny's *Beruf* may for analytical purposes be split into two parts. The first of these contained the criticisms of the natural law codes with their arbitrary disregard of the real character of the people. The second attempted to show the ways in which legislation might become a valid source of law. In this section, Savigny laid out a set of principles which might be used to construct a successful code. Such legislation would contain a complete set of systematically organized basic legal principles, while leaving adequate room for local variations. Rigorous historical study was the key to the discovery of these basic principles and it was precisely in that area that Savigny considered contemporary jurisprudence to be deficient. . . .

"The emergence of a separate Germanist branch of the Historical School of Law in the 1840s has long been regarded as a major event in the history of nineteenth-century German jurisprudence. It derived in large part from the often noticed paradox in the work of Savigny and his principal followers—their emphasis on the search for the true traditions of German law through the investigation of predominantly Roman law sources. In fact, Savigny had called for study of the German as well as the Roman legal tradition in 1814. . . .

"There can be little doubt about the connections between the growing Germanist movement and the upsurge of nationalism in the early 1840s. . . . In part, the difference between the Germanists and Romanists lay in their attitude to political reform and the process of legislation. . . . In 1842 Anton Christ . . . published an important work calling for a national code. His concern for legal unity was rooted in his desire for national unity and the strength of the nation in relation to other countries. Like the Germanists, he accepted that the historical method was 'the only one which is suitable and beneficial' in the preparation of legislation, but he went on to argue that the primacy of historical law lay in its source—the collective will of the people. . . .

"The acceptance of Savigny's theory of the origins of law had important implications for the way in which a codification might be attempted. In particular, it meant lengthy study of the legal sources and the collection of materials from the different parts of Germany so that justice might be done to regional variations. . . .

"By the early 1860s, then, there was widespread agreement on both the possibility and the desirability of national legislation in the sphere of the civil law. This was a question in which political considerations had determined policy. . . .

"By the 1840s . . . resurgent liberal nationalism of that decade began to cast aside Savigny's negative assessment of the potential value of legislation, while broadly accepting his theories about the nature of the law. This implied a further set of opinions about how legislation should proceed, involving lengthy historical study of the sources of law and close attention to specific historical institutions. This was the position adopted by the majority in the Frankfurt Parliament, and was decisive in heading off radical demands for an immediate start on the work of codification. . . .

"There can be little doubt that the selective appropriation of Savigny's theories by the supporters of legal unification had considerable influence here. . . . Considerable differences on these important, essentially political questions existed throughout the 1860s and early 1870s, and were only partially concealed by the powerful consensus in favour of national legislation in the field of civil law. Accordingly, it was in these terms that the debate was principally conducted after Prussia's victory in 1866 overturned the institutional framework of the German Confederation."

Ibid., Ch. 3 ("The Politics of Legal Unity, 1867–1873"), pp. 42, 44, 46–48, 63–64, 68: "The campaign for a unified legal system thus enjoyed widespread support in Germany by 1867. The foundation of the North German Confederation in that year and the establishment of the Reichstag as a national forum for debate entirely changed the context of the discussions. . . .

"Those who wished to see the creation of a national system of civil law had first to contend with the restrictions on the legislative competence of the new state enshrined in Art. 4, No. 13 of the 1867 and 1871 constitutions. This clause restricted the new state's legislative competence to 'the law of obligations, criminal law, commercial law, the law of bills of exchange and court procedure'. . . . [T]he period after about 1840 saw a growing acceptance of Savigny's historical theory of law by the supporters of national legal unification. In the 1860s and 1870s, supporters of the Lasker-Miquel motions tended to deny the validity of Savigny's hostility to codification, but on the whole they did so from within the historical camp. . . .

"This technical argument was frequently buttressed by statements to the effect that Savigny's objections to codification were no longer valid, that it was precisely as a result of his work that German jurisprudence was now capable of successful legislation, and even that he was a covert supporter of a national code. These were favourite themes of Miquel in particular, but gained their credibility from the re-evaluation of Savigny's work. . . . [O]ne of Savigny's pupils, M. A. von Bethmann-Hollweg, was arguing by 1876 that Savigny's opposition to Thibaut did not reflect hostility to the ideal of legal unity and that codification was 'unavoidable'. It would be correct to say that this view of Savigny's heritage dominated the German legal community by this time. Its importance in depriving the opponents of the Lasker-Miquel motions of a powerful argument against legal unification would be difficult to overestimate. . . .

"Another National Liberal, Ludwig Enneccerus, went even further in claiming Savigny for the cause of national legal unity against the particularist designs of the states. . . .

"Enneccerus . . . accepted the *Volksgeistlehre*, but also stressed that law was rooted in a nation's will rather than in its consciousness (*Bewusstsein*), as Savigny had believed. A reforming legislator might well, he said, be ahead of the development of his nation's consciousness. . . . These conceptions of the potentially innovative role of legislation and of the will of the legislator coexisted uneasily with the *Volksgeistlehre* and with Savigny's views on an ideal code.

"Once again, these developments were important in relation to the political battles of the period. . . .

"It was also important that the debates concerning the Reich's legislative competence came at a time when current procedures for the preparation of laws were already the subject of close scrutiny as a result of the codes of civil and criminal procedure and of court organization. . . .

"Moreover, developments in Prussian legislation provided cause for concern. The Prussian legislation of 5 May 1872 relating to the acquisition of landed property [etc.] . . . had progressed considerably further in a liberal direction than was the case in the south. In addition, liberal publicists were openly applauding Prussia as the source of 'organic laws', and tended to emphasize that Prussian legislation was an important step towards legal unity. To that extent, the choice between codification and special legislation was not merely a question of legislative technique or even of the states' right to participate. . . . Special legislation meant the possibility of liberal reform through the imposition of Prussian institutions with the support of the Reichstag majority. To that extent, the fear of 'Prussianization' and of 'modern ideas' were two sides of the same coin."

Ibid., Ch. 4 ("The Approach to Codification, 1874–1888"), pp. 73, 82, 84–85, 98–99: "The Bundesrat's final acceptance of the Lasker-Miquel motion in December 1873 began a new period in the history of the Civil Code. It had been agreed that work on a code should be started immediately, but beyond that there had been remarkably little discussion about how the task should be approached. Proposals did exist within the Prussian government . . . but they aroused the southern states' fears of the twin dangers of 'modern ideas' and 'Prussianization'. . . . An important feature of these discussions was once again the realization that the method by which a code was prepared would be vital in determining what sort of code was prepared. . . .

"The important issue at stake here was the relationship between formal systematization and the preservation of the historical peculiarities of the different regions of Germany. That relationship was implicitly a difficult one despite the roots of both elements in Savigny's work. . . . In addition, the old battle between 'Romanists' and 'Germanists' had largely disappeared in the quarter century after 1848, although it was to revive in very different political circumstances in the late 1880s. By 1870 at the latest, conceptual jurisprudence—the basic technique of legal positivism—more or less had the field to itself as far as the technical approach to legislation was concerned. . . . Far from involving a rejection of the historical theory of the origins of law, it was really part of the reassessment of Savigny's theories in the middle of the century. . . . Planck . . . agreed with the Historical School that a code should essentially deal with existing law, and that 'innovation was only justified if the trend of developments was unmistakable. . . .'

"This view of conceptual jurisprudence as determining legislative form and technique rather than the content of laws was both correct and misleading. Its mid-century founders—academic lawyers such as Puchta and Gerber—had effectively abandoned Savigny's notion of the organic relationship between law and society, putting in its place an emphasis on the productive development of new law out of concepts derived from study of the sources. . . . Instead, following the work of the late Savigny (the Savigny of the *System des heutigen römischen Rechts*, rather than the Savigny of the *Beruf*), jurisprudence should seek to develop a system of rationally interrelated concepts. . . ." Cf. ensuing discussion of Savigny's Romanist theory of associations as "fictitious persons" in distinction to Gierke's Germanist theory of associations as "real collective persons."

Ibid., Ch. 5 ("The Public Response and the Campaign for Legal Reform, 1888–1896"): pp. 108–109, 154–155: "Of all the writers associated with this type of criticism of the 1888 draft code, Otto von Gierke [who was treated in our Vol. IV, Pt. I] was by far the most famous. His achievement was to place the widespread criticisms of the social consequences of the commission's emphasis on Roman law within a systematic social and political theory. Gierke was keen to influence the national and Prussian governments through his work. . . .

"A favourite accusation against Gierke was that his demand for a truly 'German' code, which largely excluded Roman law elements, ignored the fact that Roman law had become part of the German legal tradition in the period since the Middle Ages. . . .

"On balance, the influence of the various interest groups on the final version of the Code was disappointingly small in relation to the amount of attention they devoted to the matter. . . . In part, it was because of the limited responsiveness of the government and political parties to the frequently dubious claims made by sectional interests. . . .

"A second . . . feature of the debates is that they tended to reveal the disunity of opinions among the groups commenting on the draft code."

Ibid., Ch. 6 ("The Wilhelmine State and the Revision of the Code, 1888–1896"), pp. 160, 170–171, 181, 190–191, 194, 196: "The nature of the Wilhelmine state occupies a prominent position in the modern historiography of this period of German history. . . .

452 / Notes to Chapter VI

"A . . . consequence of this method of procedure was the loosening of the control of Prussia and the larger states over the work. It is true that the Reich justice office continued to be closely linked to Prussia, and never obtained the power to present legislative proposals without the prior agreement of the Prussian ministry of state in the 1890s. Nevertheless, it would be wrong to conclude from this that the office merely acted as the agent of Prussian policy. . . . In the 1870s, the question of legal unity was generally considered by governments to be a question of the location of sovereignty, and there are signs that such matters were uppermost in the minds of many ministers after 1888. . . .

"Of all the states involved, Prussia probably devoted the greatest attention to the task of revising the Code. . . . The controversy over the draft code had sharpened antagonisms between two alternative conceptions of nationalism: the concern for German/Christian traditions, emphasized by Gierke and the agrarians; and the older governmental/liberal nationalism, which stressed the unity of the State and its law and the concern with systematic precision and 'legal certainty'. . . .

"The Kaiser's involvement was part of a broader set of policies designed to link the Code with symbols of national unity and progress. . . .

"An important feature of the government's standpoint was that codification was a special type of legislation, which was not equivalent to the whole of the legal order. The claims of previous codes, most notably the *Allgemeines Landrecht*, to cover the whole of the legal order were rejected by legislators in the late nineteenth century. By the 1890s it was standard procedure for bureaucrats to divert calls for major legal reforms into other types of legislation. On the one hand, there was the possibility of using legislation by the individual states to achieve reforms which were not considered suitable for the whole of Germany. . . .

"The Civil Code was a very unusual piece of legislation, in terms both of its scope and of its complexity. For that reason, it would be wrong to infer too much about the operation of the Prussian and Reich governments in the 1890s from the Code's history."

Ibid., Ch. 7 ("The Final Stage: The Civil Code in the Bundesrat and Reichstag, 1895–1896"), pp. 199, 204–205, 231, 234–235, 238: "The months between October 1895 and July 1896 gave the Reich's legislative institutions the chance to discuss the Code at length for the first time. This in turn generated considerable levels of public interest. . . . The Code now became a pressing issue for politicians. . . .

"The . . . influence of the Bundesrat and Reichstag on the final content of the Code . . . was relatively limited. . . . [M]ost of the possible debates had been pre-empted in the second commission, where both the major states and the larger political parties . . . had had their say. A speedy conclusion to the work thus relied on the willingness of the states and political parties to renounce their constitutional rights to subject the Code to a fundamental revision. . . .

"In the end . . . the Code was accepted by a majority of two hundred and thirty-two votes to forty-eight on 1 July 1896. . . .

"Bismarck's involvement in this campaign was self-evidently opportunistic and seems to have been highly unpopular in Reichstag circles. . . . [T]he government had succeeded in gaining the support of all three liberal parties, the Centre party, and most of the two conservative parties for the Code. All of these groups recognized the advantages of legal unity, and the Code was in any case generally seen as an improvement on existing law. . . . [T]he general theory of legislation . . . [argued] that special legislation was the proper place for contentious reforms. . . .

"The conclusion of the Civil Code was a political event of great importance, and contemporaries recognized it as . . . a major piece of legislation and an honour to both the nation and the Reichstag. . . . The high degree of party unity in the final division suggests the ability of the Reichstag parties to overcome their members' other loyalties, for example to interest groups."

Ibid., Ch. 8 ("Conclusion"), pp. 241–242, 248–249: "From 1815 until 1896, the campaign for a Civil Code always depended on answers to those broader questions—the nature of the nation, the location of sovereignty, the definition of the proper role of the state *vis-à-vis* the different interests which made up 'civil society', and so on. . . . [I]n . . . 1866–71 . . . the political and constitutional hindrances to unified legislation were removed by Bismarck's 'revolution from above'. . . . [T]he major feature of the debates about legal unity in the 1860s and 1870s was the controversial nature of that 'revolution'. . . . Savigny's . . . emphasis on the *Volksgeist* as the true source of law . . . downgraded the role of legislation . . . because of the extent to which the state bureaucracies were attempting to solve the political problems of the post-revolutionary period by extensive use of their legislative powers. Yet in the long run these political aspects of Savigny's work had far less influence than the jurisprudential, technical aspects—the insistence on an historical approach to the law, the *Volksgeistlehre*, and so on. . . . Savigny's theory of the origins of the law tended to be separated from his hostility to codification, and Savigny was gradually transformed into a supporter of national codes. By the mid-1860s it would be fair to say that support for codification on the basis of historical legal traditions was the position adopted by most of the German political nation. . . .

"The widespread acceptance of the *Volksgeistlehre* was important in undermining fears that codification would involve the introduction of radical legal reforms. It also had important consequences for the way in which the Civil Code was prepared, where emphasis was placed on lengthy historical research, respect for regional peculiarities, and systematic precision in the formulation of legal norms. The work of the first codifying commission between 1874 and 1888 provides much evidence . . . of the . . . connection between the procedures adopted in the preparation of legislation and the eventual contents of that legislation. . . .

"Throughout the nineteenth century, codification had been a favourite method of political integration for the state bureaucracies. Indeed, it would be correct to suggest a certain consonance between the bureaucrats' drive towards rationalization of the law and the liberals' campaign for codification. . . . The departmental priorities of the Reich justice office and the Prussian ministry of justice involved an emphasis on clarity and systematic precision which successfully worked against demands from other ministries for social and economic reforms through the civil law."

On codification, with sporadic further relation to Savigny *et al.*, see esp. the following: Helmut Corng and Walter Wilhelm (eds.), *Wissenschaft und Kodifikation des Privatrechts im 19. Jahrhundert* (6 vols., Frankfurt, 1974–1982), yet with relatively little on legislation directly except for Vol. III in other contexts; P. Caroni, "Savigny und die Kodifikatione: Versuch einer Neudeutung des 'Berufes'," *Zeitschrift der Savigny-Stiftung für Rechtsgeschichte, Germanistische Abteilung* 86 (1969), pp. 97–176; H. Kiefner, "Thibaut und Savigny: Bemerkungen zum Kodifikationsstreit," in *Festscharift für Rudolf Gmür zum 70 Geburtstag 28. Juli 1983* (edited by A. Buschmann *et al.*, Bielefeld, 1983), pp. 53–85.

54. Eikema Hommes, *Major Trends*, pp. 193–194. Also cf. Hallowell, *Main Currents*, pp. 331–332.

More extensive and intensive bibliog. on the Pandectist School, with particular regard to the German *Civil Code* of 1900, can be found in the brochure of publications produced under the auspices of Keip Verlag to commemorate the hundredth-year anniversary in 1996 of the completion of the *Civil Code* in 1896. The publisher's brochure is entitled *Bürgerliches Gesetzbuch und Pandektenrecht*. I am grateful to Prof. Hans Erich Troje at Frankfurt University for supplying a copy of this brochure, with its rich secondary as well as primary bibliog. refs. I regret that I was not able to make better use of it here. It calls attention to the importance of the *Civil Code* as well as the Pandectist School. Its bibliog. refs. also suggest the key background role of the Historical School. The roles of Savigny

454 / Notes to Chapter VI

and Puchta are thus intricately interwoven in these contexts. The evident early place of Thibaut in the Pandectist movement—which subsequently centered on Savigny's Berlin pupil Puchta, whose work was greatly compatible with Savigny's—further serves to show indirectly the various common aims and methods shared by Savigny and Thibaut.

55. Otto Pflanze, *Bismarck and the Development of Germany*, Vol. II, *The Period of Unification, 1871–1880* (Princeton, 1990), Ch. IV, "Nationalism and National Policy," pp. 93–94: "After 1866 he [Bismarck] . . . [depicted] himself as a German patriot whose aim . . . had always been to unify Germany. Yet it would be wrong to conclude that his later expressions of German national sentiment were purely tactical. . . . The problem is not whether Bismarck was moved . . . by German national sentiment, but by what kind. Did he conceive the German nation as an ethnic and cultural entity, formed and animated by a *Volksgeist*? Or was the German nation for him an entity shaped by the state and associated with its social and political institutions? Was the German Reich a 'nation-state' or 'state-nation'?

"As used here, these terms identify two conflicting traditions in Germany. In the tradition of Herder, on the one hand, the nation is a spiritual force creating the unique forms of cultural life that characterize and differentiate peoples. . . . In the tradition of Hegel, on the other hand, the state is the vessel of the *Weltgeist* and as such a divine creation embodying morality—a conception that gave to the state a status never before attributed to it in western political thought. Hegel himself never invested the state with the power to produce ethnic homogeneity, but the Hegelian tradition assumed new forms as Germany passed from the age of the restoration to that of national unification. Divested of its metaphysical trappings, the state remained a *Machtstaat* in the era of *Realpolitik*. Earlier regarded as the product of spirit, the state was now assumed to have the moral authority to enforce conformity of spirit. . . .

"The traditions of Herder (nation-state) and Hegel (state-nation) were both alive in modified forms during the Bismarck period, but the German experience conformed more to the latter than the former. Although some German historians have been prone to identify the Hegelian tradition exclusively with liberalism, this is manifestly a distortion."

56. *Ibid*., pp. 93n, 95, with useful bibliog. refs. It perhaps is telltale that the main body of Pflanze's Ch. IV on "national policy" bears a rather vague relationship to his initial discussion of "nationalism," the two parts of the ch. title.

57. Hawgood, *Modern Constitutions*, Ch. XVIII; *Dokumente*, Vol. 2, pp. 267 ff.

58. *Modern Constitutions*, Ch. XVIII; *Dokumente*, pp. 318 ff.

59. Pflanze, *Bismarck*, Vol. III, *The Period of Fortification, 1880–1898* (Princeton, 1990), Ch. VI. Many other secondary sources could be adduced, needless to say, on such topics.

60. *Ibid.*

61. *Ibid.*

62. *Ibid.*

63. John, *Politics and the Law*, cf. index under "Bismarck."

64. Pflanze, *Bismarck*, Vol. I, *The Period of Unification, 1815–1871* (Princeton, 1990), Ch. IV.

65. On Bismarck and his era more broadly, concerning political realism, the state, nationalism, and so on, one can also consult the miscellaneous works to follow: Hans Rothfels (ed.), *Bismarck und der Staat* (2nd edn., Munich, Stuttgart, 1953, 1st. edn. 1925), on the state in connection with power, nation, church, society, etc., but with little concerning legislation in itself; Wilhelm Rössle (ed.), *Bismarcks Politik nach seinen Staatsschriften und Reden* (Jena, 1943), with many documents concerning the state in general terms but again with little on legislation *per se*; Theodore S. Hamerow (ed.), *The Age of Bismarck: Documents and Interpretations* (New York, 1973), a richly presented

collection with much inclusion of topics in legislation, showing its importance, but usually within other broader contexts; Leonard Krieger, *The German Idea of Freedom: History of a Political Tradition* (Chicago, 1957), with much pre-Bismarckian material relating to sovereignty, nationalism, and national liberalism, not to mention Hegel and Kant, but with esp. useful discussions on the liberal state (1830–1870) leading through the early Bismarckian era up to the Empire; Gustav Seeber (ed.), *Gestalten der Bismarckzeit* (2 vols., Berlin, 1978, 1986), an East German perspective from the Communist era on Bismarck's unification of the German state; George Steinmetz, *Regulating the Social: The Welfare State and Local Politics in Imperial Germany* (Princeton, 1993), primarily on social policy; Fritz Stern, *Gold and Iron: Bismarck, Bleichröder, and the Building of the German Empire* (New York, 1964); Otto Friedrich, *Blood and Iron: From Bismarck to Hitler* (New York, 1995), the Bismarck-Hitler progression being a much debated issue among historians, centering here on the impact of the von Moltke family; Carole Fink, *et al.* (eds.), *German Nationalism and the European Response, 1890–1914* (Norman, 1985), with inclusion of William II's efforts to bridge Prussian and wider German society; John C. G. Röhl, *Kaiser, Hof und Staat: Wilhelm II und die deutsche Politik* (Munich, 1987), arguing that William II by century's end established a crown-centered autocracy; Rich, *Age of Nationalism*, pp. 126, downplaying Bismarck's political realism or *Realpolitik* as unique to him in distinction to other political leaders more generally, while also stressing his realistic recognition of the limits of power and doctrine; Theodore S. Hamerow, *Restoration, Revolution, Reaction: Economics and Politics in Germany, 1815–1871* (Princeton, 1958), e.g. Ch. 14, "The Road to Unification" (p. 262: ". . . it was under the auspices of a policy of blood and iron that Central Europe finally embraced the machine age."); Gordon A. Craig, *Germany, 1866–1945* (New York, 1978), with chs. on unification, institutions, ideology, socialism (both in the forms Bismarck opposed and in those he developed), etc.; Robert C. Binkley, *Realism and Nationalism, 1852–1871* (New York, 1935, etc.), Chs. IX–XII passim on Germany; Thomas G. Barnes and Gerald D. Feldman, *Nationalism, Industrialization, and Democracy, 1815–1914* (Boston, 1972), Ch. 6 ("The Politics of Power, 1852–1871"), with a Bismarck speech to the *Reichstag* in 1863; and Boyd C. Shafer, *Nationalism: Myth and Reality* (New York, 1955), Sect. IV ("The Age of Nationalism, 1815–1955"), with inclusion of Germany but with such wide chronological scope to the supposed "age" of that "ism" as to render precise analysis difficult.

Perhaps the best survey concerned with legislation in Germany from numerous angles including codification (but not sovereignty and state *per se*) is in Helmut Coing (ed.), *Handbuch der Quellen und Literatur der neuren europäischen Privatrechtsgeschichte*, Vol. III, *Das 19. Jahrhundert*, Bk. 2 (Munich, 1982), Pt. II, Sect. VIII, pp. 1403 ff.

Finally, it is interesting to note Bismarck's characterization of the Prussian constitution in the 1860s. For him, the (non-absolutist?) essence of power held by both parliament and crown was ultimately legislative. This factor was often underscored by him throughout his career. Hence *Bismarck: The Memoirs*, Vol. II (translated by A. Butler, New York, 1966, repr. of 1899 edn.), p. 77: "I do not consider absolutism by any means a form of government that is desirable or successful in Germany in the long run. The Prussian Constitution, disregarding a few meaningless articles translated from that of Belgium, is in the main reasonable. It has three factors, the King and two Chambers, each of which by its vote can prevent arbitrary alterations of the legal *status quo*. This is a just apportionment of legislative power, but if the latter is emancipated from the public criticism of the press and from parliamentary control, there is increased danger of its going astray. The absolutism of the Crown is just as little tenable as the absolutism of parliamentary majorities; the necessity for the agreement of both in every alteration of the legal *status quo* is just, and we did not need to make any important improvement in the Prussian

Constitution. Government can be carried on with it, and the course of German policy would have been littered up if we had altered it in 1866."

66. Representative "debates" on the relation of Mazzinianism to Cavourism can be found in *The Unification of Italy, 1859–1861: Cavour, Mazzini, or Garibaldi?* (edited by C. Delzell, New York, 1965), esp. Sects. 2 ("Mazzinianism in the 1850s: Hindrance or Help?") and 3 ("Cavour's Use of Plebiscites: Desirable or Regrettable?").

An illustrative division of subject matter is found in René Albrecht-Carrié's *Italy from Napoleon to Mussolini* (New York, 1950), Ch. II ("Italy Becomes a National State"), sects. 3–4 ("The Role of Ideas: Mazzini, the Apostle" and "The Triumph of Reality: Cavour, the Wielder of Power"), and Ch. III ("Italy as a National State, 1870–1915"). E.g. pp. 36–37 (Ch. II, sect. 4): "[I]n terms of practical reality, Mazzini's activity was at best a noble failure. To this, . . . the career of Cavour present[s] the sharpest contrast. . . . Perhaps the chief impression . . . is that . . . he evinced none of the romantic stress of his contemporary [Mazzini]. . . . Cavour was nothing if not modern. . . . Cavour was a practical man . . . [not given to] contemplative speculation. . . . [H]is behavior was opportunistic . . ."

According to Raymond Grew, *A Sterner Plan for Italian Unity: The Italian National Society in the Risorgimento* (Princeton, 1963), Intro., pp. ix–x: "[T]hose nationalists [like Cavour] who won . . . favored unification with monarchy. . . . [T]hey came from fear as well as realism to rely on diplomacy, Piedmont's army, and the state rather than on revolution and popular participation to direct Italy's unification. . . . [T]hey moved . . . from concern for liberty and justice to an emphasis on unanimity and the strength of the state. . . . [R]epublicans were turning to Cavour . . . [and] nationalists would accept unification under Piedmontese monarchy. . . . [T]he era of Mazzini was really over. . . . [P]lebiscites and elections . . . followed unification."

Concerning law, the following works are of general interest: Antonio Marongiu, *Storia del diritto italiano: Ordinamento e istituto di governo* (Milan, 1977, new edn.), Pt. IV ("Il diritto pubblico italiano"), Ch. I, pp. 464 ff ("Politica diritto tra il 1848 e la proclamazione del Regno d'Italia"), and Ch. II ("Lo Stato italiano dal 1861 al 1915"), on a wide range of legal subjects but to the neglect of legislation; and Aldo Schiavone (ed.), *Stato e cultura giuridica in Italia dall'Unità alla Repubblica* (Rome, 1990), a wide-ranging series of detailed essays; Carlo Calisse, *A History of Italian Law* (translated by L. Register (Boston, 1928), Bk. I ("Public Law"), Ch. XXX ("The Restoration and Risorgimente"); Enrico Besta, *Il diritto pubblico italiano: Dai principati allo stato contemporaneo* (Padua, 1931), one of many such broad historical surveys of Italian public law; and Pietro Costa, *Lo stato immaginario: Metafore e paradigmi nella cultura giuridica italiana fra ottocento e novecento* (Milan, 1986), with some discussion of public law in Italian juridical ideas on "images" of the state.

A brief but good intro. to the legislative history of Italy in the nineteenth century, esp. after unification, can be found in M. Cappelletti, *et al.* (eds.), *The Italian Legal System: An Introduction* (Stanford, 1965, etc.), Ch. I ("History of Italian Law"), sects. 19–22. The following bare outline is useful (pp. 45–47): "The proclamation of the new Kingdom of Italy in 1861 brought about a rapid and sometimes artificial process of unification of law and centralization of administration. At first the process involved the simple introduction of the codes and principal public laws of Piedmont (the Kingdom of Sardinia headed by the House of Savoy) into the annexed territories. In some cases the introduction of these codes involved a regression to local laws. The second stage was the promulgation, in 1865 and following years, of new codes for the Kingdom of Italy: the Civil Code, Code of Commerce, Code of Civil Procedure, Navigation Code, and Code of Criminal Procedure.

"The most complex and most important of these codes was the Civil Code [1865]. . . . Its general structure was modeled on the Napoleonic Code, although it varied from its model by adhering to Italian legal traditions in some places and by innovating in others. Italian doctrine in the decades following the enactment of the code, especially in the years after the German Pandectist school had become influential, criticized it for its poor analytic structure. The compilers had been moved more by practical motivations than by scientific spirit. . . .

"There were two exceptions to legislative unification . . . [i]n Tuscany . . . [and] Venetia. . . .

"Partial unification ended with the promulgation of the new Commercial Code in 1882 . . . [and with] the Penal Code of 1889. The Commercial Code, although following the structure of the French Code de commerce of 1807, was a marked improvement over its model.

"The last codification prior to the enactment of the current codes of 1930 and 1940–42 was the revision in 1913 of the Code of Criminal Procedure of 1865. . . . The Code of 1913 marked the end of the first period of codification in unified Italy. Although not marked by great originality, these codes contributed much to the consolidation of the youthful Italian state."

Perhaps the most pertinent and substantive work on "legislative unification" is by Alberto Aquarone, who treats new legislation as well as the 1865 codifications, although he mostly sidesteps the problem of the state in general. His *L'unificazione legislativa e i codici del 1865* (Milan, 1960) consists of a lengthy introduction and voluminous documents. The complex background of those topics, earlier in the nineteenth century, is also briefly handled. But this work fits into the wider historiographical pattern for *Risorgimento* Italy, according to which historians either deal with the state but neglect legislation or conversely discuss legislation and codification at the expense of the state. Lacking here is a full-length analysis of legislation and codification in relation to the state not just in terms of 1865 but the whole *Risorgimento*. Also on legislation in relation to codification, etc. in Italy, cf. Coing (ed.), *Handbuch*, Vol. III, Bk. 1 (Munich, 1982), Pt. II, Sect. I, pp. 177 ff., though not on sovereignty and state *per se*.

For Cavour on legislation, cf. e.g. *Tutti gli scritti di Camillo Cavour* (edited by C. Pischedda and G. Talamo, 4 vols., Turin, repr. 1976–1978), Vol. IV, pp. 1863–1865, *"Note sur la législation en vigueur dans les États Sardes relativement à l'exercice du culte protestant"* (1855).

Numerous other related topics in bibliography could be cited at length. On nationalism *per se*, there is e.g. Ronald S. Cunsolo, *Italian Nationalism: From Its Origins to World War II* (Melbourne, 1990). On public administration, there is, e.g. [*Istituto per la scienza dell' amministrazione pubblica:*] *L'amministrazione nella storia moderna*, in 2 vols. (*Archivio*, new ser., no. 3) (Milan, 1985), on Cavour, etc. Regarding liberalism and fascism, there is e.g. Guido Melis, *Due modelli di amministrazione tra liberalismo e fascismo* (Rome, 1988). On developments from unification to fascism, there is Zanni Rosiello (ed.), *Gli apparati statali dall' Unità al fascismo* (Bologna, 1976).

On constitutionalism and a host of other "isms," there are several notable works by Carlo Ghisalberti. Indicative headings in his *Storia costituzionale d'Italia, 1849–1948* (Rome, 1974) include the following: "Il liberalismo risorgimentale" (I, 1), "Il liberalismo moderno" (III, 7), "Autoritarismo, . . . parlamentarismo . . ." (VI), "La fine dello Stato liberale" (IX), "Gradualismo del fascismo . . ." (IX, 12), and "Fascismo, nazismo e razzismo" (X, 8). Although sporadic attention is given to "legislative activity," there is little focus on its key role regarding the state. Not oncerned with the legislative state, the author dwells on such typologies as "liberal state," "administrative monarchy," "parliamentary regime," "political unification," "parliamentary omnipotence," "unitary state," "republican constitution," "constitutional republic," and "parliamentary republic." One short section deals specifically with aspects of "legislative and administrative unification" (III, 8). Nevertheless, the author's scattered discussions on legislation need to be brought together in order to show the central role of the legislative state. The earlier period is covered in similar fashion in Ghisalberti's *Dall' antico regime al 1848: Le origini costituzionali dell' Italia moderna* (Rome, 1974, 1987). Starting with the "ancient regime" and progressing through the Napoleonic era to the revolutions of 1848, the author highlights such categories as the following: "La qualificazione della sovranità e il trapasso dallo Stato assoluto allo Stato costituzionale" (I, 8), "Dall' assolutismo al costituzionalismo" (II), "Stato e strutture politiche nel periodo napoleonico" (IV), and the like. There are brief sporadic discussions of "legislative activity" amidst broader considerations of "public institutions" and "administrative organization." However, as was seen in our preceding book, such categories as state absolutism and state constitutionalism, absolutist state and constitutional state, state liberalism and state conservatism, and liberal state and conservative state are all typically reducible to the legislative state and state legislation. Concentrating on the *Risorgimento* period in his *Stato e costituzione nel risorgimento* (Milan, 1972), Ghisalberti broadly identifies the newly emergent "modern state" of Italy during this period with the "liberal state," relating the two even more peripherally to legislation. Cf. esp. Chs. I ("Sulla formazione dello Stato moderno in Italia") and VII ("Silvo Spaventa teorico dello Stato liberale"). Closely related in approach is Ghisalberti's *Modelli costituzionali e stato risorgimentale* (Rome, 1987), highlighting such rubrics as "constitutionalism" and "*Risorgimento* state" (Chs. I–II).

Similar typologies centering around a maze of "isms," to the neglect of legislation, are in Manlio Di Lalla's *Storia del liberalismo italiano dal risorgimento al fascismo* (Bologna, 1976). Indicative headings include: "Realismo e fatalismo durante il dominio napoleonico" (II, 1), "I liberali rivoluzionari" (III), "Momenti liberali del mazzinianismo" (III, 7), "Costituzionalismo liberale" (IV), "Liberalismo e storicismo romantico" (IV, 1), "Realismo e costituzionalismo del liberali moderati" (IV, 2), "Storicismo tedesco e cattolicesimo liberale" (IV, 3), "La . . . vitalità del liberalismo cavouriano" (V, 3), "Il liberalismo unitario . . ." (V, 6), "La Carona tra la tentazione del costituzionalismo e . . . regime pseudoparlamentare" (VI, 4), "Empirismo o principio regolativo?" (VII), "Il trasformismo . . . (VII, 4), ". . . Il pluralismo agnostico" (VII, 5), and "La polemica sul parlamentarismo."

Of contextual documentary value is Denis Mack Smith (ed.), *The Making of Italy, 1796–1870* (New York, 1968), in addition to the many other notable books by him on the *Risorgimento* and its political leaders.

Notes to Chapter VII
The Growth of "Neo-*Isms*"

1. Virgilio Giorgianni, *Neopositivismo e scienza del diritto* (Rome, 1956), e.g. Ch. VI, sect. 1, a(2), "Il formalismo giuridico kelseniano come conseguenza del presupposto epistemologico della teoria pura."

2. A. S. de Bustamante y Montoro, "Kelsenism," in *Interpretations of Modern Legal Philosophy: Essays in Honor of Roscoe Pound* (edited by Paul Sayre, New York, 1947), pp. 43 ff.

3. Fassò, *Storia*, Vol. III, Ch. XIV ("Aspetti filosofici della scienza giuridica del Novecento").

4. Eikema Hommes, *Major Trends*, Ch. XIV ("Some Existentialist and Neo-Positivist Trends in Modern Legal Philosophy").

5. Thilly and Wood, *History*, Chs. XXI–XXII ("Realist Tendencies in Recent Philosophy," and "Pragmatism, Positivism, and Analytical Philosophy").

6. The account to follow, from Hallowell, *Main Currents*, pp. 343–345, is preceded by discussion of the Analytical School of law begun in Britain by Bentham and Austin. German jurists like Jellinek, influenced by positivism, treated jurisprudence as a formal legal science and were engaged especially in the examination of positive law. The account below correctly underscores the Kelsenian "norms" in their "pure" form as linking neopositivism to neo-Kantianism, in contradistinction to neo-Hegelianism. By indicating the affinity of these legal norms to universal Platonic "ideas" of law, the account also aptly serves to show the bond of idealism that formerly united more closely (in the nineteenth century) Kantianism with Hegelianism. Hence the joint treatment of works by Kant and Hegel above, in our Part One, under the rubric of "ideal*ism*," can now be considered for the early and mid-twentieth century under two different schools or branches. Hence Hallowell: "By the end of the nineteenth century jurists had split into two opposing schools: the Neo-Hegelians and the Neo-Kantians. The formalism of Gerber, Laband and Jellinek was carried to its logical conclusion by the Neo-Kantians in an effort to create a

'pure' science of law divorced completely from all political and social reality. Regarding jurisprudence as being essentially a normative science concerned with 'what ought to be' rather than with 'what is,' they removed jurisprudence by definition to a 'pure' realm of theory beyond actuality. By emphasizing norms to the exclusion of the wills that must exist in actuality in order to realize them, the Neo-Kantians postulated a realm that may have had logical but certainly no actual existence. At any rate they assumed the existence of this realm apart from social reality and acted for the purposes of constructing a 'pure theory of law' 'as if' it actually existed. . . .

"The separation of law from political and social reality, begun by jurists like Laband and Jellinek, was completed by the Neo-Kantians. In an effort to establish a 'pure' science of law, jurists like Rudolph Stammler and Hans Kelsen sought to find the *a priori* principles which underlie all law regardless of its content. They sought to isolate, in a Platonic sense, the 'idea' of law, which was universal, from the content of law which was variable. They adopted for this purpose the critical method of Kant, a method which ignores historical development and psychological motivation in favor of a deductive search for the universal and formal elements of knowledge. They sought to find the pure forms of law, the universal elements that are found in all law. They assume, of course, that the content of law is ever changing and that the form of law alone is eternal and immutable."

Such classifications agree, on the whole, with the approaches of Spahr (ed.), *Readings*, Chs. V, VII, XIV–XV, XVII. Kant's "Doctrine of Right" and Hegel's *Philosophy of Right* are used by Spahr together under the category of "German idealism." Later neo-Kantianism is handled with respect to Rudolf Stammuler under the heading of "new jurisprudence"; all this appears under the broader category of "the defense of the doctrine of sovereignty," under which in diverse different ways are also included Albert Dicey, Roscoe Pound, and Benjamin Cardozo. Under separate, more complex classifications are grouped British idealism in T. H. Green, British neo-Hegelianism in Bernard Bosanquet, and nationalism in Heinrich von Treitschke; all are grouped together under the broad heading of "end-century idealism and nationalism." Other ways of presenting neo-idealism are also used by Spahr.

7. Among the multitude of works dealing with legal positivism, the following provide a brief sampling of the many diverse ways in which history has been mixed with theory, inclusive of such writers as Kelsen, Austin, and Hart: W. J. Waluchow, *Inclusive Legal Positivism* (Oxford, 1994), a recent reaction against earlier exclusive positivism through adoption of a more comprehensive viewpoint (p. 1: "Legal-theory is in a perplexing state. Traditional boundaries between rival views have been blurred to the point where one wonders just what the issues are . . ."); Samuel I. Shuman, *Legal Positivism: Its Scope and Limitations* (Detroit, 1963), e.g. pp. 12 ff., "Some Differences between Analytical Jurisprudence and Legal Positivism"; Elspeth Attwooll (ed.), *Perspectives in Jurisprudence* (Glasgow, 1977), Ch. I, "Coercion and the Law" (esp. sect. I, "The concept of coercion as crucial to the law"), and Ch. II, "John Austin's Political Pamphlets, 1824–1839"; *Cos' è il positivismo giuridico* (Milan, 1965), esp. Ch. IX on "legal positivism and the modern state"; Walter Ott, *Der Rechtspositivismus* (2nd edn., Berlin, 1992), Pt. I, Ch. I, sects. 3–5 on Austin's analytical jurisprudence, positive law, and Kelsen's "pure" theory; Werner Maihofer, *Naturrecht oder Rechtspositivismus?* (3rd edn., Darmstadt, 1981); and John Finch, *Introduction to Legal Theory* (3rd edn., London, 1979), Chs. 2, 4–5, 7 on positivism, Bentham, Austin, Kelsen, force, and authority.

Mieczyslaw Maweli, *Judicial Positivism and Human Rights* (New York, 1981), gives some considerations to legislation. He combines extensive historical examinations of writers like Austin with discussions of neo-positivist viewpoints a la Kelsen and others, as geared toward a newer concept of positive realism in Ch. X. There he states (p. 363): "Positivist realism emerges as a theory of law adjusted to the new social conditions and political realities of the end of the 20th century." Clearly, inclusive positivism and positivist realism in law reflect the continuing vitality of positivism in newer forms, while broadening well beyond the "pure" confines of Kelsen's positivistic norms to embrace a wide variety of other subject areas, including politics and sociology.

On philosophical positivism more generally, there is A. J. Ayer (ed.), *Logical Positivism* (Glencoe, 1959), Ch. 5 (by Carl Hempel, a leading recent exponent of positivism, on "The Empiricist Criterion of Meaning"), and Pt. IV ("Analytical Philosophy"); and Richard Harvey Brown, "Positivism, Relativism, and Narrative in the Logic of the Historical Sciences" (review article), *Amer. Hist. Rev.*, 92 (1987), pp. 908 ff.

8. Hans Kelsen, *General Theory of Law and State* (Camb., Mass., 1945). Cf. Kelsen's *Allgemeine Staatslehre* (Berlin, 1925) and his . . . *Staatsrechtslehre* (1911). Also Kelsen's *Das Problem der souveränität und die Theorie des Völkerrechts: Beitrag zu einer reinen Rechtslehre* (Tubingen, 1920).

9. Kelsen, *Law and State*, Pt. I, Ch. I, pp. 3, 13, 18, 24, 29–32.

10. *Ibid.*, Pt. I, Ch. IV, pp. 62–63.

11. *Ibid.*, Pt. I, Ch. V, p. 71.

12. *Ibid.*, Pt. I, Ch. I, pp. 33–36.

13. *Ibid.*, Pt. I, Chs. X–XI (the latter ch., once again, entitled "The Hierarchy of Norms"), pp. 112–115, 122–123, 126–128: "According to the nature of the basic norm, we may distinguish between two different types of orders or normative systems: static and dynamic systems. Within an order of the first kind the norms are 'valid' and that means, we assume that the individuals whose behavior is regulated by the norms 'ought' to behave as the norms prescribe. . . . The basic norm of a dynamic system is the fundamental rule according to which the norms of the system are to be created. A norm forms part of a dynamic system if it has been created in a way that is—in the last analysis—determined by the basic norm. . . .

"The system of norms we call a legal order is a system of the dynamic kind. Legal norms are not valid because they themselves or the basic norm have a content the binding force of which is self-evident. . . .

"Law is always positive law, and its positivity lies in the fact that it is created and annulled by acts of human beings, thus being independent of morality and similar norm systems. This constitutes the difference between positive law and natural law, which, like morality, is deduced from a presumably self-evident basic norm which is considered to be the expression of the 'will of nature' or of 'pure reason.' The basic norm of a positive legal order is nothing but the fundamental rule according to which the various norms of the order are to be created. . . .

"Legal norms are created in many different ways: general norms through custom or legislation, individual norms through judicial and administrative acts or legal transactions. Law is always created by an act that deliberately aims at creating law, except in the case when law has its origin in custom, that is to say, in a generally observed course of conduct, during which the acting individuals do not consciously aim at creating law; but they must regard their acts as in conformity with a binding norm and not as a matter of arbitrary choice. . . .

"We shall distinguish between statutory and customary law as the two fundamental types of law. By statutory law we shall understand law created in a way other than by custom, namely, by legislative, judicial, or administrative acts or by legal transactions, especially by contracts and (international) treaties. . . .

"If one looks upon the legal order from the dynamic point of view, as it has been expounded here, it seems possible to define the concept of law in a way quite different from that in which we have tried to define it in this theory. It seems especially possible to ignore the element of coercion in defining the concept of law.

"It is a fact that the legislator can enact commandments without considering it necessary to attach a criminal or civil sanction to their violation. If such norms are also called legal norms, it is because they were created by an authority which, according to the constitution, is competent to create law. They are law because they issue from a law-creating authority. According to this concept, law is anything that has come about in the way the constitution prescribes for the creation of law. This dynamic concept differs from the concept of law defined as a coercive norm. According to the dynamic concept, law is something created by a certain process, and everything created in this way is law. This dynamic concept, however, is only apparently a concept of law. It contains no answer to the question of what is the essence of law, what is the criterion by which law can be distinguished from other social norms. This dynamic concept furnishes an answer only to the question whether or not and why a certain norm belongs to a system of valid legal norms, forms a part of a certain legal order. And the answer is, a norm belongs to a certain legal order if it is created in accordance with a procedure prescribed by the constitution fundamental to this legal order.

"It must, however, be noted that not only a norm, i.e., a command regulating human behavior, can be created in the way prescribed by the constitution for the creation of law. An important stage in the law-creating process is the procedure by which general norms are created, that is, the procedure of legislation. The constitution may organize this procedure of legislation. . . .

"If, within a legal order, there exists by the side of statutory also customary law, if the law-applying organs, especially the courts, have to apply not only the general norms created by the legislative organ, the statutes, but also the general norms created by custom, then custom is considered to be a law-creating fact just as is legislation. This is possible only if the constitution—in the material sense of the word—institutes custom, just as it institutes legislation, as a law-creating procedure. Custom has to be, like legislation, a constitutional institution. . . .

"Sometimes it is maintained that custom is not a constitutive, that is to say, a law-creating fact, but has only a declaratory character: it merely indicates the preexistence of a rule of law. This rule of law is, according to the natural law doctrine, created by God or by nature; according to the German historic school. . . .

"There is no difference between a rule of customary law and a rule of statutory law in their relationship to the law-applying organ. The statement that a customary rule becomes law only by recognition on the part of the court applying the rule is neither more nor less correct than the same statement made with reference to a rule enacted by the legislative organ. . . . The real difference between customary and statutory law consists in the fact that the former is a decentralized whereas the latter is a centralized creation of law. Customary law is created by the individuals subject to the law created by them, whereas statutory law is created by special organs instituted for that purpose. In this respect, customary law is similar to law made by contract or treaty. . . .

"The general norms established by way of legislation or custom form a level which comes next to the constitution in the hierarchy of law."

14. *Ibid.*, Pt. II, Ch. I, pp. 201–202: "The distinction between private and public law, in traditional jurisprudence, is made the basis of the systematization of law. Yet we look in vain for an unambiguous definition of the two concepts. Yet . . . theory designates as 'private law' the norms stipulating duties and rights between private persons, and as 'public' law the norms stipulating duties and rights between the State, on the one hand, and private persons, on the other. . . .

"This theory is obviously not satisfactory. . . . The difficulty in distinguishing between public and private law resides precisely in the fact that the relation between the State and its subjects can have not only a 'public' but also a 'private' character."

15. *Ibid.*, Pt. II, Chs. II–III, pp. 255–258, 269–270, 272, 280: "The power of the State is usually listed as its third so-called element. The State is thought of as an aggregate of individuals, a people, living within a certain limited part of the earth's surface and subject to a certain power: One State, one territory, one people, and one power. Sovereignty is said to be the defining characteristic of this power. Though unity of the power is held to be as essential as the unity of the territory and the people, it is nevertheless thought possible to distinguish between three different component powers, the legislative, the executive, and the judicial power of the State.

"The word 'power' has different meanings in these different usages. . . . The 'power' of the State must be the validity and efficacy of the national legal order, if sovereignty is to be considered as a quality of this power. . . . Legislation (*legis latio* of Roman law) is the creation of laws (*leges*). . . . Execution of laws, however, is also the function of so-called judicial power. . . . The common trichotomy is thus at bottom a dichotomy, the fundamental distinction of *legis latio* and *legis executio*. The latter function is subdivided into the judicial and the executive functions in the narrower sense. . . .

"The functions of the State thus prove to be identical with the essential functions of law. It is the difference between creation and application of law that expresses itself in the distinction between the three powers of the State. . . .

"By legislative power or legislation one does not understand the entire function of creating law, but a special aspect of this function, the creation of general norms. 'A law'—a product of the legislative process—is essentially a general norm, or a complex of such norms. . . .

"By legislation, further, is understood not the creation of all general norms, but only the creation of general norms by special organs, namely by the so-called legislative bodies. . . . The modern concept of legislation could not arise until the deliberate creation of general norms by special central organs began to take its place beside or instead of customary creation. . . .

"From a functional point of view, there is no essential difference between these norms and 'laws' or statutes (general norms) created by the legislative body. The general norms created by the legislative body are called 'statutes' in contradistinction to those general norms which, exceptionally, an organ other than the legislative body—the head of state or other executive or judicial organs—may create. The general norms issued by organs of the executive power are usually not called 'statute' but 'ordinances' or 'regulations.' . . . The function is here exactly the same as that which is ordinarily performed by the legislative body. A similar impropriety is involved when general norms created by a court are classified as decisions and referred to the judicial function.

"A law-creating function not taken into account at all by the usual trichotomy is the creation of general norms by way of custom. The general norms of customary law, although not created by the legislative power, are executed by the organs of the so-called 'executive' as well as by the organs of the judicial power. Custom is a law-creating process completely equivalent to the legislative procedure. The customary creation of general legal norms is a *legis latio* just as much as what is ordinarily designated as legislation. The general norms of customary law are applied by the executive power just as are the statutes. . . . The legislative process, that is, the creation of general legal norms, is divided into at least two stages: the creation of general norms which is usually called legislation (but comprises also the creation of customary law) and the creation of the general norms regulating this process of legislation. The latter norms form the essential contents of that normative system which is designated as the 'constitution.' . . .

"The judicial review of legislation is an obvious encroachment upon the principle of separation of powers. This principle lies at the basis of the American Constitution and is considered to be a specific element of democracy. . . .

"The concept of 'separation of powers' designates a principle of political organization. It presupposes that the three so-called powers can be determined as three distinct coordinated functions of the State, and that it is possible to define boundary lines separating each of these three functions from the others. But this presupposition is not borne out by the facts. As we have seen, there are not three but two basic functions of the State: creation and application (execution) of law. . . . [I]t is not possible to define boundary lines separating these functions from each other. . . . [T]he distinction between creation and application of law . . . has only a relative character, most acts of State being at the same time law-creating and law-applying acts. It is impossible to assign the creation of law to one organ and the application (execution) of law to another so exclusively that no organ would fulfill both functions simultaneously. It is hardly possible, and at any rate not desirable, to reserve even legislation—which is only a certain kind of law-creation—to a 'separate body of public servants,' and to exclude all the other organs from this function. . . .

"By 'legislation' as a function we can hardly understand anything other than the creation of general legal norms. An organ is a legislative organ insofar as it is authorized to create general legal norms. It never occurs in political reality that all the general norms of a national legal order have to be created exclusively by one organ designated as legislator. There is no legal order of a modern State according to which the courts and adminsitrative authorities are excluded from creating general legal norms, that is, from legislating, and legislating not only on the basis of statutes and customary law, but also directly on the basis of the constitution. . . . The habit of characterizing only one organ as 'legislative' organ, of calling the general norms created by this organ 'laws' or 'statutes,' is justified, however, to a certain extent if this organ has a certain prerogative in creating general norms. . . . Thus the so-called legislative organ is the source of all general norms, in part directly and in part indirectly through organs to which it delegates legislative competence. . . .

"Most constitutions that are supposed to embody the principle of the separation of powers authorize the head of the executive department to enact general norms in place of the legislative organ, without a special authorization emanating from this organ. . . .

"We have already seen that courts fulfill a legislative function when authorized to annul unconstitutional laws. They do so also when they are competent to annul a regulation on the ground that it appears to be contrary to a law. . . .

"Where customary law is valid, the creation of general norms is not reserved for the so-called legislative organ even in the sense that other organs can create such norms only upon authorization from the former. Custom is a method of creating general norms that is a genuine alternative to legislation. As to the effect of their legal function, custom and legislation are in no way different. Customary and statutory law are equally obligating for the individual. . . .

"Thus one can hardly speak of any separation of legislation from other functions of the State in the sense that the so-called 'legislative' organ—to the exclusion of the so-called 'executive' and 'judicial' organs—would alone be competent to exercise this function. . . .

"When courts are competent to examine not only individual administrative measures but also administrative regulations and administrative laws, then these legislative functions are actually under the control of courts. As pointed out, such a control is not compatible with the principle of the separation of powers."

16. *Ibid.*, Pt. II, Chs. IV–V, pp. 283, 298–299, 303: "The central problem of political theory is the classification of governments. From a juristic point of view, it is the distinction between different archetypes of constitutions. Hence, the problem may be presented also as the distinction between different forms of State. . . .

"The will of the State, that is, the legal order, is created in a procedure that runs, as we have pointed out, through several stages. . . .

"Democracy at the stage of legislation means—disregarding direct democracies—that, in principle, all the general norms are created by a parliament elected by the people. . . .

"At the stage of legislation it is possible to combine, to a certain extent, the principle of indirect and that of direct democracy. Such a combination is the institution of 'popular initiative,' which means that parliament must decide upon proposals for legislation signed by a certain number of citizens. Another way of combining direct and indirect democracy is the 'referendum.' . . .

"The State is, as we have found, a legal order. Its 'elements,' territory and people, are the territorial and personal spheres of validity of that legal order. The 'power' of the State is the validity and efficacy of the legal order, while the three 'powers' or functions are different stages in the creation thereof. The two basic forms of government, democracy and autocracy, are different modes of creating the legal order. . . . [C]entralization and decentralization, generally considered as forms of State organization with reference to territorial division, must be understood as two types of legal orders. The difference between a centralized and a decentralized State must be a difference in their legal orders."

17. *Ibid.*, Pt. II, Ch. V, pp. 316–317.

18. The topic of sovereignty is affirmed by Kelsen to reside at the apex of his theory of the state, but not in traditional modes of the power to issue legislative commands *per se* (as according to Austin). The context is rather the coercive normative legal order of the national state, above which there is no higher legal order (including international law). Through this context comes the authority to issue obligating legislative commands.

Hence *Ibid.*, Pt. II, Ch. IV, pp. 383–384: "The most important consequence of the theory which proceeds from the primacy of national law is that the State whose legal order is the starting point of the whole construction can be considered to be sovereign. For the legal order of this State is presupposed to be the supreme order, above which no other legal order exists. . . .

"The statement that sovereignty is an essential quality of the State means that the State is a supreme authority. 'Authority' is usually defined as the right or power to issue obligating commands. The actual power of forcing others to a certain behavior does not suffice to constitute an authority. . . . Only a normative order can be 'sovereign,' that is to say, a supreme authority, the ultimate reason for the validity of norms which one individual is authorized to issue as 'commands' and other individuals are obliged to obey. . . .

"The State in its capacity as legal authority must be identical with the national legal order. That the State is sovereign means that the national legal order is an order above which there is no higher order."

Kelsen is not wholly accurate when he says that these main points in his argument diverge fundamentally from Austin's command-theory of legislation and sovereignty. Upon closer inspection, the end result seems once more to be a different version of how Austin had, long before, conceived his command-theory to lie at the heart of legal sovereignty. Kelsen's qualified prefatory statements above on his close affinities with Austin are perhaps closer to the mark than his subsequent periodic emphases on their differences. This is not to suggest that Kelsen's state theory is merely Austinianism in a new guise despite the label "neo-Austinian*ism*" applied above. The point is rather that here as elsewhere the central content of coercive legislation remains intact, once the outer layers of a normative system are peeled away to reveal the actual operations of the state's inner legislative core. To be sure, Kelsen presents a more elaborate formalistic (neo-Kantian) system of legal logic than we encountered in Austin's *Lectures*. Here Kelsen was also influenced by German system-builders of state theory in the positivist traditions of Jhering, Jellinek, and many others. Yet the neo-Austinian no less than the wider neo-positivist end products must be duly recognized.

19. The perspectives on Kelsen given in the preceding note are further borne out in Kelsen's voluminous Appendix, which reacts in part to the "renaissance" of natural-law theories of justice in the early twentieth century. The Appendix focuses on positivistic aspects of positive law as the core problem (and as the entryway for legislation) in Kelsen's system of norms, which he relates to traditional theories of natural law and metaphysical systems. There is an interesting concluding evaluation, pro and con, of "Kant's critical idealism and legal positivism."

To be more specific, Kelsen's huge Appendix in *ibid.*, pp. 389–446 (translated by W. Kraus), bears the indicative title "Natural Law Doctrine and Legal Positivism." The titles of its four sections indicate Kelsen's focus on positive (or positivistic) law: I, "The Idea of Natural Law and the Essence of Positive Law"; II, "Natural and Positive Law as Systems of Norms"; III, "The Relation of Natural to Positive Law. The Political Significance of Natural-Law Theory"; and IV, "The Epistemological (Metaphysical) and Psychological Foundations." Included hereunder are such topics as: I, D, "The Basic Norm of Positive Law"; I, F, "The Limitation of the Natural-Law Idea"; II, A, "The Unity of Systems of Norms"; II, B, "The Static Principle of Natural Law and the Dynamic Principle of Positive Law"; II, C, "The Limitation of Positivism"; II, D, "Positive Law as a Meaningful Order"; III, A, "The Exclusive Validity of a System of Norms: the Logical Principle of Contradiction in the Sphere of Normative Validity"; III, B, "The Norm as an 'Ought' and as a Psychological Fact . . ."; III, D, "The Logical Impossibility of the Coexistence of Positive and Natural Law"; IV, B (c), "Legal positivism, law and power"; IV, B (d), "The transcendental-logical natural-law doctrine. The political indifference of legal positivism"; IV, B (e), "The ideal of justice becomes a logical pattern"; IV, B (f), "The Method of the Ideal Type"; IV, B (g), "The realization of ideal types in intellectual history"; and IV, B (h), "Kant's critical idealism and legal positivism."

In his concluding comments, pro and con, on Kant's philosophy (pp. 444 ff.), Kelsen states as follows: "The last of the types we have developed, which in contrast to the metaphysical, has been described as critical dualism, evidently bears the features of Kant's philosophy of critical idealism. Yet it will be immediately observed that Kant's philosophical system differs somewhat from our ideal picture. . . . The role which the 'thing-in-itself' plays in his system reveals a good deal of metaphysical transcendence. . . . [W]e do not find in him . . . uncompromising . . . relativism, which is the inescapable consequence of any real elimination of metaphysics [impossible for Kant because he was] . . . deeply rooted in Christianity. . . . So it happened that Kant, whose philosophy of transcendent logic was preeminently destined to provide the groundwork for a positivistic legal and political doctrine, stayed, as a legal philosopher, in the rut of the natural-law doctrine. . . . Ultimately, positivism proves itself only in discarding the particular ideology which the natural-law theory uses in its justification of positive law. . . . [However,] the overwhelming experience of the Great War [has shaken the advance of positivism]. . . . An anti-metaphysical, scientific-critical philosophy with objectivity as its ideal, like legal positivism, seems to thrive only in relatively quiet times. . . . [Our age now] augurs a renaissance of metaphysics and . . . natural-law theory."

20. Hans Kelsen, *Pure Theory of Law* (Berkeley, 1967, new edn. and transl. of 1st Ger. edn. of 1934), Chs. I, 1 and VI, 37–41.

21. Kelsen, *Law and State*, p. 201.

22. For a broad overview of the problem of norms in relation to authority, with references to Kelsen, Hart, and numerous other theorists, see George C. Christie, *Law, Norms, and Authority* (London, 1982), with some useful diagrams. For other kinds of broad general discussion on norms with respect to legislation, there is e.g. Hermann K. Heussner, *Volksgesetzgebung in den USA und Deutschland: Ein Vergleich der Normen, Funktionen, Probleme und Erfahrungen* (Cologne, 1994); Ernst-Wolfgang Böckenforde, *Gesetz und gesetzgebende Gewalt: Von den Anfängen der deutschen Staatsrechtslehre bis*

zur Höhe des staatsrechtlichen Positivismus (Berlin, 1958), with discussions on Locke, Montesquieu, Rousseau, Hegel, Jellinek, and many others; Gerd Roellecke, *Der Begriff des positiven Gesetzes und das Grundgesetz* (Mainz, 1969), with regard to Hobbes, Kant, Marx, Hegel, Kelsen and many others mostly as regards *Gesetzesbegriff* in general but also to *Gesetzgebung* more specifically; and Maneli, *Judicial Positivism*, passim on legislation, norms, Kelsen (esp. pp. 318 ff.), and related pertinent items.

23. Spahr (ed.), *Readings*, pp. 701 ff.

24. On later idealism or neo-idealism and its relationships to liberalism and Hegelianism, cf. in general the following: Sabine, *History of Political Theory*, pp. 737 ff.; Spahr (ed.), *Readings*, Ch. VII; Peter Nicholson, *The Political Philosophy of the British Idealists: Selected Studies* (Cambridge, 1990), who sympathetically discusses T. H. Green's and Bernard Bosanquet's respective concepts of common good and general will, finding in them basic common ground rather than the contrasts often made between them (neo-Kantian vs. neo-Hegelian, etc.); Avial Simhony, "Idealist Organicism: Beyond Holism and Individualism," *Hist. of Pol. Tht.*, XII (1991), pp. 515–535, who counters Nicholson by pointing out on other grounds the distinctive differences between Green and Bosanquet; and Sandra M. Den Otter, *British Idealism and Social Explanation: A Study in Late Victorian Thought* (New York, 1996), who concentrates on Bosanquet and other second-generation British idealists and explores their distinctive critical blends of British and German (including Hegelian) intellectual traditions.

Hallowell, *Main Currents*, dwells primarily on German forms of neo-Hegelianism and neo-idealism, as in the following manner (pp. 343–344): "Repelled by this highly abstract and formal endeavor [of the Neo-Kantians] the Neo-Hegelians rejected all normative criteria of law and emphasized the conception of law as a social product and instrument. Positivism had led to a complete separation of fact and standard, will and norm. It was necessary after the emergence of positivism to make one or the other absolute. The result of this separation and the focusing of attention upon either fact or standard to the exclusion of the other was to divorce the concept of law completely from any absolute idea of justice in the form of eternal and universal truths transcending individuals. The Neo-Hegelians focused their attention upon legal content to the exclusion of all normative considerations, the Neo-Kantians focused their attention upon the normative elements in law to the exclusion of all consideration of legal content. Both schools of thought, as a consequence, fostered irresponsibility; the Neo-Kantians, individual irresponsibility, and the Neo-Hegelians, irresponsibility on the part of the State. In the final analysis both placed the law beyond the boundaries of good and evil. Any action was lawful, according to the Neo-Kantians, if it conformed to certain formal, procedural requirements. . . . The Neo-Hegelians, on the other hand, distinguished the law by the physical coercion behind it irrespective of the form which that coercion took. By separating will and norm, interest and ideal, fact and standard, and by emphasizing one of these as the criterion of law to the exclusion of the other, responsibility is made impossible for the idea of responsibility requires both notions. A will, unrestrained by a recognition of transcendent standards, is limited only by its physical capacity and by the might of a stronger will. A norm, without a will to actualize it, is equally devoid of imposing responsibility, for the notion of responsibility necessarily implies *willing* to do or not to do something specific. In the last analysis justice is equated with might."

Hallowell goes on, in a section on "The Pure Theory of Power," to discuss the emergence of the German neo-Hegelian school of law and politics under Josef Kohler (1849–1919, who attacked the Historical as well as Analytical Schools), Adolf Lasson, Erich Kaufmann, and Carl Schmitt.

The lines between neo-Hegelianism, neo-Kantianism, neo-positivism, and myriad related neo-"isms," especially in Germany, are so interwoven as to render distinct lines of development difficult to distinguish. Cf. e.g. Klaus Christian Köhnke, *The Rise of Neo-*

Kantianism: German Academic Philosophy between Idealism and Positivism (translated by R. Hollingdale, Cambridge, 1991), and Ossip K. Flechtheim, *Von Hegel zu Kelsen: Rechtstheoretische Aufsätze* (Berlin, 1963), with discussions on Marx and Engels as well as totalitarianism. Primary and secondary works often also closely interconnect neo-Hegelianism and neo-Marxism along with other neo-"isms."

25. Thomas Hill Green, *Lectures on the Principles of Political Obligation* (London, 1941, 1960, repr. of the posthumous publ. of Green's 1879–1880 lectures). This edn. consists of a shorter preliminary section entitled "On the Different Senses of 'Freedom' as Applied to will and to the Natural Progress of Man" and the ensuing voluminous "Lectures on the Principles of Political Obligation." The latter is divided into 251 brief numbered sub-sections (mostly consisting of paragraphs) bearing lengthy titles of their own (pp. 28 ff.). The citations to follow are all concerned with the latter materials.

On Green, in addition to above citations, cf. Marek N. Jakubowski, "Th. Green's 'Analysis of Hegel'," *Hist. of Pol. Tht.*, XIII (1992), pp. 339–340; Avial Simhony, "Th. Green: The Common Good Society," *ibid.*, XIV (1993), pp. 226–247; Geoffrey Thomas, *The Moral Philosophy of T. H. Green* (Oxford, 1987); B. Wempe, *Beyond Equality: A Study of T. H. Green's Theory of Positive Freedom* (Delft, 1986); and I. M. Greengarten, *Thomas Hill Green and the Development of Liberal-Democratic Thought* (Toronto, 1981).

26. Green, *Political Obligation* (all *sic*), pp. 29, 39, 41, 44–45, 47 (§1, 18, 21, 25, 29): "The subject of this course of lectures is the principles of political obligation; and that term is intended to include the obligation of the subject towards the sovereign, the obligation of the citizen towards the state, and the obligation of individuals to each other as enforced by a political superior. My purpose is to consider the moral function or object served by law, or by the system of rights and obligations which the state enforces, and in so doing to discover the true ground or justification for obedience to law. . . .

"Laws of this kind have often been objected to on the strength of a one-sided view of the function of laws; the view, viz., that its only business is to prevent interference with the liberty of the individual. And this view has gained undue favour on account of the real reforms to which it has led. . . . Having done its work, the theory now tends to become obstructive, because in fact advancing civilisation brings with it more and more interference with the liberty of the individual to do as he likes, and this theory affords a reason for resisting all positive reforms, all reforms which involve an action of the state in the way of promoting conditions favourable to moral life. . . . A law is not good because it enforces 'natural rights,' but because it contributes to the realisation of a certain end. . . .

"The doctrine here asserted, that all rights are relative to moral ends or duties, must not be confused with the ordinary statement that every right implies a duty, or that rights and duties are correlative. . . . No one therefore can have a right except (1) as a member of a society, and (2) of a society in which some common good is recognised by the members of the society as their own ideal good, as that which should be for each of them. . . . Only through the possession of rights can the power of the individual freely to make a common good his own have reality given to it. Rights are what may be called the negative realisation of this power. . . .

"The capacity, then, on the part of the individual of conceiving a good as the same for himself and others, and of being determined to action by that conception, is the foundation of rights; and rights are the condition of that capacity being realised."

27. *Ibid.*, pp. 68, 80, 82–83, 85, 90–91 (§ 51, 64, 68–71, 79): "It was chiefly Rousseau who gave that cast to the doctrine of the origin of political obligation in contract, in which it best lends itself to the assertion of rights apart from duties on the part of individuals, in opposition to the counter-fallacy which claims rights for the state irrespectively of its fulfilment of its functions as securing the rights of individuals. It is probably true that the

Contrat Social had great effect on the founders of American independence. . . . That 'sovereignty of the people,' which Locke looks upon as held in reserve after its original exercise in the establishment of government, only to be asserted in the event of a legislature proving false to its trust, Rousseau supposes to be in constant exercise. Previous writers had thought of the political society or commonwealth, upon its formation by compact, as instituting a sovereign. . . . Rousseau does not think of the society, *civitas* or commonwealth, as thus instituting a sovereign, but as itself in the act of its formation becoming a sovereign and ever after continuing so. . . . Rousseau himself thinks that he is treating of the sovereign in the ordinary sense; in the sense of some power of which it could be reasonably asked how it was established in the part where it resides, when and by whom and in what way it is exercised. . . .

"The practical result is a vague exaltation of the prerogatives of the sovereign people, without any corresponding limitation of the conditions under which an act is to be deemed that of the sovereign people. . . . Thus the question of what really needs to be enacted by the state in order to secure the conditions under which a good life is possible, is lost sight of in the quest for majorities. . . .

"The incompatibility between the ideal attributes which Rousseau ascribes to the sovereign and any power that can actually be exercised by any man or body of men becomes clearer as we proceed. He expressly distinguishes 'sovereignty' from power. . . . The prevalence of particular interests may prevent there being a will at all of the kind which Rousseau would count general or truly sovereign, but they cannot be more prevalent in the magistracy, constituted by the whole people, than in the same people acting in the way of legislation. . . .

"We may try to answer this question by distinguishing sovereign *de facto* from sovereign *de jure*, and saying that what Rousseau meant was that the general will, as defined by him and as exercised under the conditions which he prescribes, was the only sovereign *de jure*, but that he would have recognised in the ordinary states of his time a sovereign *de facto*. . . ."

28. *Ibid.*, pp. 93–95 (§ 80–81, 83): "The questions then arise (1) whether there is any truth in Rousseau's conception of sovereignty as founded upon a 'volonté générale' in its application to actual sovereignty. . . .

"The first question is one which, if we take our notions of sovereignty from such writers as Austin, we shall be at first disposed decidedly to negative. Austin is considered a master of precise definition. We may begin, therefore, by looking to his definition of sovereignty and the terms connected with it. . . . Laws are further explained as a species of commands. . . . 'Every positive law, or every law simply and strictly so called, is set by a sovereign person or a sovereign body of persons to a member or members of the independent political society wherein that person or body is sovereign or supreme. . . .'

"Austin's doctrine seems diametrically opposite to one which finds the sovereign in a 'volonté générale,' . . ."

29. *Ibid.*, pp. 97–98 (§ 85–86).

30. *Ibid.*, pp. 102–103, 110–111 (§ 91–93, 100): "The answer, then, to the question whether there is any truth in Rousseau's conception of sovereignty as founded upon a 'volonté générale,' in its application to actual sovereignty, must depend on what we mean by 'sovereign.' The essential thing in political society is a power which guarantees men rights, i.e. a certain freedom of action and acquisition conditionally upon their allowing a like freedom in others. . . .

"Thus, though it may be misleading to speak of the general will as anywhere, either actually or properly sovereign, because the term 'sovereign' is best kept to the ordinary usage in which it signifies a determinate person or persons charged with the supreme coercive function of the state, and the general will does not admit of being vested in a person or persons, yet it is true that the institutions of political society—those by which equal rights are guaranteed to members of such a society—are an expression of, and are maintained by, a general will.... It is on the relation to a society, to other men recognising a common good, that the individual's rights depend, as much as the gravity of a body depends on relations to other bodies. A right is a power claimed and recognised as contributory to a common good.... It is thus the social duty of the individual to conform, and he can have no right, as we have seen, that is against his social duty; no right to anything or to do anything that is not involved in the ability to do his duty."

31. *Ibid.*, pp. 121–122, 126, 138–140 (§ 113–114, 119, 133–136), under the heading on p. 121, "Will, not Force, is the basis of the State": "Looking back on the political theories which we have discussed, we may see that they all start with putting the question to be dealt with in the same way, and that their errors are very much due to the way in which they put it.... They take no account of other forms of community than that regulated by a supreme coercive power.... They leave out of sight the process by which men have been clothed with rights and duties, and with senses of right and duty, which are neither natural nor derived from a sovereign power. They look only to the supreme coercive power on the one side and to individuals, to whom natural rights are ascribed, on the other, and ask what is the nature and origin of the right of that supreme coercive power as against these natural rights of individuals....

"To ask why I am to submit to the power of the state, is to ask why I am to allow my life to be regulated by that complex of institutions without which I literally should not have a life to call my own....

"Whether the legislative and administrative agencies of society can be kept in the main free from bias by private interests, and true to the idea of common good, . . . can be kept alive without active participation of the people in legislative functions.... [T]he term 'state' has just been applied (i.e. . . . a systematic law in which the rights recognised are harmonised, and which is enforced by a power strong enough at once to protect a society against disturbance within and aggression from without).... A word is needed to express that form of society.... The word 'state' is the one naturally used for the purpose....

"It is a mistake then to think of the state as an aggregation of individuals under a sovereign.... A state presupposes other forms of community, with the rights that arise out of them, and only exists as sustaining, securing, and completing them. In order to make a state there must have been . . . recognition of a right.... [T]he rights recognised need definition and reconciliation in a general law. When such a general law has been arrived at . . . then the elementary state has been formed.... When once it has come into being, new rights arise in it . . . rights far removed from any obvious foundation on the *suum cuique* principle.... The administration of the state gives rise to rights, to the establishment of powers necessary for its administration.... What I am now concerned to point out is that, however necessary a factor force may have been in the process by which states have been formed and transformed, it has only been such a factor as co-operating with those ideas without which rights could not exist."

32. Bernard Bosanquet, *The Philosophical Theory of the State* (London, 1930; orig. edns. in 1899, 1910, 1920). All *sic.*

33. *Ibid.*, Chs. I–II ("Sociological Compared with Philosophical Theory," "The Paradox of Political Obligation: Self-Government"), pp. 4, 8, 10, 12, 16–17, 55–56, 62, 64–65: "[S]uch a community had existed, before the beginnings of the modern world, in the Greek city-state, and in the Greek city-state alone. A political consciousness in the strict sense was a necessary factor in the experience of such a commonwealth. The demand for 'autonomy'—government by one's own law,—and for 'isonomy'—government according to equal law—though far from being always satisfied, was inherent in the Greek nature; and its

strenuousness was evinced by the throes of revolution and the labours of legislation which were shaking the world of Greece at the dawn of history. . . .

"Many writers have told the story of the change which came over the mind of Greece when the independent sovereignty of its City-states became a thing of the past. . . . From this period forward, till the rise of the modern Nation-states, men's thoughts about life and conduct were cast in the mould of moral theory, of religious mysticism and theology, or of jurisprudence. . . .

"To restore their ancient significance, expanded in conformity with a larger order of things, to the traditional formulae, demanded just the type of experience which was furnished by the modern Nation-state. . . .

"The revival of a true philosophical meaning within the abstract terms of juristic tradition was the work of the eighteenth century as a whole. . . . For it is Rousseau who stands midway between Hobbes and Locke on the one hand, and Kant and Hegel on the other, and in whose writings the actual revival of the full idea of human nature may be watched from paragraph to paragraph as it struggles to throw off the husk of an effete tradition. Between Locke and Rousseau the genius of Vico and of Montesquieu had given a new meaning to the dry formulae of law by showing the sap of society circulating within them. Moreover the revived experience of the Greeks . . . was influential with Rousseau himself. . . .

"Beginning with Vico's *New Science,* there has been more than one attempt in modern Europe to inaugurate the Science of Society as a new departure. But the distinctive and modern spirit of what is known as Sociology . . . first found unmistakable expression in Auguste Comte. . . . Its essence was the inclusion of human society among the objects of natural science; its watchwords were law and cause—in the sense in which alone Positivism allowed causes to be thought of. . . . Nevertheless the modern starting-point is wholly different from that of antiquity. . . . The work of the latter has been revived by modern idealist philosophy dating from Rousseau and Hegel, and finding a second home in Great Britain, as that of the former has developed itself within the peculiar limits and traditions of sociological research, flourishing more especially upon French and American soil. . . .

"It is instructive, therefore, to note Bentham's uncompromising hostility to all the theories of philosophical jurists. The common point of all their theories, from Hobbes and Grotius to Montesquieu and Rousseau, not to mention Kant and his successors, has lain in the fact that their authors divined under the forms of power and command, exercised by some over others, a substantive and general element of positive human nature, which they attempted to drag to light by one analogy after another. . . . Bentham . . . can understand nothing in law but the character of a command. . . . On many points indeed, when the simple protection of 'others' is concerned, Mill's doctrine leads to sound conclusions. Such, for example, is the problem of legislation after the pattern of the Factory Acts.

"But . . . under the name of freedom, Mill is led to object to interference which may be perfectly justified and effectual. . . .

"It is worth noticing, in conclusion, that in two examples . . . Mill recognises a principle wholly at variance with his own. . . . For we are entitled to argue from the essential nature of freedom to what freedom really demands, as opposed to what the man momentarily seems to wish. . . . Here we have in germ the doctrine of the 'real' will, and a conception analogous to that of Rousseau when he speaks of a man 'being forced to be free'."

Also, a number of concentrated criticisms of Green, especially in relation to Hegel, are made by Bosanquet in a later part of his *Theory of State,* Ch. X, pp. 267 ff.

34. *Ibid.,* Ch. V ("The Conception of a 'Real' Will"), pp. 96, 99–101, 104, 108–110, 112: "[F]or Rousseau's political theory everything turns on the reality of the 'moral person' which constitutes the State. When active, this 'moral' or 'public person,' or common self, is

called sovereign; and sovereignty for Rousseau consists in the exercise of the General Will; and it is in this characteristic of political society that he finds that justification for the use of force upon individuals which he set out to seek. . . . The present chapter will be devoted to explaining the idea of a General Will with reference to Rousseau's presentation of it, and the rest of the work will develop and apply it more freely. . . .

"What Rousseau means to indicate by his expression, 'the General Will,' may seem to many persons, as he clearly saw, to have no actual existence. It is of the nature of a principle. . . . Thus, it has been said that what Rousseau really aimed at, with his conception of the General Will, was the will 'in itself,' or the will as it would be if it carried out what its nature implies and demands.

"We can see that some notion of this kind floats before Rousseau's mind from the predicates which he assigns to Sovereignty and the General Will, which are for him nearly convertible terms. . . .

"Rousseau develops his idea of a General Will by the contrast which he draws between the General Will and the Will of All. . . .

"If such a theory as that just stated were to be literally pressed, it would lead to the conclusion that a law which was not *really* for the general interest was not binding on the subjects of a state. For, by the definition, such a law could not be a true act of sovereignty. No political theorist, however visionary, could accept such a conclusion as this, and Rousseau, seeing that the decision of the recognised sovereign must be final, attempts to show how and when it comes nearest to a true General Will. . . . In this aim, what is present to his mind is of course the popular idea of the ancient City-State. . . . And more especially, the very core of the common good represented by the life of a modern Nation-State is its profound and complex organisation, which makes it greater than the conscious momentary will of any individual. . . .

"The other and more fruitful direction of Rousseau's speculations upon the General Will is to be found in his remarks on the function of the Legislator. We will approach them by help of a short restatement of the problem as it now stands. . . . [W]hat Rousseau had before him in his notion of the General Will might be described as the 'Will in itself,' or the Real Will. Any such conception involves a contrast between the Real Will and the Actual Will, which may seem to be meaningless. . . .

"It is such a process of interpretation that Rousseau ascribes to the legislator. He fathers on him the whole labour of history and social logic in moulding the customs and institutions of mankind. And in agreement with our general attitude to Rousseau's historical imagination, we may take what he says of legislation and the legislator as an expression of his views on the function of customs and ordinances in the constitution of will."

35. *Ibid.*, Ch. X ("The Analysis of a Modern State. Hegel's 'Philosophy of Right' "), pp. 254–255, 258, 261–264: "The principle of the ancient State, as concentratedly expressed in Plato's *Republic*, was weak and undeveloped, and fell short of the true claims of intelligence. . . .

"The modern demand—such is Hegel's conception—is harder and higher. . . .

"The basis of State regulation is the emergence of aspects of common interest in the system of particular interests. . . . Hegel . . . was early impressed . . . with the beautiful unity of the ancient Greek commonwealths. And the first and last idea which governs his representations of the modern State is that of the Greek commonwealth enlarged as it were from a sun to a solar system. . . . As ultimate power, the State maintains on one side the attitude of an external necessity towards the spheres of private life. . . . It may intervene by force to remove hindrances in the path of the common good. . . . It is, in short, the incarnation of the general or Real Will. . . .

"The division of functions in the State is a necessary condition of its rational organisation. But, as Rousseau had insisted, it is altogether false to regard these separate functions as independent, or as checks on one another. There could be no living unity, if the functions of the State were ultimately independent and negative towards each other. . . .

"Sovereignty . . . resides only in the organised whole acting *qua* organised whole. If, for example, we speak of the 'Sovereignty of the People' in a sense opposed to the Sovereignty of the state—as if there were such a thing as 'the people' over and above the organised means of expressing and adjusting the will of the community—we are saying what is, strictly speaking, meaningless. . . . Rousseau clearly explained the impossibility of expressing the general will except by a determinate system of law. But what he seemed to suggest, and was taken to mean, by popular Sovereignty, was no doubt just the view which Hegel condemns. . . . Law and constitution are utterances of the spirit of a nation.

"The form of State which Hegel analyses is a modern constitutional monarchy. . . .

"The logical division of power, in his language, is that the Legislature has to establish universal principles, the executive has to apply these principles to particular cases, and the prince has to bring to a point the acts of the State by giving them, 'like the dot on the i,' the final shape of individual volition.

"The distinction of States into Monarchy, Aristocracy, and Democracy, Hegel refuses to regard as applicable to the modern world. At best, it could only apply to the undeveloped communities of antiquity. . . . It is at least remarkable to compare this view with the tendency to one-man government in the administration of the United States of America.

"The State, then, is on one side the external force and automatic machinery . . ."

36. *Ibid.*, Ch. VII ("Psychological Illustrations of the Idea of a Real or General Will"), p. 146: "Our purpose, therefore, is to explain what is meant by saying that 'a will' can be embodied in the State, in society, in law and institutions; and how it is possible for the individual, as we know him, to be in an identity with this will, such as continually to vary, but never wholly to disappear. How can a man's real self lie in a great degree outside his normal self, and be something which he only now and then gets hold of distinctly, and never completely?"

37. *Ibid.*, Ch. VIII ("Nature of the End of the State and Consequent Limit of State Action"), pp. 167–169: "[T]he distinction between the individual on the one hand, and the social or political whole on the other, is not relevant to the question where the 'end' of man in Society is to be sought. . . . This antithesis is really, however, absurd. There are not two opposable sets of contents concerned in the matter at all; but a single web of content which in its totality is society and in its differentiations the individuals. . . .

"For us, then, the ultimate end of Society and the State as of the individual is the realisation of the best life."

38. *Ibid.*, Ch. VIII, pp. 172–173, 175: "We have hitherto spoken of the State and Society as almost convertible terms. And in fact it is part of our argument that the influences of Society differ only in degree from the powers of the State, and that the explanation of both is ultimately the same. But on the other hand, it is also part of our argument that the State as such is a necessary factor in civilised life; and that no true ideal lies in the direction of minimising its individuality or restricting its absolute power. By the State, then, we mean Society as a unit, recognised as rightly exercising control over its members through absolute physical power. . . . But the State *de facto* (which is also *de jure*) is the Society which is recognised as exercising compulsory power over its members, and as presenting itself *qua* a single independent corporation among other independent corporations. Without such power, or where, if anywhere, it does not exist, there can be no ultimate and effective adjustment of the claims of individuals, and of the various social groups in which individuals are involved. It is the need for this ultimate effective adjustment which constitutes the need that every individual in civilised life should belong to one state, and to one only. . . . That Society, then, is a State, which is habitually recognised as a unit lawfully exercising force. . . .

"The end of the State, then, is the end of Society and of the Individual—the best life, as determined by the fundamental logic of the will. The means at its disposal, *qua* State, always partake of the nature of force, though this does not exclude their having other aspects as well. Taxation . . . can only be secured by compulsion. No State could undertake its work on the basis of voluntary contributions. . . . It is because the authority is ultimate that it must be single. Now, authority which is to be ultimate in a sphere including the world of bodily action, must be an authority which can use force. And it is for this reason that, as we said, force is involved in the distinctive attributes of the State. . . . This does not mean merely the performance of outward bodily movements, such as might be brought to pass by actual physical force. It is remarkable that actual physical force plays a very small part in the work of any decently ordered State."

39. *Ibid.*, Ch. VIII, pp. 216–217: "We may, in conclusion, sum up the whole theory of State action in the formula which we inherit from Rousseau—that Sovereignty is the exercise of the General Will.

"First. All State action is General in its bearing and justification. . . .

"And, secondly. All State action is at bottom the exercise of a Will. . . . [I]t is 'forcing men to be free'."

40. *Ibid.*, Ch. IX ("Rousseau's Theory as Applied to the Modern State: Kant, Fichte, Hegel"), pp. 218, 221: "Probably no other philosophical movement has ever focussed in itself so much human nature as the post-Kantian Idealism. . . . [T]he ethical and political theory of Kant, Fichte, and Hegel springs from the same *Evangel of Jean Jacques* from which the French Revolution drew its formulae. . . . [T]he modern abstraction of 'freedom' was blended, for Hegel, with the idea of concrete life through the tradition of the Greek city. . . . [T]he whole political philosophy of Kant, Hegel, and Fichte is founded on the idea of freedom . . . first announced—such was Hegel's distinct judgment—by Rousseau."

41. *Ibid.*, Ch. X, pp. 242–243: "Thus, it is a confusion of spheres to apply the idea of contract to the State, for the State is an imperative necessity of man's nature as rational, while contract is a mere agreement of certain free persons about certain external things. The idea of the social contract is a confusion of the same type as that by which public rights and functions were treated as private property in the Middle Ages. . . .

"This phase or view of law as, in its letter, an ultimate and absolute rule, may be illustrated, Hegel says, by the . . . Draconic conception that every offence demands the extreme penalty. . . . It might also be illustrated by Austin's theory of law as a command enforced by a penalty . . ."

42. L. T. Hobhouse, *The Metaphysical Theory of the State* (London, 1918; repr. 1922, 1926), Pref.

43. *Ibid.*, Lect. I ("The Objects of Social Investigation"), pp. 18, 22—24.

44. *Ibid.*, Lects. II–III ("Freedom and Law," "The Real Will"), pp. 37, 43, 59: "Hegel's first position is now before us. Freedom for him rests not on absence of constraint but on the acceptance of a principle expressing the true nature of rational will running through and unifying all the diverse purposes of men. The embodiment of such a principle and therefore of freedom Hegel finds in the system of right and law. . . . Moral freedom—we shall see later that Dr. Bosanquet candidly recognizes the distinction between moral and legal liberty—lies in conformity to the real will. The real will is the general will and is expressed in the social fabric. . . .

"We cannot, therefore, accept the definition of freedom suggested by Dr. Bosanquet . . ."

45. *Ibid.*, Lects. IV–V ("The Will of the State," "Varying Applications of the Metaphysical Theory"), pp. 71, 73, 76–77, 83, 96: "[There are] three main propositions of the metaphysical theory of the state. Of these three the first is that true individuality or free-

dom lies in conformity to our real will. The second is that our real will is identical with the general will, and the third—with which we have not yet dealt—is that the general will is embodied more or less perfectly in the state. . . . Dr. Bosanquet . . . passes from his conception of the real will as the foundation of our individuality to the state as the supreme object of our allegiance. . . . Bosanquet's own ideas are mostly derived from Germany. . . . Bosanquet's double definition of the state, on the one hand as the operative criticism of institutions and on the other hand as force, is an abortive union of two radically opposed conceptions. . . . Bosanquet fails to meet the real point of Green's challenge. We come back again to the central point that the institutions of society are not the outcome of a unitary will but of the clash of wills, in which the selfishness and generally the bad in human nature is constantly operative, intermingled with but not always overcome by the better elements. . . .

"The idealistic conception of the state has sometimes figured as an organic theory of society. In the form given to it by Green this description is not unjust, for to Green, the ethical basis of the state is a common good, which at the same time is the good of each individual citizen. The state rests, for Green, on a mutual recognition of rights, rights being for each the conditions under which he can live the best life. We have here beyond doubt the elements of an organic theory, or, if the term be preferred, of a harmony between the state and the individual. Now such a harmony . . . is contemplated by Hegel himself. . . . This points to the true ideal, but unfortunately there is nowhere in Hegel a clear distinction between the ideal and the actual."

46. *Ibid.*, Lect. V, pp. 100–102, 104, 108–109, 113: "The state being the individual writ large, its own independence is the primary condition of its internal life and indeed of its freedom. . . . And for this reason it imposes an absolute sacrifice on the individual when it is necessary to maintain it. Hegel finds . . . in the security of the state . . . the 'ethical moment' of war, which is to be regarded as not an absolute evil or as merely an external accident. . . . We are apparently to think it is positively good if not only our property but also the lives of those dearest to us should be destroyed from time to time by the god-state in order to teach us the vanity of earthly affections. This is one advantage of war. Another is that it inculcates discipline and moral soundness. People who will not endure sovereignty within are brought under the heel of others. . . . Kant's proposal of a League of Peace is specifically repudiated. . . . The state is a self-dependent totality . . . , and yet it cannot be an actual individual without relation to other states. . . . In only one respect has Hegel failed to anticipate the whole practice of modern Germany, and that is that he lays down that the relations of states remain in war and that in war the possibility of peace is preserved. . . . [In] the Hegelian state [lies] . . . the germ of the colossal suffering of Europe and of the backward movement that went so far to arrest the civilizing tendencies of the eighteenth and nineteenth centuries.

"Dr. Bosanquet follows Hegel in conceiving the state as necessarily one unity among others. . . . The state has absolute physical power in the sense that it can inflict imprisonment, torture or death if it has an army and a police force, but how far does it do so rightly? . . .

"Dr. Bosanquet goes on to say that every individual must belong to one state and one only. . . .

"Dr. Bosanquet's discussion brings out the contrast between the metaphysical way of regarding social problems and the way which is at once ethical and scientific, or, in a word, practical. The metaphysical method says that in the state there is a real self and beyond it there are only external and mechanical relations. . . .

"Bosanquet finds it hard to see how the state can commit theft or murder . . . , and when Bosanquet denies . . . that a country is guilty of murder when it carries on war, he overlooks the justice or injustice of that war. . . . When philosophy deserts its duty, who will fulfil it? International anarchy is not due to philosophy but to the passions of men, but the restraint which humanitarian philosophy has sought to impose has been fatally loosened by the sophistications of idealism."

47. *Ibid.*, Lect. V and Concl., pp. 117–119, 134, 136: "We have summed up the metaphysical theory in three propositions. . . . We have seen reasons for denying all these propositions. We have maintained that there is no distinction between the real will and the actual will, that the will of the individual is not identical with the general will and that the rational order, which the general will is supposed to maintain, is not confined and may be opposed to the state organization. . . . In the hands of Green, for example, the notion of the general will is stated in terms which bring it into closer relation to the facts of experience. . . . It is not my purpose here either to explain or criticize Green's *Principles of Political Obligation*, a work of great power and of some weaknesses, . . . but for the sake of fairness to Green and to living writers who have drawn their principal inspiration from him rather than Hegel, I would call attention to one or two points in which Green departs notably from the Hegelian model.

"First and above all, the right of the individual runs through Green's entire argument. . . .

"Where Green is less happy, as I think, is in his discussion of the rights which society ought to recognize but does not. . . .

"The . . . history of our time shows that if men no longer believe in God they will make themselves gods of Power, of Evolution, of the Race, the Nation, or the State. In the name of such gods will they drench a continent with blood. . . . There is no double dose of original sin which established this worship in Germany. It is the product of a combination of historic causes. . . . The idealized exaltation of the state supervened to . . . give them a creed justifying their dislike of humanitarianism. In Hegel's hands this creed had, as we have seen, its idealistic side, and events had to move before this could be shed, and the naked doctrine of Power be proclaimed by Treitschke. . . . [T]he . . . state . . . becomes a false god, and its worship the abomination of desolation, as seen at Ypres or on the Somme."

48. The edn. of Bosanquet's *Theory of State* cited above contains the various prefaces and introductions to the earlier edns.

49. In general cf. Sabine, *History of Political Theory*, pp. 857 ff., 872 ff. on Italian Fascism in political thought.

Among the numerous recent studies of Italian Fascism (and other national varieties of Fascism) relevant to the present sects. are the following. Stanley G. Payne, *A History of Fascism, 1914–1945* (Madison, 1995), includes Italian Fascism as one of several types of authoritarian nationalism in European countries. He points to the broad "end of century" cultural crisis rather than to the narrower economic "crisis of Marxism" stressed in Zeev Sternhell's *The Birth of Fascist Ideology* (Princeton, 1994). Payne also discusses the cultural background to Fascism (more "pluralist" in Italy, more "totalizing" and racial in Germany) in the Enlightenment and chiefly Rousseau (an interesting point in view of the uses made of Rousseau by Green, Bosanquet, and others). Franklin Hugh Adler, *Italian Individualists from Liberalism to Fascism: The Political Development of the Industrial Bourgeoisie, 1906–1934* (New York, 1996), stresses the role of "corporatism" among Fascist ideologues as a way to avoid the defects of both capitalism and socialism. Yet it may be that this role was less crucial to actual Fascist ideologies (of Mussolini and others) and more of propaganda value than was the case for pre-Fascist theories, as suggested in Marco Palla's *Fascismo e stato corporativo* (Milan, 1991). Emilio Gentile, *The Sacralization of Politics in Fascist Italy* (Camb., Mass., 1996), explores Fascist uses of religious political symbols. Yet Italian Fascist ideology was perhaps less monolithic than suggested, while Mussolini brought together the different ideological varieties. (The "spiritual" and even deified state in Fascist ideology could be used by some to show a neo-Hegelian background.) The author also accentuates the new totalitarian tendencies in Italian Fascism (far more so than did Arendt). Norberto Bobbio's *Ideological Profile of Twentieth-Century Italy* (translated by L. Cochrane, Princeton, 1995), includes discussions on Fascist ideology and Croce's opposition (Chs. 10–11).

A vast topic not able to be included here but nonetheless relevant is social Darwinism. It has often been cited, for instance, as a crucial ingredient in the political/military climate of thought before as well as after World War I. In general cf. Mike Hawkins' voluminous *Social Darwinism in European and American Thought, 1860–1945* (Cambridge, 1997), which includes treatment of the more sinister incorporation of the subject in Nazism and Fascism.

Other background factors include neo-positivism, on which cf. Shuman, *Legal Positivism*, "Totalitarianism and Legal Philosophy," pp. 178 ff.

50. Giovanni Gentile, *Che cosa è il fascismo: Discorsi e polemiche* (Florence, 1925).
51. In Spahr (ed.), *Readings*, pp. 689 ff.
52. *Ibid.*, 695–696.
53. *Ibid.*, pp. 698 ff.
54. Giovanni Gentile, *Los fundamentos de la filosofia del derecho* (translated by E. Campolongo, Buenos Aires, 1944), esp. Chs. IV–V with regard to law as well as legislation, and Ch. VII on the state.
55. In Spahr (ed.), *Readings*, pp. 681 ff.
56. *Ibid.*
57. *Ibid.*
58. Benito Mussolini, *The Political and Social Doctrine of Fascism* (1932, transl. 1933), as given in William Ebenstein (ed.), *Modern Political Thought* (New York, 1947, etc.), pp. 330 ff. Here, for instance, Mussolini refers to Renan, Marx, Bismarck, Napoleon III, the liberal revolutions of 1830, the Frankfurt Assembly, Mazzini, Garabaldi, Humboldt, Von Moltke, Bentham, Adam Smith, the French Revolution, and ancient Rome. As the most crucial foundation of Fascism, the state is an absolute entity based on force, will, power, and war, while having its own corporative personality. Individual citizens are relative to it; through loyal obedience to it and sacrifice for it, they achieve their highest purpose and good. "The state," Mussolini says, "is . . . the custodian and transmitter of the spirit of the people, as it has grown up through the centuries. . . . [T]ranscending the brief limits of life, it represents the immanent spirit of the nation."

Here the spirit of the people or nation that is expressed through the state is presented in a quasi-Hegelian manner, in apparent combination with German notions of the *Volksgeist* that are partly reminiscent of the German Historical School of law. (Distinctions, in fact, between the Hegelian and Historical Schools related to this subject are underscored by Carl Joachim Friedrich, *The Philosophy of Law in Historical Perspective*, published in 1958, Chicago, Ch. XV, "Law as the Expression of the Spirit: Hegel and the Historical School"). This viewpoint can be understood in connection with Mussolini's brief depictions of the authoritarian German spirit as it developed in the nineteenth century.

This appropriation of German notions of the *Volksgeist*, as compatible with the Fascist idea of the state, serves to break down a distinction sometimes drawn by historians between Fascism and Nazism. Mussolini's Fascist idea of the state is sometimes seen by historians to be more pro-Hegelian because it conversely reduces the significance of the nation and the people. Hitler's Nazi ideas are sometimes seen by historians to be somewhat anti-Hegelian because they purportedly exalt the nation, people, and *Volksgeist* above the state *per se*. In fact, both sets of ideas combined state and nation with particular regard to the demands of the national state. Some generalized differences of emphasis between state and nation can be detected at points in the views of Mussolini and Hitler on such subjects. Yet the actual implementation of the totalitarian state in both Germany and Italy (Hitler largely applying and developing Mussolini's model) shows these distinctions to be of relatively minor significance. The authoritarian tradition in German history, as cited by Mussolini with regard to the state, obviously greatly impacted Fascist as well as Nazi ideology on the state in conjunction with the nation. The Hegelian deification of the state (not unrelated to the totalitarian exaltation of its "spiritual" identity and mission) was an inescapable part of that tradition, however perversely distorted by the totalitarian ideologues.

It should not be overlooked that Mussolini (like Gentile and Rocco above, but perhaps more forcefully) stressed the *total* involvement of the lives of the citizens in the national state. For instance: "The Fascist State . . . reaches every aspect of the national life and includes . . . all the . . . forces of the nation. . . . [Its citizens] . . . are continually conscious of its power and are ready at once to serve it . . ." The uses of propaganda in creating and perpetuating this mass movement are also suggested.

The *Oxford English Dictionary* defines totalitarian(ism) as follows: "Of or pertaining to a system of government which tolerates only one political party, to which all other institutions are subordinated, and which usu. demands the complete subservience of the individual to the state." An extract dated 1929 states: "A reaction against parliamentarism in favour of a 'totalitarian' or unitary state, whether Fascist or Communist."

Based on these rather loose parameters, it does not stretch the imagination to see in the uses of traditional terms such as "absolute," on the part of earlier theorists such as Bosanquet, a prologue to the more "total" and sinister concepts of the Fascist state. Hitler's Nazi state is often typically referred to, with justification, as also the Fascist state, which can be considered to include both Italian and German varieties.

59. *Hegel and Legal Philosophy*, in 2 vols.—as Vol. 10 (1989) of the *Cardozo Law Review*.

60. Walter Kaufmann, *Hegel: A Reinterpretation* (Garden City, 1965, 1966), p. vii.

61. Tom Rockmore, *Before and After Hegel: A Historical Introduction to Hegel's Thought* (Berkeley, 1993), p. 172.

62. E.g. Nicholson, *British Idealists*.

63. V. I. Lenin, *State and Revolution* (New York, 1994, transl.; written in 1917 and published in 1918 as a long pamphlet).

64. *Ibid.*, Ch. I, sects. 2–4, and Ch. II, sect. 1 (pp. 10, 12, 17, 19–20, 22–23): "Engels develops the conception of that 'power' which is termed the state—a power arising from society, but placing itself above it and becoming more and more separated from it. What does this power mainly consist of? It consists of special bodies of armed men. . . . A standing army and police are the chief instruments of state power. . . .

"For the maintenance of a special public force standing above society, taxes and state loans are needed [quoting Engels]. . . .

"Special laws are enacted regarding the sanctity and the inviolability of the officials. . . . As a matter of fact, Engels speaks here of the destruction of the bourgeois state by the proletarian revolution, while the words about its withering away refer to the remains of *proletarian* statehood *after* the Socialist revolution. The bourgeois state does not 'wither away,' according to Engels, but is 'put an end to' by the proletariat in the course of the revolution. What withers away after the revolution is the proletarian state or semi-state. . . .

"We have already said above and shall show more fully later that the teaching of Marx and Engels regarding the inevitability of a violent revolution refers to the bourgeois state. It *cannot* be replaced by the proletarian state (the dictatorship of the proletariat) through 'withering away,' but, as a general rule, only through a violent revolution. . . .

"The replacement of the bourgeois by the proletarian state is impossible without a violent revolution. The abolition of the proletarian state, *i.e.*, of all states, is only possible through 'withering away.' . . .

"Here we have a formulation of one of the most remarkable and most important ideas of Marxism on the subject of the state, namely, the idea of the 'dictatorship of the proletariat' (as Marx and Engels began to term it after the Paris Commune); and also a definition of the state, in the highest degree interesting, but nevertheless also belonging to the category of 'forgotten words' of Marxism: *'the state, i.e., the proletariat organised as the ruling class.'* . . .

"The proletariat needs state power, the centralised organisation of force, the organisation of violence, both for the purpose of crushing the resistance of the exploiters and for the purpose of *guiding* the great mass of the population . . . in the work of organising Socialist economy."

65. *Ibid.*, Ch. II, sects. 2–3 (pp. 25–26, 31): "In this remarkable passage Marxism makes a tremendous step forward in comparison with the position of the *Communist Manifesto*. There the question of the state still is treated extremely in the abstract, in the most general terms and expressions. Here the question is treated in a concrete manner, and the conclusion is most precise, definite, practical and palpable: all revolutions which have taken place up to the present have helped to perfect the state machinery, whereas it must be shattered, broken to pieces. . . . The question as to how, from the point of view of historical development, this replacement of the capitalist state by the proletarian state shall take place, is not raised here. . . .

"The centralised state power peculiar to bourgeois society came into being in the period of the fall of absolutism. Two institutions are especially characteristic of this state machinery: bureaucracy and the standing army. . . .

"Bureaucracy and the standing army constitute a 'parasite' on the body of bourgeois society. . . . The forms of bourgeois states are exceedingly variegated, but their essence is the same: in one way or another, all these states are in the last analysis inevitably a *dictatorship of the bourgeoisie*. The transition from capitalism to Communism will certainly bring a great variety and abundance of political forms, but the essence will inevitably be only one: *the dictatorship of the proletariat*."

66. *Ibid.*, Ch. III, sect. 2 (pp. 35–39).

67. *Ibid.*, Ch. III, sect. 3 (pp. 39–41, 43): "This remarkable criticism of parliamentarism made in 1871 also belongs to the 'forgotten words' of Marxism, thanks to the prevalence of social-chauvinism and opportunism. . . .

"The way out of parliamentarism is to be found, of course, not in the abolition of the representative institutions and the elective principle, but in the conversion of the representative institutions from mere 'talking shops' into working bodies. 'The Commune was to be a working, not a parliamentary body, executive and legislative at the same time.' . . . This is so true that even in the Russian republic, a bourgeois-democratic republic, all these aims of parliamentarism were immediately revealed, even before a real parliament was created. Such heroes of rotten philistinism . . . have managed to pollute even the Soviets, after the model of the most despicable petty-bourgeois parliamentarism, by turning them into hollow talking shops. . . .

"The venal and rotten parliamentarism of bourgeois society is replaced in the Commune by institutions in which freedom of opinion and discussion does not degenerate into deception, for the parliamentarians must themselves work, must themselves execute their own laws, must themselves verify their results in actual life, must themselves be directly responsible to their electorate. Representative institutions remain, but parliamentarism as a special system, as a division of labour between the legislative and the executive functions, as a privileged position for the deputies, *no longer exists*. Without representative institutions we cannot imagine democracy, not even proletarian democracy; but we can and *must* think of democracy without parliamentarism. . . . This is *our* proletarian task, with this we can and must *begin* when carrying through a proletarian revolution. Such a beginning, on the basis of large-scale production, of itself leads to the gradual 'withering away' of all bureaucracy, to the gradual creation of a new order. . . ."

68. *Ibid.*, Ch. III, sect. 4 ("The Organization of National Unity")–5, and Ch. IV, sect. 3 (pp. 44–45, 48, 55–56): "From these Communes would be elected the 'National Delegation' at Paris. . . .

"To what extent the opportunists of contemporary Social-Democracy have failed to understand . . . these observations of Marx is best shown by the famous . . . book of the renegade Bernstein. . . .

"This is really monstrous: thus to confuse Marx's views on the 'destruction of the state power,' of the 'parasitic excrescence' with the federalism of Proudhon! . . .

"Federalism is not touched upon in Marx's observations about the experience of the Commune. . . .

"Marx deducted from the whole history of Socialism and political struggle that the state was bound to disappear, and that the transitional form of its disappearance (the transition from the political state to no state) would be the 'proletariat organised as the ruling class.' But Marx did not undertake the task of *discovering* the political *forms* of this future stage. He limited himself to an exact observation of French history, its analysis and the conclusion to which the year 1851 had led, *viz.*, that matters were moving towards the *destruction* of the bourgeois machinery of state. . . .

"The Commune is the first attempt of a proletarian revolution to *break up* the bourgeois state machinery and constitutes the political form, 'at last discovered,' which can and must *take the place* of the broken machine.

"We shall see below that the Russian Revolutions of 1905 and 1917, in different surroundings and under different circumstances, continued the work of the Commune and confirmed the historic analysis made by the genius of Marx. . . .

" 'The Commune was no longer a state in the proper sense of the word '—this is Engels' most important statement, theoretically speaking. After what has been presented above, this statement is perfectly clear. The Commune *ceased* to be a state in so far as it had to repress, not the majority of the population but a minority (the exploiters); it had broken the bourgeois state machinery; in the place of a *special* repressive force, the whole population itself came onto the scene. All this is a departure from the state in its proper sense."

69. *Ibid.*, Ch. V, sects. 2–3 (pp. 73, 75, 77–78): "Democracy for the vast majority of the people, and suppression by force, *i.e.*, exclusion from democracy, of the exploiters and oppressors of the people—this is the modification of democracy during the *transition* from capitalism to Communism. . . . [T]he need for *special machinery* of suppression will begin to disappear. The exploiters are, naturally, unable to suppress the people without a most complex machinery for performing this task; but *the people* can suppress the exploiters even with very simple 'machinery,' almost without any 'machinery,' without any special apparatus, by the simple *organisation of the armed masses* (such as the Soviets of Workers' and Soldiers' Deputies. . . .

"Finally, only Communism renders the state absolutely unnecessary, for there is *no one* to be suppressed. . . .

"The first phase of Communism, therefore, still cannot produce justice and equality; differences, and unjust differences, in wealth will still exist, but the *exploitation* of man by man will have become impossible. . . .

"And so, in the first phase of Communist society (generally called Socialism) 'bourgeois right' is *not* abolished in its entirety, but only in part. . . .

"And there is no other standard yet than that of 'bourgeois right.' To this extent, therefore, a form of state is still necessary, which, while maintaining public ownership of the means of production, would preserve the equality of labour and equality in the distribution of products. . . .

"But the state has not yet altogether withered away, since there still remains the protection of 'bourgeois right' which sanctifies actual inequality. For the complete extinction of the state, complete Communism is necessary."

70. *Ibid.*, Ch. V, sect. 4 (pp. 79–84): "Only now can we appreciate the full correctness of Engels' remarks in which he mercilessly ridiculed all the absurdity of combining the words 'freedom' and 'state.' While the state exists there is no freedom. When there is freedom, there will be no state. . . .

"The state will be able to wither away completely when society has realised the rule: 'From each according to his ability; to each according to his needs,' *i.e.*, when people have become accustomed to observe the fundamental rules of social life. . . .

"Until the 'higher' phase of Communism arrives, the Socialists demand the *strictest* control, *by society and by the state*, of the quantity of labour and the quantity of consumption; . . . and the complete subordination . . . to the really democratic state of the *Soviets of Workers' and Soldiers' Deputies*. . . .

"But the scientific difference between Socialism and Communism is clear. What is generally called Socialism was termed by Marx the 'first' or lower phase of Communist society. In so far as the means of production become *public* property, the word 'Communism' is also applicable here, providing we do not forget that it is *not* full Communism. . . .

"In its first phase or first stage Communism *cannot* as yet be economically ripe and entirely free of all tradition and of all taint of capitalism. . . .

"Democracy is of great importance for the working class in its struggle for freedom against the capitalists. . . . But democracy means only *formal* equality. . . . [T]he question [arises] of going further from formal equality to real equality, *i.e.*, to realising the rule, 'From each according to his ability; to each according to his needs.' . . .

"Democracy is a form of the state—one of its varieties. Consequently, like every state, it consists in organised, systematic application of force against human beings. This on the one hand. On the other hand, however, it signifies the formal recognition of the equality of all citizens, the equal right of all to determine the structure and administration of the state. . . .

"From the moment when all members of society, or even only the overwhelming majority, have learned how to govern the state *themselves*, . . . the need for any government begins to disappear. The more complete the democracy, the nearer the moment when it begins to be unnecessary."

71. *Ibid.*, Ch. VI, sect. 3 (pp. 91–92, 94–95): "In all such enterprises [according to Kautsky] the workers will, of course, 'elect delegates who form *something in the nature of a parliament.*'

But . . . this 'something in the nature of a parliament' will *not* be a parliament in the sense of bourgeois-parliamentary institutions . . . as imagined by Kautsky, whose ideas do not go beyond the framework of bourgeois parliamentarism. In a Socialist society, this 'something in the nature of a parliament,' consisting of workers' deputies, will of course determine the conditions of work. . . .

"Kautsky has not reflected at all on Marx's words: 'The Commune was to be a working, not a parliamentary body, executive and legislative at the same time.'

"Kautsky has not in the least understood the difference between bourgeois parliamentarism, combining democracy (*not for the people*) with bureaucracy (*against the people*), and proletarian democracy, which will take immediate steps to cut down bureaucracy at the roots. . . .

"The difference between the Marxists and Anarchists consists in this: (1) the former, while aiming at the complete destruction of the state, recognise that this aim can only be realised after the abolition of classes by a Socialist revolution, as the result of the establishment of Socialism, leading to the withering away of the state; the latter want the complete destruction of the state within twenty-four hours, not understanding the conditions under which such destruction can be carried out; . . . (3) the former insist upon making use of the modern state as a means of preparing the workers for revolution; the latter reject this."

72. E.g. *Encyclop. Brit.* and Palmer, *History*, pp. 247–248, 776–778, 781–782.

73. Webster's *New Collegiate Dictionary*.

74. *Basic Laws on the Structure of the Soviet State* (translated and edited by Harold J. Berman and John B. Quigley, Jr., Camb., Mass., 1969), pp. 3 ff.

75. *Ibid.*, pp. 30 ff.

76. Secondary literature includes the following: Theodore H. von Laue, *Why Lenin? Why Stalin?: A Reappraisal of the Russian Revolution, 1900–1920* (2nd. edn., New York, 1971), who concludes (Ch. X) with "The Stalin Revolution, 1924–1930"; Harold Shukman, *Lenin and the Russian Revolution* (New York, 1966); R. N. Carew Hunt, *The Theory and Practice of Communism: An Introduction* (Baltimore, 1963), Pt. III ("Leninism and Stalinism"), e.g. Ch. 14 ("The Background of Leninism"), p. 17, citing Stalin's definition ("Leninism is marxism of the era of imperialism and of the proletarian revolution"); Nicolas Berdyaev, *The Origin of Russian Communism* (Ann Arbor, 1973), Ch. VI on the Revolution in relation to Communism; Arthur E. Adams (ed.), *The Russian Revolution and Bolshevik Victory: Causes and Processes* (Lexington, Mass., 1972), including a variety of viewpoints on the shifting left-right political spectrum; Carl Cohen (ed.), *Communism, Fascism, and Democracy: The Theoretical Foundations* (2nd edn., New York, 1972), with selections from Lenin, Kautsky, Bernstein, and others; Stephen J. Lee, *The European Dictatorships, 1918–1945* (London, 1987), Ch. 2, sects. 1, 3 ("Lenin's Regime, 1917–24" and "Stalin's Pre-War Regime, 1924–41"); Sidney Hook, *Marx and the Marxists* (Princeton, 1955), Ch. 5 on Lenin, sect. 5 ("The Dictatorship of the Party"), and Ch. 8 on Stalin, sect. 7 ("The Triumph of Stalinism"); Christopher Read, *From Tsar to Soviets: The Russian People and Their Revolution, 1917–21* (New York, 1996), e.g. on popular revolution in relation to the soviets; Lewis H. Siegelbaum, *Soviet State and Society between Revolutions, 1918–1929* (New York, 1992), in which concepts of state are blurred with those of society more generally; Roger S. Gottlieb, *Marxism, 1944–1990: Origins, Betrayal, Rebirth* (New York, 1992), showing how original Marxism was "betrayed" by being turned into the Leninist-Stalinist one-party state; and Alfred Levin, "The Fifth Social-Democratic Congress and the Duma," *Jour. of Mod. Hist.*, XI (1939), pp. 484 ff., of interest for the duma tradition in relation to the Revolution of 1917.

77. Eduard Bernstein, *Evolutionary Socialism* (1898), as excerpted in Cohen (ed.), *Communism*, pp. 221–222, with regard to legislation and revolution.

78. It has not been possible in the scope of this book to explore in depth the many complex ideological differences between Marxism, Leninism, and Stalinism, much less between them and their opponents, over issues of the state as regards legislation. Lenin indicated that Marx came only later and incompletely to consider the subject head-on. Lenin himself was regarded by some as insufficiently thorough in his appreciation of the subject's ramifications. There remained an underlying ideological negativity of varying kinds and degrees toward the state itself, and consequently its legislative basis, whether in terms of the hated bourgeois state that was to be destroyed or the transitional proletarian state that was eventually supposed to wither away by itself. But, once again, the primary point for present purposes is the continuing albeit changing legislative orientation of the state and its sovereignty—from Marx to Lenin and to Stalin. There was indeed an increase of positive interest in the state and its legislative basis from Marx to Lenin and to the Constitution of the Soviet Stalinist era.

In the final analysis, the very "ideological" or polemical nature of Communistic attacks on bourgeois parliamentarism, especially poignant in Lenin's case, has served to sidetrack historians from paying full due attention to the issue of legislation itself, even though the Communist soviets and congresses often became (or so it could be argued) legislative parliaments in their own way. Nor should the Communist denunciation of ideology itself, as somehow antithetical to materialism, sidetrack historians in these respects. The place of law and legislation in Communist ideology or rhetoric over many decades in the Soviet Union, not to mention in Western Europe, was complicated and changeable. Yet it can be pieced together from multitudinous discussions in writings not focusing at length directly on it, but only in fragmented form, as in the writings of Marx and Lenin examined above; or it can be more fully viewed as in the case of the "constitutional" documents explored above.

79. Hans Kelsen, *The Communist Theory of Law* (London, 1955), Chs. 1–2 ("The Marx-Engels Theory of State and Law," "Lenin's Theory of State and Law"). For instance (pp. 1, 51–52, 58, 61): "[p. 1] The Marxian theory of law is inescapably concerned with the theory of state. . . . [pp. 51 ff.] [For] Lenin, [in] *State and Revolution*, . . . the proletarian state is a democracy and at the same time no democracy. . . . [T]he dictatorship of the proletariat is a state and at the same time it is no state. . . . To the extent the bourgeois law disappears, the law assumes the character of socialist law. Hence the law during the transition period is at the same time bourgeois and socialist law . . . [i.e.] still bourgeois law. . . . [I]n the first phase [of communism, in Kelsen's reading of Lenin,] the 'bourgeois law' will disappear only to a certain extent, whereas in the second phase it will disappear completely. In the first phase the law is to a certain extent already socialist law. Will it in the second phase be completely socialist law? Lenin says that in the first phase of communism the state does not altogether wither away, 'since there still remains the protection of "bourgeois law" which sanctions actual inequality. For the complete extinction of the state, complete communism is necessary.' Lenin does not refer to a complete extinction of law. Lenin's interpretation of Marx's doctrine does not remove this ambiguity with respect to the future of the law." Kelsen seems to suggest that Lenin's vision of a stateless society in the second phase of full communism—where justice rules without law, a view contradicted by Lenin himself—is no less tenable, even by his own logic, than that the proletarian state or semi-state will eventually wither away by itself. Kelsen criticizes (p. vii) Soviet legal theory for being "dominated almost exclusively by political factors." Kelsen's criticisms stem from his much earlier writings.

For a rebuttal of Kelsen, cf. S. Volfson, "A Criticism of Kelsen's Interpretation of the Marxist Theory of State, Anarchism, and Communism" (1924), *Soviet Political Thought: An Anthology* (translated and edited by Michael Jaworskyj, Baltimore, 1967), pp. 179 ff. The writer asserts that Kelsen is one of those "enemies of Marxism" who "slander the entire Marxist conception of the state," in distinction to "pseudo-Marxists who destroy the revolutionary essence of the Marxist theory of state" (p. 179). Kelsen's criticisms, he says (p. 181), begin with "a formal juridical definition of the state as a coercive legal order." He refers to "the fruitless scholasticism of Kelsenian theory."

According to I. Podvolotskii (1923), *ibid.*, pp. 114 ff., Lenin makes it clear that proletarian law would replace bourgeois law in the second phase of communism, while the task now is to prove that no law will exist under full communism. Coercive rules or legal norms a la Kelsen will also disappear. Meantime, "proletarian legislation must take into consideration only their expediency" (p. 132).

According to I. D. Ilinskii (1925), *ibid.*, pp. 216 ff., "it would be absurd to deny that respect for the law, cultivated among the masses, is one of the most powerful means for bringing about mass control in the interest of the ruling class."

484 / *Notes to Chapter VII*

In general cf. Rudolf Schlesinger, *Social Legal Theory: Its Social Background and Development* (London, 1945, 1951).
80. Adolf Hitler, *Mein Kampf* (translated by R. Manheim, Boston, 1971).
81. *Ibid.*, pp. 386 ff. (Ch. II, Vol. [Pt.] II).
82. *Ibid.*, pp. 392, 398 (II, II).
83. *Ibid.*, pp. 403, 407, 427 (II, II).
84. *Ibid.*, pp. 442–443 (IV, II).
85. *Ibid.*, pp. 450–451 (IV, II).
86. *Ibid.*, p. 329 (XI, I).
87. *Ibid.*, pp. 6–7 (I, I).
88. *Ibid.*, p. 333 (XII, I): "If we understand that the resurrection of the German nation represents a question of regaining our political will for self-preservation, it is also clear that this cannot be done by winning elements which in point of will at least are already national, but only by the nationalization of the consciously anti-national masses.
"A young movement which, therefore, sets itself the goal of resurrecting a German state with its own sovereignty will have to direct its fight entirely to winning the broad masses. . . . Even if the German bourgeoisie, for their well-known narrow-minded and short-sighted reasons, should, as they once did toward Bismarck, maintain an obstinate attitude of passive resistance in the hour of coming liberation—an active resistance . . . is never to be feared."
89. *Ibid.*, pp. 559–560 (X, II).
90. *Ibid.*, pp. 566—567 (X, II): "[I]n Germany without doubt the individual states did exist first and in the form of states, and the Reich was formed out of them. But the very formation of the Reich did not take place on the basis of the free will or equal participation of the single states, but through the workings of the hegemony of one state among them, Prussia. . . . The difference in size between the smallest of the former federated states and the larger ones, let alone the largest, shows the non-similarity of their achievements, and also the inequality of their share in the founding of the Reich, the forming of the federated state. Actually, in most of these states there could be no question of a real sovereignty, except if state sovereignty was taken only as an official phrase. In reality, not only the past, but the present as well, had put an end to any number of these so-called 'sovereign states' and thus clearly demonstrated the weakness of these 'sovereign' formations. . . .
"All this, in part at least, was taken into account by the constitution of the old Reich, in so far as it did not grant the individual states the same representation in the Bundesrat, but set up gradations corresponding to size and actual importance, as well as the achievement of the individual states in the formation of the Reich."
91. *Ibid.*, pp. 567–568 (X, II).
92. *Ibid.*, pp. 145–146 (IV, I). In addition, p. 162 (V, I): "My own position on the conflict . . . was not that Austria was fighting for some Serbian satisfaction, but that Germany was fighting for her existence. . . . The time had come for Bismarck's work to fight; what the fathers had once won in the battles from Weissenburg to Sedan and Paris, young Germany now had to earn once more."
Also, p. 127 (IV, I): "I came to these latter indirectly through the German alliance policy which from my Austrian days I considered absolutely mistaken. However, the full extent of this self-deception on the part of the Reich had not been clear to me in Vienna . . . [,] an alliance policy which after all Bismarck himself had founded and the sudden cessation of which could not be desirable . . ."
93. *Ibid.*, pp. 655–656 (XIV, II).
94. *Ibid.*, p. 155 (IV, I).
95. *Ibid.*, pp. 172–173 (V, I): "Bismarck's Socialist legislation finally failed and had to fail, in spite of everything. Lacking was the platform of a new philosophy for whose rise

the fight could have been waged. For only the proverbial wisdom of high government officials will succeed in believing that drivel about so-called 'state authority' or 'law and order' could form a suitable basis for the spiritual impetus of a life-and-death struggle.

"Since a real spiritual basis for this struggle was lacking, Bismarck had to entrust the execution of his Socialist legislation to the judgment and desires of that institution which itself was a product of Marxist thinking. By entrusting the fate of his war on the Marxists to the well-wishing of bourgeois democracy, the Iron Chancellor set the wolf to mind the sheep.

"All this was only the necessary consequence of the absence of a basic new anti-Marxist philosophy endowed with a stormy will to conquer.

"Hence the sole result of Bismarck's struggle was a grave disillusionment.

"Were conditions different during the World War or at its beginning? Unfortunately not.

"The more I occupied myself with the idea of a necessary change in the government's attitude toward Social Democracy as the momentary embodiment of Marxism, the more I recognized the lack of a serviceable substitute for this doctrine."

96. *Ibid.*, p. 269 (X, I): "The aimlessness of German domestic and foreign policy was apparent to everyone who was not purposely blind. The regime of compromise seemed to be most in keeping with Bismarck's conception that 'politics is an art of the possible.' But between Bismarck and the later German chancellors there was a slight difference which made it permissible for the former to let fall such an utterance on the nature of politics while the same view from the mouths of his successors could not but take on an entirely different meaning. For Bismarck with this phrase only wanted to say that for the achievement of a definite political goal all possibilities should be utilized, or, in other words, that all possibilities should be taken into account; in the view of his successors, however, this utterance solemnly released them from the necessity of having any political ideas or goals whatever. And the leadership of the Reich at this time really had no more political goals; for the necessary foundation of a definite philosophy was lacking, as well as the necessary clarity on the inner laws governing the development of all political life."

97. *Ibid.*, pp. 234–235 (X, I): "In proportion as economic life grew to be the dominant mistress of the state, money became the god whom all had to serve. . . .

"Unfortunately, the domination of money was sanctioned even by that authority which should have most opposed it: His Majesty the Kaiser acted most unfortunately by drawing the aristocracy into the orbit of the new finance capital. It must be said to his credit, however, that unfortunately even Bismarck himself did not recognize the menacing danger in this respect."

98. *Ibid.*, p. 681 (XV, II): "What will rank Mussolini among the great men of this earth is his determination not to share Italy with the Marxists, but to destroy internationalism and save the fatherland from it.

"How miserable and dwarfish our German would-be statesmen seem by comparison, and how one gags with disgust when these nonentities, with boorish arrogance, dare to criticize this man who is a thousand times greater than they; and how painful it is to think that this is happening in a land which barely half a century ago could call a Bismarck its leader."

99. Of particular interest, in view of their provocative titles, are Louis L. Snyder, *From Bismarck to Hitler: The Background of Modern German Nationalism* (Williamsport, 1935), and J. C. G. Köhl, *From Bismarck to Hitler: The Problem of Continuity in German History* (New York, 1970), with frontispiece portraying Hitler dressed in the regalia of Bismarck. The first book devotes chapters in Pt. I to "The Traditional Nationalism of Otto von Bismarck" (1), "The Nationalist Historian—Heinrich von Treitschke" (3), and "The Integral Nationalism of Adolf Hitler" (8). Chapters in Pt. 2 include: "The Dissolution of Liberal Nationalism" [which was inaugurated in the writings

of Bentham] (1), "Junkerdom and Nationalism" (2), "The Rise of Nationalistic Societies" (4), "Nationalistic Aspects of German Anti-Semitism" (8), and "Nationalism [under Hitler] Triumphant" (9), the last sect. of which is entitled " 'National regeneration' or 'national breakdown'?" The author views Hitler as "[t]he apotheosis of German nationalism" (p. 75).

Köhl, *ibid.*, states the following (Intro., pp. xi–xiii): "[T]he theory of continuity in German history is gaining more and more currency as an explanation of Hitler's appeal to the German people.

"Ironically, it was the Nazis themselves who first propagated the idea of continuity. It was they who claimed to be the spiritual descendants of the ancient Teutonic tribes, of Luther, Frederick the Great, Bismarck, Hindenburg and Ludendorff, . . . to justify their rule . . . [and] legitimize their regime. All the more remarkable, therefore, is the ready acceptance of the Nazi view of German history by the West. . . . [I]f Hitler had sought to claim the glory of Prussia for his dictatorship, the anti-German historians were saying that the Prussian tradition had culminated in the barbarism of the Third Reich.

"Because both interpretations were so obviously propagandist in intention, they had become almost wholly discredited in academic circles by the end of the 1950s. . . .

"It was the work of . . . Fritz Fischer . . . which reopened the debate . . . in 1961. . . . Despite the initial outcry, his basic conclusions have now been widely accepted and his influence is clearly discernible in most of the monographs now appearing in Germany. . . .

"Fischer's investigations . . . made it possible to see German history from unification in 1871 to catastrophe in 1945 as a unified whole. However, . . . [there are] a number of . . . issues raised by Fischer's discoveries: to what extent were the seeds of German expansionism implanted in the Germany created by Bismarck in the years 1862–71 . . . ? . . .

"Politically, the period from Bismarck to Hitler must be divided into three parts—the Empire, 1871–1918; the Republic, 1918–1933; and the Nazi era, 1933–45."

Among the documents presented by Köhl, *ibid.*, are two that include revealing statements by Nazi writers on Bismarck. The first document (1936) on the Nazi view of German history and the roots of National Socialism is by Friedrich Freherr von der Goltz and Theodor Stiefenhofer and includes the following (p. 1): "The triumph of the enemies of the German people seemed complete when the Congress of Vienna pushed a huge rock in front of the gate through which the Germans hoped to pass to national self-determination, freedom and unity. But Bismarck pushed this rock aside with titanic strength after the citizens' revolt of 1848, the 'revolution in dressing-gown and slippers', had failed to achieve the same aim because of its disunity and lack of realism.

"Bismarck gave us the Second Reich whose shining outline had already become visible against the dark backcloth of Germany's miserable and impotent petty States in the rise of Prussia from Frederick the Great onwards. The Hohenzollern State was strengthened in its historical mission by the revival of a German national consciousness directed against the alien elements which had entered all aspects of German life after the Peace of Westphalia."

A second document (1944) on the "true Bismarck" is by Ulrich von Hassell and includes the following (p. 181): "Germany, situated in the middle of Europe, is the heart of Europe. Europe cannot live without a sound, strong heart. During recent years I have studied Bismarck, and his stature as a statesman grows constantly in my estimation. It is regrettable what a false picture of him we ourselves have given the world—that of the power-politician with cuirassier boots—in our childish joy over the fact that at last someone had made Germany a name to reckon with again. In his own way he knew how to win confidence in the world; exactly the reverse of what is done today. In truth, the highest diplomacy and great moderation were his real gifts."

100. Cf. e.g. William Ebenstein, *The Nazi State* (New York, 1943).

101. On the above and related details cf. *ibid.*, Chs. I–II; Lee, *European Dictatorships*, Ch. 4; Gordon A. Craig, *Germany, 1866–1945* (New York, 1978), Chs. XV–XVI; John L. Snell (ed.), *The Nazi Revolution: Germany's Guilt or Germany's Fate?* (Boston, 1959); Felix Gilbert, *The End of the European Era, 1890 to the Present* (New York, 1979), Ch. 8, sect. 3; Alan Bullock, *Hitler: A Study in Tyranny* (New York, revised edn., 1962), Bk. II; and William L. Shirer, *The Rise and Fall of the Third Reich: A History of Nazi Germany* (New York, 1950 etc.), Bk. II.

In addition concerning totalitarianism there are, among the vast sea of secondary works, the following general items: Hannah Arendt, *The Origins of Totalitarianism* (Cleveland, 1964 etc., repr.); Paul T. Masson (ed.), *Totalitarianism: Temporary Madness or Permanent Danger?* (Lexington, Mass., 1967); George L. Mosse (ed.), *Nazi Culture: A Documentary History* (New York, 1981, 1st edn. 1966), Ch. 5; and G. Wright and A. Mejia, Jr. *An Age of Controversy* (New York, 1963, etc.), Ch. VI ("Totalitarianism: An Outmoded Label?"—an interesting title in view of our treatment of the subject earlier in the present chapter).

On problems of law and Nazi ideology regarding the state, there are such works as the following: Mosse, *Nazi Culture*, Ch. 9 ("What Is the State and Who Are Its Citizens?," with excerpts from Carl Schmitt, "Public Law in a New Context"); William Scheuerman, "Legal Indeterminacy and the Origins of Nazi Legal Thought: The Case of Carl Schmitt," *Hist. of Pol. Tht.*, XVII (1996), pp. 572 ff., showing Schmitt's proclivity toward German Fascism prior to the actual rise of Hitler; *ibid.*, "The Rule of Law under Siege: Carl Schmitt and the Death of the Weimar Republic," *ibid.*, XIV (1993), pp. 265 ff., concerning Schmitt's belief that the modern rule of law had become irrelevant and that an authoritarian alternative was needed; *ibid.*, *Between the Exception and the Norm: The Frankfurt School and the Rule of Law* (Camb., Mass., 1994), with various materials and discussions relating to legislative subjects in the 1920s and to Nazism; Carl Schmitt, *Political Theology: Four Chapters on the Concept of Sovereignty* (translated by G. Oakes, Camb., Mass., 1986), with Schmitt's noted definition (p. 5), "Sovereign is he who decides on the exception" (regarding superiority to law and with forced relationships to Bodin's definition of sovereignty); Renato Cristi, "Carl Schmitt on Liberalism, Democracy and Catholicism," *Hist. of Pol. Tht.*, XIV (1993), pp. 282 ff., with examination of Schmitt's *Parliamentarism*; Ingo Müller, *Hitler's Justice: The Courts of the Third Reich* (translated by D. Schneider, Camb., Mass., 1991), showing the degradation of the German jurists and courts under the Nazis; Lothar Gruchmann, *Justiz im Dritten Reich, 1933–1940: Anpassung und Unterwerfung in der Ara Gürtner* (Munich, 1988), a massive tome on the Ministry of Justice and the justice apparatus, with particular regard to the tragic ways in which people who served in the system of justice inherited from the Weimar Republic accommodated themselves to the Nazi dictatorship.

Characterizations of the Nazi state as a "police state" and a "racial state" (among many other such rubrics) are exemplified in two works. George C. Browder, *Foundations of the Nazi Police State: The Formation of Sipo and SD* (Lexington, Kentucky, 1990), enters the historiographical debate between "intentionalists," who stress the central role of Hitler's ideas and personality in shaping the Third Reich, and the "functionalists," who focus on the functional nature of decision-making. Michael Burleigh and Wolfgang Wippermann, *The Racial State: Germany, 1933–1945* (Cambridge, 1991), deal with questions about the "totalitarian" extent of German racial policies.

Further works concerning the Bismarck-to-Hitler theme and its wider contexts include the following examples. Fritz Fischer, *From Kaiserreich to Third Reich: Elements of Continuity in German History, 1871–1945* (translated by Roger Fleicher, London, 1986), draws direct if not straight lines of "continuity" in modern German history from the Prussian military state of the eighteenth century to Bismarck's Empire and to the Nazi dictatorship as regards the political system and social forces supporting it. Klaus Hildebrand, *Das vergangene Reich: Deutsche Aussenpolitik von Bismarck bis Hitler, 1871–1945* (Stuttgart, 1995), relates domestic events to foreign affairs. *Ibid., German Foreign Policy from Bismarck to Adenauer: The Limits of Statecraft* (translated by L. Willmot, London, 1989), defends Bismarckian diplomacy against its critics and portrays Hitler's designs on France as secondary to his Eastern ambitions. Geoff Eley, *From Unification to Nazism: Reinterpreting the German Past* (Boston, 1986), underscores the immediate crises and aftermath of World War I, rather than the longer trajectories of German history from Bismarck on, when explaining the rise of Nazism. In wider context, E. Earle (ed.), *Makers of Modern Strategy: Military Thought from Machiavelli to Hitler* (Princeton, 1944), includes pre-Hitlerian German materials.

Historians who argue strongly for the pre-Hitlerian roots of German "nationalism" under the Nazis have often cited such writers as Heinrich von Treitschke. The state is the focal point of his *Politics*, Vol. I (translated by A. Balfour, New York, 1916). Treitschke's first chapter ("The State Idea") of Bk. I ("The Nature of the State") begins as follows (p. 3): "The State is the people, legally united as an independent entity." Further on he declares (pp. 12–13): "Ultramontanes and Jacobins both start with the assumption that the legislation of a modern State is the work of sinful man. They thus . . . lack . . . reverence for the . . . will of God . . . unfolded in the life of the State." However (p. 65): "Without war no State could be." At the same time (pp. 89, 106): "[T]he State must necessarily be subject to the moral law . . . [and] is in itself an ethical force and a high moral good." Such recognitions of the legal and legislative as well as militaristic bases of the state, combined with his Hegelian and nationalistic ideas, were characteristic of Treitschke's outlook. His *Politics* (c. 1880), published posthumously in 1897–1898, became a kind of gospel for pre-war German nationalism. His lectures on the subject at the University of Berlin from 1874 on, drawing sizable audiences over many years, can be compared with T. H. Green's lectures on political obligation at Oxford. Treitschke's work figured prominently in the German counterpart to the British "idealist" tradition. Treitschke's *Politics* shared not only the Hegelian strain but as well the more ominous tendencies also revealed in the writings of Bosanquet.

General surveys of the history of nationalism have included the Nazi era in varying ways. A few brief examples will suffice. Hans Kohn, *Nationalism: Its Meaning and History* (revised edn., Toronto, 1965), includes such indicatively entitled chs. (in Pt. I) as "Nationalism and *Realpolitik*" (5) and "Racialism and Totalitarianism" (7). Boyd C. Shafer, *Nationalism: Myth and Reality* (New York, 1955), Sect. IV, "The Age of Nationalism, 1815–1955," gives a much broader and more extended scope to nationalism as an "age" than is often encountered in the nineteenth-century frameworks adopted by many historians. Another kind of periodization is apparent in the title *Nationalism, Industrialization, and Democracy, 1815–1914* (edited by T. Barnes and G. Feldman, 1972). Other types of works could be cited linking nationalism with questions of modernity in the development of German history.

At the same time, one sometimes encounters such press clippings as "Nazism Wasn't Nationalism," by conservative columnist George F. Will in the *Washington Post*, August 11, 1991, p. C7. It was written on the occasion of the moving of the remains of Frederick the Great from southern Germany to Berlin. Will writes: "Frederick is considered the father of German militarism, which is considered inextricably entwined with German nationalism, which is considered embryonic Nazism. Both Germany and nationalism are too important to be so misunderstood.

"Nazism was Hitler's creation and died with him.

"He was never really chief of state. He was Führer, personal leader, head of a party. . . . He despised state structures as inhibitous on his discretion. . . . Conservative nationalists predominated among those who . . . came heartbreakingly close to killing him. . . .

"Suspicion of nationalism, deriving from a misinterpretation of modern history, is weakening U.S. foreign policy. . . .

"But in the modern age, democracy presupposes nationalism. Nationalism is a sense of shared destiny based on a common history and civic culture within a particular territory. It involves wholesome pride . . ."

Needless to say, such provocative assertions are debatable.

102. John Rawls, *A Theory of Justice* (Camb., Mass., 1971), Ch. I, sect. 5, "Classical Utilitarianism."

103. H. L. A. Hart, *Bentham*; *The Concept of Law* (Oxford, 1961); and *Essays in Jurisprudence and Philosophy* (Oxford, 1983), esp. Ch. 8, "Utilitarianism and Natural Rights" (1978), and Ch. 9, "Between Utility and Rights" (1973).

104. Hart, *Concept*, p. 43.
105. *Ibid.*, p. 44.
106. *Ibid.*, p. 44.
107. *Ibid.*, p. 49.
108. *Ibid.*, p. 53.
109. *Ibid.*, e.g. p. 59.
110. *Ibid.*, pp. 62–63.
111. *Ibid.*, p. 50.
112. *Ibid.*, pp. 65, 68–69.
113. *Ibid.*, p. 69.
114. *Ibid.*, p. 70.
115. *Ibid.*, p. 76.
116. *Ibid.*, p. 77.
117. *Ibid.*, p. 183.

118. The following two titles are especially indicative here: James E. Crimmins, *Secular Utilitarianism: Social Science and the Critique of Religion in the Thought of Jeremy Bentham* (Oxford, 1990), and P. J. Kelly, *Utilitarianism and Distributive Justice: Jeremy Bentham and the Civil Law* (Oxford, 1990). Crimmins' work gives much consideration to the integral part of religion in Bentham's writing career, along with that of legislation. Kelly's Intro. presents extensive condensed rebuttals of Rawl's attacks on neo-utilitarian writers, as will be further cited below. Two passages are here particularly revealing of Kelly's positions on Bentham and Hart: First (p. 7): "The argument of this work is intended to demonstrate that Bentham not only had a utilitarian theory of justice, but also that it accommodates the liberal values of liberty, equality, and personal inviolability, and therefore that his utilitarian theory is not subject to the substantial criticisms raised by Rawls and others." Second (pp. 211–212): "In this work I have maintained a distinction between the principle of utility as the creation of moral judgement or the standard of the good from a utilitarian principle of moral obligation. However, in arguing against Hart's indirect utilitarian interpretation of the principle, the claim that the principle of utility cannot be action-guiding was rejected. Some revisionist interpretations of Mill's moral theory have tried to maintain that the principle of utility is a standard of the good and not the criterion of what is right or wrong and what one ought to do."

Cf. H. L. Pohlman, *Justice Oliver Wendell Holmes and Utilitarian Jurisprudence* (Camb., Mass., 1984), Chs. I–II, "Utility, Morality, and Liberty" and "Law, Sovereignty, and Legal Obligation."

Mieczyslaw Maneli, *Judicial Positivism and Human Rights* (New York, 1981), declares as follows on Austin and utilitarianism (p. 39): "John Austin developed and systematized utilitarianism in the sphere of jurisprudence. Although he lacked the innovative spirit of his master and teacher, Jeremy Bentham, he was a more precise jurist. . . . John Stuart Mill followed a broader humanistic path." There are chs. on Bentham (founder of judicial positivism), Austin, Jhering (who combined elements of Roman law, Comte's positivism, Bentham's utilitarianism, Austin's juridical theory, and Mill's liberalism), and so forth.

D. Weinstein, "Equal Freedom, Rights and Utility in Spencer's Moral Philosophy," *Hist. of Pol. Tht.*, XI (1990), pp. 119 ff., raises issues on the combinations of utilitarianism, moralism, and liberalism in Spencer's thought with regard to theorists in more recent times who have argued that (for good or bad) utilitarianism has traditionally excluded those other areas.

Relevant to the foregoing issues is, as its title suggests, Douglas G. Long, *Bentham on Liberty: Jeremy Bentham's Idea of Liberty in Relation to His Utilitarianism* (Toronto, 1977).

Notes to Chapter VIII
The Growth of "Anti–Neo-*Isms*"

1. Hugo Krabbe, *The Modern Idea of the State* (translated by G. Sabine and W. Shepard, The Hague, 1922, 1st pub. 1915); pp. 1–2.

2. *Ibid.*, pp. 200–201.

3. *Ibid.*, p. 3: "[T]he modern idea of the state came to dominate political practice, while political theory still maintained the old view of the state derived from absolutism. Theory has not taken account of the change in the relations between rulers and subjects which has gradually come about during the last half century, or at least has not done so adequately.

"For centuries our life has been dominated by the idea of a *sovereign*, having a subjective right to rule, and of a *people*, standing in a relation of political subordination. This sovereign was conceived as embodied either in a prince or in an assembly, and consequently its right to rule was viewed as a personal and subjective right. Since the Middle Ages political theory has continually discussed the question of the origin of this personal right of sovereignty and the purposes to which it must be applied, and the limitations which must in consequence be placed upon the sovereign's right to rule."

4. *Ibid.*, p. 6.

5. *Ibid.*, pp. 6–9: "The idea of the state which adopts as its central conception an assumed right to rule vested in a specific person, fell into disrepute with the introduction of the constitutional system, even though this right was exercised in the name of the state as a legal person. The will of the old historical possessor of sovereign authority is no longer binding in and of itself; the co-operation of parliament is required. In parliament, however, it is a changing majority, composed now of certain persons and now of others, whose co-operation suffices. Consequently the exercise of the sovereign authority, so far as it concerns parliament at least, no longer rests in the hands of specific persons. In proportion, therefore, as the decisive power in the state devolves upon parliament, it becomes evident that the positive law owes its validity to an authority which in the concrete is

constantly changing, but which in the abstract is personified as the 'legislative power.' Consequently it is also evident that the authority of positive law requires another support than that which is found in the will of particular members of parliament.

"This circumstance involves the necessity of recognizing in positive law something other than the will of the traditional sovereign. The fact that parliament is elected by and from the people favors the view that it is an organ of the people's sense of law and right. Accordingly it would be precisely this sense of right which is expressed in the positive law. Thus a completely new basis for the authority of positive law comes into view. Not the will of a sovereign who exists only in the imagination, but the legal conviction of the people lends binding force to positive law; *positive law* is valid, therefore, only by virtue of the fact that it incorporates principles of right (*Recht*).

"With this new theory of the validity of positive law, there comes also as a practical consequence of the constitutional system the possibility of subjecting the bearer of the earlier sovereign authority, the king, to the positive law. In practice it was already conceded that the state might be bound by the common civil law. This was explained by a theoretical fiction which imputed to the state a double personality; one of these, the 'state-fisc,' was subject to the law which was binding upon all other persons, while the other, the 'state-sovereign,' was not. Under the domination of the constitutional system, however, where king and parliament together decreed the positive law, this fiction was no longer necessary in order to establish the validity of common law even for the sovereign. In fact, the positive law, as a product of both the king and the popular representative body, was thus made superior to the sovereign in the original sense of the term. And consequently there was no difficulty in recognizing the supremacy of positive law even in the field of public law. Under the designation of the legal state (*Rechtsstaat*), this supremacy of the positive law has been established step by step. First it was merely a *limitation* of the sovereign authority; then it became the demand that the mere will of the sovereign be *replaced*, so far as possible, by law; and finally it brought about the unconditional victory of the law. . . .

"[W]e no longer perceive the state as localized in a sovereign, but we find it wherever we perceive the power of the law to create obligations. What is now in actual practice adorned with the old name of sovereign is a man or an assemblage of men upon whom the law has laid a task. They are not, therefore, invested with a power to be expressed through their will in independence of the law."

6. *Ibid.*, pp. 12–15, 36: "Sociological and historical investigations have shown that the reciprocal interdependence which has existed between men from the earliest times has caused them to live in organizations which were in no way imposed upon them from the outside, that is, by a sovereign, but which arose from instinctive feelings, though these feelings were clearly differentiated only at a later stage. This is the original type of community, in which duties are accepted without owing their sanction to a sovereign. . . . A sovereign first appears when the tribe, presumably for military reasons, accepts a chief and renders him obedience. In the beginning this chief derives his rights from the organization of the community. . . .

"The original relation of the prince to the community, however, could not endure. This would have been possible only in case an organized means of law-making had continued to exist, but it was precisely this which was interrupted by the disappearance of the popular assembly or representative body which provided for it. It is indeed true that there appeared at times in the organization of the state an assembly of estates, but its function was not the making of law but more especially the representation of interests. Its origin and *raison d'être* are to be found in the limitation of princely power, in the protection of the rights and privileges of the estates. This disappearance of a popular organ of legislation made it impossible for the community to preserve a connection between its own inherent legal order and the authority of the chief, such as might have kept alive the notion that this authority was an outgrowth of the communal organization. . . .

"With the appearance of a sovereign authority distinct from the authority of the law, there arose the need of giving it a legal character, though its basis was extra-legal. Down to our own day political theory has assumed this task and has made the authority of the sovereign its central point, to the almost complete neglect of the authority of the law. Indeed it may be said that since the Middle Ages political theory has been nothing more than a theory of sovereignty and that the theory of the state has devoted itself to the elaboration of the organization of powers involved in sovereignty [Krabbe goes on to discuss Plato and Aristotle on sovereignty and ethical ends.] . . . Since the French Revolution, when a legislative organ begins to be active in the community, a change has taken place. Step by step this organ has succeeded in re-establishing the validity of law as against the sovereign. Political theory finds itself confronted again with a dualism of authorities until, under the theory and practice of the legal state, this dualism is removed and the sole rulership is again assigned to law."

7. *Ibid.*, pp. 37–39: "Consequently, a careful distinction between law (*Recht*) and justice (*Gerechtigkeit*) is as important for the theory of the sovereignty of law as for jurisprudence. Usage is uncertain, especially with reference to the word *law* (*Recht*), which is not always used in contradistinction to *justice* (*Gerechtigkeit*) but sometimes as synomymous with it. When, for example, one speaks of a conflict with law or right (*Recht*), he can be understood to mean either a conflict with effective legal rules or with the idea of justice. It is necessary at the start, therefore, to insist that in investigating the basis of the binding force of law, this word *law* (*Recht*) is taken to mean the totality of effective legal rules. . . . Though the will of the legislator may be a sufficient reason for our accepting legal rules as having binding force, there is always the possibility of showing that the standard applied by the legislator does not correspond, or only partly corresponds, with the idea of justice. The investigation of this standard is not our task, but rather that of legal philosophy. We must keep our eyes fixed solely upon the law which is in force. . . . On the whole, it may be said that the theory of the sovereignty of law has gained supremacy in the practice of the western European states."

8. *Ibid.*, p. 127.

9. *Ibid.*, pp. 127–128: "It followed from this view that when the sovereign, who was personified as an imaginary 'legislator,' had not spoken there was no law. But it is impossible that there should be gaps in the law. Therefore, howsoever the sovereign might have spoken, the law which was promulgated by him must be looked upon as complete, a requirement which could be met only by developing the sovereign's law into a *system* from which any missing rules might be derived by a process of deduction. The chief task of the jurist, therefore, was the *construction of a system of ideas* to be incorporated in the law of the sovereign. Miracles of analysis and synthesis have been wrought in this field, and for many years this satisfied the need of expanding the sovereign's law into a legal system adequate to the great variety of social relationships. The law, therefore, sprang from a two-fold source. First, it was derived from the will of the sovereign, which was to be found especially in the statutes. And second, it came from the juristic system which was constructed with more or less skill to fill in the gaps in the statutes. It was assumed that the legislator had developed his law systematically, though without stating all the details. The second source of law, the system, was especially the product of a purely intellectual process."

10. *Ibid.*, p. 129: "This conception of law, as a substance produced by the legislator and worked over by the dialectical ingenuity of the jurist into a legal system comprehending all the relationships of life, was doubtless strengthened, though it was by no means created, by codification. In the main the law taken over into the codes had already been

worked together into a system by centuries of juristic manipulation. Codification merely made it easier for the jurist to work toward the architectonic completion of the law and in fact he has devoted himself to this task to the point of intellectual exhaustion. Indeed codification has been recommended as a better means for system-making, and in this respect it has answered its purpose. It was also expected, however, that it would make the law more accessible to the people. This goal has not been, and could not be, achieved, for codified law was jurists' law and has always remained, as it still does, mostly outside the layman's world of ideas and feelings."

11. *Ibid.*, p. 144: "If the law is recognized as an ultimate source of authority, it is not permissible to maintain the idea of sovereignty. Nevertheless both ideas are maintained, with the necessary consequence that neither constitutional nor administrative law, lacking a secure starting-point, is capable of being reduced to a system. . . .

"Constitutional and administrative law can be rescued from this morass only by returning to the old political theory of the police state or by going forward to the new political theory which accepts no authority as valid except that of the law. A compromise is impossible; and since political fact has outgrown the theory of the police state, the actual course of affairs can be understood and guided only by holding fast to the one title to authority which has survived the overthrow of sovereignty, viz., that of the law. If this is done, . . . the police state will be dissolved into a complex of rights and duties evoked in behalf of various public interests by the action of the social sense of right, either organized or unorganized. This sense of right is a real authority and the only real authority, because obedience to its commands is not imposed by constraint but is freely given."

12. *Ibid.*, pp. 145-147: "The old concept of the state and of the law required a sovereign placed over against the people in order that the law might be valid. . . . Now the law is admitted to be a norm which gets its binding force from the spiritual nature of man, viz., from his sense of right. . . . Under the domination of the idea of sovereignty, the law was formerly monopolized by the sovereign. In case there were gaps in the statutes, one had to take refuge in the notion of an omniscient legislator in whose subconsciousness numerous rules were concealed which might be brought to light by means of dialectic. At the present time the field controlled by statutory law is limited to those interests which actually lay within the ken of the legislator at the time the statute was enacted, and to these interests only in so far as they were envisaged by him. . . . At the present time, it is perceived that the basis for the validity of statutory law lies in a valuation of interests, which is not made merely on occasion within the walls of the parliament house; the citizenship in the full circle of its social life is continually participating in this valuation by applying the standard of its legal convictions to various interests, even to those which have already been appraised in the written law. Consequently the entire mass of the law is a living organism, whose parts die or are renewed when other legal convictions come into control than those which prevailed when the statute was enacted or the law created. . . . The present belongs to us completely and wholly. We repudiate entirely an appeal to the judgment of history. When a higher sanction is sought by means of this appeal for a law which no longer reflects the vital convictions of the people (as, for example, when it is said that God reveals himself in history), this is preaching submission when resistance ought to be urged. Resistance is necessary to liberate our feelings, thoughts, and wills from the yoke of history and tradition, which hinder the birth of a matured spiritual life."

13. *Ibid.*, pp. 208-211: "If then the ruler's title cannot be questioned on the basis of law, because it is not a legal title, the law is confronted by a sphere of power at the entrance to which the rulership of law terminates. For this sphere of power does not belong to the world of norms and hence cannot be controlled by norms. The full rulership of law cannot be reached. The theory results in a twofold power built upon different foundations, and neither power can affect the other.

"This view of the state, therefore, is untenable. . . . The relations between Duguit's 'rulers' and 'ruled' are not therefore factual relations but legal relations. And since the quality of being a ruler is bestowed by law, there is no authority which is not rooted in law. The rulership inherent in the state can therefore be traced back to a single authority, that of the law. . . . As a result of this conclusion, . . . it follows that the idea of the [modern] state must be derived from the law. . . . If only a single nationality is contained in a state, its peculiar body of legal relations is richer and more original, and all the members of the nation contribute to defining the spiritual value to be found in the feeling or sense of right. The civilized states of our own time differ chiefly in respect to the specific body of legal relations which each possesses, based on its distinct nationality. Consequently their inner force and significance as means of raising mankind to a higher spiritual existence is infinitely greater than in earlier times, when the life of the state was discernible only by the subjection of a portion of mankind to a sovereign standing apart from the people. The collective life in the field of law developed late. . . . But since the people have recovered their share in law-making, national bodies of legal relations have manifestly begun to grow up. . . . The modern idea of the state has its foundation specifically in these bodies of legal relations. . . . A state which includes many races or nationalities can be held together only by reducing centralized law-making to a minimum. This was the case particularly in Austria. On the other hand, the spiritual bonds between peoples of different states may so increase as to develop a collective body of legal relations on a more inclusive scale and thus lead to a higher organization of the sense of right. Germany may stand as an example of this process. . . .

"In all civilized states, however, we find more or less developed organs to express the sense of right residing in the state. This is the reason why the functioning of a legislative organ is the superficial mark of statehood among a portion of mankind. What this organ is, is determined by the constitution of the country in question. Nevertheless, the law contained in the constitution is, in the last analysis, as subject to change as law existing anywhere else. History is full of examples in which unorganized law has worked changes in constitutional law in order to make room for a different legislative organ or for one differently constituted.

"In every organ devoted to law-making, the idea of the state may be perceived, even in the functioning of communal councils and provincial legislatures when they possess the power of issuing ordinances. These organs, however, are products of a legal system which proceeds from the operation of another and higher source of law and by which their composition and competence are determined. The other and higher source of law, in the case of the unitary state, lies in that sense of right which has been organized and centralized for a community including the communes and provinces. For the part of mankind which occupies a given territory, this sense of right creates all legal value, including that which determines the composition of the 'legislative authority' itself. Independently of the organized method of law-making, however, the unorganized sense of right may always make itself felt. The portion of mankind included within a community which is based upon such an independently operating sense of right is a state. This, to be sure, does not mean that all law-making depends upon the state; the sense of right, whatever it may be, cannot be made to cease working. It does mean that the finding of organs for the sense of right lies within the authority of the state."

14. *Ibid.*, p. 218: "The vesting in absolute monarchy of the twofold function of preserving interests and making law has controlled the theory of the state down to our own day. On the one hand, the establishment of absolute monarchy brought forward the conception of the state as a legal community. . . . The transformation of the prince from an official entrusted with the care of certain public interests into an organ of the state conceived as a legal community has seriously hampered an understanding of the nature of the state.

"In particular the ideas of power and authority, which are necessarily connected with the state as a legal community, are transferred, in absolute monarchy, to the public interests which the prince must preserve, with the result that these interests are regarded as 'powers.' Both the older and the more recent literature is saturated with this conception."

15. *Ibid.*, pp. 218–219, 221–223.

16. *Ibid.*, pp. 269–271: "The progress of the political organization which leads to the establishment of confederations and federal states must eventually issue in an organ founded upon . . . a world-wide sense of right in every field. The right of a nation to live according to its own law will then have vanished and states will be amalgamated into a single world-empire. This world-empire, which will bring us the One State uniting the whole of mankind, may still be delayed for centuries; but . . . the process . . . is going on before our eyes. As interests of an international nature increase, the center of law-making is shifted from the states to an ever-broadening legal community. . . . The One State will never appear until an organ has developed specially designed to make international law and proceeding from the people themselves. The present states will be related to this One State as its provinces, i.e., as communities equipped, to be sure, with a special-making organ. . . .

"It is of minor importance, however, to speculate upon a world-state. . . . [T]he civilization of a nation must have developed sufficiently for it to feel that its communal life is ruled exclusively by the power of an ethical idea, like that of law. In the centuries which preceded the rise of the modern idea of the state, such a civilization was lacking in the great majority of nations."

17. Léon Duguit, "The Law and the State: French and German Doctrines," *Harvard Law Review*, XXXI (1917), pp. 1–185 (at pp. 1, 6–7).

18. *Ibid.*, pp. 10, 78–79: "This doctrine is made up of two essential elements. The State is the organized nation; the nation is a person; it possesses according to Jean Jacques Rousseau, *a common ego (un moi commun)*, a conscience, a will. It is the general will, the national will; and this will is sovereign, because it is the general will. The State is sovereign because it is the nation organized, and it is accordingly endowed with this general sovereign will. . . .

"This doctrine, the most complete and concise expression of which may be found in the Declaration of the Rights of Man and of the Citizen of 1789, is built in solid logical fashion. . . . But the premise may well be contested. The foundations of the doctrine are singularly fragile; and the guarantees that it pretends to give the individual against the arbitrary acts of the State appear very precarious. . . .

"In Hegel's *Philosophy of Mind* may be found the following: 'The essence of the State is the universal, self-originated and self-developed,—the reasonable spirit of will; but, as self-knowing and self-actualizing, sheer subjectivity, and—as an actuality—one individual . . .' . . . .

"Thus, by means of the State, the moral idea finds its complete realization. . . .

"This is the fundamental notion underlying the Hegelian doctrine of the State, the notion which is the upshot of his philosophical system and is the starting point of his political doctrine. For the latter is no more than the development of the former. Let us not think, however, that this conception of Hegel's is entirely new. It was already expressed in Rousseau's *Contrat Social* in less abstract and less philosophical but certainly clearer terms. . . .

"If the State is the realization of the moral idea, it is at the same time the rational in itself and for itself. . . ."

19. *Ibid.*, pp. 119, 123–124: "The political doctrines of Kant and of Hegel were really juridical doctrines. But neither one nor the other was a jurist by profession. They had indicated the bases for a juridical theory of the State, but they did not work it out, and

had they cared to do so, they could not have constructed such a theory. Not until the last part of the nineteenth century do we find in the legal literature of Germany a true juridical theory of the State. Up to that time public law had not completely divorced itself either from politics or moral philosophy. And with respect to public law the works of the professional jurists contain scarcely a practical explanation of the rules of positive law so far as the political and administrative organization is concerned. . . . This idea was destined to become the fundamental conception underlying later attempts to formulate the whole juridical theory of the State—the theory which finds its full development in the work of one quite worthy of admiration, namely, Professor Georg Jellinek. . . .

"Gerber was the precursor of contemporary German doctrines of public law growing out of the metaphysical conception of the State. These doctrines, so interrelated in German legal literature, have found their most complete and exact expression in the comprehensive and, indeed, remarkable work of Professor Jellinek. . . . The work of Jellinek is, as it were, a synthesis of the movement of absolutist ideas proceeding from Kant and Hegel, having for their inspiration the thought that the State is a great moral personality, which realizes and alone can realize the moral idea, and in consequence may impose its will without reserve and without restriction. But, at the same time an ingenious though sterile effort appears, having for its purpose reconciliation of this omnipotence of the State with public law upon which it has been superimposed, in order to explain how the modern State, while being all powerful, is at the same time a State under law, a *Rechtsstaat*. . . .

"The German doctrine of public law in that stage of development to which it had been raised by Jellinek . . . has not been surpassed since his death. . . .

"Can any one fail to see that we have here only a sophistry? This auto-limitation of the State is illusory."

20. *Ibid.*, pp. 181–182: "As Auguste Comte has so clearly shown, the notion of subjective right is a notion of a metaphysical order. 'There can only be a true right,' said the great thinker, 'so long as regular powers emanate from supernatural wills. . . . In the positive state, which does not admit of heavenly prerogative, the idea of right disappears absolutely.'

"There thus disappears, on the one hand, not only the sovereignty of the State, conceived as the subjective right of commanding, the incumbent of which right would be the State personified, but there also disappears the autonomy of the individual, together with his subjective rights."

21. Léon Duguit, *Law in the Modern State* (translated by F. and H. Laski, New York, 1919), pp. 3, 6, 8–12, 15, 20, 28: "During the feudal period this theory of the *imperium* was almost eclipsed. . . .

"When the feudal theory was combined with the memory of Roman ideas of *dominium* the outlines of the new system were already clear. . . .

"From these materials the lawyers of the ancient régime built up a precise and complex theory. . . .

"In its origin sovereignty was not the power of the king, it was only a special character attached to certain lordships and notably to royal lordships. . . . It was Bodin who first used the word in this sense and thus began, at least in part, the endless controversies we have inherited. He defined sovereignty as 'the absolute and perpetual power in the state.' . . .

"In the seventeenth and eighteenth centuries, therefore, sovereignty means a right to command placed in the king's hands. It is a right of the same kind as the right of property. . . .

"Every one knows the teaching of Locke, of Mably, of Rousseau and of Montesquieu. . . .

"So may be defined the basis of public law inherited from the Revolution. The nation, as a person, possesses a subjective right in that power to command which we call sovereignty. . . .

"With some rare exceptions there was no class or party in the nineteenth century which did not accept national sovereignty as a religious dogma. . . .

"Sovereignty being, like the national person which possesses it, one and indivisible, the same men and the same territory must be under unified control. . . .

"Indeed the conception of sovereignty has always been, both in theory and practice, an absolutist conception. . . . Rousseau justifies this proposition by a strange piece of sophistry."

22. *Ibid.*, pp. 32, 43–45: "The idea of public service is to-day replacing the old theory of sovereignty as the basis of public law. It is not, of course, a new attitude. . . . Sociological jurisprudence has sought to determine the facts. . . . Personally, it seems to me clear that its real basis is social interdependence. . . . There has been a vital element of political power and public law which, it is worth noting, is quite outside the realm of the social contract. That theory suggested that men united by an agreement and gave up their natural isolation; so was born a sovereignty and collective will which constitutes government. The fact, on the contrary, is that we have to start with a social group. The distinction between rulers and subjects is spontaneously produced and the former's power is imposed on the latter to a degree which varies with the belief and its utility. . . .

"I have observed above that the government must at every time perform three functions: (1) National defence; (2) the maintenance of internal security and order, and (3) justice. To-day these services are not enough."

23. *Ibid.*, pp. 48–51, 54, 58.

24. *Ibid.*, pp. 68–70.

25. *Ibid.*, pp. 71–72: "But the idea of this social rule is in no sense metaphysical. It does not transcend society. . . . We obey this rule, not because it creates a superior duty, but simply because we are, for good or ill, members of society, and therefore necessarily subject to its social discipline. . . .

"We say that normative statutes are imposed on all because they contain a rule of law every ruler recognised at a given place and time. This idea has been remarkably worked out by Prof. Dicey. . . .

"It is not true only of England but for every country in every age. It may be added that if opinion is the essential factor in the making of law it plays this rôle only when men think that a certain rule is imposed by a social sanction. In other words, public opinion only makes legislation when the individual minds that have formed it possess juristic content."

26. *Ibid.*, pp. 73–75.

27. *Ibid.*, pp. 95–97: "Other facts tend to make clear the disappearance from statute of the ideas of a sovereign command. And it is exactly here that there is to be discerned the profoundest change of modern times. The theory of a sovereign state, indeed, its emanation from a nationality, situated on definite territory, and organised into a government, was rigorously logical enough. It swept all wills save its own from the field of control. The texts bear witness to the immense influence it exerted.

"The consequence of this theory is clear. If law is the expression of the unified and sovereign will, it is evident that on a given territory there can only be one law and that the members of a nation recognising only that one law can admit the validity of no other form of statute. But we shall see that in the modern state alongside national laws there are local laws and group laws which the citizens accept and the courts enforce.

"Obviously the sovereign cannot admit a federalist organisation. . . . By federalism the convention understood what we to-day call decentralisation—that is to say, any system in which a territorial area is self-governing. . . .

"To-day all this is changed. Every impartial observer must be impressed with the variety of law and especially with its localisation. It is very striking in federal countries when on the same territory federal law and state law are both applied. . . .

"Moreover, it is not only in federal countries but even in unitary states like France that this localisation of law is apparent. Law, above all, is a rule which derives from the central government and is applicable in theory to every individual in the state; but, by its side, local laws begin to make their appearance."

28. Secondary literature on Harold Laski's political philosophy is rich and diverse, involving numerous controversies over such issues as his later tendencies to neo-Marxist ideas concerning state and sovereignty. The following works are illustrative: Peter Lamb, "Laski on Sovereignty: Removing the Mask from Class Dominance," *Hist. of Pol. Tht.*, XVIII (1997), pp. 325 ff.; W. H. Greenleaf, "Laski and British Socialism," *ibid.*, II (1981), pp. 573 ff.; and H. A. Dean, *The Political Ideas of Harold J. Laski* (New York, 1955).

29. Harold J. Laski, *The Rise of European Liberalism: An Essay in Interpretation* (London, 1936), pp. 154–155. Also cf. e.g. Laski's *Liberty in the Modern State* (London, 1930, 1948), Intro., pp. 19–21, for warnings against planned economics and public-works programs.

30. Harold J. Laski, *The State in Theory and Practice* (New York, 1935), pp. 35–40, 42–43.

31. Harold J. Laski, *Studies in the Problem of Sovereignty* (New York, 1917), pp. 6–8.

32. *Ibid.*, pp. 12–14, 16–17, 111, 261.

33. Laski, *State in Theory and Practice*, pp. 59, 64.

34. *Ibid.*, pp. 64–65, 242: "We have, in fact, to distinguish between three different senses in which the idea of law can be used. There is the formal juristic sense, which is no more than an announcement, ultimately dependent upon the sovereign authority, of the will to enforce certain decisions. There is the political sense, in which the formal announcement is validated by the acceptance of it by those to whom it applies. There is, finally, the ethical sense, in which the decision announced ought to be obeyed because it is morally right that what it proposes should be done.

"Now it is clear that in the first two of these three senses the citizen has no inherent duty to obey. . . . Nor can it, I think, be seriously claimed, either, that the political and ethical senses are identical; the commands of the Hitlerite state on June 30, 1934, were law in the sense that they went into effective operation, and were accepted by the population over whom it ruled; but most people in a position to make an independent judgment would, I suggest, regard them as ethically outrageous. Might, however profound, does not make right; effective operation of law still leaves undecided the question of ethical adequacy.

"Neither formal competence, then, nor political power can confer a just title to obedience. With what are we left? Only, I think, with the insistence that law to be ethically valid must conform with the requirements of the system of rights the purposes of which the state exists to maintain. . . . For, on the view here set out, the unity we find in our society is not one of consent, but of coercion; and the essential feature of the state is not its search for a common welfare but its power to compel the acceptance of certain class-relationships which make that common welfare peripheral, and not central, to its aim. The true end of the state is to maintain the legal principles which secure within its confines the predominance of the owners of the instruments of production; and what of common welfare it ever establishes is always subordinate to that major end. Social legislation is not the outcome of a rational and objective willing of the common good by all members of the community alike; it is the price paid for those legal principles which secure the predominance of the owners of property."

35. Harold J. Laski, *The Foundations of Sovereignty and Other Essays* (New York, 1921), pp. 17–19, 233, 236–237.

36. *Ibid.*, pp. 13–16: "Here, it may be suggested, is the permanent significance of Machiavelli. The medieval thinker grew to see that the national state was necessary to achieve the perfect life. But Machiavelli saw that to live well it must first have the means to live; and he painted in relentless phrase the arts of government. He summarized a development perhaps longer than he knew. The wearisome search for abstract right was largely impotent before concrete power and grasping ambition. . . . He saw that achievement rested with the men who, like Caesar Borgia, moved from the immediate purpose clearly seen to the power consciously at hand. He sacrificed an interest in eternal right to the practical rights that *de facto* power so easily obtained. . . .

"The state thus became the heir of the *Respublica Christiana*. . . . The state was growing free from limitations of a legal kind upon its power. . . . Luther was compelled to re-assert the divine character of princely power. When to his claim was added the plea of territoriality in religion, all the materials were at hand for subsequent events. . . . What at bottom had been asserted was the right of the state, through the person of its prince. . . . Henry VIII did no more than give the fullest expression that generation was to see of the new Erastianism in action."

37. *Ibid.*, pp. 26–29, 244: "The foundations of sovereignty are, after Rousseau's time, most largely conceived in terms of the synthesis he envisaged. Bentham and Austin, at bottom, did little more than translate the purpose he desired into the special legal institutions adapted to their time. The state, with them as with him, differs from every other form of organization in that it defines a common ground upon which the interests of men may be held identical. The lawyers present us with a state whose sovereign organ has unlimited and irresistible power. The philosophers have reinforced the legal concept by drawing attention to the greatness of the purpose by which the state has been informed. They express, so to speak, the unexplored teleology of the legal system. . . .

"But to move from that unified sovereignty which is a protective against external attack to the more complex problems of internal arrangement has no necessary validity. Internal change is movement against the interests of an existing order which the sovereignty of the state is, as a matter of history, used always to preserve. Its legal right to be merges without the necessary inquiry into ethical justification. Some, as Hobbes, may argue that the price of resistance is always greater than the value it obtains. Others, as T. H. Green, may urge that we confront the state in fear and awe because the presumption in resistance is always against us. Others again, as Bosanquet, may give the state unquestioned right upon the ground that, ultimately, it will come to summarize the best of ourselves. Yet the simple fact is that from the standpoint of internal relations the true heart of a state is its government; . . . England, France, America, mean on domestic issues a complex of interests which struggle among themselves for survival. In any realistic analysis there is no necessary unity of purpose between the groups we there discover. The wills we meet are aiming at achievement which often involves the destruction of the legal order maintained by government. . . . That is not even to argue that there may not be an objective common good transcendentally better than the private goods secured. But in actual political conflict the sovereignty of the state means the sovereignty of government. . . .

"The fact is that the state as an external unit seeking survival in a world of states is never the same to its members as that same state in the ebb and flow of its internal daily life. The relations of its parts are, in this latter aspect, unified neither in aim nor method. What the orthodox theory of sovereignty has done is to coerce them into an unity and thereby to place itself at the disposal of the social group which, at any given historic moment, happens to dominate the life of the state. . . . That is why the legal theory of sovereignty can never offer a basis for a working philosophy of the state. For a legal theory of sovereignty takes its stand upon the beatification of order; and it does not inquire—it is not its business to inquire—into the purposes for which order is maintained. . . . To this aspect the ethical side of political pluralism stands in the closest relation. Fundamentally, it is a denial that a law can be explained merely as a command of the sovereign for the simple reason that it denies, ultimately, the sovereignty of anything save right conduct. The philosophers since, particularly, the time of T. H. Green, have told us insistently that the state is based upon will . . ."

38. Laski, *Rise of European Liberalism*, p. 40: "In England, . . . the strong and popular Tudor monarchs broke the last vestiges of feudal pretensions. . . . New legislation, a new and powerful class of officials largely composed of *novi homines*, the renovation of the office of justice of the peace and its attachment by unbreakable links to the Crown, these are the main experiments of the period, and they all make for that centralizing nationalism which was the most urgent need of the age. Nor must we fail to note the significance of Parliament, different in quality from that of any continental legislature. The Tudors, no doubt, were despots; Professor Pollard has said of Henry VIII that he was Machiavelli's prince in action. But they were despots by popular consent. Whatever the divisions of the nobility, the middle classes rallied to them. The landowner and the merchant enabled them to use Parliament as the instrument of a state using political means for economic welfare. The Tudors made their law prevail by infusing it with the spirit that the new order required."

39. *Ibid.*, pp. 39–40: "The evolution of the civil law has . . . complex implications. Yet its essence is unmistakably secularization. The decline of the canon law reflects definitively the defeat of the claims of Rome. The Reception of the Roman law, in Germany . . . as well as in the Latin countries, came because its principles were far better suited than feudal rules to an age which required uniformity and strong government. The appeal of Roman law lay . . . in the fact that it exalted the state, and the prince as the embodiment of the state, as the unchallengeable sanction of political power. . . . What was supremely important was that, once the change had been made, the power of the state rested upon a different level from that of any possible competitor."

40. Laski, *Foundations of Sovereignty*, pp. 248–249: "Those who take refuge in the irrefutable logic of the sovereign state may sometimes take thought that for many centuries of medieval history the very notion of sovereignty was unknown. I would not seek unduly to magnify those far-off times; but it is worth while to remember that no thoughts were dearer to the heart of medieval thinkers than ideas of right and justice."

41. *Ibid.*, pp. 232 ff. ("The Pluralistic State").

42. Friedrich A. Hayek, *The Constitution of Liberty* (Chicago, 1966), pp. 133–134.

43. *Ibid.*, pp. 253 ff.

44. *Ibid.*, pp. 397 ff.

45. *The Essence of Hayek* (edited by C. Nishiyama and K. Leure, Stanford, 1984), pp. 63, 65.

46. *Ibid.*, p. 291 (also cf. *Constitution of Liberty*, pp. 407–408), with ref. to Laski.

47. *The Collected Works of Hayek*, Vol. X, *Socialism and War* (edited by B. Caldwell, Chicago, 1997), pp. 218–219. Also e.g. pp. 84 ff., 175 ff., 181 ff. Also pertinent is Vol. IX, *Contra Keynes and Cambridge*.

48. Friedrich A. Hayek, *Law, Legislation and Liberty* (3 vols., Chicago, 1973–1979), Vol. I, *Rules and Order*, pp. 72 ff.

49. *Ibid.*, pp. 91–92.

50. *Ibid.*, pp. 124 ff.

51. Holly Smith Goldman, "Rawls and Utilitarianism," in *John Rawls' Theory of Social Justice: An Introduction* (edited by H. Blocker and E. Smith, Athens, Ohio, 1980), Ch. 3, pp. 346 ff. (at pp. 346, 390). A slightly earlier assessment by Robert Paul Wolff, *Understanding Rawls: A Reconstruction and Critique of "A Theory of Justice"*

502 / Notes to Chapter VIII

(Princeton, 1977), referred (p. 3) to "the flood of comments that have appeared in the half-decade since its [*Theory of Justice*] publication." A key question is Rawls' relationship to Kant (Pt. III). In the last two decades, Rawls' ideas have been subjected to intense scrutiny pro and con.

Of interest is Sibyl A. Schwarzenbach, "Rawls, Hegel, and Communitarianism," *Political Theory*, 19 (1991), pp. 539 ff. The author begins (pp. 539–540) with the following observations: "From its origins in . . . revolt against the British idealists . . . , analytical philosophy [analysis of language, meaning, etc.] has defined itself in opposition to the Hegelian speculative and metaphysical tradition. . . . [H]owever, it is not altogether clear who has won the debate. Ample evidence exists that despite more than fourscore years of disparagement and ridicule, the influence of Hegel (and many of the idealist positions) has not only *not died* but may even be gaining in strength. . . . Hegel's influence [appears] in an area where one might not yet have suspected it: in the thought of the paradigmatic theorist of justice in the Anglo-American world John Rawls."

In pondering ideas of community and the just society a la Rawls and Hegel, Schwarzenbach concludes (pp. 563–564) that because of the new influx of women into crucial communal activities there can now be a new concept of the modern state less oriented to maintaining law and order, etc., and more characterized as altruistic "provider of services." This notion is perhaps not as "new" as she believes but rather an adaptation of the ideas of Duguit. In any case, the central influence of Hegel on Rawls remains important. The reemergence of focus on the individual's necessary connections with the organic social whole of the community "is only a part of the legacy of Hegel which remains alive and well in the thought of Rawls [p. 364]."

Also cf. Duncan Ivison, "The Secret History of Public Reason: Hobbes to Rawls," *Hist. of Pol. Tht.*, XVIII (1997), pp. 125 ff.

52. John Rawls, *A Theory of Justice* (Camb., Mass., 1971), Ch. I, sect. 5, p. 22.
53. *Ibid.*, pp. 23, 25–26.
54. *Ibid.*, Ch. I, sect. 6, pp. 28–33.
55. *Ibid.*, Ch. V, sect. 46, pp. 298–299.
56. Cf. e.g. Dennis Patterson, *Law and Truth* (New York, 1996), Ch. 8, and Seyla Benhabib, "Critical Theory and Postmodernism: On the Interplay of Ethics, Aesthetics, and Utopia in Critical Theory," in *Deconstruction and the Possibility of Justice*, Vol. 11, *Cardozo Law Review* (1990), pp. 1435 ff.